The Empire Strikes Out

Also by Robert Elias

The Deadly Tools of Ignorance: A Novel
Baseball and the American Dream
The Politics of Victimization
Victims Still
Victims of the System
Rethinking Peace (co-edited)
The Encyclopedia of Violence, Peace & Conflict (co-edited)
The Peace Resource Book (co-edited)

The Empire Strikes Out

How Baseball Sold U.S. Foreign Policy and
Promoted the American Way Abroad

ROBERT ELIAS

THE NEW PRESS

NEW YORK
LONDON

Requests for permission to reproduce selections from this book should be mailed to: Permissions Department, The New Press, 38 Greene Street, New York, NY 10013.

Published in the United States by The New Press, New York, 2010
Distributed by Perseus Distribution

LIBRARY OF CONGRESS CATALOGING-IN-PUBLICATION DATA
Elias, Robert, 1950–
The empire strikes out : how baseball sold U.S. foreign policy and promoted the American way abroad / Robert Elias.
p. cm.
Includes bibliographical references and index.
ISBN 978-1-59558-195-2 (hc. : alk. paper)   1. Baseball—Social aspects.   2. Baseball—Public opinion.   3. Sports in popular culture.   4. United States—Foreign relations.   I. Title.
GV867.64.E45 2010
796.357—dc22

2009033388

The New Press was established in 1990 as a not-for-profit alternative to the large, commercial publishing houses currently dominating the book publishing industry. The New Press operates in the public interest rather than for private gain, and is committed to publishing, in innovative ways, works of educational, cultural, and community value that are often deemed insufficiently profitable.

www.thenewpress.com

Composition by NK Graphics
This book was set in Bembo

Printed in the United States of America

2 4 6 8 10 9 7 5 3 1

For my children's dream:
Madeleine singing and Andre playing America's new
national anthem, "This Land Is Your Land," before
Jack's major-league debut at AT&T Park

Baseball is more like a novel than like a war. It is
like an ongoing, hundred-year work of art, peopled
with thousands of characters, full of improbable
events, anecdotes, folklore, and numbers.

—Luke Salisbury, *The Answer Is Baseball*

Contents

Preface xi

Introduction 1

1. Wars at Home (1775–1892) 5
2. Missionaries Abroad (1888–1897) 20
3. Small Wars and the Old Army Game (1898–1909) 37
4. Imperium Rising (1910–1916) 54
5. Real War (1917–1919) 77
6. From the Home Front to Horsehide Diplomacy (1919–1940) 94
7. Good War Hunting (1941–1945) 126
8. Cold War, Hot War (1946–1953) 161
9. Revolution and Quagmire (1953–1975) 189
10. Purging the Vietnam Syndrome (1976–1999) 212
11. Foreign Policy on Steroids (2000–2009) 245
12. The Empire Strikes Out 282

Notes 295

Index 393

Preface

Baseball has a richness and broad usefulness far beyond the complex pleasures it offers as a game . . . [it] provides a superb mix of people, atmosphere and action for the creation of popular myth and metaphor. Its possibilities for heroics, for humor and—naturally—for disaster have made baseball a tremendously fertile field for writers.

—Loudon Wainwright

On the field, the game of baseball provides a compelling drama, whose limitless complexities have been exhaustively documented by the sport's obsessive statistics and by its many histories. Off the field, the sport has been examined, more than any other, as a social and cultural phenomenon central to U.S. history. I'm concerned with a different story: American baseball's projection of itself abroad, for its own sake and also for spreading American influence around the globe. Several years ago, I began teaching and writing about baseball's meaning in U.S. culture, the subject of my book *Baseball and the American Dream*. But as I looked further, I realized I was leaving out baseball's external role. The more I probed, the bigger that global projection seemed to be.

The story of baseball's own foreign policy and its historic role in promoting U.S. diplomatic, military, and globalization policies has been overlooked. Yet the sport repeatedly appears in America's long history of wars, interventions, cultural missions, and diplomatic forays. Baseball has been among the main promoters of the American dream and the American way. The pieces of this story are extensive and many of them have been explored individually. But here I examine the big picture: what is the full history of this phenomenon—from its earliest days through the present?

While this story provides a rich and intriguing history featuring a long list of unlikely characters and improbable events, I've tried to offer more than simply a historical chronology. I'm also interested in what this neglected history tells us about baseball, America, and the world. I'm concerned about the emergence of an American empire, baseball's role in it, and the repercussions when dynasties begin to fall. In the end, I argue that baseball has been profoundly affected by a "national pastime trade-off," whereby in exchange for maintaining its status as the national game, the sport has pursued policies and alliances that have exacted a great price. At this point, in the early twenty-first century, baseball ought to reexamine that trade-off and consider a new direction—just as the nation itself would also be wise to do so.

To create this book's larger tapestry, I'm indebted to many writers for their more specialized contributions on various aspects of this theme. The early research of David Voigt, Richard Crepeau, Harold Seymour, Joel Zoss, John Bowman, and Howard Senzel first got me interested in baseball's global role. More recently, the work of Stephen Pope, Gerald Gems, Bill Brown, Mark Lamster, Thomas Zeiler, James Elfers, William Kelly, Wanda Wakefield, Mark Dyreson, Alan Bairner, John Krich, Peter Bjarkman, Joseph Reaves, Adrian Burgos, John Kelly, and Alan Klein has been particularly valuable. Maverick writers such as Dave Zirin, Merritt Clifton, Jim Bouton, and Bill Lee have encouraged me to rethink old perspectives. Most of all, I've been influenced by the work of Ron Briley, who likely could have written this book better than I and whose analysis of Cold War baseball in particular has been especially instructive. I appreciate his insights and collegiality.

I'd like to thank several other baseball scholars for their long-term support and for providing models of scholarly work. My gratitude goes to Roger Kahn, Jean Ardell, Lee Lowenfish, Paul Zingg, Jay Feldman, Sam Regalado, Bill Nowlin, the late Jules Tygiel, and particularly to George Gmelch, whose friendship and support I deeply appreciate. I'm grateful for the encouragement provided by Howard Nemerovski, Dan Ardell, Kerry Huffman, Will Carroll, and Rick and Tracy Ferm. My thanks for research assistance goes to Lenny DiFranza, Claudette Burke, Freddy Berowski, and Jim Gates at the Cooperstown Hall of Fame Library, and to Len Levin at the Society for American Baseball Research. I appreciate the benefit I derived from being made a member of the International Worshop on "Mapping an Empire of American Sports," sponsored by Penn State University and the University of California, Berkeley, at the Bancroft Library. I'm indebted to my New Press editors, Marc Favreau, Andy Hsiao, Sarah Fan, and Furaha Norton, and their assistants, Joel Ariaratnam and Jason Ng, and to my copy editor, Gary Stimeling, for all their work in putting the book together.

At the University of San Francisco, I'm thankful for the support of my colleagues Michael Bloch, Brian Weiner, Jeremy Howell, Dean Rader, Jeff Brand, and my fellow Politics Department faculty, as well as administrative assistants Kerry Donoghue and Spencer Rangitsch. At the Gleeson Library, Lloyd Affholter and Joseph Campi were particularly helpful with my research.

My gratitude to Pamela Organista for including me in two very productive weekend writing retreats. I'm obliged to Robert Fordham and USF's Fromm Institute Lecture Series for allowing me to explore many of the book's ideas. I'd like to thank the undergraduate and Fromm students in my Law, Politics and the National Pastime course, and, for their indispensable contributions, my student research assistants: Nicola Fraser, Rob Bachmann, Nick Miller, Stephen Lucia, Hannah Minkevitch, Stephen Rapaport, Christa Watkins, and Hannah Linkenhoker.

For their support, I'm very appreciative of my children, Andre, Madeleine, and Jack, and of my sister, Patti Barcel. I'm especially thankful to Jennifer Turpin for her love and understanding. Thanks to all of you for putting up with my long preoccupation with this project and for sustaining me through its challenges.

—Robert Elias
Mill Valley, California

Introduction

The true patriot is one who gives his highest loyalty not to his country as it is, but to what it can and ought to be.

—Albert Camus

In *Field of Dreams*, in his memorable speech at the film's end, Terence Mann reminds us that "the one constant throughout all the years has been baseball. America has rolled by like an army of steamrollers. It has been erased like a blackboard, rebuilt and erased again. But baseball has marked the time." Yet what should we make of this hallowed institution? Aren't sports often viewed as merely the background of any society—as inconsequential games? Hasn't baseball, for all its longevity, been merely bread and circuses for the American people?

For more than two centuries, baseball has shown up in surprising ways as America has emerged in the world and built itself into an empire. Baseball was played in America as far back as the Revolutionary War and was first designated as the "national pastime" in the 1850s. Since then, the sport has worked hard to maintain that status. To do so, baseball—and major league baseball (MLB) in particular—has tried to associate itself with the values of the American dream. It has also sought to equate itself with American masculinity and patriotism, and with U.S. military endeavors in particular. Baseball has also fought its own wars, pitting owners against players and one league against another.

When the United States began projecting itself as a global power in the late nineteenth century, baseball was enlisted in America's imperial quests—helping the nation colonize other lands, from the Caribbean to Asia to the Pacific. The game was regularly part of U.S. "civilizing missions" launched abroad, either militarily or economically, and sometimes bolstered by the forces of "muscular Christianity." Baseball was used to sell and export the American dream. It took its place in the globalization of the world, even if Americanization was more the objective. In America's foreign diplomacy, baseball was often regarded as the nation's "moral equivalent of war." And at home, baseball was employed to help manage immigration and the nation's own internal colonies, as well as to promote American identity and nationalism.

Affiliating itself with true-blue Americanism has had its benefits but also some negative repercussions. Routinely, patriotism has been defined not as support for the nation's ideals, but rather as loyalty to official policies. In exchange for its good standing as the national pastime, has baseball trapped itself into a blind adherence to U.S. foreign and military policies? Baseball has long engaged in a "national pastime trade-off," whereby it must religiously toe the official government or military line in return for being able to maintain its claim as the national game. At stake, of course, is far more than a symbolic designation; substantial owner profits are potentially on the line, as well as the sport's independence. Likewise, baseball has parroted America's approach to globalization in its own business dealings abroad. As MLB has become its own empire, concerns have been raised about whether it still represents the game's best interests.

With more Americans identifying football as their favorite sport over the last three decades, can baseball still sustain its claim as the national game? Despite the popularity numbers, some argue that baseball will always remain the national pastime; others believe the claim has now been lost. By pursuing the national pastime trade-off, baseball maintained its prominence for most of American history. Does the more recent challenge from football mean that baseball must redouble its flag-waving patriotism? Or does it suggest the limitations of that approach and signal baseball's need for a new role in American society and the world? What can we learn, for example, from baseball's recent response to the September 11 attacks and to America's get-tough military policies, including the wars on terrorism, Afghanistan, and Iraq—which some view, ironically, as U.S. foreign policy on steroids? Should baseball remain wedded to the U.S. empire or can it convey a different America to the world?

To understand the present, we must revisit the past. What, exactly, has been baseball's relationship to American wars and patriotism, to the U.S. military, and to the nation's burgeoning economic, political, and cultural dominance around the world? It's a baseball history that reveals a colorful, and often startling, cast of characters. It involves generals from Washington to MacArthur to Eisenhower to Powell, and presidents from Lincoln to Nixon to Bush to the Roosevelts. It's the story of foreign leaders, such as Sun Yat-Sen, Pope Pius X, the Emperor Hirohito, the Sultan of Zanzibar, the King of England, and Hugo Chávez, and politicians from Jesse Helms and Rudy Giuliani to J. Edgar Hoover and Madeleine Albright. The game has preoccupied writers from Mark Twain and Walt Whitman to Sir Arthur Conan Doyle and Tom Clancy, and featured entertainers such as Paul Robeson, Jimmy Stewart, José Feliciano, and Tim Robbins; industrialists such as Henry Ford; and media moguls such as William Randolph Hearst, Ted Turner, and Rupert Murdoch. And it's a baseball history that involves dozens of ballplayers in endlessly unexpected ways, including stars ranging from Mathewson, Thorpe, DiMaggio, Greenberg, Feller, Robinson, and O'Doul to Clemente, Seaver, Bouton, Ripken, McGwire, Sosa, and Delgado—not to mention managers and executives such as Spalding, McGraw, Mack, Landis, Griffith, Rickey, Wrigley, Chandler, Lasorda, Steinbrenner, and Selig.

Examining baseball's historic relationship with America's foreign policy establishment raises a long list of provocative questions, which we'll examine in the pages ahead. Why was a general chosen as baseball's "founder"? What interrupted the Seventh Cavalry's regular series of baseball games in the Black Hills? Why were baseball games played in Egypt at the foot of the Great Sphinx? What baseball executive was nearly court-martialed for kidnapping Kaiser Wilhelm? Which ballplayer was proposed as a peacemaker between the United States and Japan? What role did the game play in the World War II Japanese American concentration camps? Which second-string big-league catcher was really an American spy? Which Negro Leaguers played baseball at gunpoint for a Dominican dictator? How did the Mexican Revolution threaten MLB? Could the Washington Senators have signed Fidel Castro before the Cuban Revolution and changed the course of history? Who rescued the American flag in the Dodger Stadium outfield? Who saw baseball fields as evidence of Soviet subversion? Why did a major leaguer refuse to stand for the singing of "God Bless America"?

Most important: in the early twenty-first century, is baseball the sport of America's bright future? Or—perhaps reflecting the nation that created it—is baseball an empire that's destined to strike out?

1

Wars at Home
(1775–1892)

It had been a great war for baseball.

—Albert Spalding

The story of baseball's relationship to the American empire is an old one, beginning as far back as the earliest days of the republic.[1] According to baseball writer Merritt Clifton, the name of our most celebrated team, the Yankees, emerged from military sources in the pre–Revolutionary War era—in a most unflattering manner. The period's most popular song was "Yankee Doodle," whose lyrics included this verse:

> Yankee Doodle went to town
> A-riding on a pony
> Stuck a feather in his hat
> And called it macaroni.

At the time, *macaroni* didn't mean "pasta" but rather someone who was a "dandy." Viewed by the English as country bumpkins, the American colonials proudly accepted that status, making fun of themselves in the song by implying that merely a feather could make them into sophisticated gentlemen. But the real put-down of the colonials lay not in "macaroni" but rather in "Yankee Doodle."

Detailed early maps of Newfoundland show a body of water called Dildo Pond, named for its shape by the British garrison stationed in North America more than three hundred years ago. In the colonial period, the word *dildo* evolved into *doodle*, British barracks slang for male genitalia. And, to *yank* something meant back then exactly what it means now. Thus, to the British, a Yankee Doodle was one who yanked his doodle. A Yankee Doodle was a first-rate greenhorn—too thick and dim to realize the joke was on him. The Americans didn't recognize the English slang, and—to the astonishment of the British—instead made "Yankee Doodle" their anthem. Then the Americans began calling themselves Yankees generally, and eventually they gave that name to their greatest baseball club and outfitted their sons and daughters in Yankees caps and uniforms.[2] Baseball, patriotism, and the military—all together from the very beginning.

From Revolutionary War to Mexican War

Thomas Jefferson claimed that "base ball was too violent for the body and stamped no character on the mind." Nevertheless, while the sport's exact origins cannot be pinned down, repeated references to ball games were made in the eighteenth century, and during the American Revolution soldiers wrote about playing baseball to help endure their hardships. The Revolutionary War soldier George Ewing, camped at Valley Forge, wrote on April 7, 1778, that he and others "exercisd in the afternoon in the intervals and playd at base." Games among soldiers may have been played as early as 1775, and they continued through 1782, in several states.[3]

In New York City, in 1777, Americans played baseball in British prisoner-of-war compounds. In the spring of 1779, American soldier Henry Dearborn described an army expedition against the Iroquois Indians: "All the Officers of the Brigade turn'd out & Play'd a game at ball, the first we have had this yeare." Later, he wrote that "we are oblige'd to walk 4 miles to day to find a place leavel enough to play ball." Even George Washington played: in September 1779 the French legation secretary wrote about the American general: "Today he throws and catches a ball for whole hours with his aides-de-camp."[4]

While we have little record of ball playing during the War of 1812, army private Peter Van Smoot, a Battle of New Orleans veteran, did report that "I found a soft ball in my knapsack, that I forgot I had put there and started playing catch with it." During the war, some American prisoners played baseball at England's Dartmoor prison while awaiting postwar repatriation. One long base hit prompted some prisoners to enlarge a hole in the prison wall enough to retrieve the ball. But it was mistaken for an escape attempt: seven Americans were killed and thirty-one were wounded. Back home, other baseball games were reported at the U.S. Military Academy between 1818 and 1822.[5]

While Alexander Cartwright and Doc Adams were organizing the first baseball games (employing rules we'd recognize today) at New Jersey's Elysian Fields in the 1840s, America was launching its first major military foray abroad—the Mexican War. Under the pretense of repelling border incursions (Mexicans call the war the "North American Intervention"), which America had provoked, the United States attacked Mexico in 1846. Invoking Manifest Destiny, the war was rationalized for racial and religious reasons—Mexicans were "backward people" who were either heathens or practicing an inferior brand of Christianity. Therefore, they had to be saved. The war's real purpose? To try to expand slavery and to engineer a major land grab, which incorporated nearly half of Mexico's territory into the United States.[6]

While Henry David Thoreau sat in jail protesting the U.S. invasion of Mexico and Abraham Lincoln opposed it in Congress, others cut their teeth as spies, soldiers, and even ballplayers. One of them, Adolph Engelmann, wrote about playing games in Saltillo, Mexico in 1847. Another story claims the first baseball game in Mexico occurred in Jalapa that year, where the wooden leg of the defeated general, Antonio Lopez de Santa Anna, was used as a bat. A U.S. military officer and the presumptive inventor of baseball, Abner Doubleday, supposedly spread the game beyond America when he led U.S. troops stationed in Mexico City. By the end of the Mexican War, the New York Volunteer Regiment reached southern California, and "largely because of the baseball games," which the soldiers began playing, "the Spanish-speaking people of Santa Barbara came to look upon the New Yorkers as loudmouthed, uncouth hoodlums . . . [and] the hostilities between Californians and Americanos continued to fester for generations."[7]

During the 1840s and 1850s, baseball grew like wildfire in the East. By 1856, the sport was already dubbed the national pastime by the *New York Mercury* and the Native American Sport by *Porter's Spirit of the Times* in 1857. Baseball's rise was remarkable, considering how strongly entrenched its main competitor, cricket, had been. As in its many other colonies, Britain sought to implant its national sport. Dozens of cricket clubs populated the major U.S. cities before the Civil War, but they would be short-lived. Cricket carried a stigma: it was a thoroughly British game in a society that was struggling to escape its inferiority complex toward England.[8]

Civil War

The Civil War briefly stalled baseball's rising star. During the conflict, baseball clubs disbanded, star players declined, and attendance shrank. The National Association of Base Ball Players cut short its 1861 season and ball playing diminished generally. Baseball's fortunes revived, however, with stories of Abraham Lincoln's devotion to the game. It's said that when a visiting delegation was about to hand him the 1860 Republican presidential nomination, Lincoln was out on a baseball field and insisted on taking his at bat before accepting the offer. Later he took time out from prosecuting the Civil War to watch ball games. Baseball was played not only informally but also in organized contests by soldiers. While the game was not unknown in the South, Union soldiers further spread it among Confederates and Westerners. The Civil War marked the first extensive connection the game made to America's long history of wars, thereby linking the sport and military patriotism. As Albert Spalding later claimed, "It had been a great war for baseball."[9]

If the Mexican War was America's fledging imperial initiative, then its first notions of full-blown empire may have emerged during the Civil War. Cloaked in the compelling quest to "preserve the union,"[10] the war quickly launched the United States toward more ambitious and far-flung objectives. According to Secretary of State William Seward, "We are charged with responsibilities of establishing a higher condition of civilization." Baseball would often be enlisted in the cause.

About the Civil War, historian George Kirsch has written: "It was war, time to take up swords and muskets and lay aside bats and balls. . . . Instead, baseball went to war with men in blue and gray, changed as they changed, and emerged stronger than ever to help reunite them in their own national game."[11] Before the war, in 1857, the *New York Clipper* described baseball using a war analogy, indicating that the players "will be compelled to lay by their weapons of war, enter into winter quarters, there to discuss and lay plans for the proper conducting of next season's campaign." Later the *Clipper* described the war using a baseball analogy: In "the great game of iron and lead ball, between the loyal and rebellious States . . . we hope that the last innings will soon be played." The *Clipper* listed the baseball players who joined the Union Army, and the *Rochester Express* reported, "Many of our first class players are now engaged in the 'grand match' against the rebellious side," and have already made a "score . . . the rifle or gun taking the place of the bat."

While not yet formally embraced by the U.S. Army, baseball was nevertheless appreciated for promoting soldiers' morale. Some even claimed the North won the war because of baseball. It was used to "create happier and healthier soldiers for the battlefield and as a welcomed distraction and healer. Baseball [developed a] skill that would pay dividends in the heat of battle." According to Private Alpheris Parker, "ball-playing [had] become a mania. Officers and men forget differences in rank and indulge in the invigorating sport with a school-boy's ardor." As James Kushlan has observed, "Baseball, like war, was democratic. During the war, one was not a good soldier because of social or economic standing. On the baseball diamond, as on the battlefield, average men could become valiant and heroic."[12] By the war's end, baseball had been transformed from the "gentlemen's game" to a sport for all classes.

Baseball was used to break the boredom and soothe soldiers' woes, reviving memories of their school days and healing their homesickness. The "manly play of ball" prepared soldiers for challenging drills and group cohesion. A

Confederate surgeon, Dr. Julian Chisholm, claimed that baseball promoted health, strength, and agility. Doing well in the sport was not merely an indicator of good soldiering, but valued in itself: General Hartstuff of the 13th Massachusetts Regiment became a hero for his skill at catching and throwing a baseball alone.[13]

Baseball was also played in prison camps. At the Confederate prison at Salisbury, North Carolina, Northern prisoners used the game to endure their captivity. Union prisoners played at Camp Ford in 1863—possibly the first baseball played in Texas. At the Union prison at Johnson's Island, Ohio, Southerners formed a team that kept playing after the War. And when the Union's Fort McHenry was criticized for its treatment of Confederate soldiers, its commander offered its baseball games as evidence of "humane" conditions.[14]

Besides games in captivity, dozens of other military baseball contests were reported. When the 71st New York Volunteers reached Washington, D.C., they faced local teams. Playing near the White House, they defeated a Washington club, 42–13. Shortly thereafter, the Volunteers met the Confederates at Bull Run, sustaining heavy casualties. The most famous Civil War baseball game was held on Christmas Day 1862 on Hilton Head Island, when at least ten thousand and perhaps as many as forty thousand Union soldiers watched the 165th New York Infantry play a Union all-star team that included future National League president A.G. Mills. Baseball had arrived as a spectator sport.

The 8th and 114th Vermont Regiments played at Franklin, Louisiana, and another Louisiana game among Union troops was interrupted by a surprise enemy assault. As Union soldier George Putnam recalled: "Suddenly there came a scattering of fire of which the three fielders caught the brunt." The Northern soldiers repelled the Southern attack, "but we had lost not only our center field but . . . the only baseball in Alexandria." Southern soldiers had fewer baseball recollections, but at least one Rebel remembered the Confederate Baseball Club taking on the Southern Baseball Club.

Sometimes frontline truces were arranged so that baseball games could be played. An Iowa Regiment soldier, Sergeant Dryden, reported that during the siege of Vicksburg, Northern and Southern soldiers jokingly challenged each other to a baseball game. While the game never took place, the contesting soldiers "played catch" with each other from line to line across no-man's land: "We were throwing [our] ball . . . when firing suddenly broke out and the men from both sides dived into their trenches. . . . One big fellow named Halloran . . . wanted to go over and whip the Confederate soldier who had stolen our ball." The next morning, "during a lull in the firing, that Southerner yelled to us—and in a moment the ball came flying over to the Union trenches."[15]

Outside the military, baseball not only survived but also pushed out its sporting competitors. As the *New York Clipper* reported, "The game has too strong a foothold to be [discouraged] by the lowering brow of 'grim-visaged war.'" New York City remained America's premier baseball town, and the game was routinely linked to the Northern cause. William Cammeyer decorated his new Brooklyn ball field with American flags and opened it on May 15, 1862, with a band playing the "Star-Spangled Banner." Called the Union Grounds, it was the first enclosed field, allowing admission to be charged for the first time. Baseball tours were successful despite the crisis, and proceeds often went to the war effort. Young boys and college students not yet old enough or ready for military service began playing baseball, which also became popular at colleges such as Harvard University, whose first team began in 1864. The Union Club, comprised of escaped slaves, played in Manhattan. Periodicals kept the sport in the public eye, using it as a distraction from horrific accounts of battlefield carnage.[16]

"Popular memory," according to Lara Nielsen, "identifies baseball mythologies within the American traditions of military life." While generally connected to America's wars, baseball has a special affinity with the Civil War,[17] which Thomas Dyja demonstrates in his award-winning novel, *Play for a Kingdom.* As Dyja has observed:

> The Civil War marked this nation's coming of age, and baseball . . . took hold as our American game at the same time. . . . After the war, following the fortunes of [military] regiments blurred easily into following our teams, and even now millions of us use baseball and the Civil War to define our communities, and ourselves within them.[18]

In the late 1990s, *Civil War Times* asked its readers about baseball's ongoing association with the Civil War.[19] Their responses were illuminating:

> [It] seems deeply rooted in a return to what once was. The need to get on with things may be eclipsed by a yearning to reconnect with patterns of life that disappeared on a thousand battlefields. Baseball may have enabled former soldiers to regain a portion of their lost innocence.

> Americans are so passionate about [them] because [no] two things are more American. The mythical feats of the great generals and players stimulate the passions and imaginations. . . . Robert E. Lee's boldness in dividing his army at Chancellorsville and Babe Ruth's in calling his shot

in the 1932 World Series are the stories of legend. While their triumphs [transcend] the normal man, we can all envision ourselves as bit players.

Some Americans are still fighting the Civil War, and sometimes it shows up in baseball. Six decades after the war, Mississippians Gee and Harvey Walker were recruited by New York for the major leagues. But their Confederate mother could not bear seeing them in a "Yankees" uniform, so she forced them to sign instead with the Tigers.[20]

Post–Civil War Nationalism

After the Civil War, baseball was carried to America's far-flung corners, where it began earning its billing as the national game. In Denver, the Rocky Mountain Boys, a Union contingent, helped promote the sport. San Francisco teams were well-established in time to play the first professional baseball team, the Cincinnati Red Stockings. Undefeated in its grand tour of the Midwest and East, the Red Stockings ventured westward and in 1869 were among the first passengers on the just-completed transcontinental railroad. As *American Railroad Journal* editor Henry Poor suggested, the railway would fulfill America's mission "to establish our empire on the Pacific, where our civilization can take possession of the New Continent and confront the Old."[21] Baseball also helped consolidate the nation and stimulate its rise to world prominence. As George Kirsch observed, "the stage was set for the game's glory years—and the glory years of the nation itself."[22]

Baseball first helped heal sectional wounds after the Civil War. According to Albert Spalding, "It was a panacea for the pangs of humiliation to the vanquished, and a sedative against the natural exuberance of the victors." As David Lamoreaux has noted, in Spalding's eyes baseball became a national rite of conflict and reconciliation: "It is a bloodless battle, and when the struggle ends, the foes of the minute past are friends of the minute present."[23] In his novel of the period, *Our Base Ball Club and How It Won the Championship*, Noah Brooks described the post–Civil War baseball "epidemic" in northern Illinois. The townsfolk filled the ball park to watch "the mimic combat in the field below." When their team was on the road, they gathered at the newspaper office awaiting news from "the front," and according to one onlooker, "It looks as it did in the war, when the news from Shiloh and Vicksburg was coming in." When a victory occurred, the Stars and Stripes flew high above the town.

In the 1870s, according to the *New York Clipper*, "the ball players 'policy of reconstruction' [was] marked by true fraternal regard, irrespective of political opinions or sectional feelings, the National Association [of Base Ball Players] knowing . . . no North, no South."[24] To promote harmony, Northern teams launched tours to play Southern clubs, which sprung up quickly after the war. At first, not all Southerners would play their Northern visitors. When they did and won, however, it was sweet revenge.

Soon interregional games were regularly played, which helped smooth North–South relations. As the *Clipper* observed, "Maryland was fast being reconstructed on this base-is." In 1868, the Philadelphia Athletics went to play a Louisville, Kentucky, team, which wore gray uniforms. But one Athletic claimed the opponent's colors had "nothing to do with our National Game. If [former Confederate leader] Jefferson Davis was to meet me on the ball field and salute me as a gentleman, I would endeavor to prove to him that I was one." A New Orleans editorial wondered, "Would it not be pleasant to see the hatchet buried in the great national game, 'spite the efforts of politicians to keep up ill feeling between the sections?" The *Wilkes' Spirit* newspaper reported the New York Mutuals trip to the South: "This National Game seems destined to close the National Wounds opened by the late war." By the 1880s, baseball was thoroughly incorporated into Southern culture.[25]

Baseball was poised to satisfy the newly fused country's patriotic quest for national identity and its need for a new kind of hero—the self-reliant, self-made man. The thirty-one Civil War veterans who became major leaguers were lauded in particular. Professional athletes became the guardians of national morality, and baseball heroes attained the status of political and military leaders. As Ronald Story has observed, by the 1880s, "baseball became . . . a mass cultural movement, a large-scale, passionate American affair [like] . . . revivalism or temperance."[26] Soon, nationalism became a constant theme in major league baseball (MLB).

Catering to political forces behind American nationalism, baseball found itself drawn—symbiotically—to U.S. presidents. Making the patriotic connection was important, especially in times of war. This began with Lincoln and escalated through the present day. Lincoln's successor, Andrew Johnson—despite his impeachment troubles—found time to host the Washington Nationals at the White House. As president, war hero Ulysses S. Grant received the Cincinnati Red Stockings in 1869. Chester A. Arthur greeted the Cleveland club in 1883, proclaiming, "Good ballplayers make good citizens." In 1885, Cap Anson's Chicago White Stockings got to shake hands with President Grover Cleveland. In 1892, Benjamin Harrison became the first president to attend a major-league ball game. And in 1897, William McKinley entertained the Washington Senators in the Oval Office.[27]

Even then, America's nationalism went beyond merely pride in one's coun-

try. Predicated on notions of U.S. exceptionalism, it assumed America was superior to all other nations. Baseball soon shared this jingoistic spirit.[28] In his
book *America's National Game*, Albert Spalding provided a chauvinistic history
of U.S. baseball. America's internal sense of superiority cultivated external visions of how the United States should make the world over in its own image.
Describing baseball at the time, Walt Whitman proclaimed: "it's our game . . .
it has the snap, go, fling of the American atmosphere—it belongs as much to
our institutions as our Constitution's laws: is just as important in the sum total
of our historic life."[29] Whitman envisioned baseball "accomplishing the ron-
dure of the world, spreading . . . the 'American atmosphere' to Australia, Asia,
Africa and Europe," after it helped complete America's own continental manifest destiny, incorporating "forty to fifty great States, among them Canada
and Cuba."

Canada had already been a target, and Cuba would soon become one, for
both baseball and America. In Darryl Brock's brilliant baseball novel *If I Never
Get Back*, his protagonist plays for the Cincinnati Red Stockings in the 1860s
and gets ensnared in a Fenian Brotherhood plot to invade Canada and ransom
it for Irish freedom. Part fantasy but also historically true: the U.S. sought to
acquire Canada after the Revolutionary War, after thousands of American
loyalists had migrated there. Failing that, during the War of 1812, the United
States invaded Canada, hoping to annex its northern neighbor. Thousands
more loyalists fled north, mostly to southwestern Ontario; baseball may have
been brought from the United States to Canada via this migration.[30] Later the
Fenians led a U.S.-based Irish independence movement. In the 1850s, they
created a front for their political activities: the Fenian Baseball Club. After the
Civil War, Fenians (including their ballplayers) launched invasion attempts like
the one Brock describes. The White House looked the other way, and the Fenians ultimately failed, but formal U.S. government proposals for invading
Canada persisted.[31]

Had Walt Whitman lived into the twentieth century, he would have seen
baseball's manifest destiny confirmed across the continent and then "south to
Cuba for some of its finest players and then . . . north to absorb Canada." And
that would be only the beginning of baseball's globalization. According to Joel
Zoss and John Bowman, "baseball became inextricably entwined with . . . the
'mission' of America to expand and spread its form of government, by sword
if necessary, all over the world." And not merely its politics: baseball would
also be promoted for profits, just as other U.S. companies looked abroad for
new markets.[32]

But would Americans have the fortitude for imperial pursuits? Before the
Civil War, sports were scorned in favor of the serious business of earning a

living. This changed dramatically as concerns were raised about American masculinity. In 1859, the *New York Herald* warned against America's increasing feminization, recommending sports—and baseball in particular—as an antidote. After the Civil War, young men who hadn't fought questioned their manhood, wondering whether they could equal their fathers' bravery. Increasingly, baseball was deemed essential for all boys.[33] As former ballplayer turned Wild West novelist Zane Grey insisted, "All boys love baseball. If they don't, they're not real boys." Many American men concluded that their masculinity "could be saved by leading their nation into the modern imperial world."[34]

American religion had also opposed sports as a distraction from theological teachings. But this changed in the 1870s and 1880s when church leaders used baseball in their crusades to save nonbelievers abroad, especially in Asia and Latin America. "Muscular Christianity," promoted by the evangelical Young Men's Christian Association (YMCA), embraced baseball as a way to create the manly Christian gentleman, who "was the athlete of continence, not coitus, continuously testing his manliness in the fires of self-denial."[35]

After the Civil War, baseball had won the war against cricket, but two other sports emerged—football in the 1880s and basketball in the 1890s. While the latter was slow to take off, football began to make inroads. While baseball had become firmly entrenched as America's national pastime, some wondered whether it was vigorous enough to reflect the nation's emerging global aspirations. Social Darwinist theories of rugged individualism and the "survival of the fittest" would have to be embodied in our national game. Some thought football's rough-and-tumble violence might better serve the nation's needs. In response, organized baseball increasingly portrayed its sport as every bit as masculine as football.[36] Baseball would soon launch a new campaign to tout its martial spirit, but in the meantime it would simply follow the nation to war.

Indian Wars

A series of at least forty conflicts, the Indian Wars were fought by the U.S. military against Native Americans between 1775 and 1890. The earliest was the "western front" of the American Revolutionary War, when many Indians allied with the British, hoping to forestall further American expansion. These wars ended with the U.S. military massacre at Wounded Knee in 1890. The Indian Wars intensified in the post–Civil War period. The U.S. had solidified as a Union and established control over most of the territory that would fall within its current borders. But while the U.S. laid claim to its lands, actually settling them launched a new round of violence. The U.S. military turned away from the South and preoccupied itself with the Indian Wars in the West.

Conquering those lands and peoples would be the final American frontier, at least in North America. And as historian Thomas Borstelmann has suggested, "The subjugation of native Americans and their treatment as dependent wards of the state laid the groundwork for parallel U.S. actions in the Philippines a few years later."[37]

In these bloody Indian campaigns, baseball often rode along. According to David Lamoreaux, the baseball diamond could be seen as "an almost physical analogue of the country." The infield/outfield division paralleled that between civilization and wilderness, with the infield "an abstract symbol of the civilized portions of the country." The outfield, "with its theoretically illimitable reach . . . suggested the frontier."

If this was a metaphorical stretch, then baseball would also perform a more tangible role.[38] U.S. soldiers played various ball games out West as early as the 1830s. After launching the first organized baseball contests in New Jersey, Alexander Cartwright moved west in 1849. On his cross-country journey to California and then Hawaii, Cartwright taught baseball at every army post he encountered. Although many were lured to the military to combat hostile Indians, the reality was a life of drudgery. Only an occasional raid broke the monotony. Otherwise, the troops had few diversions, but baseball was the most popular. The sport boosted morale under horrible conditions, and military campaigns would have been less successful without it.[39]

After the Civil War, the 7th Cavalry was sent to protect westward railroad construction. The 7th was led by General George Custer, who became America's most famous Indian fighter. Baseball contests were the regiment's main entertainment when it was based at Fort Riley, Kansas, in 1866. On military campaigns, bats and balls were carried along with the soldiers' few other supplies. In 1868, the Kansas Volunteers joined the 7th Cavalry, and they played baseball during their harsh campaign against the Cheyenne and then again when they went after Indians in the Texas panhandle. In 1871, the Fourth of July celebration at Fort Sill, Kansas, featured a baseball game against the African American 10th Cavalry team. In 1873, the 7th played baseball in Nashville, Louisville, and then out in the Dakota territories and at Yellowstone.[40]

When gold, timber, and minerals were discovered in the Black Hills in the 1870s, U.S.-Indian treaties were broken, and Custer's 7th Cavalry was sent to secure the area for white prospectors and industrialists.[41] During this expedition, the 7th developed two teams: the Actives and the Benteens. Games were played at Harney's Peak and at "Custer's Park." The Benteen shortstop, General Andrew Burt, had established teams at posts in Wyoming, Montana, and Nebraska. Intensely hated by the Benteen players, Custer watched only the Actives ball games. While the Actives remained north and played baseball in

North Dakota, the Benteens were sent in 1874 to help suppress civil unrest in New Orleans, where they played more baseball. The 7th Cavalry baseball teams were reunited in the Dakotas in 1875. The Benteens played the Mc-Dougal club and the First Infantry team at Fort Randall. At Fort Abraham Lincoln, the Nameless played the Actives, who then faced the Modocs—named after a defeated Indian tribe.[42]

In the major leagues, on June 25, 1876, the Chicago White Sox defeated the Cincinnati Reds, 3–2. Later that day, General Custer and five companies of the 7th Cavalry were wiped out at the Battle of the Little Bighorn. Approaching an Indian encampment, Custer anticipated an easy victory and split his forces. To rob his detested subordinate of the glory (possibly due in part to a baseball rivalry), he sent Captain Benteen on a scouting mission. A final force, headed by Major Marcus Reno, attacked the Indians from one side, only to be repelled. This left Custer and 264 men vulnerable to attack by several thousand Sioux warriors. Among the casualties were most of the 7th Cavalry baseball teams. According to soldier Thomas Everts, whose diary chronicled frontier baseball, the 7th's best player, Sergeant Joseph McCurry, was expected to leave the army to play professional baseball, but he was wounded and never played again. Most other ballplayer soldiers were killed.[43]

Despite the defeat, by the 1880s the wars against Native Americans were in their final stages—concentrated around isolated posts in Texas and New Mexico. The 13th Infantry, which fought along the Mexican border against Geronimo and the Apaches, played baseball games among themselves and against local cowboy teams. The U.S. military helped spread baseball wherever it went, a practice it would soon extend well beyond America's borders.

And the military rubbed off on baseball, as well. According to Michael Bryson, the term *bullpen* likely arose during America's Indian-fighting days. A bullpen was a square log military enclosure, used to contain captured Indians. The word carried over into colloquial speech as a place of confinement and was applied to pitchers, who were restricted to their warm-up space until needed.[44] Besides this, at least three veterans of the Indian Wars went on to play professional baseball. One of them, John Grimes, played for the St. Louis Browns in 1897 and was also a veteran of the Spanish American War and World War I.

Baseball Wars

While baseball had been enlisted in America's wars and military expeditions, wars also raged within the sport itself. The first was waged through the 1860s, when the entrenched amateur game resisted the rise of professional baseball.

Founded in 1858, the National Association of Base Ball Players (NABBP) warned that professionalism (paying ballplayers) would ruin the sport: the profit motive would induce corruption and wrest baseball from the people, and pro athletes would lose their love of the game. While the NABBP had organized hundreds of amateur clubs, a few professional teams had emerged by 1870. Nicholas Young, a Civil War veteran, had converted from cricket during the war and became an active baseball player. He was instrumental in winning baseball's first war. In 1871, when the amateur NABBP threatened to expel a dozen professional teams, Young convened those clubs in revolt. They abruptly seceded from the NABBP and formed the National Association of *Professional* Base Ball *Players* (NAPBBP)—the first major league.[45]

But the baseball wars would continue. The NAPBBP was essentially organized and run by the players, at a time when American workers were viewed (as they still are today) as incompetent. The league had its ups and downs; however, it wasn't ineffectiveness but rather control that provoked further conflict. In 1875, Chicago White Stockings co-owner William Hulbert engineered a raid of Boston Red Stockings players, including its star pitcher Albert Spalding. Hulbert turned this attack into a second baseball war and ultimately a coup against the NAPBBP, after which he formed the National League of Professional Baseball *Clubs*. This revolutionized professional baseball—transferring ownership of the teams and the game from the players to new owners, who fancied themselves as industrial magnates. The baseball Robber Barons won the initial war against the players, although their policies would provoke many future battles.[46]

With the NAPBBP's demise, Nicholas Young jumped to the National League, which he eventually led. William Hulbert served as its first president, from 1876 to 1882. But soon the real power behind the National League was Albert Spalding, who led its owners in the coming baseball wars over the next two decades. In 1882 a new major league, the American Association, emerged as the National League's first real competition. In the First Association War, the Beer and Whiskey League (so called for its willingness to serve alcohol at ballgames) survived the National League's battle to destroy it, and a peace treaty—the National Agreement—was signed in 1883.[47] The National League was more successful in 1884 in fighting the Union Association War, completely beating back another competing league.

By 1885, conflict opened on another front. While the American Association initially championed the players to lure them to their new league, it abruptly reneged when it made peace with the National League. Both leagues were then accused of exploiting the players, cutting their pay, ignoring their conditions, and undermining their mobility. As a result, in 1885 the players formed the first baseball union, the Brotherhood of Professional Baseball Players. Led by the player-attorney John Montgomery Ward, the union arose amid the fierce labor-management disputes in the broader American society. Ward complained that players were being treated like "chattel" and vowed to improve their situation.[48]

Battles were fought in courtrooms and locker rooms for several years. Finally, the skirmishes provoked yet another full-scale baseball war. In 1890, under Ward's leadership, the Player's League (PL) was founded—symbolically on the historic Bastille Day of the French Revolution. The PL promoted the idea—revolutionary both inside and outside baseball—that workers could run their own workplaces, without the bosses. Inducing the best National League and American Association players to jump to the new league, the PL ran a full schedule of games, threatening the other leagues and outdrawing them in attendance.[49]

In response, Spalding formed a "War Committee" to fight the Brotherhood War. Relying on years of accumulated influence, Spalding turned the media against the Players League and poisoned popular opinion about its players. Referencing the ballplayers' working-class backgrounds, Cincinnati sportswriter Oliver Caylor applied the typical red-baiting perspective: "It is wonderful that these poor oppressed souls [the Brotherhood ballplayers] could not arrange a procession under a red flag and go through the streets shouting 'Bread or Blood!' . . . the men who kicked most against the reserve rule [blocking player mobility] are men from the slums, who were street loafers before playing ball; men who [were] a burden on the community and who would fall to the same level if baseball were wiped out tomorrow." The renowned sportswriter (and Spalding Company employee) Henry Chadwick simply called the protesting ballplayers "terrorists." Spalding accused the union leaders of "a system of terrorism peculiar to revolutionary movements."[50]

As baseball's master strategist, Spalding outmaneuvered the Player's League through some last-minute deals and dirty tricks. In the end, some PL backers were lured over to the National League with promises of new franchises. Consciously emulating Civil War General Ulysses S. Grant, Spalding demanded "unconditional surrender," and he got it: the PL folded after only a year. Flush with this victory, Spalding then launched a sneak attack in 1891 against his partner, in the Second American Association War, and conquered that rival league in what Bob Bailey has called the Forgotten War. Revealingly, National League president Nick Young observed, "Many people think the National League bought peace dearly in paying $130,000 [for the clubs it bought out], but . . . the price was cheap. We will save nearly all of that in [reduced] salaries with competition removed." Beginning in 1892, the National League would reign unchallenged for a decade.[51]

Given baseball's growing relationship with the U.S. military, it's not surprising its own conflicts would adopt a military vocabulary. One of those shared terms—*raids*—has a curious history. Beginning with William Hulbert's assault on the Red Stockings, new and existing leagues raided each other for players as a part of their ongoing battles. These early raids set the stage for future cases: the American League raids on the National League in 1900, the Federal League's raids on MLB in 1914, the Mexican League raids on MLB in 1946, and MLB's *raids* on the Negro Leagues beginning in 1947. MLB would also raid foreign leagues in the decades ahead, including those in Cuba, Venezuela, and the Dominican Republic.

In the late nineteenth century, there was one final raid of note: In 1891, before the league's demise, the American Association's Philadelphia Athletics failed to "reserve" two of its players, who jumped to National League teams. One of them signed with Pittsburgh, which had gone by the name Alleghenys. In response to the perceived raid, the Athletics angrily condemned the Pittsburgh club as Pirates, and the nickname stuck in a city hundreds of miles from the sea.[52] Baseball's attachment to U.S. wars and the American military would intensify by the turn of the nineteenth century and begin merging with the U.S. missionary impulse abroad and a long history of military interventions in foreign lands.

2

Missionaries Abroad
(1888–1897)

Although less aggressive and more modest than other late-nineteenth-century adventures in American imperialism, Spalding's gambit clearly aimed to extend an American presence in the world
—Peter Levine

America was well on its way to becoming an empire, and its new upsurge in imperialism by 1900 reached deep into American culture, economy, and intellectual life. Historian Frederick Turner announced the closing of the American frontier, and thus others were sought. Minister Josiah Strong led the church's pursuit of the missionary frontier, which sent Protestant legions abroad. The writer Brooks Adams charted an explicitly expansionist United States foreign policy. Admiral Alfred Mahan laid out the strategic basis for the American navy. And the philosopher Herbert Spencer ingrained notions of social Darwinism, including white America's superiority over other races. Economically, empire was propelled by the pursuit of overseas markets and the extraction of foreign resources—partly to ward off revolution in the United States by enlarging the economic pie. To accomplish these ends, Hawaii was pursued, for example, as the gateway to Asian markets, and Nicaragua was initially designated for an Atlantic-to-Pacific canal. Many other nations would be targeted as well.[1]

Troops, corporations, and churches were not the only U.S. emissaries overseas. American missionary zeal was also passionately expressed through baseball. According to Joel Zoss and John Bowman, "along with the confidence it had the one true religion and the one true economic system, Americans believed they had the one true sport—baseball." The sport was central, as David Voigt has suggested, to the fervent belief "that American culture is so perfect that its major elements ought to be exported so that all peoples . . . might gain by conforming to our system."[2] The resulting baseball missions were often described as "invasions of foreign territory."

The Baseball Gospel

While organized professional baseball had only emerged in 1871, already by 1874 it launched its first foreign tour to England and Ireland to spread the baseball creed. Led by Boston Red Stockings manager Harry Wright to demonstrate the "virtues of the American way," the tour fizzled. According to David Voigt, "the game of baseball and the aggressive, win-at-all costs attitude of the Americans were just too foreign for the English to accept."[3] Foreign tours were again pursued in 1879 and 1886, both to Cuba. The first also failed, but the second, featuring games between the Philadelphia Athletics and Philadelphia Phillies, was modestly successful in attracting fans.

Not long after, baseball launched a far more ambitious mission—the 1888 World Tour, organized by Albert Spalding, who, having conquered America, sought to be part of the "Great Power game of imperialism."[4] While deadly serious in his goals, Spalding was nevertheless a huckster in many ways. In turning his tour into a "grand production sure to capture the public's imagination," Spalding followed showman P.T. Barnum's rules for fooling the people and accumulating wealth.[5] Expanding his own sporting goods empire was not the least of Spalding's objectives for the tour—implant the game abroad, he reasoned, and equipment would have to be bought from someone like him.

The mission began with a crucial endorsement: "For purposes of wrapping the game in the flag," it was necessary to get President Grover Cleveland's approval. Duly validated by the White House, the tour headed to San Francisco for its first games. The trip featured a group of "working-class heroes"— ballplayers organized into two teams: the Chicago White Stockings, led by Cap Anson, and an All-American team captained by John Montgomery Ward. Curiously, players were recruited with the slogan "Join the Majors, See the World." Substitute the word *Navy* for *Majors* and you have one of today's main advertising taglines for the U.S. armed forces.[6]

The tour was permeated by racism. After its visit to San Francisco's Chinatown, an accompanying reporter, Harry Palmer, wrote that he was glad "to again breathe the air of a Christianized and civilized community." Indicative of the era's racial climate, the Chinese Exclusion Act had been passed only a few years earlier. Anson, the White Stockings captain, was already a well-known racist: his protest against African Americans drove black ballplayers from the game until Jackie Robinson's 1947 signing. The tour also carried a tangible symbol of racism: a black midget mascot, Charles Duvall, who was repeatedly baited and prodded into performing like a monkey. Spalding believed baseball was a "civilizing force" and the tour was part of America's mission to bring progress to more "backward peoples." Likewise, a *New York Times* editorial asked, approvingly, "Who shall say that baseball has not a mission for mankind?" And in *Sporting Life,* Francis Richter claimed that "baseball [reflects] the qualities that make the American man the most highly-organized, civilized being on earth."[7]

The tour's first foreign stop was Hawaii. Characterized as the "protectorate of prejudice," the Islands had become an American domain via an 1875 treaty. Secretary of State Thomas Bayard had advised, "Let the islands fill up with American planters and industries until they should be wholly identified with the U.S. It was simply a matter of waiting until the apple should fall." In 1887, the Bayonet Constitution was imposed on King Kalakaua by the white, largely American elites, who stripped him of power. Due to the exploitation of Hawaii's sugar production, the islanders were increasingly impoverished and dependent on the United States. When the king died in 1891, Queen Liliuokalani reasserted Hawaiian independence. But in 1893, a coup led by U.S. businessmen and the U.S. Marines overthrew the queen, and Sanford Dole (of the Dole fruit company) was made president in rigged elections.[8] Senator Henry Cabot Lodge supported Hawaii's annexation to the United States, proudly claiming that "we have a record of conquest, colonization and territorial expansion unequaled by any people in the nineteenth century."

When Spalding's tour arrived in Hawaii in 1888, no games could be played because U.S. missionaries had imposed Sunday blue laws there. Looking back on this brief stop, Spalding claimed the Hawaiian "heathens" were too dimwitted to understand America's pastime. Yet actually baseball had been played in Hawaii as early as the 1840s, when it was introduced at the Punahou School. Punahou students comprised a who's who of eventual business elites, including the main plantation owners (Dole, Castle, and Cooke), whose families eventually engineered the U.S. coup. Baseball was promoted for Anglos and natives alike, and in 1849 the game was further bolstered by Alexander Cartwright, who made Hawaii his final stop westward, after establishing baseball on the East Coast.[9] In 1875, the Hawaiian League was formed, and baseball was played on King Kamehameha Day between the Hawaiian infantry and cavalry. In 1879, the future Chinese revolutionary Sun Yat-sen moved to Hawaii, where he learned baseball, which he later used to help promote his political movement in China.

The troupe's next stops were in New Zealand and Australia. The local press claimed that baseball displayed "all those essentials of manliness, courage, nerve, pluck and endurance, characteristic of the Anglo Saxon race." In New

Zealand, the game had first arrived a few years earlier and, ironically, had been promoted again only weeks before Spalding's arrival by the black Hicks Sawyer Minstrel Company. Baseball may have been brought to Australia as early as 1857 by U.S. prospectors and merchants. Others claimed the first game wasn't played until 1878, by local cricket clubs. In 1879, the first Australian baseball team was formed and in 1884 Joseph Quinn began a seventeen-year career as the first Australian in the U.S. major leagues. Some worried that baseball threatened cricket and the Australian identity—challenging its strong attachment to British values. Even so, the tour was a big hit. Hundreds of new players took up the game and the Victoria Baseball League was founded. And by the time Spalding left Australia, he already had sporting goods outlets started in Melbourne, Sydney, and Adelaide.[10]

Flush with success, the tour headed for Asia. Upon arriving in Ceylon, John Tener—a pitcher and future National League president and Pennsylvania governor—complained, "They are nearly all darkies and after awhile you get tired of looking at them and hearing their funny talk." Noting the Ceylonese reception to baseball, the U.S. reporter Newton Macmillan wrote with disdain, "They regarded the whole thing as a joke, for to the Indian mind nothing is more absurd than athletics. To the Oriental, perfect repose is the ideal state. The chasing of a fly ball to him is the sheerest folly." The tourists "were happy to reduce foreign peoples and places to stereotypes."[11] It would be an attitude that would also characterize America's foreign policies.

At their next destination, Egypt, the players encountered other Americans. During the French suppression of the Algerian insurrection in 1883, a U.S. ship had landed in Algiers, where American sailors played baseball. Now, perhaps foreshadowing America's eventual Middle East obsession, the warship USS *Essex* was docked in Cairo, and Spalding's players toured the vessel. As for the Egyptians, they were described by their "general shiftlessness," which made them "the most thorough antique of all the antiquities of the nineteenth century," and either "exotic inhabitants of a beautiful and historical land, or barbarians existing in backwardness." Spalding decided the pyramids would make a good backstop, and thus a diamond was formed in the shifting sand just south of the Cheops pyramid. Besides playing the game, team members tried throwing balls over the pyramids. Then each player took a shot at hitting the Great Sphinx in the eye. Although the locals jeered the troupe, Spalding had no compunction in reporting that the spectacle had "horrified the native worshippers of Cheops and the dead Pharaohs." This demeanor reflected the Americans' "cavalier attitude toward non-Western cultures." As Mark Lamster put it, "The Americans had arrived, and they conquered.[12]

Not surprisingly, baseball didn't catch on in Egypt. Spalding blamed it on native backwardness, claiming, "In a country where they use a stick for a plow and hitch a donkey and a camel together to draw it . . . it is hardly reasonable to expect that the modern game of baseball will become one of its sports" (yet that's exactly what Spalding *had* been expecting). According to Thomas Zeiler, "Baseball players, like other white Americans, drew the color barrier inside and outside the U.S., as they dreamed of imperialism and cultural superiority." Most of the players were first- or second-generation emigrants themselves, yet they took on the racial attitudes of Anglo-Saxon elites.[13]

Meanwhile, before leaving Cairo, John Montgomery Ward—the baseball union president—received some disturbing news. While he was gone, the National League was imposing pay cuts and the Brush classification plan, a divisive hierarchy of player salaries. Ward realized he had been duped by Spalding into being absent on the home front in what was later dubbed the Plot Heard Round the World. Spalding—the "master of misrepresentation"—knew it would be convenient to have Ward thousands of miles away.[14] Ward left for home as soon as he could.

As the tour headed for Europe, a traveling reporter wrote, "Only one continent remains to be subjugated by the American baseball bat. When the Spalding party steams up New York harbor in April they will serve up the whole earth on home plate." Eagerly anticipating their escape from backwardness, the tour was surprised to discover that in Europe the Americans were viewed as inferior. At their first European stop in Italy, even the U.S. minister in Rome, John Stallo, didn't take them very seriously, saying, "I have never been interested in athletics and [will not] have my good name used for mercenary purposes."[15] Perhaps Spalding had too crassly intimated his desire for financial gain. The tour visited the Vatican, but then Spalding requested a game at Rome's Coliseum. This appalled the working archeologists there, and the tourists beat a hasty exit.

After a stop in Naples, the ballplayers moved on to France. Still smarting from their humiliating defeat in the Franco-Prussian War, the French were nursing a sense of physical inadequacy. A reward had been offered to introduce a new sport that would rejuvenate French fitness and virility. Naturally Spalding proposed baseball, arguing that it had healed wartime wounds and restored American masculinity after the U.S. Civil War. The French were persuaded to watch the tour's two teams, including games played in the shadow of the Eiffel Tower. Some Frenchmen found baseball hard to follow; others insisted France had been playing a version of the game as far back as the Middle Ages.[16]

Spalding blamed baseball's lukewarm reception on natural French and Italian shortcomings, particularly their smaller stature compared to the English, Australians, and Americans. Elsewhere, Spalding attributed it to language: "Wherever English is spoken, baseball will take root." Apparently, English equaled civilization, which in turn equaled baseball. The *New York Herald* further explained why the Continentals had resisted: They were "too impatient and impulsive to undertake that study of the game that is necessary."[17]

The tour eventually made its final stops in England and Ireland, as the mission moved into 1889. Buffalo Bill Cody's Wild West Show had enjoyed immense popularity crisscrossing the United States, reenacting the white conquest of the Indians, who were displayed as primitives.[18] The show had also just completed a sensational European tour, and Spalding was determined to turn baseball and his troupe into a similar extravaganza. He insisted that baseball, like America itself, be kept "free from the trammels of English customs," but he couldn't dispel the common British claim that baseball was merely a version of English rounders. The U.S. teams played in several British cities to a mixed reception. Reacting to the low game attendance, Cap Anson claimed that for Britons baseball "possesses too many elements of dash and danger and requires too much of an effort to play it." Even so, the Prince of Wales watched a game at the Kennington Oval, and the National Baseball League of Great Britain was soon formed—with teams sometimes coached by visiting Americans.[19] Other leagues would follow. Having the tour end in Ireland was special for the many U.S. players with Irish backgrounds. Their American baseball received a polite, if not overly enthusiastic, reception.

In April 1889, the World Tour members sailed into New York harbor, greeted by a welcoming crowd.[20] Held up as exemplars of American patriotism and exceptionalism, the players were lavishly toasted, not only in New York, but also in Philadelphia, Boston, Baltimore, Pittsburgh, and Chicago. The first celebration, at New York's plush Delmonico's Restaurant, featured three hundred celebrities—including Theodore Roosevelt and Mark Twain. The banquet was served in nine innings and seasoned by skits from the renowned actor DeWolf Hopper, famous for his theatrical renditions of "Casey at the Bat."

The all-male event was hosted by A.G. Mills, the National League president and Spalding crony, who hailed the tour as proof of how civilized Americans were compared to everyone else. Mills praised the players as "gladiators . . . covered with their American manhood." He asserted the purely U.S. lineage of baseball: "patriotism and research had established that the game . . . was American in origin." This elicited thunderous applause from a group aching to believe baseball was homegrown and not merely an English spin-off. Cries of "No rounders! No rounders! No rounders!" went up in the crowd.

In another ten years, Mark Twain would ardently oppose American aggression abroad, the bloody U.S. occupation of the Philippines in particular. Yet at the 1889 Delmonico dinner, Twain seemed to endorse American expansionism, praising the ballplayers who have "carried the American name to the uttermost parts of the earth—and covered it with glory." Instead of seeing the tour as part of the rapacious capitalism of that Gilded Age, Twain celebrated the baseball crusade as "the very symbol, the outward and visible expression of the drive, and push, and rush, and struggle of the raging, tearing, booming nineteenth century."

The attorney and lobbyist Chauncey Depew was well known for having bought more than one state legislature for the railroad industry. His Delmonico speech, "The Invasion of the Old World by the American Ball Players," lauded baseball's participation in the "manly arts": "When the American game circled the globe the effete monarchs of the East and the mighty powers of the West bowed their heads in humility and rose in acclaim." The Honorable Daniel Dougherty noted that "the tourists [had] an athletic spirit that prepared American men for the future defense of the country against foreign foes." Colonel A.K. McClure lauded baseball's code of ethics, which was "doing missionary work every day of its existence." Despite the tour's mixed success on the ground, Spalding "unhesitatingly pronounce[d] base-ball to become the universal athletic sport of the world."[21]

At the Philadelphia banquet, the politician John Rogers claimed the tour had carried baseball "where even our flag has not been, as a great American institution." In this, baseball's auxiliary role for the military would have been hard to miss. The tour solidified baseball's "place in . . . Americanizing the world through a U.S. empire of sport." On the mission's final stop in Chicago, Mayor Henry Turner urged the crowd to help "God in building up a country of men such as this. Long life to baseball. Long life to the National Guard. Long life to America, the freest land on earth."[22] God, country, the military, and baseball—all in it together.

Baseball's Early Globalization

In its attempt to promote baseball, the Spalding World Tour won some converts, but not many. Its failure to firmly implant baseball in the places it visited may have stemmed, ironically, from Spalding's success in so strongly identifying the game with America. While this shored up baseball's status in the United States, it discouraged other nations—patriotic in their own right—from adopting it as their own. And in the cultural competition between the New World and Old Europe, the Europeans may have been serving notice: the young power across the Atlantic must wait its turn at the helm of global leadership.[23]

Yet economically, the American moment was about to arrive. While financially the World Tour only broke even in the short run, Spalding dramatically expanded his empire, linking his own name unmistakably to baseball around the world. While the sport didn't immediately take hold overseas, baseball was playing a different role. Spalding's mission was an early example of globalization. By the early twentieth century, his sporting goods stores could be found in dozens of American and foreign cities—and the Spalding Company still thrives today.

At home, the World Tour was excellent public relations for baseball. In their impending battles, it helped magnates control the players and break their union. Advocating for club owners, the media condemned the players for undermining baseball—now the "global game"—with their unreasonable demands. Union head John Montgomery Ward hoped baseball would stand for justice and fair dealing, but this clashed with globalization's pseudo-free-market crassness—and globalization was the realm in which Spalding had just placed baseball. Spalding was an industrial tycoon—a dominant capitalist in a system that rolled over weaklings and competitors alike. It was the model not only for the U.S. economy but the one it would project onto the world. Many of the aggressive qualities attributed to both baseball and the military were also common to business.[24]

As Bill Brown has observed, baseball would become "a medium for eliminating differences" that would reduce other cultures to "an American global village." Spalding's trip was a model for other industries going abroad. New markets were needed, and imperial conquests offered the solution; such interventions were rationalized by social Darwinism, in the "interests of civilization and humanity" and to proliferate the American dream. As Mark Lamster has suggested, while Spalding's tourists might have been an unlikely corps of cultural diplomats, they nevertheless paved the way for a future when American products and entertainment would dominate world markets.[25]

By 1900, the *Boston Herald* claimed that "next to Abraham Lincoln and George Washington, the name of A.G. Spalding is the most famous." Besides dominating the baseball world, Spalding became a Republican senatorial candidate and even a presidential hopeful. But his most lasting legacy was his tour's symbolic meaning. Less than twenty years after hailing Spalding's world mission at Delmonico's, President Theodore Roosevelt sent the U.S. "Great White Fleet" on a similar trip. At the turn of the century, baseball teams routinely appeared at missionary outposts and military bases in resource-rich, underdeveloped nations. The players might be American or they might be natives—as the U.S. increasingly introduced baseball as a "colonial" pastime.[26]

Baseball Imperialism

While baseball began practicing its own globalization, even more so did it help expand the global reach of American corporations and U.S. military missions abroad. The best conquest would be "where there has been no conquest at all but where alien people are profoundly changed by the mere impact of American civilization."[27] Such were the words of Theodore Roosevelt, who was more likely in practice to pursue another means of American intervention: military invasions. Either way, baseball was prominently involved, not only in the training for war but in actual wars and other military conflicts. It was used as a diversion and as a means of pacification and social control by the U.S. military and American companies in those lands they assaulted and often successfully occupied.

As Thomas Zeiler has observed, baseball actually took hold more "in places the [Spalding] tour had not reached, such as Japan and the Caribbean. . . . These were nations of color (and non-English speaking) rather than the white imperial outposts so lauded by the tourists." According to Joel Zoss and John Bowman, "The countries where baseball is most popular today [are] those . . . where the U.S. has maintained a strong military, business or political presence since the late nineteenth century." In the end, Spalding adjusted his perspective: "the United States has no lands or tribes to conquer but it is only to be expected that Base Ball will invade our new possessions and [demonstrate] that possession's American-ness."[28] This might be accomplished diplomatically or by civilian missions (such as Spalding's), but more likely it would require force: U.S. military interventions "for the victims' own good." As a result, a struggle between dominance and resistance would play out in both Asia and the Caribbean.

In Asia, the United States set its sights eventually on the Philippines, but first on China and especially Japan. In 1853, U.S. Commodore Matthew Perry forced a Japanese opening to the West, and Japan absorbed various Western influences. Baseball was among the earliest cultural intrusions. American expatriates began promoting the game informally in 1863, and in 1872 Horace Wilson, a U.S. Civil War veteran, introduced baseball at Tokyo University. American teacher Albert Bates ran the first formal game the following year. Practicing the game was viewed as an entrée into the American fighting spirit. Baseball quickly caught on because it embodied the spirit of *wa*—the willingness to sacrifice oneself for the group.[29]

In 1877, future (U.S.) National League president Nick Young was asked to develop the first Japanese league and become its commissioner (he declined). The first formal Japanese ball club wasn't formed until the following year, when Hiroshi Hiroaka—formerly a student in the United States—organized the Shinbashi Athletics. While Albert Spalding left Japan out of his World Tour, he nevertheless sent baseball equipment in 1884 to address the shortage and help market the game. Despite the sometimes democratic rhetoric, racism still permeated America's treatment of the Japanese: in 1891 an American team in Japan, the Yokohama Athletic Club, rebuffed challenges from Japanese teams, calling them inferior and unworthy. When a Japanese team—the First Higher School (Ichiko)—finally got a game against Meiji Gakuin—an American school run by Christian missionaries—it suffered a humiliating loss, which came to symbolize America's unwelcome intrusion into Japanese culture. The large U.S. presence, protected by the long-term docking of the U.S. Pacific Fleet, promoted baseball's widespread diffusion. Spreading through the increase in trans-Pacific maritime traffic, baseball was the first American cultural export in this early era of globalization.[30]

Gradually, more U.S. teams played Japanese clubs in the 1890s. In 1896, Ichiko finally got its contest against the Yokohama Athletic Club and beat it badly, the same year Ned Hanlon's Orioles were winning their third straight pennant in the U.S. National League and Wee Willie Keeler was pioneering the Baltimore chop. The Japanese triumph "against a proud foreign team produced all the glory of a military victory." Japanese students believed the humiliating legacy of foreign settlements required retribution; baseball could provide their revenge.[31] Ichiko beat Yokohama in three rematches, and in 1897, another Japanese club beat the team from the USS *Olympia*, which would soon become Admiral George Dewey's flagship in the U.S. invasion of Manila.

While Americans still viewed the Japanese condescendingly, these victories were significant to the Japanese. They owed a great debt to warrior traditions; skilled baseball batters emulated samurai swordsmen. Baseball embodied the Japanese civic values of order, harmony, perseverance, and self-restraint. "The aggressive character of our national spirit is well-established," it was claimed, "as demonstrated first in [our 1894–95] Sino-Japanese War [victory] and now by our great victories in baseball." This began Japan's use of baseball to establish a national identity—its use to its own advantage of a mechanism intended for its own control. As Gerald Gems has suggested, baseball "provided a comparative tool [for] the Japanese to measure their worthiness to assume Asian leadership and a place among the world's powers." As the U.S. and European nations colonized the globe, "Japan developed imperial visions of its own," which it later imposed in places such as Taiwan, Korea, Manchuria, and Pearl Harbor.[32]

Halfway around the world, the United States had long since claimed imperial rights over the nations of the Western hemisphere. The U.S. had an early obsession with Cuba, in particular, and baseball played a central role. By 1850, America had already made three attempts to annex Cuba from Spain, whose stubborn grasp did little to deter the continuing U.S. business and military quest for control. In 1864, after studying in the United States, Nemesio Guillo introduced baseball to Cuba. In 1866, baseball was given a bigger boost when sailors from a U.S. naval ship docked in Matanzas Bay and demonstrated the game. It caught on quickly among Cuban dockhands, even though they resented repeated American attempts to sell them baseball equipment.

In 1868, the Havana Baseball Club was formed, partly for baseball's ability to produce "virtuous, robust citizens adept at struggle" and to help prepare young boys to fight for the nation. Home-grown wars for Cuban independence from Spain had already begun. In 1869, the Spanish government imposed the first of several bans on baseball, which competed with bullfighting as the Cuban national sport and which symbolized "dangerous" notions of freedom and egalitarianism. Indeed, baseball caught on partly because it was anti-Spanish and could be given a uniquely Cuban flavor. Of course, while most Cubans had their eyes on one imperial power (Spain), another one (the United States) was sneaking up behind it. As Adrian Burgos has observed, "Baseball's [existing] popularity among the new subjects in the Spanish-speaking Caribbean worked hand in hand with the [American] imperial project."[33]

Esteban Bellan became the first Cuban to play in the U.S. major leagues in 1871 when he joined the Troy Haymakers. In 1874, the first official professional baseball game was played at Matanzas and in 1878, the Hop Bitters from Rochester, New York, barnstormed Cuba, distributing American flags at each stop. The Spanish authorities quickly intervened, worrying that it would encourage the Cubans to rebel.[34] They were right, though it was not so much the flags but rather the baseball that lent concrete support to the rebellion.

In 1878, the Cuban Professional League was formed—the first baseball league outside the United States. Besides playing baseball, the new league had a startling political purpose: profits were funneled to guerrilla groups fighting for Cuban independence. It was baseball as *lucha*, or struggle. The league contributed not only money but also soldiers: many top players joined the revolutionary army as officers, and at least two ballplayers (and future Cuban Hall of Famers), Jose Pastoriza and Ricardo Cabaleiro, gave their lives as rebels.[35]

According to Peter Bjarkman, "building national pride on the battlefield [of] the baseball diamond . . . enjoys a rich history [and] . . . the island's professional league and its status as a sovereign nation were born hand in hand" in the late 1870s, well before Cuba's actual independence. Through the 1880s and beyond, Cubans associated baseball with freedom and democracy, if not

in practice, then at least as an ideal. The game was inimical to the inherited social privilege of the Spanish regime. Some worried that the growing baseball
professionalism might compete too much with the sport's larger objective, the
nationalist cause. According to Aurelio Miranda, founder of the Havana Base
Ball Club, the game was a classroom—teaching patience, tactics, and strategy.
Cuban teams adopted revolutionary names or those of national heroes. Team
meetings and practices fomented revolutionary fervor, and in 1881 the Spanish government disbanded the Cardenas ballclub for such activities.[36]

During the next decade, a slew of U.S. companies entered Cuba, quietly
launching operations in the shadow of the Spanish regime. By the mid-1880s,
while Spain still held political control, Cuba was—according to U.S. Consul
Ramon Williams—"already inside the commercial union of the United
States." In this period, U.S. Protestant missionaries descended on Cuba in
great numbers, challenging Spanish Catholicism. American ballplayers began
to arrive, seeking spots on Cuban teams. For many Cubans, America represented possible liberation from Spain, although some worried about allowing
U.S. players on their baseball clubs. In 1886, the Philadelphia Athletics became
the first major-league team to tour Cuba. In 1887, the Key West League in
Florida was formed by exiled Cubans who supported the revolution.

In 1890, the New York Giants toured Cuba, followed by many other barnstormers. In 1892, Carlos Ayala, *Sporting Life*'s Cuban correspondent, wrote
that baseball could unite the Cuban masses on the island and in exile against
Spanish despotism by acting as a social leveler, to bind Cubans across race,
class, and gender. Women were encouraged to participate as players and fans,
thus bringing them into the nationalist cause. But in the 1890s, U.S. companies intensified their island invasion, with a different purpose for baseball in
mind. Shipping and sugar firms proliferated, as well as the American Gas Light
Company, Bethlehem Steel, and Pennsylvania Steel. American corporations
promoted baseball to build popular support and as a diversion from the exploitative labor conditions they had imposed. For the Spanish regime, however, baseball meant revolution, not social control. In 1894, Cuban émigré
Augustin Molina lived in Key West and traveled to Cuba ostensibly to play
baseball, but he was actually a spy, carrying secret nationalist documents.
When he was caught later that year, Spain again banned baseball, canceling the
Cuban League's 1894–95 season.[37]

In 1895, Louis Someillan, another Cuban *Sporting Life* reporter, was arrested
as an insurgent collaborator, provoking a strong editorial: "A Cuban patriot of
Havana has been unjustly and barbarously condemned by a biased Spanish
Court to imprisonment for life for participating in the Cuban rebellion."[38]
This was not the first foray by the normally apolitical U.S. sporting press into

the Cuban revolutionary situation. Nor was Someillan alone. That same year, Emilio Sabourin, a Cuban League founder and revolutionary predecessor to Fidel Castro, was sentenced to life in prison in Morocco, where he died of malnutrition two years later.

Another Castro forerunner was José Martí, the Cuban revolutionary leader in the 1890s. While in exile in the United States, he became fascinated by baseball: "In every neighborhood there is a baseball game. Children in New York like baseball and pistols more than they like books. They go into the streets and hide from the police to play baseball in the courtyards." Back in Cuba, baseball contests were held to raise funds for Martí's movement. In 1897, on the eve of the Spanish-American War, Abel Linares—a Cuban League official—led an all-white Cuban team on a U.S. barnstorming tour. Linares was also the secretary of the Martí Society, which fronted Cuba's revolutionary movement.[39] Not merely for baseball, the tour was public relations to secure American support for Cuban independence.

By the mid-1890s, baseball had become even more closely associated with Cuban national identity, if not Cuban masculinity, thus fulfilling a role the sport also played in Japan and America. While the United States had often imposed baseball as a "civilizing" influence on other nations, Cubans viewed the game as a civilizing balm against Spanish tyrants—symbolized by the barbaric sport of bullfighting. Cubans realized that through cultural practices they could wage battle against colonial rulers. A sport can promote empire and social control but can also foment liberation and nationalism. In *Beyond a Boundary*, C.L.R. James showed how cricket was used to resist British imperialism in Trinidad.[40] For Cuba, it was baseball. It's true that José Martí worried not merely about the Spanish empire, but also about the American. But to reject baseball, especially its political role, merely because of its American origins would have tossed away something important to Cuban culture.

Elsewhere in the Caribbean, U.S. economic, political, and military interventions also proliferated. In 1866, the United States recognized Dominican independence, but by 1870 U.S. President Ulysses S. Grant sought to annex the new nation. He failed, but American companies invaded nevertheless, buying up huge tracts of Dominican lands. Transplanted Americans brought baseball with them, but the sport was promoted by Cubans as well: many of them were there in exile from the Ten Year War (1868–1878) against Spain— the first attempt at Cuban independence. By 1891, a wave of West Indians had arrived as well, bringing their own game, cricket. Most Cubans and West Indians worked in the Dominican sugar industry, where the competing sports fought it out. With the sugar business almost entirely controlled by U.S. firms, baseball ultimately won. Anthropologist Alan Klein called it sugarball and observed, "Some aspects of the colonial legacy (first Spain, now the United States) are unquestionably oppressive, such as the exploitative system built around [sugar] production. In other areas foreign domination seems more benign; [such as] baseball. But baseball is inextricably bound up with [sugar] production. It's . . . a microcosm of Dominican-American relations."[41]

Exiled Cubans exported baseball to other destinations as well. Some went to the Yucatán, where they helped establish a separate baseball culture in 1890. Other Cubans landed in Venezuela; Emilio Cramer demonstrated baseball there in the early 1890s, helping form the Caracas Base-Ball Club. Puerto Rico became another baseball hotbed, with the usual complement of U.S. interventions. The American military helped implant the game when it arrived to promote U.S. business interests on the island. But again the Cubans were involved, since some had fled to Puerto Rico to escape repression at home. Baseball was played there in the 1890s, but it may have arrived much earlier. As the Puerto Rican major leaguer Rubén Gómez claimed, "Don't say the U.S. Marines [brought] baseball. Oh no, this game, it's in our blood! The [Caguana] Indians played baseball at Utuado [site of a pre-Hispanic ceremonial playing ground]."

The United States had less help bringing baseball to other parts of Latin America. In Panama, the U.S. military first intervened in 1856, after which baseball was sporadically imported and then more permanently implanted when the U.S. Navy landed again in 1885. The sport blossomed at the end of the century when U.S. intervention intensified to build the Panama Canal. Baseball may have arrived in the Virgin Islands in the 1860s when Confederate ships used the islands as a coaling station during the U.S. Civil War.[42] By 1881, baseball had spread all the way to Uruguay: officers of the USS *Brooklyn* played baseball against the cricket club in Montevideo.

In Nicaragua, the U.S. Marines first invaded in 1847 to "protect American property and interests." In 1855, the American William Walker attacked the nation and established a bloody slave republic, which the *New York Daily News* nevertheless applauded: "Los yankis have burst their way like a fertilizing torrent through the barriers of [Nicaraguan] barbarism." Several more U.S. military interventions ensued, including an 1887 incursion orchestrated by the U.S.-based United Fruit Company, which employed the Marines to secure additional Nicaraguan farmland. That same year, appalled at cricket's lingering presence, U.S. businessman Albert Adlesberg brought baseball to Nicaragua's Atlantic coast. In 1890, upper-class Nicaraguans studying in the United States introduced baseball to the nation's Pacific coast. Soon baseball took hold of Nicaraguan politics, lasting from the initial U.S. occupations well into the twentieth-century Somozan dictatorships.[43]

Baseball Militarism

In 1884, *Sporting Life* observed that while the United States, Ireland, and Great Britain had national games, the only one "known to continental nations is the game of war." Yet organized baseball asserted its martial masculinity and collectively signed on in support of America's own rapidly accumulating wars. It wanted to go even further: to become not merely an auxiliary but rather an integral part of the U.S. military system.[44]

According to Albert Spalding, "Base Ball is a combative game . . . in which every contestant is a general, who having a field of occupation, must defend it." This contrasted with cricket, which Spalding claimed was "a splendid game for Britons [which] they play . . . because it does not overtax their energy or thought. Cricket is a gentle pastime. Base Ball is War." Baseball games, according to the historian Harold Seymour, "resembled miniature wars more than athletic contests"—bloodless outlets for village-to-village warfare or battles between warring city-states.[45]

In sportswriter Henry Chadwick's 1889 book, *How to Play Base Ball*, military metaphors proliferated. He emphasized a "well-paced attack," with tactics coordinated by the captain, or "commander of the field." The "battery" (the pitcher and catcher) was to the team "what the battery of a regiment is to the line of the infantry." The pitcher, as the squad's artillerist, lays siege to the batting team's "home base" and "is the main reliance of the attacking force of the field corps," also known as infielders, who are the immediate supporting force of the battery and "the defenders of the citadel of the field." The success of the "field corps" depended on the catcher's ability "to stand the hot fire of the pitcher's delivery." The batter, too, "must face the hot fire courageously"; otherwise, the pitcher would "capture" him.[46]

While Chadwick used martial terms to describe nineteenth-century baseball, they were drawn from eighteenth-century warfare. Even though outdated, they had a dramatic effect in Chadwick's time. Athletic and martial values were merged so thoroughly that they became virtually indistinguishable. As David Lamoreaux has described, warfare was violent but also genteel. Battles were primarily sieges and tactics to occupy strategic points of enemy territory.

Likewise, in baseball the batting team pursues a constant war of maneuver. To make a successful advance, it tries to put the ball out of its enemy's reach. A hit baseball challenges the opponent's defenses, drawing his troops out of position and giving the batter a chance to occupy enemy territory; that is, the batter tries to get on base. Once on base, the runner remains close to the base for protection, occasionally feinting toward the next one and sometimes attempting to advance; that is, he tries to steal the next base and capture new territory. The "field corps" responds to hits and advances by recovering the vehicle of the assault (the ball) and getting it to the base in time. Pursuing these strategies was "mental combat," and by the 1890s they would emerge as the "scientific game" in baseball.

Success in baseball required what Chadwick called "a nine who work together with machine-like unity," which turned baseball practice into a "kind of West Point drill." A good soldier could endure a long war. Likewise, Chadwick observed that "ultimate success in a pennant race lies mainly with the team which can best stand the costly wear and tear of the campaign." This differs from football, which emphasizes a few critical battles; superior force is concentrated at a weak point to smash a hole in the enemy line. In the late 1800s, football and military strategies of this kind were regarded as uncivilized. Later, they would be commonplace, and baseball would be regarded as less manly than football.[47]

Besides flaunting baseball's martial characteristics, advocates claimed the sport developed good soldiers.[48] Newspapers praised teams for being "drilled to the perfection of soldiers" and for their "soldierly" uniforms. More instrumentally, baseball created men who could act and think "as able generals do in the life and death events of the battlefield." While the U.S. military had long viewed sports as useful for troop recreation and morale, it finally developed an athletic policy in the 1890s, injecting them into training and daily routines. Athletics helped promote physical fitness and "the heroic spirit."[49] Sports were integrated into the military academies, which quickly became competitive with the established Eastern colleges. Baseball was emphasized in particular.

According to army officer Edmund Butts, baseball taught team play and "prompt and individual action" together with "subservience to the united action of the company. . . . An able captain of a ball team will make an abler captain in the deadlier game of war." The U.S. Army adopted the Butts manual on baseball and other sports in 1893, and baseball was promoted at one army fort after another, with hundreds of contests played. Near Fort Apache, one game was stopped when the commander learned that Geronimo had escaped from the San Carlos reservation and his unit had to give chase. In 1896, U.S. Secretary of War Stephen Elkins claimed that baseball would become a "surrogate for war." A couple of years later, when the United States fought the Spanish-American War, baseball was credited for having trained American soldiers.

As David Voigt has observed, "America ranks at the top for having more time at war or military intervention than any other nation over the last two centuries," an average of at least one campaign a year for the past 230 years, and it has become baseball's "ongoing task to support every one." As the nineteenth century drew to a close, baseball championed American nationalism to enhance its claim as the national pastime. But in return, it accumulated onerous and stifling patriotic obligations. In the great conflicts yet to come, baseball was repeatedly "invoked to represent the moral and physical superiority of the U.S. and the purity of its mission. Its martial essence was resurrected in all its glory to restock the ideological arsenal."[50]

3

Small Wars and the Old Army Game
(1898–1909)

I congratulate the Army [for] showing that the great American game follows the flag, and that in addition to being mighty good fighters, [they] are equally good ball players. As a method of attracting to the service desirable soldiers, I believe it to be the greatest thing I have ever seen.
—Charles Weeghman

On the night of February 15, 1898, American sailors—including their ship's baseball team—rested comfortably on the USS *Maine* in the Havana, Cuba harbor. The team had won the Navy championship, and its players had been scouted by the major leagues. The club was scheduled to play Cuba's top ballplayers in a series of exhibitions. The African American fireman William Lambert was the star pitcher. Second baseman and team captain Bill Gorman had just written his mother, describing Cuba as *tranquillo*. C.H. Newton, the third baseman, played taps to signal "lights out" that night. A half hour later, a huge explosion ripped through the ship. Of the 353 sailors aboard, only 88 survived. Pitcher Lambert perished along with 22 other black sailors and all but one member of the baseball team, right fielder John Bloomer.[1]

The War of 1898

By the end of the 1890s, with the termination of the Indian Wars and the closing of the American frontier, the United States was in a rambunctious mood, seeking new vistas. It looked, increasingly, beyond its North American borders. Calling themselves expansionists, not imperialists, U.S. Navy Secretary Theodore Roosevelt and other American officials pushed for foreign intervention. There being no feasible outside threat with which to legitimize such an incursion, one had to be invented. The opportunity arrived in 1898 when the *Maine* blew up in Havana. Cuba's overlord became the new enemy, and the United States declared war on Spain with the additional pretext of promoting Cuban and Filipino independence.[2]

By this time, a U.S. media empire had emerged under William Randolph Hearst, whose newspapers were already notorious for their "yellow journalism"—slanting or falsifying the news to satisfy the demands of patriotism and prejudice. Spurred on by the equally sensationalist scandal sheets published by Joseph Pulitzer, no story—no matter how untrue—was spiked if it could sell newspapers and help Hearst promote his pet policies. More benignly, Hearst also pioneered the first regular sports section in any American newspaper (in his *New York Journal*) and baseball was featured in his flagship paper, the *San Francisco Examiner*. A few years earlier, the *Examiner* had published "Casey at the Bat," a baseball ballad by a young Harvard graduate, Ernest Lawrence Thayer, which has become one of America's most enduring poems.

Hearst's interest in sports, aggressively pursued, fit well with his own imperial ambitions. He lent the full weight of his publishing empire to combating American isolationism and persuading U.S. leaders to attack Spain in retaliation for America's lost ship. No matter that there was no evidence Spain had destroyed the *Maine*.[3] While the incident is disputed, Hearst allegedly dispatched a reporter to the scene, who claimed he saw no basis for a war. In response, Hearst cabled back: "You furnish me the pictures and I'll furnish the war." One of the first propaganda films, *Tearing Down the Spanish Flag*, was also produced, showing the American (not Cuban) flag replacing Spain's. Soon the Spanish-American War was launched under the slogan "Remember the *Maine*."

Americans may have been pushed into the war in part to avenge the deaths of the warship's baseball players, who were singled out as particular heroes of the "attack." Hearst's *Sunday Herald* eulogized them: "The sailors of the ill-fated *Maine* were great lovers of the national game, and [their] baseball team was the crack club of the fleet." Before and after the incident, the baseball press also weighed in. *Sporting Life* interviewed Frank Bancroft, a player who toured Cuba as far back as 1879. He claimed the barnstormers were "dyed-in-the-wool rooters for the Cubans in their struggle for independence from Spanish tyranny." Some major leaguers, such as star pitcher Clark Griffith, even claimed they'd take up arms to defend Cuba.[4]

The slogan *"¡Cuba Libre!"* became popular in the United States, including the baseball world. The support displayed little understanding of the situation, much less the ideological principles of José Martí and the Cuban nationalists, yet a certain fervor erupted nevertheless. In one incident, the Native American ballplayer Lou Sockalexis was threatened with violence on a train by U.S. servicemen, who mistook him for a Spaniard. Whatever the misconceptions, public opinion was actively cultivated to help justify U.S. aggression.[5]

The sporting press was also happy to champion the Cuban interests of baseball owners and entrepreneurs. Joining journalists, expansionists, and even religious evangelicals, prominent major league baseball (MLB) leaders advocated U.S. intervention, because "Spanish colonial rulers had been the main obstacle to the unfettered movement of baseball talent within America's transnational circuit." The prospect of opening Cuba to trade was very appealing. Like other American enterprises, sporting goods manufacturers anticipated a quick war, after which they could target Caribbean baseball aficionados. Dealers expected a booming sports market following the war.

Albert Spalding backed the war, always connecting it to the national pastime. Employing the rhetoric of empire, he wrote approvingly, "Baseball is war! It has followed the flag to the Philippines, to Porto Rico, and to Cuba." Spalding supported America's wars for expansion and was a major booster of the imperial spirit of the times, in which he hoped baseball could be enlisted. Sure enough, when Theodore Roosevelt led his Rough Riders up San Juan Hill to help "rescue" Cuba, riding with him were not only cowboys and frontiersmen but also ballplayers, whom he chose for their virility and courage. All told, at least thirty-two professional ballplayers served in the military during the war, including fourteen major leaguers.[6] Cap Huston, who would soon own the New York Yankees, played military baseball in Cuba during the war.

The war began and ended in 1898 and resembled a typical baseball season. According to David Voigt, the conflict was launched in April (when the baseball "war" also began), after the press assault on Spain, which had its counterpart in the "usual preseason breast-beating by various baseball club spokesmen." On May Day, a time of high hopes for all teams, Admiral Dewey defeated a Spanish flotilla at Manila. Over the next six weeks, a time "when writers maintained their ritual of watchful waiting in . . . a typical baseball race," Americans (on the East Coast, at least) anxiously anticipated a battle with a second Spanish fleet. In early June, "when a strong team often scores its final break-through," the American navy crushed the second Spanish fleet in the Santiago, Cuba, harbor. July ended with the surrender of Spanish arms, and August and September "found Americans occupying strong points, exploiting their victory." In baseball, these months would have "found a front-running club mopping up its opposition." October was a "time of celebration and benefits" for the baseball champs, followed by the greeting of returning soldiers, "who were flushed with easy victory."[7]

Not that the 1898 baseball season was entirely business as usual. The war upstaged baseball for a few weeks, during which there were empty stands and some financial losses—produced partly by the small war tax on ticket prices. Cincinnati owner John Brush urged local papers to post updates and war-news broadsides at ballparks, but publishers resisted this crass attempt to boost atten-dance. On the other hand, the *New York World* showed a paperboy outside a ballpark, hawking newspapers headlined *War Extra*, with a fan motioning him away: "Your true fan is not interested in such a trivial thing as war." Still, the season's final home games were poorly attended, and during the last contest in Boston, the players were jeered as "slackers" by uniformed veterans.[8] Even so, Frank Selee's Boston Beaneaters, led by Hugh Duffy and Jimmy Collins, won their third pennant since 1893.

Calling the conflict the Spanish-American War understates the prominent role Cubans played in gaining their own independence. The War of 1898 would be a more accurate name. But the United States viewed the Cubans as "squealing, watermelon-eating imbeciles and infants," akin to transplanted southern blacks or little children, who were incapable of ruling themselves. Cuba would have to become a U.S. colony, even if it "risked mimicking Eu-ropean [imperialist] behavior." Thus, the U.S. installed an American citizen, Tomás Estrada y Palma, as the first Cuban president. Congress passed the Platt Amendment, making Cuba a protectorate. Elections were carefully manipu-lated and blacks—including those in the Cuban liberation army—were ex-cluded. But one thing the United States did not withhold was baseball. Within forty-eight hours of coming ashore, U.S. soldiers had already set up a baseball diamond. Soon, sailors from the U.S. ships *Vulcan* and *Scorpion* were playing games at Guantanamo Bay. American General Leonard Wood immediately banned the Spanish sport of bullfighting. The U.S. military didn't introduce baseball, but its presence helped ingrain it in Cuba; stationed there for long periods, American troops played the game and often faced the Cuban locals.[9]

The early progressive potential of Cuban baseball was soon compromised. While Cubans might have used the sport to promote revolution leading up to the War of 1898, the aftermath was more ambiguous. Baseball's possible func-tions began entering into U.S. policy calculations, and Americans began using it to promote political order and social control. And in 1899, when the All Cuban team barnstormed the United States to celebrate their country's liber-ation from Spanish colonialism, their tour was cut short because they were an integrated club trying to play baseball in segregated America.[10]

In 1900, a Negro League team, the Cuban X Giants, barnstormed Cuba, and the Cuban League opened its doors to American black players. An array of interracial and international talent was hosted. The Brooklyn Dodgers were early visitors, and after 1904 more major-league teams played winter ball in Cuba. In 1905, Americans were playing at several ball fields near Guantanamo Bay.[11] By 1906, Cuban League teams redoubled their efforts to beat the U.S.

clubs, as the reality of continuing American control began to set in. Beginning in 1907, the Cincinnati Reds entered a tournament with Cuban teams and the Negro League's Brooklyn Royal Giants. That same year, the Cubans ousted the puppet president Estrada, but U.S. domination of the Cuban economy and property persisted. American companies owned most of Cuba's arable lands, and they invested even more heavily in baseball teams as a way of managing the natives and diverting them from their mounting grievances.

In 1909, a Cuban team beat the visiting Detroit Tigers, the defending American League champions. By 1910, after decades of Jim Crow practices, a color line had been drawn through American society—dashing abolitionist hopes of a free and equal society. Similarly, by then the United States had hijacked the hopes of Cuban independence. Americans withdrew their support when they learned how many Cubans were black, which meant they were "too childlike or uncivilized to join the white masculine nations." That same year, the Tigers returned and split their games with Cuban teams. The Tigers' star, Ty Cobb, did well but was still outhit by three Negro Leaguers playing with the Cubans; he vowed to never play against blacks again.[12]

In 1911, the Cincinnati Reds signed two Cuban players, Rafael Almeida and Armando Marsans, thus opening the major-league door for at least some lighter-skinned Cubans. But darker Cubans, such as the pitching star José Mendez, could sign only with the Negro Leagues. This period began MLB's first acquisition of new, cheap workers for its ranks, but it required a delicate balance between the American ban on blacks and the temptations of Cuban talent. Writing in *Baseball Magazine*, Ira Thomas acknowledged the Cubans' recent wins over the visiting World Series champion Philadelphia Athletics: "The time will come when the island will be a most favorable recruiting ground for our big leagues." America's increasing integration into the world market produced a growing dependence on foreign peoples as workers and consumers.[13] This began to play out in the American baseball industry as well.

Yet after the Philadelphia Phillies became yet another barnstorming American team in Cuba, MLB's National Commission chair Gary Herrmann protested such visits because they clashed with organized baseball's unwritten law against playing with or against blacks. American League president Ban Johnson prohibited barnstorming by single teams in 1911, allowing only teams with players from several clubs to tour. MLB had a dilemma: according to social Darwinian presumptions of white superiority, black players were banned because they could never be good. Yet black Cubans and Americans (from the Negro Leagues) were regularly beating the major-league teams. So although restrictions were imposed, opportunities were still sought to spot light-skinned talent in Cuba and lure it stateside. To make it easier for the major leagues to focus on Cuban "whites," the United States proposed that Cuba segregate its teams to mirror America's own apartheid.[14]

Meanwhile, baseball's czars sometimes had to navigate the political meaning the sport had acquired for Cubans. The family of Armando Marsans, for example, had been forced to flee Cuba for revolutionary activity *after* the U.S. takeover of the island. Marsans continued supporting the independence movement (now focused against the United States) after he was signed by the Reds. But if anyone doubted who controlled Cuba, the U.S. Marines settled the question: in 1916, they began an eight-year occupation of the island.

The spoils of the 1898 war included another Spanish possession, Puerto Rico. It gained independence right before the war, but U.S. Marines landed, and the island was soon annexed.[15] Baseball had been brought to Puerto Rico a few years earlier by Cuban refugees and U.S. business interests, but it took off with the U.S. military occupation. Most Puerto Ricans opposed U.S. control, and an independence movement was launched. By 1910, the YMCA was engaged in baseball missionary activities, but it lost favor when it banned Sunday games and promoted racial segregation. Another prize of the war with Spain was Guam, which the United States annexed in 1898, installing a white government. The islanders embraced sports as a small means of reclaiming lost honor, and soon Guam baseball teams were playing U.S. military clubs.

Spurred by the war to consolidate its Pacific possessions, the United States finally annexed Hawaii, also in 1898. The continuing U.S. military presence promoted baseball there and helped develop the Oahu Plantation League and the Maui Athletic Association. The Hawaiian Baseball League was formed in 1900. When California's Santa Clara College team toured in 1908, the Hawaiians were described as "going baseball crazy." In 1910, the Chinese Hawaiian baseball team toured the United States, and Hawaii's Overseas Chinese Club defeated the New York Giants in San Francisco in 1911. In 1914, the U.S. 25th Infantry Regiment—the former Philippine Islands champions—began a string of four Hawaiian baseball championships. The University of California team toured Hawaii, and John Williams became the first Hawaiian in the major leagues, pitching for the Detroit Tigers.[16]

The YMCA and Hawaiian plantation owners used baseball for social control and for its "civilizing" influence. It defused protest and trade union militancy and helped divert workers from alcohol and prostitutes. And it buffered U.S.-Japanese relations: thousands of Japanese were being imported as workers, and baseball became a common ground. As one plantation manager observed, "Every Sunday we have games between the Filipinos and our Japanese and Portuguese boys. [Considering] the universal unrest amongst labor [yet its] absence on these islands, an unremitting endeavor should be made through baseball to keep our laborers contented and happy."[17] In 1905, the Asahi Baseball Club was organized to deter working-class boys from delinquency and social unrest.

On the other hand, Hawaiian natives and guest workers also used baseball as a form of resistance, reflecting their resentment of U.S. annexation. After the takeover, Hawaiian nationalists boycotted the pregame American flag ceremony. Likewise, baseball helped develop a sense of community across ethnic and racial lines, against U.S. cultural dominance and worker exploitation. Baseball successes helped some Hawaiians forget the shoddy way Hawaii was brought into the U.S. empire and allowed them to challenge stereotypes designed to justify colonial and racial hierarchies.[18]

The Philippine War

Theodore Roosevelt called the War of 1898 a "splendid little war," yet while the main fighting with Spain ended within months, the war was hardly little or short-lived. The United States easily captured the smaller Spanish possessions. But in the Philippines, the war got particularly ugly. The Filipinos had no intention of becoming the vassals of another colonial power, and thus for more than a decade, they fought off the United States, with tragic consequences.

In what was dubbed the Filipino Insurrection by American officials, rebels had already established de facto independence from Spain before the United States attacked. Rather than a liberation, the Philippine War was a decade-long American campaign to maintain the colony under U.S. administration. The *San Francisco Argonaut* candidly editorialized: "We want the Philippines. The islands are enormously rich, but unfortunately they are infested with Filipinos . . . and it is to be feared their extinction will be slow." Between 250,000 and 700,000 Filipinos were killed, mostly civilians. To subdue the resistance, horrendous practices were employed: burning entire villages, waterboarding and other tortures, and mass slaughter.[19]

American business had been in the Philippines since 1860, not only to exploit the colony but also to use it as a gateway to Asia. In Washington, it was thought, "If the U.S. was to achieve its manifest destiny and vie for world leadership, then it had not only a right but a duty to claim the Philippines." Protestant missionaries sought to win more souls, arguing that "morally and religiously, we should not shun an opportunity to uplift a barbarous people." President McKinley told a church group, "We could not leave them [Filipinos] to themselves . . . but [rather had] to . . . civilize and Christianize them."[20]

How could the United States rescue the Philippines? Baseball was the perfect gift. In *Outlook* magazine, William Pulliam observed that "[Rudyard] Kipling says, 'East is East and West is West and never the twain shall meet.' But Kipling didn't understand the tremendous leveling influence of baseball." The sport was introduced to help pacify an unruly and resistant population. Sailors and marines serving under Commodore Dewey brought baseball to the islands in 1898. Soon the sport gained popularity among Filipinos and helped inculcate the cultural values Americans sought to implant. It was a "tonic" for the natives "as cleansing and creative as total immersion was to a Baptist." The United States wanted to make the Filipinos into the "little brown Americans of Asia" and into "avid consumers of American ideas and ideals as [well as] American goods and services." According to U.S. Major General Franklin Bell, "Baseball had done more to civilize the Filipinos than anything else."[21]

According to historian Carl Crow, American "soldiers played baseball in intervals of peace while they were skirmishing with the insurgents." The natives were considered genetically inferior, but baseball could "strengthen their muscles and wits." Soon baseball spread to the schools, where it helped establish control and discipline. Education was an auxiliary of military conquest— sometimes provided directly by the military itself, and baseball was lauded for helping the United States "manage its new possession." One teacher of the "untamed" Moros wrote, "We first got hold of the Jolo boys through base-ball." It got children interested in going to school. Baseball also rechanneled Filipino nationalism into athletic rivalries. And at the Batangas Normal School, baseball promoted the study of English, for players who spoke anything else were removed from the field. As *Scribner's* magazine suggested, "base-ball unites all classes and conditions of men, from the White House through every layer of our population, until it enwraps the little Brown Brothers in the isles of the sea."[22]

U.S. Major (and former big-league pitcher) Arlie Pond and Reverend (and former Princeton University catcher) George W. Dunlap were among the Americans who implanted the game, making the island of Cebu a hotbed of Filipino baseball for decades. Dunlap was known as the "baseball evangelist." Another curious Filipino baseball promoter was Frederick Funston. Witnessing baseball's popularity while in Alaska, of all places, convinced Funston of its diversionary appeal. When he received a U.S. military command in the Philippines, he pushed baseball on the natives. In 1901, he also captured the Filipino rebel leader Emilio Aquinaldo and became an American hero. Funston toured the states to promote the Philippine War, claiming, "I personally strung up thirty-five Filipinos without trial. If there had been more [executions], the war would have been over long ago. Impromptu domestic hanging might also [help]. For starters, all Americans who . . . petitioned for peace . . . should be . . .

lynched." Funston returned to the Philippines in 1911, where he resumed his active baseball promotion in Luzon.[23]

Provoked by the Philippine War, Mark Twain had become an ardent anti-interventionist and vice president of the Anti-Imperialist League. Twain published a scathing critique of Frederick Funston's capture of Filipino rebels. And when the U.S. military attacked a village of Filipino Muslims in the Moro Massacre—killing at least six hundred men, women, and children—Twain lashed out again: "We have pacified thousands of the islanders and buried them, destroyed their fields, burned their villages, turned their widows and orphans out of doors, furnished heartbreak by exile to dozens of disagreeable patriots, and subjugated the remaining ten million by Benevolent Assimilation."[24]

Even so, as Albert Spalding had observed, "Wherever our soldiers and sailors go [baseball] is immediately introduced, the natives acquiring it with avidity." Filipino leagues quickly formed, although initially dominated by U.S. military teams. From 1899 through 1902, the island championships were won by the U.S. 25th Infantry Regiment—one of four African American units. The 25th began its baseball program in 1894, and when the 1898 war carried it overseas, its baseball tradition went along. The unit generated controversy, however, by fraternizing with the natives and regularly beating the white military teams.[25]

In 1903, the Paco Baseball Park was built to accommodate the Manila Baseball League. In 1908, the islands-wide Philippine League began holding regular seasons, and American military teams played the touring U.S. major leaguers, led by Al Reach. The first pitch was thrown out by the U.S. military governor, General James Smith. That same year, the Philippines public health commissioner, Victor Heiser, reported that a group of yelling Igorots (mountain tribespeople) had been seen playing baseball in a remote clearing. The catcher wore only a G-string and mask, and the runner on first started for second amid cries of "Slide, you son of a bitch, slide!" The Igorots had learned baseball watching Americans play at a local hill station.[26]

The sportswriter Ernie Harwell related a story of Philippine courtship during this time, when some Filipino men could not marry unless they presented the scalp of their bitterest enemy to their future brides. But with baseball introduced to the country, a suitor could instead win marriage by hitting a home run: "Americans, acting as muscle-bound cupids, often played simple grounders and easy outs into home runs so their Filipino friends could escape bachelorhood." Visiting major leaguer Tillie Shafer likewise concluded that "the headhunters of the Philippines have forsaken the chopping off of the heads of enemies for the excitement of the diamond." Though Americans considered them primitives, only a year later *Army and Navy Life* reported that Filipinos had tricked

U.S. soldiers into believing they knew nothing about baseball. The Americans bet heavily, and then the natives beat them—demonstrating not only Filipino cleverness but also some small resistance to their colonization.[27]

Meanwhile, the black 25th Regiment lost only three games in the Philippines between 1903 and 1905. The unit survived desperate battles against Native Americans in the West, Spanish soldiers in Cuba, and guerrilla insurgents in the Philippines. But none of that prepared them for their wounds on the racial battlefields of Brownsville, Texas, where they were reassigned in 1906. An off-base incident provoked the summary discharge of 167 African American soldiers.[28] But in 1907, the remaining black soldiers continued the fight on the baseball diamond. The regrouped 25th Regiment team returned to the Philippines, where they immediately won a tournament, suffered only two losses through 1909, and kept playing until 1912.

The 25th had many more successes in the coming years in Hawaii, on the Pacific Coast, and elsewhere. By 1918, this unit featured Hall of Famer Wilber "Bullet" Rogan and five other future Negro League stars, and soon they were raided by the Kansas City Monarchs, which became known as the army team. Another Negro League star, Oscar Charleston, blossomed while playing in the U.S. Army in the Philippines from 1911 to 1915. The success of African Americans in military baseball was one of the few bright lights amid the dramatic re-escalation of racism in Jim Crow America. But the Monarchs raid on the 25th was the final blow for black baseball in the army, just as the Jackie Robinson signing was later the death knell for the Negro Leagues. Black servicemen, such as Robinson, Larry Doby, and Monte Irvin, would eventually help open the major leagues—culminating what began much earlier in the Philippines with the 25th Regiment.[29]

By 1910, when the University of Chicago team toured the Philippines, baseball was firmly established there. According to the *Atlantic Monthly*, "Persons reluctant to canonize our Philippine policy should observe how five thousand natives will pour down upon the diamond to felicitate the author of a three bagger." In 1911, Governor General Cameron Forbes worked to extend baseball to Manila's upper classes. In 1912, Japan's powerful Waseda University team played in the Philippines and was shocked to win only two games. The Manila League had by then sent several players into professional baseball. By 1913 the Philippines had more than 1,200 teams with ten thousand players. Manila was a prominent stop on the next baseball world tour, led by the legendary major leaguers John McGraw and Charles Comiskey. In 1913, the Manila Baseball Club conducted its own tour, traveling for three months through the United States led by Alejandro Albert, "the father of Philippine baseball." Another Filipino team toured Japan. And that same year, Manila hosted the first Far Eastern Games, established by the YMCA to bring Asia into the modern world and to assimilate Filipino tribes into athletic nationalism (rather than rebellion).[30]

As Gerald Gems has observed, the American crusade in the Philippines had mixed results. It allowed the United States and its corporations to dominate the Filipino government and economy, but it undermined democracy and development and fomented future rebellion. In sports, beginning in 1915, the Philippines won the first six of the next eight Far Eastern Games baseball championships, through 1930.[31]

Thanks to the Philippine War and the War of 1898 before it, baseball significantly extended its function in the U.S. military. *Outlook* magazine claimed it was as responsible for the U.S. victories as rugby had been for the British triumph at Waterloo. These wars signaled the emergence of a U.S. empire overseas, for which the military had to change its role, size, and proper functions. Baseball—now institutionalized in formal military programs—helped the armed services make that transition.[32]

Baseball's importance was bolstered by its incorporation into military education, beginning with West Point. It soon spread to the Naval Academy, and the highlight of each season was the Army-Navy baseball game, beginning in 1901.[33] In the first of those games, future general Douglas MacArthur scored West Point's winning run. His father, Arthur, became a governor-general of the Philippines after the war, and he pushed baseball not only on his son but also on the Filipinos. In 1902, War Secretary Elihu Root ordered a dramatic increase in inter-post baseball games. Thereafter, the momentum of baseball's expanding role in the military continued, with only one important issue left to be resolved.

The Doubleday Myth

By the early twentieth century, the battle over baseball's true origins had not yet been won. While sportswriter Henry Chadwick claimed it was merely an evolution of British rounders, Albert Spalding insisted on baseball's unique U.S. ancestry. To finally settle the question, he launched an investigation; that is, he handpicked a commission guaranteed to reach the conclusion he sought. The group included Spalding employee and Amateur Athletic Union president James Sullivan, two former U.S. senators, a future National League president, and two former major leaguers. Capturing Spalding's sentiments, *Century Magazine* hoped the investigation would show that baseball was "not in any way beholden to any Foreign Power."[34]

The Commission was headed by another Spalding colleague, A.G. Mills, a past president of the National League who had already publicly condemned the rounders theory, declaring baseball purely American. In the end, the Mills Commission relied on a letter from Abner Graves, a Denver mining engineer who insisted that his friend Abner Doubleday created baseball in Coopers-town, New York, in 1839. Spalding championed this claim, and in 1907 the commission reported, "Base Ball is of American origin, and has no traceable connection whatever with 'Rounders' *or any other foreign game.*"

Of course, the Doubleday myth isn't true, and for his whopper Abner Graves may have paid dearly: soon he had a breakdown, shot his wife, and ended up in a mental institution—which suggests, perhaps, that you shouldn't mess with baseball. In any case, Doubleday could not have invented baseball in Cooperstown in 1839 because he was then a cadet living at West Point. There's no evidence Doubleday ever *played* baseball, much less created it. A.G. Mills would have known this better than most people: he was friendly with Doubleday for decades, served with him during the Civil War, and delivered the eulogy at Doubleday's 1893 funeral. Mills nevertheless perpetuated the tale, claiming: "I can well understand how the orderly mind of the embryo West Pointer would devise [baseball's rules]."

As historian Harold Peterson has indicated: "Abner Doubleday did not invent baseball. Baseball invented Abner Doubleday." Why the fabrication? The Doubleday myth performed several functions. Doubleday was a West Point general and a Mexican War and Seminole War veteran. He was also a Civil War hero, having ordered the first Union shots in defense of Fort Sumter, which later prompted Branch Rickey to claim, "The only thing General Doubleday ever started was the Civil War." He also fought at Antietam and Bull Run and helped repel Pickett's Charge at Gettysburg. Thus the Doubleday tale allowed baseball to connect itself to a military icon and the glories of American military might.[35]

This in turn allowed the sport to share in the growing sense of U.S. exceptionalism, by which Americans viewed themselves as the world's shining light. Touting the Doubleday connection and baseball's burgeoning patriotic pedigree, Albert Spalding's book, *The American National Game*, read like "an American fable, replete with a myth of origin, a pantheon of heroes, and a melodramatic narrative of good, struggling and overcoming forces of evil."[36]

Besides the military connection, the Doubleday story also helped the U.S. dispel its lingering sense of inferiority to Great Britain. In the absence of a native language and people (with most Indians now killed off), having a home-grown sport was important for America's national identity.[37] And beyond shaking off *inferiority*, baseball's creation tale was instead used to proclaim America's *superiority*. Spalding insisted the British were far too soft to have created baseball and that cricket was more appropriate for the weaker English population.

By the early 1900s, however, U.S. troops occupying Caribbean and Latin American nations were reporting back about baseball's possible roots south of the border. Descendants of various native peoples—such as Cuba's Siboney Indians and Puerto Rico's Caguana Indians—claimed they had played variations of baseball since before Columbus arrived. It was bad enough thinking the United States might have been adopting a white British sport as its own. But for Spalding and others, it was intolerable that the national pastime might have derived from nonwhite, indigenous peoples. According to James Cockcroft, not merely American superiority was on the line, but rather *white* American superiority. As a collaborator in U.S. expansionism, baseball had to be white as well. African Americans had been banned from MLB since the 1880s, and the last black played in the minor leagues in 1898—the inception date of America's rising new empire. At stake wasn't just who could *play* the game, but also who *owned* it.[38]

The Doubleday myth supplied the answer. Baseball helped reinforce the white supremacy essential for rationalizing U.S. foreign policy. Combining gunboat and dollar diplomacy, the United States occupied one Latin American nation after another, usually to promote American financial interests in sugar, bananas, mining, and banking. Glorifying the benefits of the American way for local populations, U.S. companies routinely sponsored baseball as tangible proof of *gringo* superiority, hoping to Americanize their Latino workers along the way.[39]

Commercial advantages flowed not merely to other corporations, but also to the baseball business itself. The Doubleday myth was a powerful marketing tool at home and abroad. Appealing to American pride promoted ballpark attendance. The two ballplayers on the Mills Commission, Al Reach and Harry Wright, had both established sporting goods businesses after their playing careers. Those firms profited from Americans playing (and needing equipment for) their *own*, unique game. Of course, as the quintessential sports entrepreneur, Albert Spalding eventually incorporated the Reach and Wright companies into his own business empire. He recognized the dynamics of mythmaking and patriotism's considerable financial advantages.[40]

As if this weren't enough, the Doubleday myth also helped baseball beat back football's continuing threat. While baseball players rode with Teddy Roosevelt at San Juan Hill, he preferred football. The steady rise of that sport seemed to reflect U.S. foreign policy's emerging aggressiveness, for which Roosevelt was a major champion.[41] Football renewed its rivalry with baseball just as empire began challenging America's democratic republic. Football closely resembled the pattern of imperial warfare, its teams organized like a military command structure. To Roosevelt, interventionism was not a dirty word, but rather showed toughness—from the nation and the men who ran it: "In a perfectly peaceful and commercial civilization such as ours," the Rough Rider (implausibly) claimed, "there is always a danger of placing too little stress upon the more virile virtues—which make up a race of statesmen and soldiers, of pioneers and explorers."

But had football gone too far? By the early twentieth century, football violence—which had caused dozens of deaths and many serious injuries—prompted calls for the sport's elimination. But Roosevelt defended football, including—indeed, especially—its violence: having a vital life was a matter of repeatedly "hitting the line." Roosevelt advocated football as a "game appropriate for a nation ripe for a clean, violent, virile, yet gentlemanly sport." It would immunize athletes against softness and make them responsive to command and the virtues of martial life. His support may have saved football from extinction. Maybe America needed football to cope with the dog-eat-dog world in which it sought to become a major player. As fellow imperialist Senator Henry Cabot Lodge said, "athletic contests and the injuries incurred . . . are the price the English-speaking race has paid for being world conquerers."[42]

Where would that leave baseball? According to Roosevelt's daughter, Alice Roosevelt Longworth, "Father and all of us regarded baseball as a mollycoddle game." Only violent sports, she claimed, appealed to them."[43] Roosevelt eventually became more receptive to baseball, but did others view it as "too soft"? Spalding thought they did, but the Doubleday myth allowed the sport to fight back. It helped baseball establish its military credentials and sign on for empire. This would not be the last time baseball would confront football for national supremacy and for the right to represent contemporary American values.

Not surprisingly, most Americans still think Doubleday invented baseball. The U.S. government endorsed the myth when the Postal Service issued a commemorative stamp. The National Baseball Hall of Fame and Museum used it to launch itself, in Cooperstown in 1939—on baseball's purported one hundredth anniversary. The museum still displays the "Doubleday ball," and the annual Hall of Fame game between two major league teams is held each summer at Doubleday Field. And according to Harrington Crissey, although "serious baseball research has refuted the [Doubleday story, it did] not diminish the relationship that developed between baseball and the military over the last century."[44]

The Old Army Game

Among the baseball czars, Albert Spalding was not alone in lauding the game's military connections. American League president Ban Johnson steadfastly supported U.S. wars and military endeavors, always eager to have baseball lend a hand. And in 1906 the *Chicago American* wrote: "Base Ball is one of the reasons why American soldiers are the best in the world—quick witted, swift to act, ready of judgment, capable of going into action without officers." In 1907, Charles Stewart extended the connection: "The handling of the baseball player, the observation of a property right in him, and the expectation of 'loyalty,' is comparable to the way of a nation with a soldier. The player is a public servant, a soldier of the cause."[45]

In 1912, in *The Battle of Base Ball*, C.H. Claudy picked up baseball's military metaphors where Henry Chadwick's 1889 book, *How to Play Base Ball*, left off. Claudy's book yoked the sport irretrievably to warfare and extolled baseball's military virtues. His language alone was suggestive: a pitcher was "bombed" if he gave up too many runs; a "rifle shot" described a hard throw or a line-drive hit; walked batters were given a "furlough"; fielders "gunned down" runners and turned "twin killings"; and a big lead "cripples the enemy." To Claudy, baseball had the characteristics of war, including its generals, captains, lieutenants, and rank and file. Teams pursued tactics and a grand strategy. The diamond was the battlefield, the equipment was baseball's armaments, and drills and discipline built up the team's fighting skills.[46]

As in warfare, Claudy claimed credit should be given to men who play for the team and not for their own records. In war, defense is accomplished when an army incapacitates the enemy, preventing him from carrying out his designs, rendering his strategy useless. In baseball, the defense tries to get the third out without allowing the offense to occupy even the first station on the road to the city it would hope to capture. Even as an army attacked has more than one line of defense—scouts, pickets, outriders, the main troops, and the reserves—so too has the defensive baseball army. At the first line, it has the battery: the pitcher and catcher who strive to put the batter out at the plate and, failing this, to frustrate his efforts to get safe on first base. At the second line of defense, the general has his infield and for the third, the outfield. In "inside base-ball," for every offense, there is a defense, for every act that might produce a base hit, a stolen base, or a run, there is a counterplan by which fielders may nullify the batter's efforts.

Interrupting an army's signals, stealing its intelligence by intercepting its telegraph wires, capturing its messengers, and reading its dispatches, have always been among the "romances of war." Likewise, reading the opposing team's signals, learning their plan before they do it and frustrating their attempt, is a favorite baseball strategy. Warfare has its reserves: ready and in training. So, too, with a baseball team. What soldiers are to the commander of an army, his players are to the baseball general—the manager.

When two nations go to war, it is a cruel thing. But it's not conducted, according to Claudy, without humanity. There are rules for civilized warfare, strictly observed even by two countries at war. So it is in the battle of baseball. Ironically, this truism was already being sorely challenged in real wars in Claudy's time, as well as in the baseball wars on the field. Not known for his restraint, Detroit Tigers star Ty Cobb observed that "baseball is not unlike war . . . and we batters are the heavy artillery." Baseball sought to prove it could be every bit as aggressive and martial as football. In the few years preceding World War I, the U.S. military was increasingly a feature at ballparks. By 1913, Colonel Dougherty's military police, for example, became well known at New York's Polo Grounds. More and more, military teams played major-league clubs, such as the 1914 game the 22nd Infantry team played against the New York Yankees.[47]

Besides Douglas MacArthur, other future generals became baseball prospects at West Point before World War I. Omar Bradley was one of the Military Academy's best players ever. Although another general, Dwight Eisenhower, claimed that "not making the West Point team may have been the greatest disappointment of my life," he was good enough to have played some summer minor-league baseball while enrolled at West Point. Engaging in professional athletics violated the Military Academy's honor code, however. Had he been discovered, he would have been expelled, and his and our world might have been very different.[48]

In 1915, Secretary of War Lindley Garrison acknowledged baseball's use for military recruitment: It was "the aim . . . to make the Army attractive to young men . . . athletics are encouraged and baseball is the most popular. [We need] good clean men [and] . . . there is no better [source] than among baseball players." Military teams became a viable option for men who wanted to play serious baseball, sometimes leading to a professional career. As *Baseball Magazine* writer William Kennedy suggested, "The European war has made it necessary for the U.S. to be prepared . . . [even though it] has never been a warlike nation, save in defense." The purported "lack of martial ideals" made it more challenging to develop a successful army, but baseball could help out: "Uncle Sam does all he can to make things interesting for the private. A chief thing is baseball, as a healthful outlet for animal spirits, a good nerve tonic, a method for fostering wholesome rivalry, and a possible future occupation."[49]

The U.S. Army created an extensive network of teams. The Military Baseball League, for example, was a nine-fort association that played extensively in the New York area, including Sundays—for which it often faced Sabbatarian opposition. The Military Athletic League sponsored tournaments to raise money for armed forces baseball, including the All-Star Army Team. Relationships were developed with Chicago ballclub owners Charles Comiskey and Charles Weeghman, who helped arrange games, offered coaches, and gave access to their ballparks. Writing to Secretary Garrison, Weeghman applauded the "splendid method for calling to the colors red-blooded, clean-thinking, high types of the young American athlete" and congratulated the Army for "showing the public that the great American game follows the flag."[50]

It's no wonder baseball became "the old Army game." On the field, the term had conflicting meanings. By one definition, it meant playing baseball straightforwardly, without strategy or trickery. But sometimes the phrase implied just the opposite: the use of "inside" baseball tactics to scrape together wins by any means possible.[51] Off the field, however, the meaning was clear: baseball had developed unequivocal ties to the U.S. military. These links would have implications when the United States fought in real wars but would have innumerably more applications in America's foreign interventions.

4

Imperium Rising
(1910–1916)

U.S. Marines shouldered bats next to their rifles when they imposed imperial order in a region by blood and fire. Baseball then became for the people of the Caribbean what soccer is to us.

—Eduardo Galeano

Feeling its oats after taking—in short order—Cuba, Guam, Hawaii, Samoa, Puerto Rico, and the Philippines, the United States was far from done. While it had intervened in the internal affairs of various nations for decades, the War of 1898 signaled the arrival of the United States as a serious imperial power.[1] As such, it set its sights far and wide, even while sometimes preaching isolationism. Pursuing the motto of Theodore Roosevelt's administration, the U.S. would "speak softly, but carry a big stick." Not infrequently, the speech would instead be thunderous and the stick would be a baseball bat.

The United States was motivated by several factors, including profit, control, religious conversion, the call to civilization, and the quest for virility and new frontiers. It would pursue these ends by various means—sometimes resorting to annexation, other times relying on economic domination, missionary crusades, semi-permanent U.S. military bases, or full-scale occupation. The national pastime followed: "The spread of baseball on the international scene can be plotted simply by following the expansion of the American empire."[2]

Escalating Interventionism

Writing in 1910, the historian Henry Adams gloomily predicted the end of useful human intellectual activity: "Socialism, Collectivism, Humanitarianism, Universalism, Philanthropism, and every other ism, has come [to] the End, and [American history teachers] can all just go out and play, for all it matters." And on the whole, he suggested, "baseball would be the best to play." As Leverett Smith notes, Adams wasn't endorsing baseball, but rather regarded it as irrelevant to a world whose clock had stopped.[3] As with similar predictions eight decades later about the "end of history," bold new events would never-theless unfold. Baseball might have become extraneous to the world the weary Adams saw disappearing, but it was in the forefront of the nation's new, dom-inant spirit in the coming years.

According to David Voigt, while America's War of 1898 triumph thrust the nation onto the world stage, the vainglorious assumption of "the white man's burden" soon had U.S. soldiers heading to the four corners of the globe. American ballplayers assumed the same responsibility. As major leaguer Jack Rowan observed, "Few people realize that a ball player has to be an A1 diplo-mat, politician, and hand-shaker."[4] Some Americans took the obligation even more seriously. Indiana Congressman Albert Beveridge claimed, "We will not renounce the mission of our race . . . [to] civilize the world. We will move for-ward . . . with gratitude for a task worthy of our strength, and thanksgiving to Almighty God that He has marked us as His chosen people." The YMCA and other missionary groups redoubled their efforts, even in already Christianized lands, where Catholicism was viewed as not Christian enough.[5]

As with the contemporary use of *globalization*, the word *civilization* back then usually meant "Americanization."[6] Interventionism was, according to Secretary of State Francis Loomis, a project "to Americanize the New World and perhaps the Old . . . not necessarily by force but rather by the dissemina-tion of lofty, civilizing agencies." Often it *was* by force, usually military power, but American corporations and evangelicals were aggressive as well. And the baseball industry was certainly as active as other business interests in expanding America's global influence.

To make baseball not just *originally* American, but also *currently* American, Albert Spalding defined it as part of a U.S. imperialist pageant, proclaiming that "wherever a ship floating the Stars and Stripes finds anchorage to-day, some-where on a nearby shore the American National Game is in progress." The ex-pansion of America was confirmed by the expansion of the game. Spalding noted the coincidence between baseball's emerging popularity and the Amer-icanization process: "No wonder the Japanese, so quick to adopt American civilization . . . should also grasp a pastime so particularly adapted to their alert, intelligent natures." While Americans would soon be singing a different tune about the Japanese, the spirit of capitalism and the spirit of baseball had become one. While baseball was emerging, in sportswriter Hugh Fullerton's words, as "the greatest single force working for Americanization" within the United States, so too was it helping Americanize the globe. And while this might also, if not primarily, benefit the United States, the targets of its crusade would nevertheless be bathed in the American dream.[7]

Psychological factors played a role as well. Americans were coping with the end of the U.S. territorial frontier. New frontiers required new targets. Conquering, militarily or economically, other lands—even while proclaiming more lofty objectives—was an obvious solution. As historian Carl Siger has noted, "new countries offer a vast field for individual, violent activities . . . the colonies serve as a safety valve for modern society." But an even more symbolic elixir was also emerging—big-time American sports, particularly baseball. Price Collier wrote that sport could maintain the frontier experience and that this "artificial adventure, artificial colonizing, artificial war" would sustain the "more stalwart and better formed race." More and more, the two—colonies and sports—would work together.[8]

According to Bill Brown, the promises of opportunity and rags-to-riches success embedded in the popular Horatio Alger novels were already becoming untenable. Just as the United States was poised to export the American dream abroad, serious doubts about its availability surfaced at home. Sports were emerging as a refuge against the realities of capitalism; success on the diamond provided new hope. Supplanting the Alger books were dozens of Frank Merriwell sports novels written by Gilbert Patten under the pen name Burt Standish. Patten featured baseball heroes, in particular, and almost all his books were set in the United States. Then his main character began to appear overseas. In his 1910 novel, *Frank Merriwell in Peru; or, In the Land of the Incas*, Patten's protagonist mimicked the recent adventures of Teddy Roosevelt's Rough Riders and displayed in the military sphere all the strategy he learned from playing baseball. Merriwell finds himself aiding an American entrepreneur, who's building a lucrative Peruvian railroad line, trying to fend off native "ingratitude." In this quest, Merriwell musters his baseball skills for this new task of promoting foreign capitalism.[9]

For civilization to spread, there must always be a new conquest, just as there's always another game to win, another team to vanquish. This vision of sporting practice relied on the non-American world as the testing ground for the national game's success, just as that world was also viewed as the gauge for America's national "manliness" and its national economic and political systems. In baseball, the point was not merely to implant the game abroad, but to beat the new teams and players. It didn't always work out that way, especially when local populations embraced baseball to resist U.S. domination.[10] Nevertheless, the progress of baseball promoted the progress of "civilization," and vice versa—the two narratives intertwined, slowly tying up the globe.[11] Albert Spalding never missed a chance to be involved. While baseball only slowly succeeded as a demonstration sport and then a formal sport at the Olympics, Spalding made sure he was selected U.S. Olympic Committee chairman in the early 1900s, when endless new possibilities for selling his sporting goods worldwide were there for the taking.[12]

As James Cockcroft has observed, the United States was shedding its insular past to become a predominantly urban, industrialized global giant destined, according to President Woodrow Wilson, "to finance the world and rule it" with American "spirits and minds." And, given the sport's influence, Wilson might have added, with "baseball bats."[13] When it required something more lethal than hardwood to impose American capitalism overseas, the U.S. military would be ready. Congressional Medal of Honor recipient and Marine Corps general Smedley Butler was involved in military interventions in a dozen Caribbean, Latin American, and Asian nations. A gung-ho soldier, he later expressed his regrets in his book *War Is a Racket*:

> I spent thirty-three years . . . [as] a high class muscle-man for Big Business, Wall Street and the Bankers . . . I was a racketeer, a gangster for capitalism . . . I helped make Mexico safe for American oil interests in 1914. I helped make Haiti and Cuba a decent place for the National City Bank boys to collect revenues. I helped in the raping of half a dozen Central American republics for Wall Street . . . I helped purify Nicaragua for the Brown Brothers banking house in 1909–1912. I brought light to the Dominican for American sugar interests in 1916. In China I helped see that Standard Oil went its way unmolested. . . . Looking back, I could have given Al Capone a few hints. The best he could do was to [control] three districts. I operated on three continents.[14]

Colonies at Home

While the United States established de facto colonies abroad, it constructed two more at home—one for American Indians and quite a different one for African Americans. Despite the war to free the slaves, little had changed for American blacks. While technically no longer in bondage, Jim Crow laws segregated the races, undermining black rights and perpetuating their destitution. Institutionalizing this racism in its 1896 *Plessy v. Ferguson* decision, the U.S. Supreme Court relegated African Americans to second-class citizenship and opened the door to a Ku Klux Klan revival and several decades of antiblack violence.

Blacks were treated as internal colonials who needed to be civilized and kept separate from superior white society—as reflected in the microcosm of U.S. baseball. In the historian Harold Seymour's analysis of the "House of

Baseball," African Americans were excluded as of the late 1890s, isolated to an "out-building" of their own. In their separate "colony," African Americans developed their own teams and leagues. Contact between "organized baseball" and the "Negro" leagues was sporadic at best in the early 1900s. Black teams distinguished themselves in the mostly segregated U.S. military, where they played and often beat white teams. Negro League clubs also ventured abroad, to Cuba, Hawaii, and the Philippines, and when Negro Leaguers were accepted and then played for foreign teams, it wasn't clear whether they were really blacks or really Americans. As W.E.B Du Bois observed, it didn't seem as if they could be both.[15]

Back in the United States, this "divided self" haunted Moses Fleetwood Walker. While apparently the first African American in major league baseball (MLB), he was also the last until nearly a century later. Pushed out in the 1880s, Walker—who was educated at Oberlin College and the University of Michigan—moved on to other notable accomplishments. He was a technical innovator in the emerging film industry, ran a prominent Ohio opera house, and patented an exploding artillery shell. But as U.S. apartheid got increasingly pervasive, Walker became disillusioned with integration. Anticipating by a decade the black nationalist leader Marcus Garvey, Walker joined the Back to Africa Movement. In 1908, he published *Our Home Colony,* in which he claimed that "the only solution of [U.S.] race troubles is the entire separation by emigration of the Negro from America." While blacks were treated as colonial subjects at home, Walker urged them to populate a colony of their own. Accordingly, Fleetwood and his brother Welday Walker became agents for black relocation to Liberia.[16]

In contrast, American Indians weren't exiled like blacks in Harold Seymour's "House of Baseball" analogy, but were instead relegated to the basement. For Native Americans, that meant their internal colonization in the form of reservations and Indian schools. White America was ambivalent: On the one hand, Indians were primitive and had to be kept largely, if not entirely, separate from the rest of society. On the other hand, Native Americans were sometimes also viewed as exotic, noble savages who might have a limited role within white culture. After most Indians had been vanquished, the survivors became a source of fascination and even toleration for some whites.

This played out curiously in baseball. As Adrian Burgos has observed, Indian-ness was conflated with foreignness, which placed Native Americans outside the nation—as foreigners in their own land. Baseball was widely played at Indian schools, such as the Carlisle School, which produced Jim Thorpe and other great Indian athletes. When a few of these Indian ballplayers were given access to professional baseball, some major leaguers objected. Future

Hall of Famer Ed Delahanty claimed, "The League has gone all to hell now that they're letting them damn foreigners in."

Yet baseball's doors nevertheless opened for American Indians, perhaps surprisingly, since African Americans had only recently been banned for their race. Organized baseball made this space, however, because it had painted itself into a contradiction. It wanted the best talent, but its racial barriers stood in the way. Tentatively accepting Native Americans was a safe compromise: Indians were not "black identified," and the limited number of players (drawn from a devastated population pool) avoided upsetting exclusionary racial practices. Their entry into baseball was mediated by the condescending treatment they received. Every Indian player was "Chief" and each was greeted with war whoops from the fans.[17]

Journalists mastered the racial stereotypes. Tapping a public consciousness that still remembered the Indian Wars and describing one of the first Native Americans in baseball, the *Literary Digest* observed that "Louis Sockalexis lugged his Penobscot Indian war club into our national game and started to whale the scalps off the paleface pitchers of the baseball world . . . a reincarnation of the racial proclivities [of the Native Americans] for deeds of valor in open-air sports has arisen Phoenix-like." To others the Indians were called "red menaces" yet also appreciated, since "out of this little group of so-called savages came some of the greatest athletes ever in competitive sports." Native Americans were applauded for abandoning their own, purportedly barbaric game of lacrosse in favor of the more civilized baseball.[18]

Sometimes the racism would be less subtle and more brutal. But allowing Indian access to baseball was nevertheless significant. To "pass" for an Indian could get you through the major league color barrier. In 1901, New York Giants manager John McGraw gave it a try, signing Charlie Grant, a Negro minor league star, claiming he was an Indian named Chief Tokahama. The plan failed, but others may have succeeded (we're not sure) and McGraw did sign a real Indian, John "Chief" Meyers, in 1909. Making an exception for Indians paved the way for allowing other nonwhites into organized baseball, particularly light-skinned Latinos, who provided an experimental laboratory for stretching tolerance while still policing baseball's color line.[19]

In 1915, looking for a new name, the American League's Cleveland Naps settled on the Indians. In recent years, with rising concerns over Indian names and mascots, the Cleveland club claimed its name had been chosen to honor its former player, Lou Sockalexis. Rather than racism, it was a noble gesture. Yet there's little evidence to support this. As Ellen Staurowsky has observed, the name was adopted only twenty-five years after the American military massacre of Indians at Wounded Knee and only six years after Geronimo died as a

U.S. political prisoner. It was a time when the United States was implement-
ing policies to strip Native Americans of their culture rather than celebrate it.
And the *Cleveland Plain Dealer* was writing condescendingly about having "Indians on the warpath all the time and eager for scalps to dangle at their belts."
Thus, rather than respect, the Indians name was more likely chosen for exploitation: typically equated with animals, Native American images frequently
adorned commercial products for sale. Not all Indians were forced onto reservations, but their colonization was nevertheless self-evident.[20]

Asian Invasion

Having imperial ambitions involved much more than colonizing the home
front. Already pursuing interests in Asia for some time, the U.S. stepped up its
efforts. Beyond its Philippine forays, the United States took an early interest in
China, where it demanded a treaty to protect American industry in Shanghai
and four other cities in 1845. This began several decades of U.S. Navy and
Marine presence there. Baseball also arrived early, when an American medical
missionary, Henry William Boone, established the Shanghai Baseball Club in
1863. The 1882 Chinese Exclusion Act banned Chinese entry into the United
States, but Americans kept arriving in China, bringing more baseball with
them. By 1895, the sport was played at U.S. Christian colleges there, and at
three Chinese colleges.[21]

In 1899, the Chinese rose up against foreign exploitation in the Boxer Rebellion. In response, as part of a multinational force, the U.S. military attacked,
in what it called the China Relief Expedition, which brutally suppressed the
uprising. Both British and U.S. forces occupied Beijing's sacred Temple of
Heaven grounds. After the fighting, the English planned to lay out cricket
fields there, but the American Army Baseball League had beaten them to it:
the 6th Cavalry and "Riley's Battery" were already playing baseball among the
altars. The U.S. Navy also formed two teams, the Apaches and the Sioux, and
the major leagues were also represented: soldier Dave Altizer played for the
Cincinnati Red Stockings.

In 1903, Liang Cheng starred on the Andover, Massachusetts, baseball team
as a visiting student. When he was appointed Chinese Minister to the United
States, President Theodore Roosevelt learned about his ball-playing days,
which created a rapport that helped smooth relations between their two nations. In 1904, teams based in China played in the ten-ship Asiatic Station
Baseball League. After winning the Russo-Japanese War in 1905, Japan
emerged as an Asian leader. As a result, as many as thirty thousand Chinese

youths went there to study. Besides the American baseball influence, Chinese students also began returning home with the Japanese baseball passion.[22]

By 1910 Maurice Allen, writing for *Baseball Magazine*, summarized the American attitude: "The time worn old Empire of China has been associated with all that is antique and unprogressive." Nevertheless, he continued, "even China should have the inherent power somewhere in the strange makeup of the Oriental mind to be [as] carried away . . . as the occidental by the bustling sports of the Western Hemisphere." On the Fourth of July, to set a positive example, a baseball game was held in China between the USS *Raleigh* and the USS *Elcano*, and then a second contest between the USS *New Orleans* and the USS *Monitor Monadnock*—both watched by American, British, and Chinese fans.[23]

Yet despite years of effort, baseball and other American influences failed to subordinate Chinese nationalist impulses. Never impressed with the United States as a model of civilization, China's leaders instead adapted sport to their own needs. Thus in 1911 Sun Yat-sen's revolutionary and anti-imperialist party organized a baseball association, the Changsha Field Ball Society, which served, among other things, as a cover to teach young men how to throw hand grenades. Sun had learned baseball while living in Hawaii three decades earlier. With some small help from baseball, his forces overthrew the Qing Dynasty and established modern China.[24]

In 1914, U.S. missionary Willard Nash organized the East China Intercollegiate Athletic Association, mostly to play baseball. In 1915, the Far Eastern baseball games were held in Shanghai, and China placed second to the Philippines. Meanwhile, Chinese teams began to visit the United States, their tours invariably described by *Baseball Magazine* as "Asian invasions." One Chinese team won 105 of its 144 games. After a game on his campus, one American college president proclaimed: "The Yellow Peril! We have seen it to-day on the athletic field. Let Providence give us more of this kind."[25]

Baseball became a vehicle for developing national pride in Japan, which began acting on its newfound confidence on the world stage. With both baseball and foreign policy, Japan was invaded, but then it launched invasions of its own. In the short run, Americans and Japanese were conflicted about baseball's role. From the U.S. perspective, Albert Spalding promoted the game as uniquely American, leaving little room for foreigners. Yet he also wanted to introduce baseball to distant lands. Thus he insisted that foreigners could play the game only if they became just like Americans. For the Japanese, the point was not merely to *learn* the U.S. game, but also to *beat* the Americans at their own game. The idea was not to become like Americans. Japanese students "spoke in one breath about [beating the U.S. in baseball games for] retribution for past injustices, and in another [breath] about using baseball to forge harmonious relations between the two countries."[26]

According to Donald Roden, although the two nations shared the "same culture of athleticism and manliness, [it] was inherently aggressive and . . . impossible to 'share' in amity and mutual respect. Cosmopolitan social Darwinism is a contradiction in terms." Baseball reflected America's imperial quest while it became Japan's "new bushido—the way of the warrior" in the modern age. "An international confrontation on the diamond had become unavoidable."[27] Not to mention *off* the diamond.

These incongruities spilled over into U.S.-Japanese foreign relations. The U.S. favored Japan in the Russo-Japanese War, and Teddy Roosevelt applauded the Japanese for "playing our game"—both literally and figuratively. But when he brokered the 1905 peace treaty, many Japanese wanted greater "spoils," for which Roosevelt chastised them for "getting the big head." While transnational relations between the two peoples—often fostered by baseball—seemed cordial, and while baseball interactions proliferated,[28] the feelings underneath may have been different. In 1905 the Japanese Ichiko School commemorated its historic 1896 baseball victory over the Americans with an aggressive poem, *"Yakyubuka"* ("Baseball Club Rouser"):

> The valorous [U.S.] sailors from the *Detroit*, *Kentucky*, and *Yorktown*
> Whose furious batting can intimidate a cyclone
> Threw off their helmets, their energies depleted.
> Behold how pathetically they run away defeated.
> Courageously we march twenty miles south
> To fight the Americans in Yokohama.
> Though they boast of the game as their national sport,
> Behold the games they have left with no score.
> Ah, for the glory of our Baseball Club!
> Ah, for the glitter it has cast!
> Pray that our martial valor never turns submissive
> And that our honor will always shine far across the Pacific.[29]

College and other teams from the United States and Japan kept visiting back and forth, as baseball's bid to maintain good relations. Yet in 1908 the intimidating U.S. Great White Fleet arrived in Japanese ports. Roosevelt sent it to warn Japan against any future aggressiveness even while American sailors played ball games with the Japanese on shore. That year, the so-called Gentlemen's Agreement excluded Japanese workers from the United States. Anti-American demonstrations in Japan sometimes spilled over onto the baseball fields. Americans became a target, and some Japanese ballplayers began to view themselves as warriors. Condescending and often racist descriptions of Japanese ball players and fans appeared in U.S. periodicals, such as the *Atlantic Monthly* caricature of the dim-witted "Mr. Togo," who in "his heathen blindness" can't seem to figure out what's happening during a baseball game.[30]

Still, baseball persisted. In 1908, the U.S. Navy team played the Keio University club, and U.S. major leaguer Tillie Shafer arrived in Japan to teach baseball and promote good will.[31] The Reach All-Americans brought the first U.S. professionals to Japan. Al Reach hoped his sporting goods company could get a foothold before his competitor, the Spalding Company. But both American enterprises received a blow when the Japanese firm, Mizuno, began manufacturing baseball equipment locally.

In 1909, Keio University invited the University of Wisconsin team for its second visit. Sensing political tensions, it felt the trip would "dispel rumors of enmity between the U.S. and Japan." Attendance was high, and the American consul claimed the trip did more for U.S.-Japanese relations than any previous visit. In 1910, the University of Chicago's baseball team arrived in Japan, and Prince Tokugawa claimed the sport would be a peacemaker between the two imperial nations—possibly averting a "terrible war."[32] Even so, Japan began to project itself more forcefully into the world, and baseball played a role. By this time, the proselytizing YMCA had a long history in Japan. While it produced few religious converts, the Y did excel in developing sports teams. Japan adopted the YMCA model to organize thousands of baseball clubs, which it then dedicated to nationalist and imperialist purposes—without the Christianity.

Japan, like Cuba, was the target of U.S. baseball imperialism. But both nations distinguished themselves by practicing a baseball interventionism of their own. In a sense, they acted as baseball surrogates—enhancing the U.S. quest to implant the game throughout the world. For Cuba, the object was other Caribbean nations. For Japan, it included Pacific islands such as Truk, where it used baseball to tame the natives in 1915. But Japan also pursued much bigger prizes. According to Joseph Reaves, "During the age of colonialism, the U.S. used baseball unabashedly as a tool of diplomacy, equating the game with the Great American dream. It worked. Up to a point. The Great American Game was adopted and then adapted so that it quickly became the Great Japanese Game in Asia."[33] That is, baseball was prominent in Japan's own imperial ambitions, in places such as Korea and Taiwan.

Korea had long been controlled by outside powers, such as China and Russia. But when Japan won the Russo-Japanese War in 1905, Korea became a Japanese protectorate. U.S. missionary Philip Gillett introduced baseball to Korea that year via the YMCA. But it was the Japanese occupation, lasting until

1945, that institutionalized the sport. Japanese soldiers promoted the game, and baseball was taught in the Japanese-run schools and imposed on the Koreans as an ingredient of Japanese culture.

In 1910 Japan formally annexed Korea, and the first official Korean League games were played. Still active in creating teams, one YMCA leader claimed that "a baseball mitt, if well used, may remain a potent factor in meeting young men and boys for Jesus Christ." The YMCA assumed Korean interest in baseball reflected enthusiasm for American customs, but most Koreans viewed the sport as Japanese, giving them a way to contest the indignities of Japanese rule. In baseball they both appeased and challenged their occupiers. An active exchange of baseball clubs between Korea and Japan began, and the Koreans played visiting American clubs as well.[34]

In Taiwan, baseball was part of the "Japanization" imposed when the island was annexed in 1895. Like many Chinese, many Taiwanese scorned physical exercise. According to Confucius, "Those who labor with their minds govern others, and those who labor with their strength are governed by others."[35] Thus many Taiwanese parents frowned on baseball for their children. Initially only the Japanese played the game in Taiwan, but it was then promoted among the natives to control them. When the Taiwanese began playing, however, the Japanese then worried it might incite, rather than defuse, rebellion.

They may have been correct. According to Taiwanese sportswriter Joan Chen, "As a colony, Taiwan was dominated by Japan economically and politically, but we could beat them in baseball." As Andrew Morris has observed, baseball "allowed the Taiwanese to prove their acculturation at the very moment Taiwanese baseball successes worked to subvert it . . . it was the final proof the [Japanese] colonial enterprise was bound to fail." But not for a lack of trying: in 1910, Japan—believing baseball could promote pacification—formed the first Taiwanese teams, and in 1915, it created the Taiwan Baseball Federation, hoping to further infuse baseball into its colony.[36]

Caribbean Beat

Meanwhile, America was active in its own backyard. From 1898 to 1933, the U.S. Marines hit the beaches at least thirty-four times in ten different Caribbean nations. And while other nations, such as Mexico, Venezuela, and Colombia, were never occupied by American troops, they became economically dependent on the United States nevertheless. And wherever the "big stick" of military might or the "big trick" of economic dominance went, baseball was not far behind.[37]

In 1913, the editors of *Baseball Magazine* wrote, "It is remarkable that some energetic promoter has not established in [these] fertile fields a branch extension of our national game, [to promote] its world-wide expansion [and to] exploit our South American neighbors." They wouldn't have long to wait. Baseball was strongly pushed in the Caribbean, sometimes preceding American military intervention, often accompanying it. Cuba acted as a baseball proxy, spreading the game it had adopted for its own. According to the Dominican Pedro Julio Santana, "It is much the same as with Christianity. Jesus could be compared to the North Americans, but the apostles spread the faith and the apostles of baseball were the Cubans."[38]

While the Marines and U.S. companies promoted baseball to manage local populations, the sport also assumed a life of its own in the region. As Rob Ruck has argued, "Caribbean baseball is not simply an appendage of the [U.S.] game . . . ; [it] has catalyzed national consciousness and cohesion . . . and influenced how these societies have defined themselves, their relations, and their ties to the U.S." Yet according to Roberto Gonzalez Echevarria, "American culture is [a] fundamental component of Cuban culture, [despite] painful attempts to fight it off." The same tension characterized other Caribbean nations. Has U.S. baseball influence been positive or negative? According to Samuel Regalado, it's been both: baseball "has [brought] great wealth for some but exploitation for others; stimulated great nationalistic pride for some but humiliation for others; provided racial tolerance for some but bigotry for others. Baseball has [brought] foreign [U.S.] cultural hegemony, but also provided a tool for local political tyranny."[39]

Many islanders resented U.S. dominance. Increasingly subjected to the military and economic power of the "Great Colossus of the North" and unable to free themselves from American militarization or capitalism, Latinos used baseball as a means of expression. Rather than being merely a "cultural transmission belt for North American values," the sport may have helped Caribbean peoples develop a "common cultural fabric, serving as a vent to social and political tensions, and a vehicle not only for individual mobility but for collective social affirmation."[40]

In Nicaragua, the U.S. military had already landed many times by the turn of the century. In 1902, after years of promises that Nicaragua would host an American canal, the United States instead gave it to Panama—a betrayal felt long into the future. In 1904, U.S. Consul Carter Donaldson founded Nicaragua's oldest surviving baseball team, the Boers, named after South Africa's Dutch-descended colonists, recently decimated in a brutal war by the British. This began a trend of calling Nicaraguan teams by foreign places, including clubs named Russia, Japan, Waterloo, Paris, New York, Alemania, and America. In 1909, when Nicaragua sought some independence from American control, a

U.S. businessman's response was typical: "How long will our chicken-livered government allow those damned Nicaraguan niggers to insult, humiliate and injure Americans and their interests?" In response, the U.S. military again intervened and installed an American mining executive as president. It 1910, the Dawson Pact established Nicaragua as a U.S. colony. From 1912 to 1925, the U.S. Marines occupied Nicaragua, installing a more repressive president. By 1914, American companies were effectively running the Nicaraguan economy. To take Nicaraguan minds off such matters, the Marines formed the Nicaraguan National League, involving local as well as U.S. military teams.[41]

In Panama, the initial American intervention was profound. Having decided to use it for a cross-isthmus canal, U.S. warships forced Panama's "independence" from Colombia in 1903, transforming the new nation into an American protectorate. Panama duly granted the United States the Canal Zone in perpetuity. According to U.S. minister Philippe Bunau-Varilla, American diplomacy had rescued Panama "from the barbarism of wasteful civil wars to consecrate it to the destiny assigned to it by Providence, the service of humanity, and the progress of civilization." As U.S. Senator, S.I. Hayakawa later described the Canal: "We stole it fair and square." U.S. corporations moved in, along with American soldiers (who occupied the nation through 1914), canal workers, and baseball.[42]

An Isthmian Baseball League was quickly formed, and Colonel George Goethels—who directed the canal construction—was league president. Soon the Atlantic League also began, and in 1908 the Panama Canal Zone League was created. In 1914, the Panama Canal opened and a second Canal Zone League was formed. U.S.-installed President Porras threw out the first pitch in the first game. By then the United States had established a puppet National Guard to ensure that Panamanian dictators would remain friendly to U.S. interests. American troops occupied Panamanian bases until after World War II. In 1916, reflecting baseball's corporate functions, the United Fruit Company presented the pennant to the Pan American League winner. The firm used baseball as a diversion for its otherwise exploited employees. Despite the raw relations provoked when the United States annexed Panama, baseball nevertheless received an enthusiastic reception in Colombia. By 1902, Jud Castro had already become the first Colombian in organized baseball. The sport took off when two Colombian students returned home from the United States with the bug in 1903. In 1916, the first Colombian baseball league began in Cartegena.[43]

In the Dominican Republic, the U.S. Marines landed in 1905 to protect American business interests. Americans considered Dominicans uncultured, and baseball was brought in to help "civilize" them. In 1911, the Marines arrived again to install a U.S.-backed president. In 1912, a baseball league solid-ified enough to conduct the first island championship series. With Dominican resentment against the U.S. presence rising, baseball was viewed as an ally. As the U.S. minister observed in 1913, "American baseball is an outlet for the an-imal spirits of the young men . . . they are leaving the plazas where they [had been] talking revolution, and resorting to the ball fields. It is a real substitute for the contest in the hill-sides with rifles [and] might [help save] the nation." Soon a common saying arose: "there has never been a revolution during base-ball season."[44]

But baseball could also be used for retaliation. In 1914, the Dominicans beat the sailors from the USS *Washington* and other U.S. military teams. The *Wash-ington* game was a no-hit victory pitched by Chico Hernandez, who became an instant hero. In 1916, civil war broke out between nationalists and the pup-pet government; the Marines arrived again, established a military government, and ran the country until 1924. Looking back, future Dominican president Juan Bosch—who lived through the U.S. intervention—observed that the baseball games "manifested the people's distaste for the occupation . . . [they were] a way to beat the North Americans." Many Dominican baseball afi-cionados viewed their adopted sport as a symbolic show of pride and defiance against U.S. imperialism.[45]

In Mexico, two leagues formed around Mexico City in 1904, and in the far reaches of the country, the Yucatán Baseball League also emerged. In 1907, the Chicago White Sox held spring training in the capital and barnstormed the nation. In 1910, the Mexican Revolution began and one of its socialist leaders, Carrillo Puerto, encouraged baseball because it was "singularly appro-priate to the social transition the [revolutionary] party would carry out in the Yucatan . . . the individual [in a baseball game] was part of a larger entity whose success depended upon the transformation of individualism into col-lective conscience." Although his "New Yucatán" did not entirely succeed, baseball survived.[46]

Between 1911 and 1921, the United States and Mexico fought several bor-der wars—partly provoked by America's opposition to Mexican revolutionary movements. When U.S. troops amassed in Texas in 1911 for a possible war, Floyd "Rube" Kroh, a Chicago Cubs pitcher the year before, left to fight with the Mexican Insurrectos. That same year, the U.S. passed the Canadian Reci-procity Bill, which ensured Canadian teams continuing involvement in base-ball leagues spanning America's northern frontier. In the south, however, U.S.-Mexican border clashes undermined transnational baseball interactions.[47]

In 1914, with President Woodrow Wilson considering proposals to invade Mexico, baseball initially served as a peacemaker. The Third U.S. Cavalry team at Fort Ringgold, Texas, played a Mexican club. The American and Mexican flags were flown from the same pole, and good feelings were displayed. But the United States invaded after all, and baseball fever intensified when the Marines occupied Veracruz to oust Mexican President Victoriano Huerta. According to U.S. Navy captain John Leonard, "baseball would civilize the country." When the United States invaded again that same year, the YMCA and Knights of Columbus arranged leagues and cross-border baseball games.[48]

In 1916 the U.S. military invaded Mexico yet again and would do so another nine times by 1920. This time, it launched the "Punitive Expedition" to pursue Pancho Villa, the Mexican revolutionary. Villa had cordial relations with America until it recognized his enemy Venustantio Carranza as president. In retaliation, he crossed the U.S. border to attack a military post. The White House fabricated a report that Villa was collaborating with the Germans, who sought Mexico as a World War I ally. President Wilson sent General John Pershing to capture Villa, and during the invasion, the U.S. launched its first-ever air-combat mission, sending eight airplanes into Mexico to bomb suspected strongholds. Among the U.S. soldiers in Mexico were two professional ballplayers: major leaguer Pat Flaherty and Negro Leaguer Wilber "Bullet" Rogan.

By the end of 1916, the United States had a hundred thousand troops at the Mexican border, and full-scale war was being considered. Such a large mobilization pushed the U.S. military further toward institutionalizing sports, and especially baseball, into its activities. More "wholesome" pursuits were sought in response to the escalating venereal disease rate among soldiers. *Baseball Magazine* observed, "War is supposed to hurt interest in mere games. [But] baseball acts as a national escape valve [and] on the brink of war with Mexico, the crowds at ball parks were noticeably large, [and] the most enthusiastic patrons were soldiers [headed] to the front." In 1917, Washington intervened again when the Mexican government converted—to only fifty years—the perpetual leases American oil companies had previously extracted from the country. Venting their anger, worker-ballplayers at some Mexican-based U.S. companies attacked their American supervisors. With the Mexican Revolution not yet over, almost nobody crossed the U.S.-Mexican border in either direction. It was patrolled by the cavalry on both sides, and when baseball emerged in Mexico after the revolution, it was almost exclusively Mexican in character, which would have long-term implications.[49]

The Tour to End All Tours

Baseball's worldwide diffusion has occurred in several ways, sometimes for ulterior motives outside the sport, such as for corporate, religious, military, or foreign policy objectives. Elsewhere, the game has been spread for its own sake or to enhance the global reach of baseball entrepreneurs. Thus the sport has had various ambassadors. From inside the game itself, two missions had already been launched: the modest Harry Wright tour of 1874 and the more grandiose Albert Spalding World Tour of 1888. As James Elfers has described, yet another mission sought to repeat the Spalding venture in 1913–1914: the "tour to end all tours" was led by John McGraw and Charles Comiskey. Built around their respective teams, the New York Giants and the Chicago White Stockings, the players were prominent major leaguers, including Tris Speaker, Sam Crawford, Red Faber, Christy Mathewson, Mike Donlin, Larry Doyle, Germany Schaefer, Fred Merkle, Buck Weaver, and Jim Thorpe. The mission was endorsed by the National Baseball Commission and by both the U.S. president and secretary of state.[50]

The tour's goals were described in lofty, if not questionable, terms. Comiskey biographer G.W. Axelson claimed, "The twentieth century tourists were to exhibit before the little brown men of Mikado's kingdom [the Japanese], the almond-eyed celestials [the Chinese] and the reformed head hunters of Uncle Sam's island possessions [the Filipinos]." *Baseball Magazine* observed, "The aim is to transplant . . . the game. As the world in the last fifty years has been adopting America's inventions for their commercial progress . . . they now wish to see America's National Game in action."[51]

The five-month-long tour began in Cincinnati in October 1913. The teams barnstormed to the American southwest, where the tourists were welcomed by the U.S. 9th Cavalry band. U.S.-Mexican tensions ran high, and the ballgame cheers convinced people across the nearby border that an American military invasion was imminent. Although it wasn't, the teams did cross the border, visiting Agua Prieta, Mexico. From there, they traveled up the West Coast and crossed into Canada. An Asahi team was just forming in Vancouver, with the intention of touring Japan. But the tourists beat them to it, setting sail from Canada shortly after arriving.[52]

In Japan, the mission played in Tokyo, Kobe, Nagasaki, and Yokohama. According to tour reporter Frank McGlynn, "the Japanese seemed to feel they were bound to win . . . and no doubt in time formidable professional baseball players will visit [the U.S.] to compete in a World's Series." The tour moved on to Shanghai, China, where it was met by "crews of Uncle Sam's Asiatic squadron, throwing their caps in the air and cheering." When Thomas Cobbs, the Shanghai Amateur Base Ball League president, was asked why they weren't teaching baseball to the local Chinese, he said, "There are too many of them. The Chinese sometimes get excited, and there is no telling when a riot might break out." The tour moved to British-controlled Hong Kong, where the U.S.

teams played the city's first baseball game. The spectators included Hindus from India along the third-base line, with a smattering of Chinese dispersed at the outer edges, but mostly rowdy British sailors.[53]

The tour stopped next in Manila, which had become an American tropical playground, since the Philippines had finally been pacified. By 1913, the U.S. military was running the thoroughly Americanized colony and propping up its government. Despite the repression, Filipinos embraced baseball as a great island unifier. The tourists received an extravagant welcome, which essentially shut down the country. Pulling into Manila Bay, Frank McGlynn wrote, "Memories of Admiral Dewey's famous naval achievement filled [our] minds as we passed the spot over which the *Olympia* moved on to victory." The ballplayers met Arlie Pond, the former major leaguer who remained in the Philippines after the war, where he had become a doctor, established a hospital, and also promoted baseball. U.S. Army authorities allowed soldiers to attend all the tour's games, and U.S. Governor General Franklin Bell gave the tour a formal welcome.[54]

The McGraw-Comiskey mission left East Asia for Australia, where baseball was already widespread. The Metropolitan Baseball Association was established in Sydney, and Australian teams, such as the Kangaroo Club, toured abroad. In 1908, the U.S. Great White Fleet visit consolidated baseball's growth, when Aussie teams played U.S. Navy clubs. In 1912, the Australian Baseball Council was organized, in time to receive the 1913 American tour. The visit generated proposals for the U.S. major leagues to invest in Australian baseball—so great was the potential already thought to be.[55]

In early 1914, the McGraw-Comiskey tourists arrived in Ceylon, which was dominated by Sir Thomas Lipton. The British dependency was essentially his personal fiefdom, from which he had built a fortune. His face adorned endless product labels, especially for tea. The world's richest man, he treated the tourists luxuriously. British cricket dominated the island, and without Lipton's support, attendance at the tourist baseball game in Colombo might have been quite low. Lipton's travels through America as a youth, however, had converted him into a baseball fan. He was the only person in Ceylon to have seen the New York Giants play, having attended the World Series the previous year at the Polo Grounds. The tourist game was memorable, with a large crowd from all social strata, and Sikh guards—imported by ruling British authorities—provided a unique patrol for the ballpark's foul lines.

The tourists left Asia for Egypt, where they were hosted by the nation's last khedive. A vigorous sportsman, Abbas II sat with Comiskey and the players' wives in his opulent box. He resented British rule and would soon be deposed by England, but the khedive nevertheless watched the Giants and White Sox play some of their best games. Jim Thorpe and Buck Weaver competed for Most Valuable Player honors in what the players dubbed the Desert Sands League. The tourists played another mock game beneath the pyramids, despite the rebuke the Spalding tourists had received for such behavior. The game was filmed by Frank McGlynn and staged by the tour organizer Ted Sullivan, a well-known racist who repeatedly belittled the Egyptians.

Despite their insensitivity, the players acknowledged the Egyptian accomplishments at the Cairo Museum, and they loved the nightlife, which featured clubs and exotic entertainment. After Egypt, the McGraw-Comiskey missionaries arrived in Italy, where Ted Sullivan observed, "We're now in a Christian country and should begin to behave." A memorial dinner was held in Naples, and the British novelist Hall Caine presented each team a bronze statue. The legend on the Giants figure read, "Baseball is the brother of war but its battles shed no blood." That on the White Sox statue read, "Sport is the uniter of nations and a strengthener and upbuilder of men." Besides building good will, the tour solicited the Church: several Catholic players visited Pope Pius X at the Vatican. When the tourists reached France, at least nineteen ball clubs were playing there, mostly in Paris. The tour's visit was short-lived, however, since extensive preparations had been made for a tourist game that, due to a scheduling mistake, never got played, and a riot nearly ensued.[56]

The tourists were happy to arrive in England, where baseball playing was on the rise—partly in response to warming U.S.-British diplomatic relations. While the Mills Commission was denying English roots for the U.S. game, baseball's British promoters were trying to sell the game there precisely *because* of such origins: advertising baseball as a kind of "glorified rounders" played well in England.[57] The American teams played a game for England's King George V, who appeared primarily to seek U.S. support against the German threats that would soon lead to World War I. The U.S. ambassador handed the king a baseball, and when he handed it back to a player on the field, he was treated as if he had "thrown out" the first pitch.[58]

But the good will wasn't universal. The British press condemned the tourists for their excessive American competitiveness. Tempers flared when John McGraw claimed, "American soldiers are superior to the British because of the athletic discipline in the U.S. and because every American soldier has learned to play baseball." Comiskey chimed in, observing that U.S. baseball was not only a "swift and thrilling sport, but an exhibition of American manhood which ought to enhance our prestige among the nations." These remarks intensified the British protest, and a boycott of the tourists' games was called.[59]

Even so, U.S. baseball resonated with the English fascination for the American Old West, and many Brits attended games to satisfy their curiosity. Uniting those worlds was Jim Thorpe, a "genuine Red Indian" who was also a baseball player. Popular throughout the tour, Thorpe was even more celebrated in Britain as the world's best athlete. His skills didn't impress racists, though. At a commemorative dinner for the tourists, with Thorpe sitting in the audience, Lord Desborough claimed that "the white races of the earth have completely demonstrated their superiority in every athletic enterprise." Nevertheless, the tour left behind some positive baseball momentum in Britain.[60]

The McGraw–Comiskey tourists returned home from Europe on the *Lusitania*, the ship whose sinking by the Germans a couple of years later provoked America's entrance into World War I. The tour encountered a new conflict upon arrival. Officials of the upstart Federal League, which was challenging the MLB monopoly, planned to meet the *Lusitania* with another boat to offer the players attractive contracts even before they landed. But MLB had ties to officials in New York's Tammany Hall political machine, who had the Federal League ship locked up in quarantine. Baseball executive Ban Johnson claimed, "I am now not in favor of peace-making methods. There is no need of dealing with these 'pirates.' There will be peace when the Federal League is exterminated." Johnson had no doubt forgotten how his own American League had "pirated" the National League only a decade earlier. In any case, baseball itself was back at war with itself.

But this didn't completely ruin the tourists' reception. The ballplayers were greeted by a banquet at New York's Biltmore Hotel, attended by six hundred people. Speeches were made by Ban Johnson, National League president John Tener, and National Baseball Commission chairman Gary Herrmann. A tour to South America, planned for the following year, was announced. Another banquet was held in Chicago. At these dinners and in the press, the mission was widely lauded: "The world tour is clearly one of the landmarks in baseball history." Another claimed that it "will ever redound to their (Comiskey's and McGraw's) fame, as men, as managers, and as patriotic Americans." According to Frank McGlynn, the ballplayers' "excursion had done much to cement the friendly sporting interest of the leading nations. The tremendous European war has postponed the effects of this friendly journey, but they are merely delayed."[61]

Others were not so sure. William Phelon, writing in the normally optimistic *Baseball Magazine*, called for realism:

> There aren't any new countries adopting baseball. . . . There will not be any wild curiosity to see American ballplayers in Europe, Asia or Australia. And, least of all, nobody east of Suez ever runs furiously. [While] the Cubans found baseball suited to their character, their kinsmen—the

European Spaniard—is far slower, more pompous, less eager for speed and sparkly. The English, slow, methodical, mechanical, can never revel in a game [of] incessant speed both in thinking and action.

Phelon continued, offering disparaging remarks against the Germans, French, Russians, and Italians as well. And, "as to the Orient—aw, don't make us laugh. [They] will think our noble heroes violent lunatics. [T]ry to imagine Chinese or Hindus playing baseball! They can't, they won't, and will never wish to."[62]

It wasn't clear that this and previous baseball tours had succeeded. Even so, MLB kept taking credit for spreading the game. On the other hand, to the extent the game was developed abroad rather than remaining purely "American," baseball took on different characteristics depending on the culture adopting it. Reflecting U.S. nationalism and its urge to promote the American way, a problem emerged for baseball as the mission of white America: nonwhites turned out to be just as good or better players. As David Voigt suggested, perhaps it was time to lay aside America's missionary position, put aside American superiority, and adopt a more realistic, cosmopolitan understanding of the world.[63]

Baseball's New Wars

In the early twentieth century, organized baseball was not merely helping the United States fight battles and establish foreign outposts. It was back waging new internal wars of its own. Since the early 1890s, the National League had emerged supreme. Free from outside competition, the baseball owners nevertheless squandered their gravy train and went to war against each other. As Benjamin Rader has observed, the owners, "imitating the Rockefellers, Carnegies, and Morgans of the day, [ruled] their fiefdoms with utter disregard for the public, their employees, the players, or their fellow owners." Amid the turmoil, the National League was outflanked by Ban Johnson, who took his minor league, the Western League, renamed it the American League, and had it compete with the "senior circuit." Thus was launched the "Great Baseball War of 1901–1903." Having observed the previous baseball conflicts firsthand, Johnson realized he was at war and proceeded accordingly.[64]

In April 1901, Spanish-American War hero Admiral George Dewey watched the Washington Senators play their home opener against the Baltimore Orioles. Later that year, President William McKinley was assassinated by Leon Czolgosz, a Polish anarchist living in Cleveland. In response, the dean of baseball sportswriters, Henry Chadwick, hopped on board the era's anti-immigrant and anti-radical hysteria and urged that baseball's "anarchists" be banished from the game just as the U.S. government should banish "this cursed crew of foreign murderers."[65] Trying to distinguish the American League from the National League, Ban Johnson launched his own crackdown, suspending players for rowdy behavior. At the same time, Johnson—in the short run—also exploited another round of player grievances against the National League, which had fomented another union, the Players Protective Association. He promised players better pay and conditions if they jumped to his league. One of Johnson's owner-managers was former National League star John McGraw, who observed, "A real baseball war was on. We immediately started a raid on the National League."

Besides enticing away National League ballplayers, including stars such as Cy Young, Willie Keeler, and Napoleon Lajoie, Johnson skillfully placed his league's franchises geographically to provide real competition for National League owners. While the war continued for two years, the final battle raged over Johnson's 1903 plan to add a team in New York City. Andrew Freedman, owner of the National League's New York Giants, appealed to his Tammany Hall political connections to block the new team, but Johnson reached a deal with another Tammany faction, and the club was brought in after all. The new American League team was the Baltimore Orioles, but the National League was trying to lure its manager, John McGraw, back into its fold. Doubting his loyalty, Johnson pushed McGraw out, exclaiming, "We want no Benedict Arnold in our midst."[66] Ironically, McGraw then signed to manage Freedman's Giants, and the Orioles became the Highlanders and soon the New York Yankees.

Outmaneuvered, the National League finally signed a 1903 peace treaty—the National Agreement—with the American League. The National Commission was formed and run by a triumvirate including the league presidents and its head, Gary Herrmann. But organized baseball was thereafter long dominated by Ban Johnson, who was dubbed the Czar of Baseball and whom sportswriter F.C. Lane described as running the sport "as an imperial ruler"—reflecting the driving spirit of President Teddy Roosevelt's new administration. Johnson was a fervent supporter of America's foreign ventures. A great patriot, he was always proud that his league was the "American" League.[67]

With the burgeoning U.S. urban population, the new relationship with the American League might benefit the National League after all. There would likely be room enough for more than one team in the large cities. New rivalries might develop, which could boost attendance. And even better, what if an annual end-of-the-season series was played between the two leagues? Public interest and patronage might be further enhanced. With that idea, the World Series was born in 1903.[68] But by then, the teams in the competing leagues were not only limited to the United States, but to the Northeast—hardly the world.

Certainly many believed that serious baseball could only be found stateside, even though it was played in the Caribbean, Asia, and elsewhere. Thus, the baseball "world" was viewed as the United States. And since various missions had sought to spread the sport around the globe, the "World" Series might have been only a premature label for a hoped-for future. But the name's implications likely went further, reflecting the emerging spirit of the times— outside of baseball. America was already viewing itself as a world player and burgeoning empire. So of course the U.S. baseball championship would also be viewed as the world's baseball championship.[69]

In 1910, in MLB's ongoing effort to shore up its patriotic credentials, Washington Senators owner Clark Griffith invited President William Howard Taft to become the first chief executive to throw out the first pitch of the season. It became a tradition repeated by virtually every subsequent American president. For nearly a decade, the major leagues had been at peace, but by 1913, more war clouds filled the horizon, and organized baseball faced yet another battle. The Federal League arose as a competing major league. As with past challenges, it was provoked by the ongoing exploitation of major leaguers in their pay, conditions, and mobility. While initially responsive, the American League reimposed old policies after the 1903 peace treaty. Those abuses, plus a desire by new entrepreneurs to break into baseball, prompted the Federal League War of 1914–1915.[70]

While the media focused on the McGraw-Comiskey world tour, Federal League owner Edward Steininger gave a rousing war talk: "We are going to invade the majors and take some of their players too." The raids were led by Federal League president "Fighting Jim" Gilmore, nicknamed for his fierce Spanish-American War service. More than two hundred American and National leaguers eventually jumped to the Feds, including stars such as Joe Tinker, Albert "Chief" Bender, Hal Chase, Jack Quinn, and Mordecai "Three Finger" Brown. Another jumper was Armando Marsans, one of the light-skinned Cubans signed by the National League, whose switch to the new league was described as "one of the mysteries of the summer, but not to anyone who knows the Latin temper." But it really wasn't so mysterious: Marsans came from a family of Cuban freedom fighters, and he bristled at the Latin stereotyping and reserve-clause contracts he faced in the National League.[71]

According to the *Chicago Daily News*, it was "All quiet in the base ball war— the war was being busy burning more or less merrily beneath the surface." In "Echoes of the Baseball War," W.G. Kibbey put the conflict into verse:

Oh! Hear the cannons roar,
Declaring a baseball war,
   Colors flying—
   Faith undying.

Loudly do we clamor
For the spear and armor,
   Always fighting—
   Often biting.
In a baseball war.[72]

The judiciary became a battleground for some Federal League battles. According to William Phelon, "most of the attacks and counter attacks are secret, furtive, of the law court rather than the diamond. Court proceedings, raids and counter-raids, novel schemes of attack and defense, and newspaper bombs by the million, kept the air full of smoke and flame." To protest MLB's violation of the antimonopoly laws, the Federal League took its case to the purported trustbuster, Judge Kenesaw Mountain Landis. In the end, Landis was more a baseball fan than an antimonopolist, and his intransigence in the court case was later rewarded when the major leagues appointed him commissioner.

Joining Ban Johnson against the Federal League was National League president John Tener. A former major-league pitcher and Spalding World Tour ballplayer, Tener became a U.S. congressman and then governor of Pennsylvania. Together, he and Johnson beat back the threat by promising a couple of Federal League owners their own MLB franchises. The jumping ballplayers were given amnesty, the Federal League collapsed, and the war was won. Tener had played a leading role, behind closed doors, in devising the peace settlement.[73]

In October 1915, Woodrow Wilson became the first U.S. president to attend a World Series game. Two months later, the Treaty of Cincinnati concluded the Federal League War. Sportswriter F.C. Lane celebrated the end of hostilities: with "the termination of the long and costly baseball war a new day of prosperity is at hand." Comparing this to other wars, Lane claimed, "The public never likes wars, however much it may enjoy reading about them. It didn't like the baseball war. Baseball as a national game has been battered, but you can't destroy it any more than you can destroy civilization by the great European struggle."[74] With World War I blazing across the Atlantic, that would remain to be seen.

5

Real War
(1917–1919)

The world ought to be made safe for baseball.

—Benjamin DeCasseres

Discussing what it called the "baseball battle," *Baseball Magazine* editorialized in 1914, "Kingdoms and principalities may pass away, dynasties may crumble, Hapsburg and Hohenzollern conquer or perish: what of that? A pennant race is a pennant race, and its interest is immutable . . . for a country of peace ideals, baseball is a better pursuit than war [and] any amount of martial glory achieved at terrible cost of human life."[1] Perhaps so, but baseball wasn't enough to prevent war.

By 1914 the Great War had begun in Europe. Many Americans supported neutrality, but while presidential candidate Woodrow Wilson campaigned promising to keep the United States out of World War I, he pushed the nation into the conflict after his 1916 reelection. In line with America's increasingly majestic visions of itself, Wilson claimed the nation was fighting to "make the world safe for democracy."[2] Baseball would join this crusade in some intriguing ways.

While the war would have no real meaning for most Americans until its fourth year, when the Providence Grays—a Boston Red Sox minor league affiliate—arrived in Montreal in 1914 with a nineteen-year-old southpaw named Babe Ruth, the evening newspapers were so filled with war bulletins, the baseball box scores didn't appear until the next day. As a British Commonwealth member, Canada—along with England—was already at war. When Ruth's teammate Wallace Shultz backed Germany, he was promptly nicknamed the Kaiser and taunted by practical jokes.[3]

Before the United States entered the war and arrived in Europe, Canadian soldiers were already in France, playing baseball. When they ran short of baseball gear for themselves and for the British and French (who began playing the game), American League president Ban Johnson sent them a shipment. By

1915, the U.S. government was already preparing for war. Major league base-ball (MLB) claimed the mobilization was good for America as well as for the game—as it essentially equated the two. In the short run, major leaguers usu-ally professed neutrality on the war. By 1916, however, Ty Cobb did find posi-tive similarities between the German kaiser's strategy of frightfulness in war and his own theory about running the base paths.[4]

Two military men, Colonel Tillinghast Huston and Colonel Jacob Rupert, bought the New York Yankees in 1915. After his Spanish-American War ser-vice, Huston led his reserve unit, and in 1916 he suggested military drills for all spring-training teams, even proposing that *fans* be made to march. Ban Johnson adopted Huston's initiative for all American League ballplayers, and then in early 1917—with "preparedness" as the watchword—he issued an of-ficial resolution, outlining how baseball would help protect the country. Play-ers were asked to appear on ball fields "trained in military tactics" to get other Americans "to emulate their example." Ballplayers became civilian soldiers, devoting an hour daily to military instruction, traveling to and from the ball-park in military formation, performing military drills before each game, and attending military training camps after the World Series.[5]

Regular military troops were also invited to march at baseball fields. Army sergeants trained the ballplayers, whom the media dubbed Ban and Till's tin soldiers. Johnson launched a drill competition among the teams, judged by Lieutenant Colonel Raymond Sheldon. The St. Louis Browns won the cash prize, yet they provided the fewest ballplayer-soldiers for the war. In Chicago, Charles Comiskey had his White Sox parade in khaki before a large crowd, in-cluding seven thousand soldiers and six military bands.[6] While these gestures were pomp and ceremony, the United States entered World War I for real in April 1917. Baseball geared up its own response.

Making the World Safe for Baseball

Organized baseball presented itself as crucial to the nation's morale. With the public initially ambivalent about the war, baseball's involvement made it "im-possible for even the most pronounced pacifist to escape a thrill of patriotism." Echoing President Wilson's words, *New York Times* writer Benjamin De-Casseres claimed that "the world ought to be made safe for baseball." As long as baseball embodied American democracy, "the Kaisers and Trotskys would strike out . . . the country that would win the war was the country that had produced Christy Mathewson, Ty Cobb, and Babe Ruth."[7]

Yet critics claimed that rather than for democracy, the war was actually be-ing fought "to make the world safe for capitalism" and U.S. domination. Economically, MLB worried about its profits and fought to keep the game going during the war. But it also sought to further promote the game abroad, and wherever the U.S. military and flag went, baseball was eager to follow. Likewise, baseball equipment dealers tied their products to the patriotic war effort. Posting advertisements claiming, "Athletes Make the Best Fighters," Alex Taylor & Co. received large athletic equipment contracts from the U.S. Army. Team owners expected a new surge of baseball interest after the war, but first the sport would have to survive.[8]

According to Joel Zoss and John Bowman, "Baseball was about to learn that its status as America's national game sometimes required it to be compliant while clever politicians manipulated it . . . [to advance] their military policies." Thus by early 1917, baseball was pushed into increasingly nationalistic displays. Advertisements in periodicals such as *Baseball Magazine* mixed patriotism with marketing, such as commercials for D&M Sporting Goods and Reach Athletic Goods: "As popular in the camps and rest-fields of France as on the baseball grounds of America." Ads also appeared for government bonds, war savings stamps, National War Saving's Day, and other war-related activities and products.[9]

National League President John Tener was applauded for his successful "war administration." Besides his role in winning the recent Federal League War, he supported America's ongoing border wars against Mexico and jumped on the World War I bandwagon: "This is a war of democracy against bureaucracy. And baseball is the very watchword of democracy. No other sport or business or anything under heaven exerts the leveling influence baseball does." Some wished Tener had "employed 'big stick' methods" a little more, but sportswriter F.C. Lane claimed he was "best fitted to pilot the league through the stormy period of the war."[10]

To support the war effort, Washington Senators owner Clark Griffith launched a Ball and Bat Fund to provide baseball equipment to U.S. army camps, and to "give the American soldier the kind of punch he needed to knock out the Hun." In appreciation, American Expeditionary Forces Commander John Pershing wrote from France, "The army executives from President Wilson down have been quick to see the value of baseball as recreation for those undergoing military drills." Wilson sent his own contribution and letter of support. Ban Johnson raised money to send three thousand baseball kits overseas to U.S. soldiers. And the prominent Hollywood actor Douglas Fairbanks ran a campaign to send baseball bats "over there." It was, he said, the "next best thing to having a seat at the Polo Grounds."[11]

Organized baseball paid an entertainment tax for each ballgame and promoted Liberty Bond drives. At the 1917 World Series, a vigorous bond campaign was conducted to "knock out the Kaiser." Baseballs autographed by stars such as Christy Mathewson, Art Fletcher, and Larry Doyle were sold for large sums to rich financiers such as John D. Rockefeller and agents of the J.P. Morgan Company. MLB affiliated with the Red Cross, raising money and serving on its committees. President Wilson attended a Red Cross benefit game between the Washington Senators and Detroit Tigers. Other exhibitions were played, including Sunday fund-raising games. Although sometimes held in towns banning sports on the Sabbath, in the end patriotism trumped religion and helped, in the long run, to lift the bans for good. Second only to the military's *Stars and Stripes,* the "bible of baseball," the *Sporting News,* was the favorite periodical among U.S. soldiers. Its editor, J. Taylor Spink, persuaded the American League and several teams to buy thousands of subscriptions for enlisted men abroad. *Baseball Magazine* subscriptions were donated as well.[12]

Over time, military displays at ballparks became more elaborate. "Take Me Out to the Ball Game" composer Harry Von Tilzer released the "great base ball war song" entitled "Batter Up: Uncle Sam Is at the Plate," which was widely performed. Large martial parades and extravaganzas were created, presaging the military flyovers seen today at big-league stadiums. Soon the National League joined the American League teams in adding ballplayer military drills. The Dodgers, Tigers, and Indians rebelled, however, against the mandated hour of marching, and it was discontinued by the end of 1917. In response to criticism, it was reinstated in 1918, when players began marching again—with bats, if not rifles. The drills were supposed to generate patriotic respect for baseball among spectators and soldiers and prepare players for service if they were called. Ballpark recruitment campaigns were primarily aimed, however, at the fans. Baseball sponsored "Wake Up America Days" to promote military volunteers. Wounded soldiers, and sometimes all military personnel— were admitted to ballparks for free.[13]

The major leagues grudgingly tolerated reduced reporting, as box scores got squeezed out by war coverage. Baseball accepted the game's downgrading on the field, as scarce materials went to the war effort. Equipment suffered, and the new baseballs were inferior—and teams were ordered to use each ball longer in games. Player ranks were depleted as well. In some cases, ballplayers were good-naturedly given new names: pitcher Alvin Crowder was nicknamed General because he shared the last name of the general running the military draft. In other cases, players changed their own names to ward off virulent anti-German sentiment: Heinie Zimmerman and Heinie Groh both took the name Henry. Major-league clubs began wearing American flag patches on their jerseys, the Cubs added red, white, and blue stockings, and the White Sox wore red, white, and blue uniforms for the World Series (and wore replicas in 2001 for their Sunday "throwback" home games). The American Association's Minneapolis Millers wore khaki uniforms with the Stars and Stripes embroidered across their shirts.[14]

Writing in *Collier's*, Jerome Beatty observed that "baseball contributed [most] to the war effort by recognizing how inconsequential it was compared to the 'real World Series'—the war." Yet while organized baseball displayed some genuine patriotism, it was drawn into the war as much by the "national pastime trade-off," or the need to maintain its status as the national game.[15] Although the United States was at war for most of 1917, the conflict's direct effects on baseball were relatively small. This threatened to change as the 1918 season opened. Many felt ballplayers, as athletes, were natural soldiers, who should join up. While a widespread stripping of team rosters would, in effect, have closed down the baseball season, others wanted more: a shutdown of ballparks to use them as storage depots for war supplies.

Some owners panicked or pursued preemptive strategies. Anticipating the drafting of Grover Cleveland Alexander, the Philadelphia Phillies traded the future Hall of Famer to the Chicago Cubs. Baseball leaders deflected criticism by stepping up their war support, such as sponsoring benefit games for soldier charities. At Camp Sheridan, the Cincinnati Reds spent part of spring training playing army teams. The New York Giants played the army aviators at Waco, Texas (as a Red Cross benefit), the New York Yankees played the 124th Infantry team, and the St. Louis Cardinals and Chicago White Sox played the Camp Funston, Kansas, club.[16]

Organized baseball wanted people to understand the war's economic hardship, with declining attendance, trimmed schedules, and lost players. General Manager Branch Rickey signed draft-proof Cuban players to hedge against military conscription. The war was also devastating to the minors: nine of the ten leagues collapsed or closed for at least a year. While the Pacific Coast League folded only for 1918, the North Carolina League shut down for good. According to Jim Sumner, the latter was "the first professional league to come face-to-face with the incompatibility of professional baseball and twentieth-century warfare."[17]

Working, Fighting, and Ballplaying

While the 1918 season began on time, the stakes were raised. In May, the U.S. government issued a "Work or Fight" order, subjecting all American men to the draft except those with a legitimate deferment or war-production employment.[18] Chicago Cubs pitcher Harry Weaver requested a deferment on the grounds that "we have a good chance to win the pennant." Nevertheless,

those not exempted would have to report by July 1, 1918; baseball was classified as a nonessential occupation.

The major leagues appealed. The first test was Brooklyn outfielder Hy
Myers, who left the Dodgers but whose Ohio draft board told him to finish
the season and then find war-industry work. Other states followed Ohio's lead.
But then the Washington, D.C., draft board ruled against another ballplayer,
Eddie Ainsmith. His team, the Washington Senators, claimed baseball was a
unique business that would be destroyed without its players' unusual skills.
Secretary of War Newton Baker intervened, however, and issued a blanket de-
nial of any baseball exemptions.

Although the draft had already made inroads into team rosters, baseball
wasn't ordered to shut down completely. In fact, its draft compliance deadline
was extended to September 2 in exchange for ending the regular season early,
by Labor Day. The War Department allowed an expedited World Series. Cynically, the owners exploited this by withholding a portion of the players'
salaries. A few ballplayers sued: one of them, Senators outfielder Burt Shotton,
was labeled a Bolsheviki and released by the team. The players' union, the
Baseball Fraternity, protested. Sportswriter John Foster had previously called
the union's predecessor, the Baseball Brotherhood, Bolsheviks. Now, he characterized the new union as "foreign, hostile, and injurious to sport."[19] It was
patriotic for players to take a financial loss, but not the owners.

To reinforce organized baseball's devotion to the cause, Ban Johnson went
to Washington, D.C., offering to serve in any war-related job. Instead Johnson
was made a liaison between the American Red Cross and the U.S. military. His
real purpose was to further lobby the War Department on baseball's behalf.
Johnson proposed a partial exemption for some players on each team, to maintain the leagues' competitive balance. Rather than seeking favoritism, he
claimed he was just trying to keep the national pastime going—for which he
believed he had the government's endorsement. Yet this proposal was also denied. But the war ended in November 1918, before the draft affected another
baseball season. And Johnson did get the War Department to hasten player-
soldier demobilization so they didn't miss the 1919 season's opening games.[20]

In *Outing* magazine, Albert Britt claimed the war dead should "inspire"
ballplayers, but it wasn't clear whether this meant they should enlist or merely
play better. Elsewhere, the message was more evident: to be a man one must embrace the military life. Despite demonstrating their manliness daily at the ball
park, did ballplayers possess the hypermasculinity necessary on the battlefront?[21]
In the end, more than 440 major and minor leaguers (and even some umpires)
left for the war. The baseball soldiers included at least 27 Hall of Famers, such as
Eddie Collins, Harry Heilman, Branch Rickey, Waite Hoyt, Rabbit Maranville,

Joe Sewell, George Sisler, Casey Stengel, Tris Speaker, and Negro Leaguers Oscar Charleston and Bullet Rogan.

The first ballplayer to enlist was Hank Gowdy, who was praised for neither slacking nor taking a shipyard job. His induction spurred other ballplayer enlistments. After the war, Gowdy returned to the Boston Braves and then the New York Giants. During the winters, he earned big lecture-circuit money telling war stories around the nation. Ballplayers often testified how baseball had prepared them for military life. According to Sam Rice, "the Navy gave me my first opportunity to see the world and made a ball player out of me." Johnny Evers worked for the Knights of Columbus promoting baseball in Europe. Grover Cleveland Alexander was drafted, as predicted, and was seriously wounded and shell-shocked in battle, although he recovered to pitch again.[22]

During the war, when American troops prepared their assault on Metz, Germany, the men carried only the bare essentials: no packs, no shovels, no canteens. After the battle, a dead U.S. soldier was found who had stormed the lines with nothing but his gun, his bayonet, and a worn baseball. Six major leaguers also died in World War I. Alex Burr of the New York Yankees was killed on his twenty-fifth birthday, only ten days before the Armistice. Marcus Milligan of the Pittsburgh Pirates, Larry Chappell of the Chicago White Sox, and Ralph Sharman of the Philadelphia Athletics were also killed. The others— former Philadelphia Phillies teammates—were Robert Troy and Eddie Grant. Grant's death was the most celebrated: a former New York Giant and Harvard University–educated attorney, Grant died in the Battle of the Argonne Forest. "Although close to exhaustion, there was no difference between the Grant who walked forward under shell-fire and the Grant of old, trotting out from the bench to third base." A New York City highway and American Legion Post were both named after him.[23]

The war's most famous baseball veteran was the pitcher Christy Mathewson, who at age thirty-seven didn't have to sign up but went anyway. In France, he was assigned—along with Ty Cobb—to the Chemical Warfare Service. During a drill, lethal gas accidentally entered a practice chamber. Two soldiers died, and both Cobb and Mathewson inhaled gas, but Matty got the worst of it. While he avoided actual battle, Mathewson inhaled more poisonous fumes when inspecting German ammunition dumps. About his exposure, he joked, "The only persons I know of who need gas are umpires." But soon he was sick, spending long stretches at a Saranac Lake, New York, sanitarium where he worked, when he could, with the American Legion to raise money for World War I veterans with tuberculosis. When Mathewson died at age forty-five, his wife Jane said, "He gave his life for his country, just as many boys like Eddie Grant, who was killed in action overseas."[24]

Some players, including Babe Ruth and Joe Jackson, pursued stateside war production work. During the war, Ruth clashed with Boston Red Sox owner Ed Barrow, and he jumped the club for the Chester Shipyards in Pennsylvania, where he played for the company's baseball team. The newspapers called him a draft dodger, even though—as a married man—he was legitimately exempt. Industrial leagues proliferated at the time, and some companies, such as Bethlehem Steel, aggressively lured professional players for their ball clubs. Aside from the prestige, fans paid companies to watch these stars.[25]

While war production was legitimate work under the Work or Fight Order, ballplayers were labeled as shirkers for pursuing it. The *Sporting News* published a sarcastic poem:

> Two more bold, fearless ath-a-letes of note
> Have gone to captivate the Kaiser's goat
> And save the world from Hun autocracy
> By smearing gobs of paint upon a boat.
> Men fought with spear and war clubs long ago,
> Then came the guns which laid the foreman low;
> And now the athlete takes his pot in hand
> And swings his trusty paint brush on the foe.

While initially endorsing professional sports during the war and providing regular coverage for soldiers, *Stars and Stripes* began to reconsider: "It seems beyond belief that any well trained athlete should be guilty of such yellow-hearted cowardice, traitors to their country's good, and worse than traitors to their own souls." Organized baseball's quest for special consideration tarnished the game's patriotic image, partly as a result of its own past propaganda that it was essential to national betterment and taught frontier qualities such as courage.[26]

Even Ban Johnson criticized "shipyard slackers" who played in "Shelter Leagues." But the real target was the companies, not the players. Speaking for the owners, sportswriter F.C. Lane decried the "widespread campaign of certain manufacturing concerns to lure away professional players . . . to [be] drawing cards on [their] baseball clubs." Lane scorned anything that interfered "with the maximum production of ships . . . yet baseball has become the victim of an attempt to pervert this most patriotic endeavor." Despite their patriotic rhetoric, the owners were most upset about their players escaping baseball's exploitative reserve-clause system, by playing instead in the industrial leagues.[27]

The religious community also weighed in. While he opposed baseball on the Sabbath, Billy Sunday, a former major leaguer turned evangelist, nevertheless urged MLB's continuation:

What are soldiers worth if they're not good athletes? What is a battle but a showdown of athletic skill of a terrible intensity? The idea that baseball is a luxury that ought to be postponed is ridiculous. It is just as useful to the average spectator as to the soldier . . . ; this country [must be brought] victorious through this terrible war. Baseball is A WAR GAME. We need it now more than ever.[28]

On the other hand, Sunday railed against slackers. Equating loyalty to country with Jesus Christ, he also claimed that "fellows who knock conscription ought to be lined up against a wall and shot like any other traitor."[29]

Defending the game, sportswriter William Phelon wrote that organized baseball "furnished a greater percentage of its personnel for military service than almost any other industry." Rather than slacking, some players were overworked in their war production jobs. Future Hall of Famer Albert "Chief" Bender toiled fourteen- to eighteen-hour days and suffered a nervous breakdown. In his investigation of "slackers," General Crowder found they had been minimal in baseball. According to major leaguer and Camp Logan athletic director Leslie Mann, military officers thought big leaguers served the nation better as players than as soldiers. And sportswriter Frederick Parmly claimed that "for the future of America, baseball is absolutely essential . . . BASEBALL will win the war." Ironically, this was published a month *after* the war ended.[30]

In any case, rather than the players, Jerome Beatty concluded that it was "the game that was heroic," and when "the test was applied, baseball proved its worthiness. It is truly the national game now." Former Chicago Cubs owner Charles Murphy went even further, observing, "What a pity Germany does not play baseball! If [it did] its people would never engage in a war of conquest . . . ; the grand old game is going to cement a friendship among liberty-loving peoples of all civilized nations. After the war, it is going to be the world game."[31]

An Army of Ballplayers

While professional baseball struggled to survive on the home front during the war, it had no trouble further integrating itself into America's military apparatus. The philosopher Randolph Bourne observed that "war is the health of the state." A wartime nation attains "a uniformity of feeling, a hierarchy of values," so that distinctions between society and the individual are all but eliminated. According to historian Eric Hobsbawm, military service was a powerful mechanism for "inculcating proper civic behavior, and turning the villager into the patriotic citizen of a nation." The military harnesses competitiveness and physical prowess, observed sports advocate Luther Gulick, for "more powerful social devotions."[32] In the United States, baseball played a pronounced role in this process.

In 1919, *Scientific American* observed how sports had become central to the military, as it sought to create an "army of athletes. . . . Narrow-chested clerks made three-base hits on the same ball teams with college athletes." According to Steven Pope, to develop the fighting instinct, an unparalleled athletics program—led by baseball—was devised in the military. Baseball was an "efficient means to cultivate national vitality, citizenship, and the martial spirit." Infused with athletics, military training would not only train "American men in the 'soldierly values' of obedience, citizenship, and combat, but also repair class schisms and restore social order." At the mammoth Great Lakes Naval Station, 150 baseball games were played in one day, inspiring Chicago Cubs owner Charles Weeghman to lend the navy his manager and coaches, send it equipment, and observe that "baseball has once more responded to the call and proved [it's] the sport of the hour, a true war game."[33]

Also instrumental to its war mobilization were America's public schools. Students were being prepared as cogs for America's growing industrial machinery, being trained for efficiency and obedience—the same traits valued by the nation's military machine. School sports led the way. *American Boy* magazine opined, "When Germany calculated whether to bring the U.S. into World War I, it ignored America's system of school athletics. It goes far beyond the ability—taught by playing baseball—of throwing a grenade far and accurate. Its well-organized and well-drilled teams provided a foundation for military training." Baseball in the schools "provides each American [tools to confront] the opponent's strategies. He learns to play the game on the diamond and is almost ready to play the not dissimilar game on the shell-torn fields of France."[34]

Religious institutions contributed as well. They had already used baseball to proselytize abroad, spread the American way, and bolster the U.S. military presence. In World War I, they launched a new burst of "muscular Christianity." The YMCA was enlisted to provide military sporting activities, and in September 1917 it helped select the athletic director for the American Expeditionary Forces in Europe. It organized intercompany and barracks baseball leagues, and when Americans were captured, it sent baseball equipment to German prisoner-of-war camps.

Promoting military baseball was rationalized on several grounds. Since one couldn't "put thousands of red-blooded American boys together without having an uncounted number of diamond battles," baseball's denial would have undermined morale. Not to mention morals: camp baseball would keep soldiers' minds off alcohol and women. Others felt that while baseball would help the armed forces, the military—by promoting the game among soldiers—would also help keep the game alive during the war.[35]

Most of all, baseball would enhance military training effectiveness, providing an "added quickness of brain and strength." It also developed particular skills. General Pershing claimed that, "in grenade and bomb throwing, Americans become proficient in a few days drill. I attribute this to baseball." Retired Boston Braves pitcher Bill James was so skilled at bomb throwing he was made into a military instructor. A new hand grenade had recently been invented by a former West Point pitcher, which would "enable our army to use effectively our national ability to play baseball." Replacing "the inferior European bomb," it had the size of a baseball and the thrower "delivered" it with the motion a pitcher used for an "outcurve."[36] Recruitment posters featured soldiers winding up to pitch, declaring, "That arm. Your country needs it."

Baseball also helped soldiers shoot accurately. The "batting eye" could instantly gauge distance. According to Yankees owner Colonel Huston, "marksmanship was instinctive with our soldiers. The feats of Daniel Boone and 'Buffalo Bill' were not exceptional. But it was baseball that fine-tuned the soldier and his shooting eye." In addition, the military had soldiers play mock baseball games wearing gas masks: if they could play ball that way, surely they could also make war.[37]

The sport also was believed to instill a spirit of fair play. Through the White House–created Creel Committee and other propaganda groups, Germany was condemned not only for being the enemy but for the way it fought the war. In contrast, baseball-trained American soldiers would "find no pleasure in maltreating the helpless." Sportswriter William Heylinger noted that the American boy had a national sport with a code of morals, "but the German boy has no national sport, and [thus no] code of fair play. Train boys to believe that 'might is right' and you kill their souls."[38] As War Department executive and future National League president Ford Frick suggested in verse, U.S. troops knew how to play the game:

> We may not be in the "highbrow" class
>   Our lessons have been hard knocks,
> But we're off to France to take our chance
>   With Luck in the pitcher's box.
> We may not star in the game of war,
>   Nor win a place with fame,
> But we'll fight our fight for the cause of right
>   For we've learned to Play the Game.

It was assumed the war ought to be fought fairly, under certain rules. According to *Stars and Stripes*, "the Huns aren't good sports. They try to spike the opposing runner, their pitchers only use the bean ball, and the Umpire [takes] their side." As Wanda Wakefield has observed, such reporting reassured U.S. soldiers they were on the high road. The Germans didn't even play fair in baseball, never mind that Germans probably never actually played baseball at all.[39]

A Great War for Baseball

When baseball went abroad with the war effort, the sport was used to explain the superiority of American armed forces over other Allied troops. English writer Rudyard Kipling denounced his countrymen's love for sports when those energies were needed instead for defense. But *Baseball Magazine* noted that U.S. wartime soldiers turned with "relief" to the "bloodless encounters of the diamond."[40] American troops were itching to both play and watch baseball. As one soldier wrote:

> Oh, I'm longing to be at the old ball yard;
>   But I gotta go out and drill.
> I wanna be out there, rootin' hard,
>   But I gotta get out and drill.
> I'd like to be jammed with the bleacher mob
> Lampin' [watching] Babe Ruth and Cravath and Cobb
>   But the doggone sergeant is on the job
>   And I gotta get out and drill.

This lament fell on receptive ears. The War Department's Commission on Training Camp Activities adopted the slogan "Every American Soldier a baseball player." The War Camp Community Service fought enlistee boredom to bolster "civilization" against the Huns; baseball was its prime service. At the peak of America's war involvement, between August 1918 and January 1919 alone, nearly 3 million people watched baseball in Europe and nearly eight hundred thousand played it in the American Expeditionary Forces.[41]

Baseball helped conceptualize the war as well. According to Wanda Wakefield, military leaders used baseball metaphors to "socialize diverse enlisted forces into the dominant discourse of a masculinist sporting culture." The circulation of *Stars and Stripes* rose because of its baseball coverage, but the sport was also used to present the war news, in headlines such as "Uncle Sam Pinch Hitting on Western Front," "Huns Hit .000 Against Lorraine Hurlers," "Kaiser Calls Bench Warmers into Play," "Austria Groggy at End of Fourth," "France Makes Fourth a Double Header," "Yanks Nip Hun Rally in Belleau Woods," "Ex-Yank Twirler Beaned by Bullet," and "Franco-Yanko Rally Routs Hun Twirlers."[42] These metaphors helped describe the war's progress, privileging athletic soldiers and forcing immigrant soldiers to learn the U.S. national game. Of course, most African Americans knew the baseball terms well, but in the segregated armed forces they likely sounded hollow.

Despite mass slaughters, the war was often presented as a game, which *Stars and Stripes* claimed "should hold no terrors for the average American soldier already trained in sports."[43] An editorial cartoon showed a soldier swinging his baseball bat at an incoming missile, which he hit back to the German lines: applying baseball skills to war, it proclaimed, was both "Business and Pleasure." Baseball and war were united: war was like baseball and the pleasure derived from the game could also be achieved through battle.

In 1917, the Germans became "evil" in America, even though they were widely admired only months before. *Baseball Magazine* ran anti-German poems, songs, cartoons, and advertisements. If Germany only had baseball, then it "might have saved her the stain of mangled Belgium and of the Lusitania." Brooklyn Dodgers pitcher Leon Cadore claimed, "The American Army is a thinking army, composed of men who are intelligent and have the proper spirit. In Germany everything is one vast scheme of iron discipline." According to Charles Murphy, "The Kaiser is a bum. . . . [If Germany] did not have a war, the [Crown] Prince would start one just for the sport of it. That would not [happen to] a man who loves our national game."

According to the *Boston Transcript*, "Germany is trying to steal home by spiking the catcher. And she can't understand why the bleachers are jeering at her." In a *Baseball Magazine* advertisement, Uncle Sam—hoping to "score" the Allies already "on base"—eagerly awaited a pitch from crafty "Lefty" Hindenburg. Former major leaguer Eddie Cicotte explained that Walter Johnson's fastball was "a floater compared to some of the things a Boche cannoneer can heave at you." Luckily, although "Fritz made about two runs in his inning, he couldn't get us out after we went to bat." When U.S. troops invaded German territory, *Stars and Stripes* gleefully reported the American seizure of the Kaiser's tennis courts for a baseball diamond.[44]

Baseball Magazine ran a cartoon imploring the United States to draft a staff of "wild spitball pitchers" and have them "aim at Trotsky in Russia" because "one of 'em is bound to bean the Kaiser in Berlin." No matter that until it left the war in early 1918, Russia was an American ally—anticommunist hysteria was already brewing. In fact, America *did* eventually aim at Trotsky, when it landed troops (including Philippine baseball patron Colonel Arlie Pond) in Russia to support White Russians against the Red Army from late 1918 through 1920.

While U.S. troops brought baseball to Vladivostok and Siberia in eastern Russia, other Americans—sympathetic to the "great socialist experiment"—soon brought the game to Moscow and Leningrad in the west.[45]

Other Allies were also fair game for baseball analysis. Formerly part of the Triple Alliance with Germany and Austria-Hungary, Italy switched sides to ally with Britain and France in the Triple Entente. But when it quickly suffered a devastating defeat in the November 1917 Battle of Caporetto, *Baseball Magazine* blamed Italy's loss on "their want of baseball." The Italians "were brave soldiers but lacked the athletic spirit [baseball could provide] to strengthen their mental and physical fiber." Not until two years later, when Italian immigrant Max Ott returned home from the United States, did Italy get its first ballgames, which he arranged in Turin.[46]

Eventually, *Stars and Stripes* ended its war-baseball cheerleading, suspending its sports page altogether in July 1918, pending an Allied victory: "Sport among the troops must go on. But the glorified, the commercialized, the spectatorial sport has been burnt out by gunfire. The sole slogan left is 'Beat Germany.'" Other baseball coverage survived, and the *Sporting News* got a flurry of new subscriptions. But troops also began getting wartime baseball news through the emerging new radio technology. In October 1917, Giants–White Sox World Series coverage was radioed to soldiers in Paris, Honolulu, Manila, and the Canal Zone. In 1918, radio baseball reports were sent as far away as Koblenz, Vladivostok, and Constantinople.[47]

The European Baseball Theater

Even before the U.S. got involved, *Baseball Magazine* observed that the war was popularizing baseball more "in conservative England than all the tours and propagandas of forty years [previous]. The Canadian has adopted the American game and wherever stationed, he organizes clubs and plays baseball."[48] Australian troops also played the game when deployed to Europe.

After the Americans arrived, baseball vastly expanded. Former major leaguer Bill Lange claimed the "Americans had taught the Europeans how to fight and now it would teach them how to play." And as Charles Comiskey observed, the Europeans "think the sport is responsible for the pop shown by our army. England and France seemed content [with] trench fighting, but our boys jumped in and won a victory our Allies thought would take years. The Europeans want to play the game if such advantages may be gained."[49]

While U.S. soldiers took the game to Holland and Belgium,[50] the real focus of wartime baseball was England and France. In Great Britain, the Anglo-

American League of U.S. and Canadian armed forces teams was cosponsored by American companies. Games were played for British royalty, as when the U.S. 85th Aero Squadron team appeared at Grantham Hall on the Fourth of July, 1918. For the U.S. Army-Navy championship game, the huge turnout included King George V and current and future prime ministers David George and Winston Churchill. Sportswriter J.G. Lee claimed the English themselves were playing baseball "with a [new] zest and enthusiasm [because of] the war, [where] regular playing is teaching them the game."[51]

In France, baseball was even more popular. It caught on like wildfire everywhere American troops were stationed. Within the U.S. military ("Uncle Sam's League") the "world's greatest baseball league" was launched in France—an "athletic movement [vaster than any other] in the history of sport, and numbering over two million players." According to *Stars and Stripes*, "it makes the American and National Leagues look like a chess club circuit in Rahway, New Jersey. It will have 1000 teams, which will play for the First Army Corps [championship] on ground hallowed by thousands who laid down their lives." French military commanders ordered their soldiers to learn baseball, to improve hand-grenade throwing and physical training. A Paris League for French teams included 30 clubs, and baseball was even played in the Tulieries Gardens. Leagues were formed in Touraine and on the Riviera. According to the *New York Times*, "every bare space behind the battle lines in France [has been] converted into a baseball diamond." The YMCA and Knights of Columbus coordinated the leagues and began placing orders for bats, gloves, and balls manufactured in France. Baseball instruction books were published in French—by none other than Albert Spalding's American Sports Publishing Company. As Charles Murphy observed, "Baseball fits the French temperament . . . the French took to baseball like a duck to water."[52]

But others had their doubts. The *American Legion Quarterly* claimed, "It may wound American vanity, but our beloved national pastime did not take strongly with the French . . . it is too difficult . . . it would take an evolution, not an introduction, to establish baseball abroad." The sport seemed dangerous to some French soldiers who had been hit in the head by fly balls. And as Christy Mathewson observed, "Baseball will never be popular in France. The French think it is brutal. They are more afraid of a hard-hit grounder or liner than a German shell." The skeptics were right: baseball took root in neither France nor Britain, although Yankees owner Colonel Huston believed it would have stuck had the war lasted a year or two longer.[53]

According to *Stars and Stripes*, the American Expeditionary Force's "batting average" for 1918 (and the war's end) was not a matter of hitting, but rather the number of officers and men captured, artillery pieces seized, and kilometers advanced toward the enemy. The game itself was played with a fury in Europe for a couple of years after the war. In October 1918, U.S. Army General Pershing and U.S. Navy Secretary Daniels claimed they had professional talent equal to the National and American leagues and that their teams should have a role in the 1918 World Series. They proposed that the American League–National League series victor play the winner of the Army–Navy series in Berlin, before an audience of occupation American, French, British, Italian, Portuguese, and Belgian troops: "Think of the lesson in honest sportsmanship and fair play [for] the German populace! Let's have a real World Series."[54]

The idea failed, however, and attention turned instead to the immediate postwar period in Europe. In Germany, the U.S. military established several baseball leagues: in Koblenz, Lutzel, the Moselle, and the Rhine. Optimistically, Charles Murphy wrote, "Twenty years from now we may see a box score in the *Tageblatt* or the *Berlin Lokal Anzeiger*. It would make these Prussian militarists think of something more humane." The Knights of Columbus expanded its baseball training activities to Germany and elsewhere in Europe. Another league accommodated soldiers from Brussels, Rotterdam, Hamburg, Danzig, and The Hague. Washington Senators owner Clark Griffith claimed, "America has a direct and personal interest in disseminating baseball love by the doughboys." He and other owners knew that baseball's expansion would generate more fans and talented players.

The U.S. Army of Occupation was restless, so General Pershing stepped up athletic competition, highlighted by baseball. In January 1919, he inaugurated the Inter-Allied Games, also known as the Military Olympics. The games were devised by Elwood Brown, who had successfully promoted baseball competitions since 1910 while working for the YMCA in the Philippines. Soon they spread to U.S. and YMCA operations in China and Japan, and then evolved into the Far Eastern Games, which were played in Manila in 1913 and 1919, in Shanghai in 1915, and in Tokyo in 1917. The model seemed as though it would work in Europe, as well.[55]

An extravagant Pershing Stadium was built in France to host the games. More than two dozen allies were invited to compete. Athletes from the defeated nations of Germany, Austria, Hungary, and Bulgaria were barred, but so, too, were the Russian allies, because Pershing feared their recent communist revolution would bring a "Bolshevik infection." The games were "an athletic adjunct to the Treaty of Versailles, in which war-guilt and reparations clauses treated Germany and her allies as scapegoats, lepers to be excluded from the family of nations." Besides baseball, other sports were included, such as hand-grenade throwing. The games lasted two weeks and engaged more than 1,500 athletes. The Americans took first place in several sports, including baseball, and U.S. soldier F.C. Thompson—a former baseball player—outdistanced all other competitors with a 246-foot grenade toss.[56]

The Inter-Allied Games provided physical activity for soldiers waiting to return home, a safety valve against other temptations. They instilled a sporting message, to show how "wholeheartedly the nations that had striven shoulder to shoulder on the battlefield could turn to friendly rivalry in the stadium." But they were also staged to show American superiority and to establish a United States presence for the Paris Peace Conference. Americans claimed their intervention won the war, but to the English and French it was helpful but not decisive. To prove its point, the United States tried to show that its soldiers were better in another, related arena: sports.[57]

As Steven Pope has shown, the U.S. military proselytized Europe with the athletic cause after the war, making itself the international missionary for American sports. Even though other sports had been played in Europe for centuries, Americans believed they had won Europeans over to baseball during the war. While sportswriter Ed Goewey claimed the U.S. military had revived sports worldwide and that baseball had always "followed the flag" around the globe, he noted that "the big war" had implanted the game into Europe in particular, where its popularity reflected the "increased good will toward [Americans]."[58]

Not everyone was so sure. During the Versailles peace talks, the Europeans and Americans clashed. The Yanks wanted to mandate terms to them, and military success meant a complete victory over the enemy—as in America's baseball and other sports. Thus, while the Armistice penalized Germany, it wasn't as punitive as the United States would have liked.[59] The Europeans prevailed, although even their "milder" reparations have been regarded by many historians as having provoked the next conflict: World War II.

The Inter-Allied Games displayed America's missionary zeal for baseball and other sports. It seemed to have little effect, but that didn't discourage the missionaries. Baseball historian Harold Seymour worried about American arrogance: "Those who believe they have the answer to the world's problems never tire of communicating it to others."[60] The games were grand, but their meaning was not uniformly embraced.

From the Home Front to Horsehide Diplomacy
(1919–1940)

All these far-flung ball games of the armed forces dispelled any
lingering doubts of America's global economic and imperial interests.
                                                    —Harold Seymour

The Great War reverberated back home in the United States, roiling the waters of baseball as well as domestic politics. Despite record attendance figures
in 1916, the baseball magnates blamed the war for the player salary cuts they
imposed. Player protests were regarded as wartime treason. The 1918 World
Series became a test of patriotism when players on the competing Boston Red
Sox and Chicago Cubs realized the war was again being exploited, this time to
slash their series shares. When baseball's National Commission ignored their
complaints, the players threatened to strike and halt the games. In response,
Ban Johnson promised to consider bigger bonuses and tearfully implored the
Red Sox to continue the Series "for the glory of the American League." For
the fans' sake, both teams agreed to play, but the media still treated them as in-
grates during wartime. In the end, besides being branded as traitors, the players received no additional pay and were denied the emblems traditionally
awarded to World Series participants.[1]

The High White Flame of Americanism

Patriotic nationalism arose elsewhere in that same World Series. In 1916, President Wilson had designated "The Star Spangled Banner" as the national anthem by executive order. He wanted to use the song as a rallying cry for the
nation's entry into World War I. While the anthem had been performed occasionally at baseball games as far back as the Civil War, major-league (MLB)
clubs began playing it more often after 1916. Then, in game one of the 1918
World Series, a patriotic crowd applauded wounded soldiers, and during the
seventh-inning stretch, the anthem was played with great fanfare. Accustomed to
military drilling, the Cubs and Red Sox players snapped to attention and faced

the flag flying over center field. The fans, already on their feet, began to sing along, followed by great applause. Given the rousing response, the song was repeated each game of the series. It was played increasingly for subsequent games (especially on patriotic holidays), and at every World Series ever since. When Congress finally ratified "The Star Spangled Banner" as the national anthem in 1931, its public familiarity at baseball games was given most of the credit.[2]

As Joel Zoss and John Bowman have observed, the anthem's "lyrics, which describe warfare with 'bombs bursting in air,'" reflects baseball's connection to war. Thus, it's not surprising that "this warlike melody, which gained currency in ballparks where athletes marched, bands played and fireworks burst . . . should be played before a game that promoted itself as a model of 19th century warfare, and which [American soldiers] carried to other lands." Some wonder, however, whether the anthem's long association with the game has been in baseball's best interests. According to historian David Voigt, the obligation to play the song at every contest may be "the highest price baseball has paid to secure its image as America's national game."[3] Does any other nation require such a patriotic display from its sports fans?

In 1919, the Chicago White Sox threw the World Series in exchange for bribes. They were motivated by their meager salaries, kept unreasonably low by miserly owners, particularly Chicago's Charles Comiskey. Nevertheless, only the game throwers were held responsible, for being not only cheaters but also tantamount to traitors. The *Philadelphia Bulletin* compared the Black Sox, as they were called, to "the soldier or sailor who would sell out his country and his flag in time of war." The players were the "Benedict Arnolds of baseball." Patriotism and the reinforcement of 100 percent Americanism was at a fever pitch. While President Wilson claimed he was exporting American values to make the world safe for democracy, other politicians used the war to promote the "high white flame of Americanism" at home.[4]

Labor agitation was automatically labeled a foreign idea, inspired either by "the Hun or the Bolshevik." Accusing the pitcher Dutch Leonard of not trying hard enough, Ty Cobb bellowed, "Don't you turn Bolshevik on me!" And Rogers Hornsby claimed, "Any ballplayer that don't sign autographs for little kids ain't American. He's a Communist." In his baseball novel, *Hunting a Detroit Tiger*, Troy Soos further illustrated the connection, describing a character who's just been indicted: "Emmett Siever was a baseball man, not a Bolshevik. As a journeyman outfielder he'd played for nine teams in five major leagues. So why the Bolshevik tag? Because . . . Siever had been trying to unionize ballplayers."[5]

Foreigners were automatically suspicious, and Jews were among the main targets. Leading the accusations was Henry Ford, the wealthy automotive tycoon, who also maintained White House ambitions through 1920, when he attributed all the world's problems to the "International Jew." A worldwide Jewish conspiracy, he argued, controlled finance, culture, and politics and put the nation at risk. Ford published several anthologies on the Jewish threat, which were read appreciatively in Germany by the young Adolf Hitler. In 1921, in his newspaper, the *Dearborn Independent*, Ford published "Jewish Gamblers Corrupt American Baseball," in which he condemned not only the bettors but also the Jewish attorneys who defended the Black Sox. In "The Jewish Degradation of Baseball," Ford further claimed that Jews had "soiled" the sport generally and that the American League had broken its "agreement" not to let Jews own ball clubs.[6]

In the 1920s, real Americans were white. In this period of widespread lynchings of African Americans, being white (or white enough) might save one's life. Pure Americanism was often enforced by racist groups, such as the Ku Klux Klan. In baseball, the ban on blacks was imposed by the "gentlemen's agreement" reached among the white owners to prevent major-league contamination. While some ethnicities might be melted and bleached into the white American fabric, blacks had to be kept separate. And Asians weren't viewed as much better: the U.S. Supreme Court decided the Japanese were also not white and thus were ineligible for U.S. citizenship.[7]

Patriotic America sought a "return to normalcy" after World War I, and those who stood out were labeled aliens, radicals, and outsiders. The emerging Red Scare targeted not only political activists and labor leaders but immigrants generally. Through a series of quotas and bans (such as the Chinese and Japanese exclusion acts), some were kept out altogether. For those already in the United States, Attorney General Mitchell Palmer launched brutal sweeps (the Palmer Raids) through ethnic neighborhoods, beating, harassing, arresting, convicting, deporting, and even killing thousands of people—the most infamous case being that of Sacco and Vanzetti. The nation had to be purged of impurities, just as baseball had been. In *Hunting a Detroit Tiger*, a character observes, "The attorney general feels strongly that the national pastime should not be allowed to go Red. It would tear at the very fabric of American society."[8]

Instead of exclusion or repression, some preferred purification to achieve maximum Americanism. Along with the schools, the churches, and the press, baseball played a helping role. While the sport was run for profit by elites, it was portrayed as the game of the common man pursuing the American dream. The major leagues developed a "baseball creed," which claimed that baseball promoted the public welfare by "building manliness, character, and an ethic of success" and by instilling "the proper values in America's youth as well as educating immigrants to the American way of life." In the 1920s, whether one was newly arrived in U.S. cities as a rural American or as a foreign immigrant, baseball was a common denominator. One couldn't be American without knowing the game. And as for children, baseball taught them patriotism. If a boy played baseball during the day, then "he could safely be placed upon guard at night."[9]

The Black Sox scandal was a shattering experience for most Americans. Combined with the war, it was a profound loss of innocence. There was disbelief but also a widespread fear that the world and even American society were in disarray. An example was required, and "baseball entered the twenties preparing to defend standards, ethics, morals, patriotism, and the remaining eternal verities." Although the Black Sox players were vindicated in court, the newly minted commissioner of baseball, Judge Kenesaw Mountain Landis, nevertheless banned them from baseball for life. As the "badge of Americanism," baseball had to be thoroughly cleansed.[10]

Combating Subversive Elements

While norms of patriotic white Americanism were sometimes enforced by unsavory groups, mainstream institutions were just as active. Between the two world wars, a potent veterans group, the American Legion, arose, and ever since, it has kept Congresses and presidents alert to military and patriotic needs. The Legion's mission was to "carry forward a constructive program of Americanism [for] youth so a strong bulwark may be erected against . . . radical propaganda."[11]

The Legion promoted baseball for its military implications: "Legionnaires know the value of national physical fitness in war . . . the qualities of character stressed by athletic training are the same [for] making a soldier." In 1925, American Legion Junior Baseball was created, not under the organization's Boys Programs but rather its Americanism Programs. It would help deal with the Red Menace: to "teach concrete Americanism through playing the game" and combat "subversive elements."

According to historian Harold Seymour, "these self-appointed guardians of America [tried] to impose a public orthodoxy, a kind of civil religion, on everybody." The Legion supported right-wing movements and lobbied against liberals, immigration, and civil rights. About the baseball program, the Legion admitted that "under cloak of a sports code, we would inculcate more good citizenship during one year than possible in five years of direct appeal." It would teach boys "leadership and loyalty and clean sports, and thereby [their] reaction to economic fictions from the communist tongue and pen [would never be in doubt]." It brought home the same lessons to the ballplayers' families, thus reaching millions of people.[12]

Junior Baseball was designed to "train soldiers for future wars and rear citizens who will accept the status quo without objection, willing to play the game [by] rules prescribed by the American Legion." Commissioner Landis, a confirmed militarist, was a big supporter, and the Legion received repeated MLB donations of up to $50,000 per year from the early 1930s on. By 1935, five hundred thousand boys were playing Legion ball, and by 1938, three thousand radio stations carried the National Legion Championships. By the 1940s, one of every five American ballplayers had Legion experience. Because Junior Baseball soon became an important talent source, organized baseball conformed abjectly to the Legion's definitions of patriotism.[13]

Its link to the American Legion was only one of many special connections MLB had with the military. As Richard Crepeau has observed, the sport "came away knowing that war had been good for America, good for the world, and good for baseball." War memorials were endorsed, and in 1921 the American League created Hospital Day to honor war veterans. With the war over, attendance skyrocketed, continuing a pattern of surging baseball interest after each of America's wars. People sought a relief from turmoil, and the sport welcomed back the thousands of soldiers who played it while in the military. According to Major Branch Rickey, "I don't think there is a more patriotic, virile, or enthusiastic body of men anywhere than the baseball players in the service. And they're coming back to help the game, too." The war also supposedly built better baseball men. Previously, for example, Cincinnati Reds pitcher Walter Ruether had shown little potential. But according to the *Sporting News*, "Thanks to Uncle Sam's methods of dealing with men, Ruether is now one of the greatest winning pitchers in baseball."[14]

Baseball maintained its postwar links to America's armed services. In the 1920s, the New York Giants collaborated with the U.S. Military Academy, playing a series of games and offering two players, Hans Lobert and Moose McCormick, to coach the cadets. The Naval Academy signed Albert "Chief" Bender from the Philadelphia Athletics to coach. The two academies faced each other annually for decades. The 1922 game was attended by Washington elites, and reporting on the contest, the *Baltimore Sun* provided a now startling description: "Navy beat the Army at baseball, 8 to 6, this afternoon, in front of the President [Warren Harding] and the Secretary of War [John Weeks], both of whom sat on the Army side and turned out to be jinxes instead of swastikas."[15] The army employed Babe Ruth for troop morale and reenlistment efforts. National Guard camps were baseball hotbeds, and dozens of military leagues emerged, often with former players, like Buck Herzog, as instructors. Some major leaguers, such as the Hall of Famer Dizzy Dean, first developed in these camps.[16]

Militarizing the Commissionership

As we've seen, most of baseball's czars or defining figures, from Doubleday and Spalding to Johnson and Tener, had notable military ties. Each was a U.S. military policy booster. This pattern continued as organized baseball moved to its new commissioner system in 1920. The three-man National Commission wasn't working, and a player's strike was only narrowly averted. The *New York Times* compared the truce to the recent Treaty of Versailles: "The great baseball war has been called off. This [is] the new fashion in international relations. . . . After peace on the Adriatic, peace on the diamond."[17]

Many military leaders have been sought as commissioner. World War I heroes General John Pershing and General Leonard Wood were serious contenders for the first opening. "Black Jack" Pershing fought in the Indian wars, in the War of 1898, in the U.S.-Mexican border wars, and in World War I, where he commanded the American Expeditionary Forces in Europe. Leonard Wood had similar experience, helping Teddy Roosevelt create the Rough Riders, serving as military governor in Cuba and the Philippines, and holding America's second highest rank in World War I. If baseball could not entice high-profile military commanders like these, then perhaps someone from the White House? Former president William Howard Taft was a candidate: he was a big fan, and his brother had owned the Chicago Cubs and Philadelphia Phillies.[18]

Unable to hire a general or a president, the owners instead appointed Judge Kenesaw Mountain Landis as the first commissioner. The owners could have found nobody more fiercely militant in his American loyalties. Landis had been named for a famous Civil War battle. His father was a Union surgeon, badly wounded at the Battle of Kennesaw Mountain, Georgia. Grateful for surviving, he gave his son the battle's name, slightly misspelled.[19]

Landis was also selected by baseball because he had been the compliant judge in the Federal League court challenge. While the major leagues had obviously violated U.S. antitrust laws, Landis delayed his decision for nearly a year, long enough to allow organized baseball to win the Federal League war. After the upstart league's collapse, another challenge reached the U.S. Supreme Court, where Justice Oliver Wendell Holmes ruled that organized baseball was exempt from America's monopoly laws. Thanks to Landis and Holmes, other competing leagues would be less likely to emerge. The national pastime was given special status, reaping enormous benefits for the owners. It also helped impose actual or perceived obligations on baseball that would further link it to American patriotism and foreign policy.

Landis was virulently jingoistic and firmly backed America's World War I involvement and the anticommunist Palmer Raids. He was also violently anti-German; when administering the citizenship oath to eighteen Chicago soldiers, Landis encouraged them to kill the Kaiser's sons. Later, Landis claimed that "justice to the world and Germany" required their execution, along with the Kaiser and "the 5000 leading German militarists." In late 1917, at age fifty-one, Landis tried to enlist for combat duty in France. Refused, he then led President Wilson's war at home. Landis railed against slackers and dissenters, and as a federal judge he threw the book at antiwar protesters, including "Big Bill" Haywood, who got twenty years in federal prison.[20]

Landis likewise gave stiff penalties to Eugene Debs and other Socialist Party officials for speaking against the war. He sentenced Milwaukee's socialist congressman, Victor Berger, for obstructing the nation's war preparation, later lamenting to Chicago's American Legion post members, "It was my great disappointment to give Berger only twenty years in Leavenworth [instead of] having him lined up against the wall and shot." Landis also cracked down on saloons, endorsing the curious connection the temperance movement made between alcohol and German aggression: "Kaiserism abroad and booze at home must go." After the war, Landis tried to extradite the Kaiser for a Chicagoan's death in the sinking of the *Lusitania*, until the secretary of state reminded him it would violate existing treaties.[21]

When asked why he took the commissionership, Landis answered, "My son Major Reed Landis flew [as a World War I fighter ace]. We went to a World Series game in Brooklyn. Outside was a bunch of little kids. Reed turned to me and said, 'Dad, wouldn't it be awful to take baseball away from them?'"[22] Landis demanded total control as commissioner and was determined to protect the game from outside threats. To do so, he launched his own foreign policy.

The 1919 World Series was the first since World War I ended, and nationalist zeal remained high. According to the press, the World Series could unite America, "amidst the new wars against Bolshevism, race riots and labor agitation." Instead, amid rumors of gambling, the series was more divisive than unifying. When the Black Sox scandal reached Landis in 1920, he decided only a purge would do. Yet his ban of the White Sox players was heavy-handed and arguably unjust.[23] The Black Sox were scapegoats. Landis banned them to send a message, not only about gambling, but also to signal his martial rule.

A New Frontier at Home

While the 1920s began with a moralistic crackdown, it ended as the Roaring Twenties. Alcohol consumption went up, not down, during Prohibition. Sex in the movies was only driven underground, soon emerging as the pornography industry. Driven by the black market in booze, crime escalated rather than declined. And despite the Black Sox purge, gambling continued in baseball. Few figures reflected the era's unruliness better than Babe Ruth. With his drinking, womanizing, and gluttony, Ruth was the antithesis of the behavior sought by "straight arrows" like Commissioner Landis. Aside from living "bigger than life," Ruth provided something Americans respected much more than purity: he represented *power*.

Until the 1920s, hitting the ball to the *right* place, rather than to the *farthest* place, distinguished a great hitter. Baseball was played as the "inner" or "scientific" game, and the few players who pursued home runs were initially regarded as uncouth, unsophisticated brutes. The real long-ball revolution came with Ruth, who hit 29 home runs in 1919 to set a new record. In 1920, likely aided by MLB's livelier baseball, he hit an astounding 54 home runs, more than any *team* that year. The fans loved it, and baseball began moving from the "scientific game" to the "power game."[24] After the war and the Black Sox scandal, Americans sought a way to feel good about themselves again. Instead of Landis's heavy-handed moralizing, Ruth filled that void with exuberance. His flamboyance was scandalous but also appealing, and he likely saved the national pastime. What Ruth said about his baseball playing also applied to his life: "I swing big, with everything I've got. I hit big or I miss big. I like to live as big as I can."

The lure of Babe Ruth and the home run represented a change in American values. Baseball, according to David Lamoreaux, became "less an exercise in collective precision and more a spectacle of power [and] muscle." As Larry Stone has noted, the home run has been baseball's glamour event, searing "itself into national consciousness, invoking epic journeys of Homer in the Odyssey and the Iliad." Ruth allowed America to "emerge from the powerless days of the early twentieth century with a larger than life spirit of the Roaring Twenties." People no longer believed in Horatio Alger myths, according to Mark Dyreson, or in illusions about controlling their own destinies. Sports were a release from the inhuman conditions of mass society. People craved excitement, and Ruth was the ideal hero for a world of consumption. The attitude was: "We were rich. We were strong. We were ready to play, with truly American force. While the market soared, we knew God loved America, and sent us the Babe to prove it."[25]

Baseball Magazine observed that "heavy artillery" won in baseball as well as on the battlefield, and it used the recent world war to illustrate how the "big hitters" win the game. The home run was dubbed the "siege gun of the diamond." It was said that Ruth "carries the heaviest war club on the field and his wallops have more potential TNT behind them than any other batter."[26]

Batting a ball might be primordial, but hitting it hard and far might be particularly American. It suggested a preference for brawn over finesse, and emerged as a metaphor for American society and even the U.S. role in the world.

Historians have noted America's long preoccupation with "conquering space." In the 1920s, America had only recently conquered its first frontier—the West. The U.S. sought new boundaries to subdue and admired those with the power to project the nation in new directions. Teddy Roosevelt was celebrated for promoting U.S. expansion beyond its national borders. America was leaving its childhood as a nation and becoming an adult, and a powerful one at that.

But if other nations served as the new frontier abroad, what supplanted the Old West at home? According to Frederick Paxson, sport provided a "new social safety value to replace the one closed by the Western frontier."[27] Among America's sports, football's aggressive violence might have seemed like the best fit. But baseball's longstanding relationship with U.S. militarism and expansionism instead filled the bill. It couldn't have done so, however, without the titanic shots off Babe Ruth's bat and the brute force he brought to the game. It was no coincidence that power was suddenly admired and even demanded in our national pastime and the broader society. America was flexing its muscles, and the ballpark became America's new frontier at home. Much as a later generation got off on watching smart bombs zero in on faraway targets, people of the twenties thrilled to see the baseball vanquish, like a cannon shot, the great green expanses of the outfield. It wouldn't be the last time.

The Moral Equivalent of War

Of course, symbolic power at home was only a shadow of real military power abroad. After World War I, not everyone was satisfied with the German surrender and Armistice agreement. Kaiser Wilhelm II had escaped to the Netherlands, where he was ensconced in a Dutch castle. Several enterprising U.S. soldiers decided to do something about it. In January 1919, they arrived at the castle, posing as journalists, and gained entry. On the brink of kidnapping Wilhelm, the Americans were chased off. Leading the would-be kidnappers were Captain Luke Lea and Captain Larry MacPhail. During the hasty retreat, MacPhail grabbed an ashtray bearing the Kaiser's crest. It occupied an honored place in each of his future offices: MacPhail would soon become a leading baseball innovator and the general manager of the Cincinnati Reds, Brooklyn Dodgers, and New York Yankees.[28]

About MacPhail, famed manager Leo Durocher observed, "There is a thin line between genius and insanity, and in Larry's case it was sometimes so thin you could see him drifting back and forth." Although MacPhail and his compatriots escaped back to France, they found the Allies in an uproar. The Dutch government protested the breach of its neutrality, and the U.S. State Department ordered the soldiers arrested. Eventually, the case came to General John Pershing, who had the men released and the escapade hushed up. Pershing later admitted, "I am not a rich man, but I would have given a year's pay to have been with those boys in Holland!"[29]

MacPhail's little adventure was a metaphor for America's post–World War I international relations. Should it rely on diplomacy to handle the world's problems or instead pursue aggressive unilateral actions? While it did launch some diplomatic initiatives, its foreign policy was more often conducted via military raids. Sometimes they didn't work; other times, they succeeded in the short run, only to haunt the U.S. later. The period after the Great War tested the world's ability to avoid such a terrible conflict ever again. Baseball would be involved in the ensuing developments over the next two decades. Could horsehide diplomacy help prevent the next war?

In 1919, Harvard psychologist William James published a groundbreaking essay, "The Moral Equivalent of War," which argued that nations maintained civic unity primarily by inventing enemies, against which the population could be rallied. Unfortunately, this often provoked wars, which also united citizens but at a horrible cost. James proposed mandatory national service as the moral equivalent of war. But philosopher Morris Cohen claimed to have a better idea: baseball. The game "cultivates hope and courage when we are behind, resignation when we are beaten, fairness to the other team when we are ahead, charity for the umpire, and above all the zest for combat." The sport could undermine Germany's martial spirit, and international baseball would "arouse more national religious fervor than the monotonous game of armaments and war." A close international pennant race would fuel national aspirations, "and yet such rivalry would [help establish] the true Church Universal in which all men would feel their brotherhood in the Infinite Game of baseball."[30]

When the American Expeditionary Forces remained in Europe after World War I, they helped spread baseball to some unexpected destinations, such as Hungary, Finland, and Czechoslovakia.[31] Baseball also had a tentative grip in England when Sir Arthur Conan Doyle put aside his Sherlock Holmes mysteries to visit the United States in 1922. He fancied himself a shortstop, returned home a baseball enthusiast, and declared, "I know baseball is the game England needs." Duly encouraged, in 1924 John McGraw and Charles Comiskey launched yet another world baseball tour. *Time* magazine wrote that "instead of Bibles and hymn-books, these missionaries will carry with them balls, bats, and mits [*sic*]. Instead of love and light, they will shed baseball fanaticism all over Europe." *Baseball Magazine* observed, "The infusion of that spirit [of baseball] in other nations and races would help [solve Europe's] complex problems." The British press emphasized the game's economic advantages: "Financially it is much better to be a first-class pitcher on the White Sox than prime minister of England and a much safer job, too."[32]

Unfortunately, the 1924 tour, which began in Great Britain, was turned back by low attendance. It probably hadn't helped that McGraw's New York Giants had recently donated heavily to the Irish relief fund, which aided those suffering under British rule and which likely helped finance the militant Irish Republican Army. In 1926, major leaguer Bucky Harris led another European tour, which was well received only in Ireland. The International Baseball Board of England and Wales was formed in 1927, and British professional teams had some success in the early 1930s.

In 1936, however, the Bishop of Liverpool condemned baseball, claiming it was no game for saintly individuals or even sinners: "The backchat and calls of players and spectators at a baseball match in America are [deplorable]. If English spectators learn them then soon they will be seen at association football matches." But the bishop's concerns were largely dispelled, and that same year, baseball was made compulsory at England's Royal Air Force Cadet Training College, so highly touted was the sport's military value. In 1937, the International Baseball Federation was created, and in 1938 England won the first-ever World Amateur Baseball Championship, defeating a U.S. team.[33]

Between the world wars, baseball made unexpected connections at both ends of the political spectrum. On the one hand, Benito Mussolini began using baseball as an athletic experiment at Rome's Fascist Academy in the late 1920s. Could Il Duce have been the "father of Italian baseball"? In 1931, Italy announced it was sending instructors to the United States to learn baseball so it could become the Italian national game.[34]

On the other hand, baseball also came to the Soviet Union. After the 1917 Russian Revolution and through the 1920s, anti-Soviet and anticommunist hysteria was widespread in America. In response, in 1925 the Soviet magazine *Smena* (*Change*) insisted baseball was a version of the old Russian village game *laptá*, which "was played when the United States was not even marked on the maps." Thus it claimed the unthinkable: that the American national pastime was actually a Russian invention. Five decades later, *Time* magazine writer John Leo dated *laptá's* U.S. arrival in the 1840s, citing a story from *Pravda* (*Truth*), which speculated that *laptá* had been "stolen by a Marine guard at the U.S. embassy in Moscow, who scurrilously wheedled crucial *lapta* information out of an unwary Russian cook during an evening of illicit and probably drug-induced lovemaking." Recalling Jacques Barzun's famous dictum about America and baseball, Leo reminded readers of Vladimir Lenin's purported admonition about the Russian psyche: "Anyone who wishes to understand the Russian soul had better learn *lapta*."[35]

In the early 1930s, a U.S. Navy squadron landed in the Soviet Union and played baseball, with Russians watching in the stands. Upset about the game, Russian leader Joseph Stalin sacked the admiral who allowed the Americans to come in. Even so, increasingly the U.S.S.R. was seen as a possible ally against the rising Japanese threat, and the United States finally recognized the Soviet government in 1933. That same year, 25,000 spectators watched an Anglo-American baseball contest in Moscow, and Americans in Russia began trying to spread the game. In 1934, Russian teams sprang up in several Soviet cities, and the first intercity baseball game was played between the American workers at the Gorki Auto Plant and the Moscow Foreign Workers Club. The Stalin Auto Plant workers took up baseball in 1935, the same year the Soviet government, apparently seeking to reclaim ownership of the game, sponsored a program for promoting baseball as a national sport.[36]

Fear of the Reds occasionally had comic effects in baseball back in America. Beginning in the mid-1930s, the Cleveland Indians featured a player many regarded as the next Babe Ruth. But this power-hitting first baseman had a name, Hal Trosky, that made him instantly controversial. On a bad day at the ballpark, fans would implore Trosky to "go back to Russia," referring to the Russian revolutionary Leon Trotsky. According to sportswriter Jack De Vries, "Trosky thought his Russian-sounding name might have had some fans concluding he had 'revolutionary' ideas about inciting his fellow players."[37]

Shifting Frontiers Abroad

Baseball's frontiers abroad began to shift. As Barbara Keys has observed, in the 1920s, foreigners began developing a "voracious appetite for U.S. popular culture," eagerly consuming "fast food, jeans, Hollywood movies, jazz, and American slang."[38] Outsiders seemed more indifferent to American team sports. After some initial enthusiasm, baseball seemed to fizzle in post–World War I Europe, but this may be misleading. According to Mark Dyreson, "the effort to globalize American culture through sport, [to prepare] the world for American products, began long before Michael Jordan, Nike and other athletic empires. Baseball began this process." U.S. leaders knew other cultures would consume U.S. goods only if foreigners became Americanized. As in many other economic endeavors abroad, the U.S. departments of Commerce and State collaborated with the U.S. military to open new markets and promote American lifestyles around the world. However unrealistic, U.S. officials embraced baseball as their primary vehicle for invading other cultures.[39] Besides promoting U.S. products, baseball was also drawn into a moral crusade to spread peace and democracy—on American terms. According to Richard Crepeau, "Baseball saw itself as a game of peace, played by a peaceful people, and capable of promoting peace wherever it went. However, if provoked to war, baseball was ready."[40]

Sports, and especially baseball, demonstrated Christian brotherly love and a bridge of understanding between nations. According to the YMCA, Eastern European and Far Eastern countries could best be brought within the "respectable, democratic camp" through athletic programs. Baseball in particular would ward off the "radical democracy" emanating from communist Petrograd like a "cloud of poisonous gas." Asian and African troops serving in the Allied forces were targeted for baseball by religious groups, including the Chinese Labor Corps, the Indian troops in the British corps, and the Arabs, Senegalese, and Tunisians in the French military. As the Reverend Harold Martin, the Canadian-American Baseball League president, noted, "We can thank Almighty God we have baseball to take our minds off the tragedy of the world . . . no institution outside the church can accomplish what baseball has for the good of God, country and fellow men."[41]

While the United States feigned political isolationism, it instead promoted an "aggressive, idealistic internationalism in the cultural sphere." According to William Stead, America exported its competitive values, training techniques, and moral underpinnings, as well as its more tangible sports. As U.S. international sports participation grew, it helped shape foreign views of the U.S. and the American way of life. U.S. athletes traveling abroad were emissaries of American culture. Some foreigners resisted the influence, concerned about U.S. brutality, hypercompetitiveness, and even mindlessness, but much about American life was absorbed. Promoting peace and democracy was equated with exporting materialism and consumer culture. Sports were used to sell products abroad, including athletic merchandise. Various sporting goods manufacturers began to compete with Albert Spalding's old empire.[42]

Of course, wherever the U.S. military roamed, it was happy to help baseball take hold. In the 1920s, the U.S. army ran a Philippines Baseball League, a league in Tientsin, China, teams in Puerto Rico, and a club that won the Far Eastern Games. The U.S. Navy became a National Amateur Athletic Federation (NAAF) member, used the sport to recruit, and played baseball in the Hawaii League, in Haiti, Calcutta, Riga (Latvia), London, Tunis, Holland, Ceylon, Panama, Guantanamo, and Brazil, and against the Samoans in Tutuilla. The Pacific and Atlantic fleets each had championships and then played each other for the navy crown. The U.S. Marines also joined the NAAF and played in Puerto Rico, Haiti, Santo Domingo, and China. The U.S. Coast Guard followed the same pattern. Championships were also held across militaries, with the army, navy, and marines each developing "super-teams" and playing, for example, for the "championship of the Orient" before large foreign audiences.

The U.S. armed forces also fielded teams in the national leagues of countries where its troops were stationed, such as the Philippines, the Canal Zone, El Salvador, Cuba, Japan, Guam, and Nicaragua. According to historian Harold Seymour, "All these far-flung ball games of the armed forces dispelled any lingering doubt of America's global economic and imperial interests," and exposed the real intentions of America's "cultural diplomacy" during this period.[43]

Baseball hadn't abandoned its quest to conquer the world. MLB was as active as other large industries in expanding American influence in the decades between the wars. For the game to take root abroad, however, baseball could not be transplanted by "hothouse" methods. According to Irving Sanborn, "Not until baseball is taken up by the kids of a nation will it gain sufficient vogue to [influence] the physical and mental traits of a foreign country." For example, baseball had long been played in Japanese schools, and thus Japan was beginning to compete with Cuba in the development of the game. When baseball stalled in post–World War I Europe, the crusade shifted precisely in those directions—to the Caribbean and Far East, where the sport made significant inroads in the decades ahead.[44]

The Emerging Caribbean Mecca

America's control over Latin America and the Caribbean grew significantly after World War I. As before, baseball accompanied U.S. troops and corporations, but now MLB began taking the region more seriously as a source of ballplayers and markets. In Cuba, Babe Ruth's 1920 barnstorming visit "elevated" the game: "I am happy to have known Santiago," he declared. "The Cubans had good reason to fight for their independence half a century ago." In fact, they still had good reason to fight—now against U.S. rather than Spanish rule. Rebellion erupted again, as many Cubans resented having their lands taken from them. Some of their ballplayers were being taken, as well, for U.S. baseball executives, like Branch Rickey and Clark Griffith, began signing inexpensive Caribbean talent. One of the recruits, Baldomero Acosta, pitched for the Washington Senators but left the team to lead rebel forces in western Cuba. As usual, when the uprising began to succeed, U.S. Marines arrived to suppress it and "protect American interests."[45]

In 1930, Hack Wilson of the Chicago Cubs drove in 191 runs, setting the major-league record. That same year, the Amateur Baseball World Series was arranged in Havana by the faltering, U.S.-installed Cuban dictator Gerardo

Machado, to distract public attention from civil unrest and poverty. By this time, American blacks, barred from the major leagues, had begun playing in the professional Cuban League, and some black Cubans tried their luck in the U.S. Negro Leagues. In 1933, the United States replaced Machado with another tyrant, Fulgencio Batista, who launched a military coup to tighten the repressive clampdown. The island lost outside communication for a week; when it was restored, Cubans wanted—before all else—to know the American baseball scores they had missed. Both U.S. and Cuban politicians used the sport as social control, but other baseball clubs organized for political resistance. And in the late 1930s, Cuba hosted a St. Louis Cardinals barnstorming series, and former major leaguer Les Mann coordinated an international baseball championship in Havana.[46]

In Haiti and the Dominican Republic, the U.S. military occupiers were already widely despised. Employing the usual stereotypes, the *Sporting News* observed, "The military occupation by Marines is regarded by the natives as a bum decision" because it interfered "with their national sport of revolution."[47] While U.S. forces helped infuse baseball into the Dominican Republic, some Americans felt the invasions undermined baseball's goodwill efforts. By 1918, various Dominican politicians tried to ban baseball as a corrupting Yankee influence. Dominican rebels pushed for national emancipation, and hundreds of clashes with the U.S. Marines took place.

In the 1920s, Dominicans resisted Americanization when the U.S. tightened its economic grip. Marcus Garvey's black nationalism movement spread throughout the Caribbean, radicalizing many islanders. The Dominican pitcher Fellito Guerra was offered a big-league contract but, protesting the American military presence, became an instant hero when he refused to sign with the "occupiers." Most Americans simply assumed U.S. benevolence. About baseball's influence, William Pulliam claimed it was teaching Dominicans English and proper values: "Youthful minds, weaned away from sordid things like rum, cockfights and lottery tickets, engage in the exhilarating sport."

Pulliam also acknowledged their growing baseball competence: "Perhaps it is the Spanish inborn love for the spectacular, as evidenced by the matador striving for plaudits in the bull ring, that explains the skill of Dominican ball players in their truly sensational fielding stunts." According to Alan Klein, Dominicans excelled because they played in the industrial leagues, where U.S. sugar refineries fueled fierce baseball rivalries and rewarded their best ballplaying workers. By 1923, the Dominicans regularly beat the U.S. Marine teams. But when the occupation ended and U.S. military forces declined, Pulliam claimed the Dominican game suffered: "Just another example of the lack of sustained effort [by] the average Latin-American in anything calling for perseverance."[48]

In 1930, the United States installed the brutal, West Point–trained dictator Rafael Trujillo in the Dominican Republic. Trujillo used baseball to help maintain control and to distract the masses from his government's rigged elections, repression, and murder. With the help of the American Sugar Company, he organized teams, built ball fields, and revitalized the Dominican League. "It's good to have people [watch] baseball [so] they don't pay attention to politics," Trujillo observed. "Always, dictatorships do that." Left initially on its own, the Dominican game developed its own style, soon dubbed "baseball *romantico*."[49]

By 1937, Trujillo had decided he must have the island's best team. In a raid on the Negro League's Pittsburgh Crawfords, Trujillo paid stars such as Satchel Paige, Josh Gibson, and Cool Papa Bell to play for him and elevate his public status. When his team lost games, Trujillo had Dominican soldiers threaten the American black players at gunpoint. The Caribbean Winter Leagues began pursuing other U.S. black stars more aggressively as well. And light-skinned Latino players were increasingly plucked, on the cheap, from the Caribbean to play in the major leagues.[50]

In 1940, Venezuela barely beat the Dominican team in a Caribbean championship game, ending on a close play. When the Dominicans protested, the Venezuelans offered to replay the game. The Dominicans refused, hurling insults against their opponents and then against Venezuelans generally. Offended, the Venezuelans staged rallies and demanded action. Their government severed relations with the Dominican Republic, but many Venezuelans wanted war. Cooler heads prevailed, but diplomatic relations were not restored for several years.[51] Baseball got a big boost in Venezuela when oil was discovered there. The Standard Oil Company quickly moved in and began sponsoring baseball teams to keep exploited local workers diverted. The game spread rapidly, and Venezuela's national teams were soon competitive in Central American championships.

Elsewhere in the Caribbean, baseball and international politics again mixed. In 1917, the American navy brought baseball to the Virgin Islands shortly after the United States purchased them from Denmark. That same year, Puerto Ricans were granted U.S. citizenship, but nationalists opposed the move; many wanted their independence back, and they clung fiercely to their language and lifestyle. By 1920, major-league and Negro League teams were barnstorming Puerto Rico or playing winter ball there. Poverty deepened under U.S. administration, and more Puerto Ricans sought refuge up north. In 1923, one group formed the socialist Puerto Rican Workers Alliance, which then began the Porto Rican Baseball League in New Jersey. In 1924, New York City's San Juan Baseball Club entertained the visiting Puerto Rican All-Stars.

With dissent simmering in Puerto Rico, the Nationalist Party sponsored an independence march in 1936. In the Ponce Massacre, the demonstration was

brutally suppressed by the U.S.-controlled government. Despite the continuing repression, poverty, and exploitation, baseball helped Puerto Ricans maintain their self-esteem. The Cincinnati Reds held spring training on the island,
and when they lost to a Puerto Rican club and a visiting Cuban team, it was
front-page news in San Juan. Historian Samuel Regalado later reflected the
prevailing sentiment: "Latins viewed their passion for the game as not solely
based on financial gain, but as a labor of love, whereas the Yankee baseball
players came always for speculation." By 1938, the amateur American Baseball
Congress and the National Baseball Congress began sending teams, and the
Puerto Rican Winter League was formed. By then, Puerto Rico was largely
Americanized, but its race policies were still significantly different. The island
regularly hosted integrated games by the late 1930s.[52]

In Nicaragua, also under American military occupation, a U.S. Marine team
joined the local league in 1919.[53] Another team, Club Managua, was sponsored
by the U.S.-controlled Nicaraguan military. Clifford Ham, the Collector General of Customs and the American who ran Nicaragua's economy, exclaimed,
"Three cheers for the American Marine who is teaching baseball and sportsmanship! It is the best step towards order, peace and stability." The dominant
U.S. agribusiness firm, W.R. Grace, promoted baseball "to control and civilize
the locals." While baseball helped pacify the masses, it was sometimes used by
Nicaraguans to resist U.S. dominance—substituting for deadly wars and helping to construct a Nicaraguan national identity. Even if it was only a symbolic
victory, it was satisfying to beat the Americans at their own game.[54]

After the marines left in 1925, a revolt broke out against the American puppets, and U.S. troops returned in 1926 to occupy the nation for another seven
years. According to Secretary of State Frank Kellogg, a "Nicaraguan-Mexican-
Soviet" conspiracy to inspire a "Mexican-Bolshevik revolution" made the reoc-
cupation necessary. U.S. Undersecretary of State Robert Olds claimed, "There
is no room for any outside influence other than ours in the region." During this
intervention, the marines enraged the locals by commandeering a cherished
Managua ball field for a landing strip. In 1927, to fortify the marines, the United
States created the brutal Nicaraguan National Guard, which, along with U.S.
troops, targeted Augusto César Sandino, who was leading a guerrilla war against
the American occupation and its repressive Nicaraguan collaborators. Sandino
claimed, "This is a struggle . . . to expel the foreign invasion. [It seeks] . . . su-
pervised elections by representatives of Latin America instead of American
Marines." He protested "the exploitation of the country by the money powers of Nicaragua and Wall Street."[55]

When American forces left Nicaragua in 1933, the United States installed
Anastasio Somoza Sr. to head the National Guard, which killed thousands

sympathetic to the Sandino rebellion. While the guard directed the government, the United States controlled three fourths of the Nicaraguan economy.[56] In 1934, Somoza tricked Sandino into a truce and had him assassinated—making him a martyr and later the inspiration for the 1979 Sandinista revolution. In 1936, Somoza, with American help, launched a coup, became president, and opened the doors wider to international investment, thus deepening Nicaragua's economic dependence. He remained closely tied to the U.S. military and stepped up his repressive campaigns.

Somoza had studied in Philadelphia and had returned as a Philadelphia Athletics fan to Nicaragua, where he often officiated as an umpire. After snatching the presidency, Somoza declared baseball Nicaragua's national sport, built a national baseball stadium (named after himself), and subsidized the Cinco Estrellas team, which began competing in international baseball championships. In the early 1940s, despite resenting American interventions, Nicaraguans eagerly tuned in the first direct radio transmissions of U.S. big-league ball games. For the now baseball-crazy Nicaraguans, the new greeting for all male babies became "Born with a glove and ball in his hand."

In Mexico in 1920, General Alvaro Obregón overthrew the U.S.-backed regime of Venustiano Carranza, and U.S. Senator Albert Fall (representing American oil interests there) tried to provoke a declaration of war. U.S.-Mexican tensions remained heated, but in 1921 President Warren Harding suggested baseball as a peacemaker and American League President Ban Johnson led a baseball tour south of the border. In 1923, Johnson presented a baseball trophy (for the annual Mexican championship) to Obregón, a gesture some claimed had helped prevent war. In 1925, the first professional summer league, the Mexican Baseball League, was founded. In 1928, Johnson visited Mexico City again and brought another trophy—Obregón stole the first one when he left office. An amateur championship was held, for which the American League provided free uniforms, on "Ban Johnson Day." For once, baseball was credited with *reducing* militarism, elevating a nonmilitary man to the Mexican presidency for the first time in four decades. And in 1929, industrial baseball leagues were launched, with U.S. companies sponsoring several teams.[57]

Elsewhere in Mexico, in the Yucatán, socialist revolutionary Felipe Carrillo Puerto took control in the early 1920s. Besides agrarian and other social reforms, he developed a regional sports program to make the Yucatán into "a baseball mecca." The game was central to grassroots mobilization, while also featuring characteristics that "preserved personal accountability within a structure of fellowship." The teams were organized into "resistance leagues," with such club names as Soviets, Agraristas, Marx, Zapata, Gorki, and Los Martires (the Martyrs) de Chicago. Baseball arrived to even the smallest Yucatán towns, with a focus on getting children hooked on the game. The Yucatán government ordered $18,000 worth of baseball gear from the United States for the public schools, where youngsters used it for free. And tracts of land were set aside for baseball fields. Thus baseball made rapid headway that lasted a few years, until Carrillo Puerto was assassinated.[58]

In 1937, the Philadelphia Athletics held spring training in Mexico. Accompanying the team, sportswriter Red Smith got an unusual interview. Fleeing a murder contract from Stalin, Leon Trotsky had gotten asylum in Mexico City. In his report, "Red Smith Meets Red Trotsky," Smith poked fun at Trotsky's revolutionary fervor, inadvertently showing his own ignorance of the Russian revolution and world politics. When Trotsky was assassinated by a Stalinist thug in Mexico in 1940, the story was covered by U.S. newspapers sometimes using baseball metaphors. Referring to the ice pick that killed him, the *Boston Globe* observed, "Trotsky's career as a Red ends due to a 'deceptive pick-off move.'" The *Washington Post* suggested that Trotsky had died as a result of "a freak accident in the Mexican League." While American reporters were amused, the Mexican League was taken very seriously elsewhere. In the early 1940s, All-Star Negro League shortstop Willie Wells gave up on U.S. race relations and left to play in the Mexican League, where he became a star player and manager. Wells observed, "I was branded a Negro in the United States and had to act accordingly. Everything I did, including playing ball, was regulated by color. Here, in Mexico, I am a man."[59]

The final Caribbean enclave for baseball and American foreign policy was Panama, which the U.S. military invaded again in 1918. That year, the Canal Zone was recommended as a spring training site for MLB. But by the mid-1920s, Panamanians had begun questioning U.S. control over the zone, demanding their sovereignty back. Baseball grew despite the domestic political turmoil, and Panama began sending teams into international competition by the 1930s.[60]

Not limited to the Caribbean, baseball advanced further into South America. In Brazil, the national telephone company began a baseball league in the 1920s, featuring American and Brazilian players. In 1922, according to the *New York Times*, "South America has been made safe for the democracy of baseball. The people of Brazil have mastered the lingo of the bleachers and [have adopted] the Yankee game [and] credit must be given to the United States Battleship *Nevada* [sailors who] have their duties no less than diplomats . . . to spread their message of baseball." The U.S. military couldn't take all the praise, however: since 1908, Japanese immigrants had been settling in Brazil, bringing their own version of baseball.[61]

Baseball even made its way to Africa, again with a mission. In 1921

Dr. C. Guyer Kelly formed the Baseball Club of Africa in Tunis, which spawned a league of sixteen teams. The French government supported the program to cope with Tunisian unrest against its colonial rule, and in 1924 Kelly was made an international delegate to the new French Baseball Federation. In 1932, the first game occurred between North Africans and North Americans, as Tunis League players faced sailors from the U.S. warship *President Johnson*. By 1933, Kelly worked to revive European baseball interest and to promote the game elsewhere in Africa, including Morocco, Algeria, and Libya. Dubbed the "baseball missionary" by the Methodist Church, Kelly advocated baseball to promote American values and international peace. By 1951, he had created 160 ball clubs and organized more than 200 international games, many involving U.S. servicemen.[62]

Keeping the Far East Peace

As in Latin America, baseball proliferated along with U.S. foreign policy endeavors in the Far East, where Americans "had long felt they had a special civilizing mission." As gateways to the Far East, Hawaii and Australia played intermediary roles. Hawaii was now a U.S. territory, and sovereignty conflicts were common. In 1920 a huge plantation-workers strike shook the white-controlled islands. Agribusiness owners redoubled their efforts to integrate baseball into the workers' lives to distract them from labor grievances. In 1923, Hawaii was used to launch a U.S. baseball tour headed for Asia, led by former major leaguer Herb Hunter. In 1924, the Meiji University team arrived in Hawaii to play the local Asahi club, which during the next two decades would win fifteen Hawaiian championships and conduct frequent Far East tours. In the 1930s, the Dole Corporation gave some Negro League stars, including Newt Allen and "Bullet" Joe Rogan, easy jobs to play for its plantation team. More major leaguers arrived, en route to Japan, including Babe Ruth. In Australia, troops returning from World War I Europe brought their baseball enthusiasm back home. In the 1920s, Australia hosted many U.S. and Japanese baseball tours. In 1934, the Australian National League was formed, giving professional baseball its start down under.[63]

Much more extensive was baseball's role in Japanese life and politics. As Robert Sinclair has suggested, "Baseball promised the maturation of Japanese national identity and dissolution of cultural barriers between the Orient and Occident . . . the Japanese discovered the importance of physical fitness to the Social Darwinist code of competition . . . the fittest nations embraced manliness, athleticism, and patriotism." Baseball was adopted partly to force Westerners to reassess stereotypes of Japanese inferiority. Excellence in playing the game, particularly against U.S. opposition, helped redefine Japan's international image.[64]

In 1917, the Japanese won the third Far Eastern Games, held in Tokyo. Observing the games, YMCA director Elwood Brown noted, "On the battlefield Western civilization may be scattering its good-will to the four winds, but on the athletic field the East is welding a great amulet which will encircle the Far East in international fellowship." This rosy picture ignored Japan's own fledgling imperial ambitions and the way it would use baseball to promote them. But it was still early. In 1918, besides baseball, Japan was "adopting the military, business and industrial methods" of Western nations. This was taken as an indication that Japan had traveled "pretty far in the right direction, on the highway of civilization!"[65]

Following World War I, officials in Washington and Tokyo realized baseball's significance for peace and goodwill. According to Sinclair, "While diplomatic talks often stalled, exchanges through baseball better legitimized the activities of American and Japanese political elites." President Harding endorsed baseball tours to Japan as having "real diplomatic value." The *Literary Digest* predicted "baseball would be more important to peace between the U.S. and Japan than all the efforts of diplomats combined." In 1920, the University of Chicago baseball team toured Japan and invited Japanese clubs back to U.S. campuses. Even sumo wrestlers began developing a passion for baseball. And Herb Hunter's major-league tour of Japan arrived—Hunter was headed for a West Point military career but then "decided that bombarding the fences of a baseball park was a more thrilling and civilizing pastime than battering down a beleaguered city."[66]

Optimistically, Japanese reporter Kinnosuke Adachi observed that while anti–American fever existed in Japan, younger Japanese brushed it aside: "When American baseball stars drove into sight our half-ripe manhood forgot about international politics [and] all such nonsense as a possible American-Japanese war. . . . There is [more to] this diplomacy through international baseball than the old fossils in the world's chancelleries [possibly know]." Others observed that "men who cross bats with each other will not exchange them for heavier artillery. In baseball, the American conquest of Japan was complete. But there is to be a [baseball] reprisal—a sure-enough invasion of the Pacific Coast." In retrospect, these glib assessments were chilling, given the eventual turn in U.S.-Japanese relations.[67]

In 1921, more baseball exchanges were arranged, and the American missionary school played the Higashi Hongwanji temple team in Japan. The score was reported: Christians 2, Buddhists 1. Another University of Chicago tour in 1922 attracted seventy thousand people for contests against Japanese universities, which won most of the games. Nels Norgren, Chicago's coach, even felt, "Baseball is more the national sport of Japan than it is of America." In 1922, Herb Hunter launched his second tour, featuring major leaguers Casey Stengel, Herb Pennock, and Waite Hoyt. For the trip, Japan was targeted, along with China, the Philippines, Australia, Ceylon, Egypt, and Europe, as the nations that were "most in need of [baseball] enlightenment." American ballplayers "discovered the Nipponese did not wear horns or live in caves; [and] that Filipinos were not all head-hunters." The *Sporting News* claimed such baseball tours would "promote friendship and understanding between the two nations." According to sportswriter H.G. Salsinger, baseball's popularity among the "children of yellow races" opened the possibility of a true World Series one day, which would "increase the prospects for world peace," since nations with much in common were not prone to war with one another.[68]

On the other hand, the U.S. Supreme Court had by then made the Japanese ineligible for American citizenship. *Baseball Magazine* claimed "good sportsmanship" around baseball would smooth things over. Yet on the field, the Japanese teams played particularly hard against Hunter's All-Stars—in retaliation, some believe, for America's policies. For the first time, a U.S. professional team lost to a Japanese club. Rather than a vehicle of peace, Japanese baseball emerged with another purpose. According to Gerald Gems, it fueled nationalistic sentiments and reaffirmed Japanese masculinity, emphasizing patriotism, conformity, obedience, and toughness. In response to American racism, Japan used baseball to challenge the cultural superiority preached by U.S. Protestant missionaries. In the schools, the sport was increasingly employed to inculcate fascist rather than democratic ideology. Baseball was increasingly a "resistive force"—not a surrogate for war but rather a preparation for it.[69]

More fuel for the fire was added in 1924, when the U.S. Congress passed the Japanese Exclusion Act, which banned Japanese entry altogether. Some felt the Japanese wouldn't resent this, since Hunter's tours had allowed them to befriend American ballplayers, which showed "that some of Uncle Sam's folks are good square sports, free from racial prejudice." That was wishful thinking: Japan reacted strongly to the insult, organizing consumer boycotts of American goods and cultural practices. The Japanese didn't abandon baseball because they now regarded the sport as their own. Even so, U.S. sportswriter Francis Richter lamented U.S. exclusionary policies, claiming that baseball advances in Japan were now destroyed and had been wasted.[70]

Still, the baseball exchanges continued. In 1925, the semiprofessional women's team, the Philadelphia Bobbies, toured Japan. The Tokyo Six University

League was formed, and its Waseda University team defeated the visiting University of Chicago. Waseda was coached by Suishu Tobita, "the god of Japanese baseball," who imposed rigid discipline known as "death training." Tobita viewed baseball as war: "If the players do not try so hard as to vomit blood in practice, then they can not hope to win games." Going beyond the martial spirit often encouraged in American baseball, Tobita's methods mirrored modern elite military training, akin to contemporary U.S. Navy SEALs "hell week." Comparing baseball and war in the United States and Japan reveals close parallels in their masculine war metaphors and imperial impulses.[71]

In 1927, Waseda University played the Quantico Marines in Virginia. Japan again won the Far Eastern Games baseball championship. The Negro League's Philadelphia Royal Giants played twenty-four games in Japan, and the Fresno Japanese-American team barnstormed the country. In 1928, Ty Cobb led a U.S. tour to Japan, and in 1930 the U.S. Marine team also visited. Enamored with baseball, Japanese Prince Hirohito donated the Regent's Cup to celebrate each year's Japanese champion. Some still held out hope for baseball playing a peaceful role. The editors of *Literary Digest*, however, worried about Japanese expansionism: "There is no more assurance the ethical code Japan displays in her sporting life will function in dealings with China than that the sportsmanship of England's or America's playing fields will hold good in their dealings with India and Nicaragua." And what about direct relations between the U.S. and Japan?[72]

In 1931, Japan invaded eastern China, seized Manchuria, and began running it with a puppet government. The League of Nations protested, and Japan abruptly dropped out; thus both Japan and the United States were out of the world's only peacekeeping institution. This signaled Japan's move toward fascism and further militarizing its sports for war and intervention. Meanwhile, Herb Hunter conducted another Japanese tour despite concerns by Commissioner Landis, who chastised him for allowing the Japanese to beat U.S. professionals on his last trip. Another mission, led by Lou Gehrig and Lefty O'Doul, played seventeen games, including a sold-out Tokyo contest at which Japanese Education Minister Tanaka Kotaro threw out the first pitch to U.S. Ambassador Cameron Forbes. The black Royal Giants returned for another tour, reportedly building greater good will than the "more arrogant" white major leaguers. Meanwhile, back home, the Pacific Coast League's Sacramento Senators and Oakland Oaks held their own widely advertised "Sino-Japanese War," when they pitted Japanese pitcher Kenso Nushida against Chinese pitcher Lee Gum Hong.[73]

In 1932, the Rikkyo University team toured the United States, claiming that college contacts promoted better international relations. Bunshir Itom, a

University of California Japanese alumnus, stated, "All Japanese love peace and will never dare fight America. If some people say there may be trouble, tell them we want to settle it on a baseball field!"[74] Accompanied by Ted Lyons and Moe Berg, Lefty O'Doul led another visit, this time staying three months to coach Japanese teams. O'Doul, America's premier baseball ambassador to Japan, returned convinced that the Japanese game would soon be competitive with U.S. baseball. National League president John Heydler expressed his hope that a Japanese team would someday play in the World Series.

The most spectacular U.S. tour of Japan (and other Far East destinations) was led by O'Doul, Babe Ruth, and Connie Mack in 1934, the year the St. Louis Cardinals "Gas House Gang" electrified the baseball world.[75] Already a legend in Japan, Ruth didn't disappoint his hosts, hitting fourteen home runs as his team won all seventeen games played. Millions lined the streets and more than 65,000 fans crammed Tokyo's Jingu Stadium to see him. The 1934 U.S. tour inspired the formation of Japan's first professional team, the Dai Nippon Tokyo Yakyu Kurabu (the Great Japan Tokyo Baseball Club).

The *Sporting News* hailed the O'Doul tour as a missionary crusade: "We all are brothers under the skin and sons of one Adam, and if left to our natural impulses without greed of exploiters and machinations of politicians, we could in live in peace." The tour would "prove to Americans that the so-called 'yellow peril' wears the same clothes, plays the same game and entertains the same thoughts." Sportswriter Bill Dooley believed the 1934 visit promoted respect for America much more effectively than any politicians, preserving diplomatic stability by "sublimating tensions and hostilities otherwise released in battle." The touring major leaguers were greeted enthusiastically even by anti-American university audiences. Connie Mack claimed it was "one of the greatest peace measures in the history of nations." Because the United States was blocking agreement on parity in a naval treaty it was negotiating with Japan, there was, according to Mack, "strong anti-American feeling throughout Japan . . . but then Babe Ruth smacked a home run and all the ill feeling and war sentiment vanished." According to the *New York Times*, "the Babe's big bulk blotted out such unimportant things as international squabbles over oil and navies." Perhaps it was naive, but many thought baseball and Japanese national hero Babe Ruth really could preserve the peace.[76]

Others weren't sure the peace would hold. The 1934 tour was tarnished when Matsutaro Shoriki, the Tokyo publisher who had arranged it, was stabbed by a member of the Warlike Gods Society, a rebel group that claimed Shoriki was draining money from Japan's depressed economy. Also, during a tour game, young Kyoto pitcher Eiji Sawamura achieved the amazing feat of striking out future Hall of Famers Charlie Gehringer, Babe Ruth, Lou Gehrig, and Jimmie Foxx in succession. Sawamura was offered a contract by the Pittsburgh Pirates but refused to sign. An outspoken anti-American critic, he explained, "My problem is I hate America and cannot make myself like Americans."[77]

The news wasn't good back home, either. At its December 1934 winter meetings, MLB discouraged any further Japanese tours. Upset, *Sporting News* editors claimed baseball should remain active in promoting sportsmanship and brotherly love. It acknowledged the "jingoists" who dwelled on strained U.S.-Japanese relations but felt the tours would either delay or prevent conflict. Organized baseball had to acknowledge, however, that the White House had refused to recognize the new Japanese government and that baseball no longer necessarily signaled peace. According to Henry Chauncey, America could "expect that the problem of parity will involve baseball as well as battle-ships." As Merritt Clifton has observed, "even as jingoistic Japanese generals urged a return to the code of the samurai . . . baseball was not only tolerated but even encouraged. Baseball and military preparations were perhaps the only two realms in which Japanese leaders urged the population to learn from the West right up to the war's outbreak."[78]

Even so, the U.S.-Japanese baseball relationship survived a few more years. In 1935, after winning 92 of its 102 games in its U.S.-Canada tour, Japan's only professional team changed its name to the Tokyo Giants and adopted uniforms like that worn by their American hero, Lefty O'Doul, when he played for the New York Giants. The Yale University team toured Japan, not to be outdone by the Harvard University tour the year before. Former big leaguer Les Mann led another U.S. tour to Japan, hosted by Meiji University.[79] And despite their misgivings about tours, major-league executives again raised the U.S.-Japanese World Series idea. President Franklin Roosevelt gave his blessing, indicating that perhaps the Japanese could be won over through athletic competition rather than military conflict.

In 1936, the Japanese Professional League was formed, with Lefty O'Doul's considerable help. The Tokyo Giants signed future star Victor Starfin, the son of Russian aristocrats who found refuge in Japan after the Bolshevik Revolution.[80] That same year, the Tokyo club played its spring training in the United States. After this visit, however, the U.S. baseball press wrote little about Japan for several years. Instead, it focused on Europe, where—as it smugly noted— "nations that did not play baseball were headed into war." Yet a year later, Japan launched the Second Sino-Japanese War, as a result of which it controlled most of China until its surrender after World War II.

Elsewhere in the Far East, U.S. and Japanese baseball competed for attention as the two nations jockeyed for diplomatic and military control. The two imperial powers maintained an uneasy peace, each using baseball to compete for Asian "hearts and minds." In China, the 1922 Herb Hunter tour played games against both Chinese and U.S. Marines teams. In 1924, the U.S. Congress excluded not only the Japanese but also the Chinese, which fueled similar anti-American sentiment. The Chinese again showed their resentment of U.S. Christian missionaries and U.S. corporate exploitation of Chinese labor and resources. In 1927, a civil war erupted between the corrupt Nationalist government and Communist rebels, lasting for decades. Baseball was strongly promoted in 1931 when Manchuria was invaded by Japan, which quickly arranged a baseball tournament there among itself, Taiwan, Korea, and the Philippines. Not to be outdone, the 1934 Babe Ruth–Connie Mack All Star tour stopped in Shanghai for several games, including one against the Pandas, the team led Liang Funchu, the "grandfather of Chinese baseball."[81]

The Chinese Communist revolutionaries also embraced baseball, challenging the U.S. sporting influence in China by incorporating women and diverse races into the games. The 511 Unit of the People's Liberation Army (PLA) formed a team, as did the Eighth Route Army in the northwest, one of the main units, after 1937, in the war of resistance against Japan. During that conflict, baseball was also played in the prisoner-of-war compounds. PLA leader, Marshal He Long viewed it as ideal training for soldiers: "Baseball and other sports are the pillars of national defense and development." He gave preferential treatment to Japanese prisoners-of-war so they could help teach his troops baseball, and he had a special factory designated just to supply baseball equipment. Communist baseball continued until the 1960s. Marshal He was made Commissar for National Sport but then fell out of favor. Without his support, baseball was denounced by the Red Guards as Western decadence.[82]

Japan's firm control over Taiwan continued after World War I. To integrate the Taiwanese into Japanese culture and to defuse armed resistance to Japanese rule, baseball was introduced into the schools. But in the early 1920s, native Taiwanese youth formed their own team, which challenged Japanese hegemony on the baseball field. The Japanese government seized the team in 1924, renaming it Nenggao, after a Taiwanese mountain. Explaining the move, the local Japanese governor, Saburo Eguchi, stated, "Teaching barbarians to play baseball is an astonishing thing. . . . I want to correct these barbarians born with violent blood and let them feel the sport's true spirit."[83]

Taiwan kept forming its own teams, and in 1929 one of them upset a Japanese team in Japan, initiating a groundswell of pride and even fanaticism. Into the 1930s, while Taiwan increasingly used baseball to confront its Japanese overlord, it nevertheless played the Japanese game—stressing small ball in contrast to

America's emerging power game. As it went further down the fascist path, Japan began to retighten its grip on Taiwan, intensifying the Japanization of Taiwan and relying partly on the shared experience of baseball. In 1936, a Japanese professional team signed a Taiwanese player for the first time. In 1940, Taiwan was transformed into a major Japanese munitions producer in preparation for war, and a new dose of imperial nationalism was introduced to the island.

As yet another target for U.S. and Japanese control, Korea began resisting Japanese rule in 1919, only to be violently subjugated. The second Herb Hunter tour stopped for games in Korea in 1922. The next year, the Japanese-controlled Korean government launched a baseball campaign to undermine subversive impulses. It created the Chosen Amateur Athletic Association, which promoted teams and publicized games. In 1934, the Americans arrived again, led by Babe Ruth and Connie Mack. Their so-called bonsai barnstorming was a model of sports transcending politics, but a geopolitical competition simmered underneath, and the U.S.-Japanese baseball rivalry had more than mere game outcomes at stake.[84] The U.S. All Stars played Korean teams and also a U.S. Marines club—a visible sign of American interests in the region. By the late 1930s, with Japan and the United States increasingly preoccupied by the impending war, baseball began to fade in Korea.

In the Philippines, the roles were reversed. The United States ruled, and Japan sought to make inroads—often through visits by its baseball teams. By 1919, the Filipino teams excelled: the national team won the Far Eastern Games championship that year, and again in 1921, 1923, 1925, and 1930. The 1922 Herb Hunter tour also hit the Philippines, then governed by U.S. General Leonard Wood, who had turned down the MLB commissionership to take this command. Colonial exploitation again incited general anti-American rebellion in the Philippines, which spilled onto the baseball field. But by 1923, baseball began losing favor there: it was implicated in the U.S. quest to impose the American lifestyle. In response, the *Sporting News* recommended U.S. withdrawal from the Philippines, because any people who refused to embrace baseball "will never be suited to live under the Stars and Stripes." The U.S.-Japanese baseball influence in the Philippines waxed and waned for the next several years, until Japan attacked and occupied the islands in 1941, in the early stages of World War II.[85]

War Clouds over Europe

While the U.S. followed Far East developments, it was more alarmed in the mid-1930s about the war threat in Europe. Despite the extraordinary economic dislocation, ideological conflict, and nationalist extremism of that decade, global sports nevertheless grew remarkably. Baseball became embroiled in the politicized world of international athletics, centered on the Olympic Games. Illustrating the initial limits of baseball's diffusion around the world, the game was played at the 1904, 1912, and 1928 Olympics but only as a demonstration sport and not by real baseball players. Even with Albert Spalding heading the U.S. Olympic Committee in the early years, baseball wasn't adopted for regular Olympic Games.

By 1936, baseball was ready to try again but got entangled in the racial politics of the times. As National Baseball Congress head, former major leaguer Les Mann was challenged by the Japanese, who wanted a demonstration game against the United States at the Olympics. To find players, Mann ran advertisements urging Americans to "bear the name of your country and carry your flag" by trying out for the U.S. team. But the games were scheduled for Berlin, and Mann's efforts were confronted by the anti-Nazi boycott movement. When asked to support Mann's team, MLB declined, trying to insulate itself from Olympic politics.[86]

Reports about Nazi persecution of Jews and others were already common. Wouldn't participating in the Berlin Olympics implicitly endorse that bigotry? Or could involvement instead be used to challenge theories of racial superiority? And what about America's own record on race? In baseball the color barrier was still firmly entrenched and would remain so until the Jackie Robinson breakthrough a decade later. The spirit of Robinson appeared at the 1936 Olympics, however, as Jackie's brother Mack won the 200 meter silver medal, a close second to the black superstar Jesse Owen. The sterling performance of African Americans at the Berlin Games sent a message.[87]

For those concerned about the Nazis, the implicit idea was that American sports could beat other ideologies or transform them. Ironically, just before the games began, Japan pulled out, forcing Les Mann to send two U.S. baseball teams to Berlin, where they played each other. A local German newspaper tried to decipher the sport for the German people, and the American ballplayers spent several days teaching baseball "to the eager young Hanses and Heinrichs." Carson Thompson, a Temple University four-letter man, appeared as a reliever in the game. A few days earlier, he had been selected to explain baseball to an Olympic documentary film narrator—"a charming woman" with whom Thompson spent an entire day: she was Eva Braun, the mistress of Adolf Hitler.[88]

The Olympic ball game turnout was huge: 125,000 spectators, including the Führer. Controversy arose over how the ballplayers should wave to the crowd, some fearing the wrong motion might resemble a Nazi salute. Otherwise, the game went well, and the reception was so enthusiastic that a World's

Tournament of baseball (involving at least nine nations) was planned for the 1940 Olympics. As Mark Dyreson has suggested, convinced of the "power of their national pastime to transform the globe . . . Americans mapped a pacific empire united by a common faith in baseball."[89] With World War II's outbreak, however, the games were cancelled. As Pete Cava has observed, "In ancient times, wars were postponed so the Olympics could take place. In this century, it's been the opposite."[90]

A Failure of Baseball Diplomacy?

Back in the States, the celebration of baseball as an alternative to war continued into the late 1930s, the ballpark a sanctuary from war hysteria. Each spring, as Richard Crepeau has observed, America preferred the call of "Batter up" and screaming against the umpire to the call of "Shoulder arms" and the screaming of men dying on the battlefields. According to the *Feather River Bulletin*, "American boys are not conscripted into army service, they play baseball. 'Play ball' is their battle cry, not 'Heil Hitler.' While little Fascists are learning to toss hand grenades, little Americans are learning to groove one over the plate. But woe betide the enemy when an American boy finds it needful to throw hand grenades!" The 1930s Great Depression challenged American masculinity, with unemployment and destitution often blamed on individual failures. In the U.S. military, athletics were again bolstered to supply a proving ground for men. The lure of athletics and war worked together, and the emerging military museums displayed martial exploits alongside sports accomplishments—especially in baseball.[91]

By 1940, the mental preparation for war had increased. While the Cincinnati Reds were heading toward their second straight pennant, the *Sporting News* rallied baseball around Flag Day, advocating flag-raising and "The Star-Spangled Banner" for all games, not merely special occasions. As Richard Crepeau has observed, this was accomplished by 1941, "to make baseball fans . . . more nation-conscious, in preparation for possible entry into World War II."[92] Even so, in response to German aggression, Americans remained largely isolationist. The Jewish plight under the Nazis didn't mobilize war fever, and America refused to provide sanctuary. President Franklin Roosevelt decided, however, that the United States must enter the European war. Ironically, however, it was his policies toward Japan, rather than Germany, that launched a sequence of events that turned American public opinion around and mobilized the U.S. Congress to declare war immediately after Pearl Harbor.[93]

By 1940, changes in Japanese baseball foretold an imminent U.S.-Japanese clash. Baseball radio broadcasts ended, English baseball terms were replaced with Japanese words, and U.S.-style uniforms were rejected. In August 1941, baseball itself was significantly curtailed in Japan. This dismayed the *Sporting News*, which noted again the goodwill baseball had created between the two nations. Referring to Japanese Emperor Hirohito as Mr. Herohater, it observed that tyrants can't tolerate sports like baseball because the game's values clash with dictatorship, and only when the spirit of sport reigns over international affairs will human life emerge from the jungle. A few months later, when the Japanese attacked Pearl Harbor, organized baseball took it very personally. It was a failure of baseball diplomacy. The sport had had a greater impact on Japan than on any other country. How was it possible that a people who took so well to "democracy's game" would turn out to be the archenemy of the "greatest democracy on earth?"[94] Had the empire struck out?

Explaining this alarming turnaround required some considerable rewriting of history. The *Sporting News* noted how the Japanese quickly became first-class fielders but their small size limited them as power hitters. This weakness was "always a sore spot with this cocky race of yellow-skinned, almond eyed players," whose attitude only disguised their "national inferiority complex." Apparently, despite appearances, the Japanese were never fully converted to the game. The people of this "treacherous Asiatic land" couldn't understand the American practice of questioning the umpire's authority and harassing opponents. Americans, the *Sporting News* observed, would never say "so sorry" through a "grimacing yellow mask," nor would they ever "stab an honorable opponent in the back" or "crush out his brains with a bat while he is asleep." The careful observer could see that the Japanese had never acquired the "soul of our National Game," for if it "had ever penetrated their yellow hides," they could never have committed that "infamous deed" of December 7, 1941.[95]

According to *Sporting News* editor J.G. Spink, MLB should confess its error in allowing the Japanese "to share the game's benefits and God-given qualities." The attention of all "civilized, democratic peoples of the world" should be called to Japan's "unworthiness" to retain baseball. He claimed the gift of baseball should be withdrawn, and that more care be taken in determining "who should be given the gift in the future."[96] Others chimed in similarly. Pittsburgh Pirates manager Frankie Frisch hoped, if the draft took any of his players, that they would hit ".400 against the Japs and Nazis alike." Major-league umpire Bill Klem, a veteran of several Japanese tours, claimed "the Jap is a constitutional kleptomaniac"—whatever that meant.

Sportswriter Dan Daniel said the Japanese had been just going through the motions and didn't know any more about baseball than Hitler. "The dirty japs" were "white-livered punks," "thugs," "crooks," "skunks," and a "lot of cockeyed Joe Yoshaharas." They would "never beat the USA at war, baseball or marbles," and soon they would realize they had slipped themselves a 'Mickey Finn'" when they attacked Pearl Harbor. "Mr. Tojo will wake up some night with two strikes against him and [Hall of Fame pitcher Bob] Feller having one hell of a day." Before a person can take part in "the give and take," and accept the decisions "the umpire gives them on the ball field," Daniel noted, "he has to have the American way of living in him." As he admitted, "I am especially sore about this because it is the first *failure* of baseball."[97]

As Robert Sinclair has observed, organized baseball had convinced itself that America had been created to serve mankind and that the sport would spread fellowship worldwide "as if a vehicle of American foreign policy." While the First World War bred some disillusionment, which humbled American internationalism, "it also stimulated a moral arrogance." Conveniently ignoring its own Black Sox scandal, baseball felt its unequaled moral reputation gave it a responsibility to foster global harmony. Thus, to baseball's true believers, Pearl Harbor was a cruel blow. When baseball wasn't blaming Japanese weakness or treachery, it instead wondered whether baseball had failed in its "self-appointed mission to save the world and export the American dream."[98]

But had baseball also "failed" by having let itself get dragged into America's far-flung military adventures? U.S. political and military leaders had used the game to further imperial policies, and thus baseball became associated with American aggression. For Japan, baseball was a symbol of U.S. intervention as much as it was a common denominator and peacekeeper. It served as a model for Japan. But rather than being controlled by the sport, as had other targets of U.S. invasions, Japan instead controlled baseball and then used it in its own increasingly imperialistic foreign policies in Taiwan, China, Korea, the Philippines, and eventually against the Americans.

Baseball's overseers and many American political leaders thought the Japanese loved baseball because they loved the "American way of living." But according to Joseph Reaves, while the Japanese embraced "the gospel of baseball," they "heard the Good Word differently." For them, baseball wasn't a coveted model of the American dream, but rather a "perfect outlet for Japanese values." As Robert Whiting observed, "Baseball provided the Japanese an opportunity to express their renowned group proclivities on an athletic field." But it also "tapped [their] militaristic tendencies [rewarding] self-discipline, loyalty, a fighting spirit, filial piety, and the ability to endure adversity." The sport, as Reaves has noted, provided a reservoir "for Japan's immense national pride—a way to measure Japan's place in the world through a game invented by the very people who forced the Japanese to surrender centuries of blissful isolation." As Richard Crepeau has suggested, this helped promote Japan's hypernationalism, which may have enhanced its proclivity toward expansionist wars.[99]

In light of Pearl Harbor, organized baseball was forced to mute its extravagant claims for the sport, at least for a while. Idealism would have some tough years ahead. However much baseball sought fellowship with other nations, it had an even bigger obligation, as the national pastime, to stand behind the United States in war. It would do so rather dramatically with the outbreak of World War II.

7

Good War Hunting
(1941–1945)

Think of these men who now play, but soon will fight, and remember that they will take Baseball with them, in their hearts—that, if through the fortunes of war and the will of God, they fall; that spot where they will lie will be forever American, and Baseball.

—J.G.T. Spink

As everyone knows, in the early morning of December 7, 1941, Japan launched an unprovoked sneak attack on the United States at Hawaii's Pearl Harbor, killing 2,333 Americans. The ambush shook the country out of its isolationism and launched it into World War II. This shameful blow assaulted America not only physically but also symbolically. As the 2001 movie *Pearl Harbor* showed us—on film and in advertising posters—the Japanese Zeros first flew in over a sandlot, where boys were playing baseball. Along with everything else, the Japanese attacked the quintessential American icon, the national pastime.

After the onslaught, President Franklin Roosevelt claimed it would be a "day that will live in infamy." Most deservedly, it has. Seeking revenge against Japan and defeating the evils of Nazi Germany would turn World War II into the "Good War." An endless array of books, reports, miniseries, and movies have put the war in a good light, including recent films, such as *Saving Private Ryan*, *The Greatest Generation*, *Band of Brothers*, *Flags of Our Fathers*, *The War*, and, of course, *Pearl Harbor*. But with baseball's assistance, the ongoing campaign to keep World War II on a pedestal may be misleading. What "everyone knows" about the war may not be entirely true.[1] Was the Japanese attack really unprovoked? Was the White House really unaware of the impending assault?[2]

Raising these and other such doubts is blasphemy, of course, especially now that the Good War is being used not only to justify itself, but also to help legitimize American wars of the early twenty-first century—in response to another Pearl Harbor: 9/11. According to World War II veteran and Hall of Fame pitcher Bob Feller, left-wing revisionists and bureaucrats are now trying to rewrite American history.³ Yet doubts about the Good War story of Pearl Harbor are not just being considered now but were raised immediately after the attack. Members of Congress proposed an investigation but retreated under attacks against their patriotism. More recently, the main "revisionist" on Pearl Harbor is not left-wing or a bureaucrat, but rather a conservative journalist who served in World War II with George H.W. Bush and who was awarded ten battle stars and the Presidential Unit Citation.⁴

Whatever the truths or misconceptions about Pearl Harbor and the war, one thing we know for sure: boys were *not* playing sandlot baseball at daybreak on December 7, 1941, as much as movie directors and others would love Americans to make that emotional connection. But baseball would be inextricably involved in World War II in many other ways.

When Everything Changed

In response to Pearl Harbor, organized baseball sang a different tune not merely about Japan, but about war and peace generally. Until then, World War II didn't look like a "good war," and thus Americans adopted a holier-than-thou attitude about the warmongering of others. The 1941 baseball season opened with America still at peace, and the *Sporting News* ran cartoons proclaiming, "Europe's national pastime seems to be war; America's is baseball." The editors commented, "War broke loose in America this week—but instead of rifles, bayonets, cannon, machine guns and airplanes, it is a battle of bats and balls. That is the American way—the Baseball way. God has blessed America, and baseball offers a place where rivalries can be settled without bloodshed or slaughter of innocents."⁵

As the 1941 season unfolded, baseball began developing a wartime consciousness, emphasizing battle analogies. On its front page, the *Sporting News* showed "the entire Yankee team trying to steam across the Atlantic as if it were a freighter facing enemy torpedoes." A photo caption read, "Battered Yankee Raider Being Rearmed for Flag Fight" to make the team the "Terror of the Seas" again. A piece examining relief pitching was headlined "Convoys for Starters." Under "Daily Box Scores," tallies were kept of German planes shot down.

Like a chameleon, baseball changed its official feeling about the war. One symbol of the transformation happened on the ball field, as Michael Seidel described in his book *Streak*. America was transfixed in 1941, watching New York Yankees slugger Joe DiMaggio's fifty-six-game hitting streak unfold. On May 15, the day DiMaggio's streak began, world headlines announced the bizarre solo flight and parachute jump of Nazi leader Rudolf Hess into Scotland. Three days later, "I Am an American Day" brought thirty thousand fans to Yankee Stadium, where servicemen were admitted for free, the 7th Regiment Band played martial tunes, and speeches lauded the American way. African American dancer Bill Robinson entertained and guaranteed the crowd he would personally stop Hitler if the "crazed Führer" ever marched on Harlem.[6]

On May 27, 1941, at the Polo Grounds, with the score tied in the seventh inning, the umpires stopped the game, and both teams left the field. It was almost ten thirty. For the next forty-five minutes, the crowd heard President Roosevelt declare the United States to be in a state of unlimited emergency, for which he was stationing American forces strategically, in case of war with Germany. The speech got rousing applause, the teams took the field, and the Giants went on to win the game. Baseball continued.

Some advocated a more isolationist stance. Yankees general manager Ed Barrow claimed the European conflict was holding baseball hostage: the Selective Service Act of 1940 was drafting players without knowing whether they'd be needed. As DiMaggio's streak began to heat up, the "increasingly strident nationalism and German sympathies" of the American hero Charles Lindbergh shared the ballplayer's headlines: "Our civilization," Lindbergh argued, "depends on a Western wall of race and arms to hold back either a Genghis Kahn or the infiltration of inferior blood." Former baseball commissioner candidate General Leonard Wood led the America First Committee— a xenophobic, pro-German, and largely anti-Semitic organization, for which Lindbergh was a prominent spokesman.[7]

But Brooklyn Dodgers general manager Larry MacPhail rejected its appeal, instead chairing the Brooklyn division of the Committee to Defend America by Aiding the Allies. As Michael Seidel observed, the days of DiMaggio's streak recorded the energies of a land increasingly "preoccupied by war but as yet untested and unscarred by it." America was "excited by heroic prospects and frightened by bleak realities; fascinated by air power and horrified by the saturation bombing in Europe." With DiMaggio's streak still going, on June 22 Hitler launched the largest military campaign in world history against America's ally Russia, and the United States deployed troops to a war zone for the first time. On the day DiMaggio broke George Sisler's forty-one-game hitting streak, Nazi airplane production surpassed American output. But as Seidel notes, "At a time when the preparation for war could not be severed from the threat of falling just short, the performance of Joe DiMaggio helped buoy a nation forging a new myth of its own potential."[8]

Admired to this day as an almost superhuman accomplishment, DiMaggio's streak was finally broken on July 17, 1941. It ended at the same time Lindbergh's status bottomed out, his fascist sympathies all too evident. The 1941 season finished before the United States went to war. Pearl Harbor came as a surprise to most Americans, their eyes having been focused largely on Europe. After the attack, people talked about "when everything changed." It's a lament that echoes eerily in our own times but may have had even more meaning back then. As Seidel suggested, DiMaggio's streak closed an American era. It was "the last year before our full immersion into an awful conflict, a year that both forges and closes the myth of an epoch to which DiMaggio's streak contributes its bounty of energy, endurance and grace."[9]

No Baseball, No Victory, No America

While the English playwright George Bernard Shaw called baseball "the great American tragedy," to most Americans it was instead a saving grace for a nation at war. According to William Mead, "No institution voiced [patriotic jingoism] more loudly, nor identified itself more with the war effort, than organized baseball," which was one of the institutions American boys "were fighting to preserve." Reading the era's baseball propaganda, "you'd have thought Kenesaw Mountain Landis was leading U.S. troops, wearing spikes, down the main street of Tokyo."[10]

Baseball went beyond being the national pastime, to become the national religion in the war years.[11] Arguing that baseball should play an even bigger part in this war, *Baseball Magazine* reprinted the article that Billy Sunday had written promoting the game's role in the previous world war. And the *Sporting News* editors preached:

> Just think if somebody in Germany had evolved this sport and today its virtues were confined to the terrain Adolf and his Gestapo terrorize. Baseball thanks a heavenly Protector for giving it to America . . . thanks an all-pervading Providence for its abiding faith in God. . . . And as Baseball thanks the Lord and thanks America, this great country thanks our Heavenly Father for the glories of its achievements, the justice of our cause, the might of the right—and Baseball.[12]

In response to the September 11, 2001, terrorist attack, President George Bush told Americans to fight back by going shopping. After the 1941 Pearl Harbor attack, sportswriter Dan Daniel implored Americans to buy tickets to ball games: "Old Glory is hoisted and the stirring strains of our national anthem set your blood a-tingling. 'This is MY AMERICA' you say to yourself, as you stand with head bowed in an American ball park, your appreciation of living in this country keener than ever. Baseball is doing its part. But, Baseball's war effort cannot live without every fan coming through the turnstiles."[13]

The sport was placed on a pedestal as never before, even equated with our most sacred institutions: "Baseball is not just baseball. Baseball is a piece of America. As the Declaration of Independence says, 'We hold these truths to be self-evident.'" What also seemed self-evident was that the United States couldn't win the war without baseball. It couldn't prevail if professional baseball were suspended or if U.S. soldiers didn't have it to train or entertain themselves. Echoing Albert Spalding a half century earlier, sportswriter James Gould claimed, "Baseball is a War!" although real "war is a baseball game raised to the nth power of seriousness." Dan Daniel put the game in an old hymn: "Baseball marches on in martial tread, cognizant of its duties and the hazards which confront it on land, sea and in air. Onward baseball soldiers, marching to the fray."[14]

This involved more than merely patriotism. Major League Baseball (MLB) and everyone associated with it were also fighting to survive. Baseball had nearly been shut down during World War I. This new war might be an even greater threat unless the sport could convincingly justify itself. Some claimed it offered a "comeback spirit."[15] Conveniently, those with a commercial stake in continuing baseball chimed in. In St. Louis, the Columbia Brewing Company ran a large ad:

> Listen to the little Red Bird, Adolf . . . it's saying YOUR LEAD ISNT BIG ENOUGH! That foul-play combination, Hitler to Hirohito to Benito, worked like a charm in the early innings because you started playing *your* game before anyone else had a fair chance to field a team. [But] a *fighting spirit can overcome any lead*. The United Nations are hitting their stride. They have started smashing your pitchers all over the lot. Soon they'll be scoring on your home plate! There's only one flag you are going to run up in the game *you* started: the white flag of surrender. In the World Series that lies ahead, it's in the Cards to *win*, as surely as it's in the cards for Hitler, Hirohito and Benito to *lose*.

Similarly, the Wilson Sporting Goods Company declared:

> [Among the] things overlooked in [the attempt] to make the world Germany's Oyster . . . was *baseball*. . . . But Hirohito and Hitler will know before the "ninth inning" of this war, what those roars of protest from the stands have meant in America. They are going to bat in that greater world's series—where the "pennant" means the life of our nation and

the world's future peace—where teamwork counts as never before—where thousands of "sacrifice hits" are being made by courageous "players" to speed the United Nations team on to Victory. So, a salute to Baseball, the great American game that has taught the will to win to millions of our boys and loyalty to millions of our people.[16]

Baseball became integral to war mobilization, garnering countless military endorsements. Pacific Commander Ernest King said, "Baseball has a rightful place in America at war." Colonel Theodore Bank, the U.S. Army athletic director, argued that baseball was "not a supplement to [the Army's training] program" but rather a basic part of it.[17] General Omar Bradley observed, "Every member of our baseball team at West Point became a general." As in World War I, the skill of American soldiers in throwing grenades was attributed to their baseball backgrounds. And the U.S. military relied heavily upon baseball to instill a "common sense that the American athlete, like the American warrior, was superior."[18]

Despite having just signed a five-year general-manager contract with the Dodgers and despite being in his fifties, Larry MacPhail tried to enlist. Instead, he was hired by the War Department and became baseball's closest link to the armed forces. MacPhail was on the Normandy invasion flagship and toured the European front, flew with Roosevelt, Churchill, and Eisenhower, and met with Pope Pius XII, who gave him religious medals for the Dodger players. MacPhail was an aide to Commander General Brehon Somervell, whose speech he delivered at the 1944 Baseball Writers' Association dinner. They, too, considered baseball a military exercise:

The successes of the British Army can be traced to the cricket fields of Eton. And the sandlots and big league ballparks of America have contributed to our military success. Nearly 70% of all major league players are wearing the uniform. Besides, a million and a half kids from junior sandlot teams sponsored by the major leagues and American Legion are in the Armed Services. They learned the teamwork it takes to win a battle or war. We never dare forget that a campaign can be upset by a ninth inning rally. We dare not relax until the last man is out.[19]

MacPhail later added his own conflation of baseball and military metaphors, in a letter he wrote to soldiers:

You fellows going "over there" will be batting in a tough league . . . on the road [where] the parks resemble ploughed fields planted with busted pop bottles. The bunch you'll be [facing] have as much sportsmanship as sons of rattlesnakes who mass-married a pack of black widow spiders. If they can use rusty razor blades instead of spikes they [will]. Every sack is "booby-trapped" and every beanball that skins your kisser didn't get there by accident. Those bastards aren't playing for pennants—nor even a cut of the game. They're out after the gate, the parks, and anything else they can grab. If they don't win this series, they'll start over again next season—if you let them stay in the league. Their managers know every lousy trick . . . a ball's a ball and a strike's a strike only if it adds up right for them. When you step up to the plate, take a real cut, and blast it out of the park. Anything short of straight over the center-field wall will be called a foul. [And] carry that bat with you on the way "round the bases." It might come in handy.[20]

According to Wisconsin Congressman La Vern Dilweg, "our fighting forces—men who achieved glorious victory in Africa, who are battling the Japs in the Pacific, and who are poised for the victorious invasion of Europe—want spectator sports to continue [at] home and hungrily await the sporting news." This belief was reflected in wartime films, where baseball was a unifying force and a symbol "for patriotism, mom's apple-pie Americana, and unabashed flag waving." Movies like *Guadalcanal Diary*, *Wake Island*, and *Lifeboat* were set in the Pacific and typically featured William Bendix, who played a U.S. Marine and fanatical Dodgers fan from Brooklyn: "If I was back home, I wouldn't be on no boat. Ebbets Field. That's for me. Watchin' them beautiful Bums." Inevitably, Bendix is shot and dying but hears the Dodgers game on a nearby shortwave radio. With his last gasp, he asks for the score, and with the Marine Hymn playing in the background, he dies smiling, knowing the Dodgers have won and the American dream remains intact.[21]

Journalist Quentin Reynolds pleaded, "Hitler has killed a great many things. Do not let him kill baseball." Public opinion polls consistently supported MLB's continuation. In a survey of wounded soldiers at Walter Reed hospital, sustaining wartime baseball was favored 300–3. As Sergeant Louis Eanes expressed it, "Without baseball we would sink back to the dark ages." Baseball was also promoted more matter-of-factly as a needed diversion for a people at war. According to Illinois Representative Melvin Price, baseball "not only lifts morale on the home front, but also the morale of our armed forces [around] the world." Looking back, New York Senator Kenneth Keating characterized baseball as a "great and certain tranquilizer that was as vital to our security as the sword and shield of our armed might."[22]

Baseball also meant fitness, as the Hillerich and Bradsby Company reminded Americans. Together with the American Legion, it ran ads claiming its equipment aided the war effort. "Play Ball, Keep Fit," the ads advised: "American boys and men must be healthy—strong—industrious. To work hard and get results, Americans must have time to relax and baseball, the All-American game, builds healthy bodies. Choose your baseball bats as Champions do and insist on the Louisville Slugger Trademark." The company also turned part of its bat-making operation into producing stocks for the M1 carbine.[23]

Using patriotic appeals to sell baseball and other products was common, and manufacturers happily concluded that selling more would help win the war. According to Wilson Sporting Goods, the sport was "vital to the American way. In times of WAR, baseball is even more important to the health of our youth, our workers, and those on the home front." Baseball card companies, such as Gum, Goudey, Donruss, and Bowman, sold patriotic, pro-war baseball cards, decorated in nationalistic symbols and wrapped in red, white, and blue paper, as well as military card sets such as "America at War," "Allies in Action," "Power for Peace," and "U.S. Naval Victories." The *Sporting News* redoubled its pitch for sales and subscriptions; Hollywood actor Joe E. Brown's All-Pacific Recreation Fund bought fourteen thousand subscriptions for men overseas. While existing baseball periodicals successfully survived, one new magazine, *Baseball Digest*, used the war to get itself started. Launched in 1942, it has been a consistent flag-waver for more than six decades.[24]

Publishers, sportswriters, and baseball officials all had a financial stake; remembering the sport being called a shirker during the last war, they determined not to repeat that mistake. If baseball hadn't participated intensely in World War II, it would have lost its status as the national pastime. Baseball could even help our Allies. Oblivious to Japan's own obsession with the game, sportswriter James Gould asserted, "If there had been baseball in Europe and Asia, there wouldn't have been any World War II—or any World War I, for that matter." But since war was here, the United States would be not only in a "war of rifles" but also a "battle of bats and balls," and America's Allies would grow to appreciate baseball as a symbol of freedom in a way the Japanese never could.[25]

Against this wave of support for wartime baseball, a few wondered whether soldiers had other things to worry about. And maybe baseball players were *not* better prepared to be soldiers than other people. According to war correspondent Stanley Frank, "You are asked to believe that men overseas are fighting for the privilege of calling the umpire a blind bum. This romantic, unrealistic thinking infuriates the soldier and convinces him civilians have no [idea] the enormous sacrifices he is making. The soldier is not fighting to see a ball game, to taste Mom's cooking, or to hear the latest juke-box recording. He is fighting for his life."[26]

In January 1942, in his "Green Light" letter to Commissioner Landis, President Roosevelt claimed it would be "best for the country to keep baseball going." Although he assumed all players eligible for military or government service would enlist, he felt the game would remain worthy, despite its depleted ranks. This preserved baseball not only during the war but perhaps from extinction altogether. Fortunately, Roosevelt was a fan and often used baseball terminology: "I have no expectation of making a hit every time I come to bat. What I seek is the highest possible batting average, not only for myself, but for my team." In the end, Roosevelt felt "baseball would help win the war." The president was politically astute enough to understand baseball's relationship to official ideology. When Roosevelt died during the war, his successor, Harry Truman, also quickly endorsed wartime baseball.[27]

The green light didn't come from any friendship between Roosevelt and Landis; they hated each other. Landis opposed Roosevelt's New Deal policies, thought the president was a socialist, and questioned the U.S. entrance into World War II. According to Frank Graham, "The game's relations with Washington, like Red China's today, were uneasy and unofficial." Sportswriter Shirley Povich claimed that "Landis wasn't much more welcome at the White House than the Japanese ambassador." It must have particularly irked Landis when the *Sporting News* named Roosevelt Player of the Year for his letter.[28]

If Roosevelt needed persuading to give baseball the go-ahead, then it came from others. National League president Ford Frick smoothed tensions, and Washington Senators owner Clark Griffith maintained a clandestine pipeline between baseball and the White House. Despite his personal views, Landis pledged MLB's support: "We want the same rules applied as on anyone else." American League president Will Harridge said Roosevelt's letter confirmed baseball's "definite place in the welfare of our country, particularly in times of stress." Frick promised his "complete cooperation," indicating he would "not [be] going to Washington with any appeal [for] the players."[29]

Baseball Pitches In

While organized baseball didn't keep its pledge of noninterference, it did fulfill its other commitments. On baseball's behalf, the *Sporting News* declared, "Uncle Sam, We Are at Your Command!" Referring to "Czar" Landis, *Look* magazine warned that "baseball's monarch faces the ticklish task of gearing his empire to the exigencies of an all-out war." Portrayed as a dictator, even one prone to "Gestapo methods," what actions would Landis have baseball take?[30]

Even before the United States entered the War, a March 1940 all-star game raised money for the Finnish Relief Fund. Baseball exhibitions were played at military camps, and soldiers were admitted free to major-league games. Benefit contests were played for the USO, the Red Cross, and other humanitarian groups. In 1942, every major- and minor-league team played a benefit for the Army and Navy Relief Fund. The winner of that year's All-Star Game played the U.S. Service team in a second game, dubbed the Patriot Game. Held in Cleveland's Municipal Stadium, it featured military bands, a Marine Corps drill team, a tank parade, and a V-formation of U.S. Coast Guard and Navy personnel. Sportswriter Fred Lieb covered the game: "As though it were a contagion, one could feel the patriotic feeling of the 65,000 fans, it sent needles shooting down one's spine, started honest tears trickling down the cheeks, and made one murmur to one's self 'Thank God, I am an American.' . . . the service men lost [the game] but their victory will come later."[31]

A second Patriot Game, the Negro League's Benefit Game, was played a month later to raise additional money for Army and Navy Relief. That game matched the East All Stars against the West All Stars. Before the contest, members of the Elks, the Home Guards, the American Legion, the Veterans of Foreign Wars, the Veterans of the Spanish-American War, and assorted military dignitaries took part in ceremonies.[32] Another game matched the Kansas City Monarchs against a servicemen's team and drew 30,000 fans.

In Louisville, on Waste Fat Night, fans donated 2,587 pounds of grease, which was converted into glycerin to make powder for 75-millimeter shells. In Cincinnati, a "Smokes for Servicemen" Game was held, where fans paid admission with cigarettes, which were sent to the troops. In July 1943, a Yankees–White Sox game was interrupted to announce Benito Mussolini's resignation as Italian prime minister; fans began dancing in the aisles. On June 6, 1944, all baseball games were cancelled when Allied forces invaded France at Normandy. Two weeks later, a three-way game was played at the Polo Grounds between the Yankees, Giants, and Dodgers. Getting tickets required a war-bond purchase, and the game raised nearly $6 million. In another game, the 1945 Washington Senators home opener, the U.S. soldiers who raised the flag on Iwo Jima were honored. Kids who brought scrap metal and rubber recyclables were often admitted free to ballparks. Chicago Cubs owner Phil Wrigley sent soldiers free gum and stopped using aluminum foil in his gum manufacturing, so it could go instead to war production.[33]

Baseball equipment was donated to the American and Canadian Ball and Bat funds. The major leagues authorized $25,000 to purchase baseball gear for the U.S. Army and Navy sports programs. Fans threw back foul balls so they could be donated to the military. Following Dodgers general manager Larry

MacPhail's dictum that "every war bond kills a Jap," ballplayers hawked them at lunch halls, industrial plants, and town meetings. Some were sold based on performance: $2,500 for each single made by a buyer's player, $5,000 for each double, $7,500 for each triple, $10,000 for each home run, $35,000 for each pitching victory, and $50,000 for each shutout.[34] The Baseball Writers Association of America joined big-league teams in a "Keep 'Em Slugging" campaign to provide bats and balls for U.S. military bases.

MacPhail pushed the major leagues to fund an Army Flying Fortress. The huge, state-of-the-art bomber would be named the Kenesaw Mountain Landis and crewed by major leaguers. Ballparks were proposed as bomb shelters. According to Yankees owner Ed Barrow, fifteen thousand people could be protected under the stadium bleachers and another forty thousand under the grandstand. Mayor Fiorello LaGuardia proclaimed, "If we are to be hit, I'd just as soon get hit in Yankee Stadium, the Polo Grounds or Ebbets Field. . . . I am for baseball now, more than ever."[35]

Promoting patriotic symbols was also important. Commissioner Landis ordered American flag patches for all player uniforms.[36] Teams wore the insignia of the "Hail America, Hale America" campaign, sponsored by the Federal Security Administration to promote a stronger America. During a 1942 doubleheader, the Philadelphia Phillies and Boston Braves wore poppies on their uniforms, donated by a local American Legion post. The Chicago Cubs put a War Department emblem on the uniforms of their players returning from military service. The St. Louis Cardinals players wore the U.S. Marine insignia on their caps. Military pilots, in turn, donned baseball hats when they weren't flying.

During the war, players marched to the flagpole before each contest to raise the flag and sing "The Star Spangled Banner." Kate Smith began her legendary renditions of "God Bless America" at the ballparks. As Richard Crepeau has observed, "It would be nice to say all of this was pure patriotic expression, but much of it was created by PR-conscious owners to make sure no one questioned the patriotism of [their] athletes. . . . Four years of war, followed by the Cold War and the emergence of the American Empire, solidified the practice [of playing the national anthem] and made it into a national ritual."[37]

As a throwback to World War I, Philadelphia Phillies players marched with their bats, simulating rifles on their shoulders during 1942 spring training. The drills were inspired by Phillies manager Hans Lobert, a former major leaguer who ran the U.S. Military Academy baseball team from 1918 to 1925. At the Chicago White Sox spring training camp in Pasadena, pitchers often threw at four-by-six-foot cardboard caricatures of bespectacled Japanese soldiers. Elsewhere in California, soldiers-in-training played baseball with gas masks, preparing for possible chemical attacks.[38]

Radio broadcasts brought baseball to the troops. The U.S. Army helped provide the games, and the Office of War Information sent scores to the soldiers. Commercial sponsors of game broadcasts agreed to deliver government messages for things such as the USO, war bonds, and Coast Guard recruiting. The 1942 World Series—whose proceeds were partly donated to the Army's Emergency Relief Fund—was the first one broadcast by shortwave radio to American armed forces around the world. But the Wartime Censorship Code also limited radio transmissions. In interviews, announcers were told to avoid questions about a soldier's unit, or previous or future location. The regulations also banned talk about the weather, which confused Dizzy Dean, by then a broadcaster, who could never explain a rain delay: "I ain't sayin' nothin' about the weather," he said during one game, "but I'd advise you women listenin' to get your washes off the clothes line."[39]

Though often being merely the backdrop of wartime films, baseball was sometimes featured. The 1942 release of *The Pride of the Yankees*, the late Lou Gehrig's life story, "reminded Americans of a sad but profound truth, that even heroes can die young."[40] Baseball appeared in the newsreels preceding feature presentations. Typically, a clip of Bob Feller, Joe DiMaggio, or Hank Greenberg in military uniform was shown to reinforce the patriotic commitment to baseball heroes, apple pie, and the United States.

In some cases, the baseball idols appeared in person. Probably no ballplayer crusaded more than Babe Ruth. Retired and in his late forties, Ruth was a patriotic symbol, ranking just below the flag and bald eagle. He was photographed promoting remote battles or wartime relief programs. He canvassed door-to-door for the Red Cross, umpired benefit ball games, donated baseball films to the navy and Red Cross, and sold war bonds. Ruth appeared in a photograph in the *Detroit News* holding $100,000 worth of Defense Bonds, under a headline exploiting his hitting prowess: "Babe Invests Fruits of the Home Run." Ruth toured the country for the Ford Motor Company and the American Legion—for which he became the youth baseball director after the War.[41]

But when Congress asked Ruth to tour combat zones abroad and manage professional teams that would play for the troops, he was stopped by his declining health. He was well enough in August 1943, however, to meet Hall of Fame pitcher Walter Johnson in a special pregame fund-raiser at Yankee Stadium. According to sportswriter James Dawson, "Babe Ruth hit one of his greatest home runs yesterday in the interests of freedom and the democratic way of living."[42]

Ruth was legendary, if not mythical, for curing children with his home runs and hospital visits. But baseball might have been good for the health of soldiers, as well. Besides breaking the monotony and preventing homesickness for healthy soldiers, baseball also helped injured GIs. Wounds took soldiers out of the group; baseball let them back in. In one case, doctors gave up on a shell-shocked soldier, but he recovered after reading the *Sporting News* from cover to cover. When soldiers returned from the war, the thing they wanted most was baseball tickets. When freed from military prisons, their first question was "Who won the World Series?"

Baseball was also enlisted for wartime political campaigns. It was used to confront absenteeism and labor agitation, carrying the message that the soldier "hates, with a vengeance, the scum who promote strikes." While World War II might have been the Good War, it nevertheless witnessed fourteen thousand strikes, involving 7 million American workers. Why were they condemned while war profiteers were given a free pass? Despite the enormous resources the war effort pumped into the U.S. economy, real wages steadily declined. Some companies used patriotic appeals to convince workers to take "voluntary" pay cuts. Baseball supported this crusade, criticizing worker selfishness. The major leagues pursued the same ends in their own industry. Owner Ed Barrow used the war to justify salary freezes for his 1941 World Series champion Yankees, including Joe DiMaggio, on the heels of his fifty-six-game hitting streak. St. Louis Cardinals owner Sam Breadon chastised pitcher Mort Cooper for returning his contract unsigned: "I don't think it makes very good reading for people who have their boys on the fighting fronts." Rather than exceeding the typical worker's pay, ballplayer wages fell below the average. Yet it was the owners rather than the players who were applauded for their wartime financial contributions.[43]

Ballplayers Go to War

Signaling the players' readiness to participate in other ways, the *Sporting News* claimed, "Born in America, propagated in America, and recognized as the National Game, . . . all those engaged in the sport are Americans first, last, and always. . . . In all the history of baseball there never was a conscientious objector, or a slacker in its ranks." That's debatable, but more than 1,700 major leaguers (and 3,700 minor leaguers) did serve during the war. As Steve Bullock has suggested, they were a "highly visible aspect of the military war machine" and became "symbols for their fellow Americans to follow."[44]

Other ballplayers were criticized because they didn't serve or because they delayed or reduced their commitment. As Robert Burk has noted, despite organized baseball's claims of noninterference, each team "retained its own officer charged with keeping players out of the draft." In one case, infielder Irv Dickens was exempted for varicose veins, prompting a medical examiner and draft board to resign in protest. On the other hand, Hal Newhouser, the two-time MVP Detroit Tigers pitcher, was rejected for his bad heart yet had to constantly fend off slacker accusations. New York Giants outfielder Morrie Arnovich was ineligible (4F) because he had horrible teeth; when criticized, he held a news conference to show his bridgework. An Arnovich spokesman stated, "He never asked for a deferment, and tried to enlist. As a Giant, he doesn't like being called a dodger, particularly a draft dodger."[45]

Other players avoided the military through war production work, including Sal Maglie, Val Picinich, and Lefty Gomez, as well as Negro Leaguers Buddy Burbage and Vic Harris. Some took such jobs because the military rejected them, but some general managers, such as Bill DeWitt of the St. Louis Browns, secured defense jobs for players to keep them out of the service. A Good War should have generated no dissenters, but in fact thousands of Americans resisted military service. Among the conscientious objectors was Tom Ananicz, who played in the American Association. Likewise, major-league pitcher Bill Zuber filed for CO status, although he was instead kept out by a 2B (war production) classification, and then a 4F.[46]

Players who did join the armed forces were sometimes accused of having easy assignments, amounting to as little as playing military baseball. While true for some players, their baseball role in the military was often rationalized as the best use for their services. Others, like Ted Williams, played key roles (in his case, as a flight instructor), even if he didn't see combat. FBI director J. Edgar Hoover defended baseball, saying, "our records show few if any such cases [of dodging service] among ballplayers." Some believed ballplayers suffered *worse* treatment than others. Yankees pitcher Red Ruffing was drafted even though he was missing four toes. Players initially classified as 4F were sometimes drafted later, even after failing one or more physicals. While War Mobilization Director James Byrnes assured MLB he wouldn't single out ballplayers, he nevertheless began reclassifying exempt major leaguers.[47]

Some ballplayers, including high-profile stars, had significant combat action. The most prominent was Cleveland Indians pitcher Bob Feller, who enlisted right after Pearl Harbor. According to Harrington Crissey, "With the U.S. entry into the war, it was highly desirable that the Navy enlist an American sports hero to induce others to sign up." Feller asserted, "There are many things more important than baseball. . . . I can throw a few strikes for Uncle Sam." Feller felt that "being in sports had nothing to do with being a good sailor." Nevertheless, he earned eight battle stars in the Pacific aboard the USS *Alabama* and became a leading spokesman for the U.S. military for decades thereafter.[48]

Others who served under fire included Washington Senators player Buddy

Lewis, who told his teammates he was "aiming at a new slugging record against the Japs." According to the *Sporting News*, "Lewis doesn't see how the little brown men can be any harder to hit than the American League's southpaw chuckers." Yogi Berra, Tommy Byrne, and Ralph Houk landed at Normandy; Warren Spahn and Harry Walker served in the Battle of the Bulge; and Hank Greenberg and Jerry Coleman saw battle in the Asia–Pacific Theater. Phil Marchildron joined the Canadian Air Force, was shot down, and was held in a German prisoner-of-war camp for nine months.[49]

Some suffered serious injuries. Lou Brissie, a promising prospect, was gravely wounded in the leg and amputation was planned. Begging the doctor to hold off, he recovered, pitched for the Athletics for seven years, and succeeded Babe Ruth as American Legion youth baseball director. Gene Bearden's ship was blown up in the Pacific by a Japanese torpedo. Clinging to wreckage for ten days, he barely lived and was nearly crippled. Yet he returned to the Indians after the war and helped them win the 1948 World Series. Even more remarkable, Bert Shepard was shot down over Germany and woke up in a prison hospital, where his mangled leg had been amputated. Fighting back, he got an artificial limb and returned to pitch for the Senators in 1945.[50]

Others suffered psychological wounds. Like other soldiers, ballplayers witnessed unspeakable things that often haunted them, if not causing an outright breakdown. Pitcher Murry Dickson was in the Normandy invasion and the Battle of the Bulge and was among the first Americans to enter the Dachau concentration camp. He returned to the big leagues but apparently never got over the war—much like another Dachau liberator, Phillies star Bob Savage. Of course, some experienced an even worse fate. Nearly fifty ballplayers lost their lives, including three major leaguers. One of them, Elmer Gedeon, played for the Senators and was missing in action over occupied France. Another, Harry O'Neill of the Athletics, was killed on Iwo Jima.[51]

Conspicuous Ethnic Patriots

Amid all the others, the World War II experience of two ballplayer soldiers, Hank Greenberg and Joe DiMaggio, stood out. By the late 1930s, Jews and Italians were already baseball fans, but when stars like Greenberg and DiMaggio broke through, the fan base soared, and MLB got the message. More than an increase in paying customers was involved. Racism was tainting national policymaking in Europe. To portray itself as morally superior to Germany and Italy, the United States tempered its ethnic commentary both inside and outside baseball.

As a result, DiMaggio and Greenberg were transformed into "American" (rather than merely ethnic) role models. They were portrayed as humble, hard-working patriots who took their ethnic heritages seriously but didn't exhibit stereotypical characteristics. They were not only star players but also the poster boys for America's melting-pot theory of ethnicity. But was their acceptance genuine, or were they merely "useful ethnics" for the time? Historian Edward White has asked, Was their apparent patriotism, evidenced by their U.S. military enlistment, appreciated for its own sake or were DiMaggio and Greenberg more so applauded for being "conspicuous ethnic patriots?"[52]

When Hank Greenberg joined the Detroit Tigers, the media praised his decision to play baseball on Rosh Hashanah, and when he hit two home runs, the *Detroit Times* claimed they "were propelled by a force born of pride of a young Jew who turned his back on the ancient ways of his race and creed to help his teammates." Greenberg was praised for discarding his religion and ethnicity in order to be "more American." But when he decided to honor a holier Jewish holiday, Yom Kippur, he became a national issue. He went from being fairly unconscious about his heritage to "resenting being singled out as a *Jewish* ballplayer, period." Except for Jackie Robinson, no ballplayer took more abuse than Greenberg, who asked, "How the hell could you get up to home plate every day and have some son of a bitch call you a Jew bastard and a kike and a sheenie without feeling the pressure?" Greenberg began understanding the international implications of being Jewish: "I didn't pay much attention at first [but then] I came to feel that if as a Jew I hit a home run, I was hitting one against Hitler." In 1940, Greenberg was classified as ineligible for the military. When the media accused him of bribing the doctor, Greenberg insisted on a new physical and was inducted for a one-year term. After Pearl Harbor, he reenlisted and was out of baseball until 1945. Despite having served (and having won four battle stars and a Presidential Unit Citation), he was still baited after his return.[53]

Joe DiMaggio was the first big Italian star. He interrupted his New York Yankees career to enlist, although not until 1943. DiMaggio's military involvement and its ethnic implications transformed his public image, even though he served largely by playing baseball. Before the war, his Italian background generated the usual caricatures. But when the United States entered the war, with Italy as one of its enemies, DiMaggio's commitment to the Allied cause was proof that Italian immigrants could become good Americans. Congress had been considering the reclassification of Italian Americans as enemies and restricting their movements. Thus it's no wonder that when another Italian ballplayer, Cookie Lavagetto, was asked by the *Brooklyn Eagle* about the war, he snapped, "Don't call me an Italian; I'm an American." DiMaggio's case was influential in resisting U.S. government proposals to relocate Italians to detention centers, as the Japanese Americans had been in 1942. In congressional testimony, a San Francisco attorney used Joe's father, Giuseppe DiMaggio, as an example. Although neither DiMaggio's father nor mother was an American citizen, eight of their children were U.S.-born. To evacuate the parents, the attorney indicated, "would, in view of the splendid family they have reared, present a serious injustice." In October 1942, the plan was called off.[54]

By muting his background, DiMaggio gained the label of the hero and "good ethnic." Since Greenberg wasn't entirely willing to "play ball" with his ethnicity, his reputation suffered, even though he was the battle-tested soldier of the two. Nevertheless, both played a role for the national pastime, confirming the notion that baseball made people into American patriots.

Fighting the Race War

Ethnic tolerance, however, had its limits when it spilled over into race. At the edge of the ethnic-race line, organized baseball was willing to sign light-skinned Latino players, mostly from Cuba. Ten of them had been signed by the Washington Senators by 1944, including Gil Torres, Alejandro Carresquel, Bobby Estalella, and Roberto Ortiz.[55] For African Americans, however, MLB and the U.S. military practiced Jim Crow. In supporting the war, the *Sporting News* gushed about baseball being God's blessing and the by-product of American democracy, thus distinguishing the United States from the evil Axis powers. Yet it supported segregation at home, suggesting in one headline that it was "No Good Raising the Race Issue."

Commissioner Landis—second to no one in his patriotism—praised the national pastime as the "symbol of America as the melting pot. The players embrace all national origins and the fans make only one demand on them: Can they play the game?" This fit well into the wartime theme of national unity, but hypocritically ignored organized baseball's continuing ban on blacks, for which Landis was directly responsible. This was particularly nauseating since MLB was obviously shorthanded for good talent during the war years. As Negro League star Chet Brewer asked, "How do you think I felt when I saw a one-armed outfielder?"[56]

The United States was not in the war to fight bigotry—against the Jews or other targets of Nazism. Not only was America practicing its own virulent racism; it was a *model* for how to do so. Describing his foreign policy, Adolf Hitler claimed, when subjugating other races, "he would not repeat the mistake of the Spanish conquerors of Latin America, whose intermarriage with Indians and Africans led to racial degradation." Rather, he would "follow the

North American model of annihilating indigenous peoples to ensure 'Aryan' racial domination."[57]

In the U.S. military, blacks were treated as second-class soldiers, despite being subject to the draft. Some were conscripted; many others volunteered. As for the draft, black pitcher Nate Moreland complained, "I can play in Mexico, but I have to fight for America, where I can't play." Among the enlistees, however, were many of the Negro League's finest ballplayers, including Josh Johnson, Russell Awkard, Frank Duncan, Joe Black, and Buck O'Neil. They came from teams such as the Homestead Grays, the Pittsburgh Crawfords, and the Kansas City Monarchs. The Negro Leagues not only *supplied* soldiers, they entertained them. The Newark Eagles invited the all-black, twenty-five-hundred member 372nd Infantry Regiment for opening day and also the black members of the Free French forces stationed at nearby Fort Dix.[58]

But the contributions blacks had made to winning the previous world war (not to mention previous wars) had been forgotten, and military racism continued. African American stars, such as Larry Doby, were blocked from playing baseball for the Great Lakes Navy team. Another black star, Monte Irvin, pointed out, "I took basic training in the South. I'd been asked to give up everything, including my life, to defend democracy. Yet I had to ride in the back of a bus, or not at all on some buses."

Despite his stellar athletic career at UCLA, no professional baseball, basketball, or football team in the United States would take Jackie Robinson. Instead, he signed with the Honolulu Bears, a Hawaiian minor league football team. He returned home just two days before the Pearl Harbor attack. Robinson enlisted but had to fight for admission to the all-white Officer's Candidate School at Fort Riley, Kansas. He was promoted to second lieutenant and transferred to Fort Hood, Texas. In July 1944, Robinson refused a driver's order to sit in the back of the military bus. He was arrested, and although most charges were eventually dropped, he was nevertheless court-martialed for insubordination. Robinson was ultimately acquitted and honorably discharged, but as he observed, "I had learned I was in two wars, one against the foreign enemy, the other against prejudice at home."[59]

During the war, black ballplayers were rarely allowed to play with whites in the United States but were allowed to when stationed abroad. When America was more visible to outsiders, it was important to avoid racist displays—at least against its own people. Thus in Hawaii, Calvin Medley pitched for the Fleet Marine team and Hal Hairston pitched in the Service World Series. U.S. troops displayed little racism *against* the enemy Germans and Italians, and they didn't express much sympathy *for* the Jews until their fight against Hitler showed them where racism could lead. This may have muted their discrimination against blacks, although U.S. soldiers remained quite racist against the Japanese. According to Thomas Bortelsmann, "Fighting a war with nonwhite enemies and allies forced" U.S. authorities to try to educate Americans "about distinguishing 'good Asians' (Filipinos, Chinese, Indians) from 'bad Asians' (Japanese)."[60]

Baseball Struggles On

The game itself changed during the war. President Roosevelt sought more night games to allow more people to attend. The Chicago Cubs planned to install lights for the 1942 season but donated them instead to the war effort.[61] Night baseball emerged elsewhere, except in coastal cities, where the lights might—however improbably—have helped the enemy. Curfews were strictly enforced, sometimes adversely affecting games. When it jeopardized the Dodgers, it was said that "Hitler better beware, because [manager] Leo Durocher won't stand for it." As a compromise, twilight games were inaugurated.[62]

Commissioner Landis reaped public relations rewards by voluntarily reducing baseball travel to conserve fuel. As the Office of Defense Transportation indicated, "baseball's cooperation might serve as a pattern for the nation." Longer and fewer road trips were scheduled, and spring training in the South was canceled. Beginning in 1943, Landis required teams to train north of the Potomac and Ohio rivers and east of the Mississippi, prompting one reporter to remark, "It sounds like a treaty with the French and Indians."[63] Before the ban, Connie Mack's Philadelphia Athletics went to California for their usual spring training but had to brave the new challenge of air-raid drills. After the travel ban, teams targeted alternative camps, including the Brooklyn Dodgers, who trained at West Point. In 1945, the All-Star Game was canceled, partly due to travel restrictions. The Allies were about to triumph over the Axis powers and travel by troops returning home was given first priority.[64]

Baseball made other concessions as well. As in the broader society, rationing was imposed—and inferior equipment was introduced. Sportswriter Dwight Freeburg described how baseball would lose the power game for a while and instead have to play the "inner game." A wood shortage affected the quality and quantity of baseball bats. But most altered were the baseballs, whose covers had been made from Belgian horsehide. When the war cut off that supply, the major leagues turned to Bolivian horsehide, which was quickly depleted. The balata ball was then substituted, made from the latex material used for golf-ball covers. Cincinnati Reds general manager Warren Giles compared ballplayers using these balls to "asking our soldiers, sailors and marines to win the war with blanks instead of real ammunition."[65]

As for the overall skill level, it had declined. But when Cleveland Indians owner Alva Bradley wondered about shutting baseball down, the other owners angrily defended the game's integrity. Yet in retrospect, baseball analyst Bill James lamented, "With most good players in the service, a collection of old men and children, and men with one arm and seven dependents gathered and battered around a dull spheroid and this was called MLB for four years." Old players, such as Babe Herman, Pepper Martin, Ben Chapman, and Jimmie Foxx came out of retirement. Boys, such as fifteen-year-old Joe Nuxhall, were allowed to play. Disabled players also took the field, and not only the 4Fs who failed their physicals.[66]

The most prominent was Pete Gray, the one-armed outfielder who joined the majors after winning the Southern League's Most Valuable Player award. This prompted North Dakota Senator William Langer to propose legislation to require each major-league club to have 10 percent of its roster comprised of athletes missing a hand, an arm, or a leg. Some viewed Gray's story as a testimony to the American dream and an inspiration for disabled people everywhere. Others felt it mocked the game and insulted the excellent, able-bodied black ballplayers who remained banned even with a player shortage.

Similar misgivings arose over the miraculous rise of the perennial doormat, the St. Louis Browns. The Browns were planning to move to Los Angeles in 1942, but because of the war, they stayed, and within two years were the American League champions. In the World Series, the Browns faced their crosstown rivals, the St. Louis Cardinals, and nearly won. For the Browns to have made it to the Series seemed like a travesty to some observers. Others felt baseball during the war years reflected national values, and the Browns' success demonstrated the Horatio Alger work ethic and the glories of the American dream. Major-league attendance in 1945 was 11 million, 2 million more than when the War began. World Series patronage had increased by a hundred thousand fans. Thanks in part to its dedicated support for the war effort, baseball's patronage would further skyrocket in the next few years.[67]

To compensate for dwindling men's teams, women began playing baseball during the war. Chicago Cubs owner Phil Wrigley believed baseball's survival relied partly on women, and thus he created the All-American Girls Professional Baseball League (AAGPBL) in 1943. The AAGPBL was a part of the trend in America—symbolized by "Rosie the Riveter"—of women entering the workplace while men were away at war. According to a Grand Rapids Chicks player, Jeanie Des Combes Lesko, the AAGPBL "gave local communities a place to go to have a good time, be with people and forget about the hard times. People needed local heroes . . . and we provided them." It was important, however, that women remained ladylike, and thus they wore skirts and attended charm school. They were expected to look like Betty Grable—to remind American men what they were allegedly fighting for. Despite the frills, the women played serious and entertaining baseball. Some thought a woman might break into a major league lineup.[68]

The AAGPBL operated primarily in the Midwest, and in 1944 it played the first night game at Wrigley Field—long before the Cubs, under a portable lighting system. The women's teams sold war bonds and played exhibitions at military training camps. They recruited for the Women's Army Corps and gave free admission to Red Cross workers and blood donors. They visited military hospitals and taught children how to play ball. In their pregame routine, the women lined up in a V-for-victory formation to rally the troops, and "The Star Spangled Banner" was played. The AAGPBL women began generating a following among GIs overseas. In June 1944, Mickey Maguire took the field for the AAGPBL's Milwaukee Chicks and began "the most dramatic exhibition of courage." She had just heard that her husband had been killed fighting in Italy but Maguire decided to play anyway in his honor.[69] In August 1945, the All-American teams celebrated the end of World War II at their ballparks.

Elsewhere, the American Legion program celebrated its fifteenth anniversary in 1942. H.L. Chaillaux wrote that Legion baseball "had provided the needed physical training, coordination of mind and muscle, and teamwork so vitally important to our fighting men today." More than 1,500 former Legion players were minor leaguers by the time the United States entered the war. While many of them were drafted, more American Legion kids were getting a shot at the majors than ever before. It was another way the Legion promulgated its martial values and solidified its longstanding relationship with organized baseball.[70]

At baseball's grass roots, patriotism motivated Carl Stotz when he launched Little League Baseball on the eve of World War II. Established in 1939 in Williamsport, Pennsylvania, the need for workers and war matériel initially limited the league's growth. In 1941, the original Little League field was seized for war production. Still, the league persisted during the war, which helped shape the objectives it maintains to this day: not only citizenship and physical well-being, but also patriotic, religious, and quasi-militaristic values. While a keystone was the original emblem, local Little League branches often adopted martial symbols resembling army patches.

With fathers off to war and mothers replacing fathers at the workplace, children grew up with less parental supervision. Little League helped fill the void and became an alternative for teaching American values. In 1944, Stotz received his draft notice, but was somehow allowed to remain in Williamsport. Was it in recognition of Little League's contribution to American patriotism?

Not surprisingly, on August 14, 1945, the scheduled Little League games were suspended to acknowledge the war's end.

Stateside Service Baseball

Military conscription and enlistment drained organized baseball of its players, who didn't merely join the armed services; they also played baseball there. The influx was the "impetus for a colossal explosion in military baseball." At least 75 percent of the men played baseball during the war. Ballplayer-soldier Warren Spahn felt sorry for American GIs who weren't baseball fans; they stood out so conspicuously. The military viewed the game as good for training and morale. As Captain Robert Emmet described it, soldiers "discuss an exciting game for days . . . there's no room for homesickness or depressive thoughts." According to Captain H.A. McClure, military baseball was "pointblank proof to our enemies that they cannot overhaul our way of life." Women also played: army nurses created softball teams and leagues. At key U.S. installations, such as the Canal Zone, baseball was the rage. The local San Blas Indians quickly learned baseball from GIs stationed there.[71]

But military baseball wasn't merely recreation. Top-notch baseball was played under competitive circumstances, and powerhouse armed-services teams developed. Two navy clubs stood out: the Great Lakes Training Center and the Norfolk Training Station teams. They were coached by Hall of Famers, such as Mickey Cochrane, and featured major-league stars, such as Bob Feller, Sam Chapman, Fred Hutchinson, Phil Rizzuto, and Vince DiMaggio.[72] The Great Lakes Team played all comers, routinely defeated major-league clubs, and accumulated a 188–32 record during the war years.

Some accused the military of protecting star ballplayers, shielding them from dangerous duty for fear that national heroes might be shot. Or they might be hoarded to strengthen the company baseball team. These charges were denied, and examples of stars going into battle were offered as proof. Even so, having major leaguers around had significant celebrity value. According to Steve Bullock, "Many military leaders viewed a winning team as a reflection on their command and attempted by means bordering on the unethical to secure desired athletes." Regardless of how much some baseball stars were coddled, most soldiers wanted baseball continued, not only outside the military but also inside.[73]

Hawaii became a center for military baseball. After the Pearl Harbor attack, martial law was declared, which lasted until October 1944. Baseball served as a refuge. A Honolulu League and other new circuits were created. The Hawaiian League, which had been established in 1925, created a playoff series named after Alexander Cartwright. Except for the U.S. Navy team, the Hawaiian League had been organized by ethnic background, including Filipinos, Chinese, Hawaiians, Braves (Portuguese), Elks (whites), and Asahis (Japanese). But after Pearl Harbor, everyone felt they had to stand together, and thus the ethnic barriers fell. To protect itself against anti-Japanese sentiment, the Asahis changed their name to the Athletics; the Chinese became the Tigers. By the war's end, the league was overshadowed by American military teams, but it had brought a higher caliber of baseball to the Islands.[74]

From his post in Hawaii, U.S. Fleet Admiral Chester Nimitz commented, "We are all in a bigger league now. We plan to keep the Japs in the cellar until they learn to play ball with civilized nations." Nimitz took an interest in the U.S. Navy baseball team and agreed to a Service World Series in Honolulu. A Navy World Series had already been held stateside in 1943. But the Hawaii Series was much bigger, matching top army players, such as Joe DiMaggio, Red Ruffing, Johnny Beazley, and Joe Gordon, against navy standouts, such as Johnny Mize, Pee Wee Reese, and Dom DiMaggio. Of the fifty players in the series, thirty-six were major leaguers. For many people, the Service Series was the real 1944 World Series—it went eleven games and was won by the Navy team. Then in 1945 another Navy World Series was held, featuring more stars, such as Ted Williams, Johnny Pesky, Stan Musial, Billy Herman, and Bob Lemon. Absent a major-league All-Star Game that year, this series—which went seven games—was considered an appropriate, if not superior, substitute.[75]

Various warships and Liberty Ships were named after famous ballplayers. First launched in 1943, the S.S. *Lou Gehrig* thrilled soldiers in North Africa and transported cargo and soldiers for the D-Day invasion, as did the USS *Abner Doubleday*. The USS *Christy Mathewson* visited Bombay, Tasmania, and the Pacific Islands. The USS *Edward L. Grant* was on hand when Antwerp was taken from the Nazis. The USS *John J. McGraw* was transferred temporarily to the British, then flew the American flag in India, the Suez, the Persian Gulf, the South Pacific, and in Murmansk, Russia—where the sailors played in the White Sea Baseball League.[76]

The European War

Service baseball flourished in both the European/North African and Asia/Pacific theaters. Soldiers not only followed the major leagues; they played the game themselves—a distraction indispensable to fighting the war. Although the British baseball leagues were suspended in 1939, the Canadians returned the game to England in 1940. They sponsored two London teams, and began playing the Americans in 1942. The U.S. Air Force team in England was led by Washington Senators pitcher Monte Weaver. More than fifty thousand U.S. infantry troops arrived in Northern Ireland, and baseball helped maintain morale; the Irish Duke of Abercorn was a big fan. Soon these troops were sent to Africa, where they were thrown into battle against Field Marshall Rommel's Afrika Korps in Tunisia.[77]

In 1943, the London International Baseball League was formed. It created an all-star team, the CBS Clowns, which faced challengers in Britain, Northern Ireland, and France. A spectacular game was played that year at London's Wembley Stadium, featuring several U.S. pro ballplayers. The Wings for Victory campaign to build more fighter planes was promoted through a Britain-wide series of baseball games. Holidays at Home was a morale-boosting event, followed by a Salute the Soldier campaign and Red Cross benefits—all of them featuring baseball games. Soon, one million Americans were stationed in Britain, and baseball was everywhere—and steadily spreading on the Continent. According to *Stars and Stripes*, American servicemen had done more to promote baseball in Europe "than all the peacetime all star teams could ever have hoped to do."

Meanwhile, Nazi propaganda minister Joseph Goebbels announced, "There are fresh atrocities in the U.S. The Yankees, not content with their pious interference all over the world, are beating up their own cardinals in St. Louis."[78] This was a veiled reference to the 1943 World Series, in which the New York Yankees clobbered the St. Louis Cardinals. More seriously, U.S. airmen in England accused the Luftwaffe of bombing their baseball diamonds.

An ETO (European Theatre of Operations) World Series was played in 1943. The 116th Infantry Regiment Yankees were the winners, but their euphoria was short-lived. The players, including major leaguers, were among the first troops to land at Omaha Beach during the 1944 Normandy invasion and were sitting ducks—nineteen men from the regiment and three of their ballplayers were killed. Another invasion casualty was Joe Pinder, who was awarded the Medal of Honor for establishing vital radio communications while seriously wounded, before dying on the beach. Pinder, a minor leaguer, was not alone among those whose big-league aspirations were undermined by the war. Back in the United States, major-league games were all canceled as the nation awaited the D-Day outcome. "Let's Make the Axis Lose the Game: No Huns; No Blitz; No Terrors" was announced as a prize-winning anti-Nazi slogan. Allegedly President Roosevelt made a phone call to America's new ally, the Russian premier Joseph Stalin, greeting him with, "Hello, Joe? It's Frank. Giants three. Dodgers nothing."[79]

When American troops began making headway against the Nazis, baseball accompanied each new advance. Ball fields were built everywhere U.S. soldiers were posted. Games were played in unusual places, such as beneath the Leaning Tower of Pisa. Airmen adopted baseball names for their planes, such as Ott's Big Bat (after the New York Giants slugger) and Winning Run. John Downs of the 100th Bomb Group compared his flak suit to "a baseball umpire's chest pad." Captain Eddie Waitkus, only recently the Chicago Cubs first baseman, described how an amphibious invasion was "like stealing home in baseball. If it worked, swell. If it didn't, you looked idiotic."[80] Private David Dennis said he put his minor-league experience to good use the day he heard his buddy yell "slide" and did so just in time to avoid a strafing Nazi airplane.

While pushing forward into Europe, U.S. troops worried that the Germans were sending spies dressed as American GIs and speaking American English to infiltrate U.S. lines. To guard against this, U.S. soldiers asked suspected agents baseball questions "no red-blooded American boy would have any trouble answering." A guard might ask, "Who's the second sacker for the Bums?" First, you had to know *what* a second sacker [baseman] was. Then, you had to know who the *Bums* [Brooklyn Dodgers] were, and then you had to know *who* the second sacker was [Billy Herman in 1942–43; Eddie Stanky in 1944–45]. The *Chicago Herald American* described the case of two men who wore U.S. Army uniforms but whose English was not very good. When asked their favorite sport, both said baseball. But then a GI asked, " 'Did you hear, Connie Mack pitched a shutout against Brooklyn and Tommy Harmon got two homers for the Bums?' " Not having learned in their indoctrination that Mack was the octogenarian Athletics manager and Harmon was a football hero, the infiltrators answered yes. The result, the newspaper reported: "Two defunct Nazi parachutists." In another incident, three Germans posing as U.S. soldiers were exposed by their baseball ignorance and were shot. During the Battle of the Bulge, a woman appeared without proper ID, claiming to work for the Red Cross: "I finally convinced the major I was an American when I rattled off the Brooklyn Dodgers lineup for the 1941 World Series."[81]

Current and former major leaguers who weren't in the military got together to bring baseball to the troops. USO baseball tours brought stars and games to dozens of locations, from Alaska to New Guinea. They would tell stories, supply World Series films, and otherwise entertain the troops. Al Schacht, the ballplayer–turned–baseball clown, performed his comedy routines.[82] One of the tours, the Foxhole Circuit, sailed the Bering Sea, rode half-trucks across the Sahara, sat on coral in the New Guinea jungles, traveled to the Battle of the Bulge, climbed the Burmese mountains, and bounced through the frozen mud of Italy. This group included Leo Durocher, Nick Etten, and former St. Louis ballplayer Joe "Ducky" Medwick, who, when he met Pope Pius XII, said, "Your Holiness, I'm Joseph Medwick. I, too, used to be a Cardinal."[83] Another tour, Batter

Up, was sent to the Persian Gulf command, where a twelve-team baseball league was already operating. Yet another expedition included Frankie Frisch, Mel Ott, Bucky Walters, and Dutch Leonard. At a stop in Luxembourg, generals George Patton and Omar Bradley showed up to see the World Series film. At the end, Patton rose to say, "Gentlemen, I'm sorry but I have to get some rest. I've got a lot of killing to do in the morning."

Crucial to the war's outcome was the Allied campaign in North Africa, where baseball again played a role. The military code words to launch the U.S. invasion were "Play Ball." During the 1942 Battle of Tunisia, U.S. First Division troops adopted the Brooklyn Dodgers as their team and followed the club during the Sicilian campaign in Europe. The *Sporting News* reported an Italian broadcast "explaining the debacle [Axis loss] in North Africa," claiming the U.S. won because the "Americans threw too many baseballs." This was a grudging admission that skills developed on the diamond had been transformed into hitting and pitching power, as well as teamwork, which drove U.S. soldiers on to victory.

Baseball was played extensively in North Africa. Former major leaguer Zeke Bonura promoted sports programs from his Oran, Algeria, headquarters. As a ballplayer, Bonura was a great slugger but a horrible first baseman whose futile swipes at ground balls were dubbed the Mussolini Wave. Much more successful in organizing baseball, Bonura got local Arabs involved in the game and gave baseball lessons in exchange for Arabian stallion rides. But his big accomplishment was the North Africa World Series, which he created in 1944 and which culminated the games played by more than 1,500 players on 150 teams. This series was broadcast via radio to soldiers throughout the Mediterranean. The field had no fence, and thus long fly balls would roll into the sea until Italian prisoners-of-war were stationed around the outfield to stop them.[84] The series drew 3,000 fans to the Eugene Stadium in Algiers, where the Casablanca Yankees defeated the Algiers Streetwalkers. Bonura, the so-called Czar of North African Baseball was decorated for his efforts by General Dwight Eisenhower with the Legion of Merit.

If Zeke Bonura seemed like an odd character, he was nevertheless overshadowed by an even more unusual figure: Moe Berg graduated from Princeton University, received his law degree from Columbia University, and studied philosophy at the Sorbonne in Paris. He was a genius who spoke and read Sanskrit and a host of other languages. With this unlikely background, Berg played MLB, mostly with the Boston Red Sox and Chicago White Sox, for 15 years from 1923 through 1939—during which time he also passed the New York bar exam. Berg was a poor hitter. The phrase "good field, no hit" was invented to describe him, and his teammate Ted Lyons once observed, "He can speak twelve languages but can't hit in any of them." Thus, Berg's value was primarily as a reliable backup catcher. But the main reason he hung on so long in the majors was that he was using baseball as a cover: Moe Berg was an American spy.[85]

In his fictional story, "Fuhrer Furor at Fenway!" former major league pitcher Bill Lee imagines a visit to the United States by Adolf Hitler in August 1939, where Berg and Ted Williams collaborate to assassinate the German dictator. When the Fuhrer throws out the first pitch at a Red Sox game, Williams can't lay off the German's perfect strike. He leans in and smashes the ball, which crowns Hitler between the eyes, kills the tyrant, and spares the world a terrible war. Baseball did its part in World War II, but it didn't go that far. In real life, however, Moe Berg ended his major-league playing days in September 1939, the day before the war began in Europe, but he continued as a coach. He was increasingly upset the United States wasn't involved in the war: "Europe is in flames, withering in a fire set by Hitler. All over that continent, men and women and children are dying. And what am I doing? I'm sitting in the bullpen, telling jokes to the relief pitchers." Soon he would do much more.[86]

After the United States entered the war, Berg was hired by the U.S. Office of Latin American Affairs. Purportedly working to help U.S. troops, Berg was instead infiltrating governments and collecting information about Latin American leaders and their relations with Germany and Japan. He was then sent to Europe by the Office of Strategic Services (OSS), the predecessor of the Central Intelligence Agency. Berg traveled to the Black Forest in 1944 disguised as a Swiss student to attend a lecture by German scientist Werner Heisenberg to determine whether he was helping Hitler develop atomic weapons. If so, Berg's orders were to assassinate him. He carried a Beretta revolver and a cyanide pill to kill himself if necessary. Berg determined that Heisenberg wasn't a threat. Berg then parachuted into Italy to contact Antonio Ferri, a scientist who gave him insider information about the German atomic program. Berg learned the Nazis weren't close to developing nuclear weapons. Berg taught Ferri's children baseball and convinced him to defect to America, where he made valuable contributions to the National Advisory Committee on Aeronautics, the forerunner of NASA.[87]

The Pacific War

What were Moe Berg's credentials for taking on European spy missions? Why did he win a Medal of Freedom, and why—at the CIA Exhibit Center in Langley, Virginia, on display above the pistol once owned by OSS director Wild

Bill Donovan—are there two worn baseball cards of Moe Berg, flanked by a tribute to his service? The rest of the story dates back to Berg's baseball-playing days.[88]

Most major-league tours of foreign lands featured star players. Yet in 1934, the mediocre Moe Berg joined Babe Ruth and Lefty O'Doul for his second of several Japan visits. Because of his language skills, Berg delivered a speech in Japanese and conversed extensively with the people he met. Secretly, he also took military-sensitive photographs of Japanese cities. When a teammate was hospitalized at St. Luke's, Berg made his way up to the roof wearing a ceremonial kimono, pulled out a motion picture camera, and filmed shipyards, industrial and military sites, and downtown Tokyo.[89] Filming strategic locations was strictly prohibited, so Berg could have been executed by Japanese authorities.

With baseball as his disguise, Berg was a U.S. spy long before his European espionage. He compiled photos and information America might need if U.S.-Japanese tensions ever led to war. Early in 1942, Lieutenant Colonel Jimmy Doolittle led bombing raids on Tokyo in retaliation for Pearl Harbor. Coming in low, the raiders flew over a sandlot baseball game, and an American pilot mockingly shouted, "What's the score?" The U.S. planes also flew over Tokyo's Meiji Stadium, where only a few years earlier, American stars had played baseball. Supplementing other strategic information, Moe Berg's photographs were credited for Doolittle's success, bolstering American morale and proving Japanese vulnerability. Berg also made OSS radio broadcasts in Japanese, urging Japan to cease hostilities. In one of them, he asked, "What sound basis is there for enmity between two peoples who enjoy the same national sport?"[90]

With the European war winding down, the "Big League War" shifted to Japan. As the *Bomb Bay Messenger* suggested, "The Japs have been running wild on the bases in the Asiatic League but now are up against big league pitching by the [U.S.] Army, Navy, and Marines." Baseball played by American servicemen was "paying off in the Pacific by making Americans better fighters," according to Marine Captain O.W. Todd, who was also the general manager of the Pacific Coast League's San Diego Padres. Thirty years earlier, an all-star U.S. Marine team had toured Japan to promote good relations and celebrate Christmas there. In 1944, a member of that team, Lieutenant Colonel Roscoe Arnett, yearned to return to Nagasaki again on Christmas Day—presumably not for a quick doubleheader.[91] Dodgers general manager Branch Rickey observed, "To live hopefully and joyfully is the American objective and our fighting to live must match the religious frenzy of the Japs who fight to die."

Amid the fury of fierce Pacific combat, baseball persevered. Many major leaguers were involved, including owner Bill Veeck, who lost a leg in the war.

Virgil Trucks and other ballplayers signed baseballs (often "To Tojo with Love") that were later dropped from B-29s on bombing missions.[92] Realizing baseball's importance to U.S. soldiers, Japan tried to jam Armed Forces Radio ball-game broadcasts. On Japanese radio in 1943, the impending battle of the Philippines was compared to "the final game of the World Series," pitting General Tomoyuki Yamashita against General Douglas MacArthur: "the choice of the American League." American troops who might be listening were informed that "the fate of the whole world hinges on the outcome and Yamashita is ready to lead East Asia to victory in the big game."

A contemporary *Victory at Sea* television episode showed the United States retaking the Philippines from Japan, with tanks roaming through a baseball park. The field was Manila's Rizal Stadium, and the tanks were blowing up the grandstands, where Japanese soldiers were holed up. According to Richard Goldstein, "the ballpark became a field of death in the savage fighting between American and Japanese troops. Eight hundred booby traps and the bodies of dead Japanese soldiers had to be removed before ball games could be played again."[93]

Elsewhere in the Pacific war, painstaking preparation and practice—which some compared to baseball training—determined whether bomber pilots would return from their runs. According to David Cataneo, many pilots wore baseball caps to shield their eyes from the tropical sun. But such hats—"like Cokes, Rita Hayworth pinups, and fresh strawberries—were rare." Thus, Marine Major Gregory (Pappy) Boyington made an offer during the 1943 World Series: "His squadron would shoot down a Japanese Zero in trade for each baseball cap from the winning team." The winners were the New York Yankees. Not to be outdone, a B-24 outfit in the U.S. 8th Bomber Group was known as Cronin's Kids (after Boston manager Joe Cronin) because they all wore Red Sox caps. Even in war, the Yankees–Red Sox rivalry was kept alive.[94]

If team hats provided a kind of baseball magic, then how do we explain an even more fantastic scenario? During the 1944 Tulagi invasion in the Solomon Islands, U.S. Marine Sergeant Dana Babcock stumbled—from a distance—on what looked like a pickup baseball game played by weary Marines. One soldier had "torn a dead branch from a jungle tree to use as a bat," and the players ran the bases, hit home runs, got caught in rundowns, and argued with the umpire, "calling him every name in the book." But as Babcock moved closer, he noticed the Marines were playing without a ball! Unable to locate one, they invented a "ghost" ball, with the umpire calling balls and strikes as the "pitcher delivered his phantom pitch." Baseball was "deep in the hearts" of American servicemen; even an imaginary game was "a bit of sanity in an atmosphere rife with insanity."[95]

Among the things contested in the Pacific were baseball diamonds. The Americans and Japanese built ball fields wherever they landed. They were valuable prizes: the Japanese might play a game on a particular field, only to have the Americans take it and then play ball there themselves. In the South Pacific, there were three U.S. leagues, including thirty teams playing on twenty-one diamonds. In New Guinea, U.S. soldiers—including major leaguers Hugh Mulcahy and Ken Silvestri—played baseball waiting to launch the Philippines invasion. In the North Pacific's Marianas Islands, there were ten baseball leagues, with sixty-five diamonds. On one island, Tinian, games were played in the shadow of a secrecy-shrouded hangar belonging to the 20th Air Force Composite Group. In August 1945, the B-29 Enola Gay rolled out of that hangar to drop the atomic bomb on Hiroshima.[96]

Near the war's end, when most Pacific islands had been retaken from the Japanese, the navy sponsored a Pacific Tour featuring two All-Star baseball teams sent to entertain the troops. The players included major leaguers Gene Woodling, Barney McCoskey, Johnny Rigney, and Mickey Vernon. And in the China-Burma-India theater, yet another USO baseball tour—the Over the Plate Circuit—was conducted, including big leaguers Dixie Walker, Paul Waner, and Luke Sewell. They arrived in Calcutta, where fourteen teams were already playing, and in Shanghai, where clubs were competing in the Rice Paddy Conference.

Prisoner-of-War Baseball

Baseball played a significant role in World War II prisoner-of-war camps. In the German prisons, baseball provided U.S. prisoners entertainment and a reminder of home. The Germans tolerated it and allowed equipment to be supplied by the YMCA and Red Cross. When a Louisville Slugger shipment reached an Upper Silesia camp, American prisoners dumbfounded their captors by crying at the sight of the bats. In some German prisons, there were dozens of teams and even a Bad Nauheim Baseball League. In Stalag Luft III in the summer of 1944, two hundred teams played in six compounds. The Germans thought baseball would keep the Americans out of trouble.[97]

That was not always the case. As Tim Wolter indicates, prisoners spent considerable time preparing for escape. In some cases, baseball played a "cameo role," when ballgames were scheduled as diversionary tactics while escape tunnels were being dug. Occasionally, baseball equipment was used for escape activities, such as a bat found at Stalag Luft III, which had been turned into a pick handle.[98] Sometimes the United States tried to smuggle escape equipment into the prison camps. The MIS-X program used doctored baseball gear, including bats and balls. The Goldsmith Company manufactured baseballs for the U.S. government with miniature radio components built in. Because the Germans knew nothing about baseball gear, some items got through. In all, in the German and Japanese camps, at least 130,000 Americans were imprisoned. Umpires and professional ballplayers, including major leaguers, were among them.[99]

Japan was condemned for violating Geneva Convention rules in its prison camps.[100] Among the less serious mistreatments: the Japanese sometimes banned Americans from playing baseball and were accused of confiscating bats provided by the Red Cross. Sometimes, though, Americans were given access to the baseball infrastructure the Japanese had built for themselves, not only in Japan but in other places GIs were imprisoned. The *New York Post* featured an American who recalled that Japanese guards selected "the nine most anemic-looking" prisoners, instructing them to form a team "against the hand-picked Jap jerks. The idea was a psychological one, monkey-man style, to prove to the banana skins that the yellows are better than the whites." On the other hand, according to another American prisoner, "On the diamond, prisoner-guard relationships were forgotten." An ex-POW described a ball game in the Philippines in which the Americans had to ease up to allow their Japanese captors to save face.[101]

Many other ball games were played by the Americans among themselves. In Manila, at the Santo Tomás prison camp, the Japanese allowed U.S. prisoners to form thirty teams, divided into American and National leagues, which had their own World Series. The *Sporting News* even ran a photo of POW ball, which it published under the caption, "Yank War Prisoners at Ball Game." Through their underground network, Americans also received reports about major-league games.

At home, Americans applauded themselves for the decent treatment provided in their own prison camps. No doubt there were some exemplary conditions. Yet like Germany, the United States imprisoned not only the enemy, but also its own people—incarcerating more of them (primarily citizens) than all the Americans held in Axis prison camps combined. As for enemy prisoners, the Japanese were allowed to play baseball in U.S. camps, in places as far apart as Texas and Guam. As for the Germans, the U.S. military tried to indoctrinate them through psychological programs, claiming it was countering Russian communist brainwashing of its German prisoners.[102] The Americans also used baseball to try to inculcate democracy in their captives—such were the deep-seated assumptions about the sport.

The Germans were not very receptive, with one remarkable exception. During the war, a young Brooklyn Dodgers prospect, Gene Moore, was assigned by the U.S. Navy to guard German sailors held in American prison camps in Louisiana. Moore convinced his commander to let him teach the Germans baseball, claiming it would bolster the Americans and distract the Germans, who would otherwise plan escapes: "We would be playing with the enemy, but using them too." Despite huge obstacles, the experiment worked. After weeks of practices and scrimmages, a successful camp Friendship Game was held in 1945. While it was marred by a devastating ankle injury that kept Moore out of the major leagues, his contribution to baseball diplomacy was remarkable.[103]

Enemy combatants were not the only ones interned in America during the war. Germans and Italians (mostly American citizens) were among the millions designated as enemies under the Alien Registration Act. Lists of dangerous foreigners were compiled, and their movements and property ownership were severely restricted. Under the Alien Enemies Act, more than thirty thousand people were arrested, including eleven thousand Germans—dashing the dreams of at least one baseball prospect.[104]

Worse, in February 1942, Executive Order 9066 interned 120,000 Japanese, 75 percent of whom were American citizens, to ten prison camps around the country. The imprisonment robbed Japanese Americans of their freedom, property, and dignity, and packed them into cramped quarters—oftentimes abandoned animal stalls. As Sam Regalado has suggested, before the internment, baseball was played by the Japanese because they loved the game and it was the American thing to do. While they played other ethnicities, Japanese communities were large enough for them to form their own leagues.[105]

Most notable in this regard was the work of Kenichi Zenimura. In 1920, he organized the Fresno Athletic Club, a Japanese American baseball team, and built a field. He established Japanese American leagues throughout the West, led three all-star teams to Japan, and played with Lou Gehrig and Babe Ruth when they barnstormed California. Zenimura was interned temporarily in Fresno, where he started more teams and built a field. When his family was relocated to the Gila River camp in Butte, Arizona, Zenimura built another ballpark, under almost impossible circumstances. By 1943 he had established thirty-two teams.

At Zenimura Field and other fields at other camps, baseball sustained people and provided entertainment. It demonstrated Japanese American allegiance to the United States, dulled the reality of incarceration and social loss, and provided an outlet for anxiety and frustration. According to Zenimura's son, Howard, "Baseball was the only thing that kept us going." It helped interned Japanese avoid labeling themselves as prisoners. As camp resident George Omachi indicated, "Without baseball, camp life would have been miserable. It was humiliating and demeaning—being incarcerated in our own country." Japanese

Americans were a part of America and baseball proved it. But for U.S. authorities, it was a valuable control measure: "Baseball, as a small social system, helped quell the urge for resistance in the internment camps." When released in 1945, instead of being paralyzed by bitterness, Zenimura returned to Fresno and created a new baseball team to try to "speed up the mutual good feeling between the Americans and the Japanese."[106]

In his novel *Suitcase Sefton and the American Dream*, Jay Feldman tells the story of a baseball scout who finds a once-in-a-lifetime pitching talent on the eve of the war. He can't sign him, however, because he's been interned. The tale could well have described the real-life experience of Henry Honda. A Japanese American from San Jose, Honda was signed by the Cleveland Indians in 1941, but his contract was yanked after the Pearl Harbor attack, sinking his chances of making the major leagues, as well as those of other Asian Americans for many years to come.[107]

Japanese Americans were considered enemy aliens, but if they played baseball, they could sometimes escape the barbed wire, at least temporarily. While teams such as the Arizona state champions visited the camps to play the prisoners, some Japanese ballplayers were also allowed to take road trips to other prison camps or other outside diamonds. Baseball uniforms symbolized a certain freedom. While not without racist resistance, away games were nevertheless played against high school, college, and other teams.[108]

The only other Japanese escaping the camps were those serving in the U.S. military. Somehow it was dangerous to let Japanese Americans free in the United States, but it was okay for them to fight to keep other Americans free. The Japanese American troops were among the most decorated units in the war. The Japanese American 100th Infantry Battalion landed in North Africa, where they fought the Germans and played baseball against other U.S. military teams. After the war, when Japanese Americans tried to put their lives back together, baseball was one of the things that kept their communities going.

A Ruthian Blow

Initially, most U.S. soldiers didn't know their Japanese enemies played baseball. As Thomas Gilbert has noted, "One American pilot recalled his shock, while flying over Japan on a bombing mission, when he noticed baseball fields, which somehow brought home to him the humanity of his enemy; until then he had never thought of the far-away objects of his bombs as fellow human beings." Soldier and Hall of Famer Enos Slaughter marveled, "When we got to Saipan [the Japanese] were holed up in the hills. I'll be damned if they didn't sneak out and watch us play ball [and then] fade back into their caves . . . they could have got themselves killed. Talk about real fans."[109]

On the other hand, Japanese officials continued to downplay baseball due to deteriorating conditions and to further distinguish their game from the American game. Japan had to use inferior baseballs, baseball caps took on a military style, and uniform letters were converted from Roman to Japanese characters. The Tokyo Giants were renamed Kyojin Gun (Giant Troop). The stellar Waseda University and Keio University teams played a "farewell" game before thirty thousand fans in October 1943, after which most players were drafted. By 1944, Taiwanese men were inducted into the Japanese army, which closed down their leagues. In Japan, only six professional teams competed for the championship, each playing only thirty-five games that year. The 1945 season was canceled altogether. Former American umpire Hap O'Conner, who had officiated games in Japan, thought the Japanese abandoned baseball because "they would never beat us at it anyway," for he had "never seen an Oriental capable of hitting a home run."[110]

While some American ballplayers died in the war, most of the ballplayers who perished were Japanese, including Eiji Sawamura, the celebrated pitcher who struck out several Hall of Famers and rejected a Pittsburgh Pirates contract. Another casualty was the former 20-game winner, Shinichi Ishimaru, who died in a kamikaze plane. According to Thomas Gilbert, "Before he took his fatal flight, Ishimaru spoke a brief farewell to baseball and life, got out a glove and baseball, and after asking a newspaper reporter to umpire, threw ten strikes" and then boarded his plane.[111]

The Japanese were conflicted about their baseball link to America. They revered Babe Ruth, who recalled his 1934 Japan tour thus: "They lined the streets of Ginza, the Broadway of Tokyo, for miles and greeted us as real heroes. No doubt there were plenty of stinkers among them, but it is only another example of how a crackpot government can lead a friendly people into war." Yet for all he was respected, Japanese soldiers were known to yell, "To Hell with Babe Ruth!" or even "Fuck Babe Ruth" in battle with the Americans. To insult baseball's greatest player was to mock all of America. Hearing about this, Ruth destroyed most of his Japanese souvenirs, saying: "I hope every Jap that mentions my name gets shot. To hell with all Japs anyway."[112]

By midsummer 1945, with Japan on the brink of defeat, it was proposed that Ruth fly to Guam to broadcast a translated radio message urging the Japanese to surrender. To have even considered Ruth for this mission suggested how strong a grip the U.S. intelligence community believed baseball still held over Japan. The game and its biggest name were considered viable tools of diplomacy more than fourteen years after the last U.S. barnstorming tour of Japan. Nothing came of the plan, however, and instead, soon thereafter, President Truman ordered the atomic bombing of Hiroshima and Nagasaki.[113]

Of course, "as everyone knows," the bombings, which immediately killed more than 220,000 people, were justified. The Japanese were a cruel enemy and deserved no mercy. And the bombings saved tens of thousands of American soldiers who would have died had an invasion been required. Yet many have questioned the morality and necessity of the atomic explosions, not only in retrospect but also at the time of the bombings. Many military leaders, including six of the seven wartime five-star generals, criticized the attacks. Joint Chiefs of Staff chairman William Leahy bluntly stated that "the use of this barbarous weapon was of no material assistance. The Japanese were already defeated and ready to surrender . . . we adopted an ethical standard common to the barbarians of the Dark Ages."[114]

If they weren't necessary to end the war, then why were the bombs dropped? Perhaps it was to send a signal to the next in America's endless parade of foreign enemies, the Soviet Union—"We have the bomb and we're willing to use it." Whatever the motivation, we shouldn't underestimate the psychological effects the bombings wrought. How the war ended, at the very least, questioned the "Good War" myth, despite the campaign to keep it alive. Underneath the triumphalism, profound doubts had been raised about U.S. morality. As Tom Engelhardt has put it, Hiroshima marked the beginning of the end of America's "victory culture."[115] But it wasn't the end of Babe Ruth's Japanese connection: after the surrender, Japan sought Ruth as a sympathetic mediator in the upcoming peace talks. But that plan fell through as well.

8

Cold War, Hot War
(1946–1953)

While the marching hordes in China are spreading communism, officials
of the national pastime are helping democracy work.

—Senator John Bricker

General Dwight Eisenhower returned to the States from World War II in 1945
as a conquering hero. He was honored in Washington and New York by
politicians, plutocrats, and movie stars. A reluctant celebrity, he finally broke
away to do what he missed most during the war: attend a ball game at the Polo
Grounds. An Eisenhower Day game was designated, and in his pregame chat,
Eisenhower revealed his professional baseball days in the Kansas State League
before his military career. Lamenting his lost aspirations, he later wrote,
"When I was growing up in Kansas, a friend of mine and I went fishing, and
as we sat there we talked about what we wanted to do when we grew up. I told
him I wanted to be a major-league baseball player, a genuine professional like
Honus Wagner. My friend said he'd like to be president of the United States.
Neither of us got our wish."[1]

Eisenhower would soon get his friend's wish, but it was Harry Truman who
presided as president over the war's end. On September 8, 1945, the Japanese
having surrendered six days earlier, Truman got to resume a decades-old tradition. The war had interrupted the practice of U.S. presidents throwing out
the Opening Day first pitch. Better late than never—Truman, flanked by Admiral William Leahy, threw out the first pitch at the game that day between
the Washington Senators and St. Louis Browns. He resumed the Opening Day
ritual the following April. In the meantime, Truman commended *Sporting
News* editor J. Taylor Spink for his wartime service: "News from home was vital [and] our forces were most keenly interested [in] baseball. . . . The military
editions made an effective contribution to the morale of our troops."[2]

Postwar America

In the 1946 film *The Best Years of Our Lives*, soldiers returning from the war discussed the local baseball team on the ride home. From then on, the "enemy" they'd be rooting against wouldn't be the "German U-boat commander or Japanese *kamikaze* pilot" but rather the slugging first baseman and slick-fielding shortstop who played for the home team's archrivals.[3] It was a comforting, yet perhaps fleeting, thought. Despite being heroes of the Good War, each of the veterans found his return rough going—including Harold Russell, who lost both hands in the Pacific and played himself in the movie.

The movie's mixture of triumph and loss characterized not only the broader society, but the baseball world as well. Some ballplayers returned to the big leagues with great fanfare. Bob Feller, Hank Greenberg, Ted Williams, and Joe DiMaggio were given hero's welcomes. All had lost valuable time from their careers, but each became a star again.[4] Overjoyed, Warren Spahn observed, "what a great way to make a living. If I goof up, there's going to be a relief pitcher. Nobody's going to shoot me." And the St. Louis Cardinals were ecstatic when their returning star Enos Slaughter scampered home with the winning run to clinch the 1946 World Series.

Others weren't as happy. The women of the All American Girls Professional Baseball League (AAGPBL) did their part during the war. They were professionals who wanted to retain their jobs and assumed their fans would keep supporting them. But after the war, the women were quickly replaced and expected to return to their wifely duties—just as they were in other occupations. Women were now portrayed as "pinch hitters" both inside and outside baseball. The *Sporting News* captured the sentiment in its headline "Women's Place Is in Grandstand."[5] While the AAGBPL limped along for a few more years, women's baseball was killed by the men's return.

Yet the homecoming for the men didn't necessarily go smoothly either. Some couldn't come back. They were killed or too badly wounded, or their skills had deteriorated too much. The Washington Senators' Cecil Travis suffered severely frostbitten toes and was forced to retire. Other ballplayers were able-bodied and tried to come back, but were refused. Under the Veterans Act of 1946, all returning servicemen were guaranteed their previous jobs back for at least one year at no less than their previous salary. But organized baseball didn't go along. Only about 300 of the more than 1,000 major leaguers who left during the war got their old jobs back. Philadelphia first baseman Tony Lupien sued, and, fearful that he might challenge the reserve clause and baseball's antitrust exemption, the Phillies offered a settlement. All told, more than 140 major leaguers and 900 minor leaguers filed complaints, sometimes backed by the American Veterans of World War II (AMVETS). Almost all of them failed.[6]

Communists and the Color Line

African American soldiers returned home with high expectations as well. Color lines began to weaken, antidiscrimination laws were passed, and white soldiers shed some of their fears. Organized baseball refused to allow black ballplayers during the war, yet cracks began to show. Nazism helped discredit white supremacy, especially with blacks fighting and dying to defeat the Germans. Just as emerging Third World nations began agitating for independence abroad, African Americans sought freedom at home.

Yet in the South, efforts were made to reinforce Jim Crow practices. Washington only tentatively addressed discrimination. And in baseball, the major leagues went through a series of charades. They created a Committee on Baseball Integration—which never met and conducted phantom tryouts, such as the one the Boston Red Sox announced for Jackie Robinson, with no intention of really considering him. In 1944, when staunch segregationist Commissioner Landis died and he was replaced by Albert "Happy" Chandler, the former Kentucky senator claimed the owners knew "I was a Southerner, and thought I'd be all right on the nigger thing."[7]

Breaking the baseball color barrier remained an uphill battle. It was accomplished, nevertheless, by Jackie Robinson under a plan devised by Brooklyn Dodgers president Branch Rickey. But he certainly didn't act alone. The original initiative to integrate major league baseball (MLB) came from the Communist Party of the USA (CPUSA). This "threat" to America's national security had campaigned against racism since the 1920s. A black activist and athlete, Paul Robeson, had joined protesters at Yankee Stadium during the war and asked, "If we are able to stop bullets, why not baseballs?" Black sportswriters and newspapers—such as Wendell Smith and the *Pittsburgh Courier*—also lobbied to end baseball's color line, applauding the sports antidiscrimination work pursued by the Communists.[8]

Leading that effort was Lester Rodney, who for a dozen years agitated for baseball integration as the *Daily Worker*'s sports editor. Rodney first challenged the "gentlemen's agreement" among the owners. After denying the exclusionary policy, officials blamed the players and managers. Yet when Rodney interviewed the players, many of them had no objections to blacks. Joe DiMaggio and Bucky Walters observed that Satchel Paige and other black ballplayers were "some of the best [they'd] ever seen." Johnny Vander Meer said, "I don't see why they're banned." And manager Bill McKechnie claimed that "I'd use Negroes if I were given permission." Rodney noted that owners such as Clark Griffith had already hired Latinos, so why not blacks? This reporting was instrumental in breaking down the barrier. Lobbied by Rodney and the Communist Party, the Pittsburgh Pirates scheduled what would have been the first black tryout, for Roy Campanella in 1942.[9] But baseball officials pressured owner William Benswanger, and he backed out. Even so, Campanella acknowledged the Communist Party's work on his behalf, and how Rodney had "pounded hard and unceasingly against the color line in organized ball."

While Commissioner Chandler had no integration plans, he surprised the baseball owners by asserting, "If they [blacks] can fight and die on Okinawa, Guadalcanal, and the South Pacific, they can play baseball in America." It provided a small opening, and in 1945 Rickey signed Robinson to a minor-league contract. He was sent to the Dodgers' Montreal Royals affiliate because Rickey felt the Canadians would be less racist than the Americans. For the same reason, Rickey took the Dodgers (with Robinson) to play exhibitions in Panama and then to its 1947 spring training in Cuba rather than Florida. Robinson soon broke the color barrier when he was promoted to the big club. Larry Doby integrated the American League when he joined the Cleveland Indians. Both Robinson and Doby gained baseball credibility by having been military veterans. In turn, with baseball providing evidence that integration could work, the U.S. military was desegregated in 1948 (although the change wasn't enforced until after the Korean War).[10]

A virulent anticommunist, Branch Rickey vehemently denied being influenced by outside pressures. He ordered Arthur Mann—a sportswriter and close friend whom Rickey authorized to break the official integration story—to deny any credit to the Communist Party. As Jules Tygiel suggested, "Since the Robinson story played itself out against the backdrop of the post–World War II Red Scare and the repression of the Communist Party, suppressing the Party's role . . . proved relatively easy."[11]

While international politics had challenged baseball on race issues, the major leagues nevertheless stood firm as the American military's loyal friend and as a hard-line supporter of aggressive U.S. foreign policy. Shortly before his 1944 death, Commissioner Landis endorsed American unilateralism. In response to the proposed UN, he claimed it was "all bull to talk about a United States of the World." With Landis gone, the U.S. lost one its fiercest cheerleaders for reflexive American patriotism. To replace him, the major leagues again looked first to the U.S. military, seeking to further burnish its national pastime credentials.

Among the commissioner candidates was Undersecretary of War Robert Patterson, Coast Guard admiral Robert Donoghue, American Legion head

Erle Crocke Jr. and War Mobilization Board director James F. Byrnes. Even though the war hadn't ended yet, General Dwight Eisenhower, General Douglas MacArthur, General George C. Marshall, General Maxwell Taylor, and General Clifton Gates were also discussed, along with FBI Director J. Edgar Hoover. In 1945, the owners instead chose former U.S. senator Happy Chandler, whose credentials were close enough. Chandler supported baseball during the war: "I'm for winning the war—and for keeping baseball. We can—and must—do both." In 1943, he brought President Roosevelt and club owners together to buoy the game's wartime status. In 1944, he blocked a House Military Affairs Committee bill that would have shut baseball down. Superpatriot Yankees general manager Larry MacPhail nominated Chandler for commissioner, claiming Happy's Washington ties would guarantee government support for the game.[12]

In the Senate, Chandler was an influential Military Affairs Committee member who toured five American military bases, successfully lobbying to strengthen Pacific defenses. Because of his folksy, down-home demeanor, Chandler was sometimes taken lightly. But not, according to the *Stars and Stripes*, by the U.S. military. Aside from baseball integration (for which he sought more credit), Chandler would have a chance to prove himself: during his reign, he and organized baseball would confront the Cold War and the Korean War. But before those, Chandler had another battle: the Mexican League War.

The Mexican League War

After the Second World War, besides its refusal to restore players to their jobs, organized baseball also depressed player wages—despite record profits in the war's final year. The new players union, the American Baseball Guild, pushed for reforms. Then in late 1946, the major leagues faced an unexpected new challenge: the Mexican League began signing major-league players. To baseball owners, the Guild seemed like a revolution but with the Mexican League incursion, it now felt more like a war. The first shots were fired in 1940, largely under organized baseball's radar, when Negro League players Cool Papa Bell, Leon Day, Ray Dandridge, Martin Dihigo, Josh Gibson, and Willie Wells helped the Veracruz Blues win the Mexican League pennant. The team's owner, Jorge Pasquel, had begun recruiting African Americans to his league. Jackie Robinson was solicited, and Roy Campanella actually played in the Mexican League, as did Monte Irvin, who ended up enshrined in both the Mexican and the American baseball halls of fame.[13]

In 1942, two African Americans in the Mexican League, Theolic Smith and Quincy Trouppe, were drafted into the U.S. military. But using his government contacts, Pasquel arranged a loan of eighty thousand Mexican workers to the U.S. in a "trade" for the two players. This was a little-known part of the "Bracero Program," created to attract Mexican labor to keep American railroads, mines, and farms running at full capacity during World War II—a program its chief U.S. administrator later called "legalized slavery."[14]

In 1946, Pasquel shifted his sights to organized white baseball. The Mexican League offered U.S. ballplayers better pay, with no reserve clause. Beginning with a few Latino major leaguers, Pasquel then targeted top stars, such as Ted Williams, Bob Feller, Hank Greenberg, Stan Musial, Phil Rizzuto, and Johnny Pesky. While none signed, several used the Mexican offers for better deals from their U.S. clubs. Pasquel did lure twenty-three other major leaguers to Mexico, including lesser stars, such as Vern Stephens, Sal Maglie, Max Lanier, and Mickey Owen. He signed the Hall of Famer Rogers Hornsby to manage, and lavishly hosted Babe Ruth in Mexico City, exploiting the snub the major leagues had given Ruth's managerial aspirations.[15]

Big league baseball fought back. The Yankees' Larry MacPhail got a restraining order against Mexican scouts. U.S. sporting goods companies were pressured to stop selling equipment to the Mexican League. Commissioner Happy Chandler created a blacklist and ultimately banned eighteen jumpers for five years, justifying his decision using the "rhetoric of loyalty and subversion, which was becoming prevalent in American life" (in these, the emerging years of McCarthyism), labeling the jumpers as "disloyal" and urging all supporters to "stand by the flag of Organized Baseball."[16]

By late February 1946, the baseball war was headline news. The *Sporting News* called the Mexicans "outlaws" and ran a cover showing a stereotypical "bandido" with a six-shooter sticking up an honest-looking American in a business suit. The victim was labeled Organized Baseball. A United Press International report commented, "Pancho Villa's raids over the border looked like pale stuff compared to the peso-happy caballero promoting big-time baseball in Mexico and using bona fide Brooklyn Dodgers for bait." According to John Phillips, "Mexico and the U.S. were allies during World War II. [But] when it ended, the baseball hierarchies of the two countries went to war."[17]

Militaristic rhetoric permeated the 1946 season: wars, battles, besieged owners, and exploited American workers were hot topics. "What baseball's war lacked in blood and tears, it made up for in Churchillian posturing and oratory. There was talk of truces, amnesties, peace conferences and tripartite agreements." By April, the U.S. and Mexican governments were drawn in. Mexican officials wanted their nation treated as an equal. Concerned that the dispute was harming U.S.-Mexican relations, American officials urged MLB to settle its differences with the Mexican League: "Baseball is making it tough on us.

We try to build up goodwill and this sort of thing tears it down." Mexican diplomats in Washington and at the United Nations wondered, "We exchange students, professors, artists, workers . . . so why not ballplayers?" Defending MLB's lordly attitude, Commissioner Chandler posed a revealing analogy: "Suppose the Mexican government did not recognize American oil concessions. Don't you suppose [the State Department] would protest?"[18]

Nationalism—not merely baseball—was a driving force behind the conflict. Pasquel was a proud Mexican patriot, who resented his maltreatment by the major leagues. By labeling itself "organized" baseball, MLB implied that everything else was chaotic and inferior. And if there were any "outlaws," Pasquel claimed, they were U.S. clubs, attempting to monopolize the game. He wondered why the two U.S. leagues acted like the world's governing body for the sport when fine baseball was being played in Mexico and elsewhere. How could the Americans hold a *World* Series without playing against foreign leagues? The U.S. champion should have to play the Mexican League champion to win the crown.

But the dispute cut deeper. Pasquel had close ties to Mexican presidential candidate Miguel Alemán. Because Mexicans loved baseball and followed MLB, it was thought that luring Americans to the Mexican League would help his election campaign. Indeed, Aleman won and credited Pasquel for his assistance. Yet Pasquel had still other political motives. In 1942, before Mexico's entry into World War II, the U.S. State Department had placed him on its blacklist for allegedly trading with the enemy (Germany). And when he and Alemán were young boys, they experienced firsthand the 1914 U.S. bombing and seizure of their hometown, Veracruz, in retaliation against the Mexican government's plan to nationalize its own oil industry. Hundreds of Mexicans were killed. This and other American interventions left a bad taste in Pasquel's mouth. The Mexican League was used to fan the flames of nationalism. About Pasquel—an admirer of Napoléon Bonaparte, it was said—"Nobody really likes Jorge—but he's a national hero, nevertheless." The conflict escalated, and even Cuba was drawn into the dispute.[19]

By 1947, the Mexican League challenge began to fizzle. Jumpers reconsidered and attempted reinstatement. When refused, some switched to the independent Quebec League. But the owners feared the blacklist would only result in dangerous court cases, and their concerns were confirmed when one jumper, Danny Gardella, targeted his suit at baseball's heart and soul, claiming the reserve clause was illegal. Before a congressional panel, Branch Rickey called the case "a communist plot," but Gardella responded, "I was no communist for exercising my American rights."[20]

The owners portrayed the challenge as the sport's potential death knell.

Commissioner Chandler hinted at amnesty for the other jumpers, and thus some of them disavowed any connection to Gardella. The whole affair sounded a lot like the broader U.S. society, as Americans were pointing fingers, naming names, and dissociating themselves from their past affiliations in the growing Cold War climate. In 1949, MLB settled the Gardella case and reinstated the jumpers.[21]

Meanwhile, although Pasquel lost, this episode helped bolster the Mexican League in the long run. While not gaining the major-league designation Pasquel sought, it did secure the highest minor-league (AAA) status and survived as a relatively protected summer league. Back in the United States, however, Mexicans were soon blamed for America's 1954 recession after the Korean War and were scapegoated as the cause of the job shortage faced by returning veterans. In response, Washington launched Operation Wetback, in which a million Mexicans—a third of them American citizens—were rounded up and deported to Mexico. Could this have occurred, in part, as retaliation against Pasquel's Mexican invasion?[22]

Postwar Baseball Diplomacy

After the war, baseball was an ambassador for democracy and American values. According to Wade Lewis, an international baseball league would ensure world peace because "no time would be found for war if our leaders had important baseball games to discuss."[23] Baseball became important to America's foreign diplomacy in Europe and Asia, as the U.S. sought to shore up its new superpower status. The U.S. exported the sport with the eager collaboration of organized baseball and the American press. According to Bryan Price, "Similar to the way Europeans planned to civilize the untamed savages of the New World with Christianity, Americans attempted to democratize any willing client state with the game of baseball." It was thought that "the introduction of American baseball would help assist the U.S. image." In *Baseball Magazine*, Clifford Bloodgood observed, "The seed of baseball has been planted in every country American troops have been. So eventually we shall have practically world coverage." And in response to baseball's use as a tool of Cold War policy, Communist China and Czechoslovakia banned the sport.[24]

The 1947 President's Committee on Civil Rights urged the United States to address its rights abuses because they were damaging American foreign relations: "Countries with 'competing philosophies' have tried to prove our democracy an empty fraud and our nation an oppressor of underprivileged people." Thus, Jackie Robinson's integration that year had some international value. It inspired some white South African baseball teams to play some clandestine ball games against black clubs in the early 1950s. The integrated Dodgers drew Crown Prince Aduaye Emeni, the Nigerian emissary to the UN, to the games. Impressed by strides made by African Americans, he claimed Nigerians were developing more positive feelings for the United States. Another Dodgers fan was Iraq's King Faisal II, one of America's few Middle East friends, who attended games at Ebbets Field in 1952. And an American foreign-service officer described the relationship baseball helped him create with the Sultan of Zanzibar when the U.S. Navy staged games there.[25]

The State Department began sending athletes abroad through its Bureau of Educational and Cultural Affairs baseball exchanges, especially to nonaligned Third World nations. U.S. Cold Warriors sought to compete against Soviet incursions into black Africa using baseball as a pro-American, anticommunist propaganda tool. In the early 1950s, a world tour by the Brooklyn Dodgers and Cleveland Indians was organized to showcase the new black players, Jackie Robinson and Larry Doby, "as living evidence of the opportunity to reach the top which America's No. 1 sport gives all participants regardless of race." Baseball was praised as a peacemaker in Tunisia, where the game united different peoples "better than any other tie." It could "join together men who were fierce enemies yesterday." And reports from Africa's Gold Coast claimed that copies of the *Sporting News*, with pictures of black baseball players, "have done much to make the work of the U.S. Catholic missions easier."[26]

The incoming Eisenhower administration also recognized sports' international propaganda value. In Latin America, U.S. Ambassador Walter Donnelly was lauded for promoting baseball diplomacy in Venezuela. *Life* magazine routinely sent stories of baseball diplomacy home to American readers, including baseball games in Africa and Saudi Arabia.[27] Baseball's role in America's postwar occupations of Europe and the Asia–Pacific region was of particular interest.

Postwar Europe

In Britain, baseball was rejuvenated by the large holdover of American and Canadian troops. The English championships were revived in 1948. The European Baseball Confederation was formed in 1954, with its first championship held a year later. And so grateful was American soldier Bill Arce for surviving the Battle of the Bulge, he decided to use baseball to spread goodwill. His first target was Holland, but the U.S. State Department spurned his funding bid, offering instead to finance a Czechoslovakia trip, where it "wanted to use baseball as a political tool."[28]

In Germany, the day after VE Day in 1945, U.S. engineering units stopped constructing combat bridges and airfields and began converting European battlefields into ball fields, using German prisoner-of-war labor. American officers launched huge baseball leagues, and soon more than two hundred thousand soldiers were playing in Germany and elsewhere in Europe. An All-Star Army team toured Germany, France, Italy, and Austria.[29] Major leaguers in the military played games at sites such as Hermann Goering Stadium in Koblenz.

Segregation still afflicted military baseball at home, but some African Americans were permitted on American forces teams abroad. Thus, the Negro Leaguers Leon Day and Willard Brown played for General George Patton's Third Army team. And while the Chicago Cubs and Detroit Tigers were battling for the 1945 World Series crown back in the United States, the GI World Series was held at Soldier's Field in Nuremberg, Germany, before fifty thousand servicemen. Six years earlier, at the same location, a similar-size crowd had cheered Adolf Hitler and a parade of Nazi armaments. But in 1945, Day, Brown, and former National League pitcher Sam Nahem led the Overseas Invasion Service Expedition All Stars to a thrilling five-game victory over the mighty 71st Infantry Division team.[30]

The 1948 film *A Foreign Affair* was set in the rubble of postwar, U.S.-occupied Berlin. While watching German kids playing baseball, a U.S. congressman remarked, "One thing they don't have to worry about around here is breaking windows." Yet the locals embraced the game and got better at it, and Germany led the way in organizing a European baseball league. U.S. soldiers taught baseball to German children and helped establish leagues in Frankfurt, Mannheim, Munich, and Marburg. By 1948, Germany had 140 teams, and a German baseball championship was launched in 1951. To de-Nazify the Germans, a healthy dose of baseball was prescribed. According to the *Sporting News*, "Americanization" was required, incorporating "our good old American sport of baseball. The [German] kids like the Americans and they're not as war-minded as some would think." The State Department published a list of approved sports for occupied Germany: baseball was described as the most civilized and democratic.[31]

Among the Germans who learned baseball were Klaus and Hanjorg Helmig, who started their own team in Mannheim in 1952. Watching the Americans play and then joining street teams, the Helmig brothers got very good. In 1956, about the time Don Larsen threw the only no-hitter in World Series history, a Baltimore Orioles scout arrived in Germany to offer them contracts. Sent to the minors, they had some success and lots of publicity but were released later that year. These two German white boys then signed with the Baltimore Elite Stars of the Negro Leagues. They soon returned home, with most of their baseball behind them, and the sport began to die out in the mid-1950s in Germany, as service baseball began to fade and American troops began to leave.

In Italy after the war, baseball was very unfamiliar: when one Italian boy first saw American GIs breaking out the equipment, he thought the bats, balls, and gloves must be some clever new fighting devices. But soon baseball caught on; for many Italians it represented rebirth amid so much death. In 1947, U.S. Lieutenant Colonel Charles Butte used Italian workers to build a cemetery for American war dead in Nettuno, Italy. When they showed interest in baseball, Butte felt the game would help build good relations. He had equipment sent and got permission to allow the Italians to build their own stadium. Some of the grandstand came from the steel planking the Americans used to land at Anzio during the war. A local nobleman donated the land, and the ballpark was eventually named after Butte. The cemetery workers formed a team, then helped spread baseball around Italy, starting the first professional league in 1948. Soon youngsters were being given baseball bats and gloves for their first communion, a tradition that continues to this day, as baseball remains huge in Nettuno. Officially calling itself the City of Baseball, it even hosted a visit by Joe DiMaggio.[32]

American soldiers taught baseball in Milan and elsewhere in Italy, and they helped build one of the first permanent fields, in Trieste in 1951. The Italian Baseball Federation was formed, dozens of teams blossomed, and baseball became Italy's second largest spectator sport. In the early 1950s, the U.S. Information Agency sent baseball rule books and training films in Italian. As Blake Erlich claimed, "Baseball teaches individual initiative keyed to team responsibility, a lesson Italy greatly needs. It is an outlet for youthful energies [otherwise] largely absorbed by political marching and rioting." Besides U.S. government initiatives, Baseball for Italy, Inc. was launched, because "there is nothing more American than baseball, and it can serve as a bridge over which people can be brought together."[33]

Postwar Asia and the Pacific

The postwar U.S. occupation of Japan disarmed the nation, purged it of war criminals, established a new constitution, launched an anticommunist crusade, and sought the Americanization of Japanese society. For the latter, baseball was considered instrumental: the two cultures shared this more than anything else. Looking back on their Tokyo raids, American flyers recalled feeling guilty about dropping their bombs after passing over children playing sandlot baseball. During the 1945 World Series, loudspeakers and a giant scoreboard were erected outside a leading Japanese newspaper office, where Japanese civilians and American occupation troops stood side by side to follow the games.[34]

General Douglas MacArthur, the supreme allied commander in Japan, recognized baseball as a common bond. While MLB touted its martial qualities, MacArthur actually favored baseball because he thought it had the *fewest* military overtones and might serve as the best peacemaker. While the sport may have failed to prevent the war, it was important afterward for healing its wounds. The Japanese had commandeered Korakuen Stadium, the Tokyo Giants home field, as an ammunition depot, but MacArthur immediately restored it as a ballpark.[35] And the Japanese professional leagues were revived only three months after the war's end.

Sharing MacArthur's baseball enthusiasm was his right-hand man, Major General William Marquat, who administered the M Fund, a large reserve for rebuilding Japan. Besides wanting to revive baseball, both men sought to suppress sumo wrestling, a favorite sport of Japanese militarists and right-wing nationalists. M Fund monies were generously devoted to baseball, and Ryuji Suzuki, the Japan Central League's future president, sought the sport's rapid revival: "Baseball is the national sport of America. That's why we need to reorganize the game here. We have to use diplomacy, not weapons . . . baseball is the way to go." He made a similar appeal to Japanese foreign minister Takizo Matsumoto: "America is occupying Japan. We wonder what will happen if we fail to get along. Baseball will build a bridge." Japanese newspapers endorsed baseball to promote better understanding: "The different customs of the two nations could be more easily reconciled on the baseball field than by Japanese officials meeting with American authorities." According to U.S. sportswriter Fred Lieb, "It may take America a long time to forget the treachery of Pearl Harbor, the march from Bataan, the horror of the prison camps, but the baseball field may furnish some future meeting ground with our erstwhile foe." Remarkably, in 1947 Japan declared an annual Babe Ruth Day.[36]

Writing in *Collier's* magazine, Weldon James cautioned, "Our military-government people don't think baseball in itself will make the Japanese more democratic. But compared with the schools' old military drill, it's practically Jeffersonian." As John Duvall has noted, this smacked a bit of cultural imperialism: "What to do with an essentially undemocratic race? Give them baseball, and get them to act more like Americans." Perhaps it worked, for according to Norman Cousins, razzing the umpire was on the rise: "The Japanese are as baseball crazy as ever, and the way they now treat umpires is probably the best proof that democratization has succeeded." As for their baseball skills, the Japanese players were viewed as good, but weak. Their shortage of power hitting was oddly linked to U.S. firepower. As Duvall put it, "American postwar confidence [derived from] our exclusive possession of the 'big blast'—where the home run and atom bomb metaphorically merged."[37]

To enhance Americanization, U.S. films were tailored for the Japanese, often featuring values and themes conveyed through baseball. A 1946 comedy *Carefree Father* featured twenty-five pro baseball players. In the 1948 film *Bridal Champion*, the Center for International Exchange had a baseball sequence inserted, claiming it "would add a good deal to the spirit of democracy." That same year, *The Age of Baseball Fever* emphasized Japan's and America's common love of the game. The film *Enoken's Home Run King* featured Japan's most famous comedian and scenes of professional baseball games. In 1949, an RKO Studios promotional campaign distributed baseball bats and gloves as presents from Gary Cooper on the Japanese release of *The Pride of the Yankees*. Japanese fans were also excited to see a baseball stadium scene in Akira Kurosawa's 1949 film noir masterpiece, *Stray Dog*.[38]

Postwar baseball was so effective that some felt it could rebuild Japan from the ground up. Japanese boys were playing baseball only a mile from Hiroshima's ground zero. Yet MacArthur sensed a certain weariness emerging in the war-ravaged country. In response, he called on Lefty O'Doul, who had often visited Japan before the war. In 1949, the year Casey Stengel began managing the New York Yankees to five straight World Series victories, O'Doul brought his San Francisco Seals to Japan, where they were greeted by a parade of one million people. The Seals conducted clinics and raised money for charities, and their eleven-game tour drew another half million fans.

After six weeks of O'Doul, morale was bolstered, and the Japanese were crying "Banzai" again. As O'Doul reflected, "I knew [our] baseball team . . . would cement a friendship between these people and us." MacArthur exulted: "This is the greatest piece of diplomacy ever." His successor, General Matthew Ridgeway, concurred: "Words cannot describe Lefty's wonderful contributions through baseball to the post–war rebuilding effort." Tokyo Giants owner Toru Shoriki called the tour "the most successful goodwill event ever made on an international scale." Emperor Hirohito was so impressed he summoned O'Doul to the Imperial Palace to thank him personally.[39]

O'Doul made many more trips to Japan in the next decade, often with stars like Joe and Dom DiMaggio. The 1950 tour seemed focused, in particular, on preventing the spread of communism. According to Seals coach Del Young, "When we got there the communists were on soap boxes on almost every street corner. But before long they disappeared in the crowds." O'Doul's popularity steadily rose, and "you would have thought [he] was the emperor." Along the parade routes, there was a deafening chant: "Banzai, O'Doul." Restoring their American-style uniforms, he also engineered a Tokyo Giants visit to the

United States. In the end, O'Doul was regarded as a great peacemaker and the father of Japanese professional baseball, for which he was inducted into the Japanese Baseball Hall of Fame. When he died, the Japanese consul led a delegation to his funeral.[40]

By 1950, the M Fund built a new stadium in Osaka and Japan's professional leagues expanded to fifteen clubs. Under the Nippon Professional Baseball Organization umbrella, Pacific League and Central League teams competed for pennants and a chance to meet in the Japan World Series. In the next few years, the Hawaiian Wally Yonamine became the "Jackie Robinson of Japan"—the first Japanese American to play professionally in Japan. Initially resisted for not speaking Japanese and for his aggressive American style of play, he was eventually accepted, had a sterling career, was inducted into the Japanese Baseball Hall of Fame, and received the Imperial Order of the Sacred Treasure for strengthening U.S.-Japan friendship.

Elsewhere, two black U.S. minor leaguers were "loaned" by the St. Louis Browns to the Hankyu Braves of the Japanese Pacific League, and Boston Braves pitcher Phil Paine became the first ex–major leaguer to play in the Japanese big leagues—while still serving in the U.S. Air Force. The American occupation ended in 1952, but many U.S. troops remained in Japan, causing increasing resentment, some of it directed at Paine. And while manager Leo Durocher was deemed a "great ambassador" for his tour the following year, his repeated flouting of local customs was regarded by the Japanese as a symbol of imperialism and cultural insensitivity.[41]

Having lost the war, Japan was ousted from its Pacific and East Asian territories. In Taiwan, the Chinese nationalists took control as the civil war with the Chinese Communists entered its final phase. Taiwanese baseball had been shaped largely by the Japanese, yet it persisted, also claiming Chinese roots, for the game on the mainland dated from 1863. The Nationalists sought to "de-Taiwanese" the island, to purge Japanese influences and consolidate the "one, true China." They were less prepared for the Taiwanese independence movement, which sought autonomy from all outside powers. That movement achieved its identity with the help of baseball, which it had used to resist Japanese imperialism before the war. With U.S. troops now stationed on the island, the Taiwanese began emulating American baseball—emphasizing slugging power. In 1947, the Chinese Nationalists carried out anticommunist massacres that indiscriminately victimized the independence movement as well, killing at least one of its ballplayers. Soon, however, Mao Tse-tung's Communist revolution overran the Nationalists and forced them to retreat permanently to Taiwan, where they established a dictatorship. Baseball continued under martial rule, and by 1954 the Taiwanese Army, Navy, and Air Force all had active teams.

On mainland China, baseball was played in the Chinese and Japanese prisoner-of-war camps during the Sino-Japanese War, which lasted until the end of World War II. American troops were stationed in China after the war, and wherever they established bases, "baseball diamonds sprung up overnight." Major Roger Doulens wrote glowingly about Chinese baseball, encouraging the U.S. military to further ingrain the game, especially among the nation's 75 million boys. While Mao's revolution forced the Americans out, baseball remained. By 1950, Chinese Communist revolutionary hero Marshal He Long was crediting the sport for his accomplishments and incorporating it into People's Liberation Army training: "Baseball and sports are the pillars of national defense and development. It made better soldiers, and our pitchers could toss a grenade faster and farther than anyone else . . . and with a curve on it." Baseball was played throughout China after the revolution and embraced by thousands of Chinese soldiers in particular. In 1952, the Chinese Red Army held a baseball competition: the winners were awarded American guns captured in the Korean War.[42]

In the Pacific, the Philippines were liberated from the Japanese, gaining formal independence. Yet the country remained deeply dependent on and thoroughly dominated by the United States, which established long-term military bases there. Filipino baseball had all but died out, but it began making a comeback after the war. In 1951, an All-Taiwan team toured the islands, and in subsequent years, Japanese and U.S. clubs also did so—including the black San Francisco Sea Lions team. Filipino Little League teams rose to international prominence. And the Philippines won the 1954 Asian Amateur Baseball Championship.[43] But growing anti-U.S. resentment and the emerging Filipino independence movement helped undermine the sport. Potential Filipino baseball talent was distanced from its major training ground—the U.S. Army. Rather than becoming a source of postwar resistance and identity, baseball was largely abandoned for other sports.[44]

The Korean War

In another former Japanese colony, Korea, baseball had begun to fade by the 1930s, and then stopped altogether during World War II. It rebounded after the war, fueled by the U.S. military presence and the new Taehan Baseball Association. But a civil conflict was brewing, again interrupting baseball, and war finally erupted in 1950. The UN Security Council approved a "police action," with the United States providing most of the forces. But the American troops in South Korea needed help. Baseball played a role in providing it and may have even changed the course of the war.

The American forces closest to Korea were those occupying Japan. Besides the logistical problems of moving them, it was feared a troop reduction would invite Japanese unrest. What could pacify the population? William Marquat, Japan's International Baseball Commissioner, planned an amateur series, matching the Japanese national team against the National Baseball Congress (NBC) champions. His invitation—at General MacArthur's behest—to the 1950 NBC champion Fort Wayne Capeharts was the first interhemispheric baseball series, but also an elaborate military diversion to help hide the impending U.S. invasion of Korea.[45]

Although the Fort Wayne team had neither passports nor inoculations, Marquat sidestepped the regulations. MacArthur provided scarce military air transport to fly the team to Japan, where they were under U.S. Army temporary duty orders. Former military officer and NBC executive Charles Cookson was restored to active duty for the event, which was presented as merely a goodwill gesture between the two nations.[46] Actually, as Marquat confided to Cookson, the series was "of vital importance to the interests of the U.S."

The turnout at the games, parades, and pep rallies was overwhelming, and virtually took over Tokyo and the rest of the country. The five-game series drew bigger crowds than the Yankees-Phillies World Series that year. Behind the pitching of former Negro Leaguer Pat Scantlebury, Fort Wayne won games one and two in Tokyo. On September 12, 1950, the teams traveled to Osaka, while MacArthur secretly boarded the USS *Mount McKinley*. The Japanese won the third game, but the Americans took the fourth. The teams returned to Tokyo on September 15, where Fort Wayne won its fourth game and the tournament. But the big news in the world that day happened across the Yellow Sea. MacArthur had unleashed thirteen thousand marines in a land-and-sea surprise attack at Inchon, Korea. The North Koreans were routed and forced to retreat. As sportswriter Bob Broeg reported, the games were "a militaristic red herring against the Communistic Reds." That is, the series not only preoccupied the Japanese but was publicized so grandiosely in the region that the North Koreans didn't suspect a military operation against them was about to be launched.[47]

On October 6, 1950, a *New Orleans Statesman* cartoon showed Russian premier Joseph Stalin dressed in a baseball uniform. Behind him was a character with folded arms, peering eyes, and a world globe for a head. Representing public opinion, the character leaned over the outfield fence looking at a broken baseball bat labeled "Korea." Stalin scratched his head and stared at a collection of new bats—each labeled with a political powder keg of the day—Greece, Turkey, Finland, India, Berlin, Austria, Formosa, Indochina, and Japan. Against gloomy assessments that the Korean War and perhaps other conflicts might claim all of America's bats and close down baseball, Chicago White Sox general manager Frank Lane, argued, "Next to religion, no other agency [besides baseball] maintained our morale at home and at [World War II] battlefronts. . . . [Short of] enemy attacks on the U.S. shore . . . , professional baseball should continue [during the Korean conflict]." But AMVETS National Commander Harold Russell complained to baseball owners, "We remember the strange crop of deferments during World War II to keep baseball going and profits rolling in." The *New York Post* editorialized that "the public does not readily associate courage with a game children can play, especially when they read the latest casualty lists from Korea."[48]

More supportively, *Sport* magazine argued that baseball should continue but with no special privileges. The *Sporting News* agreed: "Baseball, as always in its history, is proud to send its players to their appropriate places in [the war] effort." According to Ron Briley, this meant that "baseball should do its duty in the shooting war as well as in the ideological Cold War, asking no favors but continuing its role of indoctrination and maintaining morale." As a U.S. senator, Happy Chandler championed baseball during World War II, but as commissioner, he said it might have to stop for the Korean conflict. For many owners, this took baseball patriotism too far. Chandler's speculation was the last straw, and he was removed. American Legion head Erle Crocke Jr. was a possible replacement until he, too, suggested baseball's possible suspension.[49]

To deflect accusations that they didn't support the war and to keep their military connections, the owners next turned to Douglas MacArthur. By April 1951, MacArthur had been dismissed by Harry Truman for insubordination yet was being celebrated in New York City by a huge ticker-tape parade. When the ambidextrous Truman threw out the first pitches (one with each hand) of that season at Washington's Griffith Stadium, he was booed for firing the general—the first ball-game heckling of a president since the "We Want Beer" chants against Herbert Hoover during prohibition. At Ebbets Field, MacArthur—in full-dress military uniform—was ceremoniously delivered via limousine to home plate for a lavish tribute. He would thereafter be a regular Dodgers guest. MacArthur was also toasted at Yankee Stadium and the Polo Grounds, where a wounded Korean War veteran threw out the first pitch. To the crowd, MacArthur said, "It is wonderful to be here, to be able to hear the baseball against the bat, ball against glove, the call of the vendor, and be able to boo the umpire." By the end of 1951, MacArthur could have done more than taunt the umpires; he could have been their boss.[50]

But MacArthur declined the commissionership. The baseball owners instead selected yet another military man, Major General Emmett "Rosy" O'Donnell. Besides being a World War II hero, he was a big baseball fan and was viewed as a check against any calls to halt the games because of the Korean War. Truman blocked the appointment, however, claiming the country couldn't afford to release O'Donnell from active duty. More likely this was retaliation against O'Donnell, who like MacArthur had been a critic of U.S. policy in Korea.[51] Other military men were on MLB's candidate list, including General Dwight Eisenhower and General Maxwell Taylor; both declined. Frustrated, MLB finally gave the job to National League president Ford Frick.

During the Korean conflict, the major leagues suffered some setbacks. Baseballs were scarce, as the use of horsehide was curbed; fans were asked to return foul balls. Baseball salaries were affected by the government's wage controls. The Red Scare atmosphere tainted some baseball relationships, as when Dodgers owner Walter O'Malley accused Cardinals boss Fred Saigh of being a socialist for proposing revenue sharing for television contracts. To bolster troop morale, MLB sponsored tours to the front by stars such as Joe DiMaggio. Nevertheless, ballpark attendance dipped. According to Leigh Montville, "Baseball's response to the Korean War sent a mixed message. While prominent players were called to service, . . . the draft [didn't] seriously alter major league rosters."[52]

At least sixty-six professional ballplayers served in both World War II and the Korean War—the most prominent being the major leaguers Jerry Coleman and Ted Williams. Larry French pursued a military career after thirteen years in the majors. Another doing double duty was Bob Neighbors, the only major leaguer killed in Korea. An additional ninety ballplayers served only during the Korean conflict, including stars Whitey Ford, Billy Martin, Don Newcombe, Ernie Banks, Johnny Antonelli, Dick Groat, Willie Mays, and Eddie Mathews. Bobby Brown joined up as an army doctor, and Curt Simmons—bemoaning his defeat by the Cincinnati Reds before he departed for the military—said, "I hope I have better luck against those Reds in Korea." And while he never made the majors, the 1944 Little League batting champion, Mark Lindenmuth, was a Korean War hero. Wounded four times, he remembered that "in the Marines I began thinking of the battlefield as a huge baseball diamond. In Korea I fought to live, because in Little League I was taught how to play the game."[53]

Not so positive about his experience was Ted Williams. Despite his troubled relations with Boston fans and sportswriters, a Ted Williams Day was held at Fenway Park on April 30, 1952, to say good-bye to their star, who was shipping out to the war. While he appreciated the gesture, Williams resented being recalled after having served in World War II. He felt he and Jerry Coleman were targeted for their publicity value.[54] Williams appealed; when he was denied, he became a reluctant warrior. He claimed policy makers weren't trying hard enough to win the conflict, calling it the forgotten war. He grumbled about poor facilities and equipment, including planes too dangerous to fly: "I expect to be killed, of course." He was even accused of undermining morale, from which rumors of a possible court-martial arose. Even so, Williams flew thirty-nine heroic combat missions, was hit three times, and ultimately crashed in a badly damaged jet. He inspired thousands of young men and flew with future astronaut and U.S. senator John Glenn, who said, "Ted may have batted .400 for the Red Sox, but he hit a thousand for the Marines and the United States."[55]

Much later, Williams spoke publicly about his situation: "If it were an emergency, fine. Everybody goes. But Korea wasn't an all-out war. They should have let the professionals handle it. Vietnam was another undeclared war. If I had had a kid [there] I'd have been screaming. The unfairness of the Selective Service is obvious." Williams wasn't against American involvement in Korea or Vietnam, but complained about how it was done. Even this small departure from official military policy among ballplayers was remarkable, however. Ted Williams, the Marine hero, a war resister? But once he got the anger off his chest, Williams put it behind him and was proud to have been a marine. He always said his three favorite songs were the "Marines' Hymn," "The Star Spangled Banner," and "Take Me Out to the Ballgame." And in 1991, Williams accepted the Medal of Honor from President George H.W. Bush for "an especially meritorious contribution to the security and national interests of the U.S."[56]

As with World War II, Korean War soldiers were always reminded why they were fighting. Not everyone bought it: at least one soldier complained about being "fed pap that the war was fought for the privilege of munching a hot dog at Ebbets Field." As Christopher DeRosa has shown, baseball was used repeatedly in political indoctrination. Sometimes, to lighten the atmosphere and soften the more explicit political content, some military instructors would play the "Baseball Game," in which they'd divide the troops into opposing teams and ask questions based on the previous lecture. Military chaplains also used baseball to teach lessons. In their Duty, Honor, Country pamphlet series, the "unsportsmanlike" Russian premier Vladimir Lenin was contrasted with the apocryphal, quasi-religious tale of Babe Ruth healing a sick child with a home run. The military also used the sport to distract soldiers from the arbitrary and unpleasant aspects of army life—aided by the Armed Forces Radio Service, which kept up a steady diet of baseball.[57]

In 1953, a cease-fire was declared in the Korean conflict, a war that has still not officially ended. After the hostilities, some Chinese and North Korean prisoners in UN custody refused repatriation. But Americans were shocked to discover that twenty-one U.S. soldiers held by the enemy also refused to come home. Complete strangers wrote letters to these soldiers trying to change their minds, warning that baseball would be among the important things they'd lose.

According to DeRosa, by the mid-1950s, the looser, sports-laden propaganda for soldiers was increasingly replaced, amid Cold War hysteria, by a more strident, militaristic indoctrination. The South Korean national team regrouped quickly enough after the war to be admitted into the International Baseball Association and to earn its first big regional win against Japan in the fifth Asian Amateur Baseball Championships. While the U.S. military featured some top-notch ballplayers for a couple more years, baseball was increasingly replaced by softball in the armed forces after Korea—a potentially ominous sign for the sport's future.

A Patriot's Purgatory

While the hot war of the Korean conflict was brewing between American and Russian surrogates on the battlefield, the Cold War of the U.S.-Soviet rivalry was heating up behind the scenes. The National Security Act of 1947 created the Central Intelligence Agency and began turning almost every aspect of American life into a national security issue. Some claimed the final act of the U.S. war with Japan, the bombings of Hiroshima and Nagasaki, were actually the first shots in America's next war with the USSR. And concerns were raised that communists were beginning to infiltrate all walks of American life.

But if, for example, communists might be influencing U.S. sports, could sports also be enlisted in the fight against communism? Such a question arose in 1949, when Paul Robeson stated, "It would be unthinkable that American Negroes would go to war on behalf of those who have oppressed us for generations against the Soviet Union." Robeson, an African American, was a Renaissance man: a world famous actor and singer, a writer and lawyer, a civil rights and antiwar activist, and an All-American football player. He was also a communist who questioned black loyalty to a racist society. From then until his death almost three decades later, the FBI and other agencies used various surreptitious methods to sabotage his work.

To rebut Robeson's charges against America, Jackie Robinson was singled out. Two years after breaking baseball's color barrier, Robinson had proven himself and was viewed by white Americans as a "good Negro" who had "succeeded the right way," without divisive protests: a veteran, a star ballplayer, and a model for African Americans. Amid the Cold War's competing accusations, the U.S. needed a symbol like Robinson to tell the world that America was a just society.[58]

With MLB's blessing, Robinson went before the notorious House Un-American Activities Committee (HUAC) to counter Robeson's contentions. A jingoistic anticommunist, Branch Rickey pushed Robinson to testify, but there was a dilemma. If Robinson did so, then he might be viewed as a black pawn in a white man's game. If he didn't, then Robeson's statements would not be rebutted. Robinson was in what journalist Carl Rowan called a "patriot's purgatory." While his own negative U.S. military experience might have curbed his enthusiasm, Robinson finally decided to testify in July 1949. He said blacks would "do their best to help their country stay out of war; if unsuccessful, they'd help their country win the war—against Russia or any other enemy. . . . Americans of many races and faiths have too much invested in our country's welfare to let it be taken from us."[59]

Robinson also observed that the "American public ought to understand that because it is a Communist [Robeson] who denounces injustice in the courts, police brutality and lynching, doesn't change the truth of the charges." On the other hand, "Negroes were stirred up long before there was a Communist party, and they'll stay stirred up long after the party has disappeared." Even though they had helped him and other blacks break the color barrier, Robinson asserted that "we [Negroes] can win our fight [against discrimination] without the Communists and we don't want their help." The day after Robinson's testimony, the *New York Times* ran a front-page article featuring two photos: one showing Robeson lecturing and one showing Robinson sliding into home plate. That is, *The communists have ideology; we have baseball.* The story conveyed the intended message: that Robeson didn't represent black America. Baseball had scored a big run in the Cold War game against the Soviets and homegrown dissidents.[60]

For his testimony, Robinson received many honors, including the Veterans of Foreign Wars gold medal for good citizenship, the Catholic War Veterans Commander's Citation, and a Freedom Foundation Award in a presentation by Dwight Eisenhower to those contributing the most to the American way of life.[61] Years later, however, Robinson described his HUAC testimony as "the greatest regret of my life." He noted, "I have grown wiser [about] . . . America's destructiveness. I have an increased respect for Paul Robeson who sacrificed himself . . . sincerely trying to help his people." By the end of his life, Robinson shared Robeson's critical views of American racism and U.S. foreign policy: "I wouldn't fly the flag on the Fourth of July or any other day. When I see a car with a flag on it, I figure the guy behind the wheel isn't my friend."[62] A remarkable crack in baseball patriotism, for anyone who was paying attention.

The Shot Heard 'Round the World

On October 3, 1951, Bobby Thomson hit the "shot heard 'round the world." Tied for first place, the New York Giants and Brooklyn Dodgers were forced into a playoff. With the Giants down by two runs in the ninth inning of the deciding game, Thomson hit a dramatic three-run home run to give New York the National League pennant. Four decades later, Thomson's shot provided the foundation for Don DeLillo's epic novel *Underworld*, whose prologue (also published separately as *Pafko at the Wall*) marked that afternoon as a crucial turning point in American history.[63]

As Jules Tygiel has recounted, the entire 1951 baseball season was "played out against the backdrop of Cold War and Korean War tensions." The United States had weathered Paul Robeson's challenge, and troops (including black soldiers) had been committed against the Soviet-backed North Koreans. Truman and MacArthur had parted ways, Red Scare hysteria had escalated, and anti-Soviet tensions were in the air. Referencing his new National League record for walks, sportswriters began calling Giants second baseman Eddie Stanky "Gromyko," for the Russian diplomat who had recently walked out of the United Nations in protest.[64]

During the playoff, antiwar radicals at the City University of New York interrupted their political discussions for the ball games. Unable to choose between the Giants and the Dodgers broadcasts, they decided to switch stations every inning, suspending their protest strategy meetings altogether to listen to game three. They and many others, either tuning in or attending the game in person, soon witnessed Thomson's climactic blast. But it wasn't the only dramatic explosion that day: the Soviets announced they had successfully tested a second atomic bomb. This confirmed it: the U.S. nuclear monopoly was over. But the next day, the Soviet test had to share the *New York Times* front page with Thomson's home run. In its editorial on "The Russian Bomb," the *Times* called it "news of the gravest import in the whole world." It was followed by a second editorial, which began, "Well, the Giants exploded a bomb, too," and then invoked the image of a "home run heard 'round the world."[65]

The notion that events in baseball might intersect with Cold War politics had already been seen. But, as John Duvall asks, "Why does one cultural event, a baseball game, eclipse [or at least compete with] a moment crucial to the construction of the Cold War? If October 3, 1951 exists as part of American consciousness, it is for Bobby Thomson's heroics, not Russia's atomic bomb."

Later, in *M**A*S*H, television's Korean War retrospective, the characters in one episode listened to the game and then saw Thomson's home run again on a newsreel. But as Duvall notes, "Presumably, that same newsreel would detail the Soviet blast, yet this piece of history—surely pertinent to anyone serving in the Korean War—[was] invisible."[66]

Partly in response to this odd construction of American cultural memory, Don DeLillo's *Underworld* offers a stunning chronicle of the events of the next few decades, beginning with Thomson's 1951 blow and threaded together by the home run ball as it leaves the ballpark and passes from hand to hand. In his epilogue, DeLillo fast-forwards to a near future in which ruthless capitalism, the Internet, and a new, hushed but tentative faith in America's prospects have replaced the Cold War's blend of dread and euphoria.

In an earlier novel, *End Zone*, DeLillo explored how difficult it was to distinguish the language of football from the language of nuclear strategy. In *Underworld*, however, his prologue showed that baseball's language has also been available for the "figuration of nuclear war."[67] In DeLillo's version of the final playoff game, Thomson's home run unleashed not only agony and ecstasy, but also a mock apocalypse with torn paper fragments flying around the ballpark like confetti—as the fallout. Among the fallen pages was a *Life* magazine photo of Pieter Bruegel's 1562 painting *The Triumph of Death*, which showed a macabre panorama of doom, dying, and destruction. This symbolic foreshadowing of the nuclear age landed in the lap of one of the game's actual spectators, FBI director J. Edgar Hoover, who only a few minutes earlier had received word of the Soviet atomic test. The blast gave Hoover the "ammunition" to pursue his anticommunist agenda even more ruthlessly. With an adversary large enough to sustain postwar paranoia about threats to U.S. national security, this day became crucial to the Cold War's escalation.

As Ron Briley has observed, instead of being able to "bask in the sunshine of peace and prosperity" after the Good War, Americans "were frustrated by the emergence of the Cold War . . . and a shooting war in Korea. . . . Baseball had fought the war against fascism, now it would be enlisted in the struggle against communism." America emerged from World War II with an exaggerated sense of exceptionalism, for which baseball was called into service. Purportedly the sport was why we defeated Germany and Japan; now baseball would be a justified form of cultural imperialism that defined America's difference from communism and the Soviet Union.[68]

But Don DeLillo wasn't so sure. He was concerned about how U.S. mass culture—including sports such as baseball—might distort America's understanding of the world. In *Underworld*, he juxtaposed the jubilant crowd with nuclear annihilation. An intoxicated fan storms the field and in slow motion giddily circles the bases. As Duvall notes, "The drunk is frozen in the last moment of euphoria over America's long-ball power, our exclusive possession of the big blast." David Holmberg has suggested, "DeLillo subverts the modern conception of baseball as a hopeful, redemptive symbol. The postmodern collapse of culture [brought on by the nuclear age] *is* baseball . . . [and] the [Thomson] ball commemorates the failure of [the sport], and all the dreams with which it is inexorably fused."[69]

America wasn't alone in injecting baseball with meaning. After World War II, the Soviet press deemed it a "bad imperialist game." But if the sport had been introduced as a peacemaker to the USSR through a series of annual Russian-American games—as South Dakota Congressman Karl Mundt had proposed—could Cold War relations have been positively affected? Instead, a less friendly approach was promoted, as suggested by Dan Parker in the *New York Mirror*: "If more ambassadors used sports, the world would be much better off, and to test the theory, I'd like to see the new envoy to Moscow introduce himself by fetching Uncle Joe Stalin a resounding whack on the noggin with one of Joe DiMaggio's castoff bats."[70]

Unfazed, the Soviets struck back. In September 1952, the Russian magazine *Smena* [*Change*], under the title "Beizbol," explained that American baseball (with teams like the "Tigers" and the "Pirates") was a "beastly battle, a bloody fight with mayhem and murder" and ultimately a tragic Yankee perversion of the ancient Russian village sport of *laptá*. Embellishing its earlier claims in 1925 that Russians had invented baseball, *Smena* observed that rich capitalists ingrained the now-distorted sport into impressionable young boys and that despite high team profits, the players "are slaves . . . bought and sold like sheep and then, when they are worn out and usually crippled [by] injuries, they are thrown out to join the army of American unemployed or die of starvation."[71] While an exaggeration, this cut rather close to the bone of reality for American ballplayers under MLB's reserve clause, which—remarkably—became yet another contested issue of Cold War politics.

By the early 1950s, despite its World War II triumph, the United States had already lost confidence in itself. The mood was defensive, the Cold War was intensified, and the House Un-American Activities Committee was hunting for scapegoats. Ohio Senator John Bricker "sought to enlist baseball in the Cold War, maintaining that [it] was essential to the American way of life." Commissioner Happy Chandler signaled his willingness to comply, in what remained of his reign. Bricker enthused, "While the marching hordes in China are spreading communism, officials of the national pastime are helping democracy work." He saw baseball as "indoctrinating American youth and combating the alien influence of communist ideology."[72]

Cold War Culture and the American Way

As cultural indoctrination, baseball played a varied role. The sport appeared routinely in American films, television, and novels in the early Cold War years and in later depictions of that period. As Ron Briley has observed, Hollywood responded to insecurities about the Soviet Union, and a reassuring baseball theme was common. In *Strategic Air Command*, Jimmy Stewart played the St. Louis Cardinals star third baseman. A former flyer, Stewart was called back into the Air Force to work with the Strategic Air Command (SAC). In real life, SAC was headed by Curtis LeMay who, despite the SAC motto, "Peace Is Our Profession," always endorsed aggressive military action, advocating a nuclear first strike against Russia during the Cuban Missile Crisis and then the use of nuclear weapons to "bomb the Vietnamese back into the Stone Age." Both on and off screen, it was presumed that only a strong, aggressive military could keep the peace. In the film, the SAC team worked effectively because it had the "discipline of a baseball team." Other baseball metaphors fostered patriotism and sacrifice, such as when the crew kept "them in there pitching."

Conjuring up the real-life experience of Ted Williams, Stewart's character sacrificed his baseball career and piloted his B-36 while wearing his Cardinals cap. When Stewart was transferred to the new B-47 bomber, he was told the plane was "on third base, waiting for you to bring it home." In the movie, MLB does without Stewart, suggesting that it was doing its part to guarantee the nation's security—never placing profit above the national interest. In real life, as Briley notes, organized baseball exaggerated its contribution to the Korean conflict. *Strategic Air Command* tried to resurrect the victory culture of World War II with strong, authoritarian male figures embracing militarism and patriarchal values, and it put baseball in just the light the major leagues sought.[73]

Similarly, many 1950s science-fiction movies were only thinly disguised anticommunist propaganda films, in which godless, tyrannical "aliens" had to be stopped from threatening America. On television, one of the most popular programs was *Father Knows Best*, which promoted family hierarchy and helped rationalize women's postwar return from the workplace to the household. The program's cast was recruited by the U.S. Treasury Department to produce one of its many propaganda movies. The film, *Twenty Four Hours in Tyrantland*, showed what would happen under Soviet rule. As a prime illustration, the son Bud was blocked from joining his friends in a baseball game. His equipment was confiscated, and he was told there was no time for frivolous pursuits. Communism would mean the end of baseball![74]

Looking back, Philip Roth lampooned the era's anticommunist hysteria. In *The Great American Novel*, he explored the communist infiltration of

America—revealed most dramatically in baseball, of all places. In Roth's plot, unbeknownst to the subsequent generation, a third major league, the Patriot League, had existed until the postwar Red Scare. One of its teams, the Rupert Mundys, was forced to become an all-road team when its ballpark was commandeered for the war effort. By 1946, besides their presumed infiltration of the State Department and the War Department (as Senator Joseph McCarthy so vigorously insisted), communists had—through the Mundys—insinuated themselves into the very heart of American life: they were running the Patriot League and trying to destroy "America's religion—baseball." According to one of Roth's characters, "when baseball goes . . . you can kiss America goodbye." The Patriot League president testified before HUAC to try to save it, but he failed. As a result, the "greatest cover-up in U.S. history" was then perpetrated: the Patriot League was not only dismantled but expunged from history. The narrator, an aging sportswriter who knows the secret, can't get America to face the truth. While humorous today, baseball's role as a bulwark against communism was no laughing matter in the Cold War's darkest days.[75]

Russell Crawford has argued that "sports became the primary vehicle for reifying the Cold War and villainizing the Soviet Union." They were used explicitly by the Eisenhower and Kennedy administrations as Cold War tools. Sports were integral to "the American way," a phrase first devised for the 1920s consumer culture, which assumed a new ideological weight in the early 1950s. The American way embodied fundamental values of U.S. life, and as Benjamin Rader put it, "attained such a broad consensus that dissenting views were driven out of the mainstream, which sought to homogenize American culture." In 1956, a Sports in Art exhibit began an international tour, but before leaving the country, anticommunist protesters appeared at its Dallas showing, demanding the removal of four pieces, including a Ben Shahn baseball drawing, *National Pastime*. These efforts by the Communism in Art Committee of the Dallas Patriotic Society were resisted, but the exhibit was nevertheless kept out of the 1956 Olympics in Australia.[76]

The *Saturday Evening Post*, the period's most influential magazine, viewed baseball as a unifying force in American society. Its frequent baseball and national security stories, covers, and commentaries constantly posed the question: "What would October [the World Series] be like under Soviet domination?" While capitalism and the future of the American way were intensely scrutinized during the depression years, by the 1950s, such questioning was "playing into Soviet hands." For the first time, the word "God" was inserted into the Pledge of Allegiance, as religion was also enlisted in the anti-Soviet campaign.[77] Speaking about the U.S. Armed Forces, the Reverend William Cousins proclaimed, "We are not a military nation, but the spirit of those serving our country's cause [is] a secret weapon. You can't beat men who . . . believe the game isn't over till the last out . . . [or] discourage men who keep swinging for the fence even after two strikes . . . [or] frighten men who will never quit until God Himself pulls them out of the lineup."

Little League Baseball also emerged as a potent symbol of the American way, promoting sport, religion, and patriotism. The organization spread rapidly during the Red Scare years, and its values attracted prominent Cold Warriors. In 1948, the U.S. Rubber Company began sponsoring Little League, injecting the organization with corporate values. In a 1950 letter to its management, FBI director J. Edgar Hoover wrote, "Little League Baseball is providing a splendid way for young people to . . . bolster Americanism." The Little League newsletter, long produced by Army Colonel W.H. "Cappy" Wells, "mixed League news with advice on current social ills and patriotic prose reflecting the era of the red scare." The February 1951 newsletter congratulated "the individuals who launched the [Little League] movement [for] . . . the promotion of Americanism." According to the 1954 Little League World Series Official Program, "The young Americans who compose the Little League will provide a hitless target for the peddlers of godless ideology."[78] Soon thereafter, the organization adopted the Little League Pledge, which asked (as it still does today) young ballplayers to recite verses, half of which have a questionable connection to baseball but an obvious link to other objectives:

> I trust in God
> I love my country
> And will respect its laws

As Michael Carriere has written, "On the Little League field, the ideals of consensus, equality, and fairness were displayed for all the world to see." Youth baseball became a "symbol that many used not only to further" corporate liberalism at home, "but also as a valuable tool in the Cold War struggle against Communism." U.S. and foreign political and military leaders, as well as Little League officials and even parents, began to see Little League's promotional potential. As United Nations president Carlos Romulo once noted, Little League was a "sort of UN in miniature, advancing the cause of democracy in greater freedom." While the first Little League outside the United States was created in Canada in 1951, the organization was also viewed as capable of "bringing democracy to postwar Europe and Asia by introducing youngsters to distinctly American values." With support from the U.S. State Department and Armed Forces, Little Leagues were established in many other nations, specifically to "battle the Red Menace." An army officer who helped bring Little League to

Italy claimed it would "instill good American principles in the [Italian] boys at an early age."

In the Pacific, the U.S. Army Signal Corps translated a popular Little League promotional from English into Japanese and distributed it throughout Japan as part of Douglas MacArthur's plan to Westernize Japanese culture. When Little League reached South Korea in 1951, U.S. Captain Richard Hutchins explained that "we've introduced the game to teach the American way of life and help cement American–Korean relations." For many Cold Warriors, Little League targeted those most susceptible to Communist rhetoric, the impressionable young, and countered the anti–Western discourse spread by Communist agents.[79]

In 1955, George W. Bush began his first of four years playing Little League in Texas, and would become the first graduate ever elected president of the United States. By this time, Little League was already huge and having a significant influence. There were over 3,300 leagues, not only in the United States, but also in many nations abroad. Many other countries would also be targeted, as Little League accompanied American foreign policy for decades to come.[80]

9

Revolution and Quagmire
(1953–1975)

We were Reds before they were.

—Bill DeWitt

While baseball loomed large in postwar culture, major league baseball (MLB) sought a particular niche. But who would lead the sport through the Cold War? When MLB failed to replace Happy Chandler with a military man, it settled on National League president Ford Frick as its new commissioner. In Frick, the owners got a man who knew baseball but who wasn't the kind of professional soldier they'd wanted. But if baseball didn't get what it wanted from the military, the armed forces did get what they needed from Frick and the major leagues. Before entering baseball, Frick developed some early ties while working in the War Department rehabilitation division. During World War II, Frick smoothed relations between baseball and the War and State departments, warding off concerns about special wartime treatment. Frick's warm relationship with the military persisted throughout his time as commissioner.[1]

The United Nations of Baseball

During the 1950s, as Ron Briley has noted, "Frick proclaimed that organized baseball would support the ideological Cold War as well as the shooting war in Korea." He said the national pastime would indoctrinate youth about democracy and "remain a proud part of our ideal way of life." Such patriotic rhetoric helped make baseball central to the American national consensus. Frick supposed that "if Russia had a sports program like the Americans, there would be no danger of Communism." America was safe, he argued, as long as boys went to bed with catcher's mitts under their pillows. While this was fine-sounding oratory, some considered it merely platitudes designed to ingratiate MLB to ensure continued club profits.[2]

Frick's major leagues created an environment in which red-baiting might be used to attack an opposing player. San Francisco Giants manager Alvin Dark claimed, "Any pitcher who throws at a batter and tries to hit him is a communist." Sometimes baseball was proposed as a weapon against the Soviet threat, as when White Sox general manager Frank Lane suggested, "All you have to do is sit [Soviet foreign minister] Molotov down between [Brooklyn Dodgers general manager] Branch Rickey and [New York Yankees manager] Casey Stengel, and in four years Russia will have nothing left but Siberia and a couple of left-handed pitchers." The advent of a new Red Scare during Frick's reign created some name problems. The Decatur Commies team in the Three-I League took some heat for their name, although it was actually short for Commodores. Likewise, the Cincinnati Reds owners were concerned that their club's nickname would link them to the dreaded Red Menace. So the uniforms were altered and the team name was changed in the mid-1950s from Reds to the Redlegs. The name wasn't switched back to the Reds until the 1960s, when Cincinnati general manager Bill DeWitt explained, "We were Reds before they were."[3]

A major anticommunist ally of Frick's was Branch Rickey, who wasn't the first to call baseball "the moral equivalent of war," but he took it much further: he turned his Brooklyn Dodgers into baseball's fiercest bastion of anti-radicalism. As historian Carl Prince observed, unlike the Cincinnati Reds, "the Dodgers didn't change names, but the team's commitment to conservative American values was impressively complete. Anticommunism permeated the Dodger locker room as well as the front office." Rickey's "personal brand of red-baiting" pushed Jackie Robinson into testifying against Paul Robeson. While Robinson later realized he had been manipulated into being the "good, anti-communist Negro," at the time he played along, saying, "Can you sit down in Russia and say the head man is a louse? [No], not unless you want to play center field in the Siberian League." Rickey led his team in a relentless patriotic campaign, believing that the schools and Christianity must "mark an end to subversion, secret cells, and false isms." He had Happy Felton, host of the Dodgers *Knothole Gang* children's television show, lead the Alert America Convoy, part of a New York parade dedicated to establishing civil defense requirements for bomb shelters.

Rickey welcomed servicemen to Ebbets Field with great fanfare, repeatedly hosting military organizations, such as the American Legion, the Veterans of Foreign Wars, the Disabled American Veterans, and Catholic and Jewish veterans groups. Upon his return to the United States, Rickey immediately snared Douglas MacArthur "as a continuing symbol at Ebbets Field of the Dodgers' commitment to patriotic values," and was the general's biggest advocate for the baseball commissionership. Rickey also "played hardball in defense of the sacred reserve clause," condemning the "avowed communist tendencies" of the players union. The same atmosphere continued when Walter O'Malley gained control of the Dodgers in the early 1950s. Vice president and anticommunist crusader Richard Nixon was made a kind of team mascot and given regular access to the Dodger locker room. According to Prince, the Dodgers were "a remarkable reflection of the conservative politics of the time."[4]

In his autobiography, Frick gave an example of "baseball's real value" in world affairs: In 1958 Vice President Nixon traveled to Venezuela, where his limo was pelted with stones by an angry mob. Shortly thereafter, the U.S. State Department asked Frick to organize major leaguers for a Venezuelan tour to teach youngsters baseball. A clinic was held at the very spot where Nixon had been attacked. While the players worried about the reaction, instead a huge crowd of kids and parents gave the American ballplayers a rousing welcome. The group toured the country for two weeks without incident, and the Venezuelan president expressed his personal thanks. Former U.S. ambassador to Venezuela Walter Donnelly claimed the "tour did more to clear the atmosphere than a dozen top-echelon conferences." From this, Frick concluded, "Maybe Mr. Rickey was right. Maybe baseball can help solve the problems that harass the world today."[5]

In telling this story, Frick said, "Our relations with Venezuela were not good at the time," but he forgot to mention why, or even baseball's own role in the ill will. Nixon was attacked because the United States had been supporting Latin American dictatorships and cutthroat foreign and economic policies that had impoverished Venezuelans and their neighbors. The protesters opposed U.S. intervention and their puppet government's anticommunist crusades launched against local groups trying to improve the lives of the people. While baseball wasn't necessarily blamed by the activists, it was implicated. Ambassador Donnelly had organized a Chico Carrasquel Day, on which preaching anticommunism seemed more important than celebrating the noted Venezuelan major leaguer. U.S. press attaché Frederick Kuhn chased protesters away from the American embassy with a baseball bat.

By 1953, sportswriter Fred Lieb noted the growing "United Nations of baseball," and lauded the game's diverse national backgrounds. Increasing numbers of foreign-born players entered the major leagues as the decade unfolded, sometimes the first ever signed from their respective nations. Besides taking American blacks, teams were signing players like Ozzie Virgil, who became the first Dominican major leaguer when he joined the New York Giants in 1953. While seemingly a positive development, racism still plagued the process at home and interventionism tainted these developments abroad.

Baseball's international initiatives were not always well received. With the U.S. State Department's help, former major leaguer Lou Brissie led an American Legion all-star team to Latin America, where it played in seven countries. And as a goodwill gesture to nations where the White House was unpopular, Richard Nixon proposed a true World Series, saying the major leagues should add teams in Havana and Mexico City. Pointing to the Pittsburgh Pirates' visit to Mexico, Nixon encouraged other teams to tour South America, which would "contribute to international understanding and make the State Department's job easier."[6] Instead, such initiatives were sometimes viewed as only thinly disguised attempts to extend American influence.

According to Adrian Burgos, "From the perspective of Latin American baseball, Commissioner Frick's tenure resembled a foreign leader pursuing an imperial agenda, [establishing] formal agreements that . . . subsumed Latin American winter leagues under the dictates of organized baseball." The pacts restricted which players from organized baseball could participate in the Latin leagues. This limited their talent pool, and—with MLB in control—adversely affected Latino players who wanted to perform outside their native countries.

Sometimes these incursions were resisted. As Alan Klein has noted, in baseball colonialism there has been a tension between hegemony and opposition: "Whereas there is little resistance elsewhere in the cultural interaction with North Americans, Dominicans have used baseball to express their resentment." Thus in 1955, when MLB converted the Dominican professional league into a winter league so that U.S. players could use it in the off-season, Dominicans protested. While they couldn't wrest back control, Dominicans instead asserted themselves through their talents, developing a distinctive Dominican style and learning to play as well as the Americans. Some Dominicans also used baseball to react to U.S. economic domination, attempting to "find opportunity in a sea of inopportunity created by American policies."[7] Soon this resistance bubbled over into the nation's own politics, finally toppling the U.S.-backed Trujillo dictatorship.

But not before the dictator ordered one emerging Dominican star, Juan Marichal, to join Trujillo's hand-picked Dominican Air Force team in 1957. The so-called Dominican Dandy and future Hall of Famer had been playing for the Grenada team. Its sponsor, the United Fruit Company (and other companies like it), was tremendously influential in the Caribbean. Resisting the economic exploitation (low wages and poor conditions) by such U.S. multinationals was central to the Latin opposition. Agribusiness firms also dominated Cuba. In 1946, an aspiring twenty-year-old pitcher named Fidel Castro tried out for the Washington Senators. When he was turned down, he "returned to Cuba to pursue other interests."[8] Revolting against outside corporate dominance was one of them. A Cuban United Fruit Company worker described the resistance: "we couldn't meet in public, so we had to meet during our baseball games." Teams formed by multinationals to control labor agitation instead sometimes promoted it.

Besides the company teams, the Pittsburgh Pirates held their 1953 spring training in Cuba, where they faced the Cuban national team. In 1954, the Havana Sugar Kings were added to the International League, generating a raucous game environment: a "patriotic spirit—yells, songs, explosions of delirious support for the players who defended . . . the national flag as if in full war and it was actual combat between two armies." In 1955, the only year the Brooklyn Dodgers ever won the World Series, future Dodgers manager Tommy Lasorda witnessed just how seriously the Cubans took their baseball. While pitching against the Sugar Kings, he approached the home plate umpire to question a call and was subtly shown a handgun stuck in umpire Orlando Maestri's pants. Lasorda returned to the mound praising Maestri as "the best damn umpire I've ever seen."[9] It wouldn't be Lasorda's last brush with Cuban feistiness.

Elsewhere in Latin America, two Puerto Rican nationalists had tried to assassinate President Truman in 1950, the year the Puerto Rican Winter League became a new launch pad for U.S. major leaguers. In 1954, another Puerto Rican nationalist attack was made on the U.S. House of Representatives. But other Puerto Ricans turned their nationalism toward baseball, entering their own teams (rather than being subsumed within U.S. clubs) at the Caribbean Championships and the Pan American Games. In the face of often harsh racism, Puerto Ricans like Roberto Clemente and Orlando Cepeda began entering MLB. In Nicaragua, the U.S.-backed Somoza dictatorship was still using baseball as a distraction from harsh conditions, and in 1954 it provided a training base for the CIA invasion of neighboring Guatemala, toppling its democratically elected government. After his father's assassination in 1956, the new dictator, Luis Somoza, established the Nicaraguan Professional League, which became another major-league resource for winter baseball.[10]

In Asia, the NBC Fort Wayne–Japanese series during the Korean War launched a string of Japan tours, often involving major leaguers, every year from 1951 to 1958. A 1955 film, *Three Stripes in the Sun*, depicted the U.S. and Japan as trusted allies, with stereotypical cultural differences: aggressive Americans matched against polite Japanese. In 1958, the St. Louis Cardinals toured Japan, whose prime minister Nobusuke Kishi said it had promoted "the good will of the people of Japan for the U.S. Only through baseball could we have this kind of understanding." In Australia, the Baseball Council reported over seven hundred teams and ten thousand players by 1953. More than 110,000 fans in Melbourne watched the Australian team play a U.S. military club in

1956. And in 1959, thirty teams competed in the New China Baseball Tournament, before baseball was disbanded in the Great Leap Forward. In the United States, with anticommunist sentiments raging, the *Sporting News* ran a cover cartoon portraying a gigantic Chinese coolie character hanging over a ballpark fence. It was a commentary on the short left field wall at the Los Angeles Coliseum, where the Dodgers played until the Chavez Ravine ballpark was completed. The cheap home run in the cartoon was called a "Chinese homer," and the left field fence was the "Chinese wall."[11]

But what were the Dodgers doing in Los Angeles? As Steven Bullock has observed, during the 1950s, "football had begun to erode baseball's preeminent position." While baseball was expanding abroad, it was having some problems at home. One symptom was the collapse of service baseball. In 1957, when the All-Army Baseball Championship was discontinued, high-level military baseball was over. Others felt the sport had become too subdued, and no longer what Leo Durocher called a form of warfare. Robert Daley lamented, "Baseball has fallen behind. The pitcher-batter conflict is, in this age of hydrogen bombs and probes to the moon, no longer gripping enough. The game is too tame. We long to be absorbed by the spectacle . . . fans seem to thrill to 260-pound [football players] crashing into each other."[12]

Of course, MLB wasn't about to give up. According to Neil Sullivan, it "set off a wave of expansionism akin to the European imperialist scramble for African colonies in the late nineteenth century." The Brooklyn Dodgers moved to Los Angeles, and the New York Giants moved to San Francisco. In retrospect, the major-league shift west didn't bring unqualified progress. And baseball's conquest—its expansion in search of lucrative new markets—left a legacy that has "encouraged baseball management to seek a safety net in frontier expansion and avoid dealing with its problems."[13] Even so, it was on the move.

The Cuban Revolution

With the big leagues expanding by the early 1960s, some wondered whether the talent supply would keep up. Beyond homegrown U.S. players, Cubans had been the primary foreign-born players, and Dominicans were fast emerging. Yet Cold War politics challenged both of these sources. While organizing his rebel forces in Cuba's Sierra Madre mountains, Fidel Castro listened to Buck Canel's Spanish-language radio broadcasts of the 1958 World Series. On January 1, 1959, Castro's revolution reached Havana and overthrew U.S.-backed Cuban dictator Fulgencio Batista. Days later, Canel interviewed Castro, who wanted to know "why [Milwaukee Braves manager Fred] Haney pitched [Warren] Spahn instead of [Lou] Burdette in the sixth game [of the

World Series]." While Castro's baseball prospects have been exaggerated (including purported Yankees and Giants tryouts), he was nevertheless a serious baseball aficionado who ended up using the game in his many battles with the United States.[14]

Looking back, U.S. Senator Eugene McCarthy observed, "Among the early finds by Senators scouts [in Cuba was a] prospect named Fidel Castro. He was turned down because . . . he didn't have a major league fast ball. An aspiring pitching ace spurned can be a dangerous man with a long memory." So true, although it was hardly inevitable he would become America's nemesis. Castro-the-enemy was as much a U.S. creation as anything else, as the Cuban leader—whose hero was Thomas Jefferson—was pushed into the arms of the Soviets. McCarthy felt the U.S. was foolish not to recognize the "potential of baseball to transcend ideological barriers, trade conflicts, racial and national differences."[15]

The Cuban Revolution was celebrated at the first game played at the Gran Stadium after Castro's 1959 triumph. Joining the party, with a big cigar in his mouth and a rifle in his hand, was that great American patriot Tommy Lasorda, the future Dodgers manager, who was playing for the Almendares team at the time. The rebel soldiers attended the game for free and received a stirring ovation by the crowd and the players. Castro formed a barnstorming team, Los Barbudos (the Bearded Ones), which toured the country to help solidify the revolt. Prior to a scheduled International League game in Havana, Los Barbudos played a Cuban military police team. Castro pitched and had two strikeouts in two innings.[16] The next day was the anniversary of the 26th of July Movement, named after Castro's abortive revolution in 1953. During some rowdy revelry, at the anniversary-day game between the Rochester Red Wings and the Havana Sugar Kings, Rochester coach Frank Verdi and Havana shortstop Leo Cardenas were slightly grazed by gunshots. The teams were pulled off the field, although Cuban authorities claimed the fireworks were no different than typical U.S. Fourth of July celebrations.

When the Sugar Kings began having money problems in 1959, rather than turning on baseball and shunning the team as a "capitalist tool," Castro provided financial backing. The Sugar Kings won the International League pennant, then faced the American Association winners, the Minneapolis Millers, in the 1959 Junior World Series. Before the games in Havana, Castro proclaimed, "After the triumph of the revolution, we should also win the Little World Series." Future major-league manager Gene Mauch claimed the soldiers intimidated the players: after a Miller player made a catch, "a soldier made a slicing motion across his throat." Before the last game, Castro strolled by the Millers bullpen, patted a large revolver at his hip and said, "Tonight, we win."[17] While these stories might be apocryphal, the Sugar Kings did win.

But the triumph was short-lived. In July 1960, the Sugar Kings were yanked from Cuba and the International League without notice and relocated to New Jersey. Commissioner Frick blamed security concerns and then banned U.S.-born ballplayers from playing in the Cuban winter league. The *Sporting News* supported this "emergency action" as the "only reasonable" response yet provided no evidence of any threat.[18] The driving force behind these decisions was pressure put on Frick by Secretary of State Christian Herter. While Castro had demonstrated, as far as Cuba was concerned, that baseball could transcend ideology, the United States wouldn't let it. The Cuban revolution couldn't be tolerated, and Cuban baseball would become a Cold War victim. In his book *Baseball and the Cold War*, Howard Senzel chastised MLB and the United States for its persistent anticommunist paranoia—shunning repeated opportunities for baseball détente.[19] But while organized baseball realized it would lose Cuban talent, it knew it could compensate for it elsewhere in the Caribbean, and keeping in the U.S. government's good graces seemed more important.

Sugar Kings owner Bobby Maduro protested his team's elimination but to no avail. Castro denounced the move as aggression against the Cuban people. It helped radicalize him, and in the face of increasing American hostility, pushed Castro toward protective alliances elsewhere. In 1960, the year Bill Mazeroski's dramatic home run won the World Series for the Pittsburgh Pirates, Castro began nationalizing U.S. businesses, blaming them for his nation's poverty and exploitation. Writing in the *Sporting News*, Dan Daniel advised, "International baseball in Havana is an island of freedom in a sea of communism, Soviet affiliated and Castro terror. . . . Commissioner Frick should bar all players, even natives of Cuba, from competing in the Cuban [winter] League." That's just what Frick did.[20]

In 1961, with tensions escalating, Cuba asked the U.S. government to reduce its bloated embassy staff. Intending to overthrow the revolution and resume control, the United States refused. When Cuba insisted, Washington broke off diplomatic relations, forbidding American travel to the island. Later that year, the U.S. backed the Bay of Pigs invasion, launched by right-wing Cuban exiles. It failed badly but provoked the stationing of Soviet missiles to shore up Cuban defenses. Castro escalated the nationalization of U.S. companies, including IT&T and the United Fruit Company. The United States then imposed an embargo on Cuba in 1962, prohibiting all economic activity between the two nations.

Castro decided to take the fight, at least in part, to baseball. He called professional baseball *la pelota esclava* (slave baseball)—the exploitation of man by man, where athletes were sold or traded like simple merchandise. So Castro converted the Cuban League from a professional to an amateur league. The Cuban baseball star Martin Dihigo—the only player in the baseball halls of fame in the United States, Cuba, and Mexico—had been exiled by the Batista dictatorship. Dihigo used his baseball earnings abroad to help support Che Guevara and the revolution, and when he returned home, he became Minister of Sport in charge of Cuba's new concept of athletics.[21]

As Castro put it, "imperialists have tried to humiliate Latin American countries, to instill an inferiority complex; [and] to present themselves as superior . . . [often] using sport for that purpose." Unable to compete with the United States economically or militarily, Cuba turned sports into a political tool. Determined to beat America at its own game, Cuba put baseball at the service of the revolution. By 1962, Cuba was making its own baseball equipment under the Batos label—a name taken from the bat-and-ball game played by Cuba's Taino Indians before the Spanish arrived. Then in 1963, Cuba began demonstrating its baseball prowess, with one regional and international championship after another in the ensuing decades.[22]

Professional baseball in Cuba was undermined as much by U.S. foreign policy as by Castro, with organized baseball's complicity. With restrictive American laws and rising U.S.–Cuban tensions, Cubans who were already playing American ball worried whether they'd be able to reenter the U.S. if they spent the winter at home, and thus some considered playing in other Latin American winter leagues. In response, Commissioner Frick prohibited foreign players from playing outside their native country during the off-season. Cuban professional baseball was made nearly impossible. For this, Cuba usually receives the blame, but as Peter Bjarkman has asked, "Is Fidel Castro . . . a contemptible baseball villain (responsible for [subverting] the island's pro leagues) or a certified baseball hero (and the architect of a nobler flag-waving rather than dollar-waving version of the sport?)"[23]

After the postrevolutionary cutoff of Cuban players, MLB shifted its focus to the Dominican Republic. Since he had outlived his usefulness, the CIA had the dictator Rafael Trujillo assassinated in 1961. Pittsburgh Pirates scout Howie Haak observed, "You'd never sign anyone who Trujillo wanted playing for *his* team. It wasn't until [the CIA] got rid of him that the doors were opened." In its efforts to seduce Dominicans, the U.S. Information Agency launched neighborhood youth baseball leagues, securing baseball equipment donations from local U.S. corporations. But in 1965, trouble brewed again when the Dominicans rejected the U.S.-supported right-wing presidential candidate in favor of the social democrat Juan Bosch. The U.S. Marines landed to protect American sugar and other interests, toppling Bosch and leaving a puppet government behind. The turmoil canceled the Dominican Winter

League season, but baseball limped on, and the island became a growing reservoir of major-league talent.[24]

The Vietnam Quagmire

The U.S. embargo of Cuba and the Bay of Pigs invasion, as well as the 1961 Berlin Crisis, all escalated America's Cold War with the Soviet Union, but the 1962 Cuban Missile Crisis threatened the outbreak of real war. A nuclear confrontation was avoided, but the ideological battle raged on. On the "soft" side of U.S. diplomacy, the Peace Corps was created, to assist poor nations but also to spread the doctrines of Americanism. Director Sargent Shriver promised that the corps would "be operated like a baseball team, with the manager empowered to yank a player before he ruins the game." The Corps also exported baseball to help promote the American way, which also motivated the U.S. State Department's plan for a Cleveland Indians baseball tour of the Soviet Union.[25] On the "hard" side of American diplomacy, the U.S. advocated sports to promote "physical fitness and impart 'combative' values to individual citizens." It pursued a "cult of toughness [and a] highly social Darwinist, survival-of-the-fittest competition with possible international rivals."[26] Aggressive games and sports became central to Cold War culture.

In 1962, when President Kennedy stood up the Laotian ambassador so he could attend the Washington Senators' opening day, he seemed buoyant. Yet according to George Rable, "appearances deceived. The president [had] little time for following a leisurely sport that seemed quaintly out of place in the nuclear age." Suggesting the higher value of other sports, Senator Robert Kennedy noted in 1964, "Part of a nation's prestige in the Cold War is won in the Olympic Games." Resuscitating Teddy Roosevelt's quest for the "strenuous life," a vigorous physical culture was emphasized.[27] Football best fit this combative mode and the nation's increasing escalation of the Vietnam War. President Johnson ended his perfunctory visits to Washington's Griffith Stadium, signaling baseball's declining grip on officials and on Americans generally.

To respond to its latest challenges, MLB was again looking for change by the mid-1960s. As Ron Briley has suggested, while some baseball officials used Cold War rhetoric to shore up their profits, "to many other Americans baseball remained a symbol of traditional values in a confusing world." To better tap this sentiment and to toughen its exterior, baseball again sought military leadership. General Curtis LeMay, the bellicose Strategic Air Command director who wanted to nuke Vietnam, was again a top candidate. So were retired Air Force general William Eckert and former secretary of the air force General Eugene Zuckert. Richard Nixon was also nominated for the post.

In the end, the owners selected General "Spike" Eckert, whom the press quickly dubbed the unknown soldier since he was unheard of, a poor leader, and knew essentially nothing about baseball. But if baseball was lagging as the national pastime, then the military connection might provide a patriotic boost. Interviewed by sportswriter Dick Young, Eckert outlined some baseball-military ties:

> In baseball you've got the clubs. In the Air Force you've got the wings and squadrons . . . they're [both] highly mobile and their personnel change a lot . . . it's highly competitive . . . one Air Force squadron against another in gunnery perfection, bombing . . . in Vietnam you want excellence [in] fighting units . . . and it is measured statistically, like batting averages, and you get awards, just like in baseball, for the best squadron, the best fighter pilots. . . . In baseball, there are many rules to be made, to be changed, to be interpreted; in the military, you also have many regulations. Then there is the matter in the military of opening and closing bases. In baseball, you may have franchises moved from one place to another, new franchises in some cities.

Young asked, "Do you [think] baseball expects your Washington connections to help [pass] bills through Congress?" Eckert responded, "No one has suggested that it would." But this was not what the owners thought or expected.[28]

Eckert joined MLB in 1965. Using false reports of an unprovoked attack on U.S. ships, President Lyndon Johnson had just secured the Gulf of Tonkin Resolution, a blank check to vastly intensify America's involvement in the Vietnam War. The new commissioner immediately moved baseball closer to the war. The *Sporting News* urged MLB to reassert itself amid the growing protests against the war and "reaffirm the game's support for traditional values such as patriotism." In turn, organized baseball donated *Sporting News* subscriptions for a hundred thousand servicemen, and Eckert urged ballplayers to volunteer for military service.[29]

Flogging the theme "Where soldiers and veterans are, baseball will be," the American League premiered its 1966 official film at Walter Reed Medical Center for an audience of soldiers wounded in Vietnam. That same year, the commissioner was honored by General William Westmoreland, commander of U.S. forces in Vietnam, for the tour he arranged to war zones featuring major leaguers Harmon Killebrew, Brooks Robinson, Joe Torre, Hank Aaron, and Stan Musial. In 1967, Eckert received an Air Force meritorious award for sending baseball players—including Ernie Banks, Pete Rose, Tony Conigliaro, and Joe DiMaggio—to entertain the troops and raise their morale. As the Tet Offensive fighting raged in Vietnam, Eckert and American League triple-crown winner Carl Yastrzemski visited the White House, where the beleaguered President Johnson commended the commissioner for supporting the war.

Baseball's relationship with Congress wasn't as cordial. While MLB beat back threats to rescind its antitrust exemption, it was under scrutiny for its draft policies. George W. Bush wasn't the only one who avoided Vietnam War service by securing a National Guard position; organized baseball was also accused of protecting its players that way. Michigan Congressman Lucien Nedzi observed that "people are complaining about the fairness of the draft . . . [having] athletes getting preferred treatment undermines public confidence in the system." A 1967 Defense Department report found that 360 athletes were serving in draft-exempt units, 311 of whom had joined after turning professional. As the body bags returning from Vietnam piled up, the number of deferred ballplayers was embarrassing for MLB and the Pentagon.[30]

Baseball officials denied any interference with local draft boards, yet the evidence suggested otherwise. For example, Detroit Tigers prospect George Gmelch was allowed to use his team's executive offices to complete correspondence courses to maintain his college draft deferment. Late one night, he stumbled on a room where "the names of all 125-odd players in the Tigers organization were posted. Each had a star by his name, color coded by draft status." Management was carefully monitoring each player's eligibility. Soon thereafter, while playing in the Florida State League, Gmelch and two teammates were called for military physicals. One, a fringe player, passed, but Gmelch and the other player failed for no apparent reason.

To avoid favoritism, Defense Secretary Robert McNamara ordered all reserve and guard vacancies filled on a "first-come, first-served basis," but most ballplayers got them when they wanted them, anyway. Organized baseball sought to protect its investments, and its close military-government relationship didn't hurt. According to the *Sporting News*, baseball clubs were as patriotic as any other business or sport, and they had the canceled checks to prove it. For expenses such as transportation costs and paying salaries in absentia, MLB claimed the military reserve program was costing it $1,300,000 per year.[31]

Of course, some ballplayers were actually drafted, including at least fifty major leaguers. Among the more recognizable were Bobby Murcer, Jerry Koosman, and Thurman Munson. But most others were not top players or prospects, and few had their careers seriously interrupted. Only a handful actually went to Vietnam, including Garry Maddox and Al Bumbry—who won a Bronze Star. No major leaguers were killed in the war, although a dozen minor leaguers died. Some players were severely injured. The most tragic case was Roy Gleason. A top Dodgers prospect, he got bad advice and was drafted.

The Dodgers never communicated with him while he was on the Vietnam front lines, where he was wounded and received the Purple Heart. Struggling to recover, his 1969 comeback attempt failed. Gleason's abandonment wasn't acknowledged until 1983, when he was finally recognized at Dodger Stadium in a ceremony he dedicated to all neglected veterans.[32]

While some ballplayers were caught up in the war, most were not. Baseball officials signed on to the Cold War, claiming the sport symbolized American values in contrast to Soviet totalitarianism. Energy and lip service were extended to goodwill tours, hospital visits, and troop morale boosters, but major leaguers didn't flock to the colors. Even the reserves or national guard were often viewed as a troublesome interference, despite having little effect on baseball as usual.[33] Commissioner Eckert made a final gesture when he flew Captain John Q. Williams, a wounded Army Special Forces soldier and Congressional Medal of Honor winner, to Boston's Fenway Park to be his guest for the 1967 World Series. But overall, Eckert showed he couldn't cope: among other things, he was blamed for baseball losing further ground to football and for bungling baseball's reaction to the Robert Kennedy assassination (by not canceling games). Thus, after only three years, MLB was seeking a new commissioner again in 1968.[34]

As with Ford Frick, organized baseball turned to an insider—Bowie Kuhn, the longtime National League attorney. Kuhn was in a college naval officer training program, although he never entered the armed forces. But his aides, National League president Charles Feeney and American League president Lee MacPhail, had both served in World War II. The lingering Vietnam War led the list of Kuhn's many challenges. Like his predecessor, he encouraged ballplayer excursions to Southeast Asia. The 1968 delegation was led by Ernie Banks, and in 1969 Kuhn joined other players sent to Vietnam, including Reggie Jackson, Milt Pappas, and Denny McLain. The visits expanded in 1970 when four groups were sent to the war zone. Besides Hall of Famers Bob Feller and Waite Hoyt, the other players included Bud Harrelson, Willie Stargell, and Phil Niekro. As the war began to wind down, so did the baseball tours. Following the 1971 season, two groups were sent to Vietnam, as well as to hospitals in Japan, Guam, and the Philippines. They included Bob Gibson, Graig Nettles, and Bobby Bonds.

Organized baseball was happy to have returning ballplayers talk about their visits. Touring players praised the troops for their courage. Cincinnati's Pete Rose, a reservist who avoided the draft and Vietnam, claimed his group went to dangerous locations ignored by the Bob Hope USO shows. He was impressed with troop morale, observing, "Most of them are boys of nineteen or twenty but, believe me, they're men." Chicago's Ernie Banks also cheered the soldiers, griping, "You see a lot of young people complaining, who hang out in the streets and don't want to work." But in Vietnam, he noted with approval, young men were piloting helicopters and twenty-one-year-old lieutenants were leading men into combat. St. Louis Cardinals executive Al Fleischman claimed the "clean-cut young men" knew "why they were fighting in Vietnam." He didn't mention the reasons, nor did many others associated with baseball seem to understand much about American foreign policy. Most were merely awed. Cleveland's Sam McDowell exclaimed, "Believe me, it was the most gratifying experience of my life. I'll never forget it."[35]

Counterculture Baseball

While the baseball establishment and most ballplayers were united behind the war, not everyone was. Some eventually spoke out. An environment had arisen that challenged baseball from several directions. As a recent Baseball Reliquary retrospective exhibition put it, "The Times They Were A-Changin'." It was "Baseball in the Age of Aquarius." In the late 1960s, baseball encountered not only the war but also declining attendance, the rise of football, and the counterculture's critique of business as usual. According to psychologist Rosalind Cartwright, "Baseball is very much 'establishment'—'as American as baseball' has always been a popular cliché—and as youth become more anti-establishment, they become more anti-baseball."[36]

Of course, organized baseball fought this notion. According to the *Sporting News*, "If you think the hippies and yippies represent young America, you're wrong. For every rabble-rouser on a college campus, there are hundreds of others finding a wholesome outlet in sports." Baseball positioned itself on behalf of other besieged American institutions as a defender of conventional standards. The *Sporting News* viewed America gloomily: "We have dissension over the War in Vietnam, racial discord, college rioting, profiteering, religious irreverence, flagrant pornography, and rampant crime." It acknowledged that the 1969 World Series champion New York Mets had caught "the spirit of a youth rebellion sweeping the world [but] the sports version seems highly preferable to [other] forms of revolt."

The Vietnam War generated greater ambiguity than America's other wars and interventions. According to historian David Zang, a contest developed in the 1960s between "traditional values and a counterculture which questioned whether sport contributed to character building or provided a level playing field." As Zang argued, "For many reasons—its perceived injustice; its overtones of racism and genocide; its charges of corruption, bullying and impotence— the war in Vietnam held loaded meanings for American institutions." Through the Korean War years, the tradition of masculine heroism required combat service. But when it encountered the 1960s, it foundered. While most went along, some athletes began associating organized sports with the killing in Vietnam. They dropped sports or avoided military duty, or both. As Russell Crawford has observed, one's views on athletics became a pretty good predictor of one's stance on the nation's foreign policy. Opponents of sports often had a different vision of the American way.[37]

Ironically, while football absorbed the brunt of the counterculture attack, it also received a boost in the process. While previous military generations used *home base* or *home run* to describe their activities, by the early 1960s, Stanley Kubrick's film *Dr. Strangelove* was portending nuclear destruction using football terms, such as *drop kick, the bomb, field general,* and *the trenches.* In Don DeLillo's novel *End Zone,* a college athlete confronted the urge to dominate, and the violence of football was linked to the nuclear policy of mutually assured destruction. To the counterculture, the mixed language of sport and war reflected American violence at home and abroad. As David Zang noted, to its critics, football represented an imperialistic and bullying society, a "soulless mindset that typified everything from male chauvinism to American manifest destiny." By the 1970s, few supporters could refute claims that American football and aggression in Southeast Asia were linked.[38]

Yet this may have been a reason why, by 1970, professional football had become so popular and why it began to unseat baseball as the national pastime. Some men began to drop out, growing their hair long, piercing their ears, and experimenting sexually. Traditionalists found it "harder and harder to tell the boys from the girls." In response, the Super Bowl, football's national championship, emerged to reassert American masculinity by cheerleading for the war and patriotically backing U.S. policies. According to Warren Farrell, the Super Bowl's early days demonstrated that for men, as in Vince Lombardi's dictum, "winning is the only thing." At the Big Game, fighter jets flew over the field; the national anthem was sung; red, white, and blue blanketed the stadium; and national unity was solidified. And everybody was assured that men, not girls, were down on the field (except at halftime).[39] Sports remained a metaphor for a masculine war against communism—"the athletic ideal meshed with the demands of national defense." But where did that leave baseball?

MLB responded to the war and U.S. foreign policy more cautiously. After the war became controversial, baseball acted halfheartedly. Commissioner Kuhn later claimed that "there was no comprehensive support of the war effort through anything baseball did." Yet others saw it differently. Historian David Voigt found that players who spoke against the war received the "chill of official disapproval" and were deterred from joining peace movements. Players who engaged in small subversive actions were often sanctioned by managers and coaches. According to Ron Briley, while dissent increasingly permeated American culture, organized baseball was "less tolerant of those who questioned authority or military policy. Baseball officials embraced the Vietnam War," although it provided few of its soldiers.[40]

Some ballplayers made special efforts to support the war. Detroit catcher Bill Freehan rescued a team official and army general Samuel Marshall from an antiwar demonstrator—an ex-marine who was trying to block the induction of three hundred men and women into the army before a Tigers ballgame. New York Yankees rookie John Ellis was called upon to confront a Yale University antiwar protest while in the Connecticut National Guard. "Would I fire at demonstrators?" he asked rhetorically. "I would have to find myself in a spot similar to Kent State . . . there are things which must be changed, but I can't imagine bearded, dirty young radicals accomplishing it."[41] The Kent State soldiers had fired at unarmed students, killing four of them.

Beneath the surface of MLB support and its efforts to crack down on dissent, antiwar voices began to break through. When army public relations officials pressured Pittsburgh Pirates pitcher Dock Ellis to go on television with what he called "some bullshit" about Vietnam, he told them he would instead talk about the black market and drugs he saw on his visit. At a rally during spring training, St. Petersburg's mayor lauded the Mets as "a symbol of Americanism in the battle against hippies and demonstrators." In reply, pitcher Tug McGraw flashed the peace sign. Another Met player, Ron Swoboda, felt he had been manipulated by the Nixon administration, which asked him to support the president's reelection after Swoboda had praised the troops. He said that nothing "has changed us as a country more in squandering our living capital and assets . . . and we just decimated the [Vietnamese] culture. I feel a big guilt about that."[42]

Swoboda's teammate, the star pitcher Tom Seaver, was more outspoken during the war. His father and his corporate executive friends, as well as most Mets sponsors, all supported the war. Despite his own marines service, Seaver did not. He dissociated himself from the Vietnam Moratorium Day protesters outside Shea Stadium during the 1969 World Series, but only because they used his name in unauthorized leaflets. Future baseball commissioner Bart Giamatti wrote glowingly about Seaver, comparing him positively to the era's protesters and flower children. But Seaver sympathized with those people far more than Giamatti knew. New York mayor John Lindsay supported the 1969 moratorium and thousands of antiwar marchers. He ordered the flag flown at half-mast at all city properties, but a near-riot ensued at Shea Stadium, including protests by an honor guard of 225 wounded veterans. Commissioner Kuhn intervened and had the flag raised up to full staff.[43] Seaver refused to discuss Vietnam until after the World Series. Later he did comment, "If the Mets can win the World Series, then we can get out of Vietnam," but his promised *New York Times* ad didn't protest but merely asked people to pray for peace. He deflected New Left recruitment attempts, but Seaver's star status and cautious approach allowed him some dissent from the baseball establishment.

In contrast, Jim Bouton, the former Yankees star, went much further. In 1970, Commissioner Kuhn ridiculed Bouton's controversial book *Ball Four* for exposing the real behavior of ballplayers inside and outside the clubhouse. More seriously, Bouton accused organized baseball of hypocrisy, of portraying a squeaky-clean image while ignoring burning social issues. Bouton condemned the Vietnam War and baseball's support for it. He attacked the Reverend Billy Graham for his claim that communists were organizing the antiwar protests, and insisted that flag-waving wasn't real patriotism. Kuhn claimed no players were ostracized for their dissent, yet Bouton was repeatedly heckled at games for his antiwar views by players and fans. "They wanted to know if I was working for Ho Chi Minh." While Bouton's book became a bestseller, he paid dearly in baseball, for he was blacklisted from playing and even excluded from many ballparks.[44]

Other kinds of dissent were also sanctioned. In 1968, guitar legend Jimi Hendrix performed a raucous, psychedelic version of the national anthem, which some regarded as anti-American. That same year, the blind recording star José Feliciano played a Puerto Rican soul version of the "Star Spangled Banner" in Detroit before a World Series game. It also drew hot criticism, charges of subversion, and calls for his arrest for treason. Although the performance was arranged by Hall of Fame Tigers broadcaster Ernie Harwell, one critic fumed, "Anybody who'd let that long-hair hippie ruin our 'Star Spangled Banner' has got to be a Communist." MLB then mandated that teams play only conservative versions of the national anthem. Spokesman John Holland said the Chicago Cubs would comply "due to the situation in Vietnam and the world." According to Russell Crawford, singing the anthem and saluting the flag showed baseball's privileged (although some would say, subservient) place in American life. The ritual cemented "the implicit link between patriotism and sport."

A few ballplayers defended Feliciano's creativity; some challenged the use of the national anthem generally. Ken Smith observed, "For Christ sakes, we're running a business here. Does Macy's play the 'Star Spangled Banner' before opening its doors every day?" Jim Bouton confessed, "The whole anthem-flag ritual makes me uncomfortable . . . I'd usually go into the dugout during the anthem."[45] Then in 1972, Kansas City Royals owner Ewing Kauffman reserved the national anthem at his ballpark for Sundays, holidays, and special occasions. In response to the enormous backlash from the Veterans of Foreign Wars and many others, Kauffman simply said he thought it was disrespectful to play the anthem every day.[46] Among his few defenders was sportswriter Robert Creamer, who remembered when the anthem was special, before baseball turned it into a relentless patriotic gesture. He wrote that "we need less flag waving and more attention to the Constitution."[47] Nevertheless, Kauffman was forced to respond to wartime protests and reinstate the anthem at every game.

Looking back on his early 1970s challenge to baseball's reserve clause, black St. Louis Cardinals outfielder Curt Flood evoked the spirit of the times: "I'm a man of the sixties, [when] this country was coming apart at the seams. We were in Southeast Asia. . . . Good men were dying for America and the Constitution . . . we were marching for civil rights and Dr. King had been assassinated. . . . And to think that merely because I was a professional baseball player, I could ignore what was going on outside the walls of Busch Stadium?"[48] While Flood was protesting against being treated like "a high priced slave," the Vietnam War was being linked to racism as well. Resisting induction, professional boxer Muhammad Ali asked, "What has any Vietnamese ever done wrong to me?" Martin Luther King Jr. worried about minorities being used as the war's cannon fodder.

After his son returned home from Vietnam as a troubled drug addict, Jackie Robinson—who had faithfully supported the government and military establishment—could no longer hold back his own war protest: "American society, whose white rulers spend so much time cautioning black people to be nonviolent, is one of the most violent 'civilizations' on the map, and the rest of the world knows it."[49] In 1972, right before his premature death, Robinson went even further: "There I was the black grandson of a slave, the son of a black sharecropper, part of a historic occasion, a symbolic hero to my people. The band struck up the national anthem. The flag billowed in the wind. It should have been a glorious moment for me. [But] as I look back on that opening game of my first World Series, it was Mr. Rickey's drama and I was only an actor. As I write this twenty years later, I cannot stand and sing the anthem. I cannot salute the flag."[50]

Counterculture protests against the war affected some baseball fans, as well. It was a radicalizing experience, which put the sport in a different light. Howard Senzel reminded us, "In 1970, a young [antiwar] radical named Theodore Gold . . . joined the Weathermen, went underground . . . and was killed in a townhouse explosion. [He felt his] society, institutions and human relationships were so bankrupt, corrupt, and awful that it was worth risking his life to change them. . . . At the same time, Gold was a fanatical follower of the Giants. He read the box scores every morning [and said] he'd have to wait until Willie Mays re-tired before he could become a true revolutionary."[51] Obviously he couldn't wait.

Among the others distanced from baseball was Howard Senzel himself, who wrote, "In the process of forming my grand moral attitudes, baseball got closed out. The functions baseball served in my life were taken over by another drama—politics. Racism, Imperialism, Anti-capitalism, Revolution, Drugs, and Rock and Roll Music replaced baseball as arenas where I could define myself as an insider. Baseball was dying inside me, but I saw it only as an awak-ening into the world of serious things." According to Senzel, "professional baseball's . . . effect was to divert people from their natural inclination to think about their lot. It was an opiate [that] gave people room to tolerate intolerable circumstances."

Government officials felt support for the Vietnam War would continue as long as domestic routines weren't disrupted, including people's ability to keep watching their favorite baseball stars. So Washington asked little from the sport. But with its identity still firmly pro-war, baseball gave anyway. It was a diversion for Americans during troubled times. At the Vietnam Moratorium, sportswriter Robert Lipsyte noted how baseball had remained "strongly re-lated to the military [with] service bands always performing at ball parks and troupes of ballplayers visiting the battle zones." According to David Zang, "though the Vietnam era pushed the nation's reality a few degrees . . . it did not unseat the feeling about what sports ought to provide,"[52] even if baseball did feel challenged—by football—as the best sport to provide it.

Commissioner Bowie Kuhn aligned baseball with President Richard Nixon, who fancied himself as the game's number one fan. During the 1969 All-Star Game, played at Washington's RFK Stadium during professional base-ball's one hundredth anniversary, the commissioner convinced Nixon to open the White House to baseball dignitaries. With this, Kuhn achieved a signifi-cant coup, given football's emerging challenge to baseball. More than four hundred ballplayers were invited, including those named by fans as the "great-est living players." Kuhn lauded Nixon's performance, and the president was awarded a "greatest team member" plaque.

To strengthen baseball's links to the war, Nixon encouraged teams to feature freed prisoners of war to toss out the first pitch at ball games. He enlisted one of them as his surrogate in 1971, and two years later the New York Mets staged a Prisoner of War Day for 133 soldiers and their families. The Merchant Ma-rine Academy band played, military color guards paraded, the world's largest flag was unfurled in center field, and the ballplayers hosted a party for the sol-diers. The California Angels had a POW Day as well, with Nixon as honored guest. Bowie Kuhn announced that Vietnam POWs would get Gold Lifetime passes to all professional baseball games. Embracing the president and his war, MLB sided with patriotic nationalism against growing popular dissent.[53]

President Nixon tried to use his love for baseball to connect with the common man, constantly asking servicemen, for example, which baseball team they supported. Brandishing a baseball cap, he told U.S. embassy employees in Bangkok that "while you can take American boys out of the U.S., you can never take baseball out of an American boy." These feeble gestures and Nixon's history of corruption made him ripe for ridicule. In 1972, Nixon sought reelection to the White House. His unpopular war escalation and his remoteness from the people sparked a campaign to "humanize" the candidate. This began with a question a reporter asked Nixon about his favorite baseball players, which prompted the president to compose his All-Time, All-Star Team. An obvious publicity stunt, the media nevertheless gave Nixon enormous exposure. Through baseball, Nixon came across to the gullible as a regular guy, possibly helping his reelection. Nixon's triumph was short-lived; scandal overtook his administration, forcing him to resign. Commissioner Kuhn distanced himself from the disgraced president. Perhaps sympathizing with Nixon, however, Philadelphia Phillies manager Danny Ozark recognized how easy it was to fall from power, remarking that: "Even Napoleon had his Watergate."[54]

Tragedy, Conflict, and Decline

Largely preoccupied by the Vietnam War, organized baseball nevertheless cast its net elsewhere abroad, as dictated by Cold War politics. Characterizing baseball as a potent American foreign policy tool, Bobby Maduro was appointed Coordinator of Inter-American Baseball. The exiled Cuban pursued a brash new version of America's missionary myth. He lobbied the U.S. State Department to donate baseball equipment to Latin American countries to curry goodwill. He believed the sport softened anti-*Yanqui* feelings: "Wherever baseball is played, there is pro-U.S. sentiment. Put a glove and ball and bat in the hands of a Latin American, and it makes him think indirectly of the U.S. and Democracy." Maduro claimed that where baseball is played, Americans are liked; "but in Bogota, where it is not played, there is more anti-Yankee feeling."[55]

Maduro's assessment didn't necessarily hold up. In Nicaragua, a third U.S.-backed Somoza had taken the reins of the nation's dictatorship. A member of the West Point class of 1946, Anastasio Somoza Jr. initially cut baseball spending and thus canceled the Nicaraguan Winter League season after eleven years of operation. The Nicaraguan amateur team thrived, however, and by 1972, it was led by Dennis Martinez and Tony Chevez, who would soon become

Nicaragua's first major leaguers. Reminded of baseball's political uses, Somoza launched a campaign to host the World Amateur Baseball Championship (WABC) in Managua, to help distract Nicaraguans from his miserable rule.[56] While the Nicaraguans fell short in the tournament, they nevertheless had the satisfaction of beating the U.S. team. The dictator basked in the victory but only briefly, before disaster struck.

A week later, a massive earthquake hit Nicaragua, killing ten thousand people and destroying half of Managua. Major-league star Roberto Clemente had just managed the Puerto Rican team at the WABC Championship and made many friends in Nicaragua. Back in San Juan, he decided to help the recovery. It was soon discovered that Somoza was siphoning off the international aid and stockpiling it for his corrupt government, yet President Richard Nixon was the first to call the tyrant to offer his support. A friend of the president since the 1950s, Somoza had been hosted at a White House dinner in his honor only a year earlier, when Nixon congratulated the brutal dictator for "a quarter-century of service to the cause of peace and freedom." Later, even Henry Kissinger's Central America Commission claimed Somoza's regime gave "new meaning to the term kleptocracy." Nevertheless, U.S. paratroopers were dispatched to Managua, serving only to help Somoza further loot the country. Nixon claimed he was preventing the earthquake from providing opportunities for communists.

When Clemente learned that aid wasn't being distributed, he was enraged and vowed to personally deliver the relief he had gathered. On December 31, 1972, the thirty-eight-year-old ballplayer boarded a broken-down and overloaded plane. Some warned him against making the trip, but he said, "Babies are dying. They need these supplies." Clemente and four others were killed several minutes after takeoff when the plane crashed into the Atlantic Ocean. The president proposed a Roberto Clemente Memorial Fund, even though Nixon's support for the Nicaraguan dictatorship was substantially responsible for Clemente's death. The "Great One" was a casualty of U.S. foreign policy.[57]

Halfway across the world, other Cold War baseball dramas were unfolding. In Japan in 1962, the great slugger Sadaharu Oh began his professional career, honing his game through principles of *aikido*, "the way of spirit harmony." Unfortunately, U.S.-Japanese baseball relations would soon be anything but harmonious. In 1964, Masonori Murakami became the first Japanese-born major leaguer when he signed with the San Francisco Giants. But while the Giants claimed Murakami was contractually theirs, his old team, the Nankai Hawks, insisted it was only a one-year lease. Murakami was initially celebrated in the United States, but this conflict transformed him from a model minority person into a disenchanted athlete, with racist overtones. The *Sporting News* implied that the Japanese were ungrateful and foolish for ignoring the "benefits" brought by internationalizing the reserve clause. While obviously a one-sided deal, organized baseball—backed by the American baseball press—nevertheless threatened to suspend relations with the Japanese leagues and impose economic sanctions.[58]

To make matters worse, U.S. major leaguers, such as Johnny Logan, Pete Burnside, Daryl Spencer, Jim Marshall, and Chuck Essegian, began arriving in Japan to play in its professional leagues. They were expecting to be received with open arms, but instead some Japanese complained that the Americans were too old and too well paid. Even so, the Hawks and the Japanese leagues relented, allowing Murakami to play again with San Francisco in 1965. But when Murakami and his family sought his return to Japan the next year, the *Sporting News* backed off on the grounds that it was better not to antagonize a Cold War ally. The incident tainted U.S.-Japanese baseball relations, however, which blocked further Japanese integration into the big leagues for another thirty years.[59]

Even baseball at the grass-roots levels had international implications in the overheated Cold War context. By the late 1950s, National Little League Week had been intentionally designated by President Eisenhower to coincide with Flag Day. And as David Zang has noted, Little League had been spreading "the gospel of American baseball" for decades and had been a "showcase for American victory until the late 1960s." In 1967 and 1968, however, Japanese teams won the Little League World Series. And while the Taiwanese Red Leafs didn't win the tournament, they nevertheless upset the Japanese champion team in an earlier round. A huge psychological victory against its former colonizers, this marked the birth of modern Taiwanese baseball. Now a baseball-crazy nation, Taiwan won the 1969 Little League championship and took the crown again in four of the next five years.

The team also figured prominently in Taiwan's national independence movement. Taiwan's legitimacy was undermined in 1971 when President Nixon pursued "Ping Pong diplomacy," which normalized U.S. relations with the People's Republic of China, allowing it to replace Taiwan on the UN Security Council. Little League was incorporated into Taiwan's strategy for boosting its morale in response. The Nationalist government began providing financial assistance to teams, including baseball scholarships. According to Junwei Yu, "The boys were considered 'surrogate warriors' for a country that could not succeed on political and diplomatic fronts."[60]

But although a string of Little League championships helped Taiwan's international image, it also stirred up old conflicts. While the Nationalists hoped to recapture the mainland and become the "true China," others opposed the government's despotism and corrupton. They sought independence from all foreign masters. When protesters against the Chiang Kai-shek dictatorship appeared at the Little League World Series with political signs and banners, he hired thugs from New York's Chinatown and activated Nationalist cadets who were training in the United States, and they both arrived in Williamsport to rough up and shout down the independence activists. With competing Taiwanese forces both rooting for their national team while clashing in the stands, Little League and U.S. government officials worried that the games were becoming politicized.

The "baseball diplomacy" that Little League was supposed to be promoting was also compromised when U.S. fans and policy makers began resenting the tournament outcomes: Asian teams were repeatedly beating American teams and winning the championship. After routinely defeating Japanese professional teams for years, the touring American major-league clubs also began losing.[61] A threatening shift was afoot. In response, in 1975, the year the Boston Red Sox kept their World Series jinx alive and the year the U.S. military left Vietnam in ignominy, Little League Inc. barred all foreign teams from competition. This solution proved too blatant, however, and the resulting protest forced a lifting of the ban. But when Asian teams resumed their Little League dominance for the next six years, it was particularly galling "to Americans already undone by the U.S. military's inability to defeat the North Vietnamese."[62]

A year after the Vietnam War ended, the film *Bad News Bears* was released. According to David Zang, the movie provided "a blow to conventional wisdom about sports: they don't build character after all, even in kids." In some ways, the film's high-stakes championship game "replicated the Vietnam War, muddling the sense of right and wrong, the value of victory, and the means of obtaining it." Was it a coincidence that the film came out the same week U.S. Lieutenant William Calley was finalizing his appeals against charges of war crimes in the My Lai massacre? In any case, the *Bears* film seemed to have "little regard for the sense of special time and space that baseball had enjoyed prior to the Vietnam era."[63] In the early 1970s, in terms evoking empire, former president Harry Truman proclaimed, "May the sun never set on American baseball." Yet although U.S. foreign policy had finally been extracted from its quagmire in 1975, the future of American baseball remained uncertain.

10

Purging the Vietnam Syndrome
(1976–1999)

Major league baseball, never to be confused with the U.S. State Department, nonetheless has its own evolving foreign policy.

—Claire Smith

Only by the mid-1970s, with the Vietnam War finally ended, did baseball and
the nation feel they could return to normalcy. As club executive Bill Veeck
suggested: "In the 1960s there was unrest, speed and violence . . . the war in
Vietnam . . . mugging, meanness. In this spirit, football and basketball were
natural sports. [Then] suddenly, people were tired of violence. They were
seeking stability and escape . . . [and] a sport to be savored . . . that's [why
baseball] attendance is up all over the country."

But would it last? All political dissent in America had not died, but where
it arose, baseball did its part to quell the protest. Typical was broadcaster Jerry
Coleman, who mockingly announced the San Diego Padres pitcher by saying,
"On the mound is Randy Jones, the lefty with the Karl Marx hairdo." In April
1976, two people ran onto the Dodger Stadium outfield and tried to light an
American flag on fire to protest the treatment of American Indians during the
bicentennial year. Chicago Cubs centerfielder Rick Monday swooped in to
rescue the flag, the protesters were arrested, and the plan was foiled. When the
crowd realized what happened, Monday received a standing ovation, and fans
began singing "God Bless America." A few minutes later, the huge Dodger
scoreboard read, RICK MONDAY, YOU MADE A GREAT PLAY! In the end: Americans
1, Native Americans 0.

Soon thereafter, Dodger executives presented Monday the flag in a ceremony at Chicago's Wrigley Field. He was chosen grand marshal of Chicago's
Salute to the American Flag parade, and both the Cubs and the state of Illinois
declared Rick Monday Days. Monday received thousands of calls and letters
from politicians and patriotic fans around the country. The Veterans of Foreign
Wars and American Legion honored him, and every place he'd go, Monday

was awarded another citation or plaque. *Sporting News* writer Richard Dozer gushed that Monday's accomplishment was "Francis Scott Key, Betsy Ross, Verdun and Iwo Jima—all wrapped up in one fleeting instant of patriotism." Monday had "swooped in—like Paul Revere at full gallop." Fellow outfielder José Cardenal commented, "Now we have three great patriots: Lincoln, Washington, and Monday." He had become an icon to millions of American veterans and their loved ones.[1]

Monday explained, "If you're going to burn the flag, don't do it around me. I've been to too many veterans' hospitals and seen . . . the guys who tried to protect it." That feeling was reinforced by the six years Monday served in the U.S. Marine Corps Reserves. "Whatever their protest, what they were attempting to do to the flag was wrong." Monday said. "There isn't anybody telling you not to leave if you don't like it here." On the day of Monday's flag rescue, the ubiquitous Dodgers manager, Tommy Lasorda, stormed out of the dugout and claimed he would have killed the protesters, had the police not reached them first.[2] Thirty years later, Monday's heroism was recognized at major-league ballparks, where video tributes were played and Monday threw out the first pitch. One reporter, reflecting on 9/11, said Monday had performed his own "Patriot Act," and Major League Baseball (MLB) designated the flag rescue as one of its 100 Classic Moments in baseball history.

Baseball led the flag-waving during the Bicentennial celebrations. On June 10, 1975, Army Day was held at Shea Stadium to celebrate the two hundredth birthday of the U.S. Armed Services. A sea of flags unfurled, and an ear-splitting cannon barrage shattered windows and blew away part of the center-field fence. In 1976, the National Baseball Congress was given Bicentennial status for the role it was playing "in the continued international growth of our country's greatest pastime." And National League teams wore a flag patch for the Bicentennial, in part to celebrate its own one hundredth anniversary—a coincidence of dates MLB eagerly publicized.[3]

Paying Tribute

Besides protecting the American flag, MLB continued paying tribute to the military during Commissioner Kuhn's reign. In 1979, the U.S. Embassy staff in Teheran was taken hostage, and during the long crisis, the commissioner attended a game with former Vietnam prisoner-of-war Jeremiah Denton. Reminded that he had already granted lifetime major-league passes to all Vietnam POWs, Kuhn expanded the offer, and upon their return from Iran the fifty-two hostages were given passes—to which football announcer Beano Cook responded, "Haven't they suffered enough?"[4] Baseball's battle with football was by then in full swing, as if the major leagues weren't challenged enough by the recent emergence of free agency, which would revolutionize baseball economics.

As in the past, *Sporting News* editor J.G. Taylor Spink was celebrated for supporting American foreign policy, this time in 1980 by President Reagan: "Your newspaper [was] an important source of information to our hostages in Iran. . . . [It] made a great contribution."[5] Commissioner Kuhn sought ties with presidents Gerald Ford and Jimmy Carter, but he was more successful with Ronald Reagan in reviving the MLB–White House connection.[6] Reagan began as a radio announcer, re-creating Chicago Cubs games off-site from wire reports and thereby mastering the art of impromtu fabrication that later served him so well in Washington. As an actor, he played Hall of Famer Grover Cleveland Alexander in the film *The Winning Team*. As president, Reagan was very visible, throwing out first pitches and appearing in radio and television play-by-play booths, sometimes calling an inning or two. On Opening Day 1984, Reagan became the first president to sit in a dugout during a game. In the 1980s, there was a trend toward the old-fashioned in ballparks and in baseball movies—such as *The Natural* and *Field of Dreams*—along with a renewed interest in vintage baseball cards. This mirrored the era's nostalgia, prompted by Reagan's rhetoric about the good old days. It was, according to John Bloom, an attempt to recover power for a masculine past—a longing for innocence, often invoking America's benevolent motives in fighting World War II. It wouldn't be the last revival of the "greatest generation."[7]

In 1984, when Kuhn departed as commissioner, the world and baseball had changed. Football challenged baseball not only as the national game but as the sport best reflecting America's aggressive role in the world, as the saber-rattling Reagan administration risked a nuclear confrontation with the Soviet Union. But baseball might not have been up to playing a part in a final confrontation with the so-called Evil Empire.[8]

Before Kuhn left office, he helped launch baseball's globalization. In many ways, it began with Curt Flood's reserve-clause challenge in the 1970s. The resulting free agency for U.S. ballplayers pushed the major leagues toward foreign sources of cheap labor. In addition to Europe and the Caribbean, Kuhn said he was "working with international amateur baseball and the International Olympic Committee to expand baseball, . . . [also] in China. . . . We had pieces of the communist world—Nicaragua, then under the Sandinistas, and Cuba—on our side." The commissioner felt Japan was crucial, and "the day after I left office I flew to Korea, where I met the Japanese and Korean commissioners. [These were] the underpinnings of a great international growth of baseball."[9]

That growth received a big boost in 1981, when "Fernandomania" hit the Los Angeles Dodgers. The Mexican pitcher Fernando Valenzuela became an overnight star, electrifying Mexicans on both sides of the border. President Reagan invited Valenzuela to the White House to join the Mexican president, José López Portillo, in a publicity stunt to portray the United States as racially progressive and as Mexico's "good neighbor." Valenzuela was a symbol of pride and hope for Mexicans, but he was also yet another example of talent drained from a less developed nation. America's use of him as a poster boy for assimilation was further tainted by the Dodgers' stinginess in Valenzuela's next contract, despite his brilliant season. Without irony, Dodgers manager Tommy Lasorda described Valenzuela's contract demands: "He wants Texas back."[10]

The Mexican connection portended a dramatic new role for Caribbean and Latin American players. As John Krich pointed out, "*El beisbol* [became] the Monroe Doctrine turned into a lineup card, a remembrance of past invasions."[11] But were Americans ready for the influx? During one of his Yankees broadcasts, Phil Rizzuto complained, "They've [the Montreal Expos] got so many Latin players, we're going to have to get a Latin instructor up here in the booth." And during an interview, San Diego Padres announcer Jerry Coleman asked, "Hector Torrez, how can you communicate with Enzo Hernandez when he speaks Spanish and you speak Mexican?"

Beginning in the mid-1980s, organized baseball saw a quick succession of three commissioners in eight years. The first was Peter Ueberroth, who replaced Bowie Kuhn in 1984. A businessman, Ueberroth had profitably managed the just-concluded Los Angeles Olympics. There, in another attempt to add baseball to the Olympics, the game was played as a demonstration sport. Owners were slowly recognizing that what organized baseball had done globally but only haphazardly up until then should be pursued more systematically.[12] Initially, Ueberroth's international sports experience seemed well tailored to baseball's needs. It also didn't hurt that he was a close family friend of George H.W. Bush, who was an avid baseball fan, a former Yale University first baseman, and the current vice president of the United States.

Ueberroth was flanked by National League president A. Bart Giamatti, a Renaissance scholar and former Yale University president, whose college union-busting policies didn't go unnoticed by team owners in their continuing struggles with the MLB Players Association. Robert "Bobby" Brown was appointed American League president. A frontline Korean War doctor, Brown maintained organized baseball's strong connections with the military establishment.[13]

Low-Intensity Warfare

In the 1980s, still suffering from the "Vietnam syndrome," the United States was reluctant to commit its own troops to yet another foreign war. The last war's wounds, bitterness, and defeat were still too fresh in the minds of the American people. Nevertheless, the Reagan administration was determined to escalate its surrogate wars against the Soviet Union and its purported allies. When the 1979 Sandinista Revolution toppled the U.S.-installed Somoza dictatorship, Nicaragua became a target for U.S. "low-intensity warfare." The Central Intelligence Agency created the Contras, largely from mercenaries and former Somoza National Guard members, thus provoking a civil war. There was no high-profile war on which the major leagues might take a stand, but Commissioner Ueberroth's Republican loyalties and unquestioning support for the president were well known.

Baseball loomed large in the Nicaraguan crisis. The latest of three U.S.-backed Somoza dictatorships had used baseball to promote itself, but now the tables were turned. Leading up to the revolution, future Nicaraguan vice president Sergio Ramirez wrote subversive short stories, such as "The Perfect Game" and "The Centerfielder," and also the revolutionary novel *To Bury Our Fathers*, which was structured in nine innings. Albert Williams, a Nicaraguan in the Pittsburgh Pirates farm system, returned home to become a Sandinista guerrilla for sixteen months. Williams later played for the Minnesota Twins. *Under Fire*, Hollywood's version of the Nicaraguan uprising, established its authenticity with a scene showing a boy throwing a hand grenade copying the pitching motion of hometown idol Dennis Martinez, who led his Baltimore Orioles on a visit to Nicaragua the following year.

Unsuccessful in preventing the revolution, the United States sought to undermine it. Soon to be indicted in the Iran-Contra scandal, Marine Colonel Oliver North played a central role. North sought evidence—manufactured, if need be—of the Sandinista government's relationship with the Soviet Union and Cuba. In a press briefing, recalled by NBC news anchor Tom Brokaw, North presented satellite photos of Nicaragua showing the outlines of baseball fields. Hoping to drum up support for overt U.S. military action, North pointed excitedly to the images, claiming they proved Cuban influence because, as everyone knows, "The Nicaraguans play soccer, not baseball. The Cubans play baseball!" Of course, North was ignorant or lying, or both. The Nicaraguans were wildly passionate about baseball and had been playing it for nearly a century, thanks in part to a twenty-two-year U.S. Marine occupation of the country.[14]

Like Castro's Cuba, rather than rejecting baseball as an imperialist game,

Baseball follows the flag and accompanies U.S. military interventions and occupations around the world after the Civil War. *The New York Public Library, the A.G. Spalding Baseball Collection, Miriam and Ira D. Wallach Division of Art, Prints and Photographs, Digital ID 56643*

In an early example of baseball globalization, Albert Spalding took two teams of Major Leaguers on an 1888 world tour that included a controversial game played at the Egyptian pyramids. *The New York Public Library, the A.G. Spalding Baseball Collection, Miriam and Ira D. Wallach Division of Art, Prints and Photographs, Digital ID 56641*

Baseball team of the USS *Maine*, a Navy ship blown up in Havana harbor in 1898, precipitating the Spanish American War. *Library of Congress, Prints and Photographs Division, Reproduction No. LC-USZ62-26149*

A World War I motto derived from the U.S. military using baseball to train soldiers in throwing grenades. *Library of Congress, Prints and Photographs Division, Reproduction No. LC-USZC4-10320*

Early twentieth–century portrayal of the world as baseball's oyster. *Courtesy of Transcendental Graphics / theruckerarchive.com*

OH LORD, WHY DO I
THROW LIKE A GIRL?

PARENTS – PLEASE!
LET YOUR SON PLAY
LITTLE LEAGUE!

Worth 1000.com

Little League plays an
important role in building
men, support, and skills
for the U.S. military.
http:fx.worth1000.com/
entries/223322/little-league;
artist unknown

Ballplayers raise the flag on opening day at Ebbets Field in Brooklyn, New
York. The flag and "The Star Spangled Banner" were used at ballparks to
promote public support for World War I. *Library of Congress, George
Grantham Bain Collection, Prints and Photographs Division, Reproduction
No. LC-DIG-ppmsca-19501*

U.S. General Leonard Wood throwing out the first pitch at a 1917 ballgame to help build support for U.S. involvement in World War I. *Library of Congress, George Grantham Bain Collection, Prints and Photographs Division, Reproduction No. LC-DIG-ggbain-24197*

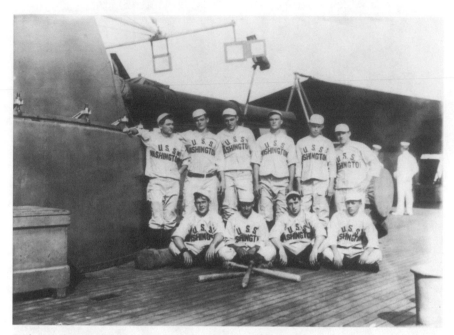

Sailors of the USS *Washington* pose for a team photo during World War II. *Library of Congress, George Grantham Bain Collection, Prints and Photographs Division, Reproduction No. LC-USZ62-78263*

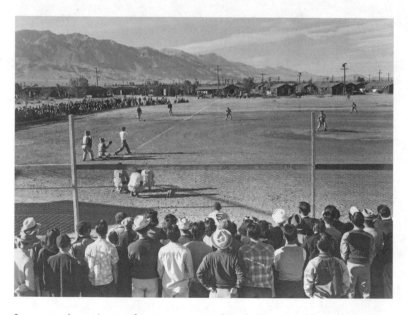

Japanese Americans observe amateur baseball at the Manzanar prison, a World War II internment camp. *Library of Congress, Prints and Photographs Division, Reproduction No. LC-DIG-ppprs-00369*

Moe Berg, pictured here with manager Casey Stengel and Manhattan Project head Lieutenant General Leslie Groves, was a Major League ballplayer and an American spy in Japan and Europe before and during World War II. *Courtesy of Neil Farkas, "My Time with the Catcher Spy, Morris Moe Berg," 2008 (Casey Stengel Estate; Charlie Hoof, New York News, September 1959)*

Lefty O'Doul, Major Leaguer and Pacific Coast League manager, helped establish professional baseball in Japan and was enlisted by General MacArthur for postwar Japanese recovery. *San Francisco History Center, San Francisco Public Library*

A *Saturday Evening Post* cover captures the attitude of U.S. military baseball abroad, as well as its relationship to American foreign policy objectives.

As a devoted fan and former ballplayer, Fidel Castro often incorporated the sport into his foreign policy and his many battles with the United States. *Courtesy of Prensa Latina*

The President throws out the first grenade at the opening invasion of the season.

A commentary on the Reagan administration's promotion of "low-intensity warfare" in Central America. *Artist unknown*

Major League ballparks have long been the sites of extensive patriotic displays, a practice that grew more common after the 9/11 terrorist attacks. *Ryan C. Tandy / bronxbrasstacks.com*

President George W. Bush throwing out the first pitch during the 2001 World Series, amidst cries of "USA! USA!" The jingoism around the games primed the nation for wars on terrorism, Afghanistan, and Iraq. *Photo by Eric Draper, courtesy of the George W. Bush Presidential Library*

Baseball arrives in Afghanistan in 2002 as a U.S. mechanism of social control, repeating a long-standing pattern from previous American military occupations. *Photo by Eric Lippmann, USN, U.S. Department of Defense*

One of many U.S. military flyovers at Major League ballparks, a practice that exploits patriotism as a marketing tool and legitimizes military policies and a militarized culture. *www.highgallery.com/UniqueAircaftPhotos.html; photographer unknown*

Censored from many newspapers, this cartoon depicts a profiteering U.S. military contractor bulked up on steroids during the Iraq War.
JD Crowe, Crowetoons.com

Architects of the Iraq War and other post-9/11 foreign policies, U.S. Defense Department officials Donald Rumsfeld and Paul Wolfowitz, on steroids.

While all Major League teams courted the U.S. military, the San Diego Padres had a particularly strong relationship. A soldier throws out the first pitch at one of many games where the Padres wear camouflage baseball uniforms. *Photographer unknown*

A huge baseball fan, Venezuelan President Hugo Chávez has been the target of U.S. attempts to overthrow his government and restrain his socialist reforms and protection of Venezuelan oil. *Photographer unknown*

Following the trend of corporate globalization, Major League baseball has harvested low-cost workers from south of the border. © *Anita Kunz*.

revolutionary Nicaragua further embraced the sport. Nicaraguan Sports Institute director Yamil Zúñiga said, "It would be absurd if the revolution turned against baseball just because it is North American." Nicaragua pursued the "massification" of baseball playing, along with a quest to perform better in international competitions. The Sandinistas used the sport to integrate society and promote values such as equality, community, sacrifice, and even some ingredients of the *American* dream. While the front pages of the Sandinista newspaper *Barricada* might attack U.S. imperialism, its sports pages carried detailed accounts of MLB. Sports editor Edgardo Tijerino explained, "Baseball doesn't just belong to the United States. It's our game, too." Interior Minister Tomás Borges observed, "Our favorite sport might be anti-imperialism, but we also love baseball." And Defense Minister Humberto Ortega proclaimed, "The only way we want to compete with the United States is through baseball. If the U.S. presence has left us something beautiful, it's baseball."[15]

In 1984, the year the San Diego Padres played in their first World Series, the Sandinistas built the Dantos Sports Factory in Nicaragua to produce baseball equipment, thus avoiding expensive imports. Making baseballs was a patriotic means of asserting independence from the United States. Well aware of baseball's role in maintaining morale, the U.S.-backed Contras ambushed truckloads of native hardwoods that were meant to be turned into baseball bats. On the other hand, under a white flag, a pickup baseball game was reportedly played between Nicaraguan soldiers and Contras at the Honduran border—so devoted were both sides to their national sport.

Beginning in December 1985, Baseball for Peace tours used the American and Nicaraguan love for baseball to generate goodwill. Led by Jay Feldman, the tours were "baseball diplomacy and war reparations. We've done such destruction to that country. I've wanted to atone in a small way to the Nicaraguan people." The traveling team played ball games around Nicaragua, delivered baseball gear (donated by the Giants and Athletics) and construction equipment, and helped rebuild war-damaged ballparks. The second Baseball for Peace tour was described at length in the book *El Beisbol*, in which John Krich wondered, "In what other firmament could we find sworn revolutionaries who interrupt their dialectics to remind us their favorite player is Ernie Banks?" But rebellion against the United States always has a cost: by 1986 at least 170 ballplayers had been killed by the Contras, in addition to thousands of others Nicaraguans.[16]

Elsewhere in the region, Panamanian dictator and former CIA operative Manuel Noriega had exhausted his value to America by the late 1980s, so the U.S. military invaded Panama to replace him. During the attack, U.S. troops stormed the home of Nicaragua's ambassador to Panama. This convinced many Nicaraguans that the United States would invade their country next, especially since the new U.S. president, George H.W. Bush, had campaigned strongly against the reelection of President Daniel Ortega and the Sandinistas.

While the Nicaraguan Revolution initially shunned the U.S. major leagues, its position had softened. Ortega encouraged visits by big-league teams and hoped his nation could settle its differences with the United States on the ball fields. Like most Nicaraguans, Ortega grew up rooting not only for a local team but also for a U.S. major-league club. Ironically, his favorite was "the Yankees, of course." Meanwhile, having been dubbed "El Presidente," major leaguer Dennis Martinez was repeatedly courted back to lead Nicaragua. Instead, Martinez worked for the U.S. State Department Speaker Program to promote youth baseball in Central America.[17]

Similar baseball developments played out elsewhere in America's sphere of influence during the 1980s. In South Korea, the decade began when the U.S.-backed dictatorship killed two thousand people in a brutal crackdown. This coincided with baseball's rise, as South Korea upset Cuba to win the World Baseball Championship and then beat the United States for the World Youth Baseball gold medal. The sport quickly became a mania and a tool of government control. The Korea Baseball Organization (KBO) provided an outlet for rebellious elements of society. According to Joseph Reaves, "The start of pro baseball in the country did much towards diverting the public's interest from politics to sports." The first KBO commissioner was Suh Jyong-chul, former defense minister and Korean Anti-Communist League president, who had previously managed the Korean Army baseball team. Seeking to salvage his sinking popularity and distract attention from the nation's political tyranny, the dictator Chun Doo Hwan began throwing out the first pitch at ballgames, at least once while sitting with Commissioner Bowie Kuhn.[18]

By the mid-1980s, South Korea had twice won the Little League World Series, and the Korean Samsung Lions were invited to Florida during spring training. In 1986, the South Korean government rescheduled a professional baseball game, for which it provided free admission, prizes, and a postgame rock concert—all to lure people away from political protests against government repression. Soon, Chan Ho Park became the first Korean-born player in MLB, although his participation clashed with his nation's mandatory military-service requirement. Baseball had been used by Japan and the United States to impose neocolonial control, but the South Korean government itself then took up the game as a channel for the energies of political and social unrest. As Reaves has noted, "Opposition leaders may have exaggerated when they accused the government of using baseball as a tool of political repression." But only slightly.[19]

The Spirit of Hiroshima

Baseball played a different role in Japan, Korea's former colonial master. Americans had been playing professionally in Japan for several years, but to mixed reactions. One Japanese player, for example, after expressing his distaste for American players, later revealed that his father had been killed by the United States in World War II. Claims about U.S.-Japanese cultural differences and each nation's baseball style fueled further conflicts, as Japanese *wa*, or harmony, was contrasted with American individualism. Some of this was captured in the film *Mr. Baseball*, based on the Japanese experience of U.S. player Leron Lee. Some initiatives were launched to generate goodwill, but hiring the abrasive Leo Durocher to manage a Japanese team might not have been the best one. Characterizing the appointment, Dodgers broadcaster Vin Scully quipped, "It took the United States 35 years to get revenge for Pearl Harbor." Of course, some believed the U.S. had already accomplished that with the atomic bombings ending World War II.[20]

To revitalize the spirit of Hiroshima, baseball played a central role. Hiroshima Stadium, home to the Hiroshima Carp, was built three hundred yards from the epicenter of the 1945 explosion. By the late 1980s, the Carp had two American players, and its outfield bleacher fans, peering toward home plate, could see the A-Bomb (Genbaku) Dome directly over the stadium roof. Baseball—despite being the attacker's national pastime—had helped revive both the city and the nation, provoking the observation, "This country has its national flag all wrong. Instead of a rising sun in the center, there should be a baseball."[21]

In 1989, Japan began recruiting in the Dominican Republic. A reporter described the players signed by the Hiroshima Carp: "Forty years after the fateful attack with the atomic bomb, Hiroshima is the target of another transcendental bombardment from the Americas. Only this time there will be no radioactive consequences, and the Pentagon will not have to worry about international criticism." While Japan's arrival was viewed by some Dominicans as an opportunity, to others it was only more of the same—"the Caribbean story in a nutshell: to accommodate the dreams of independence to one external influence after another, from the Spanish to the British, the French, the North Americans, and now East Asia."[22]

Back in America, in 1990 Heidi Koga became the first Japanese manager of a U.S. sports team when he was hired by the California League's Salinas Spurs, which gave Japanese players minor-league experience before they were called up to the Nippon Professional League (NPL). In 1992, Americans were in a frenzy over the "Japanese invasion"—Japan's alleged takeover of the U.S. economy. A bitter battle emerged when the Japanese company Nintendo sought to purchase the Seattle Mariners. The commissioner's office worried about "foreign ownership" in MLB even though Canadians already owned the Expos and Blue Jays. The Mariner sale to Nintendo saved the team, but majority owner Hiroshi Yamauchi was only allowed a minority vote. Rather than being a threat, the deal opened a huge new Japanese market for U.S. baseball. Japanese fans got a team to follow in America, but the NPL justifiably worried that such developments would make it into merely an MLB minor league. This feeling escalated in 1994 when Hideo Nomo quit his Japanese team to play for the Los Angeles Dodgers. Japanese players were increasingly targeted, provoking the NPL to tighten its regulations.[23]

In 1996, the New York Mets and Chicago Cubs opened their campaigns at the Tokyo Dome—the first regular-season games played outside North America. Not all Americans got into the spirit, however. The St. Louis Cardinals were scheduled to play the series, but their star Mark McGwire led his team's opposition, claiming that baseball "was already too international. This game belongs here. People come to America to watch our game. [MLB wants] to copy what the NFL and NBA are doing. [But they're] not the American pastime."[24]

In another former Japanese colony, Taiwan, the U.S.-backed dictatorship blocked the Cincinnati Reds from signing two former Taiwanese Little Leaguers because they had not served their mandatory military service. By the 1980s, Little Leaguers had become the "messiahs of the nation," but pressures to succeed were so intense that Taiwanese kids were beginning to turn away.[25] In 1987, martial law was lifted after four decades. By 1990, the Chinese Professional Baseball League (CPBL) was formed, and foreign players were brought in to strengthen and internationalize the game. Taiwan took the silver medal at the 1992 Barcelona Olympics, and when the Los Angeles Dodgers visited in 1993, the Taiwanese beat them two games out of three. By the mid-1990s, the ruling Nationalist party eagerly employed baseball as propaganda for Chinese nation-building.

In 1997, while the upstart Florida Marlins were winning their first World Series, a gambling scandal rocked the CPBL, undermining public support. But a second professional league, the Taiwan Major League (TML), was formed, which limited foreigners and tied teams to particular cities, thus restoring fan loyalty. In 2000, new Taiwanese president-elect Chen Shui-bian's first public address was given at the TML opening-day ceremony, where he described baseball as a "symbol of the Taiwanese spirit" and announced that 2001 would be "Taiwan Baseball Year." According to Chen, "history has passed the bat to us and it is now our turn to stand at the plate. The twenty-first century will undoubtedly throw us several good pitches, as well as one or two dusters. Regardless what is thrown, we must concentrate all our strength and willpower for our best swing."[26]

On mainland China, baseball had been officially "rehabilitated" after the Cultural Revolution and reincorporated into Maoist philosophy: "Baseball could help build the Communist party by promoting the diligent study of Marxism, Leninism and Mao Zedong Thought." In 1986, the Los Angeles Dodgers built a baseball field in Tianjin, and in 1988 the People's Republic of China hosted its first amateur baseball tournament, the Beijing International. Competing with baseball-crazy Taiwan, it tried to use baseball as the "Ping Pong diplomacy" of the 1980s.

By the late 1990s, baseball had grown, but the Chinese were influenced more by the Japanese, rather than the American, version of the game. Lawrence Lee of the Hong Kong Baseball Association observed, "[Since] the Americans do not practice all the time, we cannot learn from them like we can from the Japanese." Even so, the United States kept sending goodwill baseball missions to China, which further embraced the game, not to emulate American culture but rather because it might produce better soldiers and better diplomacy. It may have worked: Noting Chinese leader Deng Xiaoping's death in 1997, the Cincinnati first baseman, Hal Morris, joked: "As Reds, I believe we have to observe the customary six-day mourning period."[27]

By the end of the 1980s, dramatic changes were transforming the other Reds, the Soviet Union. While President Reagan took credit for bullying the "Evil Empire" into submission, other forces more convincingly explained the Russian collapse and the Cold War's culmination. But to the end, the Soviets maintained their claim on baseball. Written by Sergei Shachin in *Izvestia*, yet another Soviet story appeared insisting that baseball was originally *laptá*, a Russian game. Now it was argued that baseball had been "brought to California by Russian émigrés long before the American sport appeared." In response, *Time* magazine quipped that in *Izvestia*'s opinion, "the first American team was not the Cincinnati Reds but the Los Angeles Engels" and that "*lapta* fans deeply resented President Reagan's recent remark about *lapta*'s 'Evil Umpires.'"[28]

Even before the fall of communism, the Soviet Union began taking baseball seriously. An All-Union Baseball Federation was formed, and the Red Army offered military exemptions to servicemen who volunteered to play baseball. Soviet coaches toured the United States for baseball training tips, and Little League began organizing Russian teams. The International Baseball Association accepted the USSR as a member, and Cuban and Nicaraguan coaches arrived to provide instruction. Columbus Clippers manager Stump Merrill led a tour. The Johns Hopkins University baseball team played the

Mendelayev club, which then visited the U.S. in return. The Soviet national team toured America, playing the U.S Naval Academy squad and other college teams. And the Soviets played baseball at the Goodwill Games, organized by Ted Turner.[29]

In 1989, with the Berlin Wall about to be torn down, former major leaguer Bill "Spaceman" Lee led a visit to the Soviet Union sponsored by Baseball International. In his games there against Soviet teams, Lee kept picking off runners. The Russians had been waiting in long lines for so long that "going backward just wasn't possible." Lee said that "had Czar Nicholas been a left-handed pitcher, Russia would still be an autocracy. He would have picked off Lenin and Trotsky long before the revolution."[30]

The Moscow Red Devils won the Soviet baseball championship and then barnstormed the United States. The Soviet national team entered the European Baseball Championships. Rudolf Razhigaev became the first Russian native to join organized baseball since 1921. The Anaheim Angels began scouting Russia, calling it "baseball's last frontier," and the *Wall Street Journal* was thrilled to learn that most Russian ballplayers had no concept of a "contract." Even so, there may have been more Americans interested in Soviet baseball than Soviets interested in Soviet baseball.[31]

The Persian Gulf War

Having fallen short of the global leadership baseball could have used at the time, Commissioner Ueberroth was succeeded by Bart Giamatti in 1989. But Giamatti died of a heart attack only six months into the job and was replaced by his right-hand man, Fay Vincent, who didn't last that much longer. Vincent had a stormy relationship with the baseball owners.[32] One exception was Texas Rangers boss George W. Bush, whose uncle William "Bucky" Bush had been Vincent's college roommate. Vincent was close to the entire Bush family, attended ball games with them, and invested in the oil company Bush Jr. owned before buying into the Rangers. In 1991 Vincent flew to the All-Star Game on Air Force One with Joe DiMaggio, Ted Williams, and President George H.W. Bush. Given this relationship, it's not surprising that Commissioner Vincent supported Bush Sr. generally and his Gulf War in particular, offering baseball's assistance.

Anticipating baseball's interest in a centralized corporate structure with which to promote the game at home and abroad, Vincent launched MLB Inc. and proposed future secretary of state Condoleezza Rice as the CEO. Rice declined, saying she'd rather be the National Football League commissioner. Despite such initiatives, the owners resented Vincent's unilateral style, and thus after only three years, he was asked to resign in 1992. George W. Bush was proposed as a possible successor, but Vincent warned Bush he was only being strung along by Vincent's eventual replacement, Bud Selig, who coveted the position for himself. Bush Jr. withdrew his name when he was asked to run for the Texas governorship. A few years later, Vincent was one of the first people Bush Jr. called to ask whether he should seek the U.S. presidency.[33] In his memoirs, Vincent hit the usual sentimental notes in support of baseball's role as a focal point of patriotism. "When you see the American flag, you flash back to your childhood; you see your former self saying the Pledge of Allegiance in school. . . . Going to the ballpark nourishes the same emotions. . . . They who play and we who watch are all heroes of the game. In these perilous [post-9/11] times, we need all the heroes we can get."[34]

By the late 1980s, despite the Reagan administration's triumphalist posturing, the conservative British magazine the *Economist* described America as having all the signs of a declining civilization, increasingly frantic to retain its greatness. Although the Soviet Union was unraveling and America viewed itself as having "won," the magazine compared the condition of the United States to the British Empire's decline, earlier in the twentieth century. One common denominator, it observed, was an escalation in literal and symbolic flag displays, including an explosion of flags on commercial products. The editors noted that America was celebrating, with pronounced flag-waving, even little victories and wondered whether, in desperation, the United States would erupt in one final burst of power.[35]

The *Economist* may have underestimated the final spasms, one of which took place in 1991. Oakland Athletics president Sandy Alderson had been trying to debunk the notion that only big-market teams could win in baseball. Noting the success of his small-market club (three pennants and one World Series crown in the late 1980s), he said, "I was in Vietnam. And the big payroll doesn't always win." Yet in the world of American foreign policy, that lesson was already forgotten. Unchallenged by any other superpower and now apparently freed from public opposition to American interventionism (with its possibility of American casualties), the United States was ready to purge the Vietnam syndrome. Francis Fukuyama announced the "end of history," and President George H.W. Bush soon declared, "The specter of Vietnam has been buried forever."[36]

Later that year, the United States unleashed a "burst of power" in the Middle East: Under the pretext of rescuing Kuwait's "democracy," America launched the Persian Gulf War against Iraq. Former CIA operative and Iraqi dictator Saddam Hussein had overstayed his welcome and was now impeding U.S. access to "our oil." Uncertain how long the war would last, MLB made plans for a shorter season, roster cutbacks, and other strategies to keep the games going. They needn't have bothered: the Gulf War was a high-tech slaughter that ended within a few weeks.[37]

In the buildup to the war, moments before the first pitch of the 1990 World Series, Cincinnati Reds owner Marge Schott grabbed the microphone and called for a moment of silence for the U.S. troops "in the Far East." Never mind her sketchy geography; Schott was an outspoken bigot who at one point declared that "Hitler had the right idea, but he went too far." Her presence embarrassed the major leagues, but perhaps even more alarming to baseball owners were the daily press briefings once the Gulf War began: General Norman Schwarzkopf and other military spokesmen repeatedly used football rather than baseball metaphors to describe America's progress in the conflict: not strikeouts and home runs but rather pass blitzes and Hail Mary strategies.[38]

The major leagues supported the war, but only two professional ballplayers ended up in the military. Los Angeles Dodgers star pitcher Orel Hershiser did join a hundred celebrities in the Fox Network's singing video, "Voices That Care," which supported U.S. soldiers in the Gulf. Some objected to the hoopla, however. Sportswriter Tony Kornheiser believed the ball games would act as a balm. But, he implored, "Spare us the American dream theme park, the jet flyovers, the orchestrated anthems and the omnipresent flags. Can't anyone have a sense of decorum about the flag decals on the helmets and the flag patches on the jerseys? You cheapen patriotism by selling it like laundry detergent." Even so, precisely such displays were promoted.[39]

After a quick victory in a war costing few American lives (although hundreds of thousands of Iraqi deaths), the United States was brimming with patriotism. The jingoistic self-congratulations could barely be contained. As Jack Curry noted, "When the first pitch is thrown the urgency to revel in the charms of baseball [will] be fervent. There is reason to stand and rejoice, with the U.S. beaming over its Persian Gulf War [victory]." Opening Day 1991 was a big extravaganza, with every team "offering some tribute to the troops; from flag ceremonies, to having [soldiers] throw out the first ball, to singing the national anthem the way Whitney Houston would."[40]

Marine Corps General Richard Neal was a prominent spokesman during the war. When it ended, he and other military leaders were sent out to the ballparks. When Neal, dressed in fatigues, threw out the first pitch at Fenway Park, he glowed. "Did you hear that applause? That was for all of us." Sportswriter Joe Gergen said "baseball offered itself as a welcome wagon for returning servicemen." In Texas, Rangers owner George W. Bush asked the commander in chief, his father, to toss out the first ball. Vice President Dan Quayle and Secretary of Defense Richard Cheney did the same in Baltimore and Atlanta. The Yankees secured General Colin Powell, and Air Force pilot Steven Tate received the loudest ovation in Detroit when the crowd learned he had scored the first kill against Iraq. The New York Mets gathered four staff sergeants for its ceremonies and added a second Banner Day to salute the troops in Operation Desert Storm.

According to Gergen, "If this wholesale recruitment of servicemen seemed heavy-handed for baseball, it suited a country flushed with patriotism . . . two [Gulf War] generals even quoted that revered military strategist, Yogi Berra." Baseball rushed "to identify with the successful war effort, to tie a yellow ribbon around this season. Johnny is marching home again and baseball is standing in tribute." If baseball should catch some rays of reflected glory, "that wouldn't upset the [major league] hierarchy. After all, according to [baseball's] hoariest myth, the sport was created by Abner Doubleday, an officer trained at West Point." The circulation of Operation Desert Shield trading cards, however, might have gone too far, for many reached the Middle East and helped fuel the hatred of Americans there today.[41]

Overcoming the Wimp Factor

At least through the 1990s, Americans remained more highly regarded farther north, in Europe, where the U.S. national game made some surprising strides. The fall of the Berlin Wall boosted America's status and, among other things, it translated into an upsurge of baseball interest not only in Western, but also Eastern Europe. But although America's main Gulf War ally, the United Kingdom, jumped on the war bandwagon, it still lagged behind in absorbing America's pastime.

If baseball was still lost on the mother country, it had nevertheless taken hold in another former British colony: not only had Canada played the game as long as America, but since 1977 it had two major-league teams.[42] In 1988 a game was played in Beachville, Ontario, to celebrate the 150th anniversary of Canada's first baseball game. In 1991, Ferguson Jenkins became the first Canadian inducted into the Hall of Fame. Yet ambivalence about baseball's role in U.S.-Canadian relations had been longstanding. Having played for U.S. teams as well as the Montreal Expos, Ken Singleton observed, "From the first day they go to school, Americans are taught the U.S. is the best country. So playing in Canada is subconsciously viewed as somehow inferior."[43] That changed in 1992, when the Toronto Blue Jays became the first Canadian team to win the World Series.

Some Americans resented the Blue Jay triumphs, complaining—ironically— that the *World* Series wasn't the same with a Canadian winner. The Toronto wins challenged America because it showed that a non–U.S. team could be the best. During the series, the U.S. Marines displayed the Canadian flag upside down, and the Atlanta Braves' David Justice said he didn't go out in Toronto because he didn't know any French. Rather than condemn these blunders, the Canadian press laughed them off. Canada's politeness, according to Mark Kingwell, was "not defensive or submissive, but rather a subversive response to imperial domination."[44]

Not merely Torontonians but all Canadians cheered the World Series wins, partly because they were victories over America. Elsewhere, in less developed nations, baseball triumphs over the U.S. had been celebrated as "beating the imperialists at their own game." But Canada, no less developed than the United States (and in many ways, *more* developed) still suffered an inferiority complex. Canada wanted to win "America's game" yet also sought some distance, insisting on its differences from American culture.[45] As Kingwell notes, Toronto's World Series victories showed how a "baseball team can become a national institution" and yet how it could also reflect Canada's sense of inadequacy as a "political and economic colony of the U.S." If Canada had "a more comfortable national self-image," says Kingwell, then "we wouldn't be *insisting* on [having differences from the United States]; instead we would, [like the U.S.], be forcibly exporting them to weaker nations."

Actually, baseball *is* Canada's national pastime, yet the country has had to act as if the sport is America's game. The creation of a *Canadian* Baseball Hall of Fame was an apparent "admission of colonial inferiority and self-doubt." Certainly Canada should be able to have its own Hall, but—in contrast—the Cooperstown baseball shrine is not the American but rather *the* Hall of Fame. A year after Toronto's second World Series win, the Canadian Parliament designated lacrosse as its national game, not baseball (or even hockey). Canadians bristle at being merely extensions of American culture.[46]

Meanwhile, in 1992 Bud Selig became acting commissioner. During his first few years, many candidates for the permanent job were nominated— military leaders, in particular. Among them were Gulf War heroes General Norman Schwarzkopf and General Colin Powell, who became media celebrities and who both began signing baseballs for adoring fans. Powell instead became chairman of the Joint Chiefs of Staff and then secretary of state, in which job he was instrumental in launching the Iraq War. Former secretary of state and future secretary of defense Donald Rumsfeld was also a commissioner candidate and an architect not only of the Gulf War but later also the wars in Afghanistan and Iraq. And as mentioned, George W. Bush was also a nominee.[47] All told, the commissioner candidates were a virtual who's who of the U.S. foreign policy and military establishment. None ultimately served, but the eventual commissioner, Bud Selig, a military veteran himself, maintained close relations with all of them.

During this time, President Bill Clinton replaced George H.W. Bush, and the United States emerged from the Cold War as the lone superpower. Rather than pursue the so-called peace dividend, Clinton answered accusations that he couldn't be tough in his foreign policies. To overcome the "wimp factor"— the accusation of weakness that had bedeviled the first President Bush until he made his war on Iraq—Clinton launched bombing raids on already-defeated Iraq and tightened the economic boycott. Clinton then sent troops to escalate the drug war and counterrevolution in Colombia, fight warlords in Somalia, and prop up Haiti's military dictatorship. He ordered the U.S. bombing of Bosnia under the guise of a "humanitarian" multilateral NATO operation. Few would thereafter accuse Clinton of being "soft" as commander in chief.[48]

Baseball provided background support for these actions. In 1996, the Baseball Club Donat in Zadar, Croatia, received baseball equipment to allow it to keep playing during the Bosnia war. In 1998, a Little League was started in Bosnia-Herzegovina for a mixed group of Croats, Muslims, and Serbs, to help soften "all the things those kids have had to go through." In 1999, American ambassador to Greece Nicholas Burns used baseball diplomacy to temper Greek hostility to U.S. involvement in the Kosovo war. While the Cooperstown Hall of Fame was sponsoring a new exhibit, "Baseball Enlists," to celebrate baseball's World War II role, ballplayers weren't volunteering for 1990's military operations. The exceptions were minor leaguer Al Pepper and major leaguer Bobby Madritsch, both veterans of the Somalia, Iraq, and Bosnia wars. Steve Reich, who also enlisted, was the first West Point graduate to make the major leagues. But after he signed with the Baltimore Orioles, the army decided it would be a bad precedent to excuse him from his military commitment, so he returned to his unit, where he likely served in one of President Clinton's many military initiatives.[49]

The president also endorsed globalization, promoting the World Trade Organization and the North American Free Trade Agreement. Likewise, while baseball globalization had a couple of false starts, Commissioner Selig climbed on board. Observing professional basketball, which was already several years ahead, MLB began designing a more systematic global effort.[50]

The New Globalization

For its first century, MLB played economic hardball as a colonizer, with the backing of U.S. political and military power. Baseball's colonial legacy began in America, when eighteenth-century colonists and then nineteenth-century immigrants adopted a version of the British game rounders. Then in the early twentieth century, St. Louis Cardinals general manager Branch Rickey launched an internal colonization. By establishing the "farm system," Rickey helped baseball exploit untapped talent in the U.S. South and West. As Robert Lewis has noted, this allowed major-league clubs to build exclusive working relationships with minor-league teams (colonies) populated by poor white players (raw materials), and signed cheaply by scouts. The colonies developed the players (processed resources) for use by big-league clubs to sell their finished product (themselves) to the fans.[51]

Next, as Brooklyn Dodgers owner, Rickey invaded black America, extracting the best talent from the Negro Leagues and ultimately destroying them, leaving widespread black ballplayer unemployment in his wake. With black teams eliminated, their fans were also co-opted by the major leagues. But Rickey went even further: as Pittsburgh Pirates GM, he also helped pioneer player recruitment in the Caribbean, where baseball has always been rooted in colonialism. Along with Washington Senators owner Clark Griffith, Rickey began signing Cubans and then hundreds of other Latin players, largely to "desk contracts" (nonbinding agreements kept by scouts). Rickey called this his "quality out of quantity" strategy.

As Peter Bjarkman described it, "For the first time it is truly 'foreigners' [serving] as replacement players for the indigenous Iowa or Arkansas farm boys and California and Connecticut phenoms. This is true internationalization . . . and no longer simply the homogenizing force of a rampant Americanization." It created what Lara Nielsen has called "an outsourcing structure that pits domestic against international talent the same way NAFTA naturalizes a transnational labor conflict." While early baseball campaigns excluded nonwhite races, later ones took advantage of them. According to Robert Lewis, the major leagues have pursued a class-based approach to race in the Caribbean, adopting the "super-exploitation" of racial minorities rooted in Western colonial capitalism.[52]

Besides benefiting from U.S. colonial incursions, organized baseball practiced its own neocolonial interventions, before the practice became known as globalization. Baseball teams shared the same objectives as all large corporations: cheap resources (players), reduced competition, and expanded markets. In exploiting labor, MLB targeted a series of U.S. ethnic and racial backgrounds, inexpensively milking their baseball talent, while marketing itself to fans from those same communities. Late in his life, Jackie Robinson observed, "Baseball poses as a sacred institution dedicated to the public good but is actually a big, selfish business with a ruthlessness many businesses would never think of displaying." While baseball became the country's most racially diverse sport, this may have resulted more from MLB's profit-motivated neocolonial strategies than from its social leadership in integration.[53]

By the 1990s, however, some believed baseball was changing its approach. Joseph Nye has distinguished the "soft power" of cultural and ideological enticement from the "hard power" of economic and military force in international affairs. Perhaps belied by America's continuing belligerence, Nye nevertheless claimed that U.S. leaders increasingly relied on attraction and persuasion rather than command and coercion. The former arises from "the attractiveness of a country's culture, political ideals, and policies." While difficult to distinguish from cultural imperialism, Nye's model suggested a new direction for MLB in the world. James Quirk and Rodney Fort argued that American sports, including baseball, had hard-power weapons, such as monopolization, media leverage, and celebrity player influence. Their use, however, was increasingly viewed as abusive, and thus the major leagues pursued more "softball" approaches abroad, portraying themselves as champions of cultural and international diversity.[54]

As noted by sportswriter Claire Smith, phrases like "international competition in a non-confrontational, global, geo-political sense" began turning up among baseball officials. Through Major League Baseball International (MLBI), organized baseball launched new programs, including Play Ball and Junior Elite Camps. It sponsored baseball festivals around the world, and its Pitch, Hit and Run program—begun in 1994 to teach basic baseball skills—reached more than seven hundred thousand youngsters in Germany, Australia, South Africa, and other countries in 1998. The MLB Envoy Program sent baseball coaches to thirty-two nations. In Canada, organized baseball launched its first international clinics for girls. And proposals were made for a World Baseball Day.[55]

The Peace Corps—with help from MLB, Little League, and Rawlings Sporting Goods—stepped up its baseball promotions, developing programs and distributing equipment in places as diverse as Albania, Armenia, Bulgaria, Cameroon, Costa Rica, Estonia, Hungary, Jamaica, Kyrgyzstan, Latvia, Namibia, Romania, Sri Lanka, Thailand, Tonga, Tunisia, Uganda, Ukraine, and Zimbabwe. Via the Internet, overseas fans got the power to help choose the annual MLB All-Star teams. And the major leagues sought to restore a team to Washington, D.C., viewing it essential to its international marketing.[56]

As always, organized baseball's financial interests remained paramount. By 1993, MLB was targeting Europe not only for ball playing but also for merchandise: baseball goods appeared on souvenir stands, and European sales surpassed $100 million that year. The Major League Baseball Players Association endorsed the game's internationalization and began marketing U.S. players outside the country. And the commissioner's office created a task force on the "Japanese question," that is, the new Nippon Professional League's competition for Caribbean ballplayers.[57]

Profitable new television deals were vigorously pursued. As of 1997, MLB broadcasts reached two hundred nations. In South Korea, MLB's package with Inchon TV for a hundred games was worth $3 million for the 2000 season. Regular-season games were scheduled abroad to increase MLB's visibility, building bases for marketing, retailing, and talent recruitment. Media mogul Rupert Murdoch's purchase of the Los Angeles Dodgers gave new meaning to baseball "going global." The media–baseball synergy he created was not only a huge new profit center but also a marketing tool for his other corporations. Who won and lost on the baseball field seemed secondary to the team's other functions. The test, according to Lara Nielsen, was how MLB would survive "significant transitions in the globalizing process without shifting its own method of governance" or without losing central control.[58]

As Commissioner Bud Selig noted, "We're doing what anyone would do in the twenty-first century. It's a global economy." Still, baseball faced big challenges. In 1999, *Newsweek* suggested, "Sports may be America's most successful export to the world." But people around the globe didn't necessarily agree. American football, for example, was a very minor sport in Europe and viewed by many as a "testosterone-fueled freak show." And as Mike Marqusee notes, the habit of calling "the finals of the North American baseball competition the 'World' Series is viewed as typical American arrogance—more amusing than bombing Third World countries but cut from the same cloth."[59]

MLB struggled to portray a more international identity. The Olympic Games offered a possibility, but baseball had only been played there as a demonstration sport. In 1984, however, while the ball games remained unofficial, an actual tournament was held at the Los Angeles Olympics, in which the United States lost to Japan. In 1988, the United States avenged its loss by defeating Japan in Seoul, Korea. Baseball was first played as a formal medal game at the 1992 Barcelona Olympics, where Cuba beat Taiwan for the gold. The Team USA training that year took place at a U.S. Navy base, which got the team "thinking in a military way." It didn't help; the United States finished fourth.[60]

In 1996 Cuba again won the gold medal, this time beating Japan, with the United States getting the bronze.[61] Explaining America's disappointing play, U.S. coach Skip Bertman said, "This isn't like nuclear war, where if it's the U.S. against Grenada, the U.S. wins every time." At the 2000 Sydney Olympics, Team USA—led by Tommy Lasorda—beat Cuba to finally get the gold medal. While potentially a triumph for organized baseball, the major leagues didn't seem very committed to the Olympics after all. In many ways, a World Cup began to look more attractive. To pursue that possibility, MLB had to solve more immediate problems, especially in Latin America.[62]

Harvested on the Cheap

Once, when asked about accusations that he used an illegal *foreign* substance on the ball while pitching, Hall of Famer and reputed spitball pitcher Don Sutton replied, "Actually, that's not true. Vaseline is manufactured right here in the U.S." But the baseballs were not. Nor was most other baseball equipment and apparel. As manufacturers exploited cheap labor abroad, professional baseballs were initially made in Puerto Rico. Then in 1969 the Rawlings Company moved its ball-manufacturing operations to Haiti, where it could pay even lower wages.

By 1990, some 90 percent of the world's baseballs were made by 3,500 Haitian laborers. Besides Rawlings (a division of the U.S. military contractor Figgie International), other Haitian ball makers were employed by the Wilson, Spalding, and MacGregor companies. The U.S.-backed, "Baby Doc" Duvalier dictatorship attracted new corporate operations such as these baseball manufacturers, which were promised cheap workers, low taxes, and labor controls. A Haitian woman had to work four days to earn what million-dollar sluggers were making in forty seconds of work. MacGregor's CEO defended his labor practices, however, even calling his meeting with Duvalier the highlight of his operation. In 1994, the United States launched yet another military invasion of Haiti, promising a new era of assistance but delivering the same old imperialism. Reporter Jim Rice wondered, "The people there have suffered decades of dictatorship—for what? So our national pastime may be kept supplied in hand-stitched baseballs?"[63]

The American intervention was rationalized as necessary to protect U.S. interests, but what were they? Sarcastically, commentator Barbara Ehrenreich noted that the United States was "almost totally dependent on Haiti for its baseballs . . . [which] are stitched together by Haitian women for five to ten cents an hour, apparently out of sheer love for the game." Ball makers worked ten hour days, six or seven days a week, for a dollar a day. Labor organizing was forbidden. The chemical dips used for many balls were toxic. The U.S. invasion gave "the Haitian military a refresher course in clean, hi-tech methods of crowd control—that is, labor suppression." "We like our baseballs cheap," Ehrenreich observed, "but they shouldn't actually be dripping with blood."[64]

According to the U.S. Agency for International Development, 85 percent of every dollar of profit made in Haiti went back to the United States. A starving island, Haiti was exporting food to the United States, but the baseball firms were doing very nicely. The Rawlings Company viewed itself as a leader in baseball's global development: It sponsored Peace Corps programs, Olympic baseball demonstrations, and starter kits for Little League abroad. It publicized its baseball-equipment manufacturing overseas, but never mentioned its workers' exploitation: its operations were just a lot of happy globalization.[65]

The Caribbean provided cheap labor not only for manufacturing baseballs and other equipment but also for playing the game. While Latino major-league pioneers dated back to the early twentieth century, they began attracting particular attention in the late 1970s. Immigration to the United States was fueled by the steady availability of low-wage undesirable jobs Americans were unwilling to do themselves. In one sense, playing professional baseball might have fit into that category. Shortly before his death in 1972, Jackie Robinson bitterly lamented what little progress had been made for blacks in organized baseball. While an influx of African American players followed him into the majors in the 1950s and 1960s, by the early 1970s no blacks could be found in baseball's executive ranks, including field managers. Perhaps worse, this period began a decline in the number of black players as well. Big-league racism and other factors caused African American athletes to opt increasingly for football and basketball. If this development illustrated a job that (African) Americans were "unwilling" to do, then it helped explain why Latino immigrants moved in to fill the void. As the *New York Times* editorialized, "With the supply of homegrown talent in decline, it's possible that baseball could someday become one of those activities, like manual labor and voting, that Americans tackle a lot less enthusiastically than foreigners do."[66]

Of course, the baseball jobs Latinos filled were not undesirable. But that doesn't mean they were well paid. For the few, the eventual riches from playing professional baseball would be significant. But for the vast majority, the rewards would be meager. That is, while it set up programs to target African Americans, such as RBI (Reviving Baseball in the Inner City), the Baseball Tomorrow Fund, and a baseball academy in Compton, Los Angeles,[67] organized baseball only halfheartedly addressed the decline in black major leaguers because it had tapped into a much larger and cheaper supply of high-quality players. While African Americans and other Americans were subject to the annual baseball draft and while they increasingly had agents to protect their interests, Caribbean and Latin American players were excluded from that system. Thus they could be harvested on the cheap, not only replacing the declining numbers of blacks in the majors but increasingly displacing other Americans as well. In America generally, companies fled cities and regions with unionized workforces, first for nonunionized areas of the United States and then abroad for even less expensive workers. Similarly in baseball, the major leagues fled from player unionization and free agency to pursue unprotected workers south of the border.

As early as the late 1970s, major-league clubs set up Caribbean baseball academies, run much like plantations. Ballplayers were corralled in large numbers and signed for a pittance. Few or no rules existed, and conditions were substandard. Young people were lured from their schools, sacrificing their education. Overwhelmingly poor, the players were tempted by even small amounts of money for prospects that were dim at best. For major-league teams, "mining" for the few gems who might actually make it as professionals was very inexpensive. Hundreds of ballplayers could be signed for a couple thousand dollars each. Even if only one or two succeeded, it would be a steal.[68]

In the Dominican Republic, MLB established a Summer League in 1985 for its academy players. This helped it cope with the limited number of visas available each year to bring players into the U.S. summer minor leagues. But in doing so, it helped undermine the Dominican's own leagues, because most of the best talent was drained away, in effect turning the whole country into an American minor league. As Alan Klein put it, "North Americans [were] destroying the local tradition by making it completely dependent." According to Marcos Breton, "The academy is the baseball counterpart of the colonial outpost, the physical embodiment overseas of the parent franchise. It operates like the subsidiary of any foreign company: it finds raw materials (talented athletes), refines them (trains the athletes), and ships abroad finished products (baseball players)."[69] Of course, as the major leagues well knew, most Dominican players would never make it out of their country, even as "products."

The Dominicans struggled to retain baseball for their own development and likewise used it to express their resentment of the American invasion. But it was a losing battle. The United States encountered some small competition when the Japanese leagues began Dominican operations in the late 1990s.[70] And complaints were lodged for many years against the oppressive Dominican situation. But little changed in the short run.

Back in the United States, the situation looked very different. In 1998, MLB was applauding the home run heroics of Sammy Sosa to help revive baseball's popularity and to tell a much rosier Dominican story. In his dramatic battle with Mark McGwire, Sosa was the modern-day embodiment of the Horatio Alger American dream and the poster boy for the glories of Americanization. In 1999, Sosa was seated prominently next to Bill Clinton and featured in the president's State of the Union address to Congress, even though Sosa had been signed in the Dominican Republic "for peanuts" and was the rare success story.[71]

A similar situation emerged in Venezuela.[72] The Houston Astros established the first baseball academy there in 1989, and others followed. As in the Dominican, the major leagues created a Venezuelan Summer League for its academy players, producing similar abuses. In their book *Stealing Lives*, Arturo Marcano Guevara and David Fidler told the story of Alexis Quiroz, a Venezuelan boy who signed with the Chicago Cubs at age seventeen and began a harrowing ordeal of exploitation. Quiroz was acquired for practically nothing, repeatedly deceived, cheated out of portions of his pay, shuttled from team to team, blocked from adequate equipment and facilities, and subjected to substandard food and housing in military-style barracks. His career was ended by the poor medical treatment he received from the Cubs after an injury.

In 1989 the UN Convention on the Rights of the Child was signed by 190 nations. It sought to protect children from neglect, discrimination, exploitation, mistreatment, and physical and mental violence. According to Marcano Guevara and Fidler, the major leagues violated this convention in their treatment of ballplayers in Venezuela and elsewhere in Latin America. They pursued kids under eighteen and sometimes as young as ten and eleven years old, who were too immature to protect their own interests. Rather than giving children special care, MLB exploited their dire circumstances. Much of the discrimination against Latino youths was written right into MLB's own rules: They forbade certain practices against U.S. players but allowed them against Latinos—such as permitting big-league clubs to sign high-school players. Try-outs and facilities weren't regulated, Latinos weren't given credit toward free agency, contracts weren't required, and Spanish wasn't mandated when contracts were used.[73]

As recently as 2000, Venezuelan Baseball Players Association president Angel Vargas stated that "everything about the globalization of baseball that comes out of MLB is one-sided propaganda . . . [it] mistreats Latino children and their parents every day." According to Vargas, youth baseball in Venezuela was undermined, as good players were removed early from local play. Baseball academies signed underage players or hid prospects who were too young to sign, as if they were in concentration camps. When the Los Angeles Dodgers were caught doing this with their future star Adrián Beltré, manager Tommy Lasorda explained that *all* the teams did the same thing. MLB sanctions against the Dodgers were only symbolic. Using a "boatload mentality," players were signed en masse as commodities, and most were released despite extravagant promises about their potential. Signing bonuses often went undelivered. While some major-league camps were an exception, conditions at most academies were substandard.[74]

MLB recruiting in Latin America was compared to the "lawlessness of the Wild West." Others called it "neocolonialist," "racist," and "reminiscent of West African slave trading techniques." Organized baseball defended itself, claiming it provided unique opportunities for which "the players had to be hungry." According to Atlanta Braves scout Rene Gayo, "These guys [are] not playing for fun; they're playing for lunch . . . that's when they give you everything they've got." And as Astros scout Andres Reiner noted, "There is no difference between General Motors and the Houston Astros. One product is to be sold, and the other is to be used in the major leagues. It's just like making Cadillacs."

But this raised ethical issues for MLB like those confronted or ignored by other multinational corporations operating abroad. What responsibilities were there when recruiting in poor, often corrupt societies for an industry wielding enormous power over a vast pool of unsophisticated teenagers? Did giving a few boys an opportunity justify labor, discrimination, and child-rights violations? Were foreign workers merely a cheap natural resource to be cast aside when new profit centers emerged?[75]

Some felt MLB wasn't doing enough to globalize the game, despite its aggressive initiatives to secure Latin American players. Ironically, Mexico was largely spared from player raids and exploitation, thanks to Jorge Pasquel and his 1946 Mexican Revolution. While he lost the war, Pasquel nevertheless secured a protective agreement for Mexican players. Rather than plucking them for free from the Mexican League, major-league clubs were forced to negotiate selling prices for player contracts with Mexican teams. Thus, instead of just taking him, the Dodgers had to buy Fernando Valenzuela's contract.[76]

In 1990, Valenzuela and the Dodgers visited Monterrey, Mexico, for an exhibition series against the Milwaukee Brewers. But it was the San Diego Padres who launched the first systematic globalization initiatives in Mexico, seeking fans more than players. San Diego CEO Larry Lucchino said, "We're a baseball team with a foreign policy." In 1995, the Padres began turning themselves into a San Diego/Tijuana team. In 1996, San Diego played the New York Mets in Monterrey, in the first regular-season games held in Mexico. By 1998, San Diego had direct relationships with Mexican League teams. In 1999, it played the first MLB Opening Day game in Mexico against the Colorado Rockies. That same year, the Anaheim Angels arranged a game against Aguascalientes, the first time a major-league stadium hosted a Mexican League team. Soon, the Angels also had the major leagues' first Mexican American owner. While a poor economy limited the possibilities, Monterrey, Mexico, was often cited as the next likely major-league baseball city outside the United States.[77]

But Not with Its Puppet

Organized baseball could not successfully conquer the Caribbean until it dealt seriously with Cuba. Long wedded to official U.S. policies, which stubbornly persisted in treating Cuba as an enemy, would MLB dare to break ranks? In the early 1970s, the State Department blocked Cuban-born San Diego Padres manager Preston Gomez from taking an All-Star team to Cuba. In 1975, Senator George McGovern was hosted by Fidel Castro in Cuba and returned recommending baseball diplomacy. Castro tried using the sport to thaw U.S.-Cuba relations, as when he sent Luis Tiant Sr. to the United States to see his son, the Boston Red Sox pitcher Luis Tiant Jr., play for the first time.

In 1975, Cuba invited the New York Yankees to play in Havana. Commissioner Kuhn endorsed the idea as a potential goodwill effort, promising that the U.S. team wouldn't try to recruit Cuban players.[78] Alluding to the recent U.S. "Ping Pong diplomacy" with China, Assistant Secretary of State William Rogers said, "Basically, Bowie [Kuhn] wanted to be the ping-pong diplomat of Cuba." The commissioner met with Cuban officials in Mexico to discuss the game but ultimately called it off. Kuhn blamed Secretary of State Henry Kissinger, who was angry at Cuba for sending troops to fight U.S.-backed right-wing forces in Angola and who feared baseball might improve American public opinion toward Cuba. When another Cuban-Yankee game was proposed, the commissioner flip-flopped again, ultimately blocking it to avoid giving the Yankees an advantage in luring Cubans defectors.

In 1977, Houston Astros players and their manager visited Cuba to hold clinics, through which they also sized up Cuban talent. A third try at a ball game occurred that same year at the suggestion of President Jimmy Carter. But Kuhn called off this game (planned for spring training between U.S. all-stars and a Cuban team) as well, dropping all pretenses and stating that if Cubans kept blocking their players from signing U.S. contracts, then there would be no game. While Kuhn blamed the State Department and then the Cubans for his stance, the commissioner's own anticommunist and anti-Cuban sentiments were just as much responsible. Calling it "the best act since Casey Stengel," even the conservative *Wall Street Journal* deplored the situation, wondering why the United States was willing to deal with the Soviet Union but not with its puppet, Cuba.[79]

Trying to ease tensions, the Carter State Department gave Cleveland Indians general manager Gabe Paul permission to try yet again to arrange a game with Cuba in 1978. Broadcaster Howard Cosell got a rare live interview with Castro, who was sympathetic to the idea. But Cosell kept getting interrupted by his television producer, who wanted to cut to the ongoing speed-skating competition at the Lake Placid Olympics. Furious, Cosell resisted but finally relented. Naturally Castro was insulted by the aborted interview, and the Cleveland game never happened, either. Commissioner Kuhn made it worse when he cabled the Cuban sports director: "We are unable to schedule exhibition baseball. Our principal incentive has been to facilitate the availability of star Cuban players to American baseball," a raid the Cubans were obviously not going to permit. These rejections helped push Cuba toward a baseball relationship with Japan, which the latter exploited while the United States wallowed in Cold War politics. Meanwhile, Cuba further established itself as a baseball powerhouse, winning its fourth Intercontinental Cup in 1979. It would win eight of the next eleven cups as well.[80]

In 1980, responding to criticism that its citizens couldn't leave, Cuba launched the Mariel Boatlift, by which thousands of Cubans departed for the United States. Ballplayer Barbaro Garbey was banned from Cuban baseball for cheating, so he joined the boat refugees. According to a Cuban sportswriter: "no doubt U.S. propagandists will use Garbey to tell the world a rags-to-riches story without mentioning that he seriously violated the ethical and official rules here" (by gambling and run shaving). Sure enough, Garbey was portrayed exactly that way in the United States when he was signed by the Detroit Tigers.[81]

In the mid-1980s, the Toronto Blue Jays offered to sign the Cuban Omar Linares and skirt U.S. embargo policies by having him play only home games, in Canada. Linares declined, saying, "We are not going to be overrun by the U.S. We prefer to die in our country before we submit." Other U.S.-Cuba games were planned, but they were all blocked, either by the State Department or the commissioner, including a contest slated for Minneapolis and even one proposed in Mexico, between the Seattle Mariners and the Cuban national team.[82]

In 1991, Rene Arocha became the first defector from the Cuban team, thus increasing U.S.-Cuban tensions. The Cubans approached international competition more carefully thereafter but still won the first Olympic baseball gold medal in 1992 in Barcelona. In 1995, the Baltimore Orioles made their first attempt to play games against the Cubans. President Clinton's national security advisor, Anthony Lake, met with Orioles owner Peter Angelos and admitted, "I'm to the right of Attila the Hun on Cuba. But I'm soft on baseball." Even so, the U.S. Treasury Department rejected the plan, claiming it would violate the Trading with the Enemy Act. Besides Lake, other Clinton administration advisers kept creating roadblocks, denying baseball's role in improving relations with Cuba.

The White House remained a hostage of the anti-Castro lobby, whose past initiatives included dozens of CIA assassination attempts, one of which tried to lure Castro into catching a baseball loaded with explosives. But former senator Eugene McCarthy proposed a dramatic shift in the opposite direction: offer Fidel Castro the MLB commissionership and give him a big-league franchise for Havana in exchange for Cuban reforms. Fat chance! In 1996 Cuba again won the baseball gold medal at the Atlanta Olympics, and when U.S. ambassador to the United Nations Bill Richardson negotiated the release of three Cuban political prisoners, he got Castro to lower his guard by talking baseball. In 1997, the major leagues got a second Cuban defector, Livan Hernandez, who starred for the Florida Marlins. But U.S. scouts faced obstacles in trying to lure other Cubans.[83]

In 1998, Joe DiMaggio learned that Castro had always dreamed of having his autograph. At first he hesitated, but Joe finally sent Fidel a signed ball. According to a spokesman, DiMaggio "doesn't approve of Castro's politics. But he figured, if it helps relations between Cuba and the U.S., then okay." But relations didn't improve, because that same year, Orlando "El Duque" Hernandez also defected from the Cuban team. "Casting his lot with Yankee imperialism," as Andre Codrescu described it, El Duque's story was played up as another triumph of the American dream until it was discovered that he fudged his escape tale. In any case, Hernandez initially refused American asylum because it would have subjected him to the U.S. baseball draft and forced him to sign with whichever team picked him. Instead, he was taken—with the help of the U.S. Coast Guard (in violation of the U.S.-Cuban repatriation treaty)—to Costa Rica, where Hernandez established residency and then started a bidding war, which was won by the New York Yankees. Talk-show host David Letterman quipped, "He's a very lucky man. He escaped the dictatorial reign of a tyrant and ended up working for George Steinbrenner."[84]

But Castro wasn't amused. He responded by blocking Cuban players from extended tours overseas, which meant no more Cubans in foreign leagues. Some players were held back from international travel altogether. Cuba resented America's selective enforcement of the repatriation treaty, which otherwise would have blocked the defections. Making matters worse, a few U.S. baseball agents, such as Joe Cubas—a self-described "enemy of the Castro government"—began provoking defections, stationing themselves in the Caribbean to help rescue star ballplayers. The defections were also reinforced by the Kuhn Directive of 1977 (amended in 1991), which prohibited any major-league team from negotiating with, discussing, or signing Cuban players. This reflected U.S. foreign policy directives rather than the interests of organized baseball, yet the major leagues felt compelled to play along. When the Los Angeles Dodgers violated the directive by conducting secret tryouts and helping two Cuban players defect, they were punished by having the players declared free agents.[85]

One possibility for thawing relations was raised by the bid the Baltimore Orioles again made to arrange games with Cuba in 1999. The last teams to visit Cuba had been the Cincinnati Redlegs and Los Angeles Dodgers, forty years earlier. Orioles owner Peter Angelos finally succeeded in bringing MLB back, but it wasn't easy. As Owen Perkins observed, the games were a "fantasy-league replay of the Cold War, with Kennedy-style dirty tricks and anti-Castro agitation. Fans of baseball like to tout the game's seamless links to history but this might be too much. Bay of Pigs: get over it." The Clinton administration sought to grant permission without appearing to approve or sponsor the games. Instead of staying neutral, however, Secretary of State Madeleine Albright almost sabotaged the series when she described it as a Clinton policy to "provide the people of Cuba with hope in their struggle."[86]

While Castro had to be placated, Thomas Carter correctly observed that the baseball exchange was nevertheless "aimed at easing the plight of Cubans while maintaining sanctions against the Castro government." It wasn't Ping Pong diplomacy designed to enhance relations, but rather "gesture diplomacy." As Janine Delay suggested, it "signaled the constituency favoring dialogue that American Cuban policy was changing; at the same time it showed the constituency opposed to change that the contact was, after all, 'only a game.'" The U.S. government had no stake in the games' outcomes but they were important to Cuban nationalism. Following an initiative proposed by Pope John Paul II during his 1998 Cuba visit, the Clinton administration allowed the games only after reassurances that profits would go to Cuban humanitarian groups and not to the government. Castro bristled at Clinton's "people-to-people diplomacy," viewing it as a thinly disguised tactic to support dissidents.[87] Even so, he went along.

According to Jeff Stein, "The games were supposed to break the ice between Havana and Washington but apparently the first game, in Cuba, went so smoothly (with the Orioles winning by a run) the State Department got frightened about its implications and thought it would make trouble for the second game."[88] Thus, although the U.S. government blocked the "Brothers to the Rescue" group from "booting" the tires of the airliner carrying the Cuban ballplayers to Miami, it nevertheless permitted the organization's hostile flyovers and allowed protesters to buy blocks of seats close to the field. Initially, it denied visas for much of the Cuban delegation and greased the way for Cuban defections by asking Baltimore police to set up a system to process them. Even so, Florida representative Ileana Ros-Lehtinen claimed the games were part of "an anti-democratic festival the Clinton administration is putting on in honor of Castro."

The U.S. media criticized Peter Angelos for kowtowing to Castro, because he pledged not to pursue Cuban players or encourage defections. Baseball agents representing defectors were particularly upset, for this deprived them of potential business. In the other direction, Angelos was also accused of unfairly promoting the Orioles, so that Cuban ballplayers would all want to play for his club. Senator Jesse Helms, a lifelong opponent of racial equality, nevertheless called for an Immigration and Naturalization Service inquiry, claiming the Orioles were discriminating in violation of the 1964 Civil Rights Act—legislation Helms had opposed. Helms spokesman Mark Thiessen criticized "Mr. Angelos' love affair with the Cuban dictator."[89]

At Baltimore, in the second game, the Cubans avenged their loss with a sizable win over the Orioles. The contest was riddled with political demonstrations, with Castro haters and defenders trying to outduel each other with chants and placards. The clashes reached the field when a Cuban umpire body-slammed an anti-Castro demonstrator who ran out holding a sign that read, "Freedom—Strike Out Against Castro." Despite the controversy, the games might have been a breakthrough in U.S.-Cuban relations—had it not been for 9/11.[90]

In 1999 New York Congressman José Serrano introduced the Baseball Diplomacy Act, which would have provided special visas for Cuban athletes to play in the U.S. major leagues without having to defect. The visa was to last only one season and would have had to be renewed each year. Players could return, without sanction, to Cuba with their earnings. Cuba indicated it would allow its players to go and that only U.S. policy prevented it. Anti-Castro Cubans, such as the Cuban American National Foundation, objected. On the other hand, supporters asked, if Yao Ming—the star National Basketball Association player—can return to a Communist China, then why not treat Cuban baseball players the same? Even so, Serrano's bill languished in congressional committees, awaiting serious consideration.

In 2000, tensions rose again when the American team beat the Cubans to win its first baseball gold medal at the Sydney Olympics. U.S. coach Tommy Lasorda didn't hesitate to taunt the Cubans about their loss. That same year, a new U.S.-Cuban crisis arose when a Cuban boy, Elian Gonzalez, was rescued at sea during an escape attempt. His mother died in the ordeal, but instead of returning him to his father (who remained in Cuba), the anti-Castro exile community wanted to keep the boy in the United States. It condemned the Clinton administration when it prepared to return Gonzalez, in part to avoid a diplomatic incident. On the heels of the Cuban-Orioles series, Joe Robbie Stadium, home of the Florida Marlins, became a site of political protest. Major leaguers were enlisted in a general strike called by the anti-Castro forces. Several Marlins sat out a game, and the Latinos on the visiting San Francisco Giants were excused from playing as well. According to the Giants management, this wasn't a political statement but only a matter of the players' safety—although no apparent threats were identified. Baseball's Cuban prospects held out some dim hope, but the future remained uncertain.

Destroying the Village?

Besides baseball's problems abroad, political challenges in the United States roiled the sport as well. Many of them were the vestiges of MLB's "colonial policies" at home, notably toward Native Americans. While natives were not banned outright from organized baseball, they were nevertheless stigmatized. In the century since they first appeared in the majors, a few stood out, including Jim Thorpe, John Meyers, and Hall of Famer Charles Albert Bender. But Native Americans have been more conspicuous in baseball as mascots and team logos than as players, thus provoking accusations of degrading treatment. Indignation first arose in the 1970s and 1980s for Cleveland's and Atlanta's use of the names Indians and Braves for their major-league teams.

The protests came partly from the American Indian Movement (AIM), whose leader, Russell Means, wondered what the reaction would be to teams called the Cleveland Negroes or the Cleveland Aunt Jemimas. The Cleveland American Indian Center sued the Indians ball club over its logo, arguing that the Indian mascot, Chief Wahoo, and the team symbol, a grinning Indian caricature, were insulting. Concerns were also raised about the Atlanta Braves mascot, Chief Noc-A-Homa, who responded to each Atlanta home run by jumping out of his tepee, doing a dance, and setting off a smoke bomb. Some claimed it falsely stereotyped Indians as warlike.[91]

Most sportswriters ridiculed these complaints, claiming that team names and mascots portrayed Indians as honorable happy warriors. They observed that Chief Noc-A-Homa was a real Indian, Levi Walker Jr., who didn't mind the portrayal. Besides, Walker was using his celebrity to publicize Native American problems. But when the Braves displaced Walker from the stands to sell more seats, the team went into a tailspin and didn't recover until his tepee was restored. This superstition insulted Indian groups even more.[92]

The resistance revived in the 1990s. When Chief Noc-A-Homa asked the Braves for health care benefits, he was fired, but the fans stepped in, wearing Indian headdresses and "war paint," and devising their own "war chants." Things sacred to Native Americans were made comical or quaint in the ballpark. Native Americans picketed Atlanta Stadium during the 1992 World Series to protest the "tomahawk chop" and "Indian-style chanting" in the stands, often led by Braves owner Ted Turner. Most Native Americans felt the portrayals were racist—perpetuating stereotypes, depicting Indians as animals, and mocking their ceremonial traditions. The Chief Wahoo ("Red Sambo") logo of the Cleveland Indians was protested as grotesque, resembling the grinning, bucktoothed, watermelon-eating portrayals of Negroes in the past.[93]

Outrage over the issue peaked in 1995 at the "politically incorrect World

Series," which featured *both* the Atlanta Braves and the Cleveland Indians, neither of which had taken the protests seriously. In response, picketers carried
signs saying "Racist Mascots Must Go" and "Indians Are People, Not Mascots." Michael Haney, director of the National Coalition on Racism in Sports
and Media, wore a Ku Klux Klan robe and hood to a game to dramatize the
effects of Indian logos. More demonstrations occurred at Cleveland's 1997
All-Star Game. And in 1999 at Cleveland's home opener, a wooden Chief
Wahoo sculpture in a coffin was burned in protest, but to no avail.[94]

Several years later, the controversy resurfaced when MLB inaugurated an annual Civil Rights Game. Set in Memphis near the Civil Rights Museum to
honor Martin Luther King Jr. and other civil rights pioneers, the tribute created a protest when the Cleveland Indians were chosen for the first game. In
1838, the U.S. Army forcibly stripped the Cherokee Indians of their lands and
marched them along the Trail of Tears, so called because four thousand Indians
died en route. Memphis was on the trail and many Indian descendants still lived
in the area. Having the Cleveland team playing in the game, with its red-faced
Native American caricature as its logo and mascot, was compared to "having a
9-11 benefit game, and asking Khalid Sheikh Mohammed [the attacks' alleged
mastermind] to throw out the first pitch." As *Deadspin* editor Will Leach asked,
"If the Indians win [the game], do Native Americans get civil rights?"[95] The
contest was played as planned, and the Indians lost to the Cardinals.

Elsewhere, MLB wouldn't escape so easily. Its plantation system at home
was dramatically overthrown by the 1970s free-agency breakthrough.[96] But
instead of facing the inevitable and sharing baseball's riches, the "lords of baseball" dug in for battle against the ballplayers and the Major League Baseball
Players Association, led by Marvin Miller. Because it had always beaten back
unionization before, MLB was confident it would triumph again.

During the Vietnam War, reporter Peter Arnett recorded one U.S. soldier's
excuse for a recent massacre: "We had to destroy the village in order to save
it." The stigma of such an attitude was among the things America had to overcome to throw off the Vietnam syndrome. U.S. foreign and military policies in
the 1980s and 1990s substantially purged such albatrosses. Yet the catharsis typically meant not the elimination of past practices but rather only their rehabilitation. A generation later, America was still quite willing to "destroy the
village," illustrated by the Gulf War slaughter and the indiscriminate Bosnia,
Sudan, and Iraq bombing campaigns.[97] When asked about sanctions that had
killed a half million Iraqi children, Secretary of State Albright answered, "We
think the price was worth it."

MLB seemed willing to destroy the village as well. By launching a war
against its own players, it risked bringing down not only them but also the en-

tire sport. Historian Robert Burk astutely described 1980s baseball as "The Empire Strikes Back" and 1990s baseball as "Armageddon," or the final battle. After losing court cases and arbitration decisions, the owners provoked the 1981 players strike, trying to roll back free agency. When that failed, they colluded, agreeing not to compete for free agents in the mid-1980s. But arbitrators ruled for the union, forcing owners to reimburse players millions in unpaid salaries. Still convinced they could win, the owners demanded a salary cap in 1993 in violation of the baseball contract.[98] The players refused, and the owners withheld pensions and benefits, daring the union to strike. It did just that, in August 1994. To the owners' surprise, the players didn't break ranks. But MLB gambled with more than merely another lost labor dispute. This one forced the cancellation of the World Series, America's sacred rite for ninety years. Though fans and sportswriters blamed the players more than the owners, in the end the whole enterprise was threatened. Many fans flocked to minor-league baseball, swearing they'd never again support the major leagues. The final battle had been waged, and both sides had lost. Some claimed baseball was dead, especially with football's continuing rise in popularity.

When MLB resumed again in 1995, attendance, merchandise sales, and media contracts were all in decline. Later in the season, when Cal Ripken replaced Lou Gehrig as baseball's consecutive-game "iron man," it drew some fans back but not nearly enough. Looking for an answer, the major leagues limped through the next couple of seasons until people began noticing an unprecedented increase in home runs. Some suspected that the baseballs had been juiced, but big-league officials denied the charges. By 1998, nobody much cared about the reasons, as two players, Mark McGwire and Sammy Sosa, were on pace to challenge baseball's most sacred record: the single-season home-run mark set by Roger Maris in 1961. The home-run race captured the nation's imagination, bringing back old fans and generating millions of new ones. People's daily routines hung on the latest home-run tallies.

The British Broadcasting Corporation (BBC) covered the McGwire-Sosa race but wondered why all the fuss: "Can baseball consider itself a major sport, when so many parts of the globe are bewildered by [a game that] looks like an exotic form of rounders? Surely it is the poor relation to genuinely worldwide sports like cricket, football, and rugby?" Football (soccer), yes; but cricket and rugby? This was a blow to baseball's global aspirations. But more important for the moment was the game's status in the United States, and with the home-run fireworks, baseball was back. It had reclaimed America.[99]

Commissioner Bud Selig's reign resembled the trajectory of President Bill Clinton. Early on, Selig was viewed as ineffectual, and the 1994 World Series cancellation stained his record. As with Clinton, however, the commissioner

overcame the "wimp factor," consolidated his power base, secured the permanent commissionership, and was credited with revitalizing baseball. The sport's
situation in the late 1990s was reminiscent of early 1920s baseball. Under the
cloud of the Black Sox scandal, baseball nevertheless survived and even
thrived. As with Bud Selig, the commissioner then, Kenesaw Mountain Landis, was lauded for getting the sport back on track—even if it was Babe Ruth
who really rescued the game.

As we've seen, Ruth captured the public's imagination with his prodigious
slugging. The home run mirrored the American psyche. Its rise in importance,
via Ruth, paralleled America's ascent as a world power after World War I. The
United States has been addicted to that power ever since. For the most part, it
has characterized both America's foreign policy and America's national sport.
Occasionally, however, there's been a power deficit, as in the aftermath of the
Vietnam War fiasco. There have been similar lulls in baseball. Thus, if America's military power could break out of its shackles, then baseball could do so
as well. For the latter, it came not from Commissioner Selig (despite being its
main cheerleader) but rather from McGwire and Sosa. So compelling was the
home-run competition that fans, both old and new, even began rooting
against their home teams if they could see these sluggers add another big blow.
Divisions and team rivalries receded "in favor of national community, providing a kind of primitive solidarity."[100] Even more stirring, perhaps, were
McGwire's repeated references to the American dream and Sosa's calls for a new
Dominican-American dream. One was left with misleading but nevertheless
profound messages about American greatness and strength.

Most of all, Americans were awed by the power McGwire and Sosa generated with each mighty shot. Hitting more home runs—harder and longer—
fascinated people. Even sexual politics were involved: signs at ballparks all over
the country read, "Chicks Dig the Long Ball." And as Richard Ben Cramer
has noted, in Babe Ruth's era, as well as in more recent times, Americans "love
power. It's about how we see ourselves. It's how we're 'good' when we're very
good—with overwhelming force."[101] Reinvigorated, baseball seemed stronger
than ever. Of course, the question was *where* did all that newfound power actually come from? MLB didn't *want* to know, and even though it *did* know, it
certainly didn't want to tell.

11

Foreign Policy on Steroids
(2000–2009)

Nobody has ever called an air strike from the pitcher's mound, the proximity of military jets notwithstanding.

—Bill Littlefield

If players want to strike, they ought to just pick September 11, because that's what it's going to do to the game. . . . Let [union head] Donald Fehr drive the plane right into the building.

—Jim Bowden

On June 14, 2000, the Pentagon commemorated the Korean War's fiftieth anniversary with a ceremony at Arlington National Cemetery. Of all people, the honored guest was baseball Commissioner Bud Selig, who was joined by Korean War–era big leaguers and by Joint Chiefs of Staff chairman Henry Shelton, who noted that ballplayers served in Korea "not as privileged celebrities, but as common patriots befitting their status as genuine Americans." Selig and major league baseball (MLB) staged memorials at every ballpark and at the 2000 All-Star Game and World Series.

The commissioner described ballplayers like Jerry Coleman and Ted Williams as "heroes of the baseball diamond and battlefields of the skies. MLB sacrificed much [to] support the Korean War effort. Players like Willie Mays, Whitey Ford, Don Newcombe, Don Larson, Dr. Bobby Brown, Bob Kennedy, Curt Simmons, and Whitey Herzog . . . served with distinction . . . in defense of freedom." Coleman, who flew sixty-three missions, claimed his experience "turned me into the person I am today. I've always felt that anybody . . . who goes into the service, is better off when they get out." At the commemoration, Selig emphasized the link between baseball and the military, which he hoped "to strengthen and improve in the years ahead."[1]

Shelter During the Storm

Both baseball and America entered the twenty-first century brimming with confidence about their bright futures. The first Little League graduate to make it to the White House, the newly elected president George W. Bush, felt it wasn't enough the *last* century had been the "American century."[2] The *next* one would be, too. Flush with baseball's rebound via its late-1990s power surge, Commissioner Selig likewise foresaw good things for the game. Yet both empires were perhaps more fragile than they were willing to acknowledge.

In an eerie premonition, the historian John Lewis Gaddis wondered in the late 1990s whether the future had been foreshadowed by the 1989 San Francisco earthquake and by the Candlestick Park reaction, as the Oakland Athletics and San Francisco Giants were about to begin World Series game three. As the ground shook, the astonished crowd had a "Shakespearean insight: that there were more things in heaven and earth than had been dreamt of." As Gaddis observed, "we can prepare ourselves for Candlestick Park surprises: reinforce the bleachers, back up the communications, mark the exits, and keep the emergency squad close at hand. We may even [want to] expand our philosophy . . . to accommodate more of the things that are happening, if not in heaven then at least here on earth."[3]

Nevertheless, the United States was not prepared for the surprise when terrorists struck on September 11, 2001. Nor did Americans "expand our philosophy" beforehand to possibly avoid the attack, or afterward either, in a way that might have more sensibly guided the U.S. response. In the months leading up to 9/11, only three years after Mark McGwire set the new single-season record of 70 home runs, Barry Bonds was on pace to break it again. A consistent home-run hitter, some nevertheless wondered about Bonds' power burst and his recent bulk compared to his earlier playing days. But the chase was too exciting for most people to care.[4] After the terrorists struck and America sought to get back on track, the Bonds home-run quest was a welcome distraction. How he got there didn't seem to matter. But if Bonds was "juiced" on his way to setting a new record of 73 home runs, then it only foretold an America on juice as well—an emerging U.S. foreign policy on steroids.

Reflecting on the 9/11 attacks, Middle East scholar Ziauddin Sardar observed that "terrorism breeds in the swamp of injustice." Calling a military response counterproductive, Sardar explained that you could kill a million mosquitoes in a swamp, but as long as the swamp remained, another million mosquitoes would be back tomorrow. While sympathizing with this perspective, journalist Tarek Atia wrote that what was already back was baseball and "that's the way it should be . . . to say [the attacks] will profoundly effect America belittles the very thing that makes us Americans . . . the simple just-ness of our being. Baseball is an expression of that." That is, as Mike Marqusee has observed, there's a powerful "belief that America is not one nation among many but the unique embodiment of an idea." Yet that self-righteousness might blind the United States to an uncomfortable possibility: that it might not be fostering "just-ness" but rather the "swamp of injustice." After 9/11, Americans asked, "Why do they hate us?" but they didn't really want to hear the answer.[5]

Writing shortly before September 11, Ron Briley said it would be "difficult to envision baseball . . . as a symbol around which a leader could rally the American people in times of crisis such as Franklin Roosevelt [did] during the Great Depression and World War II." Nevertheless, Commissioner Bud Selig and assorted politicians—especially Rudy Giuliani and George W. Bush—would try. After the terrorist attacks, Selig ordered all ball games postponed. Yet he also invoked Roosevelt's "green light," claiming baseball was "woven too deeply into the national fabric" to stop the games completely. MLB embraced the flag and led the call to "support the troops." Former Commissioner Fay Vincent claimed that "after September 11, 2001, . . . many things brought us together and baseball was not the least of them." Having the games soon proceed indicated, symbolically, that America would be fighting back. Some even posted survival tactics fans could use if a terrorist attack came at a ball game.[6]

According to Rebecca Kraus, baseball served as a "shelter during the storm, . . . [bearing] much of the burden for healing the nation after September 11." As the Baseball Hall of Fame's John Odell observed, each game "became a kind of village green where people could talk and deal with their fears." The games supplied the primary stage for stirring displays of patriotic unity. As one fan noted, "We all have to continue on and support our president. And the Red Sox." When he was given the first Philadelphia Phillies game start after the attacks, Robert Person said, "I am pitching for the whole nation."[7]

Arizona Diamondbacks pitcher Curt Schilling joined the chorus: "We will proudly wear the great flag of this country on our uniforms and it's something I hope baseball will adopt forever. When the nation sings 'God Bless America,' we do so because men and women have died so we can continue as a free nation." Schilling was particularly vocal in supporting President Bush (and eventually his reelection) and a military response to 9/11—not surprising, as the hurler said he "relaxes by going to war." Schilling is a long-time military history fan and was president of Multi-Man Publishing, which supplied war games for toy manufacturers. He credited war gaming for his own success on the mound.[8]

Every major-league ballpark was awash with patriotic gestures. Moments of silence were religiously observed, and patriotic music punctuated games. Fields and stands were blanketed with red, white, and blue. Silent auctions were held and benefit games were played for the Red Cross. At Pittsburgh's PNC Park, players wore caps honoring New York's police, firefighters, and emergency crews. Fans at San Francisco's Pac Bell Park held candles, prayed and sang, and chanted "USA! USA!" Yankee Stadium held a memorial service, and manager Joe Torre took his players to shelters and firehouses. At Shea Stadium, Liza Minelli turned "New York, New York" into a fight song, Mets players raised money for the Twin Towers Relief Fund, and Diamondback players honored rescue workers at ground zero.[9]

At Busch Stadium, seventy-seven-year-old St. Louis Cardinals announcer Jack Buck, a World War II Purple Heart recipient, mesmerized the crowd with his verse:

> Since this nation was founded . . . under God
> More than 200 years ago
> We have been the bastion of freedom
> The light that keeps the free world aglow
> We do not covet the possessions of others
> We are blessed with the bounty we share
> We have rushed to help other nations
> . . . anything . . . anytime . . . anywhere
> War is just not our nature
> We won't start . . . but we will end the fight
> If we are involved we shall be resolved
> To protect what we know is right.
> We have been challenged by a cowardly foe
> Who strikes and then hides from our view.
> With one voice we say, "There is no choice today.
> There is only one thing to do."

The terrorist attacks immediately politicized baseball. President Bush "used baseball as a major patriotic statement" at the World Series and elsewhere. Maverick Media, the president's image maker, later repackaged footage from Bush's baseball appearances, playing them repeatedly during his reelection campaign. New York mayor Rudy Giuliani used 9/11 and baseball to revitalize his sagging political fortunes. Rallying the city wearing his ubiquitous Yankees cap, the mayor spent more time at the ballpark than at ground zero, and later used baseball as a backdrop for his presidential campaign.[10]

Sports have been described as a "civilizing project" for the modern nation.

Yet for a nation *at war*, there's a "functional bonding of sport and violence."[11] Thus the 2001 World Series games, broadcast by the conservative Fox network, were framed by images of U.S. flags and tanks, and the national anthem's almost nonstop performance. Pitting the Yankees against the Diamondbacks, the series was scripted as "nationalist patriotism in support of U.S. military action."[12] When the series arrived in New York for game three, President Bush prepared to throw out the first pitch. When he saw where Bush was practicing, Yankees shortstop Derek Jeter told him, "This is New York. If you throw like that from the base of the mound, they're going to boo you." Taking Jeter's advice, he walked to the top of the mound, threw a perfect strike, and then heard the roar of "USA! USA!" Bush explained that he wanted to throw the pitch "with a little zip" because he "didn't want people to think their president was incapable of finding the plate." Later he said that pitch was the highlight of his presidency.

Political pundit Chris Matthews claimed this showed Bush's military and leadership prowess: "Some things you can't fake. Either you can throw a strike from sixty feet or you can't. This is about knowing what to do at the moment you have to do it—and then doing it," presumably with a little help from your friends. Surely this proved our president would lead us out of our national nightmare. Sportswriter Bill Littlefield claimed he didn't mind having politicians show up at ball games, where they "are less likely to engage in dangerous mischief. Nobody has ever called an air strike from the pitcher's mound, the proximity of military jets notwithstanding."[13] But in effect, President Bush's World Series appearance did just that.

At the game was a torn American flag retrieved from ground zero and flown over Yankee Stadium. In the outfield, fans cheered a reenactment of New York City firefighters raising another flag over the World Trade Center debris, recalling the staged photo on World War II's Iwo Jima. "The game of baseball," according to Lara Nielsen, "was narrated by an image that endorsed the moral victory of war, [promoting] the conclusion that military retaliation . . . was the only appropriate response." It undermined any script that might have allowed fans to debate the subject. Until then, baseball's consciousness of terrorism was likely limited to what sportswriter Tom Boswell had called the "balance of terror" between pitchers and batters. Thereafter, "the sanctioned exhibition of violence and trauma most commonly associated with a militarized society emerged again on the athletic field."[14]

Some initially questioned baseball's relevance after the attacks. Jason Scheller claimed it meant nothing like it had during World War II. *Sporting News* writer Ken Rosenthal declared that "the sport no longer holds as cherished a place in our society." Yet baseball's central role in pulling New York and the nation out of the 9/11 shock and priming the country for war could not be denied. As captured in the film *Nine Innings at Ground Zero*, so profound was the connection that even the widely hated Yankees were suddenly transformed into America's team.[15]

Fittingly for the days to come, the Yankees were owned by George Steinbrenner, MLB's leading jingoist, whose idol was World War II hero General George Patton. Addicted to the movie *Patton*, Steinbrenner wrote the preface to *Patton Leadership: Strategic Lessons for Corporate Warfare*, praising the general as the "ultimate warrior"—the phrase he also used to describe his favorite Yankee ballplayers. A Culver Military Academy graduate, Steinbrenner worshipped Sun-tzu, the ancient Chinese military strategist who wrote *The Art of War*. "It's like a Bible to me. I give it to my people and say, 'This is what you must remember when you go forward.' Because we basically go to combat—whether it's baseball . . . or whatever it's in."[16]

Although Arizona's World Series victory ruined the Yankees' fairy-tale ending, the military response the games had helped legitimize emerged full force. President Bush announced the War on Terrorism and the impending attack on Afghanistan. Longtime *Baseball Digest* editor John Kuenster proclaimed, "While events of last September shocked the nation, no such . . . random luck applies in what promises to be a protracted war against those who perpetrate mass killings of innocent civilians." Thus did America quickly squander the national sense of community and international goodwill the attacks had initially engendered, and like a nation crazed with "steroid rage," the United States lashed out with wave after wave of indiscriminate violence.[17]

Curiously, some were offended that terrorists didn't play fair. Sportswriter Bill Gallo fumed: "Changeless sports events helped us regain our national equilibrium in the wake of al-Qa'ida's savagery. After all [baseball teams] still played by time-honored rules."[18] Yet with the dust settled after the 2001 season and with some people wondering about cheating in baseball, America was about to launch a wholesale assault on other time-honored rules—the U.S. Constitution and international law—a kind of cheating and rule breaking in its own right.

Muscular Conservatism

Shortly before September 11, sports diplomacy was still being advocated, as the United States continued "to impress its democratic goals on remaining holdouts such as . . . Iran and North Korea." But less than a year later, sports were downplayed except for their "imagery and rhetoric, especially [from] football, which were so heavily deployed in Pentagon press briefings." This began in the Gulf War but escalated in the war on terror and the war on Afghanistan, which by early 2002 were in full swing. In January, the stakes were further raised by President Bush's "Axis of Evil" speech, which added Iraq to Iran and North Korea, and accused those nations of fostering terrorism and stockpiling weapons of mass destruction. With the help of a fawning press, "war masculinized Bush and emasculated the Democrats," as Stephen Ducat put it, and furthered "the rise of 'muscular conservatism' and U.S. foreign policy on steroids."[19] But where would this leave baseball?

The sport's owners and patrons needn't have worried. Patriotism reigned at Opening Day in April 2002, and the military hoopla escalated further. "Whether it is 1942 or 2002," observed one commentator, "baseball and U.S. military history will always blend together." While the McGwire-Sosa home-run race of 1998 had brought in new fans, still more were generated by 9/11. As Marian Russell confessed, "I've always loathed baseball but the Boys of Summer are here and I'm glad." Dan Wachtell observed, "Baseball went on, because if we stop playing, the Taliban Terrorists win. During the offseason, Taliban management saw their major league roster decimated and their minor league systems put out of business. During spring training, missiles rained upon their outfield and now the Taliban is picked to finish [in last place and is] in serious danger of being contracted." An overly optimistic assessment of the wars, but even so, baseball, or at least baseball metaphors, could apparently help fight the terrorists.[20]

But not necessarily the ballplayers themselves. Columnist Bob Herbert remarked, "Gone are the days when a Ted Williams would interrupt a flourishing baseball career to fight the enemy . . . ; war is something for other people to fight. Waving a flag is one thing; dodging bullets is something else." Among the exceptions were the Tillman brothers. Kevin Tillman, a Cleveland Indians minor leaguer, enlisted. Pat Tillman was an Arizona Cardinals star safety who rejected a three-year contract to join the U.S. Army. The White House and Pentagon jumped all over the Pat Tillman enlistment, using him as the poster boy for patriotism.[21]

Baseball had no celebrity icon for the war, but it waved the flag in many other ways. Little League launched an "Honoring Our Hometown Heroes" program to recognize firefighters, police, and military personnel. Every professional ball game began with salutes to the troops, and baseball telecasts featured photos of soldiers in war zones watching their favorite teams. In May 2002, San Francisco honored major leaguers whose careers were interrupted by military duty, such as Giants manager Dusty Baker. The Giants also distributed desert camouflage military bucket hats at ball games and joined other teams in holding military appreciation days. Later in the season, George Steinbrenner hosted General Tommy Franks, the American forces commander in

Afghanistan, at a Yankees game. And Anaheim Angels executive Tim Mead was invited by Defense Secretary Donald Rumsfeld to the Joint Civilian Orientation Conference for a firsthand view of U.S. soldiers, their equipment and capabilities, and national defense strategies.[22]

Outsiders hoped the 9/11 attacks would shake the Bush administration's hard-core unilateralism, but instead they only intensified its "might makes right" philosophy. As for the American people, they heeded the president's call to fight the terrorists "by going shopping, [thus, the malls] remained crowded and the summer's hot topic was whether overpaid baseball players would go on strike."[23] As in past American wars, baseball's 2002 labor grievances were condemned as unpatriotic. No sport matched baseball's flag-waving after 9/11, but sportswriter Walter Shapiro brooded: "Talk about empty symbolism. Nothing would be more cynical than if the ballparks were empty on the anniversary of September 11." Shapiro scorned the rancor of the baseball negotiations "at a time when America has real enemies."[24] Yet baseball hadn't forgotten 9/11, after all. Cincinnati Reds general manager Jim Bowden compared a potential baseball walkout to the terrorist attacks: "If players want to strike, they ought to just pick September 11, because that's what it's going to do to the game. Let [union head] Donald Fehr drive the plane right into the building."

But a strike was averted, and at 9:11 P.M. on September 11, 2002, MLB paused to commemorate the previous year's terrorist attack. Commissioner Selig gave a moving tribute. ESPN broadcast twelve continuous hours of baseball. Yankee Stadium dedicated a new monument. In a letter read at every major-league game, President Bush observed, "During the past year baseball helped bring Americans together . . . and [promoted] the healing process." A few days earlier, Bush hosted the Texas Rangers, the club he previously owned. Later that day, he met with top lawmakers to plan the war on Iraq. Opposing the new intervention, protesters soon flooded the streets of America and cities around the world. At one demonstration, signs read, "Impeach Bush, Dusty Baker for President" and "Baseball, Not Bombs."[25]

One of the biggest cheerleaders for the war was New York Yankees pitcher Roger Clemens, who addressed military battalions during a mobilization farewell in March 2003. Repeating a Vietnam-era canard, Clemens recalled his brother Richard's return: "He came home and it was difficult because, as you guys know, they weren't really well received." Clemens concluded by saying, "After 20 years of playing the game I love, I consider myself a true team player. But you guys are the ultimate team. You're protecting our freedom."[26]

As part of MLB's globalization strategy, a season-opening series between the Oakland Athletics and Seattle Mariners was scheduled for April 2003 in

Tokyo. It promised to be a rousing homecoming for the Japanese stars Ichiro Suzuki, Shigetoshi Hasegawa, and Kazuhiro Sasaki, and also the first time Mariners owner Hiroshi Yamauchi would see his team play live. But because of the "tense world situation," the series was canceled: there were fears of reprisals against American players for the just-launched U.S. attack on Iraq.[27]

The Hall Protects the Troops

At home, attention turned unexpectedly to the Cooperstown Hall of Fame. While the baseball shrine had never avoided patriotic displays, such as having the American flag as the backdrop for its logo, it usually kept a low profile. In 1999, however, Dale Petroskey became the Hall's new president, and especially since 9/11, he had become a visible cheerleader for the Republican Party and U.S. military policies. Then in 2003, Petroskey canceled the twenty-fifth anniversary celebration of the landmark baseball film *Bull Durham* because two of its stars, Tim Robbins and Susan Sarandon, were outspoken Iraq War critics. Petroskey had taken the advice, at least metaphorically, of right-wing pundit Ann Coulter, who said that "a baseball bat is the most effective way [to talk to liberals] these days."

Petroskey began militarizing the Hall early on. He hired his longtime mentor, Bill Haase, an ex-Marine who created a boot-camp atmosphere. Strict military-style dress and grooming codes were imposed for Hall employees, along with a rigid top-down hierarchy of command. Free admission was offered to all active and retired military personnel, and a large, permanent podium to honor Hall of Famers who were military veterans was unveiled in a 2002 Memorial Day ceremony. Special plates were inserted under the individual plaques of every Hall of Famer who served in the military. As Eric Enders noted, some wondered whether they were visiting the Baseball Hall of Fame or the U.S. Military Hall of Fame. References to anything that might question the military's relationship with baseball, such as Jackie Robinson's court martial, were nowhere to be found.[28]

In canceling the *Bull Durham* event, Petroskey wrote Robbins and Sarandon, saying that "your public criticism of President Bush at this . . . sensitive time . . . helps undermine the U.S. position, which puts our troops in even more danger. As an institution, we stand behind our President and our troops in this conflict." All but calling them traitors, Petroskey claimed their antiwar criticism would politicize the event, as though he hadn't been politicizing the Hall for several years. A longtime Republican Party worker who had been assistant press secretary in the Reagan White House, Petroskey was also intimate with the Bush family. He gave Bush a lifetime museum pass and even nominated

him for induction into the Hall. He had a special baseball exhibit installed in
the White House. Every new Hall employee was required to watch a video of
one of Bush's political speeches, and only a year earlier, Petroskey had hosted
Bush White House press secretary Ari Fleischer at the Hall, to talk, not about
baseball, but about Republican politics and the war on terrorism.[29]

Responding to Petroskey, Tim Robbins wrote, "I was unaware that baseball
was a Republican sport. You invoke patriotism and use words like 'freedom' to
intimidate and bully. In doing so, you dishonor the words . . . and the men and
women who have fought wars to keep this nation a place where one can freely
express their opinions without fear of reprisal. . . . I wish you had . . . saved
me the rhetoric and talked honestly about your ties to the Bush and Reagan
administrations."

Petroskey's *Bull Durham* cancellation generated thousands of protests. The
dean of American baseball writers, Roger Kahn, called off his Hall appearance
scheduled for later that year: "By canceling the *Bull Durham* [celebration] for
political reasons, you are, far from supporting our troops, defying the noblest
of the American spirit." Acclaimed journalist Mitch Albom asked, "Where do
you begin with such misguided patriotism? . . . it's the *Baseball* Hall of Fame,
not the Pentagon. Who decided [its] position on the Middle East? A couple of
Hollywood types do not put bullets in our troops. Half the world already
spoke out against the war . . . hugging the flag is simple. Hugging what it
stands for is harder."[30]

Sportswriter Gwen Knapp used her critique of Petroskey to challenge baseball's broader militarism, including the ear-shattering Air Force flyovers at ball
games since 9/11: "The ritual is fundamentally disrespectful to military operations. [Having] those planes at a sporting event trivializes their real purpose.
Baseball pretends to be honoring the military . . . [but] it's really . . . aggran-
dizing itself, a commercial entity exploitatively wrapped in red, white, and
blue. It's patriotism as a marketing tool." Even so, Petroskey stuck to his *Bull
Durham* decision. Prominent baseball figures, such as Jules Tygiel, called for
Petroskey's resignation, but in the short run his job remained secure.[31]

Worshipping the Good War

As Britain's "Downing Street Memo" later revealed about the Bush administration's case for the Iraq War, "the intelligence and facts were being fixed
around the policy." That is, the president knew Saddam Hussein had no weapons
of mass destruction, wasn't close to building any, and had no connection to the
9/11 terrorist attacks. Mobilizing the nation for the war nevertheless, the White
House used the testimony of an Iraqi defector, aptly code-named Curve Ball.

Perhaps baseball should have been flattered, but this source was a former Iraqi cabdriver and well-known con artist who lied about Iraq having mobile biological weapons factories and other armaments. He was mentally unstable, and when the CIA found his fabrications in Secretary of Defense Colin Powell's planned United Nations speech to justify the U.S. attack, it deleted them—only to find the lies reinserted in Powell's actual talk. CIA officials knew Bush policy makers were "absolutely, violently committed" to using the tainted information. CIA director George Tenet was warned about Curve Ball before Powell's speech, though he later denied it.[32]

The presumed 9/11 mastermind, Osama bin Laden, had been blamed for just about everything else, so John Breneman satirically presented evidence that the terrorist was also responsible for an even deeper wound in America's heart—the "Curse of the Bambino," which had doomed the Boston Red Sox to live in the shadow of their archenemy, the New York Yankees. According to Breneman, "Appearing on videotape sporting a New York Yankees cap and swinging a Louisville Slugger instead of [his customary] Kalashnikov rifle, bin Laden demonstrated how he triggered the curse [again] in game seven [of the American League championship series] on October 16, 2003," allowing the Yankees to triumph again and advance into the World Series.[33]

Unlike bin Laden, George W. Bush had a genuine baseball connection. As Elisabeth Bumiller noted, Bush "owes much in his life, if not the presidency, to baseball . . . the game made him a multimillionaire. As a Rangers [owner, Bush built] the image and political skills to win the Texas governorship and the White House. He knew how to rally the troops using the Rangers as talking points."[34] As president, with organized baseball's compliance, Bush repeatedly invoked the sport for patriotic ends.

In his 2004 State of the Union address, Bush even discussed baseball's steroids threat, invoking it as a national security issue: "Unfortunately some in professional sports are not setting much of an example." The president didn't mention that when he owned the Rangers in the 1990s, his team was a virtual steroids crack house and the primary breeding ground for steroid proliferation in baseball. More than 20 percent of the players named in the Mitchell steroids report had been Texas Rangers.

Nevertheless, according to Carl Cannon, "one thing on which Bush lovers and haters agree is that regarding baseball, the President gets it." It showed in the president's reelection bid. Many people seemed to be paying more attention to baseball than to domestic and international politics. Perhaps this helped explain why, during the 2004 campaign, the Democratic Party challenger John Kerry couldn't win the baseball race with George W. Bush. Baseball icon Bob Feller quickly distinguished the candidates: "While President Bush's leadership in the War on Terror has made America's veterans proud of our commander-in-chief, John Kerry's changing position shows he cannot be trusted." In the words of Josh Fleer,

> Baseball's function—especially prominent in light of the terrorist attacks—became a backdrop for the 2004 election. When Kerry challenged for the presidency, he [unlike] Bush, raised important issues, [and he contrasted dramatically with Bush in his] acceptance of Vietnam War [duty]. However, when Kerry [showed] he was not proficient in the culture of baseball—where "we the people" gather to celebrate national values that unite Americans beyond their individual beliefs, America could not envision Kerry as their king, prophet and priest.[35]

Hall of Fame pitcher Bob Feller's electioneering and his war-on-terror cheerleading dovetailed nicely with his renewed efforts to remind Americans of the glories of World War II. Characterizing the 9/11 terrorist attacks as an echo of Pearl Harbor—however misleading the comparison—helped generate another "Good War" revival. In the early 2000s, Feller led a high-profile campaign for the World War II Veterans Committee, advocating veterans' rights and aggressive U.S. militarism: "Will you help me defend the legacy of World War II from left-wing revisionists who are trying to rewrite American history?" About Second World War ballplayer veterans, Feller indicated that "we were Americans first and foremost! I don't know one baseball player who . . . wouldn't do it all over again." But he bitterly resented today's America: "We changed the world. Call me a hawk if you want to. Left-wing revisionists and government bureaucrats cancelled the U.S. postage stamp commemorating the [Hiroshima] bombing [and] they denounced 'Victory over Japan' as 'politically incorrect.'" According to Feller, these events ought to be commemorated anew because they are "the stories of heroes. Yet these brave World War II vets have been forgotten and ignored."

To the contrary, World War II and its veterans have been repeatedly glorified, with the latest wave of high-profile books, movies, and documentaries coming in the early twenty-first century. Far from forgetting, America is still "worshipping the myths" of the war, according to decorated World War II veteran Edward Wood. And baseball played a central role. As historian Gary Bedingfield notes, "Baseball remains the primary athletic link to the 'greatest generation' . . . when baseball was America's sole athletic ego." The Hall of Fame played up the relationship as well, enlisting Feller as its membership spokesman and spotlighting his wartime memories in the Hall's glossy magazine.[36]

In *USA Today*, Jeff Zillgitt told readers, "Imagine the modern-day equivalent of . . . MLB during World War II: Josh Beckett informing the Florida Marlins he is joining the U.S. Navy, like Bob Feller did in 1942. Derek Jeter giving up the prime of his career with the New York Yankees to fight the war on terrorism, similar to what Hank Greenberg did. Barry Bonds and Ken Griffey Jr. leaving their teams to help the U.S., like Ted Williams and Joe DiMaggio did. These scenarios would never happen today."[37]

To augment its boosterism for the wars on terror and Iraq and to further establish the World War II connection, Fox television aired the documentary *From the Ballpark to the Battlefield: Baseball and World War II.* The film was hosted by former marine colonel and Iran-Contra conspirator Oliver North, who gushed about baseball's role in raising morale and achieving victory in the "Good War." Other tributes followed, such as the National World War II Museum conference in New Orleans on "Duty, Honor, Country: When Baseball Went to War." It featured ballplayer veterans Bob Feller, Dom DiMaggio, Morrie Martin, Jerry Coleman, Johnny Pesky, and Lou Brissie, as well as military buff and museum board member Curt Schilling and CIA Museum curator Linda McCarthy. Tommy Lasorda gave the keynote speech on "The Importance of Our National Pastime to Victory in World War II." Intentional or not, with these displays President Bush couldn't have asked for more support from baseball for his own wars.

The Stupidest War Ever

No one actually requested military recruits from baseball for the 9/11 wars, and for all of MLB's military pomp and morale-building tours to the front, essentially no one volunteered. This might have seemed hypocritical if baseball's institutional backing of U.S. military policies had not been overwhelming.[38] Commissioner Selig decided the mandatory "Star Spangled Banner" at all ball games wasn't sufficient nationalistic fervor, so he decreed that "God Bless America" also be sung during each game's seventh-inning stretch as a military tribute.[39] Explaining his decision, Selig said, "I don't honestly think [it] politicizes the issue. After all, we do have troops in Iraq and Afghanistan."

But playing the song was clearly a political statement. Professional ballplayers were reluctant to challenge this, and the one exception only underscored the norm of baseball's support for militarism.[40] That dissenter was Blue Jays first baseman Carlos Delgado, who remained in the dugout during the playing of "God Bless America." He viewed the song as cheerleading for the American attack on Iraq: "It's a very terrible thing that happened on September 11. But it's also a terrible thing that's happening in Afghanistan and Iraq. . . . I think it's the stupidest war ever."

Blue Jays president Paul Godfrey supported the Iraq War and criticized Canada for not sending troops. Another war supporter, Toronto catcher Geoff Zaun, vowed he'd never buy another Dixie Chicks CD—to protest the singing group's criticism of President Bush and his foreign policies. Nevertheless, they tolerated Delgado's right to dissent. But when the Blue Jays went to New York to play in July 2004, Delgado got a different reception. At Yankee Stadium, "God Bless America" was not optional for fans. Under owner George Steinbrenner's orders, ushers strung up chains during each seventh-inning stretch to keep people standing and block them from leaving for the bathroom or concessions until the song was finished playing.[41] During each at bat, Delgado was greeted with boos, then derisive shouts during each game's seventh-inning stretch. When he made an out, chants of "USA! USA!" went up in the crowd. About Delgado, one Yankees fan protested, "It's totally disrespectful. It's a slap in my face as a New Yorker and American." Labeling him "un-American" and unfit to collect his paycheck, some said Delgado's dissent "makes him a terrorist and he should be jailed."[42]

Well connected to his community through his Extra Bases Foundation, Delgado was not new to political protest. He campaigned for years to remove the U.S. from Vieques, an island in his native Puerto Rico used as a weapons-testing ground for sixty years. The Navy finally pulled out, leaving behind poverty, unemployment, toxic waste, and high cancer rates. Delgado wanted the United States to clean up after itself. As Dave Zirin has noted, Delgado "viewed the people of Vieques as casualties—collateral damage—from the war on Iraq because they served as guinea pigs for weapons that have wreaked havoc throughout the Persian Gulf."[43]

Eventually Delgado ended up on the New York Mets, who made it clear that "freedom of speech stops once the blue and orange uniform—their brand—is affixed to his body." Required to stand for "God Bless America," he finally relented. Delgado's silencing illustrated a larger problem. According to William Arkin, "an attitude [developed] during the Iraq war that the team—the U.S. military—can't be criticized. There is no room to call someone to task for his managing, fielding or batting errors, no matter how egregious . . . and to actually hold the team itself accountable is to be disloyal to the big team, the country."[44]

Even so, a few others questioned the "God Bless America" ritual as well. Historian Howard Zinn asked, "one wonders why we would expect that God would single out one nation, with only 5% of the world's population, for his or her blessing?" Others were puzzled why "God Bless America" was imposed in Canada, at Toronto and Montreal games, with the expectation that Canadians would sing it. And what about the 30 percent of all major leaguers and the many fans who were not Americans? Or as Dan Wachtell asked, "What about those of us who get all our patriotism out during the traditional pregame 'Star Spangled Banner'? Enough already."[45]

Of course, the national anthem was contested a bit in its own right. It bothered some people because it's a war song. The legendary Tony Bennett began substituting "America the Beautiful" when asked to perform at San Francisco's Pacific Bell Park. The Giants also played John Lennon's peace anthem "Imagine," although not for long. Sports broadcaster Bill Littlefield worried that since politicians were "considering yet another target [Iran], baseball will have to come up with another patriotic song and another place to put it: perhaps 'Yankee Doodle Dandy' after the top of the third inning."[46]

To complement the patriotic songs, Commissioner Selig mandated American flags on all major-league caps, helmets, and jerseys, even on the bases, after 9/11. Baseball wasn't the only flag-waving sport, but as Dave McKenna noted, "nobody pushes the red, white and blue like baseball. As baseball has become the most international of this country's major sports, it has only waved the flag harder." Neither America nor MLB seem to see the contradiction. Even the Canadian teams were required to wear American flags. As Paul Lukas suggested, "It was hard not to imagine Canadian fans feeling just a teeny bit resentful, a point worth considering, given that resentment over American nationalism is part of what inspired the World Trade Center attack in the first place."[47]

Beyond ballpark flags, baseball was concerned with American flags generally. While three decades had passed since Rick Monday's "flag rescue" at Dodger Stadium, it seemed fresh in Tommy Lasorda's mind. He joined Monday to campaign for an anti–flag desecration amendment to the U.S. Constitution. Lasorda claimed that "the respect we show for the nation when we face the American flag, and sing the national anthem—respect for God and country—can't just be taught for two minutes before every baseball game [but rather only] by protecting our flag from physical desecration." Lasorda argued that the Supreme Court flag decision had treated it as "just another piece of cloth that can be burned and soiled with impunity," and urged Congress to respond.[48]

Pledge Your Allegiance

Elsewhere in the nation's capital, the Montreal Expos franchise arrived in 2005, was reborn as the Washington Nationals, adopted the motto "Pledge Your Allegiance," and wasted no time in bonding with the D.C. military community. In June, the team hosted a Military Appreciation Night, featuring Operation Tribute to Freedom, in which ten new U.S. Army recruits were sworn in. President Bush and Secretary of State Rice shared the spotlight. The team then became the first to promote America Supports You, a Pentagon program "to give visibility to citizens [who] show their appreciation to America's Armed Forces." The relationship began at the July 4, 2005, game, where fans watched a Defense Department video featuring Nationals players plugging the program.

The July 24, 2005, Nationals game was designated "Armed Forces Day," and discounts were given to soldiers and the thousands of military contractors and civilian military employees swarming around the capital. Video and musical tributes to the military proliferated, often during the seventh-inning stretch. With the regular U.S. military overextended and the National Guard supplying most new Iraq War soldiers, President Bush was desperate for more enlistments. To generate recruits, the Nationals reached a naming-rights deal to call its ballpark National Guard Field at RFK (Stadium). The plan ultimately fell through, but as Dave McKenna suggested, "the Nationals have done more than their share to promote the military-baseball complex."[49]

While few other teams could match the Nationals, most other clubs paid similar devotion to the military and the wars. The Seattle Mariners held an Annual Boeing Salute to the Armed Forces Night, sponsored by the city's military contractor. The Milwaukee Brewers made their military celebration a weeklong affair, including a Navy Leapfrog parachute jump and an armed forces military display at Miller Park, where tanks and other equipment were shown off. The San Diego Padres admitted military personnel for free and divided each section by military branch. For each Sunday home game, "the Padres celebrate and give respect for our fighting troops by proudly wearing [military] camouflage uniforms . . . where GI Joe meets Abner Doubleday," thus helping perpetuate baseball's founding myth. In St. Louis, Cardinals announcer Joe Buck had one of the "most exhilarating nights of [his] broadcast career" when he connected a game live to U.S. soldiers in Iraq.[50]

The San Francisco Giants also sponsored armed forces events, such as Military Sundays. Patriotic displays were staged for the 2007 All-Star Game at AT&T Park, with a huge American flag again covering the outfield. From the Giants broadcast booth, one could see navy ships in San Francisco Bay, which the announcers regularly praised as "things of beauty." A major Giants television sponsor was the U.S. Marine Corps, which solicited enlistments, and underwrote the U.S. Marines Leaders of the Game and Honor Roll Defensive Play of the Game promotions. Along with MLB and Chevrolet, the marines also subsidized the annual Roberto Clemente Award. And the military ran ads evoking baseball, such as one that suggested, "To learn how you can make it to the big leagues, contact the U.S. Navy."[51]

Across the Bay, in Oakland, Athletics pitcher Barry Zito founded Strikeouts for Troops in 2005. With organized baseball's endorsement, the funds assisted war-wounded troops returning from Iraq and Afghanistan and recovering at U.S. military hospitals. Zito and the program's other pitchers contributed $100 for every strikeout they got during the season. Batters also signed on, pledging the same amount for each home run. Transferred from the Athletics to the Giants when Zito was traded, the star pitcher said, "Baseball is ingrained in the fabric of America, just like the military. We thought it was a good marriage."

A worthy cause without question, yet Zito also claimed: "More than anything, it's not about a partisan agenda, it's not about supporting the war or not." But the funds raised by Strikeouts for Troops were all given for distribution to the Freedom Alliance, a right-wing, pro-war organization featuring the conservative broadcaster Sean Hannity and Alliance founder Oliver North. The group's annual Defender of Freedom Award has gone exclusively to right-wing politicos, such as Jesse Helms, John Bolton, Ward Connerly, and Bob Barr. There are no Democrats on the organization's board, which is filled with Republicans and religious fundamentalists. Strikeouts for Troops received its biggest endorsement from vocal Ted Williams fan, former Vietnam War POW, and Republican pro-war presidential candidate John McCain, who enthused, "Every time Barry Zito strikes a batter out or Alex Rodriguez hits a home run we are reminded of our own duty to support those who fight for us, and our troops are reminded they have the support of a grateful nation." Because of their Strikeouts for Troops involvement, two former Athletics players—Joe Blanton and Nick Swisher—were asked to tour U.S. naval bases in Italy, Greece, and Spain.[52]

For supporting such tours and other patriotic displays, in December 2006 Commissioner Bud Selig was awarded the USO Gold Medal, which goes to the person providing the greatest support for the U.S. military. Accepting the award, Selig remarked, "There has been a long and proud relationship between baseball and the U.S. military since the Civil War. Sixty-five years ago . . . President Roosevelt decided it was best for the country to keep baseball going. Baseball . . . supports our servicemen in times of peace and times of war."[53]

Baseball hero Cal Ripken also did his part to promote America's foreign policy. Already he had been featured on a National Security Agency poster, with his knees bent and glove ready, under the headline "Security: Our Best Defense." It appeared at thousands of security briefings. Then in 2007 Secretary of State Rice appointed Ripkin Special Sports Envoy to promote baseball and improve America's global image.[54] Meanwhile, New York Yankees star Johnny Damon won the New York Baseball Writers Association's Better World Award for his Wounded Warrior Project, which assists "men and women of our armed forces who have been severely injured in Iraq, Afghanistan and other locations around the world." And in 2009, MLB launched its Welcome Back Veterans campaign to publicize the issues facing veterans returning from the Middle East and provide them employment and mental health services to assist their reentry.

Baseball also made a comeback within the armed forces. The service leagues had languished for several decades. Some blamed politics, often using the standard militarist myth: "When politicians began the systematic dismantling of our military infrastructure [after] the Vietnam War, baseball was slowly phased out and went dormant along with the decline of our armed forces." In 1990, however, organized military baseball was restored, with more than 21,000 service personnel playing on teams through the mid-2000s. The marines housed their main team in San Diego and sponsored others around the world. Also headquartered in San Diego, the U.S. Navy Baseball Club also ran three teams on the East Coast. The air force had eleven teams around the United States, mostly in the Midwest and Far West. The army's teams were based at Fort Hood, Texas, and Fort Bragg, North Carolina, but had been dormant, with so many soldiers away at the Iraq and Afghan wars. The Southern Command in Miami had the only Joint Forces team. The U.S. Military All-Star Game was played each summer immediately following a San Diego Padres game.[55]

The navy club also organized a Military All-Star Team to compete in annual Red, White, and Blue Tours of America to "raise public awareness of the men and women serving at the Tip of the Spear." In 2005, the tour barnstormed the Cape Cod League and the New England College Baseball League. The program expanded the U.S. military's visibility in the college, minor, independent, and major leagues. Professional teams hosted the All-Stars in exhibition games and wore official USA military camouflage uniforms for patriotic holidays and also for military or fan appreciation days, such as Shirt Off My Back Nights.[56]

Violence Punctuated by Committee Meetings

If baseball had been bolstering its U.S. foreign- and military-policy relationship in the early twenty-first century, then how was it faring compared to football, which had long coveted baseball's crown as the national pastime? Often sharp contrasts were drawn between the two sports. For theologian Michael Novak, football was corporate and bureaucratic, while baseball was the real America. John McMurtry lamented baseball's decline and claimed that "pro football is a sick society's projection of itself into public spectacle." In an oft-reprinted article, sportswriter Tom Boswell enumerated ninety-nine reasons why baseball is better than football.[57] Columnist George Will pointed out that "football combines the two worst elements of American society: its violence, punctuated by committee meetings." And comedian George Carlin famously compared the two sports this way:

> Baseball is played on a diamond, in a park. Football is played on a grid-iron, in a stadium called Soldiers Field or War Memorial Stadium. Baseball begins in the spring, the season of new life. Football begins in the fall, when everything's dying. Football has hitting, clipping, spearing, piling on and unnecessary roughness. Baseball has the sacrifice. In football the object is for the quarterback, the field general, to be on target with his aerial assault, riddling the defense by hitting receivers with deadly accuracy in spite of the blitz, even if he has to use the shotgun. With short bullet passes and long bombs, he marches his troops into enemy territory, balancing his aerial assault with a sustained ground attack that punches holes in the enemy's defensive line. In baseball the object is to go home! And to be safe![58]

According to Don Malcolm, "baseball, once written off as passé, gives us 'innocence' and 'order' [and a] respite from darker matters [such as global war] . . . [and] has survived the encroaching shadow of more aggressive sports."[59]

Critics, however, claimed baseball wasn't America's pastime but rather its "past tense." In his late-twentieth-century classic, *America*, British historian Alistair Cooke warned about America's signs of decline, similar to the fall of Rome. In U.S. football, Cooke saw the war and violence of empire, a vision of gladiators feverishly watched by a nation of spectators. Journalist Mary McGrory lamented, "Baseball is what we were, football is what we have become." In his 2004 gridiron history, Michael MacCambridge agreed, observing that football had become "a truer reflection of the American preoccupations with power and passion, technology and teamwork." Michael Mandelbaum saw football's intrinsic affinity with the armed forces—football games are much more like war than baseball games are. Football thrived in America (but nowhere else) beginning with the "second half of the Cold War," when the "U.S. was mobilized for international conflict, [and it] continued to prosper into the twenty-first century." Rather than football being a substitute for war, it instead seemed better suited than baseball as a preparation for war.[60]

Sportswriter Frank Deford wondered whether baseball had "forever lost that mystic ability to provide us with a sense of who we are." Instead, "never has the pigskin's preeminence been more evident, as our hideously mesomorphic gladiators head off to training camp." We might explain football's popularity by admitting that "we violent Americans just plain like smashmouth . . . [but] maybe these times are [also] most in tune with football: [in an] arrogant, unilateral and insular [America], baseball can have all its Latins and Asians, and basketball can have all its Croats and Lithuanians, but football is still ours, 100% pure American." Deford added, "Although George W. Bush is *of* baseball, he operates with none of the [sport's] patient rhythms but simply charges ahead."[61]

Of course, while football was overtaking baseball in the war for American martial superiority, the rest of the world was playing soccer. Football thrived at home, but it wasn't translating abroad. More foreigners were playing baseball, but it still remained a distant second to soccer, despite Albert Spalding's century-old prediction that "the time will come when Base Ball will become the established and recognized Field Sport of the world." In the United States, according to Alan Bairner, "soccer has never played a significant part in the construction of American national identity, except negatively perhaps by revealing what real Americans are not."[62]

Challenges from football and soccer notwithstanding, MLB pushed into the new century still clinging to the American foreign policy establishment. It authenticated itself as an international actor. As multinational corporations, Major League Baseball International (MLBI) and Major League Baseball Advanced Media generated foreign revenue for big-league clubs by selling broadcast rights, securing corporate sponsorships, licensing products, and staging events abroad. MLBI assessed the sport's status in the globalized world and decided to "grow" the game not by plugging into existing international sporting institutions but rather by devising its own model. It would be a unilateralism not unlike that reemerging in U.S. foreign and military policy. It would be international, but would it really be global? In 2007, Commissioner Bud Selig claimed the potential for globalization was unlimited. But as sportswriter Jason Stark observed, "It's not clear [Selig] has any idea what that means . . . and the whole context seems to be not the real globalization of baseball, but [rather] increasing global profits for MLB."[63]

According to Alan Klein, MLB identified three tiers of baseball nations: the established (the Caribbean, Japan, and Korea), the less developed (such as the Netherlands, Italy, and Australia), and the tentative (such as England and South Africa). Economic objectives dominated in the established nations, while development goals had greater priority in tentative nations. All major-league teams shopped in the Caribbean (although unequally), small-market teams shopped in Europe and South Africa, and large-market teams shopped in Japan and Korea.[64]

Kind of Like the Catholic Church?

Baseball became more controversial in the Caribbean and Latin America in the early 2000s.[65] After the United States drove the Sandinistas from office in the early 1990s, Nicaragua slipped below Haiti to become the Western Hemisphere's poorest country. Baseball declined, and soccer began making inroads. When the Sandinistas launched a comeback, the United States lobbied heavily against it, claiming Daniel Ortega's reelection would "bring nuclear or biological terrorism within walking distance of our undefended border." Disillusioned with U.S. intervention, in 2006 the Nicaraguans reelected Ortega anyway, and he immediately started a new baseball academy, launched a new relationship with the major leagues, and restored the Nicaraguan Professional League.

In Cuba, Fidel Castro was still using baseball to compete with America and to help shape his foreign policy. As Gerald Gems has noted, "despite outside intervention, multiple U.S. occupations and internal political upheavals, baseball has remained the one constant in Cuban life." Organized baseball would have happily harvested Cuba's ballplayers—the best of whom would likely thrive in the big leagues. But MLB has been blocked from such raids by its allegiance to American foreign policy. The Bush administration escalated the U.S.-Cuban conflict, even trying to implicate Cuba in the September 11 attacks. Belligerently anti-Castro, Otto Reich was appointed to head the State Department's Bureau of Western Hemispheric Affairs. The government further tightened travel restrictions to Cuba and harassed legal travelers. Surprisingly, this tension would soon pit MLB against U.S. Cuba policy.[66]

Meanwhile, the United States helped manufacture another nemesis for itself: Venezuelan president Hugo Chávez, a former ballplayer turned socialist, who grew up dreaming of playing for the San Francisco Giants. Castro and Chávez had in common not only their revolutions but also baseball. During their mutual visits, attending ball games together had become a ritual. Chávez was a big baseball fan, and regaining control over the sport was central to his quest to return his nation to the Venezuelan people, out of the clutches of Americans and local elites.[67] Venezuela's baseball resurgence began in 2000 when its Maracaibo team won the Little League World Series. In 2002, however, the Venezuela Winter League Season was canceled because of a U.S.-sponsored coup attempt against Chávez. He survived the attack, and during the 2004 Venezuelan presidential elections, Chávez campaigned against neoliberalism, vowing that he "would hit a home run that would soar over Cuba and land on the White House." When he won the election, despite U.S. efforts to prevent it, his supporters chanted "home run, home run."[68]

In 2005, the Cooperstown Hall of Fame created the Baseball/Beisbol: Latin American Baseball Project to highlight Latino contributions to America's national pastime. But the exhibit and its travel plans were shelved, at least temporarily, because its main sponsor was the Citgo Petroleum Corporation. Owned by Venezuela, the company had recently embarrassed the White House by providing low-cost heating oil to needy Massachusetts residents. In his United Nations address, President Chávez called Bush "the devil." Because of the politics, the Hall shut down the Baseball/Beisbol project, even though it had no qualms running an exhibit on baseball and the U.S.-Afghan war.[69]

In October 2005, the Chicago White Sox broke their long drought, winning their first World Series since 1917. Not shy about showing his pride in his native Venezuela and its leader, Hugo Chávez, Chicago manager Ozzie Guillen said he "was going to bring the trophy to Venezuela—and might not bring it back." One of Chávez's longtime baseball heroes, Guillen appeared on the president's television program after the series, when the streets of Caracas were as excited as Chicago's South Side. Speaking for Venezuela, Guillen observed, "Everybody talks about Chavez; but you've got to look at yourself [the United States] first . . . Everybody's got a different mind and nobody has to think the way the U.S. thinks."[70]

Nevertheless, in 2006, U.S. Ambassador William Brownfield began taunting Chávez, using baseball.[71] Claiming he needed to counter "anti-American messages," Brownfield began touring Venezuela, distributing funds and equipment to repair baseball fields. Knowing it would infuriate his host government, he had himself photographed playing catch with a local boy in Chávez's hometown. Brownfield was confronted at his baseball media events, however, with signs and chants of "Get out, gringo!" and "No more imperialist intervention!" One Venezuelan baseball fan asked, "Since when does the mighty U.S. give out baseballs? Do they think they will buy us that easily?" Larry Birns of the Council on Hemispheric Affairs called Brownfield "a mischief maker . . . resorting to theatrical actions to undermine the regime."[72]

Chávez resented organized baseball's exploitation of Venezuelan ballplayers and its broken promises for reform. In 2007, fifty Venezuelans were in MLB, and Chávez wanted a better deal for the thousand additional Venezuelans in the minor leagues and the baseball academies. He proposed better pay and conditions, and asked MLB to return to Venezuela 10 percent of the signing bonuses given to its players, to help maintain his nation's leagues and infrastructure. Venezuelan ambassador to the United States Bernardo Alvarez tried to ease tensions, saying that "for the future, with mutual respect on the political front, baseball could play an important role in integrating Venezuelan and

U.S. society." Chávez observed, "If George Bush and I survive all of this and we are old men, it would be good to play a game of . . . street baseball." But Washington shunned the overtures, and MLB sought baseball as usual—with maximum profits and itself firmly in control. Although Venezuelan players remained a bargain, some U.S. major-league clubs left Venezuela, focusing instead on their Dominican operations. Fearing "another Cuba" and baseball's nationalization, eight of the nineteen U.S. teams left the Venezuelan Summer League.[73]

As for the Dominican Republic, for the first time, it hosted two big-league teams, the Boston Red Sox and Houston Astros, who played part of their 2000 spring training there. MLB set up a Latin American office, saying it would prevent player exploitation. Some reforms were instituted, such as age minimums, yet reports of ballplayers as young as twelve continued. While big-league clubs and scouts complained that Caribbean ballplayers were no longer cheap, cases of stolen bonuses and underpaid players still lingered. Workers' and children's rights remained in jeopardy, but the Major League Baseball Players Association claimed it couldn't influence working conditions outside the United States. The major leagues still did little to cushion the fall experienced by most young ballplayers, who quit school to play baseball only to be routinely discarded. The 2008 film *Sugar* explores the latest conditions. While the story is fictional, it reflects the filmmakers' research findings: that abuses of Caribbean players still persist.[74]

In its own defense, MLB protested that it was a business, not a charity, and that it had nevertheless instituted a "holistic" approach to give Dominican prospects not only baseball but also food, shelter, language classes, and even religious instruction. By bringing ballplayers to its academies, it was reducing the number of mouths that had to be fed, thus helping poor households. Other family members, it pointed out, might receive secondary employment, servicing the academies. The local scouts, or *buscones*, were responsible for the worst abuses, it observed, not MLB. Former critic Alan Klein defended the big leagues, saying the academies and bonuses had improved. The Dominican economy, not baseball, was responsible for poor education and opportunities, he said, and baseball was bringing in money the country would otherwise not have. A few rich Dominican major leaguers were also building their own baseball academies to challenge those of MLB. These competing claims, of course, were standard fare in the globalization debate.[75]

In neighboring Puerto Rico, baseball—unlike in the Dominican—"has never been the exclusive ticket to the alluring Yankee dream of wealth and stardom." Peter Bjarkman notes that "the youth of San Juan are not as bound in by hopeless crushing poverty as those living [elsewhere] in the shadows of the sugar cane factories." Even so, poverty remained widespread, and the continuing U.S. military presence provoked political resistance. In 2001, MLB scheduled opening day in San Juan to test the waters for a future plan: to have the troubled Montreal Expos play twenty-two "home" games in 2003 in Puerto Rico, raising hopes that San Juan might get a permanent big-league team. Baseball remained perhaps the strongest bond between Puerto Rico and the United States, and a major factor in preserving Puerto Rican national identity. With fewer major leaguers playing in the off-season, however, the Puerto Rican Winter League was weak, and Puerto Ricans were more likely to follow big-league teams on television than watch their local clubs. Like players on the mainland, Puerto Ricans were subject to the baseball draft, but while fifty-nine of them were taken in 1989, only twenty-three were chosen in 2002. Other Latinos outside the draft were better bargains, and Puerto Ricans were paying the price. And while a Puerto Rican consortium offered to buy the Montreal Expos, MLB awarded the team to Washington, D.C., instead of allowing a Latino franchise.[76]

As we've seen, Haiti's primary major-league relationship had been as an outsourcing target for cheap labor to produce baseballs. In response to negative publicity about poor conditions and slave wages, MLB and sporting-goods companies moved most baseball production outside Haiti by the early 2000s. But the manufacturing of other baseball apparel and equipment remained, although it was now shared with Honduras, El Salvador, Bangladesh, and Indonesia, where pennies were paid to make sports jerseys that typically sold for hundreds of dollars. At the 2006 All-Star Game, a protest was launched against the host Pittsburgh Pirates by the Anti-Sweatshop Community Alliance, led by former anti-apartheid activist Dennis Brutus. Anti-sweatshop baseball cards were distributed, and demonstrations were held to publicize the poor pay, benefits, and conditions for baseball factory workers.[77]

The production of most baseballs was moved to Costa Rica, where, despite promises, conditions remained grim. Hand-stitching baseballs to machine precision is hard, crippling work. Factory temperatures rose up to 95 degrees. Laborers arrived at 6:00 A.M., worked until 5:00 P.M., and were often forced into overtime. They typically made about $55 per week. Each worker stitched four balls per hour; they were paid by the ball, about 30 cents each. Rawlings sold the balls in the United States for $14.99. The Costa Rican plants made 2.2 million balls a year and sold about 1.8 million to the major leagues.[78] Ironically, as in Haiti, barely anybody actually played baseball in Costa Rica; most who did were expatriate Nicaraguans. As former Rawlings manager Doug Kralick explained, "Costa Rica was never invaded by the U.S. Marines, so it never got baseball."

The leading company, Rawlings, came to Costa Rica to escape accusations of human rights violations in Haiti and was given a 54,000-square foot free-trade zone. It paid no taxes and imported duty-free the raw materials for producing its baseballs. As Philip Hersh has observed, "The Rawlings plant is like a pre–Industrial Revolution factory." But the Costa Rican baseball workers may not have to suffer much longer: there are plans to move the factories to Asia, where the labor will be even cheaper.[79]

Baseball globalization in Latin America generated the same problems that trouble people generally about globalization. Weak economies were targeted for cheap workers, just as they were sought for the cane fields or the textile factories. As outside corporations, major league clubs might not *cause* poverty but arguably they have been part of a system that perpetuates it, even if some of baseball's reforms have been sincere. As Sam Regalado has noted, "MLB is kind of like the Catholic Church. That is, changes in policy seem to take eras to implement." Organized baseball allows some Latinos an escape from poverty, but only briefly for most of them. Perhaps MLB should be giving back more in exchange for the gems it turns into millions.[80]

Besides harvesting baseball labor, MLB sought to establish its "brand" in the Caribbean and Latin America. Organized baseball sells more than merely what happens on the field. In 2001, Texas Rangers owner Tom Hicks was criticized for signing Alex Rodriguez to the richest multiyear contract in history, worth hundreds of millions of dollars. How could anyone be worth that much? Rodriguez had great years with the Rangers, but the team was never in contention. This missed, however, Rodriguez's bigger value. Hicks owned a multimedia empire with a substantial Latin American presence, which he sought to expand. Rodriguez was his poster boy for that market. For a time, Hicks and Rodriguez sold the Rangers as Latin America's team. Hicks made millions, not only from new fans and merchandise sales, but also from his expanding media empire.[81]

More recently, the New York Mets began their own global development plan. Led by general manager Omar Minaya, the Mets rebranded themselves as an international team. They launched an advertising blitz aimed at Hispanics, in particular, selling baseball's new multicultural face. When the Mets signed Pedro Martinez, a Dominican, they got more than a pitcher: "Pedro was as much a marketing signing as a baseball signing," according to Minaya, who also upgraded the Mets baseball academies in Venezuela and the Dominican Republic. The Mets' Rafael Perez said, "What we're doing is no different from what IBM has done for years. It's part of the globalized marketplace."[82]

Around the World

In Asia and the Pacific, ballplayers were treated differently by organized base-ball than in Latin America. A breakthrough occurred in 2001 when the Japa-nese star Ichiro Suzuki was signed by the Seattle Mariners, whose home games were thereafter televised live in Japan. Thousands of Japanese fans began flying to Seattle to attend games. Suzuki's success changed how Japanese players were regarded in the United States. That same year, President Bush hosted Japanese prime minister Junichiro Koizumi at Camp David and presented him a base-ball and glove. Spontaneously, the two began throwing the ball to each other, "which was a perfect metaphor for how they handled the relationship." In 2003, as we've seen, Iraq War fears caused MLB to cancel its planned season-opening games in Tokyo between the Mariners and Athletics. The biggest loss was in the enormous merchandise sales the games were expected to generate. The next year, the games took place, although between the Tampa Bay Devil Rays and New York Yankees instead.

In 2005, the World Children's Baseball Fair was still going strong in Japan, and cofounder Sadaharu Oh expressed his belief that "now [with] terrorism and infighting . . . this fair is meaningful because children from around the world will play baseball, and deepen their friendship." Echoing each other, President Bush and Commissioner Selig both hoped the fair would promote world peace.[83]

In 2007, President Bush hosted the new Japanese Prime Minister Shinzo Abe and continued his baseball rapport with Japanese leaders. Dominating their conversation was Japan's most recent export to America, the new Red Sox pitcher Daisuke Matsuzaka,[84] whose signing illustrated how MLB dealt with Asian countries compared to Caribbean nations. Players from neither re-gion were subject to the U.S. baseball draft, but as stronger, more developed countries, Japan and Korea negotiated better deals for their nationals. Players first have to contribute to their home teams, which are then compensated for their lost players. The winning bids for players usually range between $300,000 and $1 million, but the bid was $13 million for Ichiro Suzuki and $51 million for Daisuke Matsuzaka. For that astronomical fee, the Red Sox got far more than their pitcher; they established their brand in the lucrative Japanese mar-ket, from which the franchise expects to reap many more millions in fan sup-port and merchandising in future years.[85]

Resentments against *gaijin*, or outsiders, in Japanese and Korean baseball had declined, and quotas were fading. Would this weaken even the relatively more protected Japanese and Korean leagues? Would their losses be offset by corre-sponding gains?[86] As Jim Allen has noted, "The struggle for identity has been fundamental [to] Asia's game. Played by those threatened with oppression, baseball became an allegory for survival against materially superior outsiders." This may have been true not only for past colonies but also for those now adapting more slowly to globalization, including baseball globalization. Are Taiwan and China as vulnerable as the Caribbean nations, or can they achieve the protections Japan and Korea have established for their game? By 2004, China and Taiwan were playing baseball together, even though their governments remained relatively hostile.[87]

By the early twenty-first century, Taiwan had survived its Little League cheating fiasco and its Professional League gambling scandal, and emerged stronger. Baseball was deeply unifying and thus a help in warding off would-be colonizers. To confirm its significance, a baseball was pictured on the new Taiwanese currency. And while he wasn't the nation's first major leaguer, Chien-ming Wang became the first Taiwanese star, as a New York Yankees pitcher. Cheering his success united people across the Taiwanese political spectrum, and Yankees games had the nation's highest television ratings—thus firmly implanting the Yankees brand. But the focus on the U.S. major leagues depressed Taiwan's own professional league attendance. And major-league recruiters were prominent; as in Latin America they could sign young players and lure them out of school.[88]

Mainland China's baseball possibilities were even more intriguing. In early 2001, *Asia Week* editorialized about the Asian sports invasion of the United States. At the same time, an embarrassing invasion of China occurred when a U.S. spy plane collided with a Chinese fighter jet, sending the latter crashing into the sea. The United States claimed its plane was in international airspace, and China warned against flights so close to its borders. Tempers soon cooled; indeed, the United States had been compliantly ignoring Chinese human rights violations and other transgressions, with its eye on the nation's huge market. In 2001, MLB got on board by signing its first mainland Chinese player ever: Wang Chao. In 2002, the professional China Baseball League was formed, but the SARS (severe acute respiratory syndrome) outbreak shut down many aspects of Chinese society. When precautions were lifted in 2003, the first public event allowed was the Chinese All-Star Game, held in the baseball hotbed Tianjin. To gear up for the 2008 Beijing Olympics, the Chinese Baseball Association hired former major leaguers Jim Lefebvre and Bruce Hearst to prepare the Chinese team. MLB sent additional coaches, trained umpires, and developed youth teams. In exchange, U.S. clubs received permission to scout Chinese players. According to Jim Small of MLB, Inc., "If baseball is to be considered a global sport, it needs to be played in key countries—China is at the top of that list."[89]

Among other clubs, the New York Yankees wanted a Chinese foothold and worked hard to develop new talent there. The major leagues were looking for the baseball equivalent of Yao Ming, the Chinese basketball player whose signing got millions of Chinese hooked on the National Basketball Association. In that pursuit, organized baseball exploited China's rivalry with Japan. According to Jim Small, "It bothers them that Japan is so good at baseball and that's a tremendous opportunity for us." And as Jim Allen has observed, "The knowledge that Asian fans will watch MLB on TV and buy mass quantities of merchandise has transformed MLB owners 180 degrees—from arrogant isolationists to global thinkers." In March 2008, the first major-league exhibition game in China was played in Beijing between the Los Angeles Dodgers and San Diego Padres. Other Asian nations came to be seen as potential baseball markets as well.[90]

In the early twenty-first century, almost anywhere one looked abroad, there were new baseball initiatives. Like the Catholic Church, MLB made Africa a new target.[91] And in the Middle East, baseball made huge strides in Israel and even Iran, although its role in Iraq and Afghanistan generated greater attention, for obvious reasons. By 2002, after the American invasion, some Afghan teenagers were playing baseball, which they learned from U.S. soldiers. They had two teams—the Afghan Club and Shaheen (the Eagles)—and sandbags for bases and a tent peg for a bat. "Take Me Out to the Ballgame" blared out from army Humvee speakers. Sergeant Jay Smith explained, "Baseball is here to show the American way, to show them we're not here for any [other] reason than to help out. That's our version of beating swords into plowshares." The scene was reminiscent of past U.S. occupations in places like Nicaragua and the Dominican Republic, where baseball was used to win over the natives. While some U.S. soldiers in Afghanistan acknowledged the cultural imperialism, others disagreed: "We're not trying to force anything American on anybody. It shows we're here to support, not to attack." Curiously, Afghans were weak on most aspects of the game, except for pitching: "They're used to throwing rocks."[92]

In Iraq, in the lead-up to the 2003 U.S. attack, a tongue-in-cheek rumor claimed the CIA had devised a new covert operation to topple Saddam Hussein: "They're going to name him the Kansas City Royals manager. Inevitably, everyone in that job gets fired and is never heard from again." In the real world, it worked out a little differently. After the occupation, baseball was imported to entertain U.S. soldiers and help pacify the Iraqi population.[93] In 2004 a U.S. Marine unit offered to host the Boston Red Sox for spring training, and with good reason: at Camp Ramadi, Iraq, they had built a miniature Fenway Park— "Fenway East"—reproducing the Green Monster outfield wall.[94]

Rebuking calls to withdraw American troops from Iraq, Illinois Republican

John Shimkus protested, "Imagine my beloved St. Louis Cardinals are playing the much-despised Chicago Cubs. Who wins? We know it's the team that stays on the field." By others, baseball was championed over football as offering the best "endgame strategy." Baseball must be revived as the national pastime, it was argued, to tap the lessons it taught the "greatest generation" during World War II. That is, rather than submitting to football's artificial time constraints, the United States must instead adopt baseball's "continue until victory" approach, even if it required "extra innings." Accordingly, in 2007 President Bush ordered the "surge" to intensify the Iraq War. Leading the operation was General David Petraeus, whom Little League honored as one of its graduates and who acknowledged that youth baseball "was instrumental to my military success."[95]

By 2001, baseball was well established in at least several British Commonwealth and European nations. After the September 11 attacks, Europe overwhelmingly supported the United States. But that goodwill rapidly vanished as Europeans recoiled from America's unilateral military aggression—even souring on baseball. So crazy about America at first, for example, were young Viennese bankers, that they created teams such as the Alserstrasse Yankees and the Schwarzenberg Platz Red Sox. But the sympathy in Austria and elsewhere in Europe disappeared because, as Frederic Morton put it, America's foreign policy has "now, unmistakably, hardened into systematic global bullying. To Europeans, the statue in New York harbor brandishes not a torch but a tommy gun. [America] is the ultimate godfather, enforcing . . . a protection racket on all seven seas . . . practicing domination in the name of freedom . . . the land of milk and honey turned into the fortress of bottom line and bomb." When the French National team manager Guillaume Coste was asked whether it hurt that baseball was considered so American, he responded, "Baseball isn't American; it's a world sport." Strategically, organized baseball began saying the same thing. As MLB's Rick Dell put it: "When we first started [promoting baseball] we really put the American part in the forefront. Now we kind of put that at the back."[96]

"As Americans struggled with their nation's . . . image on the world stage," according to Mark Lamster, "baseball's status as an international sport [was] at a crossroads." The game was growing rapidly in Eastern Europe, was dominant in much of East Asia, and was perhaps even more popular in the Caribbean than in the United States.[97] As the early 2000s unfolded, MLB was gripped by two main forces: the consequences of the September 11 attacks and globalization's seductive lures. Having taken stock of the game's status worldwide, organized baseball sought some direction for itself. Other nations had focused on regional baseball tournaments, the Intercontinental Baseball Cup, and especially the World Baseball Cup—which had been contested since the 1930s.

And there was always the Olympics to display American baseball prowess. MLB could make a greater commitment to these competitions.

At the World Cup, sponsored by the International Baseball Federation, Cuba had long dominated, winning in 1998, 2001, 2003, and 2005. All told, Cuba had won twenty-five World Cups, while the United States had won only three. At the Olympics, America won its first baseball gold in 2000; Cuba and South Korea placed second and third. With its win, the United States seemed poised to remain dominant for years to come. Yet in 2003, in the qualifying round, the United States was upset by Mexico and thus eliminated from the 2004 Olympics. Former Olympic coach Tommy Lasorda said, "It's a shock and disgrace that the Americans won't be represented. Baseball is America's game. It doesn't belong to the Japanese or the Cubans or the Koreans or the Italians." In the 2004 Olympics, Cuba won the gold, trailed by upstart Australia, and then Japan. MLB's Sandy Alderson was more sanguine: "I don't think it's a setback for U.S. baseball. I think it validates the internationalization of the game."[98]

Yet it was a blow and no doubt spurred MLB to rethink its global strategy. These were not American amateurs but rather U.S. professionals losing at the Olympics. Also, although the games were only played every four years, scheduling them around the regular major-league season had become a problem. Other concerns were raised by the stringent Olympic drug testing policies, as baseball's steroid problems were coming to light. And there was the issue of who controlled the games. In 2005, the International Olympic Committee (IOC) announced its decision to eliminate baseball from the games, but MLB had already decided to move in a different direction.[99]

The Olympic announcement shook up the baseball-playing nations that relied on international competitions to attract private and public funding. Many countries didn't have their own leagues or championships. Baseball was at a disadvantage in Olympic voting because most IOC members were from nations where baseball wasn't widely played.[100] Others blamed the United States for its unwillingness to seriously address steroid use in baseball. Cuba criticized MLB for its rigid scheduling after it rejected the National Hockey League practice of taking a two-week Olympic break. Many traced Olympic baseball's elimination to a backlash against U.S. foreign and military policies since 9/11 and to MLB's often imperious approach to international baseball. Perhaps it was a small bit of "blowback" struck against the American national game. Yet organized baseball had its own games in mind: the World Baseball Classic.

Globalization American Style

In America, the land of immigrants, MLB opened its doors to one nationality after another, albeit to some of them far more slowly than equity would have warranted. Even so, immigrants did populate the teams, and a few superstars among them were championed by their respective ethnic communities. But as the national pastime, baseball was viewed as an assimilating institution, which blurred ethnic backgrounds rather than highlighting them. Recently, however, as John Kelly has suggested, it has become not only acceptable but apparently even desirable to pit nationalities against each other in American ball games.[101]

This trend began most noticeably at the Home Run Derby held before each year's All-Star Game. Derby contestants began drawing the support of ballplayers grouped by country. Players from Panama, the Dominican Republic, and other nations cheered their representative to win the competition. As Jonathan Mahler observed in 2005, "No sooner had Bobby Abreu's winning blast cleared the fence than his fellow countrymen, Johan Santana and Miguel Cabrera, rushed onto the field to drape him in an enormous Venezuelan flag." Some Americans were offended seeing other nations' flags displayed at "America's game." But MLB didn't seem to mind.

Organized baseball was already planning a tournament whose success would rely on precisely such nationalistic fervor: the World Baseball Classic (WBC) would be held in 2006, with games in Japan, Puerto Rico, and the mainland United States. Unlike the Olympics or the World Baseball Cup, the WBC would be owned and run by organized baseball. While it claimed its goal was to promote baseball's international appeal, economics were obviously paramount. The WBC's timing was favorable. As William Gould noted, "In the last five years, the U.S. has gone from being one of the world's most respected nations to the object of scorn and downright hatred." Ironically, MLB had been a major cheerleader for the policies that had put America in such a bad light, yet its WBC then became "a welcome foil to American unilateralism and xenophobia."[102]

The WBC paled compared to soccer's World Cup, matching baseball teams from only sixteen nations. Shaun Tandon observed, "As many symbols of Americana permeate the world, baseball is suffering in favor of faster, more physical sports such as soccer. It remains to be seen how global the sport wants to be." More to the point, it questioned what kind of globalization baseball sought to practice. The WBC was purposely smaller than the major leagues' own annual competition among one Canadian and twenty-nine U.S. teams, ending in the World Series. It was crafted to avoid upstaging the American championship, intentionally adopting the label *classic* so as to distinguish the two. Concerns about the World Series were such that one owner, George Steinbrenner, opposed the WBC, fearing injuries and time away from training, but he was more concerned about a Yankee championship. That is, Steinbrenner worried not only that the WBC might hamper his team's ability to *win* the World Series but that it might be a threat to the *meaning* of the World Series. To further establish a hierarchy between the two, the WBC was scheduled to start the season, during spring training, instead of after the World Series—when it might otherwise have been viewed as the culminating championship. While MLB wanted the WBC to succeed at home, it was even more important that it do well abroad. Conservatives branded as unpatriotic any major leaguers who played with their nationality team instead of with the American team. But MLB encouraged ballplayers to do so in order to equalize the competitive balance.[103]

Some controversy arose when Japan sought to run the tournament's Asia round, but MLB resisted: "If we allow Japan a separate deal, it would ruin the whole business model." That is, organized baseball wanted Japanese participation without any ownership, especially by Japan, which, more than any other baseball nation, could potentially challenge MLB's enterprise. In the games, Korea had the satisfaction of "beating the U.S. at the game they invented." Koreans also used the classic to protest against the continued (since 1953) stationing of U.S. troops in their country, against MLB's treatment of the Korean League as a minor league, and even against George Bush and the Iraq War, calling for the pullout of Korea's three thousand troops.[104]

In the end, however, Japan won the WBC, defeating Cuba in the finals. About his role on Japan's winning team, Ichiro Suzuki—already a star in two nations—exulted that it "was the biggest moment of my baseball career." As for the team he beat, Cuba was almost kept out of the tournament. In a new dose of obsolete Cold War politics, the United States tried to block Cuba's participation. The Treasury Department claimed it would violate the Trading with the Enemy Act, the White House claimed Cuba would use the games for spying, and the State Department claimed Cuba's inclusion would be rewarding a dictator. The media, including the sporting press, also chimed in. ESPN repeated claims that Cuba was the "only country here that is under a dictator." Dave Zirin noted the double standard: "The only time politics is allowed to intrude is when it's anti-Castro." Cuba was condemned while China's dictatorship and its WBC team were given a "political pass."[105]

Even so, in response to the threatened ban, Cuba had many supporters. The International Baseball Federation threatened to rescind its WBC endorsement, Puerto Rico vowed to withdraw as a host, and the IOC warned that Cuba's exclusion could jeopardize America's ability to land a future Olympics, with or without baseball. Some nations seemed prepared to pull out. Venezuela offered to host all of Cuba's tournament games outside the United States. Baseball legends Sadaharu Oh and Hank Aaron supported Cuba's participation. And in a rare departure from the official party line, even MLB protested U.S. policy. According to Baltimore Orioles owner Peter Angelos, "Once again the U.S., this huge colossus, is picking on a tiny country of 11 million. And for what? For their participation in an international baseball event? That makes us look like the big, bad bully our non-admirers say we are." The United States finally relented and let the Cuban team compete, but only if Cuba donated its game proceeds to a humanitarian cause. Ever the tactician, Fidel Castro chose the victims of Hurricane Katrina. The turmoil didn't end there, for Cuba was again targeted by right-wing exiles at the games.[106]

Despite the tensions, the World Baseball Classic gave MLB what it wanted. Its objective wasn't to reproduce the Olympic message of peace and friendship. It wasn't devising a new diplomatic mechanism, and—despite all the national flag-waving—it wasn't a statement on nationalism, either. Instead, MLB's media campaign focused entirely on individual stars. In every venue, "trailblazer" films were played on the electronic scoreboards, celebrating past major leaguers from each nation and nationality. John Kelly called this the "Jackie Robinsonization of international baseball." That is, the films told a story: that organized baseball provides opportunities for worthy individuals to partake of the American dream. The impression was that the pioneers have colonized the major leagues and not vice versa. Individual players can break down boundaries. In the real world, these were mostly fantasies, as shown, for example, by the baseball academies the big-league clubs were still running as industrial plantations in the Caribbean.

No success stories were told at the WBC about teams and leagues, for there were none to tell. To the contrary, organized baseball had always kept competing leagues subordinate, if they were allowed to survive at all. The Mexican League challenge, for example, wasn't recounted at the classic. That would have highlighted the emptiness of the *World* in World Series, which actually should be played not by U.S. pennant winners but rather by the league champions of different nations, as Jorge Pasquel had proposed in the 1940s. Other leagues in the Caribbean and East Asia haven't literally become MLB minor leagues, nor have their clubs been converted yet into big-league farm teams, but sometimes it seems that way. In MLB's empire of baseball nations, each new nation-state got its own pinnacle league. Teams in these leagues could play each other and perhaps enter regional championships, but they'd never get real championship games against the Yankees or Cardinals or Dodgers. If not exactly conquest, then it was nevertheless a kind of exclusion that wouldn't be tolerated in other international sports. Because foreign ballplayers had no chance to beat America's baseball champions, they instead had to leave home to try to join them. That's what MLB sought and celebrated: the individual migration of trailblazers and their successors in a baseball diaspora.[107]

MLB has been happy to globalize its workforce as long as it retained control and maintained its profits. Commissioner Selig declared, "Baseball may have been born in America, but now it belongs to the world." Yet while it might be played by (some of) the world, MLB insists it still owns the sport. Kelly has observed, the WBC was "a way to reclaim the game when it might have otherwise gotten away." MLB was even willing to risk losing its mastery on the field in order to reclaim ownership—a "lose to win" approach, according to a popular Japanese adage. With the Olympics' absence and the World Baseball Cup's marginalization, baseball nations have to play in the World Baseball Classic, and by MLB rules. As ESPN's Jim Caple observed, "Cheer up, fellow Americans. Our country might not have even reached the [WBC] final round, but the best players eventually all wind up here [in the U.S.] anyway." That, of course, was a prime objective: to allow MLB to audition potential new players. It was also important to manage the rules and structures of global baseball, so as to make "the world safe for our game." Through the WBC, MLB ensured itself "a highly American style of internationalization"— Americanization rather than real globalization.[108]

While not without controversy, the World Baseball Classic of 2009 was even more successful than the first.[109] The Netherlands was the Cinderella club, making it to the quarterfinals. Venezuela kept the Caribbean in semifinal contention. The championship featured a fierce Asian rivalry: Japan beat Korea to win its second WBC in a row. And Team USA did better too. But more important, MLB now controls a tremendously lucrative enterprise—"a vast, high-level tryout camp [the Daisuke Matsuzaka signing by the Red Sox was the first WBC product] and safety valve for global baseball aspirations." Under this regime, the maximum ambition for a ballplaying nation is to get chosen, possibly host a tournament round, and win—for whatever meaning the title might hold in the lingering shadow of the World Series. In the words of John Kelly, "To call it an empire, or even a monopoly, is to seriously underestimate it [and] fail to see the form of power it wields in shaping . . . its own commodious world, controlling access, avoiding and deflecting competition, limiting liability, and elaborating fictions of separate but equal." As Alan Klein has observed, "For skeptics, globalization is traditional capitalism on steroids; recognizable but grown much more muscular." If MLB's strategy holds up, it will be globalization itself on steroids.[110]

The Mighty Casey Strikes Out?

In the early twenty-first century, both America and MLB were widely viewed as empires. Sometimes, however, an empire is measured by factors suggesting strength and dominance that instead only disguise fundamental weaknesses, which better describe its decline than its ascendancy. While MLB has offered an occasional dissent, it has overwhelmingly embraced conventional American society and its foreign and military policies.[111]

So what are the prospects for America's empires? Sportswriter Dave Ring used a baseball analogy to assess the situation:

> U.S. legitimacy has waned, and [it] finds itself like Mudville's brash super-slugger Casey; our air-shattering blow against the "enemies of freedom" was . . . a whiff of thin air. The failure of U.S. foreign policy can be seen in the Administration's stance on the war in Iraq. . . . Like Casey, our nation finds itself standing at the plate, wondering where it all went wrong. . . . Like Mighty Casey, the project of America was the great hope. . . . The terrorists . . . wanted to change America and make the world turn against us. Since then we have allowed extraordinary perversions of our values [and] . . . as long as the President disregards everything that has made this country great, we'll be like the over-confident Casey, standing at the plate with an empty stadium.[112]

Has the Mighty Casey struck out?

At the 2007 Cooperstown Hall of Fame Film Festival, the top award went to *The Showdown*, a movie comparing the tense pitcher-batter confrontation to an Old West shootout. It was an appropriate metaphor for a society still drawing lines in the sand and pursuing enemies with WANTED: DEAD OR ALIVE notices. American sports were already renowned for their patriotism. The zeal further escalated when the United States became the sole superpower, then again after September 11. As Anatol Lieven has observed, it went beyond nationalism to embrace a kind of bellicose patriotism, exuding an indifference verging on contempt for the interests of non-Americans.

Sporting events such as the World Series became infected with machismo and a kind of sports militarism, yet were praised as vehicles of national healing. They conveyed a "self-absorbed, hermetically sealed sense of total supremacy, or isolation," and reinforced "all those characteristics the world finds so distasteful in Americans." When crowds began shouting "USA! USA!" at ballgames, it had a "bullying tone," as if Americans were desperate to confirm their national greatness. Steven Pope observed, "The sports context provides abundant examples of both the bravado and self-doubt of an empire in crisis." Although the United States has been an empire for more than a hundred years, Americans may be "only just beginning to understand the role their nation plays in the world and the price [it] incurs." As Pope asks, "Where better to wave the flag and lick the wounds of an aggrieved imperial power than during America's self-professed 'world championships,' such as the World Series?"[113]

By early 2008, the signs, both tangible and metaphoric, of an empire in crisis were extensive, as suggested by the U.S. Congress's oblivious obsession with steroids, about which it scheduled yet more hearings with no apparent purpose. Primed by the MLB-commissioned Mitchell Report on drugs,[114] the nation was treated to the congressional testimony of baseball's "Rocket Man," the cocky star pitcher Roger Clemens. Sadly, almost no one believed a word he said.

Another consequence of baseball's "national pastime trade-off" began to reveal itself. For its flag-waving, MLB was rewarded with its antitrust exemption, but this protective umbrella made it into an "extra-judicial entity, a society unto itself." Arguably, it bred a "culture of corruption" that allowed steroids abuse not only to emerge, but also to persist, without outside scrutiny.[115] But in response to the government's belated badgering of baseball, the *Atlantic Monthly* advised Bud Selig to provide his own analysis of performance-enhancing drugs, along the lines of this "Letter from the Commissioner":

Dear U.S. Government:
When key players in the Bush administration appeared in 2005 before [MLB] and declared under oath they had never knowingly used steroids while conducting foreign policy, they were not being truthful. Formerly classified urine samples confirm . . . that Donald Rumsfeld and Paul Wolfowitz regularly injected each other in the buttocks with anabolic steroids during the 2001 and 2002 seasons. While critics noted the two men's freakish increase in head size and sense of invincibility, we were slow to recognize the problem, despite the administration's dramatic surge in home runs and invasions in far-off lands. . . . As early as fall 2001, after the American military's success in crushing both the Taliban and the single-season home run record, [insiders] began to worry that Mr. Bush and Mr. Cheney were becoming prone to the spasmodic aggressiveness common among steroid abusers. While Mr. Bush [used] such six-shooter phrases as "You're either with us or agin' us," Mr. Cheney muscled the country into war with Iraq by [making] nonexistent links between al-Qaeda and Saddam Hussein. Then, during a hunting out-

ing . . . Mr. Cheney flew into a full-blown 'roid rage and sprayed [his partner] in the face with birdshot. . . . [Thus], retroactive to the 2001 season, every international initiative and batting statistic generated by the Bush administration shall be accompanied in the official Major League history books by an asterisk, and the 2001 to 2007 seasons will henceforth be known as the Steroid Era of American foreign policy.

Signed, Bud Selig, Baseball Commissioner[116]

Satire aside, in the real world of baseball, Commissioner Selig is scheduled to rule his MLB empire through 2012. By then, MLB will need new leadership and quite likely will again solicit military candidates. A big baseball fan, General Colin Powell has been mentioned again as a candidate. What better training could he have for coping with the Steinbrenners, Pohlads, and Linders of baseball than having already dealt with the Chiracs, Arafats, and Putins of the world? General David Petraeus, with his Little League connection, might be another commissioner possibility. With Powell or Petraeus, what could be more natural than to reconfirm baseball's long-standing relationship with the U.S. military and foreign policy establishment?

An even more intriguing candidate, given his baseball credentials, would be former president George W. Bush, who was already seriously considered for the commissionership before he entered the White House. According to a childhood friend, if Bush couldn't be the next Willie Mays, then he "wanted to be [Commissioner] Kenesaw Mountain Landis . . . legendary for his power and dictatorial style." While Bush might be too "toxic" to be commissioner immediately, things might look different by the time Selig retires.[117] Of course, if he were asked to lead MLB, then under the Bush preemptive war doctrine, batters would likely be allowed to charge the mound before pitchers actually threw at them. As a big baseball booster, and one of the most militarily aggressive presidents in American history, Bush as commissioner just might represent the confluence of interests MLB seeks—even if it isn't what it really needs.

12

The Empire Strikes Out

This field, this game, is part of our past. It reminds us of all that once was good and could be again.

—W.P. Kinsella

Prediction is hard, especially about the future.

—Yogi Berra

With the twenty-first century's first decade nearly complete, two empires stand strong but also firmly—and perhaps critically—challenged. The nation-state empire of America wields the most lethal weapons and the most aggressive economy in world history, yet in an age of terrorism and financial excess, it may be more vulnerable than ever before.[1] In a similar way, the baseball empire of the major leagues has the means to control the sport, not only at home (for record profits), but virtually around the world. Yet in an age of steroids and football frenzy, it has only a tentative hold on the future. In many regards, these empires operate apart with little connection. But as we've seen, in other ways America's empire and MLB's dynasty have been linked and often remain so to this day.

In constructing its empire, America has used its military, diplomatic, cultural, and economic resources. And its sports have played a consistent role as well. As Alan Barnier has observed, sport cannot win territory or destroy an opposing ideology or religion, but athletes can act as "proxy warriors." Sport has been a battering ram for the penetration of national economies. And according to Gerald Gems, sport can become a surrogate for war. For more than a century, baseball has been "part of the American imperial plan." In contrast to harsh, authoritarian methods, "sport is a less overt means of instilling belief in a dominant system's values." Copying the approach used by the English with cricket, America substituted its own game, baseball. "Sport not only followed the flag but often preceded it as expatriates, foreign students, and religious missionaries introduced American sport forms to other nations [sometimes] before military intervention and occupation."[2]

Baseball signed on early in support of America's imperial ambitions, partly because it had similar aspirations. The sport was drafted by the nation's empire builders, and it also eagerly enlisted. As the United States has projected its dominance worldwide, baseball lent a hand—bolstering the military, boosting the nation's global economic reach, and proselytizing for the American way. As the United States expanded, conquering new frontiers, so did baseball. Each found multiple uses for each other. And for the most part, all seemed well.

A Triumphal Air

Nevertheless, in 2007, foreign correspondent Stephen Kinzer worried about the future:

> A seemingly invulnerable power that overreaches and suddenly suffers defeats that expose its weakness and threaten its hegemony—that is the story of the U.S. as this fifth summer of [the Iraq] war begins. It is also . . . the story of America's most successful sports team, the New York Yankees. What is happening to them is also happening to President Bush, the Republican Party, and the U.S. itself. Each swaggered into the twenty-first-century with a triumphal air . . . rich and secure, looking forward to [long-term] dominance. Overconfidence lulled them into a false sense of security. Now . . . they are facing undreamed-of troubles. . . . Both need to set a different course or risk seeing their power slip away.[3]

As we consider these observations, now two year later, does the apparent resurgence of the Yankees belie Kinzer's concerns? We'll see, but not likely. For nearly two hundred years, baseball has instead aligned itself with conservative America and with an increasingly aggressive U.S. foreign, military, and globalization policy. It has helped America prepare for battle and conduct wars and interventions, and it has fought its own wars, too. It has courted and regaled presidents, generals, and assorted underlings in the foreign policy establishment. Baseball has promoted patriotism, masculinity, nationalism, and Americanism at home and helped "manage" the nation's internal, often race-based, colonization.[4] Sometimes backed by an arrogant "muscular Christianity," baseball engaged in a "civilizing mission" abroad, "enlightening" the natives, and selling the American dream. Strategically combining softball and hardball politics, baseball diplomacy helped drag other nations into the globalized world.

Through these means, organized baseball has served the nation while also advancing its own fortunes. The relationship has brought baseball many benefits. It has been regarded as the national game for most of American history. And many have gained financially from baseball's strong performance, especially team owners, who have profited from the game's special status—a monopoly exempt from antitrust regulations. Abroad, baseball has had the protection of America's armed forces, which have also helped institutionalize the game in foreign lands.

Dynasty in Decline

Even so, the alliance between baseball and America's foreign policy establishment has produced a "national pastime trade-off" that has jeopardized the sport's independence and integrity. While we'd hardly expect it to be purposely unpatriotic, MLB has instead gone to the opposite extreme, adopting an often militaristic and jingoistic nationalism that sometimes makes baseball into merely an extension of the government or armed forces. This blind patriotism has linked baseball with policies that have put the game in a bad light.

Aside from handcuffing the sport, it may have implications for baseball fans. As David Voigt has suggested, "Baseball leaders have either willingly accepted or been forced into a garrison-state mentality—forever having to defend their claim to being 'the' American sport. If [this] requires baseball officials to stand by while politicians exploit the game to support military policies, surely this must alienate fans who see this as pandering to superpatriots and warmongers."[5] Baseball has always prided itself on reflecting the best of American values, but the "national pastime trade-off" may be preventing it from doing so.

As a handmaiden of U.S. foreign policy, baseball can claim many successes. Like America's own empire, MLB has become a dynasty as well. The United States has become the sole superpower, uncontested in military strength. It has transplanted its values, culture, and products across the globe. As the saying goes, when America's economy sneezes, the rest of the world catches cold. Likewise, American baseball—and MLB in particular—dominates other baseball-playing peoples and nations abroad, substantially controlling ballplayers and baseball institutions in other lands. By these measures, America and MLB have both hit home runs.

Yet others have assessed the U.S. and major-league empires quite differently. Historians tell us the fall of Rome followed a general malaise and structural weakness that grew over time. According to sociologist Morris Berman, this describes contemporary America, where religion and plutocracy are defeating reason and democracy. In his *Dark Ages America*, Berman diagnoses large-scale processes of national collapse, such as an overextended and self-destructive U.S. foreign and military policy, which mirrors the deterioration of everyday American lives—driven by "infantile needs and impulses" fueled by schools that don't teach, news media that don't inform, obsessive shopping, mindless television, knee-jerk reactionaries, religious zealots, the frenzied acceleration of work, and the erosion of community. As the corporate consumerist juggernaut rolls on, robbing meaning from our lives, the factors that once propelled the growth of the U.S. empire—extreme individualism and inequality, territorial and economic expansion, and the pursuit of material wealth—are now becoming the nails in America's collective coffin. It's a Darwinian society that doesn't believe in Darwinism and an empire that's weaker than Americans might think. Much of the world dislikes a United States, and most Americans don't know or care. Berman predicts that within a short time the nation will be marginalized, its global hegemony replaced by that of China or the European Union.[6]

Other social critics have reached similar conclusions. They describe a state of affairs (irrespective of political party) with post–World War II origins (at the latest), characterized by the creation of a U.S. "national security state" in pursuit of foreign resources, with commitments that would almost inevitably bring the nation to the breaking point. History teaches us that if nations act soon enough, they have a choice. They can loosen their grip on empire to save themselves, or they can hang on till the bitter end. Rome made the wrong choice and perished. Britain chose more wisely and survived. What will the United States do? Will the new administration of President Barack Obama make any difference? Even if only a fraction of the alarming signs of a dynasty in decline are true,[7] then rather than hitting a home run, America's empire instead seems on the brink of striking out.[8]

Tough-Love Globalization

How, then, must we assess an institution—Major League Baseball—whose well-being has relied so long on its ties to the American empire, to whose existence the sport has made no small contribution? According to anthropologist Alan Klein it could go either way: "MLB is poised at a crossroads which invites interpretations of empire both aging and rekindled with vigor. There are those who view MLB as a colonizer, exploiting foreign players, selling itself around the world, busily generating new markets, with little or no concern for local interests. This is classic dependency theory in a baseball jersey." But as Klein also observes, "The contrasting model . . . has MLB leading [baseball's] internationalization, with other countries increasingly sharing power and finding ways to push their own national agendas." In his book *Growing the Game*, Klein roots for the latter approach, offering some cautions but mainly showing how MLB can and will maintain its domain.[9]

According to Klein, the "hyper-globalization" or "testicular globalization" advocated by boosters such as Thomas Friedman seeks only to increase America's economic dominance over other nations. Klein contrasts that with "tough love globalization," which avoids colonization and focuses on rewarding merit wherever it emerges. Endorsing the latter course for MLB, Klein says organized baseball must "take a global view in which [it] grows by reducing its dependence on strict economic and political control." While no one pursues globalization unselfishly, baseball's globalization can take a more benign direction: "It must [pursue] stewardship, not empire. In the long run, imperial notions fail, because the center cannot hold."[10]

Klein sees progressive possibilities, praising the Dodgers organization, for example, for being moral and not merely greedy: "The racial integration of baseball was built upon the same principles [as] globalization: expansion of boundaries, a relatively high degree of merit, and social openness." Klein traces this from Branch Rickey through the O'Malleys, and their forays first into new racial and ethnic communities at home and then abroad to the Caribbean, Japan, Korea, and Taiwan. Operating overseas, according to Klein, is a matter of branding and getting a product to mesh with another culture's myths. It's a matter of "how does it fit into the foreign culture?" not "play this game because we're superior to you." Klein believes MLB should market the sport more in the developing world (where people are still hungry for it) than in developed nations. Globalization would best be promoted by adding major-league franchises abroad, and even realigning MLB to create a Pan American or Pacific Rim division.

On Borrowed Time?

Yet not everyone agrees that MLB's globalization is or can be benign. As with globalization generally, it makes a big difference whether it's experienced from the bottom up by all peoples and nations or imposed from the top down by the dominant powers. The former seeks a free and equitable exchange in which everyone has a chance to benefit. The latter seems little different from colonization or imperialism. According to David Fidler, there was "a similarity between the exploitative actions of MLB teams and the neocolonial actions of U.S. companies in Central and South America during the nineteenth and twentieth centuries." And Charles Pierce claims that MLB's business activities remain intricately intertwined with U.S. foreign policy: "From Kyoto to

Baghdad, American unilateralism has alienated the world, further energizing resentments [about] American corporations and . . . the corrupting influence of American culture." Included in this condemnation is MLB's "search for cheap labor" and the use of baseball academies as low-wage maquiladoras, not to mention the "American way of being an athlete—loud, brash, and arguably arrogant," which only reflects the way the "U.S. is behaving generally in the world."[11]

Some question MLB's one-sided relationship with other nations. The interaction seems designed primarily to tap resources rather than to supply very much in exchange. Instead of developing the game abroad, organized baseball seems concerned mostly with extracting talent. This reduces other nations' baseball skill level because MLB can offer higher salaries and better working conditions than players find at home. Feeder nations are thus left with depleted native talent and can lure only second-class or rejected players back from organized baseball. As Junwei Yu points out, "Because of the distribution of wealth the asymmetrical exchange is heavily in favor of the global north."[12] Foreign *leagues* weaken, often contracting and turning into MLB surrogates. This happens even to more protected leagues, such as those in Japan and Korea, but much more to those with less bargaining power. Only Cuba has managed to remain an alternative baseball universe, but it probably cannot survive much longer.

According to Peter Bjarkman, MLB pursues such policies because it can, but also because it has become increasingly necessary to do so. Organized baseball, he argues, is in decline and just doesn't realize it. It's been kept going by a "series of gimmicks . . . and [is] apparently thriving, but it's living on borrowed time." He writes, "By no stretch of anyone's imagination is baseball qualified today to be called the American national game . . . baseball no longer reflects daily American rhythms . . . [is] no longer at the heart of every barroom or village square debate."

Had baseball been better maintained at home, the pressures to seek talent abroad might have been less compelling. This neglect may have been initiated by MLB's recognition that foreign talent would be cheaper. Thereafter, it became a self-fulfilling prophesy, with fewer Americans (and particularly African Americans) being nurtured to play the game. Unfortunately, according to Bjarkman, when "U.S. interest in the world baseball community does expand . . . the end results [are] anything but healthy for the rest of the baseball-playing world." The World Baseball Classic, for example, seems to be more a marketing tool to strengthen MLB than to promote the sport, another opportunity for U.S. baseball to plunder foreign rosters rather than nurture elite-level competition elsewhere.[13]

Even if some improvements have been made, concerns linger about the pay and conditions for ballplayers warehoused in MLB academies abroad, which still resemble the exploitative practices used by other U.S. corporations abroad. The new baseball "farms" are the modern-day manifestation of the sugar and banana plantations. The same conditions persist in the manufacture of baseballs, uniforms, gloves, and other equipment. For some foreign ballplayers, baseball has made the American dream a reality. Yet it has cruelly dashed the hopes of thousands more. Major-league hopefuls who do manage to make it to the United States are often ensnared in America's ugly immigration policies. Like illegal aliens, they're caught within the "contradictory notions of wanting to keep immigrants out, yet being unable or unwilling to do without them." For the vast majority of foreign ballplayers who never make it to the majors and who are often quickly cut even from minor league teams, Jessica Skolnikoff and Robert Engvall wonder:

> Are we creating an avenue for young people with dreams, or are we . . . creating more streets lined with 16–22-year-old young men, who already view their lives as [hopeless]? What are the ethics of hunting for talent amid squalor and poverty . . . when a search for cheap labor ends up treating human beings as disposable? What about exploiting child labor . . . [and] the ethics of putting people in a situation where they must go home, but cannot really go home again?[14]

In sum, what are multinational firms like MLB giving back to the economies from which they harvest?

Besides labor, television markets for baseball and for its lifeblood—advertising—have been nearly exhausted in the United States, and thus organized baseball seeks to replenish those markets abroad. According to Bjarkman, "The motive is . . . to extract enough talent from other countries . . . and beam their exploits . . . back to their own homelands via an MLB-owned and operated television enterprise." This alienates foreigners from their local teams and turns them instead into fans of major-league clubs. Bjarkman warns, "Corporate globalization has now come to the winnowing universe of international baseball with a frightening vengeance." Even *Sports Illustrated* has recognized the problem: baseball is "not being globalized so much as Americanized. Like the Starbucks logo and the Matrix DVDs that have popped up in remote global backwaters, the proliferation of televised American games played in American venues slathered with American signage exacts a cultural price. . . . And it's unilateral: . . . there is neither interest in nor exposure for imports." And it's not merely to sell the products of advertisers but also MLB's own merchandise.

Organized baseball wants only to market its "product" to the rest of the world, and thus it steadfastly maintains control rather than ceding power to international bodies.[15]

Arguably, MLB's internationalization policies do more to undermine than to promote baseball as a global sport. Harboring an attitude reflecting America's general approach to international law, MLB won't sign on to institutions it cannot dominate. Its recalcitrance was substantially responsible for baseball being dropped from the Olympics after 2008, which ensures MLB dominance via its own World Baseball Classic. But it's devastating to the baseball programs of most nations, whose funding has been linked primarily to Olympic competition.

Is It Really Global?

Some wonder whether baseball is really global and whether MLB is actually engaged in globalization. As anthropologist George Gmelch has observed, the game's growth has been "glacially slow and spotty" around the world. It's the national pastime of fewer than ten nations, and the National Basketball Association may be more widely followed abroad than MLB. Measured that way, it's not clear baseball will ever achieve wider international success. As Gmelch observes, "The real form baseball 'globalization' has taken is not [its] export from the U.S. to foreign countries but the migration of baseball labor to the U.S." According to William Kelly, soccer is globalized because although it has (like baseball) English origins, it has no nation-based center. It's played almost universally worldwide with little style variation. Baseball, in contrast, has a dominant center (MLB in the U.S.), is played abroad far from universally, and sometimes differs in form. Major league–dominated baseball promotes nationalism and identity (thus accounting for different styles), not globalization or even internationalism.[16]

Where baseball has diffused abroad, it was often brought by educators, missionaries, and businessmen, but almost always reinforced, if not first implanted, by the U.S. armed forces.[17] Yet if America's military has been the game's key vehicle, then why have only some of the dozens of nations U.S. Marines have invaded actually adopted the sport? Why has there been so little baseball in Haiti or Vietnam, for example? Why did the Philippines heartily embrace the game, only to later reject it? How will it fare among the children now being taught baseball by U.S. troops in Iraq and Afghanistan? However we answer these questions, we must account for the effects of MLB's own policies. Spreading the playing of baseball was not necessarily its objective. When MLB began to look seriously abroad, developing markets, importing

players, and selling merchandise were more important than nurturing baseball
for its own sake. In line with time-honored imperialist practice, organized baseball was more interested in extracting resources back to the U.S.

And yet the seeds of baseball were nevertheless planted in many nations. If
MLB was ambivalent, then often U.S. foreign and military policy makers were
not. As Allen Guttmann has suggested, baseball was sometimes promoted for
loftier reasons, such as improving health, encouraging fortitude, and diminish-
ing religious animosities in native populations. Even so, baseball was also repeatedly employed as a "civilizing force" and social control mechanism. While
occasionally baseball diplomacy failed, often its pacifying objectives were
achieved. Yet sometimes, baseball was "glocalized"; that is, it was a global phenomenon adapted for local uses. Thus, for example, while the game was an
American model for play, it became a Japanese model for work. In other situ-
ations, baseball was appropriated to develop identity and nationalist fervor.
Conversely, it sometimes was used as a form of resistance in local conflicts and
even more often, against outside intervention. In other words, baseball was
ironically one of the few ways to fight back against American imperialism.
More recently, foreign baseball has also been struggling against another outside
invasion: the "globalization" of MLB.[18]

When baseball as social control met baseball as resistance, a baseball dialogue
often emerged, which helped generate different and sometimes competing
baseball styles. As Allen Guttmann reminds us, imperial nations and multinational corporations might ultimately be dominant but they're "not all-powerful
captains of consciousness." Thus, it's worth considering how some nations
adopted and shaped baseball for the long haul. In Cuba, for example, baseball
was used to help throw off one colonial ruler, then co-opted by puppets of a
subsequent colonial ruler, but then ultimately redeployed to help throw off
and keep off the "colossus of the north." In the Dominican Republic, local
teams took advantage of U.S. racism and welcomed top-notch African American players for as long as they could. In Nicaragua, baseball became a flash
point not only for relations with the U.S. but for long-standing local political
battles between the Somozans and the Sandinistas. Thus, to a certain extent,
baseball took on a life of its own in many nations. In some cases, it developed
a style that was returned to the "mother country," such as the influx of "Latin
flair" back into MLB.[19]

Today baseball might be more grounded in the everyday lives and rhythms
of Cubans, Dominicans, and Venezuelans than of Americans, as the game has
begun to lose resonance in the United States, even though MLB remains the
world's most powerful baseball force. As Bjarkman observes, "Most American
baseball fans suffer from . . . sports-culture jingoism, . . . the narrow view that

baseball refers exclusively to the professional entertainment spectacle now being marketed to North American consumers by the capitalist powers that control MLB." It perpetuates debatable notions that baseball's "only genuine entertainment comes from watching the most talented professional stars," that the World Series rightfully represents the ultimate championship, and that the routine failure of American teams in international competition can be explained away. The jingoism raises the unnerving question of whether MLB is really good for the game. According to Bjarkman, "the emphasis is not now—nor has it ever really been—on fostering the health of the sport," except within the narrow interest of organized baseball.[20]

A Path Through the Wilderness

If some success has been achieved in "growing the game," then what does that mean? MLB has expanded and profited, yet the sport of baseball has largely stagnated in the United States and abroad. Americans are no longer the world's best ballplayers, and baseball has not become the world's game. Baseball's export abroad has brought the American dream to the few, but an American nightmare for others. And arguably, baseball hasn't even remained the national pastime in America. In the best case, MLB has prevailed but only along a very narrow dimension and quite likely only tentatively. In the worst case, assessed by more meaningful measures, the MLB empire has struck out or at least has two strikes against it. Can we begin seeing baseball without looking through the dominant lens of the major leagues? Can organized baseball reevaluate what's at stake and refocus itself toward the value of the game instead of merely the value of its portfolio? MLB's current direction might be serving its own interests far less than its leaders imagine.

Is being the loyal servant of U.S. foreign and military policy good for organized baseball? As we've seen, MLB has pursued this alliance throughout its history, but isn't it possible that the "national pastime trade-off" has outlived its usefulness? Was it perhaps overrated in the first place? Albert Camus once wrote, "The true patriot is one who gives his highest loyalty not to his country as it is, but to what it can and ought to be." That's a distinction that may be worth emphasizing at this point in American history. The United States now faces not merely the usual internal conflicts over the state of the nation and its role in the world. It also encounters a world, including its closest allies, that largely rejects its foreign, military, and globalization policies—not to mention the fact that those policies undermine the fundamental principles of American democracy and the U.S. Constitution.

Isn't it perhaps time for MLB (and all of us) to reassess what constitutes a patriotic response to these circumstances? Even from the practical perspective of merely salvaging America from the worst consequences (for itself) of its overextended empire, a reorientation might be appropriate. Does MLB really want to be viewed as the "ugly American" and remain linked with what's often regarded as a rogue nation, whose policies and government are widely hated around the world?[21] Perhaps MLB has more of a sense of this than we think. While its deviations from American policy have been rare, two have occurred recently, and both involved Cuba. In 1998, MLB challenged America's Cuba policy and the Clinton White House when it arranged a baseball series between the Baltimore Orioles and the Cuban national team. Then in 2005, MLB confronted that policy (and this time the Bush White House) again, when it sought U.S. entry for the Cuban team to play in the World Baseball Classic. Conforming to outdated Cold War politics wasn't in the best interest of MLB, and it might begin to see this in other contexts too.

What else could baseball do differently? It depends, in part, on whether organized baseball will take the lead or will have to be pushed in a new direction. All baseball fans have a stake in resisting the game's further commodification. Baseball's meaning has increasingly been contrived from above and cynically foisted on a passive public, rather than reflecting people's lived experience and their interest in engaging with the sport rather than being its passive spectators. Mike Marqusee holds out hope: "The colonization of sport, like the corporate appropriation of the Third World gene bank, can be challenged. But only if sports fans emerge from their nationalistic cocoons and begin making links across borders of all kinds." And if organized baseball shuns these overtures? Perhaps we should heed former big-league pitcher Bill Lee, who argued that fans "have to storm the commissioner's office as the peasants stormed the Bastille during the French Revolution. They have to take control. Ralph Nader had it right: sports and not religion is now the opiate of the masses. We have to shake ourselves out of that opiate-induced state and return the game to what it used to be."[22]

As with U.S.-Cuba relations, MLB might see reasons to challenge other parts of conventional U.S. foreign policy. It might recognize the value of using baseball to try to rehabilitate the world's negative view of America, but such an effort can succeed only where baseball is used for positive ends and not for social control. Will MLB remain part of the problem of American empire and of U.S. foreign and military policy, or will it become part of the solution? How about promoting genuine baseball diplomacy rather than thinly disguised gestures of self-interest? And why not reconsider baseball's longstanding association with war and militarism? Byron Price points out that baseball can serve "as a balance to or reprieve from the adrenaline of warfare, rather than its intensification." Merritt Clifton agrees: "At some point, baseball rivalry might help replace war . . . [and] nationalism, with new recognition of ourselves as members of a common species."[23]

MLB might reconsider its hoarding of the sport and try instead to genuinely spread the game. Doing so would reap financial rewards in the long run, but in the short term it might be better offered as a gift: "Here's what baseball has given us. We hope you like it. It's part of America and it's free." If MLB and the United States are serious about exporting the American dream, then it should be made a common reality, not merely a rare jackpot for the few. Roberto Gonzalez Echevarria has written that "baseball contains within it forces that oppose the advance of American-style capitalism, . . . [and] the magic of the ritual of baseball prevents the game from being appropriated by one culture or nation. Baseball is . . . human and universal . . . and now belongs to countries and cultures that are not American."[24] It could belong to many more.

Organized baseball might work to preserve and promote (rather than weaken and undermine) foreign leagues in the Caribbean, East Asia, and elsewhere, which would allow other nations to build up their baseball without having their players and fans lured away. As Peter Bjarkman has argued, "baseball's salvation depends on the continued existence of alternative baseball worlds—independent entities that can focus exclusively on their own growth and health as vibrant national cultural institutions." Accordingly, if the United States isn't weakening clubs in other nations, then it becomes more legitimate to patriotically support America's teams. And domestically, MLB could begin taking more seriously its revival as the national pastime. Rather than conceding to competing sports, it could more earnestly win back those athletes (especially African Americans) and fans it has lost—offering a new and more progressive vision of itself in American society.

Sports sociologists have shown that a nation's dominant games reflect the society that supports them. Football first challenged baseball as the national game during the late-nineteenth-century rise of American imperialism. Baseball survived this and subsequent threats but eventually lost ground, especially in the Vietnam War era. Arguably, America has become a "football society" over the last thirty years. Football's violence and other machismo may best describe the culture America has become and the way it projects itself into the world.[25] It may be the genuine sport of the American Empire. Does baseball really want to reclaim that distinction? In the house of American sports, baseball has found itself in an unfamiliar position: looking in, instead of looking out. It still labors, however, to hold on to the "national pastime" label. Should it continue to do so, and if so, how?

In the early twenty-first century, performance-enhancing drugs might seem like baseball's greatest challenge. Yet MLB's reaction to America's performance-enhanced foreign policies may matter as well. John Thorn has observed that "sometimes baseball . . . serves as a beacon, revealing a path through the wilderness." And Tim Wendel writes about how baseball offers "an alternative, a way out of all this madness."[26] Perhaps so. Ironically, for all that baseball has done, historically, to parrot America's martial and imperial spirit, it hasn't kept up. In response, should the sport redouble its efforts with a new dose of flag-waving patriotism? Should baseball compete in that way with football to regain its status as the genuine national pastime? Or should it instead recognize what it has lost, over the years, by playing that game?

Of course there are limits to how a sport can shape a nation. Even so, what kind of society does baseball really want to reflect? It might do better by letting football beat the war drums while baseball instead pushes the nation to live up to its ideals.

Notes

Chapter 1. Wars at Home (1775–1892)

1. Thomas L. Altherr, "'A Place Leavel Enough to Play Ball': Baseball and Baseball-Type Games in the Colonial Era, Revolutionary War, and Early American Republic," *Nine: A Journal of Baseball History and Social Policy Perspectives* 8:2 (2000), 15–49; David Block, *Baseball Before We Knew It: A Search for the Roots of the Game* (Lincoln: University of Nebraska Press, 2006).

2. Merritt Clifton, "Yankee Origins," *SABR-L Archives*, April 18, 2001.

3. Robert Henderson, *Ball, Bat and Bishop: The Origin of Ball Games* (Urbana: University of Illinois Press, 2001).

4. Protoball Chronology of Early Ball Play, http://retrosheet.org/Protoball/chron.

5. Altherr, "'A Place Leavel Enough to Play Ball,'" 15.

6. Gerald S. Gems, *The Athletic Crusade: Sport and American Cultural Imperialism* (Lincoln: University of Nebraska Press, 2006); Thomas Borstelmann, *The Cold War and the Color Line: American Race Relations in the Global Arena* (Cambridge, MA: Harvard University Press, 2001), 10–84; Bradford Perkins, *The Cambridge History of American Foreign Relations*, vol. 1, 1776–1865 (New York: Cambridge University Press, 1993).

7. Eric Enders, "Timeline of International Baseball," www.ericenders.com/internationalbb.htm (2000); Samuel O. Regalado, "Viva Baseball! The Beginnings of Latin American Baseball," in *Baseball History from Outside the Lines*, ed. John Dreifort (Lincoln: University of Nebraska Press, 2002), 321–36; Protoball Chronology of Early Ball Play; Walker Tompkins, "Baseball Began Here in 1847," in *It Happened in Old Santa Barbara* (Santa Barbara, CA: Santa Barbara National Bank, 1976).

8. David Voigt, *American Baseball*, vol. 1: *From the Gentleman's Sport to the Commissioner System* (University Park, PA: Penn State University Press, 1983).

9. Craig Greenham, "Outfields to Battlefields, Battlefields to Outfields: The Impact of the Civil War on Baseball in the United States," paper delivered at the North American Society for Sports History Conference, Glenwood Springs, CO, 2006; Patricia Millen, "Baseball and the Civil War" in *Total Baseball*, ed. John Thorn and Pete Palmer (Toronto: Sports Media, 2004), 47–51; George B. Kirsch, *Baseball in Blue and Gray: The National Pastime During the Civil War* (Princeton, NJ: Princeton University Press, 2003); Mark Sappenfield, "Baseball in Wartime? It's Been the American Way Since 1861; Season Opens for a Sport Uniquely Tied to Military Conflict," *Christian Science Monitor*, March 31, 2003, 2; Bill Stern, *Favorite Baseball Stories* (New York: Doubleday, 1949); Patricia Millen, *From Pastime to Passion: Baseball and the Civil War* (Bowie, MD:

Heritage Books, 2001); Arthur Bartlett, *Baseball and Mr. Spalding: The History and Romance of Baseball* (New York: Farrar, Straus and Young, 1951).

10. David Williams, *A People's History of the Civil War: Struggles for the Meaning of Freedom* (New York: The New Press, 2005).

11. George B. Kirsch, "Bats, Balls, Baseball and the Civil War," *Civil War Times*, May 1998, 30–39.

12. Allison Caveglia Barash, "Base Ball in the Civil War," *National Pastime* 23 (2003), 17–19; Jim Kushlan, "Fan Appreciation Day," *Civil War Times* 37:2 (May 1998), 4.

13. Lawrence Fielding, "Sport and the Terrible Swift Sword," *Research Quarterly* 48:1 (March 1977), 4; Lawrence Fielding, "War and Trifles: Sport in the Shadows of Civil War Army Life," *Journal of Sport History* 4:2 (Summer 1977), 154–55; Greenham, "Outfields to Battlefields, Battlefields to Outfields," 6.

14. Jim Sumner, "Baseball at Salisbury Prison Camp," in *Baseball History 1*, ed. Peter Levine (New York: Stadium Books, 1990), 19–27; Jonathan Fraser Light, *The Cultural Encyclopedia of Baseball* (Jefferson, NC: McFarland, 1997); Michael Morgan, "Bats and Bayonets," in *The Ol' Ball Game*, ed. Mark Alvarez (New York: Barnes & Noble Books, 1990), 6–8.

15. Michael G. Bryson, *The Twenty-Four-Inch Home Run* (Chicago: Contemporary Books, 1990).

16. Joseph L. Price, "'What So Proudly We Hailed': National Crisis, the National Anthem, and the National Pastime," paper presented to the 16th Cooperstown Symposium on Baseball and American Culture, Cooperstown, New York, June 2004; Jerry Malloy, "The 25th Infantry Regiment Takes the Field," *National Pastime* 15 (1995), 59–64; Protoball Chronology of Early Ball Play; Kirsch, "Bats, Balls, Baseball and the Civil War," 35; Greenham, "Outfields to Battlefields, Battlefields to Outfields," 6.

17. Doug Stewart, "The Old Ball Game," *Smithsonian* 29:7 (October 1998); Lara D. Nielsen, "Exertions: Acts of Citizenship in the Globalization of Major League Beisbol," PhD dissertation, New York University, 2002.

18. Thomas Dyja, *Play for a Kingdom* (San Diego, CA: Harcourt Brace Jovanovich, 1997); Thomas Dyja, "America's Rites of Passage," *Civil War Times*, May 1998, 38–39.

19. Kushlan, "Fan Appreciation Day," 4.

20. Dyja, "America's Rites of Passage," 38–39; Light, *Cultural Encyclopedia of Baseball*, 131.

21. Robert A. Nylen, "Frontier Baseball," *Nevada* 50 (March 1990), 27; Stephen Ambrose, *Nothing Like It in the World: The Men Who Built the Transcontinental Railroad 1863–1869* (New York: Simon & Schuster, 2001).

22. Yet this was a period that featured Jim Crow, social Darwinism, Indian wars and genocide, a brutal industrialization, and the Spanish-American War. Kirsch, "Bats, Balls, Baseball and the Civil War," 37; Jack Beatty, *Age of Betrayal* (New York: Knopf, 2007); Peter N. Carroll and David W. Noble, *The Free and the Unfree: A Progressive History of the United States* (New York: Penguin, 2001); Harvey Wasserman, *History of the United States* (New York: Four Walls Eight Windows, 1988); Howard Zinn, *A People's History of the United States: 1492–Present* (New York: HarperPerennial, 1995).

23. Barash, "Base Ball in the Civil War"; Albert G. Spalding, *America's National Game* (Chicago: American Sports Publishing, 1911); David Lamoreaux, "Baseball In the Late Nineteenth Century: The Source of Its Appeal," *Journal of Popular Culture* 11:3 (Winter 1997), 597–613.

24. John Rickards Betts, *America's Sporting Heritage, 1850–1950* (Reading, MA: Addison-Wesley, 1974); Michael Lomax, *Black Baseball Entrepreneurs, 1860–1901* (Syracuse, NY: Syracuse University Press, 2003).

25. Robert H. Gudmestad, "Baseball, the Lost Cause, and the New South in Richmond, Virginia, 1883–1890," *Virginia Magazine of History and Biography* 106 (Summer 1998), 267–300; William Ryczek, *When Johnny Came Sliding Home: The Post–Civil War Baseball Boom, 1865–1870* (Jefferson, NC: McFarland, 1998); Michael Oriard, *Dreaming of Heroes: American Sports Fiction, 1868–1980* (Chicago: Nelson Hall, 1982); E.J. Gorn and W. Goldstein, *A Brief History of American Sports* (New York: Hill & Wang, 1993), 99; Pope, *Patriotic Games*; Bairner, *Sport, Nationalism, and Globalization*, 95; D.J. Mrozek, *Sport and the American Mentality, 1880–1910* (Knoxville: University of Tennessee Press, 1983), 161.

26. Ronald Story, "The Country of the Young: The Meaning of Baseball in Early American Culture," in *Sport in America: From Wicked Amusement to National Obsession*, ed. D.K. Wiggins (Champaign, IL: Human Kinetics, 1995), 121–32.

27. Michael Mandelbaum, *The Meaning of Sports* (New York: PublicAffairs, 2004); David Voigt, *America Through Baseball* (Chicago: Nelson Hall, 1976), 84; William B. Mead and Paul Dickson, *Baseball: The President's Game* (New York: Walker, 1997).

28. Mitchell Nathanson, "Gatekeepers of Americana: Ownership's Never-Ending Quest for Control of the Baseball Creed," *Nine* 15:2 (2006), 68–87.

29. Ed Folsom, "The Manly Healthy Game: Whitman and Baseball," *Arete*, Autumn 1984, 43–62.

30. Darryl Brock, *If I Never Get Back* (New York: Crown, 1990); Some transplanted Americans joined French and English Canadians in the 1837–38 Rebellions against British rule. Canada's first recorded baseball game occurred at Beachville, Ontario, in 1838. A British militia detachment watched the game while waiting to pursue restive American settlers. It was played on King George's birthday, and another baseball game was held to celebrate the king's victory over Ontario's democratic revolt. Robert Knight Barney, "Diamond Rituals: Baseball in Canadian Culture," in *Baseball History 2*, ed. Peter Levine (Westport, CT: Meckler Books, 1989), 1–21; Robert Knight Barney, "Whose National Pastime? Baseball in Canadian Popular Culture," in *The Beaver Bites Back? American Popular Culture in Canada*, ed. David Flaherty and Frank Manning (Montreal: McGill–Queen's University Press, 1993), 152–62; Samuel R. Hill, "Baseball in Canada," *Indiana Journal of Global Legal Studies* 8 (Fall 2000), 37–72; Beth LaDow, "We Can Play Baseball on the Other Side: The Limits of Nationalist History on a U.S.-Canada Borderland," in *American Public Life and the Historical Imagination*, ed. Wendy Gamber and Michael Grossberg (Notre Dame, IN: University of Notre Dame Press, 2003), 163–82.

31. Benjamin G. Rader, *American Sports: From the Age of Folk Games to the Age of Spectators* (Englewood Cliffs, NJ: Prentice Hall, 1983), 93. By the 1880s, baseball had become integral to a shared, U.S.-Canadian borderland sporting life. U.S.-Mexican border fluidity was much less extensive. Nationalist and assimilationist sentiments heightened Anglo-Hispanic tensions, thus separating Mexican and American baseball. Colin D. Howell, "Baseball and Borders: The Diffusion of Baseball into Mexican and Canadian-American Borderland Regions, 1885–1911," *Nine* 11:2 (2003), 16–26; Barney, "Diamond Rituals"; Hill, "Baseball in Canada"; William Humber, "Canada in the Country of Baseball," in *Diamonds of the North: A Concise History of Baseball in Canada*, ed. William Humber (Toronto: Oxford University Press, 1995), 3–14.

32. Zoss and Bowman, *Diamonds in the Rough.*

33. William McKeever, *The Industrial Training of the Boy* (New York: Macmillan, 1914).

34. Michael S. Kimmel, "Baseball and the Reconstitution of American Masculinity, 1880–1920," *Baseball History 3*, ed. Peter Levine (Westport, CT: Meckler Books, 1990), 98–112; Wanda Ellen Wakefield, *Playing to Win: Sports and the American Military, 1898–1945* (Albany: State University of New York Press, 1997).

35. Steven W. Pope, "Sport, Colonialism and Empire," presented at Historians on Sport Conference, International Centre for Sport History and Culture, DeMontfort University, October 30, 2004, 1–19; Steven W. Pope, "Sport and *Pax Americana*," paper presented at the North American Society for Sports History Conference, Glenwood Springs, CO, 2006; Joel Franks, *Hawaiian Sports in the Twentieth Century* (Lewiston, ME: Edwin Mellen Press, 2002); Clifford Putney, *Muscular Christianity: Manhood and Sports in Protestant America, 1880–1920* (Cambridge, MA: Harvard University Press, 2001); Kimmel, "Baseball and the Reconstitution of American Masculinity, 1880–1920," 98–112.

36. Steven A. Reiss, "Sport and the Redefinition of Middle-Class Masculinity in Victorian America," in *The New American Sport History: Recent Approaches and Perspectives,* ed. Steven W. Pope (Urbana: University of Illinois Press, 1997), 173–97.

37. Borstelmann, *The Cold War and the Color Line,* 99.

38. In his Lewis and Clark documentary, Ken Burns tells how in 1806 the explorers taught the Nez Percé Indians to play a baseball predecessor: a stick and ball game called base. But Stephen Ambrose claims that "base" was more precisely "prisoner's base," an old Indian game. And *Baseball Magazine* described ball games played by the Creek Indians in the seventeenth century, involving "savages and threatened scalpings." Ball games have been attributed to Native Americans as far back as Columbus's arrival. Stephen Ambrose, *Undaunted Courage: The Pioneering First Mission to Explore America's Wild Frontier* (New York: Pocket Books, 2003); Paul V. Barrett, "Baseball in the Seventeenth Century," *Baseball Magazine* 5:1 (May 1910), 75; Editors, "The Baseball Idea," *Milwaukee Sentinel,* July 30, 1892, 4; Block, *Baseball Before We Knew It,* 10.

39. Harold Peterson, *The Man Who Invented Baseball* (New York: Scribner's, 1969); Harold Seymour, *Baseball: The People's Game* (New York: Oxford University Press, 1991); Larry Bowman, "Soldiers at Play: Baseball on the American Frontier," *Nine* 9:1–2 (September 2000), 35–49; Edward M. Coffman, "Army Life on the Frontier, 1865–1898," *Military Affairs* 20:4 (Winter 1956), 193–201. In 1863, Colonel "Kit" Carson attacked the Navajo Indians and imprisoned the survivors. When finally released, the Navajos kept playing the baseball they learned from U.S. soldiers. In the late 1860s, 9th Cavalry Indian War veterans played baseball against local cowboys in Big Bend and Alpine, Texas. Bowman, "Soldiers at Play"; Block, *Baseball Before We Knew It,* 289; Betty Dillard and Karen Green, "Beeves and Baseball: The Story of the Alpine Cowboys," *Journal of Big Bend Studies* 11 (1999), 171.

40. Tim Wolter, "Bats and Saddles: Base Ball with Custer's Seventh Cavalry," *National Pastime* 17 (1998), 25–28.

41. E. Randall Floyd, "George Armstrong Custer: Golden-Haired Son of the Morning Star," in *The Good, the Bad and the Mad* (New York: Barnes & Noble, 1999), 48–51.

42. Harry H. Anderson, "The Benteen Base Ball Club: Sports Enthusiasts of the Seventh Cavalry," *Montana,* July 1970, 82–87.

43. A Thom Ross story, illustrated with pen and ink drawings, shows cavalrymen and Indians dressed for war yet carrying bats and gloves instead of rifles and clubs, and baseballs instead of bullets. In the end, Crazy Horse strikes out the last five batters in relief. Final score: the Sioux/Cheyenne team (Native American League) beats the 7th Cavalry (U.S. Army League), 16–1. Thom Ross, "Custer's Last Stand Seen as a Baseball Game," in *The Dreamlife of Johnny Baseball*, ed. Richard Grossinger (Berkeley, CA: North Atlantic Books, 1987), 73–75. With his death, Custer became a martyr, and his portrait adorned saloons across America for years. When pictures of Custer were finally replaced, images of baseball's first superstar, Mike "King" Kelly, were the usual replacement.

44. Bryson, *Twenty-Four-Inch Home Run*.

45. David Voigt, "America's First Red Scare: The Cincinnati Reds of 1869," *Ohio History* 78 (Winter 1969), 13–24; William Ryczek, *Blackguards and Red Stockings: A History of Baseball's National Association, 1871–1875* (Jefferson, NC: McFarland, 1999).

46. Ted Vincent, *Mudville's Revenge: The Rise and Fall of American Sport* (Lincoln: University of Nebraska Press, 1981).

47. David Nemec, *The Beer and Whiskey League: The Illustrated History of the American Association* (New York: Lyons & Burford, 1994), 55.

48. Bryan Di Salvatore, *A Clever Base-Ballist: The Life and Times of John Montgomery Ward* (New York: Pantheon, 1999); David Stevens, *Baseball's Radical for All Seasons: A Biography of John Montgomery Ward* (Lanham, MD: Scarecrow Press, 1998).

49. Daniel M. Pearson, *Baseball in 1889: Players vs. Owners* (Bowling Green, OH: Bowling Green University Popular Press, 1993); Ed Koszarek, *The Player's League* (Jefferson, NC: McFarland, 2006).

50. Robert Smith, *Baseball in the Afternoon: Tales from a Bygone Era* (New York: Simon & Schuster, 1993), 77; Jules Tygiel, *Past Time: Baseball as History* (New York: Oxford University Press, 2000), 31.

51. Bill Brown, "Waging Baseball, Playing War: Games of American Imperialism," *Cultural Critique* 17 (Winter 1990–1991), 51–78; Enders, "Timeline of International Baseball"; Bob Bailey, "The Forgotten War: The American Association–National League War of 1891," *National Pastime* 19 (1999), 81–84; Harold Seymour, *Baseball: The Early Years* (New York: Oxford University Press, 1960); Nemec, *The Beer and Whiskey League*, 239; David Voigt, *The League That Failed* (Lanham, MD: Scarecrow Press, 1998); Harold Dellinger, "Rival Leagues," in *Total Baseball*, ed. John Thorn and Pete Palmer (Toronto: Sports Media, 2004), 678–94.

52. The reserve clause bound players to their team. At first it affected only some players, but soon was extended to all players. Sullivan, *Early Innings*, 92; Mark Lamster, *Spalding's World Tour: The Epic Adventure That Took Baseball Around the Globe—and Made It America's Game* (New York: PublicAffairs, 2006), 21.

Chapter 2. Missionaries Abroad (1888–1897)

1. Robert Kagan, *Dangerous Nation* (New York: Knopf, 2006); Walter LaFeber, *The New Empire: An Interpretation of American Expansion, 1860–1898* (Ithaca, NY: Cornell University Press, 1998).

2. Joel Zoss and John Bowman, *Diamonds in the Rough: The Untold History of Baseball* (Lincoln: University of Nebraska Press, 2004); David Voigt, *America Through Baseball* (Chicago: Nelson Hall, 1976), 92.

3. Dean A. Sullivan, *Early Innings: A Documentary History of Baseball, 1825–1908* (Lincoln: University of Nebraska Press, 1995); "International Base-Ball," *Harper's* 18:917 (July 25, 1874), 626; "Base-Ball in England," *Harper's* 18:923 (September 5, 1874), 742; Jack Kavanagh, "Brits in the Baseball Hall of Fame," *National Pastime* 12 (1992), 67–69; Neil Stout, "1874 Baseball Tour Not Cricket to British," *Baseball Research Journal* 14 (1985), 83–85; Sid Mercer, "Foreign Tours Date Back to '74," *Baseball Digest* 2 (November 1943), 21–22; George Edward Brace, "Diamond Report: The First Professional Foreign Tour," *Oldtyme Baseball News* 11:6 (1998), 18; Glenn Moore, "The Great Baseball Tour of 1888–89: A Tale of Image-Making, Intrigue, and Labour Relations in the Gilded Age," *International Journal of the History of Sport* 11:3 (December 1994), 431–56.

4. I draw extensively upon two recent and sterling portrayals of Spalding's Tour: Mark Lamster, *Spalding's World Tour: The Epic Adventure That Took Baseball Around the Globe—and Made It America's Game* (New York: PublicAffairs, 2006), and Thomas W. Zeiler, *Ambassadors in Pinstripes: The Spalding World Tour and the Birth of the American Empire* (Lanham, MD: Rowman & Littlefield, 2006). See also Ernest J. Lanagan, "Baseball's First World Tour," *Baseball Magazine*, June 1939, 300–301; Henry Chadwick, "Baseball: The Great Trip," *Sporting Life*, October 17, 1888, 4; Josh Chetwynd, "Great Britain: Baseball's Battle for Respect in the Land of Cricket, Rugby, and Soccer," in *Baseball Without Borders: The International Pastime*, ed. George Gmelch (Lincoln: University of Nebraska Press, 2006); Craig Davids, "Spalding's Baseball Tour," *American Heritage* 28 (October 1977), 46–49; Walter Evans, "The All-American Boys," *Journal of Popular Culture* 6:1 (Spring 1972), 104–21; Thom Loverro, "A Classic Baseball Road Trip Around the World: How a Nation's Pastime Became a Game for a Globe," *Washington Times*, March 17, 2006, A01; Peter Levine, *A.G. Spalding and the Rise of Baseball: The Promise of American Sport* (New York: Oxford University Press, 1985); Thomas W. Zeiler, "Basepaths to Empire: Race and the Spalding World Baseball Tour," *Journal of the Gilded Age and Progressive Era* 6:2 (April 2007).

5. Albert Spalding, *America's National Game* (Chicago: American Sports Publishing, 1911); Lamster, *Spalding's World Tour*.

6. Cynthia Bass, "The World Tour of Eighty Eight," *Elysian Fields Quarterly* 12:1 (1993), 48–58; Robert Tiemann, "Join the Majors, See the World: Baseball on Tour," *National Pastime* 10 (1990), 43–48.

7. Zeiler, "Basepaths to Empire"; Adrian Burgos, *Playing America's Game: Baseball, Latinos, and the Color Line* (Berkeley: University of California Press, 2007). While Anson is often targeted for his prejudice, we shouldn't ignore the institutional character of the racism involved. David W. Zang, *Fleet Walker's Divided Heart: The Life of Baseball's First Black Major Leaguer* (Lincoln: University of Nebraska Press, 1995); Lewis Carlson, "The Universal Athletic Sport of the World," *American History Illustrated* 19 (April 1984), 36–43; Levine, *A.G. Spalding and the Rise of Baseball*; Peter Levine, "Business, Missionary Motives Behind the 1888–1889 World Tour," *Baseball Research Journal* 13 (1984), 60–63.

8. Gerald S. Gems, *The Athletic Crusade: Sport and American Cultural Imperialism* (Lincoln: University of Nebraska Press, 2006).

9. To serenade the tourists, Spalding had a Hawaiian band play "Marching Through Georgia," a song celebrating General Sherman's bloody Civil War march. Some players called the Hawaiian leader the "King of the Cannibal Islands," and a U.S. newspaper headline read "Base Ball for Canibals." A cartoon showed bewildered natives

begging players for pointers on the game. Dan Cisco, *Hawaii Sports* (Honolulu: University of Hawaii Press, 1999); Lamster, *Spalding's World Tour*; Zeiler, *Ambassadors in Pinstripes*; Frank Ardolino, "Missionaries, Cartwright, and Spalding: The Development of Baseball in Nineteenth-Century Hawaii," *Nine* 10:2 (2002), 27–45; Frank Ardolino, "Sluggers in Paradise: Major League Visits to Hawaii, 1888–1934," *National Pastime* 12 (1992), 20–22; Monica Nucciarone, "Alexander Cartwright," http://Bioproj.sabr.org.

10. Joseph Clark, *A History of Australian Baseball* (Lincoln: University of Nebraska Press, 2003); Bruce Mitchell, "Baseball in Australia: Two Tours and the Beginnings of Baseball in Australia," *Sporting Traditions* 7 (May 1991), 2–24; Bruce Mitchell, "A National Game Goes International: Baseball in Australia," *International Journal of the History of Sport* 9 (August 1992), 288–301; Zeiler, *Ambassadors in Pinstripes*.

11. Novelist Henry James described typical U.S. tourists: "Their ignorance—their stingy, grungy, defiant attitude—their perpetual reference of all things to some American precedent which exists only in their own unscrupulous wind-bags—and then our unhappy poverty of voice, speech, of physiognomy—these things glare at you hideously. It's the absolute and incredible lack of culture that strikes you in common traveling Americans." Thus it was frightening to see Spalding and his tourists as the "harbinger of a not-to-distant-future when Americans would roam freely across the globe." Lamster, *Spalding's World Tour*.

12. Allyson Patton, "Away Game," *American History*, June 1999, 72; Zeiler, *Ambassadors in Pinstripes*; Lamster, *Spalding's World Tour*.

13. Carlson, "The Universal Athletic Sport of the World," 36; Zeiler, *Ambassadors in Pinstripes*; Lamster, *Spalding's World Tour*.

14. David Stevens, *Baseball's Radical for All Seasons: A Biography of John Montgomery Ward* (Lanham, MD: Scarecrow Press, 1998).

15. Henry Chadwick, "The Australian Trip," *Sporting Life,* August 15, 1888, 3. Ever the renegade, in 1888 the United States had neither ambassadors nor embassies, but only ministers. That this portrayed "America as a relentlessly commercial and ill-mannered nation did not serve it well in the Old World." Zeiler, *Ambassadors in Pinstripes*; Lamster, *Spalding's World Tour*.

16. At the games was Pierre de Coubertin, the father of the Olympic movement, with whom Spalding quickly connected. As a result, he headed the U.S. delegation to the Olympics in 1900 and 1904—hoping to promote his sporting goods business. Mark Dyreson, *Making the American Team: Sport, Culture and the Olympic Experience* (Urbana: University of Illinois Press, 1997).

17. Carlson, "The Universal Athletic Sport of the World," 36.

18. Richard Slotkin, "Buffalo Bill's 'Wild West' and the Mythologization of the American Empire," in *Cultures of United States Imperialism*, ed. Amy Kaplan (Durham, NC: Duke University Press, 1993); Robert W. Rydell and Rob Kroes, *Buffalo Bill in Bologna* (Chicago: University of Chicago Press, 2005).

19. Patrick Carroll, "Spalding's Tourists in Bristol," *National Pastime* 23 (2003), 64–66; "The American Baseballers at the Crystal Palace," *Sporting Life*, March 15, 1889, 1; "The American Baseballers at Leyton," *Sporting Life*, March 18, 1889, 4; Carlson, "The Universal Athletic Sport of the World"; Lamster, *Spalding's World Tour*; Martin Johnes, "Poor Man's Cricket," *International Journal of the History of Sport* 17 (2000), 153–66; Daniel Bloyce, "'Just Not Cricket': Baseball in England, 1874–1900,"

International Journal of the History of Sport 14 (1997), 207–21; "American Baseballers at Kennington Oval," *Sporting Life*, March 13, 1889, 11.

20. "The Return of the Ball-Players," *Harper's* 33:1685 (April 6, 1889), 266.

21. Howard Zinn, *A People's History of the United States: 1492–Present* (New York: HarperPerennial, 1995); Lamster, *Spalding's World Tour*.

22. Zeiler, *Ambassadors in Pinstripes*; Ron Menchine, "Tour of Duty," *Beckett's Sports Collectibles* 7 (January 1998), 44–45.

23. Zeiler, *Ambassadors in Pinstripes*.

24. Ibid.; Steven Gelber, "Working at Playing: The Culture of the Workplace and the Rise of Baseball," *Journal of Social History* 16 (June 1983), 3–22.

25. Bill Brown, "Waging Baseball, Playing War: Games of American Imperialism," *Cultural Critique* 17 (Winter 1990–91), 51–78; Kristin Hoganson, "Cosmopolitan Domesticity: Importing the American Dream, 1865–1920," *American Historical Review* 107 (February 2002), 55–83. In 1893, the baseball tourists reunited in New York to view *Ninety Days*. The play, inspired by their trip, took the heroine to Burma, where "the American athletes, in full uniform, liberated [her] from her captors by vanquishing a horde of Oriental scoundrels with their bats." At the Chicago World's Fair that same year, natives from the United States and abroad were crudely displayed to contrast backward peoples to advanced American civilization. Lamster, *Spalding's World Tour*; Zeiler, *Ambassadors in Pinstripes*; Mark Dyreson, "Nature by Design: Modern American Ideas About Sport, Energy, Evolution, and Republics, 1865–1920," *Journal of Sport History* 26:3 (Fall 1999), 447–69.

26. Levine, *A. G. Spalding and the Rise of Baseball*; Joel Zoss and John Bowman, *Diamonds in the Rough: The Untold History of Baseball* (Lincoln: University of Nebraska Press, 2004).

27. Brown, "Waging Baseball, Playing War," 63.

28. Zoss and Bowman, *Diamonds in the Rough*.

29. Harrington E. Crissey, "Baseball and the Armed Services," www.lapelota.info/puntobeisbol/history/leagues/military/armedintro.html; Sayuri Guthrie-Shimizu, "For Love of the Game: Baseball in Early U.S.-Japanese Encounters and the Rise of a Transnational Sporting Fraternity," *Diplomatic History* 28:5 (November 2004), 637–61.

30. Joseph A. Reaves, *Taking in a Game: A History of Baseball in Asia* (Lincoln: University of Nebraska Press, 2002), 49.

31. Donald Roden, "Baseball and the Quest for National Dignity in Meiji Japan," *American Historical Review* 85:3 (June 1980), 511–34.

32. "'Play Ball!'—With Samurai Trimmings," *Literary Digest* 96:11 (March 17, 1928), 34; Roden, "Baseball and the Quest for National Dignity in Meiji Japan," 530; Gems, *Athletic Crusade*, 31, 34.

33. Adrian Burgos tells us: "The game's popularity in the Spanish-speaking Caribbean arose not from U.S. military action but from cultural exchange, commercial activity, and labor migration before 1898." While Burgos correctly notes the multiple sources of baseball's migration, the U.S. military role cannot be discounted. If not providing baseball's first contact with some nations, it nevertheless often institutionalized the game. "Baseball's Spread Throughout the Spanish-Speaking Americas: Uncle Sam's New People Learning the National Game," *Sporting Life*, August 24, 1901, 1; Burgos, *Playing America's Game*, 72; Peter C. Bjarkman, *Diamonds Around the Globe: Encyclopedia of International Baseball* (Westport, CT: Greenwood Press,

2005); Louis A. Perez Jr., "Between Baseball and Bullfighting: The Quest for Nationality in Cuba, 1868–1898," *Journal of American History* 81:2 (September 1994), 493–517; Peter C. Bjarkman, *A History of Cuban Baseball* (Jefferson, NC: McFarland, 2007).

34. Roberto Gonzalez Echevarria, "The Game in Matanzas: On the Origins of Cuban Baseball," *Yale Review* 83:3 (July 1995), 62; Adrian Burgos, "Cuban Baseball Legacy Rich in American Heritage," *Memories and Dreams*, July–August 2006, 9–11.

35. Perez, "Between Baseball and Bullfighting," 493; Gems, *Athletic Crusade*, 85.

36. Bjarkman, *A History of Cuban Baseball*; Bjarkman, *Diamonds Around the Globe*, 5; Gonzalez Echevarria, "The Game in Matanzas"; James D. Cockcroft, *Latinos in Beisbol: The Hispanic Experience in the Americas* (Danbury, CT: Franklin Watts, 1996).

37. Adrian Burgos, "Entering Cuba's Other Playing Field: Cuban Baseball and the Choice Between Race and Nation, 1887–1912," *Journal of Sport & Social Issues* 29:1 (February 2005), 9–40; Michael M. Oleksak and Mary Adams Oleksak, *Beisbol: Latin Americans and the Grand Old Game* (Indianapolis: Master's Press, 1996).

38. Burgos, "Entering Cuba's Other Playing Field," 27.

39. Gems, *Athletic Crusade*, 85. The son of one of Martí's friends was Alejandro Pompez, an eventual Cooperstown Hall of Famer who was a major promoter of the Negro Leagues, providing many Cubans the chance to play in the United States. Yuyo Ruiz, *The Bambino Visits Cuba, 1920* (San Juan, PR: self-published, n.d.).

40. Louis A. Perez Jr., "Baseball and Becoming," in *On Becoming Cuban: Identity, Nationality and Culture* (Chapel Hill: University of North Carolina Press, 1999), 255–78; Perez, "Between Baseball and Bullfighting"; Paula Pettavino and Geralyn Pye, *Sport in Cuba: The Diamond in the Rough* (Pittsburgh: University of Pittsburgh Press, 1994). African American players often named their teams the Cubans (such as the New York Cuban Giants), hoping it would help them slip through the U.S. baseball color barrier and admiring the Cuban revolutionary, antislavery spirit. Lisa Brock and Bijan Bayne, "Not Just Black: African-Americans, Cubans, and Baseball," in *Between Race and Empire: African-Americans and Cubans Before the Cuban Revolution*, ed. Lisa Brock and Digna Castañeda Fuertes (Philadelphia: Temple University Press, 1997), 168–204; Thomas Carter, "Baseball Arguments: *Aficionismo* and Masculinity at the Core of *Cubanidad*," in *Sport in Latin American Society*, ed. J.A. Mangan and Lamartine DaCosta (London: Frank Cass, 2002), 117–38; Burgos, "Entering Cuba's Other Playing Field," 27; C.L.R. James, *Beyond a Boundary* (New York: Pantheon, 1983).

41. George Black, *The Good Neighbor: How the United States Wrote the History of Central America and the Caribbean* (New York: Pantheon, 1988); Gems, *Athletic Crusade*, 84; Gilbert M. Joseph, "Forging the Regional Pastime: Baseball and Class in Yucatan," in *Sport and Society in Latin America*, ed. Joseph L. Arbena (New York: Greenwood Press, 1988), 29–61; Alan M. Klein, *Sugarball: The American Game, the Dominican Dream* (New Haven: Yale University Press, 1991); Bruce Calder, *Impact of Intervention* (New York: Wiener, 2006).

42. Harold Seymour, *Baseball: The People's Game* (New York: Oxford University Press, 1991); Gems, *Athletic Crusade*, 101; Rory Costello, "Baseball in the Virgin Islands," *Baseball Research Journal* 28 (1999), 33–40.

43. Richard V. McGehee, "Sport in Nicaragua, 1889–1926," in *Sport in Latin America and the Caribbean*, ed. Joseph L. Arbena and David G. LaFrance (Wilmington, DE: Scholarly Resources, 2002), 175–205.

44. During the 1893 economic depression, Henry Chadwick implored professional ballplayers to be "patriotic" by not complaining about their slave wages.

45. Harold Seymour, *Baseball: The Early Years* (New York: Oxford University Press, 1960); David Lamoreaux, "Baseball in the Late Nineteenth Century: The Source of Its Appeal," *Journal of Popular Culture* 11:3 (Winter 1997), 597–613; Gelber, "Working at Playing," 3.

46. Henry Chadwick, *How to Play Base Ball* (New York: A.G. Spalding, 1889); Kavanagh, "Brits in the Baseball Hall of Fame"; Editors, "Football and Baseball," *Baseball Magazine* 10:1 (November 1912), 80; Gerald S. Gems, *For Pride, Profit, and Patriarchy: Football and the Incorporation of American Cultural Values* (Lanham, MD: Scarecrow Press, 2000); Zoss and Bowman, *Diamonds in the Rough*.

47. Lamoreaux, "Baseball in the Late Nineteenth Century," 597.

48. Mark Sappenfield, "Baseball in Wartime? It's Been the American Way Since 1861; Season Opens for a Sport Uniquely Tied to Military Conflict," *Christian Science Monitor*, March 31, 2003, 2.

49. Steven W. Pope, "An Army of Athletes: Playing Fields, Battlefields, and the American Military Sporting Experience, 1890–1920," *Journal of Military History* 59:3 (July 1995), 435–56; C.D. Parkhurst, "The Practical Education of the Soldier," *Journal of the Military Service Institution of the United States* (1890), 946; John Rickards Betts, "Home Front, Battle Field, and Sport During the Civil War," *Research Quarterly* 42:2 (1971), 113–32.

50. Zoss and Bowman, *Diamonds in the Rough*.

Chapter 3. Small Wars and the Old Army Game (1898–1909)

1. Jeff Arnett, "Remember the Maine! A Tragedy in International Waters Recalls the Diverse Legacy of a Little-Known Baseball Team," *Memories and Dreams*, July–August 2006, 3.

2. Walter LaFeber, *The Cambridge History of American Foreign Relations*, vol. 2, 1865–1913 (New York: Cambridge University Press, 1993); Jim Zwick, "Mark Twain's Anti-Imperialist Writings in the 'American Century,'" in *Vestiges of War: The Philippine-American War and the Aftermath of an Imperial Dream, 1899–1999*, ed. Angel Velasco Shaw and Luis H. Francia (New York: New York University Press, 2002), 38–56; Louis A. Perez Jr., *The War of 1898: The United States in History and Historiography* (Chapel Hill: University of North Carolina Press, 1998).

3. According to his deathbed confession, U.S. adventurer and (Teddy) Roosevelt protege William Astor Canler admitted to plotting the explosion. Hugh Thomas, *Cuba, or The Pursuit of Freedom* (New York: Da Capo Press, 1998), 364.

4. Adrian Burgos, *Playing America's Game: Baseball, Latinos, and the Color Line* (Berkeley: University of California Press, 2007), 80; Adrian Burgos, "Entering Cuba's Other Playing Field: Cuban Baseball and the Choice Between Race and Nation, 1887–1912," *Journal of Sport & Social Issues* 29:1 (February 2005), 9–40.

5. Kristin Hoganson, "Cuba and the Restoration of American Chivalry," in *Fighting for American Manhood: How Gender Politics Provoked the Spanish-American and Philippine-American Wars* (New Haven, CT: Yale University Press, 1998), 42–67.

6. Ibid., 80–81; Ronald Briley, "The Rhetoric of Empire: Baseball and the Spanish-American War," paper abstract for North American Society for Sport History Con-

ference, Glenwood Springs, CO, May 19–22, 2006; E.J. Gorn and W. Goldstein, *A Brief History of American Sports* (New York: Hill & Wang, 1993), 149; Amy Kaplan, "Black and Blue on San Juan Hill," in *Cultures of United States Imperialism*, ed. Amy Kaplan (Durham, NC: Duke University Press, 1993); Baseball Reference, www.baseball-reference.com; Baseball Bullpen, www.baseball-reference.com/bullpen; Society for American Baseball Research, "Armed Forces Committee," September 2004, www.sabr.org.cfm?a=cms,c,523,43.0.

7. David Voigt, *American Baseball*, vol.1, *From the Gentleman's Sport to the Commissioner System* (University Park, PA: Penn State University Press, 1983), 264–65.

8. Ibid.; Harold Seymour, *Baseball: The Early Years* (New York: Oxford University Press, 1960), 346; David Voigt, *The League That Failed* (Lanham, MD: Scarecrow Press, 1998).

9. The United States convinced itself that it alone had liberated the Cubans, on "strictly humanitarian grounds" and disparaged the largely black Cuban revolutionary army's role in defeating the Spaniards. Jay Hambridge, "The Occupation of Cuba," *Collier's* 22:2 (October 15, 1898), 12; George Black, *The Good Neighbor: How the United States Wrote the History of Central America and the Caribbean* (New York: Pantheon, 1988); *The War of 1898 and U.S. Interventions, 1898–1934*, ed. Benjamin Beede (New York: Garland, 1994); "Soldiers at Sport," *Collier's* 21:24 (September 17, 1898), 19; William A. Phelon, "Baseball in Cuba: The Great American Sport as an International Game," *Baseball Magazine* 9:1 (May 1912), 33–36.

10. Roberto Gonzalez Echevarria, *The Pride of Havana: A History of Cuban Baseball* (New York: Oxford University Press, 1999), 200; Louis A. Perez Jr., "Between Baseball and Bullfighting: The Quest for Nationality in Cuba, 1868–1898," *Journal of American History* 81:2 (September 1994), 493–517; Burgos, *Playing America's Game*, 84.

11. Harold Seymour, *Baseball: The People's Game* (New York: Oxford University Press, 1991).

12. Burgos, "Entering Cuba's Other Playing Field," 32; Lisa Brock and Bijan Bayne, "Not Just Black: African-Americans, Cubans, and Baseball," in *Between Race and Empire: African-Americans and Cubans Before the Cuban Revolution*, ed. Lisa Brock and Digna Castañeda Fuertes (Philadelphia: Temple University Press, 1997), 168–204; Michael M. Oleksak and Mary Adams Oleksak, *Beisbol: Latin Americans and the Grand Old Game* (Indianapolis: Master's Press, 1996), 14.

13. Phelon, "Baseball in Cuba"; Ira Thomas, "How They Play Our National Game in Cuba," *Baseball Magazine* 10:5 (March 1913), 61–65; Matthew Jacobson, *Barbarian Virtues: The United States Encounters Foreign Peoples at Home and Abroad* (New York: Hill & Wang, 2000).

14. Gerald S. Gems, *The Athletic Crusade: Sport and American Cultural Imperialism* (Lincoln: University of Nebraska Press, 2006), 92; Burgos, "Entering Cuba's Other Playing Field," 31.

15. Jay Feldman, "Roberto Clemente Went to Bat for All Latino Ballplayers," *Smithsonian*, September 1993, 129–42.

16. Seymour, *Baseball: The People's Game*; Joel Franks, *Hawaiian Sports in the Twentieth Century* (Lewiston, ME: Edwin Mellen Press, 2002).

17. Joel Franks, "Pacific Crossings and Baseball: Comments on Hawaii and America's National Pastime and the Great Wally Yonamine," *Nine* 8:1 (1999), 54–63; Gems, *Athletic Crusade*, 72–74.

18. Kerry Yo Nakagawa, *Through a Diamond: 100 Years of Japanese-American Baseball* (San Francisco: Rudi Publishing, 2001). The United States also intervened in nearby Samoa, which it annexed in 1899 and established as a naval base. As with Guam, the Samoans used American sports as defiance. By 1913, Samoa had gone crazy over baseball: a game between Pago Pago and Fauga-Sa lasted four days. In 1916, Samoan native guardsmen formed a league, which included a U.S. naval team. "The Crack of the Baseball Bat Goes Echoing Around the World," *Current Opinion* 55 (November 1913), 308–10; Seymour, *Baseball: The People's Game.*

19. Stuart Creighton Miller, *Benevolent Assimilation: The American Conquest of the Philippines, 1899–1903* (New Haven, CT: Yale University Press, 1982); James W. Loewen, *Lies Across America: What Our Historic Sites Get Wrong* (New York: Touchstone, 1999). U.S. soldiers indicated, "Our fighting blood was up and we all wanted to kill 'niggers.'" Some sought to "make the Samar [a Philippine province] into a howling wilderness." Daniel B. Schirmer, "U.S. Racism and Intervention in the Third World, Past and Present," in *Vestiges of War: The Philippine-American War and the Aftermath of an Imperial Dream, 1899–1999*, ed. Angel Velasco Shaw and Luis H. Francia (New York: New York University Press, 2002), 163–76.

20. Gems, *Athletic Crusade*, 46–47; Thomas Borstelmann, *The Cold War and the Color Line: American Race Relations in the Global Arena* (Cambridge, MA: Harvard University Press, 2001); Janice Beran, "Americans in the Philippines: Imperialism or Progress Through Sport?" *International Journal of the History of Sport* 6 (May 1989), 62–87. The United States claimed it was uplifting the Filipinos. William S. Bryan, *Our Islands and Their People* (New York: N.D. Thompson, 1900). Actually it brought corruption, violence, prostitution, gambling, and exploitation.

21. Tom Walsh, "Baseball in the Philippines," *Bulletin of the American Historical Collection* 23:3 (July–September 1995), 106–9; William Pulliam, "Baseball Follows the Flag—and the Thermometer," *Outlook* 144:8 (October 20, 1926), 246; Joseph A Reaves, *Taking in a Game: A History of Baseball in Asia* (Lincoln: University of Nebraska Press, 2002), 91; Charles Murphy, "Baseball as National Tonic," *Baseball Magazine*, 22:3 (January 1919), 157.

22. Reaves, *Taking in a Game*, 92–93. Baseball got Filipinos exercising, but elites initially resisted: "Baseball found its roots among the poorer community, who were not bothered with tanned complexions or roughened hands." Monroe G. Wooley, "Baseball as an Educational Influence in the Philippines: Our National Game as a Civilizing Influence," *Baseball Magazine* 16:6 (April 1916), 77–78; Monroe G. Wooley, "Batter Up in the Philippines," *Outdoor World and Recreation*, May 1913, 313–14; "Filipinos Take On American Civilization," *Leslie's Illustrated Weekly Newspaper* 120:3110 (April 15, 1915), 366; "Base-Ball and the Blue Books," *Scribner's Magazine* 48:2 (1910), 251–52.

23. Reaves, *Taking in a Game*, 95. In 1894, Funston arrived on Alaska's Hershel Island amid the Arctic Whalemen's pennant race, for which U.S. sailors and whalers were playing games in snow and ice. The contests were watched by Eskimos, who soon tried games of their own. Other Hershel Island fans included Japanese, Chinese, Tahitians, Hawaiians, and every European seafaring nationality. Frederick Funston, "Frederick Funston's Alaska Trip," *Harper's Weekly*, May 25, 1895. By 1906, Funston was the Presidio commandant during the San Francisco earthquake, whose tactics and unauthorized seizure of the city were widely criticized. Soon he was off to Nevada, lead-

ing U.S. army assaults against Industrial Workers of the World labor strikes. Eventually, Funston ended up in Mexico, hunting Pancho Villa and heading the U.S. troops occupying Veracruz. In line to lead the American Expeditionary Force in World War I, he died unexpectedly in 1917. Black, *Good Neighbor*.

24. Mark Twain, "A Defence of General Funston," *North American Review* 174 (May 1902), 1; Zwick, "Mark Twain's Anti-Imperialist Writings in the 'American Century'"; Mark Twain, "Comments on the Moro Massacre," in *Voices of a People's History of the United States*, ed. Howard Zinn and Anthony Arnove (New York: Seven Stories Press, 2004), 248–52; Howard Zinn, "Can We Handle the Truth?" *Utne Reader*, September–October 2007, 53; Mark Twain, "To the Person Sitting in Darkness," in *Vestiges of War: The Philippine-American War and the Aftermath of an Imperial Dream, 1899–1999*, ed. Angel Velasco Shaw and Luis H. Francia (New York: New York University Press, 2002), 57–68.

25. Reaves, *Taking in a Game*, 94. Campaigns were eventually waged in Congress to eliminate African Americans from the U.S. military. Gems, *Athletic Crusade*, 58.

26. Seymour, *Baseball: The People's Game*.

27. Ernie Harwell, "Baseball Among the Headhunters," *True*, November 1947, 17; Arthur Shafer, "Baseball All Around the World," *Leslie's Illustrated Weekly* 393 (April 4, 1912), 407–8.

28. A bartender was killed and a police officer was wounded, for which the black soldiers were unjustly blamed. They weren't vindicated for another fifty years.

29. Jerry Malloy, "The 25th Infantry Regiment Takes the Field," *National Pastime* 15 (1995), 59–64.

30. Rolin Hardt, "The National Game," *Atlantic Monthly* 102:2 (August 1908), 220–29; Reaves, *Taking in a Game*, 98, 99, 102.

31. The rebellion came first as a new independence movement and then as a communist movement. The U.S. churches also had mixed results, converting some but alienating others. Gems, *Athletic Crusade*, 60; Reaves, *Taking in a Game*, 41.

32. "Baseball Players and National Defense," *Outlook* 115:9 (February 28, 1917), 342; Wanda Ellen Wakefield, *Playing to Win: Sports and the American Military, 1898–1945* (Albany: State University of New York Press, 1997); Alan Bairner, *Sport, Nationalism, and Globalization: European and North American Perspectives* (Albany: State University of New York Press, 2001), 93; "Baseball in the Navy," *American Boy* 5:12 (October 1904), 368.

33. Steven W. Pope, "Sport, Colonialism and Empire," paper presented at Historians on Sport Conference, International Centre for Sport History and Culture, DeMontfort University, October 30, 2004, 1–19.

34. Charles Stewart, "The United States of Baseball," *Century Magazine* 74:2 (June 1907), 307–19.

35. Alan Bairner, *Sport, Nationalism, and Globalization*, 96; Stephen W. Pope, *Patriotic Games: Sporting Traditions in the American Imagination, 1876–1926* (New York: Oxford University Press, 1997), 71; Richard C. Crepeau, *Baseball: America's Diamond Mind, 1919–1941* (Orlando: University Presses of Central Florida, 1980).

36. Peter Levine, *A.G. Spalding and the Rise of Baseball: The Promise of American Sport* (New York: Oxford University Press, 1985); David Lamoreaux, "Baseball in the Late Nineteenth Century: The Source of Its Appeal," *Journal of Popular Culture* 11:3 (Winter 1997), 597–613; Albert Spalding, *America's National Game* (Chicago: American

Sports Publishing, 1911); Francis D. Cogliano, "Baseball and American Exceptionalism," in *Sport and National Identity*, ed. Dilwyn Porter and Adrian Smith (New York: Routledge, 2004), 145–67.

37. Bill Brown, "The Meaning of Baseball in 1992," *Popular Culture* 4 (Fall 1991), 43–69.

38. James D. Cockcroft, *Latinos in Beisbol: The Hispanic Experience in the Americas* (Danbury, CT: Franklin Watts, 1996).

39. Gerald R. Gems, "Sports, Colonialism, and United States Imperialism," *Journal of Sport History* 33:1 (Spring 2006), 3–25; Gerald R. Gems, "Sports, War and Ideological Imperialism," *Peace Review* 11:4 (1999), 573–78.

40. David C. Ogden, "Major League Baseball and Myth Making," *Nine* 15:2 (2007), 66–78; Paul J. Zingg, "Diamond in the Rough: Baseball and the Study of American Sports History," *History Teacher* 17 (1982), 388.

41. Stephen J. Ducat, *The Wimp Factor: Gender Gaps, Holy Wars, and the Politics of Anxious Masculinity* (Boston: Beacon Press, 2004).

42. Theodore Roosevelt, *The Strenuous Life* (New York: Scribner's, 1906); M.V. Lyons, "The Tremendous Popularity of Football and Its Cause," *Baseball Magazine* 12:2 (December 1913), 77–80; Michael Mandelbaum, *The Meaning of Sports* (New York: PublicAffairs, 2004).

43. William B. Mead and Paul Dickson, *Baseball: The President's Game* (New York: Walker, 1997).

44. Harrington Crissey, "Abner Doubleday Would Have Been Proud," *Baseball Research Journal* (1976), 33–36.

45. Stewart, "United States of Baseball," 307.

46. Carl H. Claudy, *The Battle of Base-Ball* (Jefferson, NC: McFarland, 2005).

47. Burt Solomon, *The Baseball Timeline: The Day-by-Day History of Baseball from Valley Forge to the Present Day* (New York: Avon, 1997); "Baseball's Army of the Unemployed," *Baseball Magazine* 17:1 (May 1916), 76.

48. Seymour, *Baseball: The People's Game*; James Elfers, *The Tour to End All Tours: The Story of Major League Baseball's 1913–1914 World Tour* (Lincoln: University of Nebraska Press, 2003).

49. William Kennedy, "The All-Star Army Team," *Baseball Magazine* 15:2 (June 1915), 45–49.

50. Charles Weeghman, "Playing Ball for Uncle Sam," *Baseball Magazine* 19:4 (August 1917), 19.

51. Paul Dickson, ed. *The Dickson Baseball Dictionary* (New York: Facts on File, 1989), 280.

Chapter 4. Imperium Rising (1910–1916)

1. Robert Kagan, *Dangerous Nation* (New York: Knopf, 2006).

2. Walter LaFeber, *The Cambridge History of American Foreign Relations*, vol. 2, 1865–1913 (New York: Cambridge University Press, 1993); Akira Iriye, *The Cambridge History of American Foreign Relations*, vol. 3, 1913–1945 (New York: Cambridge University Press, 1993); Joel Zoss and John Bowman, *Diamonds in the Rough: The Untold History of Baseball* (Lincoln: University of Nebraska Press, 2004); Mark Dyreson, "Sport and Visions of the 'American Century,'" *Peace Review* 11:4 (1999), 565–71;

Clarence Jenkins, "Baseball During America's Search for Order," paper presented at the Society for American Baseball Research Annual Conference, Louisville, Kentucky, 1997, 1–13.

3. Leverett Smith, *The American Dream and the National Game* (Bowling Green, OH: Popular Press, 2004).

4. Benjamin G. Rader, "The Quest for Self-Sufficiency and the New Strenuosity," in *The New American Sport History: Recent Approaches and Perspectives*, ed. Steven W. Pope (Urbana: University of Illinois Press, 1997), 402–16; Michael S. Kimmel, "Baseball and the Reconstitution of American Masculinity, 1880–1920," *Baseball History 3*, ed. Peter Levine (Westport, CT: Meckler Books, 1990), 98–112; David Voigt, *The League That Failed* (Lanham, MD: Scarecrow Press, 1998); "Ballplayer Diplomats," *Baseball Magazine* 13:1 (May 1914), 90.

5. Paul A. Kramer, "Empires, Exceptions and Anglo-Saxons: Race and Rule Between the British and United States Empires, 1880–1910," *Journal of American History* 88:4 (March 2002), 1315–53; Gerald R. Gems, "Sports, Colonialism, and United States Imperialism," *Journal of Sport History* 33:1 (Spring 2006), 3–25; "Baseball as America's Contribution to Religion: An Argument Which Stresses the Civilizing Influence of Our National Game," *Current Literature* 67:5 (December 1919), 318.

6. William Stead, *The Americanization of the World* (New York: H. Markley, 1902).

7. Albert Spalding, *America's National Game* (Chicago: American Sports Publishing, 1911); Bill Brown, "The Meaning of Baseball in 1992," *Popular Culture* 4 (Fall 1991), 43–69; Peter Levine, *A.G. Spalding and the Rise of Baseball: The Promise of American Sport* (New York: Oxford University Press, 1985); Kristin Hoganson, "Cosmopolitan Domesticity: Importing the American Dream, 1865–1920," *American Historical Review* 107 (2002), 55–83.

8. Carl Siger, *Essai sur la colonization* (Paris, 1907), cited in Bill Brown, "Waging Baseball, Playing War: Games of American Imperialism," *Cultural Critique* 17 (Winter 1990–91), 51–78; Levine, *A.G. Spalding and the Rise of Baseball*.

9. Burt Standish, *Frank Merriwell in Peru; or, In the Land of the Incas* (New York: Street & Smith, 1910).

10. Ibid.; Donald Roden, "Baseball and the Quest for National Dignity in Meiji Japan," *American Historical Review* 85:3 (June 1980), 511–34; Thomas Boswell, "How Baseball Helps the Harvest, or What the Bay of Pigs Did to the Bigs," in *How Life Imitates the World Series* (New York: Penguin, 1983), 81–96.

11. Brown, "Waging Baseball, Playing War," 51; Norbert Elias and Alan Dunning, *The Quest for Excitement: Sport and Leisure in the Civilizing Process* (London: Blackwell, 1994); Michael Oriard, *Dreaming of Heroes: American Sports Fiction, 1868–1980* (Chicago: Nelson Hall, 1982).

12. Frank Norris, "The Frontier Gone at Last," in *The Literary Criticism of Frank Norris*, ed. Donald Pizer (Austin: University of Texas Press, 1964), 111–17; David Osinski, "Baseball and the Olympics," in *Total Baseball*, ed. John Thorn and Pete Palmer (Toronto: Sports Media, 2004), 802–4; Pete Cava, "Baseball in the Olympics," *National Pastime* 12 (1992), 2–8; Kristen Jones, "The Game Goes for Gold: A History of Olympic Baseball," *Memories and Dreams*, July–August 2006.

13. James D. Cockcroft, *Latinos in Beisbol: The Hispanic Experience in the Americas* (Danbury, CT: Franklin Watts, 1996).

14. Smedley Butler, "War Is a Racket," in *Voices of a People's History of the United States*, ed. Howard Zinn and Anthony Arnove (New York: Seven Stories Press, 2004), 252–55.

15. Kevin Gaines, "Black Americans' Racial Uplift Ideology as 'Civilizing Mission,'" in *Cultures of United States Imperialism*, ed. Amy Kaplan (Durham, NC: Duke University Press, 1993), 437; Harold Seymour, *Baseball: The People's Game* (New York: Oxford University Press, 1991).

16. Moses Fleetwood Walker, *Our Home Colony: A Treatise on the Past, Present and Future of the Negro Race in America* (Malabar, FL: P.E. Rieger, 1993); David W. Zang, *Fleet Walker's Divided Heart: The Life of Baseball's First Black Major Leaguer* (Lincoln: University of Nebraska Press, 1995); William C. Rhoden, *Forty Million Dollar Slaves: The Rise, Fall, and Redemption of the Black Athlete* (New York: Crown, 2006).

17. Adrian Burgos, *Playing America's Game: Baseball, Latinos, and the Color Line* (Berkeley: University of California Press, 2007), 76, 85.

18. "The American Indian's Warpath on the Diamond and Gridiron," *Literary Digest* 73:9 (May 27, 1922), 53; Glenn Warner, "Red Menaces," *Collier's* 88:18 (October 31, 1931), 16; C.M. Sarchet, "Baseball as Played by Indians," *Baseball Magazine* 1:5 (September 1908), 26; Ed Goewey, "The Case of 'Chief Myers' Proves the Live Redskin Can Be a Good Indian," *Leslie's Illustrated Weekly* 115:2966 (July 11, 1912), 32.

19. Burgos, *Playing America's Game*, 79; "Baseball's Spread Throughout the Spanish-Speaking Americas: Uncle Sam's New People Learning the National Game," *Sporting Life*, August 24, 1901, 1.

20. Ellen J. Staurowsky, "Sockalexis and the Making of the Myth at the Core of Cleveland's 'Indian' Image," in *Team Spirits: The Native American Mascots Controversy*, ed. Richard C. King and Charles Fruehling Springwood (Lincoln: University of Nebraska Press, 2001), 82–106; Jeffrey Powers-Beck, *The American Indian Integration of Baseball* (Lincoln: University of Nebraska Press, 2004).

21. James Elfers, *The Tour to End All Tours: The Story of Major League Baseball's 1913–1914 World Tour* (Lincoln: University of Nebraska Press, 2003); Jeffrey Wilson, "Chinese History, Even in Baseball, Stretches Back Far in Time," *International Baseball Rundown* 5:7 (August 1996), 16–17; Gerald S. Gems, *The Athletic Crusade: Sport and American Cultural Imperialism* (Lincoln: University of Nebraska Press, 2006), 17; Joseph A. Reaves, "A History of Baseball in China: How America's Game Helped End Educational Exchanges in the Late Qing Dynasty, Taught Sun Yat-sen's Revolutionaries to Throw Hand Grenades, and Endured the Cultural Revolution," paper presented to the North American Society for Sport History Annual Conference, Windsor, Ontario, May 22–25, 1998; Joseph A. Reaves, "Silk Gowns and Gold Gloves: The Forgotten History of Chinese Bat Ball," *Nine: A Journal of Baseball History and Culture* 7:2 (Spring 1999), 60–74; John B. Foster, "International Base Ball," *Spalding Official Base Ball Guide* (1912).

22. Reaves, "Silk Gowns and Gold Gloves," 60.

23. Maurice Allen, "Baseball in China," *Baseball Magazine* 7:5 (September 1911), 57–59.

24. Reaves, "A History of Baseball in China," 10; Gems, *Athletic Crusade*, 21, 28.

25. "A New Feature of the Yellow Peril: Baseball as a Factor in the Progress of Civ-

ilization," *Baseball Magazine* 8:6 (April 1912), 80; S.H. Hoe, "America Invaded by Oriental Foes," *Baseball Magazine* 12:5 (March 1914), 67–72.

26. Some Japanese opposed baseball as harmful. In "The Evil of Baseball," the newspaper *Asahi Shimbun* quoted educators and physicians who claimed baseball caused lopsided body development and mental pressure that distorted personality development. Yet the sport also nourished traditional Japanese virtues of loyalty, courage, and honor. Spalding was happy to see the Japanese adopt the game but concerned it might elevate another nationality. Roden, "Baseball and the Quest for National Dignity in Meiji Japan," 517, 532; Rob Rains, *Baseball Samurais: Ichiro Suzuki and the Asian Invasion* (New York: St. Martin's, 2001); Robert Fitts, *Remembering Japanese Baseball* (Carbondale: Southern Illinois University Press, 2005).

27. Roden, "Baseball and the Quest for National Dignity in Meiji Japan," 519, 520, 532; Gus W. Everberg, "Baseball Beyond the Pacific," *Baseball Magazine* 9 (August 1912), 93–94.

28. Sayuri Guthrie-Shimizu, "For Love of the Game: Baseball in Early U.S.-Japanese Encounters and the Rise of a Transnational Sporting Fraternity," *Diplomatic History* 28:5 (November 2004), 637–61.

29. Joseph A. Reaves, *Taking in a Game: A History of Baseball in Asia* (Lincoln: University of Nebraska Press, 2002).

30. When Japan's Waseda University team visited the United States, however, the American press coverage often mocked the "little brown men." The Keio University team also toured abroad, while the Americans sent the University of Washington and Hawaii's Asahi club. "Brown Boys Nettle High," *Los Angeles Daily Times*, May 18, 1905; "Japanese Baseball Invaders, Without Treaty," *Collier's* 47:21 (August 12, 1911), 25; J.J. Pegues, "Japan Invades America," *Collier's* 47:4 (April 15, 1911), 21; S.E. Ulford, "Baseball in the Pacific," *Baseball Magazine* 8:6 (April 1912), 81–84; Guthrie-Shimizu, "For Love of the Game"; Gems, *Athletic Crusade*, 35; Rolin Hardt, "The National Game," *Atlantic Monthly* 102:2 (August 1908), 220–29.

31. Rhea Mansfield, "The Man Who Made Baseball in Japan: Arthur Shafer," *Baseball Magazine* 9:3 (July 1912), 26–30.

32. In 1914 the McGraw-Comiskey world baseball tour stopped briefly in Japan, and in 1915, when the University of Chicago team returned to Japan, U.S. Ambassador George Guthrie attended the games. Seymour, *Baseball: The People's Game*; "Baseball May Some Day Avert War Between America and Japan," *New York Tribune*, May 15, 1910, 2; Philip Block, "A Japanese Baseball Odyssey: Keio University's 1911 Tour to the U.S.," paper presented to the Society for American Baseball Research Annual Conference, 2000, 1–9.

33. To combat native "savagery," the Japanese introduced baseball to Truk, substituting ball fields for battlefields. "The natives don't play baseball, they wage it," thus providing a manageable outlet for their aggression. George Peter Murdock, "Waging Baseball in Truk," in *Culture and Society* (Pittsburgh: University of Pittsburgh Press, 1965), 290–93. But "the real story might be waging war *on* Truk rather than *in* Truk." Baseball helped the Japanese oppress the Truk population, violating the local culture and masking imperialist aggression—turning the island into a Japanese naval base. Brown, "Waging Baseball, Playing War." Truk was seized by the United States after World War II. A Truk team soon beat a U.S. Navy team in baseball, thus showing that

the island was "already essentially American" and "not really being occupied." The United States soon decided to use the island for nuclear testing. Joseph A. Reaves, "Asian Invasion," *AsiaWeek*, November 9, 2001, www.asiaweek.com/asiaweek/magazine/life/; Yoichi Nagata and John B. Holway, "Baseball in Japan," in *Total Baseball*, ed. John Thorn and Pete Palmer (Toronto: Sports Media, 2004), 789–93.

34. Reaves, *Taking in a Game*, 119, 122.

35. Junwei Yu and Dan Gordon, "Nationalism and National Identity in Taiwanese Baseball," *Nine* 14:2 (2006), 27–39.

36. Ibid., Andrew Morris, "Taiwan: Baseball, Colonialism, and Nationalism," in *Baseball Without Borders: The International Pastime*, ed. George Gmelch (Lincoln: University of Nebraska Press, 2006).

37. In 1913 in *Baseball Magazine*, a short fictional piece, "Insurrection at La Boca," told how the U.S. Navy helped American capitalists suppress an uprising in an unnamed Caribbean nation. Karl Decker, "The Insurrection at La Boca," *Baseball Magazine* 11:6 (October 1913), 85–90. See also Rob Ruck, "Baseball in the Caribbean," in *Total Baseball*, ed. John Thorn and Pete Palmer (Toronto: Sports Media, 2004), 796–801; Zoss and Bowman, *Diamonds in the Rough*.

38. "Baseball in South America," *Baseball Magazine* 8:6 (April 1912), 76; Peter C. Bjarkman, *Diamonds Around the Globe: The Encyclopedia of International Baseball* (Westport, CT: Greenwood Press, 2005); Adrian Burgos, "Entering Cuba's Other Playing Field: Cuban Baseball and the Choice Between Race and Nation, 1887–1912," *Journal of Sport & Social Issues* 29:1 (February 2005), 9–40; Eric Enders, "Through the Looking Glass: The Forgotten World of Cuban Baseball," *Nine* 12:1 (2003), 147–52; "Baseball in Cuba," *Collier's* 22:2 (October 15, 1898), 5.

39. Roberto Gonzalez Echevarria, *The Pride of Havana: A History of Cuban Baseball* (New York: Oxford University Press, 1999), 12; Samuel O. Regalado, "Viva Baseball! The Beginnings of Latin American Baseball," in *Baseball History from Outside the Lines*, ed. John Dreifort (Lincoln: University of Nebraska Press, 2002), 321–36.

40. Ruck, "Baseball in the Caribbean," 801.

41. Others claim the Boers were named after a Nicaraguan indigenous group. Lester D. Langley and Thomas Schoonover, *The Banana Men: American Mercenaries and Entrepreneurs in Central America, 1880–1930* (Lexington: University Press of Kentucky, 1995), 41; Gems, *Athletic Crusade*, 139; Michel Gobat, *Confronting the American Dream: Nicaragua Under U.S. Imperial Rule* (Durham, NC: Duke University Press, 2005), 99; Michael David Rice, "Nicaragua and the United States: Policy Confrontations and Cultural Interactions, 1893–1933," PhD dissertation, University of Houston, 1985.

42. Michael M. Oleksak and Mary Adams Oleksak, *Beisbol: Latin Americans and the Grand Old Game* (Indianapolis: Master's Press, 1996), 11.

43. Seymour, *Baseball: The People's Game*; Oleksak and Oleksak, *Beisbol*, 12; H. Gardner, "The Pennant in Panama," *Baseball Magazine* 18:1 (November 1916), 42; Eric Wagner, "Sports," in *Handbook of Latin American Popular Culture*, ed. Harold Hinds and Charles Tatum (Westport, CT: Greenwood Press, 1985), 135–150.

44. Gems, *Athletic Crusade*, 117; Alan M. Klein, *Sugarball: The American Game, the Dominican Dream* (New Haven, CT: Yale University Press, 1991).

45. Regalado, "Viva Baseball." Chileans were playing baseball by 1912, and U.S. companies introduced the game to Brazil in 1913, the same year the New York High-

landers (soon to be the Yankees) took spring training in Bermuda to free themselves from distractions. "Baseball in Chile," *Baseball Magazine* 9:3 (July 1912), 56; Ralph S. Graber, "When the Highlanders Trained in Bermuda," *Baseball Research Journal* 10 (1981), 15–16. By 1910, the United States controlled the Haitian railroads and banks. The U.S. Marines intervened again in 1914, removing gold off the island from the national bank, then occupying the nation for several years, and installing a puppet government. Yet for all this U.S. intervention, baseball never took hold. Given Haiti's overwhelmingly black population, the color line in America and organized baseball no doubt had an effect.

46. William Beezley, "The Rise of Baseball in Mexico and the First Valenzuela," *Studies in Latin American Popular Culture* 4 (1985), 3–13; Gilbert M. Joseph, "Forging the Regional Pastime: Baseball and Class in Yucatan," in *Sport and Society in Latin America*, ed. Joseph L. Arbena (New York: Greenwood Press, 1988), 29–61.

47. H. Levine, "Ballplayers in Foreign Militaries," *New York American* (March 24, 1911); Colin D. Howell, "Baseball and Borders: The Diffusion of Baseball into Mexican and Canadian-American Borderland Regions, 1885–1911," *Nine* 11:2 (2003), 16–26; Christopher P. Wilson, "Plotting the Border: John Reed, Pancho Villa, and *Insurgent Mexico*," in *Cultures of United States Imperialism*, ed. Amy Kaplan (Durham, NC: Duke University Press, 1993).

48. Ed Goewey, "Baseball as Peacemaker," *Leslie's Illustrated Weekly* 119:3070 (July 9, 1914), 34; James W. Loewen, *Lies My Teacher Told Me: Everything Your American History Textbook Got Wrong* (New York: Touchstone, 1996).

49. Steven W. Pope, "Sport and *Pax Americana*," paper presented at the North American Society for Sports History Conference, Glenwood Springs, CO, 2006; Steven W. Pope, "Sport, Colonialism and Empire," paper presented at Historians on Sport Conference, International Centre for Sport History and Culture, DeMontfort University, October 30, 2004, 1–19; Steven W. Pope, "An Army of Athletes: Playing Fields, Battlefields, and the American Military Sporting Experience, 1890–1920," *Journal of Military History* 59:3 (July 1995), 435–56; Editorials, *Baseball Magazine* 17:4 (August 1916), 13–14; Cockcroft, *Latinos in Beisbol*.

50. Allen Guttman, *Games and Empires: Modern Sports and Cultural Imperialism* (New York: Columbia University Press, 1994); David Voigt, *America Through Baseball* (Chicago: Nelson Hall, 1976), 98–99; Elfers, *The Tour to End All Tours*; "The World Tour of the Chicago White Sox and New York Giants," *Baseball Magazine* 12:4 (February 1914), 47–48.

51. G.W. Axelson, *Commy: The Life Story of Charles A. Comiskey* (Chicago: Reilly & Lee, 1919); Clifford Bloodgood, "Giants and White Sox, Major League Pioneers," *Baseball Magazine* 47 (June 1931), 303–4; "To the Patriotic Lovers of America's Game," in *Baseball As America: Seeing Ourselves Through Our National Game* (Washington, DC: National Geographic, 2001), 38.

52. Elfers, *Tour to End All Tours*; Bruce L. Prentice and Merritt Clifton, "Baseball in Canada," in *Total Baseball*, ed. John Thorn and Pete Palmer (Toronto: Sports Media, 2004), 542–46.

53. Frank McGlynn, "Striking Scenes from the Tour Around the World—Part I," *Baseball Magazine* 13:4 (August 1914), 59–68.

54. Frank McGlynn, "Striking Scenes from the Tour Around the World—Part II,"

Baseball Magazine 13:5 (September 1914), 69–78; Tom Walsh, "Baseball in the Philippines," _Bulletin of the American Historical Collection_ 23:3 (July–September 1995), 106–9.

55. J.B. MacKay, "A Neglected Baseball Field: The Remarkable Headway Baseball is Making in Far Off Australia," _Baseball Magazine_ 11:4 (August 1913), 73–75.

56. Baseball had arrived elsewhere in Africa. The anthropologist Allen Sangree described the game as "a primitive instinct—a mystery in ethnology. In Zululand we handed a baseball to a young chief and first he 'played catch' with it. After that, he threw as far as he could and then sock[ed] it with his war-club. He felt the seams, hooked his fingers around it like McGinnity or Chesbro, rubbed it over his cheek and finally offered an ingénue from his harem in exchange." Jonathan Light, _The Cultural Encyclopedia of Baseball_ (Jefferson, NC: McFarland, 1997); George McManus, "If the World Tourists Play in Venice," _Baseball Magazine_ 12:3 (January 1914), 48; "The Crack of the Baseball Bat Goes Echoing Around the World," _Current Opinion_ 55 (November 1913), 308–10; Franz O. Messerly, "Base Ball in France," _Spalding Official Base Ball Guide_ (1913).

57. Association football (soccer) clubs created baseball teams to generate off-season income. The Derby Baseball Club played at the "Baseball Ground." An American-led league was created in London, and then a British Baseball Association began in 1906, inaugurating the British Baseball Cup. The London Baseball League imported American players. In 1907, an "international match" was played between English-born and American-born players. By 1909, baseball again declined in Britain, and press coverage began to dwindle. Daniel Bloyce, "'Just Not Cricket': Baseball in England, 1874–1900," _International Journal of the History of Sport_ 14 (1997), 207–21; Martin Johnes, "'Poor Man's Cricket': Baseball, Class and Community in South Wales, 1880–1950," _International Journal of the History of Sport_ 17 (2000), 153–66; Daniel Bloyce, "A Very Peculiar Practice: The London Baseball League, 1906–1911," _Nine_ 14:2 (2006), 118–28; Bill Kirwin, "The Prince and Baseball," _Nine Journal of Baseball History_ 13 (Spring 2005), 118–19; David Porter, "Untold Saga of Europe's Big Leaguers," _National Pastime_ 12 (1992), 70–76.

58. Frank McGlynn, "Striking Scenes from the Tour Around the World—Part V," _Baseball Magazine_ 14:2 (December 1914), 85–88; Elfers, _The Tour to End All Tours_.

59. Voigt, _American Through Baseball_. The contests proceeded anyway, but only provoked competing barbs between the British and American press. H. Allen Smith and Ira L. Smith, _Three Men on Third_ (Halcottsville, NY: Breakaway Books, 2000), 81; "Done in the English Way," _Baseball Magazine_ 17:4 (August 1916), 27–28.

60. Richard Slotkin, "Buffalo Bill's 'Wild West' and the Mythologization of the American Empire," in _Cultures of United States Imperialism_, ed. Amy Kaplan (Durham, NC: Duke University Press, 1993); Robert W. Rydell and Rob Kroes, _Buffalo Bill in Bologna_ (Chicago: University of Chicago Press, 2005); Elfers, _Tour to End All Tours_. According to _The Nation_: "If they had only developed the love of baseball forty years ago, the German behavior in the present war might have been less detestable . . . if the Russians were devoted to baseball, football, tennis, and track athletics, some barriers between Slav and Saxon might fall. Most Russians obtain their exercise in conversation. The Anglo-Saxon releases the violence inherent in every man through the outlet of sport." William Phelps, "Sporting Blood," _The Nation_, 107:2773 (August 24, 1918), 197–98. See also Ed Goewey, "London's Lord Mayor Becomes a Baseball Fan," _Leslie's_

Illustrated Weekly, 124:3193 (November 16, 1916), 544. While the 1913–14 tour skipped the Netherlands, baseball (*honkbal*) had already been introduced in 1901 by J.C.G. Grasse, a Dutchman returning from a U.S. visit. In 1912, the first Dutch baseball federation was formed, and the U.S. and Sweden played a demonstration game at the fifth Summer Olympics. Harvey Shapiro, "Holland: An American Coaching *Honkbal*," in *Baseball Without Borders: The International Pastime*, ed. George Gmelch (Lincoln: University of Nebraska Press, 2006).

61. McGlynn, "Striking Scenes from the Tour Around the World—Part V," 85.

62. William A. Phelon, "Baseball Around the World," *Baseball Magazine* 12:3 (January 1914), 15–21; "The Expansion of Base Ball," *Spalding Official Base Ball Guide*, 1915; John B. Foster, "Base Ball Around the World," *Spalding Official Base Ball Guide*, 1917.

63. James Elfers, "World War I Overshadowed Baseball's 'Tour to End All Tours,'" *University of Delaware Daily*, July 10, 2004, 1; Voigt, *America Through Baseball*.

64. Benjamin G. Rader, "The Great Baseball War," in *Baseball: A History of America's Game* (Urbana: University of Illinois Press, 2002), 71–81; Warren N. Wilbert, *The Arrival of the American League: Ban Johnson and the 1901 Challenge to the National League Monopoly* (Jefferson, NC: McFarland, 2007); Eugene C. Murdock, *Ban Johnson: Czar of Baseball* (Westport, CT: Greenwood Press, 1982); Leonard Koppett, *Concise History of Major League Baseball* (Philadelphia: Temple University Press, 1998).

65. Murdock, *Ban Johnson*, 109.

66. Joseph Durso, *Baseball and the American Dream* (St. Louis, MO: Sporting News, 1986), 63–64.

67. John E. Bruce, "The Chief Justice of Baseball's Supreme Court: Garry Herrmann, Prince of Baseball Magnates," *Baseball Magazine* 8:4 (February 1912), 53–54; Eugene C. Murdock, "Winning the War," *Ban Johnson: Czar of Baseball* (Westport, CT: Greenwood Press, 1982).

68. End-of-season competitions had been held since the late 1880s, with prizes such as the Dauvray Cup, the Temple Cup, and the Chronicle Telegraph Cup. While none were called the World Series, the Spalding Guide claimed that "the base ball championship of the United States necessarily includes the entire world, though the time will come when Australia will step in as a rival, and after that will come Great Britain; but all that is for the future."

69. Alan Bairner, *Sport, Nationalism, and Globalization: European and North American Perspectives* (Albany: State University of New York Press, 2001), 95.

70. George C. Rable, "Patriotism, Platitudes and Politics: Baseball and the American Presidency," *Presidential Studies Quarterly* 19 (Spring 1989), 363–72; Harold Seymour, *Baseball: The Golden Age* (New York: Oxford University Press, 1971).

71. Elfers, *The Tour to End All Tours*; Mark Okkonen, *The Federal League of 1914–1915: Baseball's Third Major League* (Garrett Park, MD: Society for American Baseball Research, 1989); Durso, *Baseball and the American Dream*, 120; William A. Phelon, "The War of the Leagues," *Baseball Magazine* 13:4 (August 1914), 33–40.

72. W.G. Kibbey, "Echoes of the Baseball War," *Baseball Magazine* 12:6 (April 1914), 47.

73. Ban Johnson overshadowed other baseball executives in this period. The chair of the National Commission, Garry Herrmann, served from 1903 until 1920 but was ineffectual. William A. Phelon, "War and Rumors of War," *Baseball Magazine* 14:3

(January 1915), 15–16; Okkonen, *The Federal League of 1914–1915*; F.C. Lane, "Has President Tener Made Good?" *Baseball Magazine* 16:6 (April 1916), 62–66.

74. William A. Phelon, "The Treaty of Cincinnati: How the Great Game Came to a Close," *Baseball Magazine* 16:4 (February 1916), 15; F.C. Lane, "Peace and Prosperity," *Baseball Magazine* 16:4 (February 1916), 23–30, 106.

Chapter 5. Real War (1917–1919)

1. "The Baseball Battle," *Baseball Magazine* (November 1914), 74.

2. Susan M. Matarese, *American Foreign Policy and the Utopian Imagination* (Amherst: University of Massachusetts Press, 2001).

3. Joel Zoss and John Bowman, *Diamonds in the Rough: The Untold History of Baseball* (Lincoln: University of Nebraska Press, 2004).

4. Ed Goewey, "Steals and Slides," *Leslie's Illustrated Weekly*, 121:3127 (August 12, 1915), 163; Walt Wilson, "Yankees, Giants, and Dodgers Met in 1913," *You Could Look It Up* 5:2 (Winter 2004), 1; Michael Mott, "Making the World Safe for Baseball: World War I, the National Pastime, and *Baseball Magazine*," (April 2, 2006), www.sfsu.edu/~mpmott/public_html/baseball&wwi.htm.

5. Leonard Koppett, *Concise History of Major League Baseball* (Philadelphia: Temple University Press, 1998); Walter Trumbull, "Sport," *American Legion Weekly* 1:7 (August 15, 1919), 15; "Baseball Players and National Defense," *Outlook* 115:9 (February 28, 1917), 342.

6. Joseph Durso, *Baseball and the American Dream* (St. Louis, MO: Sporting News, 1986); William Henry Wright, "The Drift in Baseball," *Outing* 70:2 (May 1917), 274; Harrington Crissey, "Baseball and the Armed Forces," in *Total Baseball*, ed. John Thorn and Pete Palmer (New York: Sports Media, 1989), 616–17; Eugene C. Murdock, "Winning the War," *Ban Johnson: Czar of Baseball* (Westport, CT: Greenwood Press, 1982). Harrington Crissey, "Baseball and the Armed Services," www.lapelota.info/puntobeisbol/history/leagues/military/armedintro.html.

7. Mott, "Making the World Safe for Baseball."

8. Critics viewed it as a war among imperialist powers for profit and control of the world's resources. One opponent, Eugene Debs, inspired a father to name his son after the fiery socialist: Debs Garms became a National League batting champion. Robert W. Creamer, *Baseball in '41: A Celebration of the Best Baseball Season Ever in the Year America Went to War* (New York: Viking Penguin, 1991); Wanda Ellen Wakefield, *Playing to Win: Sports and the American Military, 1898–1945* (Albany: State University of New York Press, 1997); Leon Cadore, "Baseball in the U.S. Army," *Baseball Magazine* 21:4 (August 1918), 343–44.

9. Zoss and Bowman, *Diamonds in the Rough;* Paul J. Zingg, *Harry Hooper: An American Baseball Life* (Urbana: University of Illinois Press, 1995), 154.

10. F.C. Lane, "Has President Tener Made Good?" *Baseball Magazine* 16:6 (April 1916), 62–66.

11. Don Warfield, *The Roaring Redhead: Larry McPhail—Baseball's Great Innovator* (South Bend, IN: Diamond Communications, 1987); Ted Farmer, "Hank Gowdy and the Call to Arms: Major League Baseball and World War One," *Nine: A Journal of Baseball History and Social Policy Perspectives* 5:2 (1997), 265–87; "Baseball for Our Soldiers and Sailors," *Baseball Magazine* 19:3 (July 1917), 372; F.C. Lane, "The Griffith Bat and

Ball Fund," *Baseball Magazine* 21:5 (September 1918), 396; Harry Brand, "A Royal Baseball Booster," *Baseball Magazine* 20:6 (April 1918), 462.

12. A.H. Tarvin, "Baseball and the War, Again," *Baseball Magazine* 70:1 (January 1943), 369–71; Bill Stern, *Favorite Baseball Stories* (New York: Doubleday, 1949); George C. Rable, "Patriotism, Platitudes and Politics: Baseball and the American Presidency," *Presidential Studies Quarterly* 19 (Spring 1989), 363–72.

13. "Ball Games Free to Wounded Men," *Stars and Stripes* 2:15 (May 16, 1919), 7.

14. Ed Goewey, "The War and Baseball," *Leslie's Illustrated Weekly Newspaper* 125:3239 (October 6, 1917), 483; "The Council of War," *Baseball Magazine* 17:6 (October 1916), 25–26; Zoss and Bowman, *Diamonds in the Rough*; Paul Lukas, "Flag-Waving," *Village Voice* 46:39 (October 2, 2001), 165; Richard Goldstein, *Spartan Seasons: How Baseball Survived the Second World War* (New York: Macmillan, 1980).

15. Jerome Beatty, "Baseball Goes to War," *Collier's*, 62 (September 14, 1918), 13; Ron Briley, "Ambiguous Patriotism: Baseball and the Vietnam War," in *Cooperstown Symposium on Baseball and American Culture, 2005–2006*, ed. William Simons (Jefferson, NC: McFarland, 2007), 165–78.

16. Wakefield, *Playing to Win*; "A Corner in Horsehide," *American Legion Magazine* 20:4 (April 1938), 34.

17. David Voigt, *American Baseball*, vol. 2, *From the Commissioners to Continental Expansion* (University Park, PA: Penn State University Press, 1983), 121; Jim Sumner, "The North Carolina League and the Advent of World War I," *Nine* 4:2 (1996), 237–47.

18. "Khakis or Overalls for Ballplayers," *Stars and Stripes* 1:25 (July 26, 1918), 6; "Uncle Sam at the Bat," *Collier's* 59:5 (April 14, 1917), 1.

19. Durso, *Baseball and the American Dream*; J.V. Fitz Gerald, "Baseball Players Must Work or Fight, Baker Rules, Dooming National Sport," *Washington Post*, July 20, 1918; Robert F. Burk, *Never Just a Game: Players, Owners and American Baseball to 1920* (Chapel Hill: University of North Carolina Press, 1994), 214, 222; Steve Steinberg, "World War I and Free Agency," *Nine* 16:2 (2008), 84–92.

20. Warren N. Wilbert, *The Arrival of the American League: Ban Johnson and the 1901 Challenge to the National League Monopoly* (Jefferson, NC: McFarland, 2007).

21. Briley, "Ambiguous Patriotism," 165; Albert Britt, "From Playing Field to Battle Field," *Outing* 73 (1919), 3.

22. Society for American Baseball Research, "Armed Forces Committee," September 2004, http://www.sabr.org.cfm?a=cms,c,523,43.0; "Playing the Greatest Game of All," *Collier's* 62 (September 14, 1918), 12; "The Month in War," *Baseball Magazine* 21:4 (August 1918), 355, 372; Hank Gowdy, "Why I Enlisted," *Baseball Magazine* 19:5 (September 1917), 507; John Tener, "Hank Gowdy, the Man Who Blazed the Trail," *Baseball Magazine* 20:5 (March 1918), 401. When World War II was declared, Gowdy—then fifty-three—tried to enlist again and was commissioned to run the infantry school's baseball program at Fort Benning, Georgia. Stevens, "Hero of the AEF—Hank Gowdy"; Frank Ceresi, "Hank Gowdy: Baseball Player and War Hero," FC Associates (www.fcassociates.com/id44_m.htm); Clifford Bloodgood, "The Ballplayer and the War," *Baseball Magazine* 70 (May 1943), 525–27; Tod Sloan, "Letters from Major Leaguers in the Service," *Baseball Magazine* 21:3 (July 1918), 276; Sam Rice, "How the U.S. Navy Made Me a Ball Player," *Baseball Magazine* 25:3 (August 1920), 430; Hugh Bradley, "Trenches and Dugouts," *Baseball Magazine* 64:3 (February 1940), 391.

23. David Cataneo, *Peanuts and Crackerjack: A Treasury of Baseball Legends and Lore* (Nashville: Rutledge Hill, 1991); Steve Grosshandler, "Baseball & the Great War," *Oldtyme Baseball News* 3:6 (1991), 25; Society for American Baseball Research, "Armed Forces Committee"; J. Kent Steele, "A Tragic Link," *National Pastime* 17 (1997), 117. The Polo Grounds plaque for Grant was stolen after the Giants final game in 1957. Missing for forty-seven years, it turned up in a New Jersey attic and is now preserved at the Baseball Reliquary. Joseph Tekulsky, "N.Y. Giants Hero Died Valiantly in France," *USA Today Baseball Weekly* 2:1 (April 1, 1992), 56; Jay Gauthreaux, "Eddie Grant: Player On Two Fields, *Oldtyme Baseball News* 2:4 (1990), 12; Fred Lieb, "Eddie Grant a Baseball War Hero," *Baseball Magazine* 27:2 (July 1921), 346; J.L. Ray, "Introducing the War's Greatest Hero to Baseball," *Baseball Magazine* 9:23 (May 1919), 292; Damon Runyon, "Captain Eddie Grant," *Philadelphia North American*, October 23, 1918; Joseph Wayman, "Grant Plaque Still Relevant," in *Grandstand Baseball Annual* 17 (2001), 135–37; Grantland Rice, "Eddie Grant," in *Out of Left Field*, ed. Jeffrey Lyons (New York: Three Rivers Press, 1998), 251.

24. Michael Hartley, *Christy Mathewson: A Biography* (Jefferson, NC: McFarland, 2004), 141; Philip Seib, *The Player: Christy Mathewson, Baseball, and the American Century* (New York: Four Walls Eight Windows, 2003). Mathewson had chest pains before the war, and thus his illness may have been tuberculosis. The media may have adopted the gas story because it portrayed him as a war hero. Ray Robinson, *Matty, An American Hero: Christy Mathewson of the New York Giants* (New York: Oxford University Press, 1993).

25. Peter T. Dalleo and J. Vincent Watchorn, "Baltimore, the 'Babe,' and the Bethlehem Steel League, 1918," paper presented at the Eighth Cooperstown Symposium on Baseball and American Culture, Cooperstown, NY, 1996; Murdock, "Winning the War," 126.

26. Wakefield, *Playing to Win*; Alfred Cornebise, *The Stars and Stripes: Doughboy Journalism in World War I* (Westport, CT: Greenwood Press, 1984), 3–6; Marshall G. Most and Robert Rudd, *Stars, Stripes and Diamonds: American Culture and the Baseball Film* (Jefferson, NC: McFarland Publishers, 2006).

27. There professional ballplayers might shelter themselves from the draft. Crissey, "Baseball and the Armed Forces," 616; "Baseball Wonders Where It Gets Off," *Stars and Stripes* 1:23 (July 12, 1918), 6; "Ballplayers Say They're Productive," *Stars and Stripes* 1:21 (June 28, 1918), 2; F.C. Lane, "A Rising Menace to the National Game," *Baseball Magazine* 21:4 (August 1918), 345–47, 372; Harold Seymour, *Baseball: The Golden Age* (New York: Oxford University Press, 1971).

28. James Gould, "War and Baseball," *Baseball Magazine* 68:3 (February 1942), 389.

29. Frederick Giffin, "Billy Sunday: The Evangelist as 'Patriot,'" *Social Science* 48:4 (Autumn 1973), 216.

30. William A. Phelon, "Big League Players in the Army and Navy," *Baseball Magazine* 22 (January 1919), 143–47; Farmer, "Hank Gowdy and the Call to Arms"; Richard C. Crepeau, *Baseball: America's Diamond Mind, 1919–1941* (Orlando: University Presses of Central Florida, 1980), 2; Murdock, "Winning the War," 130; Leslie Mann, "What the Soldiers Think of Major League Baseball," *Baseball Magazine* 22 (December 1918), 79–81; F.C. Lane, "Baseball's Bit in the World War," *Baseball Magazine* 20:5 (March 1918), 386; Sol Metzger, "Regards Athletics as Patriotic Duty," *New*

York Times, July 22, 1917, sec. 3, p. 4; Frederick Parmly, "Baseball Will Win the War," *Baseball Magazine* 22 (December 1918), 106–10.

31. Jerome Beatty, "Baseball Goes to War"; Charles Murphy, "Baseball a Wartime Necessity," *Baseball Magazine* 22:2 (December 1919), 87; Charles Murphy, "Why I Believe Professional Baseball Should Continue During the War," *Baseball Magazine* 22 (November 1918), 21–23.

32. Steven W. Pope, "An Army of Athletes: Playing Fields, Battlefields, and the American Military Sporting Experience, 1890–1920," *Journal of Military History* 59:3 (July 1995), 435–56; Randolph Bourne, "War as the Health of the State," *Annals of America* 14 (Chicago: Encyclopaedia Britannica, 1968), 135–39; Eric Hobsbawm, *The Age of Empire* (London: Peter Smith, 1997), 304–5; Luther Gulick, "Physical Fitness for the Fighting Armies," *American Physical Education Review* 23 (1918), 348–51.

33. "How Uncle Sam Has Created an Army of Athletes," *Scientific American* 126 (1919), 114–15; Steven W. Pope, *Patriotic Games: Sporting Traditions in the American Imagination, 1876–1926* (New York: Oxford University Press, 1997); Pope, "An Army of Athletes," 435; Timothy P. O'Hanlon, "School Sports as Social Training: The Case of Athletics and the Crisis of World War I," in *Sport in America: From Wicked Amusement to National Obsession,* ed. D.K. Wiggins (Champaign, IL: Human Kinetics, 1995), 189–206; "The New Recruit," *Baseball Magazine* 17:1 (May 1916), 71–72; Charles Weeghman, "Playing Ball for Uncle Sam," *Baseball Magazine* 19:4 (August 1917), 19.

34. Samuel Bowles and Herbert Gintis, *Schooling in Capitalist America* (New York: Basic Books, 1977); Walter Kellogg Towers, "Athletics Aid to War," *American Boy* 18:11 (October 1917), 13.

35. J.C. Kofoed, "Why Athletics Are So Essential in an Army Training Camp," *Baseball Magazine* 21:3 (July 1918), 285–86; Wakefield, *Playing to Win,* 13; Alex Sullivan, "Baseball's Service to Army Morale," *Baseball Magazine* 7:23 (March 1919), 165.

36. Farmer, "Hank Gowdy and the Call to Arms"; "The 'Baseball Grenade,'" *Youth's Companion* 91:17 (April 26, 1917), 240.

37. T.L. Huston, "The Batting Eye and Shooting Eye: Baseball Helped Win the War," *American Legion Weekly* 1:4 (July 25, 1919), 11; Wakefield, *Playing to Win,* 26; "Gas Mask Game Good as Farce," *Stars and Stripes* 1:17 (May 31, 1918), 6.

38. Kofoed, "Why Athletics Are So Essential in an Army Training Camp"; William Heylinger, "Why the Germans Can't Play Fair," *American Boy* 19:8 (June 1918), 12.

39. Wakefield, *Playing to Win,* 30.

40. Thomas Connery, "World War I Baseball," *Baseball Magazine* 76 (May 1946), 419–21; "Majors in Last War," *Sporting News* 112:19 (December 18, 1941), 8; Editorials, *Baseball Magazine* 17:4 (August 1916), 13–14.

41. Ed Goewey, "Where the Baseball Stars Twinkle," *Leslie's Illustrated Weekly Newspaper* 125:3231 (August 9, 1917), 201; John Stevens, "Hero of the AEF—Hank Gowdy," *Timeline* (Ohio Historical Society) 13:2 (March 1996), 50; Robin Baily, "Making Things Pleasant for Our Soldiers and Sailors," *Baseball Magazine,* 22:1 (November 1919), 35; "Baseball Close to Doughboys Hearts," *Stars and Stripes* 2:3 (February 21, 1919), 6.

42. Wakefield, *Playing to Win; Stars and Stripes,* April 12, 1918, 1; *Stars and Stripes,* July 26, 1918, 1; *Stars and Stripes,* June 21, 1918, 1.

43. Pope, "An Army of Athletes," 449; Cornebise, *The Stars and Stripes.*

44. Cadore, "Baseball in the U.S. Army," 343; Charles Murphy, "Baseball as National Tonic," *Baseball Magazine* 22:3 (January 1919), 157; "Yanks Use Kaiser's Tennis Courts for Baseball Diamond," *Stars and Stripes* 2:8 (March 28, 1919), 6; Heylinger, "Why the Germans Can't Play Fair." *Boche* is the French derogatory slang for "rascal," which they called the Germans. "Baseball Behind the Trenches," *Baseball Magazine* 15:4 (August 1915), 75–76. Among its wartime spoofs, *Baseball Magazine* helped solve the umpire shortage: a fictional German prisoner of war, Baron Von Zunnermann, writes the German High Command: "It is impossible for us to conquer a nation that plays baseball. I am in despair, yet happy. I am umpiring, and today I ran seven of them [out of the game]. Do not offer any exchange for me till the wind-up of their baseball season." "Over There," *Baseball Magazine* 21:4 (October 1918), 366.

45. Mott, "Making the World Safe for Baseball"; Crissey, "Baseball and the Armed Forces," 616.

46. Harold Seymour, *Baseball: The People's Game* (New York: Oxford University Press, 1991), 29; Alan M. Klein, *Growing the Game: The Globalization of Major League Baseball* (New Haven, CT: Yale University Press, 2006); Dave Bidini, *Baseballissimo: My Summer in the Italian Minor Leagues* (Toronto: McClelland & Stewart, 2004).

47. "The Sporting Page Goes Out," *Stars and Stripes*, July 26, 1918, 6; Pope, "An Army of Athletes."

48. Editorials, *Baseball Magazine* 17:4 (August 1916), 13.

49. Wakefield, *Playing to Win*, 2; Ed Goewey, "Fewer Fans and More Athletes," *Leslie's Illustrated Weekly*, February 1, 1919, 168; Ed Goewey, "Will Form French Baseball League," *Leslie's Illustrated Weekly* 124:3212 (March 29, 1917), 356; J.C. Kofoed, "The Grand Revival of Sport Interest in Europe," *Baseball Magazine* 7:23 (March 1919), 153; Seymour, *Baseball: The People's Game*, 286; "The Open Field," *Stars and Stripes* 1:5 (March 8, 1918), 4; Clyde Forsythe, "The Great American Game," *Leslie's Illustrated Weekly* 126:3268 (April 27, 1918), 565; F. Messerly, "Baseball in France," *Baseball Magazine* 19:6 (October 1917), 564.

50. Harvey Shapiro, "Holland: An American Coaching *Honkbal*," in *Baseball Without Borders: The International Pastime*, ed. George Gmelch (Lincoln: University of Nebraska Press, 2006).

51. "2,000,000 Men Join Uncle Sam's League," *New York Times*, March 11, 1918, 8; "Baseball on the Hoof," *American Legion Monthly* 11:2 (August 1931), 34; "What London Thought of Its Fourth of July Baseball Game," *Literary Digest* 58:6 (August 10, 1918), 41; "The Fourth in England: The King at the American Baseball Match," *Living Age* 298:3868 (August 24, 1918), 494; "English Views of Baseball," *Baseball Magazine* 20:1 (January 1918), 283; J.G. Lee, "Baseball in England," *Baseball Magazine* 19:2 (June 1917), 309.

52. "2,000,000 Men Join Uncle Sam's League"; "World's Greatest Baseball League to Be in France," *Stars and Stripes* 2:6 (March 14, 1919), 6; "Baseball League Blossoms Out of Paris," *Stars and Stripes* 1:10 (April 12, 1918), 6; Messerly, "Baseball in France"; Editors, "Tuileries Sees Its First Ballgame," *Stars and Stripes* 1:4 (March 1, 1918), 6; "Touraine Circuit is Real Big League," *Stars and Stripes* 1:24 (July 19, 1918), 6; "Baseball as She is Politely Played in France," *Literary Digest* 60:10 (March 8, 1919), 111; H.C. Witwer, "From Baseball to Boches," *Collier's* 61:26 (August 31, 1918), 11; Ed Goewey, "The Poilu to Play the Doughboy's National Game," *Leslie's Illustrated Weekly Newspaper* 128:3313 (March 8, 1919), 335; Ed Goewey, "Europe Welcomes American

Athletics," *Leslie's Illustrated Weekly Newspaper* 129:3339 (September 6, 1919), 372; John Evers, "Teaching the Poilus How to Play Baseball," *Baseball Magazine* 22:5 (March 1919), 259; "Bats and Gloves Being Made Here," *Stars and Stripes* 1:20 (June 21, 1918), 6; John B. Foster, *Comment on joue à la balle au camp (How to Play Baseball)* (Paris: Societé Française de Publications Sportives, 1919).

53. William H. Crawford, "How Baseball Is 'Catching On' in Other Lands," *Baseball Magazine* 23:2 (June 1919), 101; John Evers, "Carrying Baseball to France," *Baseball Magazine* 21:5 (September 1918), 413; E.A. Batchelor, "How France Endorses American Sports," *Baseball Magazine* 22:4 (February 1919), 230; Alex Sullivan, "International Baseball of the Future," *Baseball Magazine* 22:5 (March 1919), 287; Heywood Broun, "Baseball in Paris, 1918," *Baseball Digest*, March 1943, 14; Murphy, "Baseball as National Tonic"; "French Reject Our National Games: Baseball and Football Will Leave with Last U.S. Soldiers," *American Legion Weekly* 1:7 (August 15, 1919), 13; "It's Dangereux, but What of It?" *Stars and Stripes* 1:13 (May 3, 1918), 6.

54. Wakefield, *Playing to Win*, 29; "The 1918 Series," *Baseball Magazine* 21:6 (October 1918), 510–12; "The Real World's Champions," *Baseball Magazine* 21:3 (July 1918), 315, 319–20.

55. Games Committee, *The Inter-Allied Games* (Paris: American Sports Publishing, 1919); Walt C. Johnson and Elwood S. Brown, *Official Athletic Almanac of the American Expeditionary Forces, 1919: A.E.F. Championships, Inter-Allied Games* (New York: American Sports Publishing, 1919).

56. Pope, "An Army of Athletes," 453–54; William Baker, *Sports in the Western World* (Totowa, NJ: Rowman & Littlefield, 1982), 210.

57. Games Committee, *Inter-Allied Games*, 154; Pope, "An Army of Athletes," 452.

58. Pope, "An Army of Athletes," 450; Steven W. Pope, "Sport and *Pax Americana*," paper presented at the North American Society for Sports History Conference, Glenwood Springs, CO, 2006; Ed Goewey, "World's Series Commanding Attention," *Leslie's Illustrated Weekly Newspaper* 125:3239 (October 6, 1917), 483.

59. Wakefield, *Playing to Win*; Klaus Schwabe, *Woodrow Wilson, Revolutionary Germany, and Peacemaking, 1918–1919: Missionary Diplomacy and the Realities of Power* (Chapel Hill: University of North Carolina Press, 1985).

60. Seymour, *Baseball: The People's Game*, 349.

Chapter 6. From the Home Front to Horsehide Diplomacy (1919–1940)

1. Paul J. Zingg, "Bitter Victory: The World Series of 1918," *Nine* 1:2 (March 1993), 121–41.

2. Joseph L. Price, "'What So Proudly We Hailed': National Crisis, the National Anthem, and the National Pastime," paper presented to the 16th Cooperstown Symposium on Baseball and American Culture, Cooperstown, NY, June 2004; Ward Harkavy, "Carrying a Tune," *Village Voice* 46:43 (October 30, 2001), 165; Richard C. Crepeau, "The Sports Song of Patriotism," May 29, 2004, www.poppolitics.com/articles/2003-02-28-flagprotest.shtml.

3. David Voigt, *America Through Baseball* (Chicago: Nelson Hall, 1976), 87.

4. The scandal made the Black Sox label stick as a description of the White Sox players. The name actually emerged earlier: when Comiskey announced that the team would no longer launder players' uniforms for free, the disgruntled players decided to

wear them dirty. Robin F. Bachin, "At the Nexus of Labor and Leisure: Baseball, Nativism, and the 1919 Black Sox Scandal," *Journal of Social History* 36:4 (2003), 941–62.

5. Richard C. Crepeau, *Baseball: America's Diamond Mind, 1919–1941* (Orlando: University Presses of Central Florida, 1980); Troy Soos, *Hunting a Detroit Tiger* (New York: Kensington, 1997), 1–2.

6. Ford did business with Hitler even after the United States entered World War II, and a portrait of Ford was found in Hitler's Berlin bunker after his suicide. Ford was referring to Red Sox owner Harry Frazee, who was incorrectly assumed to be Jewish.

7. David Shiner, "Forces of Darkness and Light: Transitions into and out of the Babe Ruth Era," unpublished paper, 1–15; "Baseball Invades the Far Off Orient," *Baseball Magazine* 1:30 (February 1923), 355.

8. Robert Justin Goldstein, *Political Repression in Modern America* (Urbana: University of Illinois Press, 2001); Soos, *Hunting a Detroit Tiger*, 298. In 1920 Warren Harding won the presidency partly by portraying baseball as a sign of his Americanism: he owned stock in his hometown Marion, Ohio, minor-league team and staged an election-campaign exhibition game between his club and the Chicago Cubs. George C. Rable, "Patriotism, Platitudes and Politics: Baseball and the American Presidency," *Presidential Studies Quarterly* 19 (Spring 1989), 363–72.

9. Crepeau, *Baseball*, 58; Steven W. Pope, *Patriotic Games: Sporting Traditions in the American Imagination, 1876–1926* (New York: Oxford University Press, 1997), 77; Alan Bairner, *Sport, Nationalism, and Globalization: European and North American Perspectives* (Albany: State University of New York Press, 2001), 97, 99; Stephen Riess, *Touching Base: Professional Baseball in the Progressive Era* (Urbana: University of Illinois Press, 1999); Marshall G. Most and Robert Rudd, *Stars, Stripes and Diamonds: American Culture and the Baseball Film* (Jefferson, NC: McFarland, 2006); Mitchell Nathanson, "Gatekeepers of Americana: Ownership's Never-Ending Quest for Control of the Baseball Creed," *Nine* 15:2 (2006), 68–87.

10. Geoffrey C. Ward and Ken Burns, *Baseball: An Illustrated History* (New York: Knopf, 1994); Crepeau, *Baseball*, 23.

11. Voigt, *America Through Baseball*, 86; "Lace It Out, Son!" *American Legion Monthly* 5:2 (August 1928), 27; Daniel J. Doherty, "To Inculcate a Sense of Individual Obligation," *American Legion Magazine* 25:1 (July 1938), 12–13, 59.

12. Harold Seymour, *Baseball: The People's Game* (New York: Oxford University Press, 1991).

13. "The Gobs Took 'Em Over—in Baseball Too," *American Legion Monthly* 17:1 (July 1934), 34. By 2008, about 95,000 high school age youths were playing on Legion teams each year and 60 percent of professional ballplayers were Legion baseball program graduates. Voigt, *America Through Baseball*, 86; Seymour, *Baseball: The People's Game*, 89; American Legion Riders, "American Legion Baseball: Still Batting A Thousand," www.legion.org/documents/legion/pdf/actionprograms_07.pdf.

14. Crepeau, *Baseball*, 3–4; Joel Zoss and John Bowman, *Diamonds in the Rough: The Untold History of Baseball* (Lincoln: University of Nebraska Press, 2004), 93.

15. While soon the swastika was associated with Nazism and evil, it didn't yet have that meaning. An ancient sign used in several cultural and religious traditions, the word came from Sanskrit and meant "good luck sign." Raymond Tompkins, "Harding Sees Middies Defeat West Pointers," *Baltimore Sun*, May 30, 1922, C1.

16. Seymour, *Baseball: The People's Game*, 361; Mike Huber and Scott Billie, "West Point's Field of Dreams: Major League Baseball at Doubleday Field," paper presented at 16th Annual Cooperstown Symposium on Baseball and American Culture, Cooperstown, NY, 2003; David C. Ogden, "Major League Baseball and Myth Making," *Nine* 15:2 (2007), 66–78.

17. "Another Peace Treaty," *New York Times*, November 15, 1920, 13.

18. Charles Murphy, "Baseball as National Tonic," *Baseball Magazine* 22:3 (January 1919), 157.

19. Jerome Holtzman, *The Commissioners: Baseball's Midlife Crisis* (New York: Total Sports, 1998); David Pietrusza, *Judge and Jury: The Life and Times of Judge Kenesaw Mountain Landis* (South Bend, IN: Diamond Communications, 1998); A.D. Suehsdorf, "Baseball Commissioners," in *Total Baseball*, ed. John Thorn and Pete Palmer (Toronto: Sports Media, 2004), 606–12.

20. Covering the Haywood trial, John Reed observed about Landis, "His is the face of Andrew Jackson—ten years dead." "Czar Landis: At 76, Baseball's Monarch Faces the Ticklish Task of Gearing His Empire to the Exigencies of an All-Out War," *Look* 7:8 (April 20, 1943), 84.

21. Pietrusza, *Judge and Jury*, 108; Holtzman, *The Commissioners*; Andrew Zimbalist, *In the Best Interests of Baseball? The Revolutionary Reign of Bud Selig* (Hoboken, NJ: Wiley, 2006).

22. Crepeau, *Baseball*, 23.

23. Doubt remains about the players' culpability, and others were betting on baseball, too. Ty Cobb and Tris Speaker were accused that same year but let off the hook. White Sox owner Charles Comiskey and others knew about the World Series fix, yet didn't report or stop it. None of them were punished; all three are in the Hall of Fame.

24. They included Gavvy Cravath (20 home runs in 1915), Wildfire Schulte (21 in 1911), Buck Freeman (25 in 1899), Ed Delahanty (19 in 1893), Sam Thompson (20 in 1889), and Ned Williamson (27 in 1884). Leverett Smith, "The Changing Style of Play: Cobb vs. Ruth," in *Baseball History from Outside the Lines* (Lincoln: University of Nebraska Press, 2002), 123–41; William Baumer, *Sports as Taught and Played at West Point* (Harrisburg, PA: Military Service Pub. Co., 1939).

25. David Lamoreaux, "Baseball In the Late Nineteenth Century: The Source of Its Appeal," *Journal of Popular Culture* 11:3 (Winter 1997), 597–613; Larry Stone, "The Home Run, Baseball's Glamour Event," in *The Best of Baseball Digest*, ed. John Kuenster (Chicago: Ivan Dee, 2006), 434–37; Mark Dyreson, "The Emergence of Consumer Culture and the Transformation of Physical Culture: American Sport in the 1920s," in *Sport in America: From Wicked Amusement to National Obsession*, ed. D.K. Wiggins (Champaign, IL: Human Kinetics, 1995), 207–23.

26. John J. Ward, "The Siege Gun of the Diamond," *Baseball Magazine* 6:31 (January 1923), 313.

27. Frederick L. Paxson, "The Rise of Sport," *Mississippi Valley Historical Review* 4 (September 1917), 144–68.

29. Joe Williams, "Larry and the Kaiser," *New York World-Telegram* 1:20 (1938).

29. David Cataneo, *Peanuts and Crackerjack: A Treasury of Baseball Legends and Lore* (Nashville, TN: Rutledge Hill, 1991); Don Warfield, *The Roaring Redhead: Larry McPhail—Baseball's Great Innovator* (South Bend, IN: Diamond Communications, 1987).

30. Morris Cohen, "Baseball," *Dial* 67:2 (July 26, 1919), 57. While Cohen championed a baseball prescription of competition and triumph, some believed the world needed cooperation and tolerance instead. This debate emerged at the Paris Peace Conference after the war. Louis Finkelstein, "Baseball and Rivalry," *Dial* 67:7 (October 4, 1919), 313; With President Wilson abroad at the peace conference, American League President Ban Johnson gave the 1919 annual baseball pass to U.S. Vice President Thomas Marshall, who responded, "I am sure I shall get more pleasures out of the performances of the American League than I will get out of the American Senate trying to organize a League of Nations." Eugene C. Murdock, *Ban Johnson: Czar of Baseball* (Westport, CT: Greenwood Press, 1982), 88.

31. In 1919, the YMCA helped bring baseball to Plzeň (Pilsen), Czechoslovakia. In 1922, the Holland baseball series began, and Hungary played its first game—although "Hungarian writers [claimed] the game was too exciting for the Hungarian temperament, and would leave too many dead on the diamond." In Finland people found baseball too slow; they played *pesapallo*, their own faster-paced ball game. The pessimists about French baseball were vindicated, as the game passed out of favor. In 1921, the Welsh Baseball Union formed, and the sport gained favor there as the "poor man's cricket." H. Allen Smith and Ira L. Smith, *Three Men on Third* (Halcottsville, NY: Breakaway Books, 2000), 42; Jay Feldman, "Baseball with a Finnish Spin," *Sports Illustrated*, May 18, 1999, 18–19; Antii Heinonen, "Six Decades of Finnish Pesapallo," unpublished paper, 1988.

32. "The English and Baseball," *Literary Digest* 74 (August 5, 1922), 62–63; Irving Sanborn, "Baseball Crusaders and the Sporting Spirit," *Literary Digest* 84 (February 14, 1925), 66–69.

33. In 1933, Sir John Moores helped form several English leagues, including the National Baseball Association, for which National League President John Heydler donated the winner's cup. In 1935, the North of England Baseball League became the first British pro league. In 1936, it was joined by the Yorkshire League and the London Major Baseball League. Smith and Smith, *Three Men on Third*, 47; Crepeau, *Baseball*, 207; Ian Smyth, "Baseball Put to the Test: And England Beats the U.S.," *Baseball Research Journal* 24 (1995), 131; Josh Chetwynd, "The Day Britain Triumphed over the United States," *Double Play* (Spring 2002), 30; Josh Chetwynd and Brian A. Belton, *British Baseball and the West Ham Club: A History of a 1930s Professional Baseball Team in East London* (Jefferson, NC: McFarland, 2006); "The Fourth in England: The King at the American Baseball Match," *Living Age* 298:3868 (August 24, 1918), 494.

34. Dave Bidini, *Baseballissimo: My Summer in the Italian Minor Leagues* (Toronto: McClelland & Stewart, 2004).

35. John Leo, "Evil Umpires? Not in Soviet Baseball," *Time* 130 (August 10, 1987); Zoss and Bowman, *Diamonds in the Rough*, 387.

36. Zoss and Bowman, *Diamonds in the Rough*, 387; Harrington Crissey, "Baseball and the Armed Forces," in *Total Baseball*, ed. John Thorn and Pete Palmer (New York: Sports Media, 1989), 616–17.

37. Trosky was implicated in a baseball controversy as well. In 1940, the Cleveland players revolted against their tyrannical manager, George Vitt. Accused of being the uprising's ringleader, Trosky claimed he was blamed "just because of my name." James E. Odenkirk, "Not Tolstoy, Not Trotsky, but Harold 'Hal' Trosky," *Nine* 11:1 (Fall

2002), 69–80. For a fanciful version of baseball's role in the fierce battle between Stalin and Trotsky, see Robert Elias, "The Secret Life of Leon Trotsky: Baseball and the Revolution," *Nine* 9:1 (2001), 131–45.

38. Barbara Keys, *Globalizing Sport: National Rivalry and International Community in the 1930s* (Cambridge, MA: Harvard University Press, 2006).

30. Mark Dyreson, "Johnny Weissmuller and the Old Global Capitalism: The Federal Blueprint for Selling American Culture to the World," paper presented at the North American Society for Sport History Annual Conference, London, Ontario, 2001. For extensive documentation of U.S. Commerce and State department efforts to use baseball in the 1920s and 1930s to promote American business and political influence at embassies around the world, see Mark Dyreson, "Mapping an Empire of Baseball: American Visions of National Pastimes and Global Influence, 1919–1941," in *Baseball in America and America in Baseball*, ed. Donald Kyle and Robert R. Fairbanks (College Station: Texas A&M University Press, 2008), 143–88.

40. Barbara Keys cited in Steven W. Pope, "Sport and *Pax Americana*," paper presented at the North American Society for Sports History Conference, Glenwood Springs, CO, 2006. In 1924, Stanford University's David Starr Jordan won the World Federation of Educational Associations award for the best plan for world peace, claiming the military spirit was absent in nations playing baseball and other sports. "Jordan Wins Award on Peace Education," *New York Times*, December 8, 1924, 2; Crepeau, *Baseball*, 199.

41. Pope, *Patriotic Games*, 450; Keys, *Globalizing Sport*, 83; Fletcher Brockman, "Association Athletics as a Training in Democracy," *Physical Training* 17 (1919), 71–76; Seymour, *Baseball: The People's Game*, 91.

42. William Stead, *The Americanization of the World* (New York: H. Markley, 1902); Keys, *Globalizing Sport*, 79; Dyreson, "Emergence of Consumer Culture."

43. Seymour, *Baseball: The People's Game*, 355.

44. David C. Ogden, "Major League Baseball and Myth Making," *Nine* 15:2 (2007); Robert J. Sinclair, "Baseball's Rising Sun: American Interwar Baseball Diplomacy and Japan," *Canadian Journal of the History of Sport* 16:2 (1995), 44–53.

45. Yuyo Ruiz, *The Bambino Visits Cuba, 1920* (San Juan, PR: self-published, n.d.); Benjamin Eastman, "Rejected America: Adolfo Luque, American Interventionism and *Cubanidad*," *International Journal of the History of Sport* 22:6 (2005), 1136–72.

46. Peter C. Bjarkman, *Diamonds Around the Globe: The Encyclopedia of International Baseball* (Westport, CT: Greenwood Press, 2005); Samuel O. Regalado, "Viva Baseball! The Beginnings of Latin American Baseball," in *Baseball History from Outside the Lines*, ed. John Dreifort (Lincoln: University of Nebraska Press, 2002), 321–36; James D. Cockcroft, *Latinos in Beisbol: The Hispanic Experience in the Americas* (Danbury, CT: Franklin Watts, 1996), 126–27.

47. Robert J. Sinclair, "For Glory and for Grandeur: Major League Baseball and America's Approach to the Second World War," MA thesis, Queen's University, 1985.

48. Regalado, "Viva Baseball!" 332; Alan M. Klein, *Sugarball: The American Game, the Dominican Dream* (New Haven, CT: Yale University Press, 1991); William Pulliam, "Baseball Follows the Flag—and the Thermometer," *Outlook* 144:8 (October 20, 1926), 246.

49. Donn Rogosin, *Invisible Men: Life in Baseball's Negro Leagues* (New York: Atheneum, 1983). The Dominican style emphasized speed and flamboyance. In neigh-

boring Haiti, after a long U.S. occupation, the Marines finally left in 1934, for the time being. The Haitians were too uniformly black and poor to be serious candidates for U.S. assimilation, and thus they were considered unfit for baseball. Cockcroft, *Latinos in Beisbol.*

50. Michael M. Oleksak and Mary Adams Oleksak, *Beisbol: Latin Americans and the Grand Old Game* (Indianapolis: Master's Press, 1996), 29; Lawrence D. Hogan, *Shades of Glory: The Negro Leagues and the Story of African American Baseball* (Washington, DC: National Geographic, 2006), 301; Lara D. Nielsen, "Exertions: Acts of Citizenship in the Globalization of Major League Beisbol," PhD dissertation, New York University, 2002, 1–305. Bill Clark claimed America's long history of racism helped promote international baseball by forcing blacks to take their baseball skills abroad. Bill Clark, "Black Players Had a Profound Influence on International Baseball," *International Baseball Rundown* 7:3 (April 1998), 4.

51. Bill Stern, *Favorite Baseball Stories* (New York: Doubleday, 1949).

52. Regalado, "Viva Baseball!"; 332; Seymour, *Baseball: The People's Game,* 287.

53. Richard McGehee, "The King and His Court: Early Baseball and Other Sports in Nicaragua," paper presented at the North American Society for Sport History Conference, Auburn University, May 24–27, 1996.

54. Clifford D. Ham, "Americanizing Nicaragua: How Yankee Marines, Financial Oversight and Baseball are Stabilizing Nicaragua," *American Review of Reviews* 53:2 (1916), 185–91; Richard McGehee, "Sport in Nicaragua, 1889–1926," in *Sport in Latin America and the Caribbean,* ed. Joseph L. Arbena and David G. LaFrance (Wilmington, DE: Scholarly Resources, 2002), 175–205; Gerald S. Gems, *Athletic Crusade: Sport and American Cultural Imperialism* (Lincoln: University of Nebraska Press, 2006).

55. Stephen Kinzer, "It's 'Play Ball' Time in Nicaragua," *New York Times,* April 16, 1988, 5A; Ivan Musicant, *The Banana Wars: A History of United States Military Intervention in Latin America from the Spanish-American War to the Invasion of Panama* (New York: Macmillan, 1990), 333. In the late 1920s, Santiago, Dominican Republic, named its team Sandino to honor the Nicaraguan revolutionary. When the United States installed Dominican strongman Rafael Trujillo, he immediately had the name changed. Even so, many Dominican parents kept naming their newborn sons César (after Sandino's middle name), including future major leaguers such as César Cedeño and Julio César Franco. The Sandino team was renamed the Eagles, after the U.S. national bird. It partly honored Sandino anyway, as he was known in the Caribbean as the Eagle of El Chipote. Cockcroft, *Latinos in Beisbol.*

56. Lester D. Langley and Thomas Schoonover, *The Banana Men: American Mercenaries and Entrepreneurs in Central America, 1880–1930* (Lexington: University Press of Kentucky, 1995), 41; Gems, *Athletic Crusade;* Michael David Rice, "Nicaragua and the United States: Policy Confrontations and Cultural Interactions, 1893–1933," PhD dissertation, University of Houston, 1985.

57. Murdock, *Ban Johnson,* 195, 197.

58. The Martyrs of Chicago were the anarchists unjustly executed after the 1886 Haymarket Massacre. Sanborn, "Baseball Crusaders and the Sporting Spirit"; Gilbert M. Joseph, "Forging the Regional Pastime: Baseball and Class in Yucatan," in *Sport and Society in Latin America,* ed. Joseph L. Arbena (New York: Greenwood Press, 1988), 29–61.

59. Seymour, *Baseball: The People's Game*, 287; Red Smith, "Red Smith Meets Red Trotsky," in *The Red Smith Reader*, ed. Dave Anderson (New York: Random House, 1982).

60. W.G. Wilson, "Baseball in Panama," *Baseball Magazine* 20:3 (January 1918), 282. In 1929, the U.S. Army discovered a railroad tie made of lignum vitae wood, buried since 1850 when it was part of a railway across the Isthmus. A soldier dug it up and made it into a baseball bat for Babe Ruth, who received it in time for the new season. Smith and Smith, *Three Men on Third*, 105.

61. By 1929, the Japanese Brazilian community developed a baseball association and laid out its first baseball diamond. In the late 1930s, with World War II approaching, Brazil imposed some restrictions (but not internment) on Japanese activities. One activity *not* limited was baseball, which became a refuge for the Japanese, similar to its role in the U.S. concentration camps.

62. F.C. Lane, "Baseball's Apostle to Africa," *Baseball Magazine* 50:3 (February 1933), 401; "Methodists Appoint Baseball Missionary," *New York Times*, February 24, 1951, 14; "Dr. Caleb Kelly, Missionary, Dies," *New York Times*, January 31, 1960, 92; Caleb Guyer Kelly, "Baseball in the Garden of Allah," *Muslim World*, April 3, 2007, 39–47.

63. Susumu Awanohara, "Major League Gambit," *Far Eastern Economic Review* 156:51 (December 23, 1923), 50; Sinclair, "Baseball's Rising Sun," 44; Joel Franks, *Hawaiian Sports in the Twentieth Century* (Lewiston, ME: Edwin Mellen Press, 2002); Frank Ardolino, "Babe's Banyan Tree Grows in Hawaii," *National Pastime* 18 (1998), 62–63.

64. Donald Roden, "Baseball and the Quest for National Dignity in Meiji Japan," *American Historical Review* 85:3 (June 1980), 511–34.

65. Gems, *Athletic Crusade*, 38–39; Kinnosuke Adachi, "Baseball's Triumph in Japan," *Baseball Magazine* 21:4 (August 1918), 338–39, 373; Kinnosuke Adachi, "Attaboy Japan," *Everybody's* 40 (May 1919), 68.

66. Sinclair, "Baseball's Rising Sun," 44; "President Harding Sees Value in Tour," *New York Times*, October 6, 1922, 18; "Japanese Baseball Invasion Is on the Way," *Literary Digest* 69 (May 7, 1921), 48–51; Joseph A. Reaves, *Taking in a Game: A History of Baseball in Asia* (Lincoln: University of Nebraska Press, 2002), 54; Robert Obojski, *The Rise of Japanese Baseball Power* (Radnor, PA: Chilton Books, 1975).

67. Kinnosuke Adachi, "The Topknot Nine: Japan Changes Her National Game from Wrestling to Baseball," *Outlook* 146:8 (June 22, 1927), 250; "Baseball Frenzy Sweeping Japan," *Literary Digest* 94:2 (July 9, 1927), 53.

68. Cataneo, *Peanuts and Crackerjack*, 41; Henry Misselwitz, "American Baseball Conquers Japan," *Living Age*, May 1940, 225; G.W. Axelson, "Enlightening the World with Baseball," *Harper's* 58:2989 (April 4, 1914), 24; "Brotherhood and Baseball," *Sporting News*, January 25, 1923, 4; "For Peace and Good Will," *Sporting News*, March 23, 1922, 4; H.G. Salsinger, "Scribbled by Scribes," *Sporting News*, March 8, 1923, 4; "Base Ball in Foreign Lands," *Spalding Official Base Ball Guide* (1922).

69. "Baseball Invades the Far Off Orient," *Baseball Magazine* 1:30 (February 1923), 355; Gems, *Athletic Crusade*, 42–43.

70. Sanborn, "Baseball Crusaders and the Sporting Spirit"; "The Senate's Declaration of War," *Japan Times and Mail*, April 19, 1924, 4; Francis Richter, "Casual Comment," *Sporting News*, August 14, 1923, 4.

71. Behrad Hosseinzadeh, "Baseball Is War! And More? Masculinity, Nationalism, and the Old Pastime in Japan and America, 1870–1980," MA thesis, California State University, 2005.

72. Kazuo Samaya, "'Their Throws Were Like Arrows'—How a Black Team Spurred Pro Ball in Japan," *Baseball Research Journal* 16 (1987), 85–88; David A. Hendsch, "A Photo, a Tour, a Life: Harvey Iwata and a Glimpse of Japanese-American Baseball," *National Pastime* 17 (1998), 82–84; David A. Hendsch, "Fresno Shows the Japanese How to Do It: Baseball in the Making," in *Northern California Baseball History*, ed. Norman Macht (Cleveland: Society for American Baseball Research, 1998), 28–30; "U.S. Marine Baseball 'Intervention' in Japan Highly Successful," *China Weekly Review* 54:11 (November 15, 1930), 398; "'Play Ball!'—with Samurai Trimmings," *Literary Digest* 96:11 (March 17, 1928), 34.

73. I. Abe, "Fascism, Sport and Society in Japan," *International Journal of the History of Sport* 9 (April 1992), 1–28; "Herb Hunter in Japan," *Sporting News* 112:19 (December 18, 1941), 10; Zoss and Bowman, *Diamonds in the Rough*, 412; Yoichi Nagata, "The First All-Asian Pitching Duel in Organized Baseball," *Baseball Research Journal* 21 (1992) 13–14.

74. Seymour, *Baseball: The People's Game*, 187.

75. Henry Chauncey, "Japan Plays the American National Game," *Literary Digest* 118:20 (November 24, 1934), 39.

76. "Brotherhood and Baseball"; "Good Will Tour of Orient," *Sporting News*, November 1, 1934 4; Bill Dooley, "Scribbled by Scribes," *Sporting News*, January 24, 1935, 4; Sinclair, "Baseball's Rising Sun"; "Mack Hails Ruth as Peace Promoter," *New York Times*, January 6, 1935, 7. Ruth was praised for "promoting the Japanese nation's understanding of true Yankee spirit." Marshall Smelser, *The Life that Ruth Built: A Biography* (Lincoln: University of Nebraska Press, 1975); Reaves, *Taking in a Game*, 79.

77. Sawamura died in action in World War II, which prompted the Japanese Baseball Commissioner to establish the Sawamura Award—Japan's Cy Young Award—to honor the best pitcher each year.

78. "Stifling Good Will Tours," *Sporting News*, January 3, 1935, 4; Henry Chauncey, "Japan Plays the American National Game," *Literary Digest*, November 24, 1934, 118; Merritt Clifton, "Where the Twain Shall Meet: What Baseball Means to Japan—and Humanity," *National Pastime* 4 (1985), 12–22.

79. Leslie Mann, *Baseball Around the World: History and Development of the USA Baseball Congress and the International Amateur Baseball Federation* (Springfield, MA: International Amateur Baseball Federation, 1939).

80. Robert Whiting, *The Samurai Way of Baseball: The Impact of Ichiro and the New Wave from Japan* (New York: Warner Books, 2004).

81. Joseph A. Reaves, "A History of Baseball in China: How America's Game Helped End Educational Exchanges in the Late Qing Dynasty, Taught Sun Yat-sen's Revolutionaries to Throw Hand Grenades, and Endured the Cultural Revolution," paper presented to the North American Society for Sport History Annual Conference, Windsor, Ontario, May 22–25, 1998.

82. Tim Wolter, *POW Baseball in World War II: The National Pastime Behind Barbed Wire* (Jefferson, NC: McFarland, 2002); Uli Schmetzer, "Chinese Baseball Hanging In There," *Chicago Tribune*, May 3, 1991, 6.

83. Junwei Yu, *Playing in Isolation: A History of Baseball in Taiwan* (Lincoln: University of Nebraska Press, 2007).

84. Joseph A. Reaves, "Korea: Straw Sandals and Strong Arms," in *Baseball Without Borders: The International Pastime*, ed. George Gmelch (Lincoln: University of Nebraska Press, 2006).

85. Ibid.; baseball nevertheless continued in the Philippines through the 1930s. Japanese teams arrived to barnstorm, and the Japanese game was increasingly pushed on the Filipinos. The 1934 Babe Ruth–Connie Mack All Star tour stopped in the Philippines, where Ruth and Lou Gehrig hit the first home runs out of Manila's new Rizal Baseball Stadium. Crepeau, *Baseball*, 129.

86. M.E. Travaglini, "Olympic Baseball 1936: Was es Das?" *National Pastime* 4 (1985), 46–55.

87. This came at the expense of American Jews. The only two Jews on the 1936 U.S. track team were pulled at the last minute under pressure from American official Avery Brundage. Having competed in the 1912 Stockholm Olympics, Brundage became the U.S. Olympic Committee head in 1928. He fiercely resisted the proposed anti-Nazi boycott in 1936, and so the German authorities elevated him to the International Olympic Committee (IOC). Brundage was very conservative, strongly anticommunist, and pro-Nazi. Later, after becoming IOC president, he banned Tommie Smith and John Carlos from the 1968 Mexico City Olympics for their Black Power protest and kept the 1972 Munich Olympics going despite the terrorist attack that killed eleven Israeli athletes. Brundage opposed the restoration of the medals that Native American Jim Thorpe had won at the 1912 Olympics. They had been stripped because Thorpe had played some professional baseball. Thorpe had beaten Brundage in both the pentathlon and decathlon during that Olympics. After Brundage's death, it was revealed that he was the one who secretly blew the whistle on Thorpe. Keys, *Globalizing Sport*, 74.

88. Kristen Jones, "The Game Goes for Gold: A History of Olympic Baseball," *Memories and Dreams*, July–August 2006, 20–23; Pete Cava, "Baseball in the Olympics," *National Pastime* 12 (1992), 2–8.

89. In *National Geographic* magazine, J.R. Hildebrand "identified baseball as the key to his map for remaking the world through sport." Dyreson, "Mapping an Empire of Baseball," 143–88.

90. Cava, "Baseball in the Olympics," 8; David Osinski, "Baseball and the Olympics," in *Total Baseball*, ed. John Thorn and Pete Palmer (Toronto: Sports Media, 2004), 802–4.

91. Crepeau, *Baseball*, 203; Wanda Ellen Wakefield, *Playing to Win: Sports and the American Military, 1898–1945* (Albany: State University of New York Press, 1997), 61.

92. Crepeau, *Baseball*, 205.

93. For evidence that Roosevelt provoked the Japanese and then let the Pearl Harbor attack occur, see Robert Stinnett, *Day of Deceit: The Truth About FDR and Pearl Harbor* (New York: Free Press, 2001).

94. "Sport Falls as Dictators Rise," *Sporting News*, August 28, 1941, 4.

95. "It's Not the Same Game in Japan," *Sporting News*, December 18, 1941, 4.

96. J.G.T. Spink, "Looping the Loops," *Sporting News*, January 1, 1942, 1.

97. Daniel M. Daniel, "Rambling Round the Circuit with Pitcher Snorter Casey," *Sporting News*, December 25, 1941, 4.

98. Sinclair, "For Glory and for Grandeur," 44; Reaves, *Taking In a Game*, 75.

99. Whiting, *Samurai Way of Baseball*; Crepeau, *Baseball*, 124; Richard C. Crepeau, "Pearl Harbor: A Failure of Baseball?" *Journal of Popular Culture* 15:4 (1982), 67–74; Richard C. Crepeau, "The Sports Song of Patriotism," May 29, 2004, http://www.poppolitics.com/articles/2003-02-28-flagprotest.shtml.

Chapter 7. Good War Hunting (1941–1945)

1. Edward W. Wood, *Worshipping the Myths of World War II: Reflections on America's Dedication to War* (Dulles, VA: Potomac Books, 2006); Paul Fussell, *Wartime* (New York: Oxford University Press, 1990); Thomas Childers, *Soldier from the War Returning: The Greatest Generation's Troubled Homecoming from World War II* (New York: Houghton Mifflin Harcourt, 2009); Carl Boggs, "Pearl Harbor: How Film Conquers History," *New Political Science* 28:4 (December 2006), 451–66. Closely associated with the "Good War" are the Americans who fought it—the "Greatest Generation." Jim Smith, "The Greatest Generation? Not Who You Think," December 17, 2007, www.portside.org/archive.

2. Robert Stinnett, *Day of Deceit: The Truth About FDR and Pearl Harbor* (New York: Free Press, 2001).

3. From a World War II Veteran's Committee mail campaign. "Statement by Baseball Hall of Famer and World War II Veteran Bob Feller," July 5, 2004, www.freerepublic.com/focus/f-news/1165855/posts.

4. Stinnett, *Day of Deceit*.

5. William B. Mead, *Baseball Goes to War: Stars Don Khaki, 4-Fs Vie for Pennant* (Washington, DC: Broadcast Interview Source, 1998), 3; Bob Herzog, "Baseball Goes to War," *Newsday*, October 9, 2001, A74–76; John Philips, *Baseball Goes to War* (Kathleen, GA: John Phillips, 2003); Todd Anton, *No Greater Love: Life Lessons from the Men Who Saved Baseball* (Cambridge, MA: Rounder Books, 2007); Todd Anton and Bill Nowlin, eds., *When Baseball Went to War* (Chicago: Triumph Books, 2008); Clifford Bloodgood, "The Ballplayer and the War," *Baseball Magazine* 70 (May 1943), 525–27; Jason Patrick Scheller, "The National Pastime Enlists: How Baseball Fought the Second World War," master's thesis, Texas Tech University, 2002; Robert J. Sinclair, "For Glory and for Grandeur: Major League Baseball and America's Approach to the Second World War," master's thesis, Queen's University, 1985; A.H. Tarvin, "Baseball and the War, Again," *Baseball Magazine* 70 (January 1943), 369–71; Tol Broome, "Serving Their Country," *Sports Collectors Digest* 18:11 (March 15, 1991), 120; Jim Charlton, "Genuine Veteran Ballplayers," *National Pastime* 23 (2003), 81; Tom Parish, "How Was It During the War Years?" *Baseball Digest* 36 (January 1977), 68–70; Bill Cunningham, "Wartime Baseball: Who'll Win?" *Liberty* 19:16 (April 18, 1942), 26; Frank Graham, "Bats and Bayonets," *Liberty* 19:20 (May 16, 1942), 52; Eric Moskowitz, "The Sporting News During WWII," *National Pastime* 23 (2003), 44–54; "Bible of Baseball: *Sporting News*," *Saturday Evening Post* 214 (June 20, 1942), 9–10; Hugh Bradley, "Trenches and Dugouts," *Baseball Magazine* 64:3 (February 1940), 391.

6. "It's Not the Same Game in Japan," *Sporting News*, December 18, 1941, 4; Alfred W. Place, "Japs in the Third Inning" *Baseball Digest* 2:6 (August 1943), 29; Seidel, *Streak*.

7. Seidel, *Streak*; Robert W. Creamer, *Baseball in '41: A Celebration of the Best Baseball Season Ever in the Year America Went to War* (New York: Viking Penguin, 1991);

Richard Goldstein, "Life During Wartime," *Boston* 81:3 (March 1989), 73; Richard Goldstein, *Spartan Seasons: How Baseball Survived the Second World War* (New York: Macmillan, 1980).

8. Seidel, *Streak.*

9. Ibid.; Dom DiMaggio with Bill Gilbert, *Real Grass, Real Heroes* (New York: Kensington, 1990).

10. David Voigt, *American Baseball*, vol. 2: *From the Commissioners to Continental Expansion* (University Park, PA: Penn State University Press, 1983); William B. Mead, "Baseball During the War Years," *Boston Globe*, April 26, 1978, 23; Furman Bisher, "The Unforgettable Camps of '44: Training in Frostbite Belt," *Sporting News* 187:9 (March 3, 1979), 15.

11. Bryan Price, "More Than a Game: Baseball in World War II and the Cold War, 1941–1958," paper presented at National Baseball Hall of Fame Library, May 1998, 1–43.

12. Moskowitz, "The Sporting News During WWII," 44.

13. Daniel M. Daniel, "Baseball's War Effort Seeks Vast Sums for Vital Causes," *Baseball Magazine* 69:1 (June 1942), 291.

14. Daniel M. Daniel, "Major Leagues Have Proud Record in War and Relief Enterprises," *Baseball Magazine* 71 (September 1943), 327–29; Steve Bullock, *Playing for Their Nation: The American Military and Baseball During World War II* (Lincoln: University of Nebraska Press, 2004); James Gould, "War and Baseball," *Baseball Magazine* 68:3 (February 1942), 389.

15. Gene Mack, "The Come-Back Spirit," *Boston Daily Globe*, December 9, 1941, 23.

16. Wilson Sporting Goods, "Play On, Fight On, America!" *Sporting News*, August 27, 1942, 16.

17. "A Four Way Service in Wartime," *Sporting News*, November 12, 1942, 4.

18. "Baseball Makes 16th Grenade Tossers Expert," *Armodier*, March 30, 1944, 1; Wanda Ellen Wakefield, *Playing to Win: Sports and the American Military, 1898–1945* (Albany: State University of New York Press, 1997).

19. Don Warfield, *The Roaring Redhead: Larry MacPhail—Baseball's Great Innovator* (South Bend, IN: Diamond Communications, 1987); "Baseball Gets Mandate from Army to Carry On," *Recreation*, August 1944, 274.

20. Warfield, *Roaring Redhead*, 89.

21. Rob Edelman, "Politics, Patriotism, and Baseball On-Screen," in *Baseball and American Culture*, ed. Edward J. Rielly (New York: Haworth Press, 2003), 163–72; La Vern Dilweg, "Baseball and the War," *Baseball Digest* 2:6 (August 1943), 41; "Where Have You Gone, William Bendix? Baseball as a Symbol of American Values in World War II," in Ron Briley, *Class at Bat, Gender on Deck, and Race in the Hole* (Jefferson, NC: McFarland, 2003), 39–54.

22. "Baseball Men Warn Against Dropping Game Lest Japanese Morale Benefit," *New York Times*, March 26, 1943, 23. New York governor Thomas Dewey endorsed baseball, observing that "only in totalitarian countries do they try to eliminate sports in wartime." According to aviation hero Captain Eddie Rickenbacker, "When there is no more reason for self reliance in this country, then and then alone will there be no more reason for baseball." Bullock, *Playing for Their Nation*; Edelman, "Politics, Patriotism, and Baseball On-Screen," 163; Frank Graham, "When Baseball Went to War," *Sports Illustrated* 26:16 (April 17, 1967), 78; "Sport Falls As Dictators Rise," *Sporting*

News, August 28, 1941, 4; Gould, "War and Baseball," 389; Ron Briley, "Don't Let Hitler (or the Depression) Kill Baseball: Franklin D. Roosevelt and the National Pastime, 1932–1945," in *Franklin D. Roosevelt and the Shaping of American Culture*, ed. Nancy Beck Young, William D. Pederson, and Bryon W. Daynes (New York: M.E. Sharpe, 2001), 119–33.

23. "Sports Aid Preparedness," *American Legion Magazine* 32:4 (April 1942), 59.

24. Mead, *Baseball Goes to War*; Goldstein, *Spartan Seasons*; John Bloom, *A House of Cards: Baseball Card Collecting and Popular Culture* (Minneapolis: University of Minnesota Press, 1997); Andy Esposito, "Mets Memorabilia: Tributes and Fund-Raisers Raise Spirit of America," *New York Mets Inside Pitch* 19:11 (November 2001), 26; Thomas Barthel, *Walkie-Talkie Fanning Bees: Baseball Ambassadors Visit Combat Areas in World War II* (self-published, 2001).

25. Price, "More Than Just a Game," 1; Gerald Bazer and Steven Culbertson, "Baseball During World War II," *Nine* 10:1 (2002), 114–29; "Game's Part in U.S. War Effort," *Sporting News* 112:19 (December 18, 1941), 4.

26. Bill Davidson, "Sports During the War?" *Yank* 3:45 (April 27, 1945), 23; *New York Herald Tribune* sports editor Stanley Woodward didn't view sports as essential. And in the 1942 film *Woman of the Year*, Katharine Hepburn claimed baseball should be banned during wartime. But Spencer Tracy responded, "We're concerned with a threat to our American way of life. What's the sense of abolishing the thing you're trying to protect?" Stanley Woodward, "Sports Here and There," *New York Herald Tribune*, December 10, 1941, 36.

27. Bazer and Culbertson, "Baseball During World War II," 114; "Truman Endorses Wartime Baseball," *New York Times*, April 4, 1945, sec. 3, p. 1; James Gould, "The President Says Play Ball," *Baseball Magazine* 68:3 (January 1, 1942), 435.

28. Graham, "When Baseball Went to War," 78; "Fears for Great American Game Laid to Rest," *Newsweek* 19:4 (January 26, 1942), 51; Briley, "Don't Let Hitler (or the Depression) Kill Baseball," 119; J.G. Taylor Spink, "Let's Keep 'Em Playing," *Sporting News*, May 7, 1941, 1.

29. Mead, *Baseball Goes to War*; Jerome Holtzman, *The Commissioners: Baseball's Midlife Crisis* (New York: Total Sports, 1998); "O.B. Ready to Spark War Morale Again," *Sporting News*, December 11, 1941, 1; Richard C. Crepeau, *Baseball: America's Diamond Mind, 1919–1941* (Orlando: University Presses of Central Florida, 1980); James A. Percoco, "Baseball and World War II: A Study of the Landis-Roosevelt Correspondence," *OAH Magazine of History* 7 (Summer 1992).

30. L.H. Addington, "War Effort," *Baseball Magazine* 69:4 (September 1942), 469; "Czar Landis: At 76, Baseball's Monarch Faces the Ticklish Task of Gearing His Empire to the Exigencies of an All-Out War," *Look* 7:8 (April 20, 1943), 84.

31. Jim Sargent, "When the (Baseball) Stars Came Out: The Navy's Best, 1944–45," *Autograph Times*, March 1998, 19–22; Fred Schuld, "The Patriot Game, 1: The United States Service Team vs. American League All Stars," in *All-Star Baseball in Cleveland*, ed. Brad Sullivan (Cleveland, OH: Society for American Baseball Research, 1997), 51–55; Fred Lieb, "Two Twinkle Tilts Net $193,000 for Army and Navy Aid Funds," *Sporting News*, July 16, 1942, 7.

32. Brad Sullivan, "The Patriot Game, 2: The Negro League's Benefit Game," in *All-Star Baseball in Cleveland*, ed. Brad Sullivan (Cleveland, OH: Society for American Baseball Research, 1997), 61–63.

33. In the 1930s and 1940s, Germany had the world's strongest antismoking movement, whose research already linked cigarettes to lung cancer. While the Nazis pursued bodily purity, U.S. soldiers were killing themselves. Robert N. Proctor, "The Anti-Tobacco Campaign of the Nazis: A Little Known Aspect of Public Health in Germany, 1933–45," *Biomedical Journal* 313 (November 6, 1996), 1–10; Tom Knight, "Tri-Cornered Game: An Unusual War Benefit Contest," *National Pastime* 14 (1994), 89; Gary Bedingfield, *Baseball in World War II Europe* (Charleston, SC: Arcadia, 1999).

34. Steve Bullock, "Playing for Their Nation: The American Military and Baseball During World War II," *Journal of Sport History* 27:1 (Spring 2000), 67–89; Scott Patrick Dillow, "Safe at Home: World War II Baseball and the Reshaping of American Society," MA thesis, California State University, 1999.

35. Joel Zoss and John Bowman, *Diamonds in the Rough: The Untold History of Baseball* (Lincoln: University of Nebraska Press, 2004); David Pietrusza, *Judge and Jury: The Life and Times of Judge Kenesaw Mountain Landis* (South Bend, IN: Diamond Communications, 1998); Lee MacPhail, *My 9 Innings: An Autobiography of 50 Years in Baseball* (Westport, CT: Meckler Books, 1989); Briley, "Where Have You Gone, William Bendix?" 39.

36. Paul Lukas, "Flag-Waving," *Village Voice* 46:39 (October 2, 2001), 165.

37. Richard C. Crepeau, "The Sports Song of Patriotism," *Pop Politics*, May 29, 2004, www.poppolitics.com/articles/2003-02-28-flagprotest.shtml.

38. Gary Bloomfield, *Duty, Honor, Victory: America's Athletes in World War II* (Guilford, CT: Lyons Press, 2003); Fred Russell, "Army Has Helped Them," *Baseball Digest* 3:1 (February 1944), 10.

39. Jered Benjamin Kolbert, "Major League Baseball During World War II," *National Pastime* 14 (1994), 102–5; "Baseball Sponsors Carry War Plugs," *Broadcasting* 23:1 (July 26, 1942), 42; Bill Gilbert, *They Also Served: Baseball and the Home Front, 1941–1945* (New York: Crown, 1992); review of *They Also Served: Baseball and the Home Front, 1941–1945*, *American History Illustrated* 27:6 (January 1993), 22; "All References to Weather Forbidden in Covering Games During the Season," *Broadcasting* 22:12 (March 23, 1942), 12; Robert Gregory, *Diz: The Story of Dizzy Dean and Baseball During the Great Depression* (New York: Viking, 1992).

40. William C. Kashatus, *One-Armed Wonder: Pete Gray, Wartime Baseball, and the American Dream* (Jefferson, NC: McFarland, 1995).

41. "Babe Invests Fruits of the Home Run," *Detroit News*, December 21, 1941, Sports, 1; Leigh Montville, *The Big Bam: The Life and Times of Babe Ruth* (New York: Doubleday, 2006).

42. DiMaggio, *Real Grass, Real Heroes*, 71.

43. Mickey Zezima, *Saving Private Power: The Hidden History of the "Good War"* (Brooklyn: Soft Skull Press, 2000); Howard Zinn, *A People's History of the United States: 1429–Present* (New York: HarperPerennial, 1995); Robert F. Burk, *Much More Than a Game: Players, Owners and American Baseball Since 1920* (Chapel Hill: University of North Carolina Press, 2001).

44. "Uncle Sam We Are At Your Command!" *Sporting News*, December 11, 1941, 4; "O.B. Ready to Spark War Morale Again"; Mark Sappenfield, "Baseball in Wartime? It's Been the American Way Since 1861; Season Opens for a Sport Uniquely Tied to Military Conflict," *Christian Science Monitor*, March 31, 2003, 2; Bullock, *Playing for Their Nation*.

45. Burk, *Much More Than a Game*; Simon Kuper, "Stars Saved from Ultimate Pitched Battle," *Financial Times*, April 20, 1944; David Jordan, *A Tiger in His Time: Hal Newhouser and the Burden of Wartime Ball* (South Bend, IN: Diamond Communications, 1990).

46. "War Plant Workers," www.baseball-reference.com/bullpen/Category:War_Plant_Workers; Larry Gara and Lenna Mae Gara, ed., *A Few Small Candles: War Resistors of World War II Tell Their Stories* (Kent, OH: Kent State University Press, 1999); "Bill Zuber," *Baseball Reference*, www.baseball-reference.com/bullpen/Bill_Zuber.

47. Bill Nowlin, *Ted Williams at War* (Cambridge, MA: Rounder Books, 2006); William Jeanes, "Baseball in World War II," *Sports Illustrated* 75 (August 26, 1991), 5–6; "Frick Says Byrnes Won't Discriminate Against Ballplayers," *Stars and Stripes Weekly* (Mediterranean edition) 2:68 (March 24, 1945), 7; "After Byrnes, Baseball?" *Time* 45:2 (January 8, 1945), 50. The players included Ron Northey, Ray Mueller, Hugh Poland, and Danny Litwhiler. George McQuinn was also targeted but his congressman intervened, and he wasn't drafted.

48. Ed Rumill, "Battle Action," *Baseball Magazine* 76:2 (January 1946), 255; Harrington Crissey, *Athletes Away: A Selective Look at Professional Baseball Players in the Navy During World War II* (Philadelphia: Archway Press, 1984); Jeff Idelson, "An American Original: From Farm to Fame, He's a Legendary Feller," *National Baseball Hall of Fame and Museum Yearbook*, 2007, 20–30.

49. Moskowitz, "The Sporting News During WWII," 44; Bill Koenig, "The War Years: 50 Years Later, a Pastime Remembers When Its Players Came Home," *USA Today Baseball Weekly* 5:21 (August 16, 1995), 18; Denis Telgemeier, "World War II, Baseball & the Philadelphia Athletics," *Oakland Athletics Magazine* (1984), 20.

50. Rob Newell, "Boys of Summer Head to War: Baseball's Rising Stars Didn't Hesitate When Duty Called Them in World War II," *Retired Officer's Magazine* 57:10 (October 2001), 64–69; Furman Bisher, "Corporal Brissie and Dr. Brubaker," in *Strange but True Baseball Stories* (New York: Random House, 1966), 47–57; Ira Berkow, *The Corporal Was a Pitcher: The Courage of Lou Brissie* (Chicago: Triumph Books, 2009); Hal Butler, "Gene Beardon . . . War Casualty on the Mound," in *Sports Heroes Who Wouldn't Quit* (New York: Julian Messner, 1973), 99–118; Furman Bisher, "Lt. Shepard of the Big Leagues," in *Strange but True Baseball Stories* (New York: Random House, 1966), 131–37; Steven G. LoBello, "Bert Shepard: Amputee War Hero and Major League Pitcher," *Nine* 2:1 (1993), 28–39; Rick Hines, "The Remarkable Story of Bert Shepard," *Sports Collectors Digest*, September 17, 1993, 176–78; Mark McGuire, "One Leg a Minor Setback for Lt. Shepard," *USA Today Baseball Weekly*, April 21–27, 1993, 35; Rick Phalen, *A Bittersweet Journey: America's Fascination with Baseball* (Tampa, FL: McGregor, 2000).

51. Sean Peter Kirst, "Finding Peace in Images of War," in *The Ashes of Lou Gehrig*, ed. Sean Peter Kirst (Jefferson, NC: McFarland, 2003), 57–59; Joseph Tekulsky, "Elmer Gedeon," *National Pastime* 14 (1994), 68–71.

52. Edward G. White, *Creating the National Pastime* (Princeton, NJ: Princeton University Press, 1996).

53. William Simons, "Comparative Ethnicity: Joe DiMaggio and Hank Greenberg," in *The Cooperstown Symposium on Baseball and American Culture, 2000*, ed. William Simons (Jefferson, NC: McFarland, 2001), 237–56; White, *Creating the National Pastime*; Joseph Dorinson, "Baseball's Ethnic Heroes: Hank Greenberg and Joe

DiMaggio," in *Cooperstown Symposium on Baseball and American Culture, 2001*, ed. Alvin Hall and William Simons (Jefferson, NC: McFarland, 2002), 66–82.

54. David Pietrusza, "America Wanted Diamonds After Pearl," *USA Today Baseball Weekly* 2:1 (April 1, 1992), 56; Dorinson, "Baseball's Ethnic Heroes," 66.

55. Latino players entered the United States on six-month entertainment visas and had to register within three months to determine their draft status. But baseball-friendly draft boards always accepted appeals that delayed the process until the end of each season. The players then returned home and the cycle began again the following year. Adrian Burgos, *Playing America's Game: Baseball, Latinos, and the Color Line* (Berkeley: University of California Press, 2007).

56. George C. Rable, "Patriotism, Platitudes and Politics: Baseball and the American Presidency," *Presidential Studies Quarterly* 19 (Spring 1989), 363–72; Joe Bostic, "Dreamin'," *People's Voice*, March 21, 1942; Bob Herzog, "Majors Weren't the Only Game in WWII," *Newsday*, October 9, 2001, A74–76.

57. Thomas Borstelmann, *The Cold War and the Color Line: American Race Relations in the Global Arena* (Cambridge, MA: Harvard University Press, 2001).

58. Jean Hastings Ardell, *Breaking into Baseball: Women and the National Pastime* (Carbondale: Southern Illinois University Press, 2005).

59. Jules Tygiel, "The Court Martial of Jackie Robinson," *American Heritage* 35:5 (August–September 1984); Steven Wisensale, "The Political Wars of Jackie Robinson," *Nine* 2:1 (1993), 18–28. In response to racism charges, President Roosevelt opened aeronautical training to black cadets at the Tuskegee Institute. Future Negro League Hall of Famer John "Mule" Miles became a Tuskegee Airman and his unit returned from the war with hundreds of medals. After the war, even after Jackie Robinson broke the color barrier, Miles could get only as far as the Gulf Coast League—where he was subjected to things like "Nigger Night." Lisa Jackson, "Milestones: John 'Mule' Miles Reflects on Baseball, the Military, and Racism," *Current* 586 (August 8, 2001), 9.

60. Harrington Crissey, *Teenagers, Graybeards and 4-Fs* (Philadelphia: H.E. Crissey, 1981); Borstelmann, *The Cold War and the Color Line*.

61. Wrigley Field remained a daylight field for another forty-seven years—the last major-league park to install lights. Daniel Okrent and Steve Wulf, *Baseball Anecdotes* (New York: Harper & Row, 1989); David Pietrusza, *Lights On! The Wild, Century-Long Saga of Night Baseball* (Lanham, MD: Scarecrow Press, 1997).

62. Joe McCarthy, "Hitler Can't Annoy Durocher and Expect to Stay Healthy," *Yank* 1:8 (August 19, 1942), 22.

63. Pietrusza, *Judge and Jury*.

64. Stan Baumgartner, "Coast Raid Threats Don't Scare Connie," *Sporting News* 112:19 (December 18, 1941), 9; Leonard Levin, "Baseball in 1945—The Pits," *Providence Journal-Bulletin*, February 1995, 27.

65. "Baseball and/or Total War," *Time* 40:13 (September 28, 1942), 81; "War and Baseball," *Time* 40:3 (July 20, 1942), 49; Daniel M. Daniel, "Wartime Baseball 'Rationing' Find Fans Tolerant, Eager for Game," *Baseball Magazine* 81 (April 1944), 367–69; Fred Reed, "Rationed: War Put Players in Short Supply," *Beckett Baseball Card Monthly* 4 (September 1987), 28–31; Dwight Freeburg, "War-Time Baseball," *Baseball Magazine* 68:5 (April 1942), 509. The rubber for baseball cores was scarce since Japan controlled the world's rubber plantations. Balata balls were lifeless and felt like hitting concrete. By the war's end, cork and synthetic rubber were used to make baseballs live-

her again. "Big Leagues Get a War Baseball," *Popular Science*, July 1943, 46–47; Jim Charlton, "Yes, We Have No Balata," *National Pastime* 23 (2003), 121; "War Changes Baseball," *Science News Letter*, February 13, 1943, 110; Irvin Muchnick, "How Baseball Sent Its Hop to War," *Sports Illustrated* 36:17 (April 24, 1972), M3.

66. Tim Panaccio, "How It Was During The War Years," *Baseball Digest* 36:1 (January 1976), 68; Craig Allen Cleve, *Hardball on the Home Front: Major League Replacement Players of World War II* (Jefferson, NC: McFarland, 2004); Fred Lieb, "The Great Exhumation," *Collier's* 109 (May 16, 1942), 22, 60–61; Robert A. Greenberg, *"Swish" Nicholson: A Biography of Wartime Baseball's Leading Slugger* (Jefferson, NC: McFarland, 2008); David Finoli, *For the Good of the Country: World War II Baseball in the Major and Minor Leagues* (Jefferson, NC: McFarland, 2002).

67. William B. Mead, *Even the Browns: The Zany, True Story of Baseball in the Early Forties* (Chicago: Contemporary Books, 1978); Bill Borst, "The Best of Seasons: When Even a World War Couldn't Stop the World Series," *Dugout* 2:4 (October 1994), 3–7. The minor leagues were hard-hit by the war. The Pacific Coast League (PCL) survived, even though some of its best fans—the Japanese—had been taken away. For opening day 1942, it was "Remember Pearl Harbor" Day in Los Angeles, and the Veterans of Foreign Wars were honored in Sacramento. In heavily militarized San Diego, ballplayers were often criticized for not being in the service. Some PCL games were transmitted to the troops, in South America, the Caribbean, and Alaska. Donald R. Wells, *Baseball's Western Front: The Pacific Coast League During World War II* (Jefferson, NC: McFarland, 2004). Created in 1935, the National Baseball Congress (NBC) also survived the war. It sponsored annual semiprofessional championships and was used by stateside military outfits to expose their players to big-league scouts. Bob Rives, "War and the National Baseball Congress," in *Proceedings of 5th Annual Conference on War and Media—War and Sports* (Independence, MO: Graceland University Center for the Study of the Korean War, 2004), 33–42.

68. Patricia Vignola, "The Patriotic Pinch Hitter: The AAGBL and How the American Woman Earned a Permanent Spot on the Roster," *Nine* 12:2 (2004), 103–13; Sue Macy, *A Whole New Ballgame: The Story of the All-American Girls Professional Baseball League* (New York: Puffin Books, 1993); Dave Zirin, *A People's History of Sports in the United States* (New York: The New Press, 2008), 95.

69. Adam Peterik, "Women's Baseball During World War II," www.lib.niu.edu/ipo/1995/ihy950452.html, 1995; Lois Browne, *Girls of Summer* (New York: HarperCollins, 1992); Merrie Fidler, *The Origins and History of the All-American Girls Professional Baseball League* (Jefferson, NC: McFarland, 2006); Gai Ingham Berlage, *Women in Baseball: The Forgotten Story* (Westport, CT: Praeger, 1994).

70. H.L. Chaillaux, "American Legion Junior Baseball Program a War-Time Asset," *Athletic Journal* 23:10 (June 1943), 16, 32; Ed Rumill, "American Legion Kids Get a Chance," *Baseball Magazine*, May 1943.

71. Tom Fergusson, "Padgett, D. DiMaggio, McCoy, Rizzuto Among Players on Training Station Squad," *Sporting News*, April 2, 1944, 13.

72. Morris Siegel, "The Unnatural," *Regardie's* 9:10 (June 1989), 159.

73. Dan Polier, "Critics Put the Blast on Navy Big Leaguers," *Yank* 2:33 (February 4, 1944), 23; Bullock, *Playing for Their Nation*; Edgar G. Brands, "'Keep 'Em Playing,' Men in Service Chorus to Query: 'Should Game Go On During War?'" *Sporting*

News, August 16, 1942, 2; "Sailor's $500 Prize-Winning Letter Tells Why Nation Needs Game," *Sporting News*, May 20, 1942, 14.

74. Yoichi Nagata, "World War II and Local Hawaii Baseball," paper presented at the Society for American Baseball Research Annual Conference, Pittsburgh, PA, June 15–18, 1995, 1–6.

75. Frank Ardolino, "Big Leaguers Hit the Beach," *National Pastime* 16 (1996), 42–45; Bill Nowlin, "The 1945 All-Star Game: The Baseball Navy World Series at Furlong Field, Hawaii," *National Pastime* 26 (2006), 111–14.

76. "Widow Christened Liberty Vessel Named for McGraw," *Sporting News* 154:17 (November 17, 1962), 26; "Liberty Ships," *Baseball Magazine* 75:4 (September 1945), 360.

77. Gary Bedingfield, *Baseball in Wartime*, www.garybed.co.uk; "A Letter from London," *Baseball Magazine* 69:3 (August 1942), 418; "Service Diamond Stars Invade Sanctity of Wembley Stadium," *Sporting News*, September 2, 1943, 9; Gary Bedingfield, "Taking Baseball to War," *Army* 46 (September 1996), 62–63.

78. Goldstein, *Spartan Seasons*.

79. Stuart Thayer, "Baseball Goes to War: How a GI Became a Commissioner in World War II," *Sports Illustrated* 48 (April 25, 1988), 103–7; Gary Bedingfield, "When Virginia Baseball Went to War," *Roanoker*, April 1997, 46–48; Alex Kershaw, *The Bedford Boys: One American Town's Ultimate D-Day Sacrifice* (Cambridge, MA: Da Capo, 2003); Dick Thompson, "Baseball's Greatest Hero: John Joseph Pinder, Jr.," *Baseball Research Journal* 30 (2002), 3–10.

80. While escaping unscathed in war, Waitkus soon became famous as the gunshot victim of a crazed baseball groupie. John Theodore, *Baseball's Natural: The Story of Eddie Waitkus* (Carbondale: Southern Illinois University Press, 2002).

81. Thomas Gilbert, *Baseball at War: World War II and the Fall of the Color Line* (New York: Franklin Watts, 1997); Goldstein, *Spartan Seasons*.

82. Al Schacht, *GI Had Fun* (New York: Putnam's, 1945).

83. Thomas Barthel, "Ducky and the Lip in Italy," *National Pastime* 23 (2003), 115–21; "Six Answer, Opportunity for Hundreds," *Sporting News*, December 16, 1943, 8; "Game Goes Along at Oran," *Sporting News*, April 1, 1943, 6.

84. Ralph Martin, "The Yankees Win in North Africa Too," *Yank* 2:20 (November 5, 1943), 23; "Game Blooms in Tunisia," *Sporting News*, October 4, 1945, 19.

85. Nicholas Dawidoff, *The Catcher Was a Spy: The Mysterious Life of Moe Berg* (New York: Vintage Books, 1994); Nicholas Dawidoff, "Scholar, Lawyer, Catcher, Spy," *Sports Illustrated*, March 23, 1992, 76–86; Michael Shepard, "The Riddle Behind the Mask," *New Leader* 77 (August 15, 1994), 17–18; Richard Shepard, "Catcher in the Reich," *Time* 105 (February 3, 1975), 65–66; Jerome Holtzman, "A Great Companion," in *The Jerome Holtzman Baseball Reader* (Chicago: Triumph Books, 2003).

86. Bill Lee, with Jim Prime, *The Little Red (Sox) Book* (Chicago: Triumph Books, 2003); Dan Gutman, "Moe Berg: The Spy Who Came In from the Bullpen," in *Baseball Babylon* (New York: Penguin, 1992), 308–14.

87. Linda McCarthy, *Spies, Pop Flies, and French Fries: Stories I Told My Favorite Visitors to the CIA Exhibit Center* (Markham, VA: History Is a Hoot, Inc., 1999).

88. Michael Lewis, "Moe Berg's Japanese Reflections," *Baseball History* 2 (Spring 1987), 57–64.

89. Edward J. Rielly, "Baseball Haiku: Basho, the Babe, and the Great Japanese-American Trade," in *Cooperstown Symposium on Baseball and American Culture, 2001*, ed. William Simons (Jefferson, NC: McFarland, 2002), 246–59.

90. After leaving Japan, Berg took the Trans-Siberian Railway across the Soviet Union, shooting photos along the way. After the war, he thought the pictures could be used against Russia and awaited a new CIA appointment, but it never came. In the 1950s, Berg cavorted with characters as diverse as Yankees manager Casey Stengel and atomic bomb coordinator General Leslie Groves. In 1960, short of money, his plan to write his autobiography fell through when the publisher mistakenly thought Berg was Moe of the Three Stooges. Vivian Grey, *Moe Berg: The Spy Behind Home Plate* (Philadelphia: Jewish Publication Society, 1996); Carrie Muskat and Dan Abramson, "Americans Helped Japanese Game Prosper," *USA Today Baseball Weekly* 2:38 (January 23, 1993), 23.

91. Carl T. Felken, "Sports Skill Paying Off in the Pacific, Says Todd of Marines," *Sporting News*, November 16, 1944, 11; "Guam Yarn Stirs Memories of Lieutenant Colonel," *Marine Corps Chevron*, August 26, 1944, 20.

92. Shirley Povich, "In the Marianas, 1944," *Baseball Digest* May 1945, 17–18.

93. Chris Carola, "War Games: Enlist Exhibit at Hall of Fame Tells of Those Who Fought Instead of Playing," *USA Today Baseball Weekly* 5:10 (May 31, 1995), 6; Irvin K. Kawarsky, "The Manila Dodgers: A Great, Morale-Building Service Team at the Close of WWII," *National Pastime* 14 (1994), 59–60; "Baseball in Manila," *Yank* 4:9 (August 17, 1945), 22. After the victory, U.S. General Burton Reynolds sought a baseball team to entertain the troops, and Brooklyn Dodgers pitcher Kirby Higbe created the Manila Dodgers—featuring major leaguers Early Wynn, Joe Garagiola, and Jim Hearn. The team won both the Philippine Championship and the Pacific Olympic Championship. Goldstein, *Spartan Seasons*.

94. Wyatt Prunty, "A Baseball Team of Unknown Navy Pilots: Pacific Theater, 1944," *New Republic* 215:7 (July 1, 1996), 40; David Cataneo, *Peanuts and Crackerjack: A Treasury of Baseball Legends and Lore* (Nashville, TN: Rutledge Hill, 1991).

95. "Marine Veteran Tells About Ghost Baseball," *Stars and Stripes* (Mediterranean edition), March 11, 1944, 10.

96. "Pacific Marines Plan Baseball Careers," *Marine Corps Chevron*, February 10, 1945, 8; "New Guinea Baseball," *Yank* 3:22 (November 17, 1944), 23; Harold Winerip, "New Guinea Tent Talk," *Esquire* 22:6 (December 1944), 130.

97. Zoss and Bowman, *Diamonds in the Rough*; Tim Wolter, *POW Baseball in World War II: The National Pastime Behind Barbed Wire* (Jefferson, NC: McFarland, 2002).

98. Japanese prisoners of war in the Cowra, Australia, camp did use baseball equipment extensively in their attempted mass escape.

99. Wolter, *POW Baseball in World War II*. Many teams were represented, including Boston Red Sox players who were held in Stalag IIIB, Stalag 383, Oflag 64, Marlag, and Milag. Bill Nowlin, "Sox Who Served," *SABR Stars & SABR Stripes* 1:1 (June 2006), 2–5; Cort Vitty, "Mickey Grasso: The Catcher Was a POW," in *The National Pastime*, ed. Bob Brown (Cleveland: Society for American Baseball Research, 2009), 81–83.

100. Japan's reputation for prison cruelty was often deserved. Even so, distinctions between Japanese and American—or even German—policies have likely been colored by race or been a product of a victor's history of war prisons. Documented atrocities by Americans and British against the Japanese tend to be excluded. Philip Towle, *Jap-*

anese Prisoners of War (London: Hambledon Continuum, 1999); Richard Aldrich, *The Faraway War* (London: Corgi Publishers, 2006); Ben Fenton, "American Troops 'Murdered Japanese POWs,'" *Daily Telegraph*, June 8, 2005, 3.

101. Harold Winerip, "Of Baseball and Soldiers," *Baseball Magazine* 74:1 (December 1944), 222; Dan Polier, "Ex-POW Tells of Sports in Jap Concentration Camp," *Yank* 2:34 (February 11, 1944), 23.

102. Italian prisoners didn't play baseball, although the *Stars and Stripes* claimed they were at least once "treated to a look at baseball here [at Fort Meade], as the Philadelphia Athletics whipped Buffalo. The Ities raked the field before the game, then sat along the sidelines with 10,000 GIs and enjoyed the contest." Jonathan Fraser Light, *The Cultural Encyclopedia of Baseball* (Jefferson, NC: McFarland, 1997); J.G.T. Spink, "Combat Men Using Baseball to De-Nazify German Youth," *Sporting News*, September 13, 1945, 12.

103. Gary W. Moore, *Playing With the Enemy: A Baseball Prodigy, a World at War, and a Field of Broken Dreams* (El Dorado Hills, CA: Savas Beatie, 2006).

104. Among them were Eberhard "Zip" Fuhr and his family, who were sent to the prison camp for Germans in Crystal City, Texas, where no baseball was allowed. But Fuhr was American, and baseball was part of his American dream. Not released until 1947, his five years behind barbed wire produced a lifetime of disillusionment. John Christgau, "The Baseball Dreams of Eberhard 'Zip' Fuhr and the Reality of Internment Baseball, 1942–1947," *Nine* 15:2 (2006), 95–105.

105. The U.S. Supreme Court upheld the internment partly because Japanese Americans were "an isolated community." Yet this isolation was created by the Immigration Act of 1924, which blocked citizenship for many Japanese, who then sought the refuge of tight-knit communities. With this separation, they became even greater targets after Pearl Harbor than they might have been otherwise. Could baseball have better connected them to other communities, and thus resisted the push toward Japanese internment? Samuel O. Regalado, "Isolation or Assimilation? Dualism and Nisei Baseball," paper presented to the North American Society for Sport History, French Lick, IN, May 24, 2002; Frank Ardolino, "Americans of Japanese Ancestry Baseball," *Nine* 8:8 (1997), 184–89; Jay Feldman, "Baseball Behind Barbed Wire," *National Pastime* 12 (1992), 37–41.

106. David Davis, "A Field in the Desert That Felt like Home: An Unlikely Hero Sustained Hope for Japanese-Americans Interned in World War II," *Sports Illustrated* 89:20 (November 16, 1998), 44; Kerry Yo Nakagawa, *Through a Diamond: 100 Years of Japanese-American Baseball* (San Francisco: Rudi Publishing, 2001); Michael L. Mullan, "Sport, Ethnicity and the Reconstruction of the Self: Baseball in America's Internment Camps," *International Journal of the History of Sport* 16:1 (March 1999), 1–21.

107. Jay Feldman, *Suitcase Sefton and the American Dream* (Chicago: Triumph Books, 2006); Hans Greimel, "Japanese American Baseball Steps Back Up to the Plate," *Los Angeles Times*, October 11, 1998, 5.

108. The hostile environment around California's Tule Lake internment camp and the poor treatment inside made some Japanese wonder whether they should shift their allegiance to Japan, after all. Mullan, "Sport, Ethnicity and the Reconstruction of the Self."

109. Gilbert, *Baseball at War*; Donald Honig, *Baseball America* (New York: Macmillan, 1985), 247.

110. Jim Allen, "Wartime Japanese Baseballs," *SABR-L Archives*, July 17, 2000; Briley, "Where Have You Gone, William Bendix?" 39.

111. "Veterans Who Died Serving Their Country," www.baseball-reference.com/bullpen/Category:Veterans_who_died_serving_their_country.

112. Muskat and Abramson, "Americans Helped Japanese Game Prosper." Minor leaguer Ray Makepeace was a prisoner of war in the Philippines in 1942, watching Japanese soldiers playing baseball. When a ball rolled over to him, he threw a curveball back to the soldier, who asked if he knew Ted Williams and Babe Ruth. When Makepeace said yes, the soldier responded, "Fuck Babe Ruth." Makepeace showed the soldier how to throw a curveball in exchange for a pack of cigarettes. Nowlin, *Ted Williams at War*; Marshall Smelser, *The Life that Ruth Built: A Biography* (Lincoln: University of Nebraska Press, 1975); Montville, *Big Bam*; Stephen Goldleaf, "The War Against Babe Ruth," in *The Dreamlife of Johnny Baseball*, ed. Richard Grossinger (Berkeley, CA: North Atlantic Books, 1987), 84.

113. Montville, *Big Bam;* Robert Whiting, *You Gotta Have Wa: When Two Cultures Collide on a Baseball Diamond* (New York: Vintage, 1991); Joseph A. Reaves, *Taking in a Game: A History of Baseball in Asia* (Lincoln: University of Nebraska Press, 2002), 79.

114. Richard Polenberg, "The Good War? A Reappraisal of How World War II Affected American Society," *Virginia Magazine of History and Biography* 100 (1992), 295–322; Zezima, *Saving Private Power*; Howard Zinn, "Just and Unjust War," in *Declarations of Independence* (New York: HarperPerennial, 1991), 67–105; Zinn, *People's History of the United States*; Martin J. Sherwin, *A World Destroyed: Hiroshima and Its Legacies* (Palo Alto, CA: Stanford University Press, 2003); Gar Alperovitz, *The Decision to Use the Atomic Bomb and the Architecture of an American Myth* (New York: Knopf, 1995); Wood, *Worshipping the Myths of World War II*. General Dwight Eisenhower opposed the use of atomic weapons: "First, the Japanese were ready to surrender and it wasn't necessary to hit them with that awful thing. Second, I hated to see our country be the first to use such a weapon." Admiral William "Bull" Halsey, the U.S. Third Fleet Commander, who led the American offensive against the Japanese home islands in the war's final months, said, "the first atomic bomb was an unnecessary experiment." Leo Maley and Uday Mohan, "Not Everyone Wanted to Bomb Hiroshima," *History News Service*, November 7, 2007, http://www.h-net.org/~hns/articles/2007/110207a.html.

115. Wood, *Worshipping the Myths of World War II*; Tom Engelhardt, *The End of Victory Culture: Cold War America and the Disillusioning of a Generation* (New York: Basic Books, 1995).

Chapter 8. Cold War, Hot War (1946–1953)

1. Evelyn Krache Morris, "Did Ike Play Pro Ball?" *National Pastime* 21 (2001), 67–68; Bill Gilbert, *They Also Served: Baseball and the Home Front, 1941–1945* (New York: Crown, 1992).

2. "Wartime Editions Praised by Truman," *Sporting News* 154:22 (December 22, 1962), 13.

3. Rob Edelman, "Politics, Patriotism, and Baseball On-Screen," in *Baseball and American Culture*, ed. Edward J. Rielly (New York: Haworth Press, 2003), 163–72.

4. Herb Fagen, "They Came Back from the Wars: 1945 and Beyond," *Oldtyme Baseball News* 4:3, 28–29; Frederick Turner, *When the Boys Came Back: Baseball and 1946*

(New York: Holt, 1996); John L. Green, "A Review of 1946: When Johnny (Sain) and Hundreds More Came Marching Home," *Baseball Research Journal* 26 (1996), 122–24; Sherri Eng, "We Were Soldiers: Their Major League Baseball Careers Interrupted, Former Players Recall Their Days in the Military," *San Francisco Chronicle*, May 27, 2002, C9; William Anderson, "From the Ballpark to the Battlefield . . . and Back!!" *Michigan History Magazine* 79:5 (September 1995), 10.

5. Gary Bloomfield, "Big Leagues' Manpower Demands," *Veterans of Foreign Wars Magazine*, January 1993, 30; Patricia Vignola, "The Patriotic Pinch Hitter: The AAGBL and How the American Woman Earned a Permanent Spot on the Roster," *Nine* 12:2 (2004): 103–13; "Women's Place Is in Grandstand," *Sporting News*, July 2, 1952.

6. Rob Newell, "Boys of Summer Head to War: Baseball's Rising Stars Didn't Hesitate When Duty Called Them in World War II," *Retired Officer's Magazine* 57:10 (October 2001), 64–69; Rick Van Blair, *Dugout to Foxhole: Interviews with Baseball Players Whose Careers Were Affected by World War II* (Jefferson, NC: McFarland, 1994); Brent Kelley, *The Pastime in Turbulence: Interviews with Baseball Players of the 1940s* (Jefferson, NC: McFarland, 2001). The Pacific Coast League promoted itself as a third major league, but some owners were bought off with promises of compensation if the major leagues expanded to their city. Robert F. Burk, *Much More Than a Game: Players, Owners and American Baseball Since 1920* (Chapel Hill: University of North Carolina Press, 2001); Joel Zoss and John Bowman, *Diamonds in the Rough: The Untold History of Baseball* (Lincoln: University of Nebraska Press, 2004).

7. Thomas Borstelmann, *The Cold War and the Color Line: American Race Relations in the Global Arena* (Cambridge, MA: Harvard University Press, 2001), 10–84.

8. Tom Gallagher, "Lester Rodney, the *Daily Worker*, and the Integration of Baseball," *National Pastime* 19 (1999), 77–80; Irwin Silber, *Press Box Red: The Story of Lester Rodney, Communist Who Helped Break the Color Line in American Sports* (Philadelphia: Temple University Press, 2003); Dave Zirin, "It All Starts with Lester Rodney," in *What's My Name, Fool? Sports and Resistance in the United States* (Chicago: Haymarket Books, 2005), 23–52; Martha McArdell Shoemaker, "Propaganda or Persuasion: The Communist Party and Its Campaign to Integrate Baseball," MA thesis, University of Nevada, 1999; Bill L. Weaver, "The Black Press and the Assault on Baseball's 'Color Line': October 1945–April 1947," *Phylon* (Fourth Quarter 1979), 4.

9. Adrian Burgos, *Playing America's Game: Baseball, Latinos, and the Color Line* (Berkeley: University of California Press, 2007); "Beisboleros," *Newsweek* 23:22 (May 29, 1944), 90; Howard Senzel, *Baseball and the Cold War: Being a Soliloquy on the Necessity of Baseball in the Life of a Serious Student of Marx & Hegel* (New York: Harcourt Brace, 1977).

10. Roberto Gonzalez Echevarria, "Baseball at the Crossroads: The '47 Dodgers in Havana," *Spring Training Baseball Yearbook*, 1996, 20–25. The All-American Girls Professional Baseball League was in Havana the same time as the Dodgers and often outdrew them. Lois Browne, *Girls of Summer* (New York: HarperCollins, 1992). Manager Leo Durocher once told Rodney, "For a fucking Communist, you sure know your baseball." Rodney was active in the "Committee to End Jim Crow in Baseball," which made the U.S. attorney general's "Subversive Activities" list. Rodney was named as a national security threat by FBI director Hoover. When Rodney was drafted for the war, Bill Mardo and Nat Low inherited his campaign. J. Edgar Hoover, *Masters of Deceit* (New York: Pocket Books, 1959); Peter C. Bjarkman, "History's Many Shades: Tracking Jackie's Latino Predecessors," *Primera Fila*, October 1997, 12–13. Minnie Mi-

noso became the majors' first black Latino when he was signed by the Indians in 1949. See Bill Swank, "They Served with Valor: Negro League Ballplayers in the Armed Forces During World War II," *National Pastime* 28 (2008), 94–96; Adrian Burgos, "Cuban Baseball Legacy Rich in American Heritage," *Memories and Dreams,* July–August 2006, 9–11; James D. Cockcroft, *Latinos in Beisbol: The Hispanic Experience in the Americas* (Danbury, CT: Franklin Watts, 1996).

11. Jules Tygiel cited in Silber, *Press Box Red,* ii.

12. Frank Graham, "When Baseball Went to War," *Sports Illustrated* 26:16 (April 17, 1967), 78; Jerome Holtzman, *The Commissioners: Baseball's Midlife Crisis* (New York: Total Sports, 1998); Bill Marshall, "Baseball's Most Colorful Commissioner," in *Road Trips* (Cleveland: Society for American Baseball Research, 2004), 65–66; Bob Bailey, "The First Unknown Soldier: General Emmett O'Donnell, Baseball Commissioner," *National Pastime* 26 (2006), 115–18; William Marshall, *Baseball's Pivotal Era, 1945–1951* (Lexington: University Press of Kentucky, 1999); J.G. Taylor Spink, "Looping the Loops," *Sporting News,* January 1, 1942, 1; "May is Personally Opposed to Baseball," *Stars and Stripes Weekly* (Mediterranean edition) 2:59 (January 20, 1945), 7; Albert B. Chandler, *Heroes, Plain Folks and Skunks: The Life and Times of Happy Chandler* (New York: Bonus Books, 1989).

13. G. Richard McKelvey, *Mexican Raiders in the Major Leagues: The Pasquel Brothers Against Organized Baseball, 1946* (Jefferson, NC: McFarland, 2006).

14. Cockcroft, *Latinos in Beisbol;* Bjarkman, "History's Many Shades."

15. Milton Bracker, "Mexico's Baseball Raiders Ride Again," *Saturday Evening Post,* March 8, 1947, 26–27, 145–46.

16. Branch Rickey condemned Pasquel's raids, labeling the Mexican clubs an "outlaw league." Yet Pasquel noted the major leagues' long history of raiding competing U.S. leagues (in past baseball wars) and Rickey's own, emerging raid on the Negro Leagues— not to mention the raids on Caribbean leagues. As Pasquel observed, "For many years, while our Mexican League was struggling, major league scouts visited our cities and over our protests, stole our players, [despite their] Mexican League contracts." Washington owner Clark Griffith had stolen away more Latinos than any other owner. McKelvey, *Mexican Raiders in the Major Leagues;* Ron Briley, "Baseball and the Cold War: An Examination of Values," *OAH Magazine of History* 2 (Summer 1986), 15–18; Burk, *Much More Than a Game;* "Negro Club to Appeal to Chandler," *Christian Science Monitor,* October 24, 1945, 14; James Overmyer, *Queen of the Negro Leagues: Effa Manley and the Newark Eagles* (Lanham, MD: Scarecrow Press, 1998); John B. Holway, *Complete Book of Baseball's Negro Leagues* (Winter Park, FL: Hastings House, 2001); John Phillips, "The Mexican Jumping Beans of 1946," in *Grandstand Baseball Annual, 1997* (Downey, CA: Joseph Wayman, 1997), 60–63; John Phillips, *The Mexican Jumping Beans: The Story of the Baseball War of 1946* (Perry, GA: Capital Publishers, 1997); Kyle Crichton, "Hot Tamale Circuit," *Collier's,* June 29, 1946, 27; Alan M. Klein, "The Baseball Wars: The Mexican Baseball League and Nationalism in 1946," *Studies in Latin American Popular Culture* 13 (1994), 33.

17. Lewis Atchison, "How Mexican Raids Threatened to Ruin Majors 25 Years Ago," *Baseball Digest* 30:7 (July 1971), 72–75.

18. Pasquel offered to make Chandler the Mexican League commissioner, with a substantial pay raise. Klein, "The Baseball Wars"; Thomas Gilbert, *Baseball at War: World War II and the Fall of the Color Line* (New York: Franklin Watts, 1997).

19. Gerald F. Vaughn, "Jorge Pasquel and the Evolution of the Mexican League,"

National Pastime 12 (1992), 9–13. The Mexican League raids were a cultural resistance, "challenging the sense of superiority that so dominated not only MLB but other American institutions in the Third World." Because baseball had long "followed the flag" of U.S. intervention, it was an obvious target. Klein, "Baseball Wars"; Vaughn, "Jorge Pasquel and the Evolution of the Mexican League." To deter "outlaws," MLB banned American and Cuban players from Cuban winter ball if they also played in the Mexican (Summer) League, provoking cries of Yanqui imperialism. Branch Rickey went to Havana to discipline Cuban League officials against the Mexican League invasion. Other visits were made to the winter leagues in Panama, Puerto Rico, and Venezuela. Peter J. Bjarkman, *Diamonds Around the Globe: The Encyclopedia of International Baseball* (Westport, CT: Greenwood Press, 2005).

20. Colin D. Howell, "'A Tale of Two Outlaws': Jorge Pasquel, Jean Pierre Roy and the Postwar Challenge to Organized Baseball's Authority from the Borderlands," paper presented at the 34th Annual Conference of the North American Society for Sport History, Glenwood Springs, CO, May 2006. Gardella observed that Pasquel had survived the Mexican Revolution and then become a revolutionist himself, thumbing his nose at the United States: "He was a lot like Castro." Larry Moffi, *The Conscience of the Game: Baseball's Commissioners from Landis to Selig* (Lincoln: University of Nebraska Press, 2006); Thomas S. Mulligan, "Gardella's Challenge Helped Blaze the Trail for Today's Free Agents," *Los Angeles Times*, October 22, 1994.

21. Briley, "Baseball and the Cold War," 15; John Drebinger, "The 'Mexican War' Ends," *Baseball Magazine* 83 (August 1949), 291–93; Harold Rosenthal, "The War with Mexico," *Baseball Digest* 22:10 (December 1963–January 1964), 53–56; Jim Sargent, "Al and Danny Gardella," *Oldtyme Baseball News* 9:1 (1998), 30. Pasquel vowed, "I cannot lick [the baseball owners] because they are big and belong to the biggest country in the world. But I am going to make them pay." While the MLB salary increases were temporary, the Pasquel and Gardella challenges were important steps toward free agency. Pasquel's brother Alfonso said, "If major leaguers had any guts, they'd make sure my brother Jorge was elected to Cooperstown for helping them gain their freedom." Richard Goldstein, *Spartan Seasons: How Baseball Survived the Second World War* (New York: Macmillan, 1980); Richard Goldstein, "Life During Wartime," *Boston* 81:3 (March 1989), 73; McKelvey, *Mexican Raiders in the Major Leagues*; Robert Heuer, "Latin Ballplayers Load the Bases," *Americas* 42 (March–April 1990), 18–23; David Mandell, "Danny Gardella and the Reserve Clause," *National Pastime* 26 (May 2006), 41–44.

22. In the late 1940s, in Southern California groves, Mexican Americans formed their own leagues, where "baseball drills served as a front for union-organizing efforts." Ballplayers used the time together to share information and discuss grievances and strategies. Cockcroft, *Latinos in Beisbol*; Jerry Soifer, "Baseball a Triple Play to Mexican-Americans," *Press-Enterprise* (Riverside, CA), May 5, 2006. The U.S. National League All Stars played the Cuban League All Stars in Havana, and the New York Yankees and Boston Red Sox both barnstormed in the Caribbean. A strong winter league developed in Panama, and professional leagues were launched in both Colombia (Licobal League) and Brazil (São Paolo Federation of Baseball).

23. Wade V. Lewis, "Substitute Play for War," *Rotarian*, August 1947, 3.

24. William J. Miller, "The American Sports Empire," in *Sports in Modern America*, ed. William J. Baker and John M. Carroll (Montgomery, AL: River City, 1983), 147–58; Clifford Bloodgood, "Editorial Comment," *Baseball Magazine*, July 1945, 253; Bryan

Price, "More Than a Game: Baseball in World War II and the Cold War, 1941–1958," paper presented at National Baseball Hall of Fame Library, May 1998, 1–43.

25. Russell E. Crawford, "Consensus All-American: Sport and the Promotion of the American Way of Life During the Cold War, 1946–1965," PhD dissertation, University of Nebraska, 2004; Alan M. Klein, *Growing the Game: The Globalization of Major League Baseball* (New Haven, CT: Yale University Press, 2006); "Royal Visitor Looks at U.S.," *Life* 33:8 (August 25, 1952), 24; William Duggan, "The Sultan and the Baseball Game," *Foreign Service Journal* 54:6 (June 1977), 21.

26. Crawford, "Consensus All-American"; Jules Tygiel, *Baseball's Great Experiment: Jackie Robinson and His Legacy* (New York: Vintage, 1984); "Game Blooms in Tunisia," *Sporting News*, October 4, 1945, 19.

27. Thomas M. Domer, "Sport in Cold War America, 1953–1963: The Diplomatic and Political Uses of Sport in the Eisenhower and Kennedy Administrations," PhD dissertation, Marquette University, 1978; Thomas L. Altherr, "Baseball Is Life? Images of Baseball in *Life* Magazine, 1936–1972," *Nine* 5:1 (Fall 1996), 18–43.

28. "Harrow Meets Baseball: American Airmen Give an Exhibition of the U.S. National Sport to Puzzled English Schoolboys," *Life* 19:4 (July 23, 1945), 94.

29. Leslie Lieber, "François at the Bat," *Reader's Digest* 49: 292 (August 1946); Harrington Crissey, "Baseball and the Armed Services," in *Total Baseball*, ed. John Thorn, et al. (New York: Total Sports, 1999), 2513–20.

30. "Service Diamond Stars Invade Sanctity of Wembley Stadium," *Sporting News*, September 2, 1943, 9; Gary Bedingfield, *Baseball in World War II Europe* (Charleston, SC: Arcadia, 1999).

31. Edelman, "Politics, Patriotism, and Baseball On-Screen," 163; Roger C. Panaye, *European Amateur Baseball* (Antwerp: Federation of European Baseball, 1978); A.L. Marder, "350 Youths Attend Clinic Held by 71st Division Diamond Stars," *Sporting News*, October 18, 1945, 14; J.G.T. Spink, "Combat Men Using Baseball to De-Nazify German Youth," *Sporting News*, September 13, 1945, 12.

32. Frank Cerabino, "Baseball Italiano: The Great American Pastime Translated," *Palm Beach Post*, March 18, 2007; "Sports Classes to Meet Desires of Every Soldier Are Provided at U.S. Army's School in Rome," *Life* 9:17 (August 21, 1945), 52.

33. William Mahoney, "Field of Fame," *Stars and Stripes*, April 8, 1955, 10; Blake Erlich, "Slide, Luigi, Slide!" *New York Sunday Herald-Tribune Magazine*, September 6, 1953, 10; "European Baseball Head Here to Enlist Support," *New York Times*, December 1, 1958, B1.

34. Merritt Clifton, "Where the Twain Shall Meet: What Baseball Means to Japan—and Humanity," *National Pastime* 4 (1985), 12–22; Phil Storch, "Baseball Teams Again Invade Japan," *Marine Corps Chevron*, May 19, 1945, 8.

35. Robert Obojski, *The Rise of Japanese Baseball Power* (Radnor, PA: Chilton Books, 1975); Joseph A. Reaves, *Taking in a Game: A History of Baseball in Asia* (Lincoln: University of Nebraska Press, 2002), 81.

36. Reaves, *Taking in a Game*, 83; United Press, "Return of Baseball Sought in Japan," *New York Times*, September 16, 1945, 11; Fred Lieb, "MacArthur Takes Over Where Major Stars 'Took' Japanese Eleven Years Ago," *Sporting News*, August 1945, 14. Still wildly popular, Ruth was the only non-native voted in a 1955 poll as one of the most famous people in Japan in the previous half century. James Greenfield, "Year of the Babe," *Sports Illustrated* 3 (November 14, 1955), 57.

37. Weldon James, "Japan's at Batto Again," *Collier's*, August 2, 1947, 44–48; Herman L. Massin, "Baseball: The Great Americanizer," *Senior Scholastic*, May 3, 1950, 10–11; John N. Duvall, "Baseball as Aesthetic Ideology: Cold War History, Race, and DeLillo's 'Pafko at the Wall,'" *Modern Fiction Studies* 41:2 (1995), 285–313; Norman Cousins, "Slide, Fujimura, Slide!" *Collier's*, November 5, 1949, 28–29, 54.

38. Alfred Eckes and Thomas Zeiler, *Globalization and the American Century* (Cambridge, UK: Cambridge University Press, 2003). Later, other movies portrayed the baseball craziness of this period, including *Dynamite Bang Bang*, *The Ceremony*, and *MacArthur's Children* (Japanese island boys who form their own club to play a team of American soldiers). Hirano Kyoko, *Mr. Smith Goes to Tokyo Under the American Occupation* (Washington, DC: Smithsonian Institution Press, 1992).

39. Richard Leutzinger, "Banzai, O'Doul," in *Lefty O'Doul: The Legend That Baseball Nearly Forgot* (Carmel, CA: Carmel Bay, 1997), 53–66; Richard Leutzinger, "Lefty O'Doul and the Development of Japanese Baseball," *National Pastime* 12 (1992), 30–34; Richard Leutzinger, "Breaking the Ice: The San Francisco Seals 1949 Tour of Japan," *Elysian Fields Quarterly* 21:3 (2004), 33–37.

40. Ron Briley, "Amity is the Key to Success: Baseball and the Cold War," *Baseball History* 1 (Fall 1986), 4–19; Kerry Yo Nakagawa, *Through a Diamond: 100 Years of Japanese-American Baseball* (San Francisco: Rudi Publishing, 2001).

41. Red Parton, "Japanese Plan to Resume Pro Ball Next Spring," *Sporting News*, November 22, 1945, 9; William Kelly, "The Hanshin Tigers and Japanese Professional Baseball," in *Baseball Without Borders: The International Pastime*, ed. George Gmelch (Lincoln: University of Nebraska Press, 2006); Robert Fitts, *Remembering Japanese Baseball* (Carbondale: Southern Illinois University Press, 2005); Quentin Reynolds, "Giant in Japan," *Reader's Digest* 64:5 (May 1954), 3–6.

42. Roger B. Doulens, "Chinese Grabbing Chance to Learn Game," *Sporting News*, March 14, 1946, 13; Reaves, *Taking in a Game,* 39, 44, 45.

43. Andrew Morris, "Taiwan: Baseball, Colonialism, and Nationalism," in *Baseball Without Borders: The International Pastime*, ed. George Gmelch (Lincoln: University of Nebraska Press, 2006), 71.

44. Gerald S. Gems, *The Athletic Crusade: Sport and American Cultural Imperialism* (Lincoln: University of Nebraska Press, 2006), 66.

45. MacArthur learned baseball at western military posts from his army officer father and became a star shortstop at San Antonio's West Texas Military Academy. As a West Point cadet in 1901, he played in the first game ever between the U.S. Military Academy and the U.S. Naval Academy. National Baseball Congress, "First Official Inter-Hemisphere Playoff," *National Baseball Congress Guide* (Wichita, KS: National Baseball Congress, 1950), 3.

46. Price, "More Than Just a Game," 1.

47. Bob Broeg, *Baseball's Barnum* (Wichita, KS: Wichita State University Press, 1989); Bob Rives, "War and the National Baseball Congress," in *Proceedings of 5th Annual Conference on War and Media—War and Sports* (Independence, MO: Graceland University Center for the Study of the Korean War, 2004), 33–42; Douglas MacArthur, *Reminiscences* (New York: McGraw-Hill, 1964); Royse Parr, "The Korean War and Baseball: A Date with Destiny," *Nine* 11:2 (2003), 110–17.

48. Jules Tygiel, *Past Time: Baseball as History* (New York: Oxford University Press, 2000).

49. "The Story of the Year," *Sport* 9:4 (October 1950), 96; Briley, "Baseball and the Cold War," 15; Ron Briley, "Ambiguous Patriotism: Baseball and the Vietnam War," in *Cooperstown Symposium on Baseball and American Culture, 2005–2006*, ed. William Simons (Jefferson, NC: McFarland, 2007), 165–78; Briley, "Amity Is the Key to Success," 4.

50. Ron Briley, "The Myth and Reality of Major League Baseball," April 10, 2006, http://hnn.us/articles/23553.html.

51. "Emmett O'Donnell," *Baseball Reference Bullpen*, www.baseball-reference.com/bullpen/Emmett_O%27Donnell.

52. DiMaggio went, even though he was reportedly anti-Army because of his World War II experience, and even though he told Marilyn Monroe, as she also prepared to entertain the troops, "You know, you don't have to go over there." Paul Rogers, "Wartime Baseball, Medicine, and the New York Yankees: A Conversation with Dr. Bobby Brown," *Elysian Fields Quarterly*, Summer 1999, 58–75; Leigh Montville, *Ted Williams: The Biography of an American Hero* (New York: Doubleday, 2004), 151–53; Allen Barra, "Just a Bit Outside: Larger-Than-Life Ted Williams Was the John Wayne of Baseball," *Birmingham Weekly* 5:43 (July 25, 2002), 6.

53. The Simmons call-up hurt the Philadelphia Phillies in 1950, when they lost the World Series in four straight to the Yankees. Briley, "Amity Is the Key to Success," 15; Scott Patrick Dillow, "Safe at Home: World War II Baseball and the Reshaping of American Society," MA thesis, California State University, 1999.

54. At the tribute, Williams delivered a short speech, and *Boston Herald* reporter Eddie Costello whispered, "Tip your hat." Williams never tipped his hat but when the crowd kept cheering, he finally relented, tipping his cap to the right-field grandstand. The crowd went wild. Williams then tipped his hat to the seats behind home plate, and the crowd went wilder. Williams tipped his hat to the left-field grandstand, and the crowd was in a frenzy. It was a touching moment, a warm, possibly final embrace. "Center field," whispered Costello. "Don't forget center field." "Not those [expletives], too!" whined Williams. David Cataneo, *Peanuts and Crackerjack: A Treasury of Baseball Legends and Lore* (Nashville, TN: Rutledge Hill, 1991); Jerry Coleman with Richard Goldstein, *An American Journey: My Life on the Field, in the Air, and on the Air* (Chicago: Triumph Books, 2008). After the war, Johnny Podres joined the navy but was discharged as unfit because he had spondylolisthesis, a back ailment. But when he starred for the Brooklyn Dodgers in the 1955 World Series, Podres was reclassified from 4F to 1A and inducted again.

55. Philip Grant, "Ted Williams of the Boston Red Sox and the Korean War," in *Proceedings of 5th Annual Conference on War and Media—War and Sports* (Independence, MO: Graceland University Center for the Study of the Korean War, 2004), 107–12.

56. Nowlin, *Ted Williams at War*.

57. Christopher DeRosa, "OAFIE's Voice: Political Indoctrination in the Korean War," in *Proceedings of 5th Annual Conference on War and Media—War and Sports* (Independence, MO: Graceland University Center for the Study of the Korean War, 2004), 43–62; Dick Brooks, "Leo Compares Troops to Champion Yankees," *Pacific Stars and Stripes* 9:310 (November 7, 1953), 14.

58. Ronald A. Smith, "The Paul Robeson–Jackie Robinson Saga and a Political Collision," in *The Jackie Robinson Reader*, ed. Jules Tygiel (New York: Plume, 1997), 169–188.

59. Steven Wisensale, "The Political Wars of Jackie Robinson," *Nine* 2:1 (1993), 18–28; Jules Tygiel, "The Court Martial of Jackie Robinson," *American Heritage*, August–September 1984.

60. C.P. Trussell, "Jackie Robinson Terms Stand of Robeson on Negroes False," *New York Times*, July 19, 1949, 1; Nicholas Von Hoffman, "The Baseball Diaries," *Civilization*, February–March 1999, 38–41; Duvall, "Baseball as Aesthetic Ideology," 285.

61. Crawford, "Consensus All-American"; "Award to Jackie Robinson," *New York Times*, August 31, 1949, 26; "Jackie Robinson Cited by Catholic War Veterans for Testimony Against Communism," *New York Times*, August 31, 1949, 26; William Weart, "Freedom Group Honors Our Way," *New York Times*, November 22, 1949, 22.

62. Wisensale, "The Political Wars of Jackie Robinson"; David Zirin, "Jackie Robinson," in *What's My Name, Fool? Sports and Resistance in the United States* (Chicago: Haymarket Books, 2005).

63. Don DeLillo, *Pafko at the Wall* (New York: Scribner's, 1997); Don DeLillo, *Underworld* (New York: Scribner's, 1998).

64. Tygiel, *Past Time*, 155.

65. Cecil Powell, "Of Willie Mays & Joe McCarthy & Bobby Thompson," *Massachusetts Review* 32 (Spring 1991), 100–109; Tygiel, *Past Time*.

66. Duvall, "Baseball as Aesthetic Ideology," 285.

67. Ibid.; Don DeLillo, *End Zone* (New York: Penguin, 1986).

68. DeLillo, *End Zone*; Briley, "Baseball and the Cold War," 15.

69. Briley, "Baseball and the Cold War," 15; David Holmberg, "Nuclear Annihilation and the National Pastime in Don DeLillo's *Underworld*," paper presented at Cooperstown Symposium on Baseball and American Culture, June 2007.

70. United Press, "Introduction of Baseball in Russia is Suggested," *New York Times*, September 10, 1945.

71. "Russians Say U.S. Stole 'Beizbol,' Made It a Game of Bloody Murder," *New York Times*, September 16, 1952.

72. Briley, "Baseball and the Cold War," 15.

73. Ron Briley, "Baseball Enlists in the Cold War: *Strategic Air Command* (1956)," paper presented at the Society for American Baseball Research Annual Conference, Seattle, WA, June 2006; Ron Briley, "That's Right, John, You Never Did Play: Images of Masculinity and the Cold War Consensus in Baseball Cinema, 1947–1957," paper presented to the North American Society for Sport History Annual Conference, Windsor, Ontario, May 22–25, 1998. Stewart, known for his anticommunism and conservative politics, worked for J. Edgar Hoover as an informant and starred in an FBI propaganda film.

74. Erik Lundegaard, "Truth, Justice and (Fill in the Blank)," *New York Times*, June 30, 2006. Other baseball films may have highlighted the insecurities, more than the strengths, of American life, and illustrated "supernatural solutions for personal problems" rather than the opportunities provided by hard work and the American dream. Ron Briley, "Baseball and Supernatural Intervention: Cinematic Reflections on the Crisis of Confidence in Post–World War II America," in *Cooperstown Symposium on Baseball and American Culture*, ed. William Simon (Jefferson, NC: McFarland, 2002), 139–55.

75. Philip Roth, *The Great American Novel* (New York: Bantam, 1973); Richard C. Crepeau, "Not the Cincinnati Reds: Anti-Communism in Recent Baseball Literature," *Arete: A Journal of Sports Literature* 1 (Fall 1983), 87–97. A more recent novel depicts the rampant McCarthy era paranoia in New York City in 1953, when Communists were holding Union Square vigils for the recently sentenced atomic

spies, the Rosenbergs. Josh Rankin's father, a Communist newspaper editor, has gone underground, and the party has become family for Josh. At school, his classmates ostracize him for being a "Commie," and he's rejected by the baseball team. He meets a stranger who plays ball with him and takes him to see the Dodgers at Ebbets Field, but he turns out to be an FBI agent who's trying to use baseball to get Josh to rat on his parents and the party. Josh becomes disillusioned about baseball's cynical role in the Red Scare. Mark Lapin, *Pledge of Allegiance* (New York: Dutton, 1991).

76. Domer, "Sport in Cold War America"; Benjamin Rader, *American Ways: A Brief History of American Cultures* (Orlando, FL: Harcourt, 2001); Michael Manning, "Globalization of Baseball in Popular Culture," in *Baseball and American Culture*, ed. Edward J. Rielly (New York: Haworth Press, 2003), 109–19.

77. Crawford, "Consensus All-American."

78. Lance Van Auken and Robin Van Auken, *Play Ball! The Story of Little League Baseball* (University Park, PA: Penn State University Press, 2001).

79. Michael H. Carriere, "A Diamond Is a Boy's Best Friend: The Rise of Little League Baseball, 1939–1964," *Journal of Sport History* 32:3 (Fall 2005), 351–78.

80. Some worried that Little League was becoming too intense and corporate, robbing kids of the game's true joy. It was supposed to show the demise of class and race distinctions, yet some U.S. towns withdrew from Little League so they could keep blacks out. It was supposed to display U.S. superiority, but by 1957 the Monterrey, Mexico, team won the Little League World Series and repeated the following year. Others defended Little League. Gary Alan Fine, *With the Boys: Little League Baseball and Preadolescent Culture* (Chicago: University of Chicago Press, 1987).

Chapter 9. Revolution and Quagmire (1953–1975)

1. "Frick Says Byrnes Won't Discriminate Against Ballplayers," *Stars and Stripes Weekly* (Mediterranean Edition) 2:68 (March 24, 1945), 7; Ford C. Frick, *Games, Asterisks and People: Memoirs of A Lucky Fan* (New York: Crown, 1973). While Frick was successful with the military, he had trouble courting the commander in chief. President Dwight Eisenhower congratulated Frick for leading a New York Giants tour of Japan, claiming he was "in a very real sense our American Ambassador." Yet in 1953 Eisenhower was the first president in decades not to attend the Washington Senators' opening day, playing golf instead, which "seemed little short of high treason to baseball officials." George C. Rable, "Patriotism, Platitudes and Politics: Baseball and the American Presidency," *Presidential Studies Quarterly* 19 (Spring 1989), 363–72.

2. According to Hall of Famer Monte Irvin, "Baseball has done more to move America in the right direction than all the professional patriots with all their cheap words." Yet some of the cheapest may have come from baseball officials themselves. Briley, "Ambiguous Patriotism"; "Game to Ride Out All Threats, Frick Tells Rotary Club," *Sporting News*, December 12, 1951, 4.

3. As governments, the Soviet Reds began in 1917 and the Chinese Reds in 1949, while his Cincinnati Reds began in 1882 (when they were called the Red Stockings).

4. Carl Prince, "Political Culture: Reds and Dodger Blue," in *Brooklyn's Dodgers: The Bums, the Borough, and the Best of Baseball* (New York: Oxford University Press, 1996), 23–44.

5. Frick, *Games, Asterisks and People*, 117.

6. Fred Lieb, "Baseball—the UN That Belongs to Us," *Baseball Magazine*, August 1, 1953; Frank Graham, "The Legion's Good-Will Tour," *Sport* 22:5 (November 1956), 8; "Richard Nixon Advocates True 'World' Series," *New York Herald Tribune*, January 29, 1958; "Hit and Run Diplomacy," *Wall Street Journal* 151:101 (May 22, 1958), 12.

7. Alan M. Klein, *Sugarball: The American Game, the Dominican Dream* (New Haven, CT: Yale University Press, 1991); Alan M. Klein, "American Hegemony, Dominican Resistance, and Baseball," *Dialectical Anthropology* 13 (1988), 301–12; Alan M. Klein, "Sport and Culture as Contested Terrain: Americanization in the Caribbean," *Sociology of Sport Journal* 8 (1991), 79–85.

8. Burt Solomon, *The Baseball Timeline: The Day-by-Day History of Baseball from Valley Forge to the Present Day* (New York: Avon, 1997).

9. Milton Jamail, "Orioles Not First to Seek Showcase Visit to Cuba," *USA Today Baseball Weekly* 8:47 (February 10, 1999), 7; Gerald S. Gems, *The Athletic Crusade: Sport and American Cultural Imperialism* (Lincoln: University of Nebraska Press, 2006) 66; Paula Pettavino and Geralyn Pye, *Sport in Cuba: The Diamond in the Rough* (Pittsburgh: University of Pittsburgh Press, 1994).

10. People in Argentina and Brazil were playing baseball regularly, and further south, a ballgame was reported at Little America, Antarctica, in 1957 between civilians and SeaBees, which ended with the score, 11–6 after two innings, because of the −40°F degree temperatures.

11. "Value of Card Trip Apparent in Air Report," *Sporting News*, January 7, 1959, 16; Ron Briley, "The Chinese Wall and Murakami, Too: The Baseball Establishment and Post–World War II Perceptions of the Asian Other," in *The Cooperstown Symposium on Baseball and American Culture, 2003–2004*, ed. William M. Simons (Jefferson, NC: McFarland, 2005), 123–38.

12. Steve Bullock, *Playing for Their Nation: The American Military and Baseball During World War II* (Lincoln: University of Nebraska Press, 2004); Robert Daley, "Sports Explain the Nations," *New York Times*, August 23, 1959, SM66.

13. For the first time in fifty years, MLB franchises began to shift in 1953, when the Boston Braves moved to Milwaukee; then the St. Louis Browns moved to Baltimore to become the Orioles, and the Philadelphia Athletics moved to Kansas City. The Dodgers and Giants moves followed in 1958. MLB decided to conquer the West, but as Patricia Limerick has noted, vanquishing the frontier hasn't necessarily meant progress. According to Ron Briley, when "seeking El Dorado in the West, baseball ownership found lucrative financial veins to exploit." But it also brought troubling questions, such as the impact of franchise shifts on minor-league teams, disruptions of new communities, and lost identities in abandoned cities. In response to the Dodgers move, journalist Pete Hamill observed, "The three most hated men in America are Joseph Stalin, Adolf Hitler, and [Dodgers owner] Walter O'Malley." Besides the scars in Brooklyn, the "Battle of Chavez Ravine" in Los Angeles was just as devastating to the Mexican community uprooted to accommodate the Dodgers. Besides the threat of antitrust regulation, team expansion was provoked in 1959 by plans led by Branch Rickey for a competing Continental League, which was beaten back only by adding new MLB teams in New York, Houston, Minneapolis, and Los Angeles. Patricia Nelson Limerick, *The Legacy of Conquest: The Unbroken Past of the American West* (New

York: Norton, 1987); Dave Zirin, *A People's History of Sports in the United States* (New York: The New Press, 2008), 125; Ron Briley, "More Legacy of Conquest: Long-Term Ramifications of the Major League Shift to the West," in *Baseball History from Outside the Lines*, ed. John Dreifort (Lincoln: University of Nebraska Press, 2002), 231–45.

14. Samuel O. Regalado, *Viva Baseball! Latin American Major Leaguers and Their Special Hunger* (Urbana: University of Illinois Press, 1998); Samuel O. Regalado, "Viva Baseball! The Beginnings of Latin American Baseball," in *Baseball History from Outside the Lines*, ed. John Dreifort (Lincoln: University of Nebraska Press, 2002), 321–36; Roberto Gonzalez Echevarria, *The Pride of Havana: A History of Cuban Baseball* (New York: Oxford University Press, 1999).

15. Eugene J. McCarthy, "Diamond Diplomacy," *Elysian Fields Quarterly* 14:2 (1995), 12–15.

16. Tim Wendel, "Cuba: Behind the Curtain," in *Baseball Without Borders: The International Pastime*, ed. George Gmelch (Lincoln: University of Nebraska Press, 2006).

17. Senzel, *Baseball and the Cold War*; Stew Thornley, "Minneapolis Millers Versus Havana Sugar Kings: The 1959 Junior World Series," *National Pastime* 12 (1992), 42–44; Bill Weiss, "Sugar Kings Were Kings in Havana," *USA Today Baseball Weekly* 1:18 (August 2, 1991), 36.

18. Adrian Burgos, "Cuban Baseball Legacy Rich in American Heritage," *Memories and Dreams* (July–August 2006), 9–11; "Havana Shift Only Reasonable Action," *Sporting News* 149:26 (July 20, 1960), 14.

19. Senzel, *Baseball and the Cold War*.

20. Daniel M. Daniel, "Cuba's Political Climate Is Not Healthy For O.B.: Operating Club in Havana Is Called Incompatible with Ideals of America," *Sporting News* 149:24 (July 6, 1960), 10; "Latins Rhumba to Frick Tune—Fined $2,500," *Sporting News*, February 16, 1963, 4.

21. Rob Ruck, "Baseball in the Caribbean," in *Total Baseball*, ed. John Thorn and Pete Palmer (Toronto: Sports Media, 2004), 796–801; Milton Jamail, *Full Count: Inside Cuban Baseball* (Carbondale: Southern Illinois University Press, 2000).

22. Allen Guttmann, *Games and Empires: Modern Sports and Cultural Imperialism* (New York: Columbia University Press, 1994); Gems, *Athletic Crusade*, 97; Louis A. Perez Jr., "Between Baseball and Bullfighting: The Quest for Nationality in Cuba, 1868–1898," *Journal of American History* 81:2 (September 1994), 493–517; Roberto Gonzalez Echevarria, "The Game in Matanzas: On the Origins of Cuban Baseball," *Yale Review* 83:3 (July 1995), 62.

23. U.S.-Cuban relations were reflected in Max Apple's baseball short story, in which Fidel Castro describes his victory over the Cuban dictator Batista: "I lined his fascist pitch up his capitalist ass." Castro is chastised, however: "You took Cuba, our best farm [team] property, and went Commie with it." In response, he explains his revolution: "Cuba *libre* doesn't give a flying fuck for RBIs. The clutch hit is every minute here. Cuba loves you for your Cuban heart. I'll make you a colonel, a starter in the only game that counts. Your batting average will be counted in lives saved, in people educated, fed, and protected from capitalist exploitation." Max Apple, "Understanding Alvarado," in *The Oranging of America and Other Stories* (New York: Grossman, 1976); Paul Aron, "Why Didn't Castro Sign with the Senators?" in *Did Babe Ruth Call His Shot? (and Other Unsolved Mysteries of Baseball)* (Hoboken, NJ: Wiley, 2005), 121–26; Peter C.

Bjarkman, "Baseball and Fidel Castro," *National Pastime* 17 (1998), 64–68; Everardo J. Santamarina, "The Hoak Hoax: Castro and Hoak? Never Happened," *National Pastime* 14 (1994), 29–30; Peter C. Bjarkman, *Diamonds Around the Globe: The Encyclopedia of International Baseball* (Westport, CT: Greenwood Press, 2005); Don Hoak with Myron Cope, "The Day I Batted Against Castro," in *The Baseball Reader*, ed. Charles Einstein (New York: McGraw-Hill, 1983), 176–79; Peter C. Bjarkman, "Fidel on the Mound: Baseball Myth and History in Castro's Cuba," *Elysian Fields Quarterly* 16:3 (1999), 31–41.

24. Cockcroft, *Latinos in Baseball*, 129. The early 1960s was the heyday for Virgin Islands players, the Yankees and Dodgers both barnstormed Mexico, and the Nicaraguan League survived the Somoza dictatorship. In Chile, baseball was bolstered by Japanese mining engineers who played in the country's northern copper mines. Eric Wagner, "Sports," in *Handbook of Latin American Popular Culture*, eds., Harold Hinds and Charles Tatum (Westport, CT: Greenwood Press, 1985), 135–50; Horacio Ruiz, "Somoza May Revive Loop in Nicaragua," *Sporting News* 150:10 (September 28, 1960), 36; Horacio Ruiz, "Nicaraguan Winter League Folds; Loss of Government Aid Is Cited," *Sporting News* 164:15 (October 28, 1967), 30.

25. In response to Berlin Wall tensions, the *Sporting News* editors wrote: "Baseball has always been proud to do more than its share in providing physically fit young men for the military forces. If the country is preparing for an emergency, so must baseball." "Game Stands Ready to Do Its Share," *Sporting News* 152:2 (August 2, 1961), 12. Some used baseball to poke fun at the Cold War. In the early 1960s, the annual Baseball Writers of America dinner featured several skits, some mocking the Russians. In 1964 Paul Malloy published a spoof, *A Pennant for the Kremlin*, in which his protagonist dies hours after buying the Chicago White Sox. When it's learned he's left the team to the Kremlin, and when the Soviets manage the club to a major-league pennant, the Americans panic. Daniel M. Daniel, "'Taylorovich' Spink Subject of New York Writers' Skit," *Sporting News* 151:3 (February 8, 1961), 6; see also, "'Beizball' Game Big Mystery to Four Russian Scriveners," *Sporting News* 151:19 (May 31, 1961), 28; Paul Malloy, *A Pennant for the Kremlin* (New York: Avon, 1964); "Indians May Tour Russia for Series of Exhibitions," *Sporting News* 195:9 (March 20, 1965), 6.

26. D.J. Mrozek, "The Cult and Ritual of Toughness in Cold War America," in *Sport in America: From Wicked Amusement to National Obsession*, ed. D.K. Wiggins (Champaign, IL: Human Kinetics, 1995), 257–67.

27. Rable, "Patriotism, Platitudes and Politics," 363; David W. Zang, *Sports Wars: Athletes in the Age of Aquarius* (Fayetteville: University of Arkansas Press, 2001).

28. Dick Young, "Baseball's New Commissioner Sounds Off," *Sport* 41:6 (June 1966), 14; Bob Addie, "Eckert Honored for Aid to Morale in Vietnam," *Sporting News* 164:18 (November 18, 1967), 32.

29. "An Opportunity to Contribute," *Sporting News*, December 7, 1968, 14; "Baseball's Role in Our Life," *Sporting News*, March 17, 1968, 14.

30. Solomon, *Baseball Timeline*. Although Ron Fairly was in the reserves, he was nevertheless called up in 1961 and sent to Germany during the Berlin Crisis. Robert Creamer, "The Haven," *Sports Illustrated* 24:18 (May 2, 1966), 17; Robert Lipsyte, "Uniform Changes," *New York Times*, January 27, 1968, 20; "Defense Department Investigating Draft Status of 360 Pro Athletes," *Sporting News* 163:14 (April 22, 1967), 20.

31. Jason Karegeannes, "Baseball and the Vietnam War," paper presented at North American Society for Sport History Conference, Green Bay, WS, May 2005; Briley, "Ambiguous Patriotism," 4; "The Athlete and the Military Draft," *Sporting News*, January 14, 1967, 14; "Effects of War Light on Majors," *New York Times*, May 28, 1967, 28; Bill Fleischman, "Majors' Military Tab—$1.3 Million Per Year," *Sporting News* 172:5 (August 14, 1971), 21.

32. Al Hirshberg, "Carlos May: The Man Who Wouldn't Quit," *Sport* 49:6 (June 1970), 50–51, 80; Society for American Baseball Research, "Armed Forces Committee," September 2004, http://www.sabr.org.cfm?a=cms,c,523,43.0; Roy Gleason, *Lost in the Sun: Roy Gleason's Odyssey from the Outfield to the Battlefield* (Champaign, IL: Sports Publishing, 2005); Bob Hunter, "A Vietnam Hero Prizes Ted's Letter," *Sporting News* 167:10 (March 22, 1969), 12.

33. "Pro Athletes Depart for Military Service, Creating Some Skill Shortages," *Wall Street Journal* 170:36 (August 22, 1967), 1.

34. "Medal of Honor Winner Guest of Commissioner," *Sporting News* 164:14 (October 21, 1967), 8; Mickey Hershowitz, "A Farewell to General Eckert," *Baseball Digest* 27 (August 1969), 12–15; William Leggett, "Court Martial for a General," *Sports Illustrated* 29 (December 16, 1968), 24–25.

35. "Six-Man Major League Party Touring Vietnam," *Sporting News* 166:17 (November 9, 1968), 54; Stan Isle, "Vietnam Soldiers Cheer Banks, No. 1 Morale Booster," *Sporting News*, December 14, 1968, 31; Ross Newhan, "Fregosi Shaken to Bootstraps After Visiting War Casualties," *Sporting News* 164:25 (January 6, 1968), 51; "Players to Tour Military Hospitals," *Sporting News*, 168:16 (November 1, 1969), 16; Jim Ferguson, "Vietnam Trip on Bench's Jammed Slate," *Sporting News* 170:21 (December 5, 1970), 49; "Four Groups to Tour War Zones, Hospitals," *Sporting News* 170:15 (October 24, 1970), 22; Russell Schneider, "Vietnam GIs 'Are Amazing,' Says McDowell," *Sporting News*, December 5, 1970, 51; Ron Bergman, "GIs in Vietnam Cheer Blue–Bob Hope Comedy Battery," *Sporting News* 173:2 (January 22, 1972), 33; Jerome Holtzman, "Mr. Cub Doffs Lid to GIs in Vietnam," *Sporting News*, December 7, 1968, 45; "Rose Ready for Fast Helicopter Rides on Visit to GIs in Vietnam," *Sporting News* 164:17 (November 11, 1967), 42; Irvin Muchnick, "How Baseball Sent Its Hop to War," *Sports Illustrated* 36:17 (April 24, 1972), M3; Earl Lawson, "Pete's Praise Has No Limit When It Comes to GI Spirit," *Sporting News* 164:20 (December 2, 1967), 47.

36. Baseball Reliquary, "The Times They Were A-Changin'," www.baseballreliquary.com; Ron Briley, "Baseball and America in 1969: A Traditional Institution Responding to Changing Times," *Nine* 4:2 (1996), 263–81; Alan H. Levy, "Bad Dudes 'n Baseball: '60s' Culture and the Fate of Baseball's National Status," paper presented to the 19th Cooperstown Symposium on Baseball and American Culture, Cooperstown, NY, June 2007.

37. Briley, "Ambiguous Patriotism," 4; Zang, *Sports Wars*; Paul Hoch, *Rip Off the Big Game: The Exploitation of Sports by the Power Elite* (New York: Doubleday, 1973); Crawford, "Consensus All-American."

38. Robert Neyland, *Football as a Wargame* (Nashville: Falcon Press, 2002); Bob Andelman, *Why Men Watch Football* (Lafayette, LA: Acadian House, 2000). Secretary of Defense Melvin Laird referred to the escalation of bombing and the mining of

Haiphong Harbor as "an expansion ball club." Zirin, *People's History of Sports*, 184; Zang, *Sports Wars*; Michael MacCambridge, *America's Game: The Epic Story of How Pro Football Captured a Nation* (New York: Random House, 2004); Michael Rosenberg, *War as They Knew It: Woody Hayes, Bo Schembechler, and America in a Time of Unrest* (New York: Grand Central Publishing, 2008).

39. Warren Farrell, "The Super-Bowl Phenomenon: Machismo as Ritual," in *Jock: Sports and Male Identity*, ed. Donald F. Sabo and Ross Runfulo (Englewood Cliffs, NJ: Prentice Hall, 1980); Wanda Ellen Wakefield, *Playing to Win: Sports and the American Military, 1898–1945* (Albany: State University of New York Press, 1997).

40. Brett Walton, "Baseball and the Vietnam War," *Elysian Fields Quarterly* 24:2 (2007), 81–85; Voigt, *America Through Baseball*; Briley, "Ambiguous Patriotism," 4.

41. "Freehan Rescues Tiger Official from Attacker," *Sporting News* 165:26 (July 13, 1968), 33; Jim Ogle, "Ellis Helps to Cool It at Yale Demonstration," *Sporting News* 169:19 (May 23, 1970), 20.

42. Charles Feeney, "Ellis Awaiting Spring Test of Aching Elbow," *New York Times*, January 1, 1972, 31. Outfielder John Lowenstein cited a novel reason to prevent the Vietnam War's possible escalation out of control: "World War III," he worried, "would render all baseball statistics meaningless." Donald Hall with Dock Ellis, *Dock Ellis in the Country of Baseball* (New York: Coward, McCann & Geoghegan, 1976), 163; Peter Golenbock, *Amazin': The Miraculous History of New York's Most Beloved Baseball Team* (New York: St. Martin's, 2002), 205–6.

43. Robert B. Moncreiff, *Bart Giamatti: A Profile* (New Haven, CT: Yale University Press, 2007); James Tutte, "War Casualties Demand Full-Staff Flag at Shea," *New York Times*, October 16, 1969, 20.

44. Major-league officials required players to wear their hair short to show support for the war. According to Bouton, "If the choice for a pinch hitter or a relief pitcher was between a long-haired guy and a short-haired guy, the [latter] would get into the game." The hair rule has been revived today by some teams, including the New York Yankees and Los Angeles Dodgers. Jim Bouton, *Ball Four* (New York: Wiley, 1970); Briley, "Ambiguous Patriotism," 4; Zirin, *People's History of Sports in the United States*, 189; Walton, "Baseball and the Vietnam War," 81; Ron Briley, "The Oakland A's of 1972–1975 and the Counterculture in Baseball: Undermining the Hegemony of the Baseball Establishment," *Nine* 1:2 (Spring 1993), 142–62.

45. Zang, *Sports Wars*; Bouton, *Ball Four*.

46. Crawford, "Consensus All-American"; Robert Creamer, "Sacrilege," *Sports Illustrated* 36:25 (June 19, 1972), 10; Voigt, *America Through Baseball*.

47. "Royals Restore National Anthem," *Sporting News* 173:26 (July 8, 1972), 26; Robert Creamer, "Fourth of July Note," *Sports Illustrated* 37:1 (July 3, 1972), 9.

48. Curt Flood, *The Way It Is* (New York: Trident Press, 1971); Alex Belth, *Stepping Up: The Story of Curt Flood and His Fight for Baseball Players' Rights* (New York: Persea Books, 2006); Marvin Miller, *A Whole Different Ball Game: The Inside Story of the Baseball Revolution* (New York: Simon & Schuster, 1991); Brad Snyder, *A Well-Paid Slave: Curt Flood's Fight for Free Agency in Professional Sports* (New York: Viking, 2006); Charles P. Korr, *The End of Baseball as We Knew It: The Players Union, 1969–1981* (Urbana: University of Illinois Press, 2002); Dick Allen with Tim Whitaker, *Crash: The Life and Times of Dick Allen* (New York: Ticknor & Fields, 1981); Briley, "Ambiguous Patriotism," 4.

49. Arnold Rampersad, *Jackie Robinson: A Biography* (New York: Knopf, 1997), Jackie Robinson, "Violent Society: The American Way," *Pittsburgh Courier,* June 22, 1969.

50. Jackie Robinson, *I Never Had It Made: The Autobiography of Jackie Robinson* (Hopewell, NJ: Ecco Press, 1995).

51. Senzel, *Baseball and the Cold War.* Another SDS veteran complained about how difficult it was to enjoy conventional baseball as a leftist. David Jones, "I Played Right Field for the SDS," *Minneapolis Review of Baseball* 8 (January 1988), 32.

52. Walton, "Baseball and the Vietnam War," 81; Robert Lipsyte, "Only One More," *New York Times,* October 16, 1969, 58; Zang, *Sports Wars.*

53. Joseph L. Price, "'What So Proudly We Hailed': National Crisis, the National Anthem, and the National Pastime," paper presented at the 16th Cooperstown Symposium on Baseball and American Culture, Cooperstown, NY, June 2004; Jack Lang, "Stirring Mets' Program for POWs," *Sporting News* 175:25 (June 30, 1973), 31; Dick Miller, "Nixon Shares Angel Spotlight With Ex-POW," *Sporting News* 175:15 (April 21, 1973), 3; "Baseball Grants POWs Gold Lifetime Passes," *Sporting News* 175:6 (February 17, 1973), 47; Nicholas Evan Sarantakes, "Richard Nixon, Sportswriter: The President, His Historical All-Star Baseball Team, and the Election of 1972," *Journal of Sport History* 24 (1997), 190–93; Bowie Kuhn, *Hardball: The Education of a Baseball Commissioner* (New York: Times Books, 1987).

54. In 1971, Philip Roth satirized Richard Nixon in his novel *Our Gang.* To escape another crisis, the president must find a scapegoat. After considering Hanoi, the Berrigans, the Black Panthers, and Jane Fonda, he decides to blame baseball player Curt Flood, who's now living in Copenhagen. In his momentous "Something's Rotten in Denmark" speech to the nation, Nixon threatens to declare war if Denmark doesn't turn Flood over to the U.S. military, which has already landed on Danish soil. Philip Roth, *Our Gang* (New York: Bantam, 1971); Sarantakes, "Richard Nixon, Sportswriter," 190.

55. David Voigt, *America Through Baseball* (Chicago: Nelson Hall, 1976).

56. Jay Feldman, "Baseball in Nicaragua," *Whole Earth Review,* Fall 1987, 1–7.

57. Elizabeth DiNovella, "An American Story," *The Progressive,* July 2006, 43–44; David Maraniss, *Clemente: The Passion and Grace of Baseball's Last Hero* (New York: Simon & Schuster, 2006); Dave Zirin, "Roberto Clemente and the Value of a Number," *The Nation,* February 6, 2006; Bruce Markusen, "Roberto Clemente: Activist and Pioneer," in *Baseball as America: Seeing Ourselves Through Our National Game* (Washington, DC: National Geographic, 2001), 101–3; Joseph Durso, "Clemente Is in the Hall of Fame," *New York Times,* March 21, 1973, 31; Pat Jordan, "Dubious Triumph in Florida," *Sports Illustrated* 41:24 (December 9, 1974), 41.

58. In 1968, the Global Baseball League was launched to run teams in Latin America, Japan, and the United States. Tony Solaita became the first Samoan major leaguer. In 1969 the first foreign team, the Montreal Expos, was added to the majors. In China, baseball was viewed by the leaders of the Cultural Revolution as Western decadence, but some games were played in secret until 1974, the year the Guam Major League was formed. The Koreans were playing competitively in the Asian Amateur Baseball Championships, and in Thailand the Bangkok Boys Baseball Association was funded by the U.S. military and local corporations, such as Shell, TWA, and the Bank of America. Rory Costello, "The Tony Solaita Story: In Memory of Somoa's Only Ma-

jor League Player," http://members.aol.co/toliasolaita, 2000; Ross Peot, "Baseball in Bangkok," *Parks and Recreation* 7:6 (June 1972), 48; John B. Holway, *The Baseball Astrologer and Other Weird Tales* (New York: Total Sports Illustrated, 2000); "Bambino San," *Psychology Today* 25 (May–June 1992), 47, 90.

59. "Big Leaguers in Japan," *Newsweek* 63:13 (March 30, 1964), 59; Briley, "The Chinese Wall and Murakami, Too"; Commissioner Eckert saw barnstorming as effective anticommunist propaganda and secured a long-term agreement for MLB teams to tour Japan every two years, which still remains in effect. Eckert himself led the 1968 St. Louis Cardinals visit. "President Johnson Hails Dodgers' Trip to Japan," *Sporting News* 162:13 (October 15, 1966), 31; "President Sends Letter to Japan with Eckert," *Sporting News* 166:17 (November 9, 1968), 42.

60. The Nationalist support stopped at the Little League, however. In 1974 the San Francisco Giants signed Tan Shin-ming, the first Taiwanese professional ballplayer in the United States, but few other players had a shot for another two decades. Junwei Yu, *Playing in Isolation: A History of Baseball in Taiwan* (Lincoln: University of Nebraska Press, 2007); Joseph Timothy Sundeen, "A Kid's Game? Little League Baseball and National Identity in Taiwan," *Journal of Sport and Social Issues* 25:3 (August 2001), 260.

61. Morris, "Taiwan," 73; Chuck Nan, "The San Francisco Giants Spring Tour of Japan: March 1970," *Elysian Fields Quarterly*, Summer 2004, 38–42.

62. Zang, *Sports Wars*.

63. Ibid.

Chapter 10. Purging the Vietnam Syndrome (1976–1999)

1. "Patriotism Alive and Well," *Sporting News* 181:19 (May 15, 1976), 14; Jerome Holtzman, "For Monday, Spirit of '76 Never Flags," *Chicago Tribune*, April 28, 1996, D1; Richard Dozer, "Monday Earns Fans' Salute for a Flag-Rescue Mission," *Sporting News* 181:19 (May 15, 1976), 10; C. Phillip Francis, "Daddy's Flag," in *Grandstand Baseball Annual, 1996*, ed. Joseph Wayman (Downey, CA: Joseph Wayman, 1996), 182–83; Bruce Markusen, "Allegiance to the Flag," *Cubs Quarterly* 15 (September 1996), 150–53.

2. Markusen, "Allegiance to the Flag"; Joe Resnick, "Rick Monday Saved the Flag 30 Years Ago," *Washington Post*, April 22, 2006.

3. Robert Creamer, "Revolutionary Idea," *Sports Illustrated* 44:9 (March 1, 1976), 11; Paul Lukas, "Flag-Waving," *Village Voice* 46:39 (October 2, 2001), 165; Floyd Conner, *Baseball's Most Wanted* (Dulles, VA: Potomac Books, 2000).

4. Les Carpenter, "Safe at Home: 25 Years Ago, a Gift from Major League Baseball Helped Iran Hostages Reconnect with America," *Washington Post*, January 20, 2006, A01.

5. The *Sporting News* also lauded organized baseball's contribution: "For more than 30 years, MLB has purchased over 1000 copies of the *Sporting News* each week for distribution to American soldiers, sailors, marines and airmen overseas." Richard Waters, "Baseball's Service to Military," *Sporting News* 193:15 (April 10, 1982), 6.

6. The president's annual appearance as a spectator to start each season is said to "symbolically renew the bonds that unite the country, its leaders, and the game." "Baseball as Patriotism and Pride," National Baseball Hall of Fame, http://web .baseballhalloffame.org/index.jsp.

7. Carl M. Cannon, "The Cheering Never Stops," *Washingtonian,* April 2006, 70–73, 112–14; John Bloom, *A House of Cards: Baseball Card Collecting and Popular Culture* (Minneapolis: University of Minnesota Press, 1997); Edward W. Wood, *Worshipping the Myths of World War II: Reflections on America's Dedication to War* (Washington, DC: Potomac Books, 2006).

8. George C. Rable, "Patriotism, Platitudes and Politics: Baseball and the American Presidency," *Presidential Studies Quarterly* 19 (Spring 1989), 363–72. Besides the Soviet Union, the New York Yankees were also regularly called the Evil Empire.

9. Phillies broadcaster Harry Kalas once observed, "Two-thirds of the earth is covered by water. The rest is covered by Garry Maddox." Nicknamed "Secretary of Defense" for his fielding prowess, Maddox may have symbolized baseball's vision of global reach. W.B. Gould, "Baseball and Globalization: The Game Played and Heard and Watched 'Round the World (with Apologies to Bobby Thomson)," *Indiana Journal of Global Legal Studies* 8 (Fall 2000), 85–120; Larry Moffi, *The Conscience of the Game: Baseball's Commissioners from Landis to Selig* (Lincoln: University of Nebraska Press, 2006).

10. The Mexican League's Laredo club became the first binational sports team, with ballparks on both sides of the border. David G. LaFrance, "A Mexican Popular Image of the United States Through the Baseball Hero, Fernando Valenzuela," *Studies in Latin American Popular Culture* 4 (1985), 14; Alan M. Klein, *Baseball on the Border: A Tale of Two Laredos* (Princeton, NJ: Princeton University Press, 1997).

11. John Krich, *El Beisbol: Travels Through the Pan-American Pastime* (New York: Prentice Hall, 1989).

12. Bill Littlefield, "A Real World Series at Last?" *World Monitor,* November 1988, 84–86.

13. In May 1943, an OS2U Kingfisher, an observation plane, crashed off the California coast, and Brown received the Coast Guard Silver Medal for swimming out to rescue a flyer. Brown then enlisted. He joined the New York Yankees after World War II but then missed two seasons serving in the Korean War.

14. Paula Pettavino and Geralyn Pye, *Sport in Cuba: The Diamond in the Rough* (Pittsburgh: University of Pittsburgh Press, 1994); Philip Bennett, "Game Didn't Help Them Escape Long," *Boston Globe,* August 13, 1987, D2; James D. Cockcroft, *Latinos in Beisbol: The Hispanic Experience in the Americas* (Danbury, CT: Franklin Watts, 1996); Michael M. Oleksak and Mary Adams Oleksak, *Beisbol: Latin Americans and the Grand Old Game* (Indianapolis: Master's Press, 1996); "Garrick Throws a Curve," NewsBites, *Media Watch,* June 1, 1989, www.mediaresearch.org/mediawatch/1989/watch19890601.asp.

15. Robert Elias, "Exporting the Horsehide American Dream: The Hidden Side of Nicaraguan Baseball," in *The Contested Diamond: Essays on Baseball and Politics,* ed. Ron Briley (Jefferson, NC: McFarland, 2010). According to Nicaraguan pitcher Eloy Morales, "Baseball is integrated into society, a part of working, production and campesino life. Before, it was remote from the poverty and repression, like Hollywood." Eric Wagner, "Sport in Revolutionary Societies: Cuba and Nicaragua," in *Sport and Society in Latin America,* ed. Joseph L. Arbena (New York: Greenwood Press, 1988), 113–36; Ronnie Lovler, "Some Revolutionary Production: When They Play Hardball in Nicaragua, the Army Puts It All Together," *Boston Sunday Globe,* Novem-

ber 25, 1984, 55; Rob Ruck, "The View from Left Field," *Mother Jones* 10 (July 1985), 13; Jay Feldman, "View from Managua: Baseballs and News in Nicaragua," *Sacramento News & Review,* January 25, 1990, 16–17; Andy Kay Lieberman, "Baseball Diplomacy— USA/Nicaraguan Style, 1996," *International Institute for Sports Diplomacy,* February 27, 1996, 5.

16. In 1987, a U.S. charity delivered two thousand pounds of baseball equipment, toys, and educational supplies to Nicaragua. Then a "Bats Not Bombs" campaign arranged ball games for diplomacy between a Nicaraguan club and several California college teams. Bob McCoy, "Baseball for Peace," *Sporting News* 200:24 (December 9, 1985), 10; Robert Elias, "Baseball: A Force for Social Change?" *Berkeley Voice,* August 18, 1988, 13–14, 22–23; Robert Elias, "Baseball and Social Change," *Minneapolis Review of Baseball* 8 (January 1988), 24.

17. About Nicaragua, a conservative columnist complained, "I have never come across the liberal who—if he had any interest in baseball—wasn't a New York Met supporter (I take that back: Trotskyists root for Boston). The Yanks are viewed as 'proto-fascist.' Left-thinking people [back] the Mets because there are obvious parallels between it and whatever Third World communist movement is fashionable . . . both the Met ascent and the Sandinista insurgency began as people's revolts, struggling to gain popular support against Mickey Mantle and Anastasio Somoza. . . . Each engineered a revolution: the Sandinista in 1979, the Mets in 1969 . . . Somoza has gone, [so] now Yankee America is the oppressor. . . . And they don't even face a Contra insurrection." D. Keith Mano, "Baseball Politics," *National Review* 40 (August 19, 1988), 55–57.

18. Joseph A. Reaves, *Taking in a Game: A History of Baseball in Asia* (Lincoln: University of Nebraska Press, 2002), 125; Urban Lehner, "In Korea, It's Take Me Out to the Yagoo and Buy Me Some Dried Squid and Rice," *Wall Street Journal* 199:60 (March 29, 1982), 23; Peter C. Bjarkman, "American Baseball Imperialism, Clashing National Cultures, and the Future of Samurai *Besuboru,*" *Studies on Asia,* series 3, 3:2 (Fall 2006), 123–40.

19. Young Hoon Lee, "The Decline of Attendance in the Korean Professional Baseball League: The Major League Effects," *Journal of Sports Economics* 7:2 (May 2006), 187–200; "Will Park Serve?" *USA Today Baseball Weekly* 7:29 (October 8, 1997), 17; Reaves, *Taking in a Game,* 137; Joseph A. Reaves, "Korea: Straw Sandals and Strong Arms," in *Baseball Without Borders: The International Pastime,* ed. George Gmelch (Lincoln: University of Nebraska Press, 2006).

20. David Cataneo, *Peanuts and Crackerjack: A Treasury of Baseball Legends and Lore* (Nashville, TN: Rutledge Hill, 1991). Tensions mounted when Americans threatened Japanese records. When Randy Bass challenged his home-run mark, Sadaharu Oh allegedly had his hurlers pitch around Bass. While the American Warren Cromartie was dubbed the Master of Besaboru, some Japanese rooted against his bid to bat .400. William Kelly, "Blood and Guts in Japanese Professional Baseball," in *The Culture of Japan as Seen Through Its Leisure* (Albany: State University of New York Press, 1998), 95–111; William Kelly, "Baseball in Japan: The National Pastime Beyond National Character," in *Baseball in America: Seeing Ourselves Through Our National Game* (Washington, DC: National Geographic, 2001), 47–49; Robert Whiting, *The Chrysanthemum and the Bat: Baseball Samurai Style* (New York: Dodd, Mead, 1977); Robert

Whiting, "The Master of Besaboru," *Sports Illustrated*, August 21, 1989, 68–69; Robert Whiting, *The Samurai Way of Baseball: The Impact of Ichiro and the New Wave from Japan* (New York: Warner Books, 2004); Jerome Holtzman, "The Japanese Call This Baseball? *Wa* in the World Is Going On Over There?" *Chicago Tribune*, July 21, 1989, section 4, p. 3; Stephen I. Thompson, "Baseball and the Heart and Mind of Japan: The Randy Bass Case," in *Baseball History 4*, ed. Peter Levine (Westport, CT: Meckler, 1991), 39–50; Russell Field, "Beyond Mr. Baseball: The Japanese National Pastime," *Dugout*, June 1995, 20–24. Despite being a World War II prisoner of war in Japan, Bill Simmons started Protect Our Nation's Youth (PONY) for U.S. and Japanese kids, and later Henry Aaron and Sadaharu Oh launched the World Children's Baseball Fair. Roy Gillespie, "Tale of Three Men Who Shaped PONY Baseball/Softball in Asia," *International Baseball Rundown* 6:3 (April 1997), 21.

21. An abandoned Japanese rice paddy was converted into a reproduction of the field from the film *Field of Dreams*. Greg Mitchell, "Baseball at Ground Zero," *The Progressive* 51 (August 1987), 20–22; Robert Whiting, *You Gotta Have Wa: When Two Cultures Collide on a Baseball Diamond* (New York: Vintage, 1991); Michael Manning, "Globalization of Baseball in Popular Culture," in *Baseball and American Culture*, ed. Edward J. Rielly (New York: Haworth Press, 2003), 109–19.

22. George Black, "Japan Turns the Double Play: Scouting the Caribbean," *Nation*, March 20, 1989, 370–74.

23. The quest for Japanese players dramatically intensified: veteran scout Katsuyoshi Miwata of Kobe's Orix Blue Wave team committed suicide after failing to sign a top prospect. Jane Gross, "Mixing Two Cultures in a Diamond Test Tube," *New York Times*, May 15, 1990, A16; Susumu Awanohara, "Major League Gambit: Seattle Mariners Hope to Be Japan's Team," *Far Eastern Economic Review*, December 23, 1993, 50; Lara D. Nielsen, "Exertions: Acts of Citizenship in the Globalization of Major League Beisbol," PhD dissertation, New York University, 2002; Gould, "Baseball and Globalization." At the 2000 Sydney Olympics, after throwing a ceremonial pitch to New York Mets catcher Mike Piazza, Japanese prime minister Yoshiro Mori told South Korean president Kim Dae-Jung, "The Mets owner offered me a contract, but I declined because I'm more concerned about [Japan's] relations with the South Koreans."

24. Murray Chass, "McGwire Criticizes League for the Opener in Japan and Cites Greed," *New York Times*, March 21, 2000; "Japanese, S. Korean Leaders Conduct Baseball Diplomacy," *Sports Illustrated*, September 23, 2000, http://sportsillustrated.cnn.com/olympics/newswire/2000/09/23/387267115746_afp/.

25. John Holway, "Taiwan Little Leaguers Grow into Big Leaguers," *National Pastime* 12 (1992), 48–50.

26. Andrew Morris, "Taiwan: Baseball, Colonialism, and Nationalism," in *Baseball Without Borders: The International Pastime*, ed. George Gmelch (Lincoln: University of Nebraska Press, 2006), 64, 84; Andrew Morris, "Baseball, History, the Local and the Global in Taiwan," in *The Minor Arts of Daily Life: Popular Culture in Taiwan*, ed. D.K. Jordan, A.D. Morris, and M.L. Moskowitz (Honolulu: University of Hawaii Press, 2004), 326–81; "Baseball in Taiwan," *Travel in Taiwan* 11 (October 1996), 30.

27. Joseph A. Reaves, "A History of Baseball in China: How America's Game Helped End Educational Exchanges in the Late Qing Dynasty, Taught Sun Yat-sen's Revolutionaries to Throw Hand Grenades, and Endured the Cultural Revolution,"

paper presented to the North American Society for Sport History Annual Conference, Windsor, Ontario, May 22–25, 1998, 45, 46, 48. Elsewhere in Asia and the Pacific, national baseball championships were played in India, Israel, Mongolia, and Sri Lanka. Hawaii was producing more major leaguers, and in 1993 President Bill Clinton apologized for America's illegal takeover there a century earlier. New Zealand was playing serious baseball, and in 1989 the Australian Baseball League teams each aligned with a U.S. major league club. In 2000, former major league catcher Dave Nilsson led his Australian national team to the Olympic finals. Bruce Mitchell, "A National Game Goes International: Baseball in Australia," *International Journal of the History of Sport* 9 (August 1992), 288–301.

28. Ralph Summy and Michael E. Salla, eds., *Why the Cold War Ended* (Westport, CT: Greenwood Press, 1995); "Russians Taking Up Baseball," *New York Times*, July 20, 1987, 3; Steve Wulf, "The Russians are Humming," *Sports Illustrated*, April 23, 1992, 38–44; Kim Steven Juhase and Blair A. Ruble, "Soviet Baseball: History and Prospects," *National Pastime* 8 (1988), 45–47; John Leo, "Evil Umpires? Not in Soviet Baseball," *Time* 130 (August 10, 1987), 56; "Mighty Ivan at the Bat," *Newsweek* 110 (July 27, 1987), 36.

While this story is contested, baseball may have had a role in the U.S.-Soviet battle for the heavens: In 1969, when Apollo 11 commander Neil Armstrong first set foot on the moon, his comment, "That's one small step for [a] man, one giant leap for mankind," was heard by millions. But just before he reentered the lander, he made the remark, "Good luck, Mr. Gorsky." Many at NASA thought it referred to a rival Soviet cosmonaut, but no Gorsky could be found. When questioned about his remark, Armstrong always just smiled. Many years later, a reporter raised the question again. Since Mr. Gorsky had died, Armstrong finally responded. When he was a kid growing up, Armstrong was playing baseball in his backyard when his friend hit a ball over the fence. It landed in his neighbor's yard by the bedroom windows. Armstrong's neighbors were Mr. and Mrs. Gorsky. When he leaned down to pick up the ball, the young Armstrong heard Mrs. Gorsky shouting at Mr. Gorsky: "Sex! You want sex?! You'll get sex when the kid next door walks on the moon!"

29. Shelley Smith, "Diamonds in the Rough," *Sports Illustrated* 73 (August 6, 1990), 24–25.

30. With free agency flourishing by the late 1980s, it was proposed as a way of getting rid of world leaders. Gerald Rosen, "Free Agency for World Leaders," in *Writing Baseball*, ed. Jerry Klinkowitz (Urbana: University of Illinois Press, 1991), 121-23; Bill Lee and Richard Lally, *Have Glove Will Travel: Adventures of a Baseball Vagabond* (New York: Crown, 2005).

31. The Russians remained in the North American consciousness well after the Berlin Wall fell. After a big win by Montreal over Cincinnati, sportswriter Jeff Blair observed, "Nobody's gone after Reds with this much vigor since Joseph McCarthy." Bill Barich, "Going to the Moon," *New Yorker* 67 (July 22, 1991), 74–79; Adi Ignatius, "Here's the Real News: Baseball Player Asks, 'What's a Contract?'" *Wall Street Journal*, April 7, 1992, 3; Manning, "Globalization of Baseball in Popular Culture," 109.

32. "Fay Vincent Strikes Out," *National Review* 44:3 (February 17, 1992), 18.

33. Fay Vincent, *The Last Commissioner: A Baseball Valentine* (New York: Simon & Schuster, 2002); Molly Ivins and Lou DuBose, *Shrub: The Short but Happy Political Life of George W. Bush* (New York: Vintage, 2000); Kevin Phillips, *American Dynasty: Aris-*

tocracy, Fortune, and the Politics of Deceit in the House of Bush (New York: Viking, 2004); Peter Schweizer and Rochelle Schweizer, *The Bushes: Portrait of a Dynasty* (New York: Doubleday, 2004).

34. Vincent, *The Last Commissioner*, 157.

35. "Banners Yet Waving," *The Economist*, August 12, 1989, 18.

36. This echoed a similar announcement by Henry Adams a century earlier. Francis Fukuyama, *The End of History and the Last Man* (New York: Free Press, 1991); Howard Zinn, "The Specter of Vietnam," *Common Dreams*, June 26, 2003, http://www.commondreams.org/views03/0626-03.htm.

37. William Jeanes, "Baseball in World War II," *Sports Illustrated* 75 (August 26, 1991), 5–6.

38. Andrew Zimbalist, *In the Best Interests of Baseball? The Revolutionary Reign of Bud Selig* (Hoboken, NJ: Wiley, 2006); Bill Brown, "The Meaning of Baseball in 1992," *Popular Culture* 4 (Fall 1991), 43–69.

39. When Pittsburgh Pirates outfielder Andy Van Slyke removed the Canadian flag emblem from his helmet, leaving only the American one, the commissioner scolded him. Van Slyke claimed he was honoring U.S. Gulf War troops: "I didn't mean anything derogatory toward Montreal or Canada. But to be honest, I don't think anybody in Quebec will be upset. . . when we were there last year, they booed their own national anthem." Van Slyke was soon in more trouble when he complained about the Pirates fielding: "They had better defense at Pearl Harbor." Brent Shyer, "Orel Stands Tall, Stands Proud," *Los Angeles Dodgers Magazine and Scorecard* 4:1 (1991), 69; Tony Kornheiser, "When Winds of War Shift, Games Will Matter," *Los Angeles Times*, January 20, 1991, 9; Bob Nightengale, "No, Canada," *Sporting News* 211:16 (April 22, 1991), 18.

40. Michael Hiestand, "Baseball Players Wear Flags on Helmets," *USA Today*, March 8, 1991, 1C; Jack Curry, "Let the Bats and Patriotism Ring to Celebrate a New Season," *New York Times*, April 8, 1991, C5.

41. Joe Gergen, "As Johnny Comes Marching Home, Major League Baseball Stands in Salute," *Sporting News* 211:16 (April 22, 1991), 6; Andy Esposito, "Mets Memorabilia: Tributes and Fund-Raisers Raise Spirit of America," *New York Mets Inside Pitch* 19:11 (November 2001), 26. In nearby Africa, the African Baseball and Softball Association formed in 1990 in Nigeria. In 1997, the Zimbabwe Baseball and Softball Association trained players, and Dodgers owner Peter O'Malley donated a ball field. Kevin Brooks, "The Babies of International Baseball: Nigeria's Youth Team Comes to 'the Worlds,'" *National Pastime* 12 (1992), 51–54; Marty Appel, "Zimbabwe and Israeli Baseball: Two Nations of Growth," *Memories and Dreams*, July–August 2006, 28–29.

42. In Eastern Europe, baseball was growing in Poland, Romania, and the Czech Republic, where an MLB International Envoy arrived in 1992. In 1994, a Strausberg ballpark was created from a former East German army training ground, and the Sun Warriors team became the town's main pastime. In 1996, U.S. Marine Elliott Fellman introduced baseball to Lithuania while serving on a military liaison team. Gary Gildner, "The Warsaw Sparks," *Baseball History 3*, ed. Peter Levine (Westport, CT: Meckler Books, 1990), 1–32; Toby Smith, "Romania Discovers New Meaning for Pitch," *Baseball America*, December 21, 1998–January 3, 1999, 5. In 1997 the Montreal Expos began the first European baseball academy and a new team, the Amsterdam Expos.

Holland and Italy had become dominant baseball nations, winning most European base-ball championships. Italy became a popular place for American professionals to play. In France, by 1992 there were more than twelve thousand baseball players on 270 teams, as well as three international-class stadiums. MLB wasn't the only baseball promoter: the Japanese electronics giant Hitachi sponsored the University of Paris baseball club. West Germans learned baseball from American GIs and had five hundred clubs, thirty thousand registered players, and perhaps sixty thousand players in all. The best baseball in Belgium was being played by the Levis Braves in Brasschaat, where U.S. sailors had implanted the game after World War II. In 1997, the International Baseball Associa-tion, centered in Lausanne, Switzerland, boasted more than a hundred member na-tions. The Chicago Cubs and the Minnesota Twins became the first MLB teams to designate permanent European scouts. Jay Feldman, "In Holland, Honk If You Love Baseball," *National Pastime* 13 (1993), 50–52; "Montreal Expos in Europe," *International Baseball Rundown*, October–December 1997, 23; Peter Carino, "Baseball in Transla-tion: The Italian Professional League," *Nine* 7:2 (Spring 1999), 49–58; Peter Carino, "Italy: No Hotdogs in the Bleachers," in *Baseball Without Borders: The International Pas-time*, ed. George Gmelch (Lincoln: University of Nebraska Press, 2006); Rudolph Chelminski, "When the French Play Baseball, They Play It Their Way, *Smithsonian* 25:1 (April 1994), 94–101; Eliot Cohen, "The Latest Fashion in French Diamonds," *Sports Illustrated* 76 (June 15, 1992), 6–8; Ian Thomsen, "Baseball, the Belgian Pas-time," *International Herald Tribune*, August 23, 1994; Bob Rybarczyk, "The IBA and the World Amateur Baseball Movement," *National Pastime* 12 (1992), 64–66; Sherri Eng, "Baseball, European Style," *Giants Program*, April–May 2003, 14. A new British National League formed in 1991, and an MLB tour introduced baseball to English youngsters. Hosted by President Bush, Queen Elizabeth II attended her first game at Baltimore's Memorial Stadium but showed no interest. Joe DiMaggio tried getting her autograph, but she had no idea who he was and declined. David Porter, "Untold Saga of Europe's Big Leaguers," *National Pastime* 12 (1992), 70–76; Harvey Sahker, "'Snap-shots' of Britball," *Dugout*, June–July 1995, 27–30; Jim Jones, "MLBI Envoys Find Success and Happiness in Europe," *International Baseball Rundown* 1:14 (October 1992), 5; Tim Wendel, "Queen's Visit Could Allow Life to Imitate Art," *USA Today Baseball Weekly* 1:6 (May 10, 1991), 21.

43. Trent Frayne, "Opting Out of the Great White North," *Maclean's* 103 (Au-gust 6, 1990), 48.

44. Mark Kingwell, "The Toronto Blue Jays: Colonialism, Civility, and the Idea of a National Team," *Nine* 2:2 (1994), 209–32.

45. Frank Manning, "Reversible Resistance: Canadian Popular Culture and the American Other," in *The Beaver Bites Back? American Popular Culture in Canada*, ed. David Flaherty and Frank Manning (Montreal: McGill–Queen's University Press, 1993), 3–28.

46. In 1999, Blue Jays manager Tim Johnson was caught lying about having Viet-nam War combat experience. He told his players fake battle stories to get them to play harder, but his six-year marines duty was solely with the reserves. According to John-son, "I've had 30 years of guilt lifted off my back. Friends of mine were going to Viet-nam when I was going to spring training. While they were off fighting and getting killed, I was playing baseball." Robert Knight Barney, "Diamond Rituals: Baseball in

Canadian Culture," in *Baseball History 2*, ed. Peter Levine (Westport, CT: Meckler Books, 1989), 1–21; Robert Knight Barney, "Whose National Pastime? Baseball in Canadian Popular Culture," in *The Beaver Bites Back? American Popular Culture in Canada*, ed. David Flaherty and Frank Manning (Montreal: McGill–Queen's University Press, 1993), 152–62; Sean Hayes, "America's National Pastime and Canadian Nationalism," in *Sport and Memory in North America*, ed. Stephen G. Wieting (London: Frank Cass, 2001), 157–84; Murray Chass, "False War Tales Lead Jays to Drop Johnson," *New York Times*, March 18, 1999; S.R. Hill, "Baseball in Canada," *Indiana Journal of Global Legal Studies* 8 (Fall 2000), 37–72; William Humber, "Canada in the Country of Baseball," in *Diamonds of the North: A Concise History of Baseball in Canada*, ed. William Humber (Toronto: Oxford University Press, 1995), 3–14.

47. George W. Bush's candidacy continued a curious trend. Several commissioner nominees, including Bush, Richard Nixon, and Dwight Eisenhower, became president shortly after being proposed for the commissionership.

48. Stephen J. Ducat, *The Wimp Factor: Gender Gaps, Holy Wars, and the Politics of Anxious Masculinity* (Boston: Beacon Press, 2004); Noam Chomsky, *The New Military Humanism* (Monroe, ME: Common Courage Press, 1999).

49. "War-Torn Croatia One of Many Nations Crying Out for Equipment," *International Baseball Rundown*, May 1996, 8. Burns formed Friends of Greek Baseball, the first Greek pro team, and amateur clubs. This people-to-people diplomacy provoked Baltimore Orioles owner Peter Angelos to bring MLB to Greece. "Little League Comes to War-Torn Bosnia-Herzegovina," *International Baseball Rundown* 8:2 (July 1999), 22; Theodora Tongas, "An Olympian Task: Pitching Baseball to Greece," *Chicago Tribune*, January 6, 2000, C8; "Semper Fi at Work For Lithuanian Baseball," *International Baseball Rundown* 7:1 (January 1998), 21; Cynthia P. Schneider, "Diplomacy That Works: 'Best Practices' in Cultural Diplomacy," *Cultural Diplomacy Research Series*, 2003: 4–5. In 1999, several Anaheim Angels players spent a day aboard an aircraft carrier, and manager Terry Collins flew with the Blue Angels. In exchange, navy petty officer Mark Probst was made "Angel for a Day." Deron Snyder, "Navy Blue Appropriate for the Angels," *USA Today Baseball Weekly* 9:51 (March 10, 1999), 3; Chris Carola, "War Games: Enlist Exhibit at Hall of Fame Tells of Those Who Fought Instead of Playing," *USA Today Baseball Weekly* 5:10 (May 31, 1995), 6; Lisa Winston, "Uncle Sam Calls O's Pitcher to Active Duty," *USA Today Baseball Weekly* 6:5 (April 24, 1996), 25.

50. Walter LaFeber, *Michael Jordan and the New Global Capitalism* (New York: Norton, 2002).

51. Robert Lewis, " 'Soft Ball': MLB Shifts from Neocolonizer to Multinational Corporation," in *Cooperstown Symposium on Baseball and American Culture, 2005–2006*, ed. William M. Simons (Jefferson, NC: McFarland, 2007), 247.

52. Ibid.; Peter C. Bjarkman, *Baseball with a Latin Beat* (Jefferson, NC: McFarland, 1994); Nielson, "Exertions," 220.

53. Albert Theodore Powers, *The Business of Baseball* (Jefferson, NC: McFarland, 2003).

54. Lewis, " 'Soft Ball,' " 247.

55. Claire Smith, "Land of Rising Opportunities: Major Leagues Target Japan in International Marketing Effort," *Sporting News*, March 4, 1991, 24; Donald Dewey, "Making a Pitch for Baseball: The Sport Is No Longer a Curiosity in Europe," *Europe*

300 (October 1990), 34–35; Philip Seib, "The Future of Baseball," *CQ Researcher Online* 8:36 (September 25, 1998); Jeff Elijah, "World Baseball Day or Bust," *International Baseball Rundown* 4:7 (July 1995), 1.

56. "U.S. Peace Corps Volunteers Spreading Baseball Worldwide," *International Baseball Rundown*, May 1996, 8; Thomas Boswell, "Franchise for the World," *Washington Post*, April 19, 1991, B1; Seib, "Future of Baseball."

57. Erle Norton, "Baseball Hopes to Be Big Hit in Europe," *Wall Street Journal* 221:113 (June 11, 1993), B1; Murray Chass, "In the Game's Efforts to Go Global, Idea of a World Cup Gains Support," *New York Times*, January 19, 1997, S9.

58. "Major League Baseball Telecasts Shown in More Than 200 Countries," *International Baseball Rundown* 6:9 (October 1997), 23; Paul White, "Murdoch Has Owners Taking the World Serious," *USA Today Baseball Weekly* 8:1 (March 25, 1998), 8; Jeremy Howell, "Luring Teams, Building Ballparks," in *Baseball and the American Dream: Race, Class, Gender and the National Pastime*, ed. Robert Elias (Armonk, NY: M.E. Sharpe, 2001), 207–13; Nielson, "Exertions."

59. Larry Stone, "MLB's Japan Tour Another Selig Step onto World Stage," *Seattle Times*, April 2, 2000, D10; Mike Marqusee, "World Games: The U.S. Tries to Colonize Sport," *Colorlines* 3:2 (July 31, 2000), 36.

60. At the 1952 games, a Finnish version of baseball was played. In 1956, the United States played Australia at the Melbourne Olympics, drawing more than one hundred thousand spectators. In 1964, the United States played Japan in the Tokyo Olympics. Pete Cava, "Baseball in the Olympics," *National Pastime* 12 (1992), 2–8; David Osinski, "Baseball and the Olympics," in *Total Baseball*, ed. John Thorn and Pete Palmer (Toronto: Sports Media, 2004), 802–4; Kristen Jones, "The Game Goes for Gold: A History of Olympic Baseball," *Memories and Dreams*, July–August 2006, 20–22. U.S. coach Ron Fraser imposed a system of calling pop-ups and fly balls by giving the players military ranks: Pitchers had no rank. Catchers were buck privates. First and third basemen were sergeants, which allowed them to discipline pitchers and catchers. Middle infielders were captains. The left and right fielders were majors, which gave them authority over everybody except the center fielder—the general. And, "if you don't do what he says, you could be court-martialed." Rick Lawes, "Chain of Command," *USA Today Baseball Weekly* 2:12 (June 17, 1992), 39; Moffi, *Conscience of the Game*.

61. Peter C. Bjarkman, "The *Real* World Series: Cubans Again Dominate Olympic Action," *Baseball Research Journal*, 26 (1997), 28–29.

62. Rick Lawes, "For Gold Glory: USA Wrapped Up in Quest to Beat Cuba," *USA Today Baseball Weekly* 6:17 (July 17, 1996), 28. On the positive side, the Colombia Winter League and Brazilian Baseball Confederation were formed—the latter serving forty thousand players. In 1992, Jose Pett became the first Brazilian major leaguer, joining the Toronto Blue Jays. In the Virgin Islands, MLB launched a program to revitalize baseball passions there. Rory Costello, "Baseball in the Virgin Islands," *Baseball Research Journal* 28 (1999), 33–40.

63. Krich, *Beisbol*, 38; Allan Ebert, "How Rawlings Uses Haitian Women to Spin Profits off U.S. Baseball Sales," *Multinational Monitor* 3:8 (August 1982); Allan Ebert, "Un-sporting Multinationals: Baseball Manufacturers Taking a Walk on Workers' Rights," *Multinational Monitor* 6:18 (December 1985); Jim Rice, "Where Angels Fear to Tread," *Sojourner's*, November 1994.

64. Barbara Ehrenreich, "Haiti Redux," *Z Magazine*, March 1994, http://zena.secureforum.com/Znet/ZMag/articles/ehren3.htm.

65. At least some Haitians began to play baseball themselves: Baseball World Inc. introduced the sport to children in remote villages in the late 1990s. "Number-One Brand in Baseball Works to Make Baseball Number-One Global Sport," *International Baseball Rundown* 5:6 (July 1996), 7; Tracy Bengston, "Baseball Outreach Is a Hit in Haiti," *Miami Herald*, September 23, 1999.

66. "For the Love of Yakyu," *New York Times*, March 22, 2006.

67. Pat Coleman, "RBI Scores Big in Inner Cities and Overseas," *USA Today Baseball Weekly* 5:21 (August 16, 1995), 59.

68. Alan M. Klein, *Sugarball: The American Game, the Dominican Dream* (New Haven, CT: Yale University Press, 1991); Alan M. Klein, "Trans-nationalism, Labour Migration and Latin American Baseball," in *The Global Sports Arena: Athletic Talent Migration in an Independent World*, ed. John Bale and Joseph Maguire (London: Frank Cass, 1994), 82–105; Adrian Burgos, *Playing America's Game: Baseball, Latinos, and the Color Line* (Berkeley: University of California Press, 2007); Steve Fainaru, "Baseball's Minor Infractions: In Latin America, Young Players Come at a Bargain Price," *Washington Post*, October 26, 2001, D01; Steve Fainaru, "The Business of Building Ballplayers: In Dominican Republic, Scouts Find the Talent and Take the Money," *Washington Post*, June 17, 2001, A1.

69. The problems could be seen even in the apparent success stories. Marcos Breton, "Field of Broken Dreams: Latinos and Baseball," *Colorlines* 3:1 (2000), 13; Marcos Breton and José Luis Villegas, *Away Games: The Life and Times of a Latin Baseball Player* (New York: Simon & Schuster, 1999).

70. The Dominican winter league attracted top major leaguers in the off-season. But after free agency began in the early 1980s, the financial incentive and the Dominican league declined. The flow of players began going only toward the United States. While a number of Dominicans have made the major leagues, the country has done poorly in international baseball competitions. Gare Joyce, *The Only Ticket off the Island* (Toronto: Lester & Orpen Dennys, 1990); Rob Ruck, "Three Kings Day in Consuelo: Cricket, Baseball, and the Cocolos in San Pedro de Macoris," in *Sport in Latin America and the Caribbean*, ed. Joseph L. Arbena and David G. LaFrance (Wilmington, DE: Scholarly Resources, 2002), 71–88; Rob Ruck, *The Tropic of Baseball: Baseball in the Dominican Republic* (Westport, CT: Meckler Books, 1991); Klein, "Transnationalism, Labour Migration and Latin American Baseball"; Peter C. Bjarkman, *Diamonds Around the Globe: The Encyclopedia of International Baseball* (Westport, CT: Greenwood Press, 2005). One future star, Alfonso Soriano, did use the Japan Leagues to avoid the usual MLB exploitation of Dominican players. He signed with the Hiroshima Carp team and used his good job in Japan as leverage with the New York Yankees, who had to pay well to lure him away. Jim Allen, "Game Reinforces Key Cultural Values," February 26, 2007, http://sports.espn.go.com/mlb/asia/columns/story?id=2766653.

71. Will MacKenzie, "Playing Their Way Out: Dominicans in Major League Baseball," *Dugout* 1:1 (April 1993), 12–13; Milton Jamail, "Baseball's Latin Market," *National Pastime* 12 (1992), 83–86; Bill Brubaker, "Hey, Kid, Wanna Be a Star?" *Sports Illustrated*, July 13, 1981, 62–76.

72. Rob Ruck, "Chicos and Gringos of Beisbol Venezolana," *Baseball Research Journal*, 1986, 75–78.

73. Arturo J. Marcano Guevara and David P. Fidler, "Baseball's Exploitation of Latin Talent," *NACLA Report on the Americas* 37:5 (2004), 15; Arturo J. Marcano Guevara and David P. Fidler, *Stealing Lives: The Globalization of Baseball and the Tragic Story of Alexis Quiroz* (Bloomington: Indiana University Press, 2002).

74. A. Vargas, "The Globalization of Baseball: A Latin American Perspective," *Indiana Journal of Global Legal Studies* 8 (Fall 2000), 21–36.

75. Bjarkman, *Baseball with a Latin Beat*; Eric Forrest, "Major League Baseball's Efforts to Bring Latin Talent to the States: A Brief History Filled with Hardship," paper presented at the 18th Cooperstown Symposium on Baseball and American Culture, Cooperstown, NY, June 2006; Steven Kruczek, "Worldly Game: The Globalization of Baseball," *Harvard International Review* 20 (Fall 1998), 12–13.

76. Burgos, *Playing America's Game*.

77. The Padres also arranged Hawaii's first major-league game, in 1997, and a working agreement with Japan's Chiba Lotte Marines. Justin Martin, "Can Baseball Make It in Mexico?" *Fortune* 134 (September 30, 1996), 32; Barry Bloom, "Mission Accomplished: The Padres Have Practiced Globalization Without the Help of Major League Baseball," *Sport* 88:9 (September 1997), 46–50; Dan Cisco, *Hawaii Sports* (Honolulu: University of Hawaii Press, 1999); Joel Millman, "Dugouts of the Desperate," *POV Magazine*, September 1998, 96–105; Owen Perkins, "Viva Beisbol! Part Two: Our Intrepid Sportswriter Flies from Cuba to Mexico for the Rockies' Season Opener," *Colorado Springs Independent* 7:15 (April 21, 1999), 24.

78. Milton Jamail, "Orioles Not First to Seek Showcase Visit to Cuba," *USA Today Baseball Weekly* 8:47 (February 10, 1999), 7; "And Now, Baseball Diplomacy?" *Time*, May 19, 1975, www.time.com/time/printout/0,8816,945385,00.html; Michael M. Oleksak and Mary Adams Oleksak, *Beisbol: Latin Americans and the Grand Old Game* (Indianapolis, IN: Master's Press, 1996); John Stockwell, *In Search of Enemies: A CIA Story* (New York: Norton, 1978); Peter Kornbluh, "Baseball Diplomacy," *In These Times*, May 16, 1999, 15–17; "And Now, Baseball Diplomacy?" *Time*, May 19, 1975, www.time.com/time/printout/0,8816,945385,00.html.

79. "The Cuban Bunt," *Wall Street Journal* 187:5 (January 8, 1976), 12.

80. Robert DiNardo, "Can Cuba Beat the Yankees?" *Mother Jones*, August 1981, 15–16; Howard Cosell, *I Never Played the Game* (Boston: G.K. Hall, 1986).

81. Baseball remained a symbol of resistance: the Cubans renamed the Matanzas ballpark the Estadio Victoria de Giron, commemorating the American defeat at the Bay of Pigs. Russell Schneider, "Cuban Reservoir of Baseball Talent Contained by Politics," *Baseball Digest* 44 (April 1985), 93–95; Eric Enders, "Through the Looking Glass: The Forgotten World of Cuban Baseball," *Nine* 12:1 (2003), 147–52; Bjarkman, "American Baseball Imperialism, Clashing National Cultures, and the Future of Samurai *Besuboru*"; Thomas Boswell, "How Baseball Helps the Harvest, or What the Bay of Pigs Did to the Bigs," in *How Life Imitates the World Series* (New York: Penguin, 1983), 81–96.

82. Sally Stapleton, "Cuban Baseball," *Minneapolis Star Tribune*, March 29, 1987, 14. By 1990, U.S. reporters were mocking Cuba's "socialist" baseball, which had "a regimented style that has minimal non-socialist moves, such as the hit-and-run and the

stolen base . . . baseball [in Cuba] is a collective game. . . . [When there's a foul ball,] they obediently throw the ball back on the field. That's socialism in action." To the contrary, the Cubans were more likely to use the hit-and-run and the rest of the inner game than the Americans. After the revolution, when Fidel Castro said, "In Cuba, there's no stealing anymore, not even in baseball," he was making a rhetorical point; base stealing was actually more common in the Cuban game. And if throwing the ball back under economic crisis conditions was socialist, then U.S. baseball was socialist during the world wars and the Great Depression. Dave Hoekstra, "Cuban Game Is a Study in Socialism," *Chicago Sun-Times*, February 4, 1990, 20–21, 24.

83. Manning, "Globalization of Baseball in Popular Culture"; Kevin Baxter and Fernando Dominguez, "Baseball *Sí*, Cuba *No*," *Sporting News*, March 21, 1994, 12; "Cubans Excited over Possible Orioles Game," Associated Press, January 5, 1999; Kornbluh, "Baseball Diplomacy"; Eugene J. McCarthy, "Diamond Diplomacy," *Elysian Fields Quarterly* 14:2 (1995), 12–15; Peter C. Bjarkman, "Lifting the Iron Curtain of Cuban Baseball," *National Pastime* 16 (1997), 30–34; Tim Wendel, "A Full Count on Cuba: Defections, Politics Diminish a Proud Baseball Heritage," *USA Today Baseball Weekly* 6:45 (January 29, 1997), 20; "Where the Cold War Is Still Hot," http://sportsillustrated.cnn.com/events/1996/olympics/commemoration.html, 1996.

84. Andrei Codrescu, "El Duque: Fugitive from His Homeland, Hero in His New Land, Orlando Hernandez Casts His Lot with Yankee Imperialism," *Life* (1999), 56–64; Thomas R. Dominczyk, "The New Melting Pot: As American Attitudes Toward Foreigners Continue to Decline, Athletes Are Welcomed with Open Arms," *Seton Hall Journal of Sports Law* 8 (1998), 165–75; Jon Wertheim and Don Yaeger, "Fantastic Voyage," *Sports Illustrated* 89:22 (November 30, 1998), 60.

85. "Cuban Crackdown to Further Restrict Movement to USA," *USA Today Baseball Weekly* 8:2 (April 1, 1998), 41; Tom DiPace, "Super Secret Sports Agent: Joe Cubas Helps Cuban Defectors Reach the Majors," *USA Today*, December 15–21, 1999, 8. Since U.S. law prevented Cubans from applying as Cubans, it left them two options. The Arocha model skirted both the American and MLB directives, for he defected while already in the United States; such cases went into the regular June baseball draft. The El Duque model required a perilous escape, avoiding repatriation, and getting residency elsewhere before applying for a U.S. visa. Since such players weren't covered by the draft, a bidding war might occur, widening the gap between rich and poor major-league teams. It also carried the possibility of drowning, getting shot, or getting caught. Families were abandoned, sometimes forever. It required the renunciation of Cuban citizenship, and likely never being able to return home. It risked not getting U.S. citizenship, leaving the player without a country. Unscrupulous agents pushed players into defections with exaggerated promises. Players might resort to dangerous smugglers for themselves or their families. If MLB ever frees itself from U.S. Cuban policy, then these problems could be solved. Mathew Greller, "Give Me Your Tired, Your Poor, Your Fastball Pitchers Yearning for Strike Three: How Baseball Diplomacy Can Revitalize Major League Baseball and United States–Cuba Relations," *American University International Law Review* 14 (November–December 1999), 1647–1713; Matthew J. Frankel, "Major League Problems: Baseball's Broken System of Cuban Defection," *Boston College Third World Law Journal* 25 (2005), 383–428; Scott M. Cwiertny, "The Need for a Worldwide Draft: Major League Baseball and Its Re-

lationship with the Cuban Embargo and U.S. Foreign Policy," *Loyola of Los Angeles Entertainment Law Journal* 20 (Spring 2000), 391–428.

86. Gerald S. Gems, *The Athletic Crusade: Sport and American Cultural Imperialism* (Lincoln: University of Nebraska Press, 2006); Owen Perkins, "Hot Corners: An American Sports Writer in Cuba Lauds the Universal Language of Beisbol," *Colorado Springs Independent* 7:14 (April 14, 1999), 16; Thomas W. Lippman, "U.S. Ready to Play Ball with Cuba: Clinton to Ease Trade Embargo, Using Orioles as Envoys," *Washington Post*, January 5, 1999, A1.

87. Jeanine A. Delay, "The Curveball and the Pitch: Sports Diplomacy in the Age of Global Media," *Journal of the International Institute* 7:1 (1999); Thomas Carter, "The Political Fallacy of Baseball Diplomacy," *Peace Review* 11.4 (December 1999), 579–84; Paula Pettavino and Philip Brenner, "More Than Just a Game," *Peace Review* 11:4 (1999), 523–30.

88. Jeff Stein, "Foul Ball," *Salon*, April 30, 1999, www.salon.com/news/feature/1999/04/30/baseball/print.html.

89. Reporters ignored the economic similarities between Cuba's state-owned baseball enterprise (which they universally scorned) and the MLB monopoly. The sportswriter Art Thiel did observe, "Sitting side by side at the game in Havana were Fidel Castro, who hijacked a nation in 1959, and baseball commissioner Bud Selig, the used-car salesman who hijacked the Seattle Pilots in 1970. Have there ever been two men who have ascended so dubiously, accomplished so little, and stayed in power so long?" "Orioles' Cuba Policy Has Critics Seeing Red," *San Francisco Examiner*, May 21, 2000, D-5; Jason Weiss, "The Changing Face of Baseball: In an Age of Globalization, Is Baseball Still as American as Apple Pie and Chevrolet?" *University of Miami International and Comparative Law Review* 8 (1999–2000), 123–39; Henry Schulman, "Agents Assail Orioles' Cuban Policy," *San Francisco Chronicle*, May 23, 2000, E7; Timothy W. Maier, "Fidel's Baseball Players Safe in U.S. but Out at Home," *Insight on the News* 16:24 (June 26, 2000), 16–18; Andrea Kupfer Schneider, "Baseball Diplomacy," *Marquette Sports Law Review* 12 (2001), 473–86.

90. Lisette Corsa, "The Cuban Coach: Rigoberto Betancourt's Life in Baseball Takes a Seventh-Inning Stretch," *Miami New Times* 16:21 (August 30, 2001); Kornbluh, "Baseball Diplomacy"; Joel Zoss and John Bowman, *Diamonds in the Rough: The Untold History of Baseball* (Lincoln: University of Nebraska Press, 2004). After the Cuban-Orioles series, the Anaheim Angels applied for a U.S. Treasury license to play in Cuba. Former big-league pitcher Bill Lee began goodwill baseball tours to Cuba. Pastors for Peace sponsored a U.S.-Cuba Friendship Caravan. Friends of Cuba organized a humanitarian baseball trip with Global Exchange. The St. Thomas College team visited to play the University of Havana club. And a California youth team went to Cuba for baseball diplomacy. The tour was organized by Richard Murray, a member of the Veterans of Foreign Wars and the Garberville Veterans for Peace. The national VFW ordered him not to use VFW logos, but Murray was photographed with Castro wearing his VFW hat, for which he was court-martialed and stripped of his membership privileges. Lee and Lally, *Have Glove Will Travel*; John Manuel, "Visit to Cuba Enlightens St. Thomas Team," *Baseball America*, February 21–March 5, 2000, 40; Bob Doran, "Vamos a Cuba." *North Coast Journal*, June 8, 2000, www.northcoastjournal.com/060800/cover0608.html.

91. Russell Schneider, "Indians' Wahoo Symbol Facing a Legal Skirmish," *Sporting News* 173:4 (February 5, 1972), 43; David Berreby, "Baseball Team's Logo Suit May Be Settled—but How?" *National Law Journal* 4 (June 21, 1982), 3; David Stanley, "Do You Give a Tomahawk Chop About the Braves Nickname?" *Atlanta Inquirer* 31:20 (December 14, 1991), 6; David Stanley, "The Tomahawk Chop and the Eye of the Beholder," *Atlanta Inquirer* 31:14 (November 2, 1991), 5; "The Indian Sign," *Newsweek* 79:5 (January 31, 1972), 68; Marty Twersky, "Indians Always Lose—Even in Baseball," *Black Sports*, 3:3 (September 1973), 45, 65; Jane Harris, "Real Injun Is Braves' Mascot," *Sporting News* 168:13 (October 11, 1969), 8.

92. Leonard Koppett, "Trouble on the Reservation," *Sporting News* 173:4 (February 5, 1972), 5; Alan Bairner, *Sport, Nationalism, and Globalization: European and North American Perspectives* (Albany: State University of New York Press, 2001), 91–113, 163–77; Wells Trombley, "An Indian on the Warpath," *Sporting News* 173:4 (February 5, 1972), 35.

93. "Indian Activists Angered over Tomahawk Chop," *Navajo Nation Today* 27 (October 29, 1991), 11; Mark Trahant, "No Rhyme or Reason to Chop," *Navajo Nation Today* 27 (October 29, 1991), 6; Ward Churchill, *Indians Are Us? Culture and Genocide in Native North America* (Monroe, ME: Common Courage Press, 1993); John Hopkins, "Chop Doesn't Hurt Native Americans," *USA Today Baseball Weekly* 1:35 (December 6, 1991), 35; Cornel Pewedardy, "Indian Portrayals Are Often Offensive," *USA Today Baseball Weekly* 1:35 (December 6, 1991), 34; Stedman Graham, "What's in a Name—Plenty," *Inside Sports* 18:6 (June 1996), 8. Portland's *Oregonian* newspaper banned Indian team names, and the Cuyahoga County, Ohio, libraries banned the Cleveland Indians logo. Deron Snyder, "Closing the Book on Chief Wahoo," *USA Today Baseball Weekly* 9:6 (May 5, 1999), 3.

94. Paul White, "Native Americans Gaining Awareness on World Stage," *USA Today Baseball Weekly* 5:31 (October 25, 1995), 15; Mark Trahant, "'Indian' Label Alters Reality," *USA Today Baseball Weekly* 5:31 (October 25, 1995), 6; Burt Solomon, *The Baseball Timeline: The Day-by-Day History of Baseball from Valley Forge to the Present Day* (New York: Avon, 1997), 192; Tom McNichol, "A Major League Insult?" *USA Weekend*, July 4, 1997, 13; "Wahoo Burned," *USA Today Baseball Weekly* 9:3 (April 14, 1999), 48.

95. Will Leitch, "If the Indians Win, Do Native Americans Get Civil Rights?" *Deadspin*, February 13, 2007, http://deadspin.com/sports/mlb/if-the-indians-win-do-native-americans-get-civil-rights-248670.php; Filip Bondy, "Bud's Uncivil Wrong," *New York Daily News*, March 8, 2007; "The Civil Rights Game," *Sports Frog*, March 8, 2007, http://www.sportsfrog.com/2007/03/the_civil_rights_game.php.

96. Free agency meant ballplayers were no longer bound to their teams and existing salaries but instead could offer their services on the free market to the highest bidder.

97. Noam Chomsky, *The New Military Humanism* (London: Pluto Press, 1999).

98. Robert F. Burk, *Much More Than a Game: Players, Owners and American Baseball Since 1920* (Chapel Hill: University of North Carolina Press, 2001); Roger I. Abrams, "The Public Regulation of Baseball Labor Relations and the Public Interest," *Journal of Sports Economics* 4:4 (November 2003), 292–301; Steve Beitler, "The Empire Strikes Out," *Baseball Research Journal* 36 (2007), 58–60. Such demands risked the possibility that Congress might rescind MLB's antitrust exemption. But as the top spender among professional sports lobbyists, perhaps MLB felt well-enough protected. Bill King,

"MLB Tops Leagues in Lobbying Efforts," *Sportsbusiness Journal,* October 11-17, 1999, 6.

99. Mike Lupica, *Summer of '98: When Homers Flew, Records Fell, and Baseball Reclaimed America* (New York: Putnam's, 1999).

100. Did displays of baseball and military prowess indicate real American power, or were they instead last-gasp gestures by a nation in decline? A crisis of masculinity emerged at the end of the nineteenth century. Had a similar need to reclaim American virility arisen a century later? Ducat, *Wimp Factor;* Benjamin Rader, "A Bat and a Ball: Exclamation Point of Our Time: The Home Run Mystique," *Christian Science Monitor* 90:216 (October 1, 1996), 11.

101. Richard Ben Cramer, "The America That Ruth Built," *Newsweek,* June 24, 1998; Larry Stone, "The Home Run, Baseball's Glamour Event," in *The Best of Baseball Digest,* ed. John Kuenster (Chicago: Ivan Dee, 2006), 434–37.

Chapter 11. Foreign Policy on Steroids (2000-2009)

1. Mark Sappenfield, "Baseball in Wartime? It's Been the American Way Since 1861; Season Opens for a Sport Uniquely Tied to Military Conflict," *Christian Science Monitor,* March 31, 2003, 2; Anne Proctor, "Chairman, Baseball Commissioner, Honor Korean War Veterans," www.defenselink.mil.

2. David Slater and Peter J. Taylor, ed. *The American Century: Consensus and Coercion in the Projection of American Power* (Oxford, UK: Blackwell, 1999); Bruce Cumings, "Still the American Century," *Review of International Studies* 25 (1999), 271–99.

3. John Lewis Gaddis, "Living in Candlestick Park," *Atlantic Monthly,* April 1999, 65–74.

4. Andrew Zimbalist, *In the Best Interests of Baseball? The Revolutionary Reign of Bud Selig* (Hoboken, NJ: Wiley, 2006); Howard Bryant, *Juicing the Game: Drugs, Power and the Fight for the Soul of Major League Baseball* (New York: Viking, 2005).

5. Ziauddin Sardar and Merryl Wyn Davies, *American Dream, Global Nightmare* (Cambridge, UK: Icon Books, 2004); Tarek Atia, "Baseball and Swamps," *Cairo Live,* April 2, 2006, www.cairolive.com/newcairolive/dardasha/swamps.html; Marqusee quoted in Steven W. Pope, "Sport, Colonialism and Empire," paper presented at Historians on Sport Conference, International Centre for Sport History and Culture, De-Montfort University, October 30, 2004, 1–19; Susan M. Matarese, *American Foreign Policy and the Utopian Imagination* (Amherst: University of Massachusetts Press, 2001); Ziauddin Sardar and Merryl Wyn Davies, *Why Do People Hate America?* (New York: Disinformation Books, 2003).

6. Ron Briley, "Don't Let Hitler (or the Depression) Kill Baseball: Franklin D. Roosevelt and the National Pastime, 1932–1945," in *Franklin D. Roosevelt and the Shaping of American Culture,* ed. Nancy Beck Young, William D. Pederson, and Bryon W. Daynes (New York: M.E. Sharpe, 2001), 119–33; Fay Vincent, *The Last Commissioner: A Baseball Valentine* (New York: Simon & Schuster, 2002); Ron Briley, "The Myth and Reality of Major League Baseball," April 10, 2006, http://hnn.us/articles/23553.html. The only pro ballplayer killed in the terrorist attacks was Mike Weinberg, a New York City firefighter and former Detroit Tigers minor leaguer. Scott Miller, "Sports World Remains What It Should Be—the Great Escape," September 10, 2002, http://cbs.sportsline.com/print/mlb/story/5701288. Mark Lawrence devised plans to

escape a baseball stadium after terrorists attack, even writing the headlines: "Bin Laden/Al Qaeda Plants Dirty Bomb," "Terrorists Attack Baseball Stadium with Remote-Controlled Plane," and "Bio-Terror Attack Occurs at a Baseball Game." According to Lawrence, "Bin Laden wants to hit us in the heart of America, and you don't get any more American than Major League Baseball. Why [are we facing] a future that looks like a nightmare from the movie *Armageddon*? Because Bible prophecy is starting to play out . . . many Christian evangelists claim we are living in the 'last days.'" Mark Lawrence, "Terrorists Attack Baseball Game with Dirty Bomb," *Secrets of Survival*, n.d., www.secretsofsurvival.com/survival/baseball_terrorist_attack.html.

7. Rebecca S. Kraus, "A Shelter in the Storm: Baseball Responds to September 11," *Nine* 12:1 (2003), 88–101; Frank Dell'Apa, "Patriotism on Display by Fans," *Boston Globe*, September 19, 2001, E3.

8. Kevin Cook, "Schilling's War Games: World War II Ace," *Sports Illustrated* 90:21 (May 24, 1999), 34.

9. Steve Kroner, "A Game of Healing: Documentary on Baseball and Post–September 11," *San Francisco Chronicle*, September 10, 2004, D2; Jerry Beach, "Mets Bring Holiday Cheer to Families of Terrorist Attacks," *New York Mets Inside Pitch*, 20:2 (February 2002), 8.

10. Frank Ardolino, "Playing in the Bush League: *The Rookie* and the Baseball Presidency," *Nine* 12:1 (2003), 1–24; Ned Martel, "Learning After 9/11 That There Is a Balm in Baseball," *New York Times*, September 14, 2004, D1. Comparing a ball game to the recently launched Afghanistan War, Pastor Kelly Boggs observed, "Unlike baseball, it has been difficult to keep score. We want to know we are winning, and we want to know now." Because we're spoiled by speed in our everyday lives, he said the war will "push the limits of our time tolerance." According to Boggs, Hall of Famer Yogi Berra's dictum "It ain't over till it's over" has "never been more applicable than to the war on terrorism." Perhaps so, for the White House soon described it as a "war without end." Kelly Boggs, "Baseball and the War on Terrorism: Who's Ahead and What Inning Is It?" *Baptist Press News*, October 19, 2001, www.bpnews.net/printerfriendly.asp?ID=11975.

11. Norbert Elias and Alan Dunning, *The Quest for Excitement: Sport and Leisure in the Civilizing Process* (London: Blackwell, 1994).

12. Lara Nielsen, "Exertions: Acts of Citizenship in the Globalization of Major League Beisbol," PhD dissertation, New York University, 2002.

13. Edwin Chen, "Bush Gives Fear a Bronx Cheer at World Series," *Los Angeles Times*, October 31, 2001, A12; Eric Alterman, "The Many Man-Crushes of Chris Matthews," *The Nation*, April 9, 2007, 9; Bill Littlefield, "Of Baseball and Country," April 13, 2006, www.onlyagame.org/features/2006/04/country.asp.

14. Thomas Boswell, "Balance of Terror," in *Heart of the Order* (New York: Penguin, 1989), 247–52; Nielsen, "Exertions."

15. Jason Patrick Scheller, "The National Pastime Enlists: How Baseball Fought the Second World War," master's thesis, Texas Tech University, 2002; Ken Rosenthal, "Now Isn't the Time to Argue over Money," *Sporting News*, September 24, 2001, 5; Bill Gallo, "Avs Lead the Parade: Despite a Time-Out for Terror, 2001's Roster Was Full," *Westword* 25:18 (January 3, 2002), 10.

16. John Cassidy, "Yankee Imperialist," *New Yorker*, July 8, 2002, 34.

17. Instead of treating the terrorist assaults as crimes against humanity and relying on international.law enforcement, as had every other nation subjected to such attacks, the White House portrayed the assaults as acts of war and proceeded accordingly. John Kuenster, "High and Low Points of a Season Prolonged by Attack on America," *Baseball Digest* 60 (December 2001), 21–23.

18. Gallo, "Avs Lead the Parade," 10.

19. Jeremy Goldberg, "Sporting Diplomacy: Boosting the Size of the Diplomatic Corps," *Washington Quarterly* 23:4 (2000), 63–70; Stephen J. Ducat, *The Wimp Factor: Gender Gaps, Holy Wars, and the Politics of Anxious Masculinity* (Boston: Beacon Press, 2004).

20. "Baseball During War Time," www.ticketretriever.com/article-baseball-during-war-time.html; Robert J. Hughes, "Futures & Options: Play Ball!" *Wall Street Journal*, March 29, 2002, W2; Marian Russell, "The Blessings of Baseball and New Beginnings," *San Francisco Chronicle*, April 14, 2002, E2; Dan Wachtell, "Make Baseball, Not War: Returning to a Pastime," *Daily Princetonian*, April 8, 2002.

21. Bob Herbert, "Stepping Up to the Plate," *New York Times*, July 8, 2002, A19. After being deployed to Afghanistan, Tillman developed grave doubts about U.S. military policy and was formulating a response when he was killed. His death, by friendly fire, was covered up by the Pentagon so his celebrity sacrifice could be further exploited. Eventually his family learned the truth and came out against the war. Dave Zirin, "Pat Tillman: Our Hero," *The Nation*, October 24, 2005, 5.

22. Beginning in 2002, I've petitioned the Giants each year to hold a Peace Workers Appreciation Day to supplement the one honoring U.S. soldiers. According to the club, they're still studying the idea. Among the Giants military veterans was manager Dusty Baker, who joined the reserves rather than the National Guard in the late 1960s because he didn't want "to shoot or fight Americans at antiwar demonstrations." Baker claimed he applied marine tactics to the baseball diamond: "Knowing when to attack, when to retreat and how to allocate your resources." Sherri Eng, "We Were Soldiers: Their Major League Baseball Careers Interrupted, Former Ballplayers Recall Their Days in the Military," *San Francisco Chronicle*, May 27, 2002, C9. The weeklong Defense Department program for sixty civilian public-opinion leaders included Pentagon briefings. Participants went into the field with each of the military services, observing exercises, firing weapons, and joining in training. Mead visited bases, flew on military aircraft, and observed amphibious landings, urban combat techniques, and special-operations assaults.

23. James M. Lindsay, "It's Still Baseball and Apple Pie," *Australian Financial Review*, September 10, 2002.

24. Walter Shapiro, "Baseball Strike Talk Cheapens Post–September 11 Patriotism," *USA Today*, August 28, 2002, A 07.

25. Francis D. Cogliano, "Baseball and American Exceptionalism," in *Sport and National Identity*, ed. Dilwyn Porter and Adrian Smith (New York: Routledge, 2004), 145–67; Rob Morse, "The Anti-War, Pro-Baseball Alliance," *San Francisco Chronicle*, October 28, 2002, A2.

26. Adopting President Bush's wartime rhetoric, sports radio host Damon Bruce said that, on the steroids issue, "You're either with us or against us; it's time to draw a line in the sand." Yet coverage of baseball's steroids scandal focused on the hitters and ignored the pitchers—especially hurlers in their forties, like Clemens, who were per-

forming as though they were in their twenties. The cheerleading for America's hopped-up military interventions by the gung-ho, Hummer-driving Clemens would seem ironic when the pitcher's ongoing performance enhancement was exposed several years later. "Some A's, M's Jittery About Trip with War Looming," Associated Press, March 17, 2003; George Vecsey, "When Clemens Touched a Family Touched by 9/11," *New York Times*, March 16, 2008, C3.

27. Hal Bodley, "Baseball Scuttles Openers in Japan," *USA Today*, April 2, 2006, C1.

28. Was the Hall recognizing military service generally or only U.S. military service? At least one Hall of Famer served in a foreign military: Juan Marichal was in the Dominican Air Force. Eric Enders, "Petroskey Shames Hall," *Elysian Fields Quarterly* 20:3 (Summer 2003), 45; Scot Mondore, "1942: When Baseball Went to War," February 21, 2004, www.baseballhalloffame.org/news/article.jsp?ymd=20070221&content_id=1121&vkey=hof_news.

29. Ira Berkow, "Hall of Fame Will Tolerate No Dissent," *New York Times*, April 11, 2003, S4; Petroskey's previous Hall guests were all Republicans, including former Reagan staffer Ken Duberstein (talking about the 2000 elections) and New York governor George Pataki. The New York Republican State Committee held part of its annual convention in Hall meeting rooms. "Anti-War Actors Get Apology from Hall of Fame," *People's Weekly World* 17:47 (April 26, 2003), 15.

30. "Author Kahn Snubs Hall of Fame in Protest," *Detroit Free Press*, April 12, 2003, 8B; Mitch Albom, "The Lunacy of Misguided Patriotism," *Detroit Free Press*, April 13, 2003, 1E. Historian Tim Wendel observed, "Certain institutions need to stay above the fray. During the Vietnam War, it was baseball . . . that eventually brought us back together . . . in the 1975 [World Series] we were reunited . . . we should let the game work its magic." Others warned against letting the Republicans steal another American symbol—baseball. Tim Wendel, "Hall's Closed Stance on 'Durham' is Pure Bull," *USA Today Sports Weekly*, April 16–22, 2003, 63.

31. Gwen Knapp, "Bullheaded Decision by Hall President," *San Francisco Chronicle*, April 13, 2003, B2; Enders, "Petroskey Shames Hall." In 2008, however, Petroskey resigned under pressure for alleged fiscal mismanagement. He was then hired by Hall of Famer and team president Nolan Ryan for a job in the front office of George W. Bush's former team, the Texas Rangers. Ari Fleischer left the White House and became a consultant for the Don't Take My Bat Away Coalition, which lobbies against the return of wooden bats to amateur baseball despite growing evidence that metal bats are dangerous. Along with everything else, the bats apparently need to be juiced too. Grace Rauh, "Ex-White House Spokesman Now a Voice for Metal Bats," *New York Sun*, August 20, 2007.

32. Joby Warrick, "New Details on WMD 'Fabricator' Emerge," *Washington Post*, June 25, 2006, 1; Ronald Kessler, *The CIA at War: Inside the Secret Campaign Against Terror* (New York: St. Martin's, 2003). To drum up further support for broader U.S. military actions against terrorism, the president created the Bob Hope Patriot Award. Its first recipient, in 2003, was Mike Radford, whom the Missouri House of Representatives had already designated its Ambassador of Patriotism. Radford, a born-again Christian and former Kansas City Royals shortstop, organized military tributes around the nation.

33. Finally broken in real life in 2004, the curse supposedly ensured that, as punishment for having sold Babe Ruth to the Yankees in 1919, the Red Sox would never again win a World Series. John Breneman, "Bin Laden Claims Responsibility for

'Curse of the Bambino,'" *Humor Gazette*, February 17, 2004, www.humorgazette .com/osama_babe1003.html. Still tongue in cheek, Breneman had even worse news. Besides bin Laden and America's other evil adversary, Saddam Hussein, President Bush had identified another "imminent threat" to America and its national pastime: the New York Yankees dictator George Steinbrenner's "brazen acquisition of the most powerful weapon in baseball." According to Breneman, Bush claimed "the only way to deal with Steinbrenner, who shocked the nation by adding Alex Rodriquez to his already devastating arsenal," was to "'take him out.'" Since economic sanctions, like baseball's luxury tax, failed to stop Steinbrenner from "stockpiling an offensive jugger- naut so powerful that it threatens to destroy America's sacred game," Bush claimed "a preemptive strike" was the "only way to topple the Steinbrenner regime." It was "time to smoke him out" of his heavily fortified Yankee Stadium compound. Critics called for diplomacy, but Bush was "itching to attack Steinbrenner's so-called Bronx Bombers with a squadron of F/A-18E fighter jets." Government intelligence revealed that Steinbrenner also "acquired arms [El Duque Hernandez] from communist Cuba" and with Rodriquez, he had "the A-bomb," proof he was harboring weapons of mass destruction. John Breneman, "Bush Vows to Stop Yankee Madman," *Humor Gazette*, February 17, 2004, www.humorgazette.com/osama_babe1003.html.

34. Elisabeth Bumiller, "White House Letter: How Baseball Shaped Bush as the Person He Is," *International Herald Tribune*, April 18, 2005.

35. Carl M. Cannon, "The Cheering Never Stops," *Washingtonian*, April 2006, 70–73, 112–14. Foreign policy analyst William Arkin observed, "I went to a Red Sox game and couldn't help notice the press box: tiers of desks filled with print, radio, tele- vision and other media all reporting every move . . . more reporters cover the Sox, just one baseball team, than cover the Pentagon." William Arkin, "If Only War Reporting Were More like Sports Reporting," May 22, 2007, http://blog.washingtonpost.com/ earlywarning/2007/05. When Bush threw out the Opening Day first pitch for the St. Louis Cardinals, it was a strike. When Kerry tried the same thing for the Boston Red Sox, the ball bounced feebly in the dirt. While Kerry claimed to be a real Sox fan, he flubbed the players' names and had trouble portraying himself as a regular guy who could grab a beer and watch a ball game. Robert Elias, "One Curse Down," *Nine* 14:2 (2006), 133–35; "Statement by Baseball Hall-of-Famer and World War II Veteran Bob Feller," July 5, 2004, www.freerepublic.com/focus/f-news/1165855/posts; Joshua Fleer, "The Church of Baseball and the U.S. Presidency," *Nine* 16:1 (2007), 51–61.

36. Edward W. Wood, *Worshipping the Myths of World War II: Reflections on America's Dedication to War* (Washington, DC: Potomac Books, 2006); Gary Bedingfield, *Baseball in Wartime*, www.garybed.co.uk.

37. Jeff Zillgitt, "World War II Era Baseball Now a World Away," *USA Today*, July 19, 2004, C1.

38. As in America's previous wars, MLB also sent ballplayers to visit U.S. troops in Afghanistan and Iraq. Tamara Gabbard, "Retired Baseball Players Visit Troops in Afghanistan," *American Forces Press Service*, May 16, 2008, www.defenselink.mil/ news/newsarticle.aspx?id=49902.

39. Richard Crepeau, "The Sports Song of Patriotism," May 29, 2004, http:// www.poppolitics.com/articles/2003-02-28-flagprotest.shtml; Ward Harkavy, "Carry- ing a Tune," *Village Voice* 46:43 (October 30, 2001), 165.

40. Ron Briley, "Ambiguous Patriotism: Baseball and the Vietnam War," in *Cooperstown Symposium on Baseball and American Culture, 2005–2006*, ed. William Simons (Jefferson, NC: McFarland, 2007), 165–78.

41. While most people acquiesced, at least one fan has sued the Yankees for blocking his way, roughing him up, ejecting him, and having him arrested when he sought to leave his seat during the song. Sewell Chan, "7th-Inning Stretch Yields a Lawsuit," *New York Times*, April 16, 2009, A20; Dave Zirin, "A Pinstriped Patriot Act," *The Nation*, April 21, 2009, www.thenation.com/doc/20090504/zirin2.

42. William C. Rhoden, "Delgado Makes a Stand by Taking a Seat," *New York Times*, July 21, 2004, B1; Dave Zirin, "Cities Need to Care for Their People, Not Pro Sports Owners," *San Francisco Chronicle*, July 8, 2007, E1. Subjected to the chain policy, theologian Randall Balmer was shocked: "To be compelled to pay obeisance to this nationalistic deity—I find that fascist . . . this is coercion [yet] nobody seems upset that this goes on." Dave McKenna, "The Washington Nationalists: America, Love It or Leave the Stadium," *Washington City Paper* 25:29 (July 22–28, 2005), 14; Dave Zirin, "Carlos Delgado on Deck: Blue Jays Slugger Stands Up Against War," *Counter-Punch*, July 9, 2004, http://counterpunch.org/zirn07092004.html; Ron Borges, "Don't Boo Delgado for Iraq Protest," *MSNBC*, July 22, 2004, www.msnbc.msn.com/id/5482059/; "Yankee Fans Boo Delgado for Iraq War Protest," Associated Press, July 22, 2004; Richard Pollak, "Patriot at the Bat," *The Nation*, September 13, 2004, 10.

43. Marshall J. Cook and Jack Walsh, "Carlos Delgado: Hitting for Extra Bases on and off the Field," in *Baseball's Good Guys: The Real Heroes of the Game* (Chicago: Sports Publishing, 2004), 216–20; Zirin, "Carlos Delgado on Deck."

44. Steven Wine, "Delgado Cleanly Fields Questions Regarding War Protest," Associated Press, January 28, 2005; Dave Zirin, "The Silencing of Carlos Delgado," *The Nation*, December 19, 2005, www.thenation.com/doc/20051219/zirin; Arkin, "If Only War Reporting Were More like Sports Reporting."

45. Dan Wachtell, "Make Baseball, Not War: Returning to a Pastime," *Daily Princetonian*, April 8, 2002.

46. Littlefield, "Of Baseball and Country"; Bill Littlefield, "Sports Misused, and Games as Solace," *Only a Game* (Lincoln: University of Nebraska Press, 2007), 109–16.

47. Paul Lukas, "Flag-Waving," *Village Voice* 46:39 (October 2, 2001), 165.

48. Tom Lasorda, "Baseball, the Anthem and a Safe Flag: Patriotism—Even One Flag-Burning Is Too Many. An Amendment Is Necessary," *Los Angeles Times*, July 9, 1998, 9.

49. Dave Zirin, "War Games and War Names: Why the National Guard Wants the Rights to RFK Stadium," April 13, 2005, www.alternet.org/story/21739/; McKenna, "Washington Nationalists"; John R. Guardiano, "Baseball's Nationals Honor Armed Forces," American Forces Press Service, July 3, 2006, www.americasupportsyou.mil/americassupportsyou/. In response to the Nationals' quest for a new ballpark, Mark Hand proposed one for the Pentagon's east side, with views of the Potomac, the Washington, Lincoln, and Jefferson monuments, and the Capitol building, to be called Peace Park at Pentagon City. Defense Department officials would vacate the Pentagon (eliminating the city of Arlington as a terrorist target) and be relocated to Iraq to give the United States direct access to the enemy in its hundred-year crusade against Islam.

This would end the annoying media coverage of military policies. Baseball would be tapping into an international fan base that would appreciate the way America was helping foreigners by exporting U.S. military services to other countries. Mark Hand, "Peace Park? The Pentagon Solution to a Baseball Stadium Dilemma," *CounterPunch*, April 28, 2003, 2–3. The Nationals sponsored many more military projects: Wounded soldiers were honored, the Stars and Stripes Club was established, the U.S. Army Chorus and the Herald Trumpets performed patriotic songs, F-18s did flyovers, and 150 teenagers from National Guard Youth Challenge Programs unfurled a football field–size American flag. New recruits took the enlistment oath, fans were lobbied to send "support the troops" text messages, and children held giant military service emblems in the outfield, as the Singing Sergeants performed. Kathleen Rhem, "Baseball Team Honors Military," American Forces Press Service, July 23, 2006.

50. The Fox Sports broadcast of the Red Sox–Cardinals game was linked via live satellite to Camp Speicher in Tikrit, Iraq. Buck connected a soldier with his father and sisters in the stands. He said, "I hope [the soldiers were given a break and] transported to a place where who wins and who loses isn't such a dangerous proposition." Joe Buck, "Stealing Home: A Rare Glimpse of Baseball and Family Gave U.S. Soldiers in Iraq Something to Hold On To," *Sporting News* 229:26 (July 1, 2005), 7.

51. At one 2006 game, the broadcasters praised the Navy ships almost nonstop for three innings. In the fifth inning, they started again and interviewed a Navy official on air. In the eighth inning, they reported a call from a military historian, who helped them name the ships and their functions. As for the marines advertisements, they used them to associate themselves with "defense" rather than "offense," just as the Department of Defense had done decades earlier by changing its name from the Department of War.

52. Steve DiMeglio, "Zito Leads Effort to Aid Soldiers," *USA Today*, July 28, 2006, www.usatoday.com/sports/baseball/2006-07-27-soldiers-zito_x.htm; Dave Zirin, "Owners for McCain," *The Progressive*, October 2008, 11. Journalist Thomas Friedman had this advice for Barack Obama: "When negotiating with murderous regimes like Iran's or Syria's, you want Tony Soprano by your side, not Big Bird. Mr. Obama's gift for outreach would be much more effective with a Dick Cheney standing over his right shoulder, quietly pounding a baseball bat into his palm." Thomas Friedman, "Channeling Dick Cheney," *New York Times*, November 18, 2007; Gwen Knapp, "A's Pay Tribute to Troops: Naval Base Visits a Humbling Experience," *San Francisco Chronicle*, January 28, 2007, D2. Philadelphia Phillies pitcher Brad Lidge honors the U.S. troops in Iraq and Afghanistan on a smaller scale. His favorite band, Drowning Pool, has been featured in USO tours to Iraq, Kuwait, and Germany. When called in to pitch, Lidge has the band's song "Soldiers" played in tribute.

53. Masha Leon, "Saluting Those in Uniform," January 12, 2007, www.forward.com/articles/saluting-those-in-uniform.

54. Tony Capaccio, "Ripken Is a Matter of National Security," *USA Today Baseball Weekly* 6:4 (April 17, 1996), 21; "Ripken Chosen as Special Envoy to State Department," *Sports Illustrated*, August 9, 2007, http://sportsillustrated.cnn.com/2007/baseball/mlb/08/09/ripken.diplomat.ap.

55. In 2003 an episode of the television series *JAG* was based on the annual Navy–Marine Corps All-Star Game and featured Oakland Athletics pitcher Barry Zito. "United States Navy Baseball," www.usmilitaryallstars.us.

56. The Lancaster Jet Hawks, a Boston Red Sox Class A team, paid tribute. According to one player, "We were all immediately inspired the second we saw the jerseys. It made us think of the troops in Iraq and we couldn't wait to put them on." Another said, "I feel a responsibility to represent our troops and country, to play my very best. It's a sense of duty that maybe only our armed forces truly understand." A third player chimed in: "Seeing our players wearing these 'USA' jerseys makes me proud to be an American." Besides the player jerseys, official U.S. Military All-Stars merchandise was sold at all team stores, becoming "one of the most popular promotions in professional baseball." "Jet Hawks Inspired by U.S. Military All-Stars Camouflage 'USA' Jerseys," www.usmilitaryallstars.us.

57. John McMurtry, "Kill 'Em! Crush 'Em! Eat 'Em Raw!" in *The Norton Reader*, ed. Linda H. Peterson (New York: W.W. Norton, 2003), 200–206; Thomas Boswell, "99 Reasons Why Baseball Is Better Than Football," in *Heart of the Order* (New York: Penguin, 1989), 29–37; Michael Novak, *The Joy of Sports* (New York: Basic Books, 1976); Brian McKenna, "Professional Baseball and Football: A Close Relationship," *National Pastime* 26 (2006), 26–32; Murray Ross, "Football Red and Baseball Green," in *The Blair Reader*, ed. Laurie G. Kirszner and Stephen R. Mandell (Englewood Cliffs, NJ: Prentice Hall, 1992), 596–604. According to U.S. poet laureate Donald Hall: While "baseball is a country all to itself . . . football is a psychodrama, brothers beating up on brothers, murderous, bitter, ending with the incest of brotherly love, and in the wounds Americans carry all over their bodies. When the game is done, football digresses to a bar and drinks blended whiskey, brooding, its mouth sour, its belly flowing over its angry belt." Donald Hall with Dock Ellis, *Dock Ellis in the Country of Baseball* (New York: Coward, McCann & Geoghegan, 1976).

58. George Carlin, "Baseball and Football," *Brain Droppings* (New York: Hyperion, 2006).

59. Sharyn Thoma Guay, "Baseball Is War," March 25, 2002, www.baseballlibrary.com/baseballlibrary/submit/Guay_Sharyn_Thoma1.stm; Don Malcolm, "Sports and War, Baseball and Innocence," April 4, 2001, www.baseballthinkfactory.org.

60. Michael MacCambridge, *America's Game: The Epic Story of How Pro Football Captured a Nation* (New York: Random House, 2004). Michael Mandelbaum claimed the only obstacle to football's supremacy was American's growing *aversion* to war and violence—football's direct analogues. Mandelbaum viewed such violence as inevitable human nature and football as a legitimate surrogate. A century earlier, baseball was proposed to satisfy William James's call for a "moral equivalent of war." According to Mandelbaum, "At the outset of the [twenty-first] century, football could be seen as a candidate to fulfill his prescription." Similarly, some have lamented the loss of masculinity (if not patriarchy) and religion in America, and see football as a possible response. At the University of Colorado, the football coach claimed his sport was fighting the rejection of God and the challenge to virility imposed by feminism. In answer to the question Why do men watch football? Bob Andelman claims "it's because we're not allowed, in this female-dominated society, to act out our aggressions." With cases like these, some weren't so sure that war, violence, sexism, and religiosity had lost their luster in America after all. Mariah Burton Nelson, *The Stronger Women Get, the More Men Love Football* (New York: Quill, 1995); Michael Mandelbaum, *The Meaning of Sports* (New York: PublicAffairs, 2004); Wanda Ellen Wakefield, *Playing to Win: Sports and the American Military, 1898–1945* (Albany: State University of New York

Press, 1997), 103; Bob Andelman, *Why Men Watch Football* (Lafayette, LA: Acadian House, 2000); Robert R. Neyland, *Football as a Wargame* (Nashville: Falcon Press, 2002). In the words of Lee Siegel, "if an American sport were to have the quality of combat, it would be football, [where] the idea is to move down the field until the other team has no land left. Football is more violent because sacred property is at stake. [It] might be a good fit for a property-obsessed American society in denial." Concerns about baseball's future have often been "premised on a feeling that [the sport] is ill suited to the new economic order [globalization]." Football, "a form of corporate and quasi-military combat," has taken over. Lee Siegel, "Ownership Society," *New Republic*, February 7, 2005, 8; Alan Bairner, *Sport, Nationalism, and Globalization: European and North American Perspectives* (Albany: State University of New York Press, 2001), 91–113, 163–77. "In a New World Order and an era of globalization the U.S. seeks to master, imagining a Super Bowl as the premier international television sporting event is a way to [display] 'our' superiority," yet the whole world "isn't watching." Elements of NFL football are so distinctly American and alien that they don't resonate. Despite its obvious popularity, it's not even clear it really fits America's own traditions. The 2008 Super Bowl tried to show its connection to the Declaration of Independence: with a shifting patriotic backdrop of flags, sailors, warships and jet fighters, various football legends took turns reciting passages from the declaration without an ounce of conviction or any apparent relationship to their sport. The tribute ended piously at the grave of the declaration's chief author, Thomas Jefferson—a man who in real life would have immediately condemned football. Christopher R. Martin and Jimmie L. Reeves, "The Whole World Isn't Watching (but We Thought They Were): The Super Bowl and U.S. Solipsism," in *Sport and Memory in North America*, ed. Stephen G. Wieting (London: Frank Cass, 2001), 213–35.

61. Alistair Cooke, *Alistair Cooke's America* (New York: Knopf, 1973); Frank De-Ford, "How We Lost Our Pastime," *Newsweek* 128:27 (December 30, 1996), 62; Frank DeFord, "King Hut: Pro Football Rules in America," *Sports Illustrated*, July 30, 2003, http://sportsillustrated.cnn.com/si_online/news/2003/07/29/sc.

62. Bairner, *Sport, Nationalism, and Globalization*; Stefan Szymanski and Andrew Zimbalist, *National Pastime: How Americans Play Baseball and the Rest of the World Plays Soccer* (Washington, DC: Brookings Institution Press, 2005); Franklin Foer, *How Soccer Explains the World* (New York: HarperCollins, 2004), 235–48; Eduardo Galeano, *Soccer in Sun and Shadow* (New York: Verso, 1998); Michael Young, "Wide World of Sports: Soccer Mirrors Globalization and Its Discontents," *Reason* 36:11 (April 1, 2005), 61–63. One observer drew this thoughtful contrast between baseball and soccer: "You can wrap your arms around baseball and study it like a science. You can never wrap your arms around [soccer]. It is too big. Too undefinable, too nuanced. That is what makes it human. Baseball is an attempt to impose order on the universe. But it cannot be done. Baseball is a fantasy. Soccer represents mankind as it really exists." "Soccer and Baseball Attempt Diplomacy," *Parodical*, July 27, 2007, www.parodical.com/2006/05/08/soccer-and-baseball-attempt-diplomacy.

63. Thomas Boswell, "The International Pastime," *Washington Post*, March 28, 2003, H1; Jayson Stark, "Potential for Globalization is Unlimited," February 26, 2007, http://Sports.espn.go.com/mlb/asia/columns/story?columnist=stark_jayson&id=2766682.

64. Alan M. Klein, *Growing the Game: The Globalization of Major League Baseball* (New Haven, CT: Yale University Press, 2006).

65. In Colombia, the Yankees' Bernie Williams became a cultural ambassador even though the U.S. Embassy warned him about the "14,000 guerrillas who wanted to overthrow the government, 12,000 paramilitary soldiers who wanted to quell them, and an uncertain number of Colombians who were ferocious [against] anyone who interfered with their drug enterprises." This situation had been aggravated by Plan Colombia, the disastrous drug war launched by the Clinton administration and continued by the Bush White House. In Chile, baseball was being used for people-to-people diplomacy, and Secretary of State Condoleezza Rice arrived to help establish Little League. In Brazil, baseball surpassed the youth leagues, thanks to the nation's large Japanese ballplaying community. In Mexico, MLB sought to tap an additional fan base when it approved the first Mexican-American owner, Arturo Moreno, and his Anaheim Angels purchase. In Panama, the United States ceded limited control over the Canal Zone, and a new professional winter league was formed. Playing off the stardom of Yankees reliever Mariano Rivera, and with the help of former Panamanian major leaguer Elias Sosa and U.S. Ambassador William Eaton, new baseball equipment and training were made available. Jack Curry, "Plucking at Bernie Williams's Heartstrings," *New York Times*, February 18, 2005; Craig Kelly, "Baseball Diplomacy: Chile Catches Little League Fever," *State*, September 2005, 18–19; Nathan Crooks, "Baseball Changing Children's Lives," *Worldpress*, May 1, 2007, www.worldpress.org/article_id=2896; Carlos Azzoni, Tales Azzoni, and Wayne Patterson, "Brazil: Baseball Is Popular, and the Players Are Japanese!" in *Baseball Without Borders: The International Pastime*, ed. George Gmelch (Lincoln: University of Nebraska Press, 2006); "Baseball Will Have First Mexican-American Owner," *USA Today Sports Weekly*, April 23–29, 2003, 57; Hugh Dellios, "Mexico's Front-Runner Espouses Traditional, Less-Active Foreign Policy," *Chicago Tribune*, March 22, 2006, 3A.

66. Thomas Carter, "Playing Hardball: Constructions of Cuban Identity," PhD dissertation, University of New Mexico, 2000; S.L. Price, "The Big Red Machine," *Sports Illustrated*, March 3, 2008, 14–15; Gerald S. Gems, *The Athletic Crusade: Sport and American Cultural Imperialism* (Lincoln: University of Nebraska Press, 2006), 98; Jeremy Goldberg, "Sporting Diplomacy: Boosting the Size of the Diplomatic Corps," *Washington Quarterly* 23:4 (2000), 63–70. The spirit of Che Guevara lived on in baseball: on Cuban scoreboards, runs, hits, and errors (RHE) are shown as *carreras*, hits, and errors (CHE). Peter C. Bjarkman, "Waiting for Che—Chasing Illusions in the Modern-Era Cuban Ballpark," *Elysian Fields Quarterly* 21 (2004), 6–17; Matt Welch, "Foul Ball: How a Communist Dictatorship and a U.S. Embargo Has Silenced a Cuban Historian," *Reason Online*, June 2002; A baseball agent was charged with violating the embargo by illegally smuggling four Cubans into the United States. Since the early 1990s, several dozen Cuban ballplayers had defected but only a couple had succeeded in the major leagues. "Agent Charged in Smuggling of Cubans," *New York Times*, November 1, 2006; Lisette Corsa, "The Cuban Coach: Rigoberto Betancourt's Life in Baseball Takes a Seventh-Inning Stretch," *Miami New Times* 16:21 (August 30, 2001); Peter C. Bjarkman, *Diamonds Around the Globe: The Encyclopedia of International Baseball* (Westport, CT: Greenwood Press, 2005). Mark Feierstein proposed that President Bush offer the Washington Nationals to Havana in exchange for Castro holding free and fair elections: Washington, D.C., is really a football town, and having MLB in Cuba would be irresistible to Castro. If that worked, then the United States could move on to Venezuela's Hugo Chávez, who's always dreamed of pitching in the major

leagues. Mark Feierstein, "President Bush: Try a Little Baseball Diplomacy," March 27, 2006, www.greenbergresearch.com/index.php?ID=1682; Saul Landau, "Baseball—Big and Little: Its Role in U.S.-Cuba Relations," August 8, 2008, www.fpif.org/piftxt/5453.

67. David Gonzalez, "Cuba and Venezuela Engage in a Different Kind of Diplomacy," *New York Times*, November 20, 1999. It has been said that "the country without socialism would almost inevitably be a country without soccer." That seems to fit the United States, but the reverse might not be true. Nations with socialism don't necessarily play soccer, and may be among the biggest baseball enthusiasts. Curiously, Cuba (under Castro), Nicaragua (under Ortega), and Venezuela (under Chávez) all embraced socialism amid clashes with the United States, yet none abandoned baseball because of its American connections. Cogliano, "Baseball and American Exceptionalism," 145.

68. Bjarkman, *Diamonds Around the Globe*; Maria Burns Ortiz, "Politics Makes a Toxic Mix with MLB's Investment in Venezuela," *ESPN Sports*, November 18, 2007, http://sports.espn.go.com/mlb/news/story?id=3077371. On a state visit to the United Nations in New York in July 1999, Chávez threw out the first pitch before a Mets game at Shea Stadium. He donned a full uniform, complete with spikes, and had Mets infielder and fellow Venezuelan Melvin Mora warm him up. Chávez strolled to the mound and from a windup threw several pitches to the catcher. Later he joined Damaso Blanco as color commentator during the game's live broadcast on Venezuelan state TV, well past midnight. Steve Ellner, "Chávez Hits a Home Run," *In These Times*, September 20, 2004, 6–7.

69. "Baseball Donations from U.S. Military in Afghanistan Find a Home in the Hall of Fame," *Memories and Dreams*, Fall 2004.

70. David Zirin, "Over the Edge: The Year in Sports 2005," *Edge of Sports*, December 28, 2005, www.edgeofsports.com.

71. Tensions escalated when the United States began classifying Latin Americans as potential terrorists. The State Department, in cooperation with MLB, brought Venezuelan and Nicaraguan Little League coaches to the United States for training and goodwill diplomacy. They were taken to the White House for photos with President Bush, who used the occasion to instruct the leaders of their nations that the war on terrorism "will not be won by force of arms alone, but also in the battle of ideas." According to State Department undersecretary Karen Hughes, this meant "offering people throughout the world a positive vision of hope rooted in American beliefs . . . and isolating violent extremists and confronting their ideology of tyranny and hate." This would be accomplished through exchanges such as the "sports diplomacy program with Venezuela and Nicaraguan baseball players." Karen Hughes, "Long-Term Foundation for Waging Peace," *Washington File*, April 4, 2006.

72. Danna Harman, "In Chávez Country, US Ambassador Tries Baseball Diplomacy," *Christian Science Monitor*, June 7, 2006; Danna Harman, "U.S. Baseball Strikes Out with Chávez," *USA Today*, June 8, 2006, A18; Letta Tayler, "Diplomacy Running Afoul," *Newsday*, May 9, 2006, www.newsday.com/news/nationworld/world/ny-wovene094735273may09,0,589965.

73. Burns Ortiz, "Politics Makes a Toxic Mix with MLB's Investment in Venezuela"; Dave Zirin, "Owners Out at Home Base," *The Progressive*, March 2008, 11; Milton Jamail, *Venezuelan Bust, Baseball Boom* (Lincoln: University of Nebraska Press, 2008).

74. Ironically, the film's major consultant was former MLB pitcher Jose Rijo, who was later fired as a scout by the Washington Nationals for his involvement in yet another Dominican player scandal. Generally, see Steve Fainaru, "Baseball's Minor Infractions: In Latin America, Young Players Come at a Bargain Price," *Washington Post*, October 26, 2001, D1; Steve Fainaru, "The Business of Building Ballplayers: In Dominican Republic, Scouts Find the Talent and Take the Money," *Washington Post*, June 17, 2001, A1; Daniel Gabriel, "Inside Baseball's Sweatshop," *Elysian Fields Quarterly*, Fall 2003, 78–80; Arturo J. Marcano Guevara and David P. Fidler, "Baseball's Exploitation of Latin Talent," *NACLA Report on the Americas* 37:5 (2004), 15; Toby Miller, Geoffrey Lawrence, Jim McKay, and David Rowe, *Globalization and Sport: Playing the World* (Thousand Oaks, CA: Sage, 2001), 6–59; Toby Miller, Geoffrey Lawrence, Jim McKay, and David Rowe, "Playing the World," *Peace Review* 11:4 (1999), 495; Dave Zirin, "Say It Ain't So, Big Leagues: They Harvest Dominican Baseball Talent on the Cheap, and Give Little in Return," *The Nation*, November 14, 2005, 22–24; Dave Zirin, "Beisbol: How the Major Leagues Eat Their Young," in *Welcome to the Terrordome* (Chicago: Haymarket Books, 2007), 48–71; Roberto Gonzalez Echevaria, "American Dream, Dominican Nightmare," *New York Times*, August 13, 2003; Jorge Arangure and Luke Cyphers, "It's Not All Sun and Games," *ESPN: The Magazine*, May 2009, 67–72.

75. Diana L. Spagnuolo, "Swinging for the Fence: A Call for Institutional Reform as Dominican Boys Risk Their Futures for a Chance at Major League Baseball," *University of Pennsylvania Journal of International Economic Law* 24 (Spring 2003), 263–87; Alan M. Klein, "Dominican Republic: Forging an International Industry," in *Baseball Without Borders: The International Pastime*, ed. George Gmelch (Lincoln: University of Nebraska Press, 2006); Klein, *Growing the Game*; Bryan Curtis, "Baseball, Dominican-Style," *Slate*, May 9, 2008, www.slate.com/id/2190554. Dominican hero Sammy Sosa had a carefully crafted image as the likable, gracious immigrant, but this began to unravel when he was caught using a corked bat in 2003 and when he was accused of using steroids and called to testify before Congress in 2005. Other Latinos were also embroiled in the steroids controversy, although the drugs weren't banned in the Caribbean and their use may have been escalated by the players' quest to escape a lifetime of poverty. Adrian Burgos, *Playing America's Game: Baseball, Latinos, and the Color Line* (Berkeley: University of California Press, 2007).

76. Bjarkman, *Diamonds Across the Globe*; Gems, *Athletic Crusade*, 144; Harvey Araton, "Puerto Rico: No Longer an Island of Dreams," *New York Times*, April 13, 2003, 5. Worried that most failed prospects were uneducated and had little to fall back on, former major leaguer Edwin Correa helped establish the Puerto Rico Baseball Academy and High School. Rafael Hermoso, "Baseball and Books: Puerto Rican Academy Grooms Players," *New York Times*, April 13, 2003, 1.

77. Dave Zirin, "Stained Uniforms," *Los Angeles Times*, March 14, 2006.

78. Tim Weiner, "Low-Wage Costa Ricans Make Baseballs for Millionaires," *New York Times*, January 25, 2004, 3.

79. Diane M. Grassi, "Baseball and Rawlings Bring New Meaning to Free Trade," July 25, 2006, http://www.renewamerica.com/columns/grassi/060725; Philip Hersh, "Sewing Circles: The Sport of Baseball Has Little Popularity in Costa Rica, But Big-League Baseballs Are Produced Here," *Chicago Tribune*, July 15, 2003, http://chicagosports.chicagotribune.com/sports/baseball.

80. According to White Sox minor-league director Grace Zwit, "Those who make it to the States and then are released [from baseball] may remain to seek better job opportunities than they may find back home." Actually such players will be in the United States illegally and face grim economic prospects similar to those at home. They will join the waves of illegal immigrants who enter the United States chasing resources extracted from their nations by debt cycles and unfair trade policies. Eric Forrest, "Major League Baseball's Efforts to Bring Latin Talent to the States: A Brief History Filled With Hardship," paper presented to the 18th Cooperstown Symposium on Baseball and American Culture, Cooperstown, NY, June 2006. Kim Gore, a civilian Defense Department telecommuter employee, invited Caribbean ballplayers from the local Potomac Nationals minor-league team to her home. The army claimed this made her a security risk, and her privileges were canceled. Austin O'Neill, "Telecommuter Trouble with National Security," *Federal News Radio*, www.federalnewsradio.com, October 16, 2006. In 2004, the United States announced that the number of H-2B visas—required for foreigners playing in U.S. minor leagues—would be cut. But in 2006, President Bush gave the major leagues a gift: the Creating Opportunities for Minor League Professionals, Entertainers and Teams Through Legal Entry Act, which allowed an unlimited import of players. Some felt the law should have been called the African Americans Take a Hike Act. Making it easier to import cheap foreign players sent a message to black Americans that little would be done to reverse the decline in opportunities for them in baseball. Burgos, *Playing America's Game*; Ronald Young, "For Everyone Else, There's VISA: Immigration Visa Shortage Hits Minor League with Player Shortages," *Minor League News*, February 20, 2005, www.minorleaguenews.com/features/articles2005/02/20.html; J. Damu, "Full Disclosure: The Indictment of Barry Bonds," *San Francisco Bayview*, 2007, www.sfbayview.com; Joe Guzzardi, "Playing Baseball: A Job Americans Won't Do?" www.vdare.com/guzzardi/050618_baseball.htm, June 18, 2005; Jessica Skolnikoff and Robert Engvall, "Colonialism and Baseball: A Cultural Critique of Major League Baseball Academies," paper presented at the 18th Cooperstown Symposium on Baseball and American Culture, June 2006, 1–20; John Eisenberg, "To Understand Latin Players, You Must Understand Their Culture," *Baltimore Sun*, August 7, 2006, C2; Michael Kinsley, "Everybody Has the Dream: Baseball Scouting and Players' Hopes of Success in Dominican Republic," *Sporting News* 225:8 (February 19, 2001), 50.

81. Rupert Murdoch and Disney made a similar use of the Dodgers and Angels, respectively, when they owned those teams, both taking their leads from Atlanta Braves owner Ted Turner, who pioneered media-sports synergies. Jeremy Howell, "From Pac Bell Park to the Tokyo Dome: Baseball and Economic Nationalism," in *Corporate Nationalisms: Sport, Cultural Identity and Transnational Marketing*, ed. Michael L. Silk, David L. Andrews, and C.L. Cole (Oxford, UK: Berg Publishers, 2005), 175.

82. Jonathan Mahler, "Building the Beisbol Brand," *New York Times Magazine*, July 31, 2005, 22.

83. Alfred Eckes and Thomas Zeiler, *Globalization and the American Century* (Cambridge, UK: Cambridge University Press, 2003); Rob Rains, *Baseball Samurais: Ichiro Suzuki and the Asian Invasion* (New York: St. Martin's, 2001). A U.S.-Japanese diplomatic incident was caused by the negligent sinking of a Japanese boat by an American nuclear submarine in 2001. A series of Hawaiian baseball games helped mend the rift. Frank Ardolino, "The Tragedy of the *Ehime Maru* and the Role of Baseball in the

Healing Process," *Nine* 16:2 (2008), 80–83; Mark Silva, "Baseball, Elvis and the Baltic Sea: Bush-Style Diplomacy," *The Swamp*, June 28, 2006, www.swamppolitics.com; Bill King, "MLB Leaves $10M in Japan: Safety Outweighed Finances in Decision to Cancel," *Street and Smith's Sportsbusiness Journal* 5 (March 24, 2003), 1, 43; Tyler Kepner, "Yanks Rediscover Japan 70 Years After First Visit," *New York Times*, March 28, 2004, SP1; Charlie Nobles, "Players from Over There Get a Shot Over Here," *New York Times*, May 18, 2005, D3. Back in the United States, the independent Golden Baseball League featured the first all-Japanese team, the Samurai Bears. Ben Bolch, "Whole New Ballgame: The Samurai Bears, an All-Japanese Team, Are Trying to Adjust to Playing in the U.S. and to a Grueling Schedule in the First-Year Independent Golden Baseball League," *Los Angeles Times*, July 28, 2005, C1.

84. "Bush to Host Japan's Abe on Diplomacy, Baseball, Beef," *Raw Story*, April 26, 2007, http://rawstory.com/news/afp/Bush_to_host_Japan_s_Abe_on_diploma_04262007.html.

85. Japanese and Korean players must be nine-year veterans of their own leagues before they can demand to be "posted," at which time U.S. clubs submit blind bids for the right to deal with the player. The winning team gets to negotiate a contract, and if agreement is reached, then the player's team is paid the winning bid. Alexander Blenkinsopp, "Asian Invasion: Baseball's Ambassadors," *Harvard International Review* 24:1 (Spring 2002). Disagreement lingered about the differences between American and Japanese baseball. Jonathan Rauch, "Why Is Japanese Baseball So Dull?" *Reason* 24 (August 1992), 24; William Kelly, "The Hanshin Tigers and Japanese Professional Baseball," in *Baseball Without Borders: The International Pastime*, ed. George Gmelch (Lincoln: University of Nebraska Press, 2006); Gary A. Warner, "Japanese Baseball: A Whole New Ballgame," *Orange County Register*, September 28, 1997, 7; Alan Schwarz and Brad Lefton, "Japanese Are Irked by U.S. Interest in Pitcher," *New York Times*, November 20, 2008.

86. Eric Neel, "*Gaijin* No Longer Means 'Outsider,'" February 28, 2007, http://sports.espn.go.com/mlb/asia/columns/story?columnist=neel_eric&id=2766707; Naoki Chiba, "Pacific Professional Baseball Leagues and Migratory Patterns and Trends: 1995–1999," *Journal of Sport & Social Issues* 28:2 (May 2004), 193–211; Andrew Lam, "In Japan, a Fear of Foreigners Collides with Today's Economic Realities," *Athens News*, July 21, 2003, 3; Merritt Clifton, "Where the Twain Shall Meet: What Baseball Means to Japan—and Humanity," *National Pastime* 4 (1985), 12–22; Yoichi Nagata and John B. Holway, "Baseball in Japan," in *Total Baseball*, ed. John Thorn and Pete Palmer (Toronto: Sports Media, 2004), 789–93.

87. Jim Allen, "Game Reinforces Key Cultural Values," February 26, 2007, http://sports.espn.go.com/mlb/asia/columns/story?id=2766653; Caroline Gluck, "Taiwan Tries Baseball Diplomacy," *BBC News*, July 2004, http://news.bbc.co.uk/go/pr/fr/-/2/hi/asia-pacific/3502306.stm; Joseph Timothy Sundeen, "A 'Kid's Game'? Little League Baseball and National Identity in Taiwan," *Journal of Sport & Social Issues* 25:3 (August 2001), 251–65.

88. Joseph A. Reaves, *Taking in a Game: A History of Baseball in Asia* (Lincoln: University of Nebraska Press, 2002); Andrew Morris, "Baseball, History, the Local and the Global in Taiwan," in *The Minor Arts of Daily Life: Popular Culture in Taiwan*, ed. D.K. Jordan, A.D. Morris, and M.L. Moskowitz (Honolulu: University of Hawaii Press,

2004), 326–81; Junwei Yu, *Playing in Isolation: A History of Baseball in Taiwan* (Lincoln: University of Nebraska Press, 2007).

89. "The Games We Play," *Asian Week* 22:33 (April 11, 2001), 4. In 2004, the Chinese All-Star team traveled to the United States to play against Arizona Fall League teams. In 2007, MLB, Ripken Baseball, and the State Department hosted Chinese baseball coaches in America. Wang Liqiang, who runs the Shandong Zhanwang Baseball and Softball Club, was passionate about making baseball into China's pastime: "China's changing. With all this development, it's chaotic and young people have lost a sense of who they are. Baseball will bring that sense of order back." "The Whole World Is Watching," *Sports Illustrated*, June 14, 2004, 72–77, 79–80, 83–84, 86; Jim Caple, "Baseball Goes Global," *Baseball Digest* 60 (September 2001), 48–51; Adrienne Mong, "A Passion for Baseball." MSNBC, July 3, 2007, http://worldblog.msnbc .com/archive/2007/07/03/256152.aspx.

90. Jake Hooker, "Joining China to Find a Yao Who Can Hit," *New York Times*, January 31, 2007, C1; Tyler Kepner, "Seeking Edge in China, Yankees Put Baseball First," *New York Times*, January 26, 2007; Juliet Macur, "Playing at China, Chipping at a Wall," *New York Times*, March 16, 2008, Sports Sunday, 1. In the early twentieth century, Filipino baseball teams were among Asia's best, but then they fell into obscurity— a case of a newly independent nation rejecting rather than embracing the sport of its former colonial power. In the early 2000s, Filipino baseball showed some signs of revival. Tom Walsh, "Baseball in the Philippines," *Bulletin of the American Historical Collection* 23:3 (July–September 1995), 106–9. Elsewhere, First Pitch provided aid and equipment in 2004 to bring baseball to remote Manipur, India, in the Eastern Himalayas, and the Pittsburgh Pirates signed the first Indian ballplayers. Ted Simendinger, *Searching for Tedulkar: Baseball's Hunt for the Star of India* (Denver: Airplane Reader Pub. Co., 2004). Jenifer Langosch, "Bucs Sign Pair of Indian Hurlers," *Hot Stove Report* November 24, 2008, www.mlb.com/news; Bruce Reed, "The Mound Is Flat," *Slate*, December 4, 2008, www.slate.com. In 2005 in Baribor, the first Cambodian baseball field was opened, with the help of MLB, the U.S. Embassy, and the Cambodian National Olympic Committee. Charles McDermid and Chhim Sopheark. "Diamond Diplomacy Hits Home Run in Baribor," *Cambodia Daily*, August 1, 2005, www .camnet.com.kh/cambodia.daily/selected_features/cd-1-8 05.htm. In 2006, John Hattig was signed by the Toronto Blue Jays, becoming Guam's first major leaguer. Akash Shringi, "#1 John Hattig Jr. Becomes First Person from Guam to Make It to the Major Leagues," *Pacific Daily News*, 2004, www.guampdn.com/guampublishing/special -sections/top10_2006/01hattig.html). In 2006, the Vietnam Veterans Memorial Fund sent a Bringing Baseball to Vietnam delegation to introduce the game and to raise awareness (and promote the cleanup) of unexploded ordnance left by the U.S. military. The RENEW mine action program had to remove thirteen different kinds of land mines just to clear one baseball field. At least two thousand casualties still occur annually from explosions of the millions of land mines still scattered around Vietnam. The United States has still refused to sign the UN Land Mine Treaty, but MLB supported the veterans group with a Baseball Tomorrow Fund grant. Danny Graves, the first Vietnamese-born major leaguer, joined the veterans to dedicate Vietnam's first baseball field. "Fracas Over Fireworks," *USA Today Baseball Weekly* 10:45 (January 31, 2001), 3; "U.S. Veterans to Bring Baseball to Vietnam to Fight Mines," Agence France-Presse,

January 12, 2006; "Baseball Builds Bridges Between United States and Vietnam," February 2, 2006, www.teachvietnam.org/POPUP_Printing.cfm?SectionID-457.

91. Baseball developed in South Africa in particular. The Jackie Robinson story inspired people such as Bishop Desmond Tutu. Another anti-apartheid activist, Eddie Bennett, has promoted South African baseball since the early 2000s. The nation's baseball potential prompted the Kansas City Royals to establish an academy there. Baseball has also been imported to Gambia and Zimbabwe. MLB has donated equipment to the All-Africa Baseball Tournament, and invited players from Nigeria, Uganda, and South Africa to its baseball academy in Pisa, Italy. In 2007, New York Mets general manager Omar Minaya led an MLB and Little League delegation to Ghana. Henri E. Cauvin, "Baseball Gets Serious in a New South Africa," *New York Times*, June 27, 2000, A25, 28; Klein, *Growing the Game*; Josh Chetwynd, "A History of South African Baseball," *Nine* 16:2 (2008), 73–79; Jim Small, "From Australia to Zimbabwe," in *2001 World Series Official Program*, ed. Richard Levin (New York: Major League Baseball Promotion Corp., 2001), 83–89.

92. Americans recently migrating to Israel brought baseball with them. In a 2005 people-to-people diplomacy initiative, U.S. ambassador to Israel Daniel Kurtzer sponsored baseball instruction for Jewish and Arab Israeli kids at the Peres Center. In 2006, the Israel Association of Baseball was founded with former Ambassador Kurtzer as its commissioner. Led by former Red Sox general manager Dan Duquette, the association launched the first Israeli baseball academy. Former major leaguers held baseball clinics, new fields were opened, and even the UN Golan Heights contingent had a team. The Israel Baseball League (IBL) was created to promote community baseball, hoping to tap into "fans of baseball who were also fans of Israel." In 2007, former major leaguers Art Shamsky, Ken Holtzman, and Ron Blomberg agreed to manage three of the six teams. David Brinn, "Play Ball," October 19, 2003, http://www.israel21c.org; Bradley Burston, "Underground Exclusive: U.S. Ambassador Dan Kurtzer Talks Baseball," *Haaretz*, June 4, 2005; "Holtzman, Blomberg, Shamsky Set to Manage in Israeli Baseball League," *International Herald Tribune*, www.iht.com/bin/print.php??id=4729887; "Jewish Major Leaguers Introduce First Israel Baseball League," *Israel Insider*, February 26, 2007, http://web.israelinsider.com/Articles/Culture/10792.htm; "Pro Baseball League Planned for Israel," *Canadian Jewish News*, June 15, 2006, 46; Aryeh Dean Cohen, "Israeli Ball Players Say 'Batter Up,'" April 9, 2006, www.israel21c.org; Aaron Leibel, "Take Me Out to the Ball Game: Ex–Silver Spring Resident Promotes Baseball in Israel," *Washington Jewish Week* 42:8 (February 23, 2006), 1; Marty Appel, "Zimbabwe and Israeli Baseball: Two Nations of Growth," *Memories and Dreams*, July–August 2006, 5; David Buchbinder, "U.S. Troops Bring Little League to Afghanistan," *Christian Science Monitor*, August 19, 2002, 1; Donovan Janus, "How Baseball Helped Children and Saved Lives in Afghanistan," www.spiritofamerican.net; Brian Murphy, "Iran Takes Up 'Satan's' Game," *Boston Globe*, July 8, 2001; "Baseball Is Latest Afghanistan Craze," *BBC Newsround*, August 19, 2002, http://news.bbc.co.uk/cbbcnews/hi/world/newsid_22040000/2204003.htm.

93. Blair Larson, "Iraqi Children Learn American Pastime," U.S. Army Special Operations Command News Service, July 14, 2004, http://news.soc.mil; Kirk Semple, "Baseball in Iraq: As Pastimes Go, It's Anything But," *New York Times*, September 7, 2005; Joe Marusak, "He's Sent a Message to Iraqi Kids: Let's Play Ball," *Charlotte Ob-*

server, August 24, 2008; "What is Iraqi Baseball?" www.caironet.com/Iraqi-Baseball/ib10.htm.

94. Veronika R. Tuskowski, "Cannoncockers Build Miniature Version of Fenway Park in Iraq," *First Marine Division Report*, August 31, 2004.

95. Jim Wrenn, "America Re-Learns Baseball's Endgame Strategy," December 26, 2007, http://polisat.com; "Commander of Multinational Force in Iraq Began to Forge His Leadership Skills in Little League," February 8, 2007, www.littleleague.org/media/DavidPatraeus_020807.asp. Little League established two additional military programs for its players: Adopt a Platoon, http://adoptaplatoon.org and Pen Pals for Soldiers, Inc. www.penpalsforsoldiers.org.

96. Although Canada lost its Montreal team, baseball still thrived there. The Australians were developing notable talent, and in 2001 New Zealand supplied its first U.S. minor leaguer, Travis Wilson. In 2002, MLB returned to Britain but ultimately shifted from grass-roots baseball development to attracting impact athletes for its new European Baseball Academy. In the Netherlands, the Holland Major League has operated for several years. Dutch pitcher Alexander Smit signed with the Minnesota Twins, and thirty players from the Dutch West Indies island of Curaçao were in organized baseball as of 2002. By 2004, Holland's Olympic baseball team was coached by former major-league manager Davey Johnson. Italy was Europe's most developed baseball nation, its professional leagues attracting devoted fans. There was already a baseball academy in Pisa, and the major leagues targeted Rome for a regular season series. In 2001, the SUNY Cortland Red Dragons played baseball in Russia, and the sport was launched in the Ukraine in 2005. And in 2007, Little League International honored President George H.W. Bush and Barbara Bush for their "friendship with Little League and service to our country and humanity as well." The Bushes then flew to Poland with Little League president Creighton Hale to deliver the first Little League charters behind the former Iron Curtain. Martin Hoerchner, "Stoolball: Alive and Well in Sussex," *Baseball Research Journal* 27 (1999), 59–61; Josh Chetwynd, *Baseball in Europe* (Jefferson, NC: McFarland, 2008); Josh Chetwynd, "Great Britain: Baseball's Battle for Respect in the Land of Cricket, Rugby, and Soccer," in *Baseball Without Borders: The International Pastime*, ed. George Gmelch (Lincoln: University of Nebraska Press, 2006); Harvey Shapiro, "Holland: An American Coaching *Honkbal*," in *Baseball Without Borders: The International Pastime*, ed. George Gmelch (Lincoln: University of Nebraska Press, 2006); Dave Bidini, *Baseballissimo: My Summer in the Italian Minor Leagues* (Toronto: McClelland & Stewart, 2004); Peter Carino, "Italy: No Hotdogs in the Bleachers," in *Baseball Without Borders: The International Pastime*, ed. George Gmelch (Lincoln: University of Nebraska Press, 2006); Rick Hummel, "Simontacchi Gains Change-Up, Experience in Italian League," *St. Louis Post-Dispatch*, May 5, 2002, D10; Lawrence Mitchell Garrison, "Baseball Caps, the Grand Canyon are America's Best Ambassadors," *PRweek* 8:48 (December 5, 2005), 28; McDermid and Sopheark, "Diamond Diplomacy Hits Home Run in Baribor"; Frederic Morton, "From Role Model to International Bully in Three Short Years; in September 2001, Europe Wept for Us; Now It Won't Even Play Baseball," *Los Angeles Times*, September 27, 2004, B11; John Vinocur, "In Europe, Some Cry, 'Play Honkbal!'" *International Herald Tribune*, July 18, 2003.

97. Mark Lamster, *Spalding's World Tour: The Epic Adventure That Took Baseball Around the Globe—and Made It America's Game* (New York: PublicAffairs, 2006).

98. Ben Couch, "Spring Classic: International Competition and the WBC," *Memories and Dreams*, July–August 2006, 6–8; John Powers, "U.S. Baseball Is Stunned, Fails to Make Olympics," *Boston Globe*, November 8, 2003, E1.

99. In the 2008 Beijing Olympics, China's American-coached baseball team won only one game and finished last. The U.S. team finished third, with Cuba second, and South Korea taking the gold medal. Kirsten Jones, "The Game Goes for Gold: A History of Olympic Baseball," *Memories and Dreams*, July–August 2006, 20–22.

100. Chris Jenkins, "New Meaning for Moneyball: Major League Baseball's Globalization of Game Makes Dollars—Billions—and That Makes Sense," *San Diego Union Tribune*, March 18, 2006, 20–22; Christopher Clarey, "Baseball's New World Order," *International Herald Tribune*, May 16, 2005.

101. Jonathan Mahler, "A Whole New Ballgame; The World Baseball Classic Raises Issues of Patriotism and Identity," *Los Angeles Times*, March 5, 2006, M1; John D. Kelly, *The American Game: Capitalism, Decolonization, Global Domination, and Baseball* (Chicago: Prickly Paradigm Press, 2006).

102. But MLB squandered that goodwill when the WBC in some ways reflected the U.S. role in the world. Similar to U.S. defiance of international law in the Iraq War, the WBC rules favored the U.S. team. William B. Gould, "Baseball Classic Mirrors World Events," *San Jose Mercury News*, March 21, 2006, www.commondreams.org; Nancy Snow, *The Arrogance of American Power* (Lanham, MD: Rowman & Littlefield, 2007).

103. Shaun Tandon, "'World' Baseball Classic Defies Globalization," Agence France-Presse, March 1, 2006; Kelly, *American Game*. To play for a particular nation, a player had to have a parent born or with citizenship there. Alan Bisbort, "War Bonds: Bush and Barry Sitting in a Tree," *Valley Advocate*, March 16, 2006, 5.

104. Japanese owners resented the Americans for recruiting their best players and thus bargained hard over the WBC. Amy Chozick, "World Series; Global Pitch: A World Cup for baseball? It Isn't as Easy as It Sounds," *Wall Street Journal*, October 18, 2004, R6; Kelly, *American Game*. Korea also beat Japan twice, which some Koreans regarded as some payback for thirty-five years of Japanese colonialism. Donald Kirk, "Millions Rally in South Korea—Around Baseball," *Christian Science Monitor*, March 20, 2006, 12; Craig Simons, "South Korea Boasts New Patriotism, at U.S. Expense: Baseball Victory Reinforces Self-Image," *Atlanta Journal-Constitution*, March 19, 2006, C8; Reuben Staines, "Baseball Players Get Military Exemption," *Korea Times*, March 18, 2006; James I. Matray, "Global Bully: South Korean Perceptions of the United States," in *Proceedings of 5th Annual Conference on War and Media—War and Sports* (Independence, MO: Graceland University Center for the Study of the Korean War, 2004), 1–32.

105. Dave Zirin, "A Whole New Ball Game," *The Nation*, March 15, 2006, www.thenation.com/doc/20060327/zirin; Dan Le Batard, "WBC Fosters Our Passion for Patriotism," *Knight Ridder Tribune Business News*, March 5, 2006, 1; Roberto Gonzalez Echevarria, "Castro at the Bat," *New York Times*, January 11, 2006, A29. Nothing was mentioned about Venezuela either, whose democracy the United States had repeatedly tried to overthrow, so as to install the kind of dictatorship it has imposed in so many other nations. It was also hypocritical to criticize Cuba's lack of freedom when post-9/11 America had dramatically curtailed its own civil liberties and when political pundits repeatedly tried to silence outspoken athletes such as Carlos Delgado. Dave Zirin,

"The Bray of Pigs: Bush Nixes Beisbol Cubano," December 21, 2005, http://alternet .org/story/29878.

106. Banning Cuba from the WBC on the heels of baseball's Olympic elimination would have been a big blow. Paula Pettavino and Geralyn Pye, *Sport in Cuba: The Diamond in the Rough* (Pittsburgh: University of Pittsburgh Press, 1994); Duncan Currie, "Cuba May Be in the WBC, but Don't Harbor Any Illusions About Team Fidel," *Daily Standard* (UK), February 9, 2006; Jack Curry, "Baseball Set to Continue Fighting Ban of Cuba," *New York Times*, December 16, 2005; Jack Curry, "Cuba Makes Cut for the Classic," *New York Times*, January 21, 2006; George Vecsey, "Baseball Picks Wrong Battle, Again, in Fighting Fantasy Leagues," *New York Times*, May 28, 2006, C1; Klein, *Growing the Game*. Techno–spy thriller author and Orioles co-owner Tom Clancy was known as a fierce Cold Warrior and political conservative, yet after September 11, he joined Angelos in criticizing Bush foreign policy, including the Iraq War. Alan Wirzbicki, "Paperback Writer," *New Republic*, May 26, 2004. Angel Iglesias of Cuba's National Institute of Sports physically confronted a protester. Calling the demonstrations "cowardly" and "cynical counterrevolutionary provocations," he was briefly arrested. "Anti-Castro Signs Spark International Incident," *Fox Sports*, March 10, 2006; Jack Curry, "Politics Intrude, and Cubans Don't Respond," *New York Times*, March 14, 2006.

107. For gloomier assessments, see Bjarkman, *Diamonds Across the Globe*, and Mike Marqusee, "World Games: The U.S. Tries to Colonize Sport," *Colorlines* 3:2 (July 31, 2000), 36. John Kelly argues that MLB has imposed a "separate but equal" baseball system that's profoundly *unequal*: "While we don't accept separate but equal on race issues and while we understand how it [subjugated] the Negro Leagues as second class, we somehow miss the separate but equal that occurs among nation states and how it does the same thing for baseball in other countries." Kelly, *American Game*; Leonard Koppett, "The Globalization of Baseball," *Indiana Journal of Global Legal Studies* 8 (Fall 2000), 81–84.

108. When the NBA's earlier sports globalization stalled, MLB decided it needed to "own the championship." It couldn't take Mark McGwire's suggestion to "just stay home," since not only were there new fans to attract and profits to be made (WBC merchandise sales were even higher than expected), but the internationalization of its players meant it had to control the situation. As John Kelly suggested, "Under the *Field of Dreams* adage, 'If you build it, they will come,' if MLB hadn't built it, then someone else, probably Japan, would have soon tried to build it instead." Some believe the WBC may help other baseball-playing nations as well. If the WBC permanently supplants Olympic baseball, then according to International Baseball Federation president Aldo Notari, it would be "a disaster for the development of baseball in the world." But if other nations are willing to tolerate American control, they might invest in their WBC team as readily as they had in their Olympic team. Walter LaFeber, *Michael Jordan and the New Global Capitalism* (New York: Norton, 2002); Kelly, *American Game*; Robert Andrew Powell and Alan Schwarz, "Baseball's New World Order," *New York Times*, February 5, 2006, B1; Gould, "Baseball Classic Mirrors World Events"; Tim Brown, "World Baseball Classic: Let's Play Two . . . or More," *Los Angeles Times*, March 18, 2006, D1; Jong Woo Jun and Hyung Min Lee, "Enhancing Global-Scale Visibility and Familiarity: The Impact of the World Baseball Classic on Participating Countries," *Place Branding and Public Diplomacy* 3:1 (2007), 42–52.

109. While Fidel Castro ultimately accepted the blame for the Cuban team not making the finals, he nevertheless complained about Cuba being placed in the Asian (rather than the Caribbean) group, where it had to face the tournament's two toughest teams early on. According to Castro, "What mattered to [WBC] organizers was to eliminate Cuba, a revolutionary country that has heroically resisted and has remained undefeated in the battle of ideas." Fidel Castro, "We Are the Ones to Blame," *Granma Internacional,* March 20, 2009, www.granma.cu/ingles/2009/march/vier20/13reflex1-i.html.

110. Kelly, *American Game*; Klein, *Growing the Game.*

111. Stephen Kinzer, *Overthrow: America's Century of Regime Change from Hawaii to Iraq* (New York: Times Books, 2006); Michael J. Sullivan, *American Adventurism Abroad: Invasions, Interventions, and Regime Changes Since World War II* (Oxford, UK: Blackwell, 2008); William Blum, *Rogue State: A Guide to the World's Only Superpower* (Monroe, ME: Common Courage Press, 2005); Howard Zinn, *A People's History of American Empire* (New York: Metropolitan Books, 2008); Noam Chomsky, *Hegemony or Survival: America's Quest for Global Dominance* (New York: Holt, 1993); Stephen Burman, *The State of the American Empire: How the USA Shapes the World* (Berkeley: University of California Press, 2007); Chalmers Johnson, *Blowback: The Causes and Consequences of American Empire* (New York: Holt, 2000); Chalmers Johnson, *The Sorrows of Empire: Militarism, Secrecy, and the End of the Republic* (New York: Metropolitan Books, 2004); Morris Berman, *Dark Ages America: The Final Phase of Empire* (New York: Norton, 2006).

112. Ring is referencing the legendary baseball poem "Casey at the Bat." Dave Ring, "Bush's Strike Out," *Daily Toreador,* January 13, 2006, 1.

113. R.C. Wilcox, "Of Fungos and Fumbles: Explaining the Cultural Uniqueness of American Sport, or a Paradoxical Peek at Sport," in *Sport in the Global Village,* ed. R.C. Wilcox (Morgantown, WV: Fitness Information Technology, 1994), 73–102; Anatol Lieven, *American Right or Wrong: An Anatomy of American Nationalism* (New York: Oxford University Press, 2005); Steven W. Pope, "Sport and *Pax Americana*," paper presented at the North American Society for Sports History Conference, Glenwood Springs, CO, 2006.

114. George Mitchell bristled when accused of having conducted a "Cold War era interrogation." Teri Thompson and Michael O'Keeffe, "'Cold War' Allegation Makes George Mitchell Hot Under Collar," *New York Daily News,* January 8, 2008.

115. Mitchell J. Nathanson, "The Sovereign Nation of Baseball: Why Federal Law Does Not Apply to 'America's Game' and How It Got That Way," *Villanova Sports & Entertainment Law Journal* (2008); Mitchell J. Nathanson, "Major League Baseball as Enron: The True Meaning of the Mitchell Report," *Outside the Lines* (2008).

116. John Freeman Gill, "The Shots Heard 'Round the World: Inside the Bush Administration's Steroids Scandal," *The Atlantic* 299:3 (April 2007), 50–51.

117. Bruce Reed, "The Benchwarmer," *Slate,* January 17, 2008, www.slate.com/id/2180254.

Chapter 12. The Empire Strikes Out

1. Chalmers Johnson, *Nemesis: The Last Days of the American Republic* (New York: Metropolitan Books, 2007); Morris Berman, *Dark Ages America: The Final Phase of Empire* (New York: Norton, 2006).

2. Alan Bairner, *Sport, Nationalism, and Globalization: European and North American Perspectives* (Albany: State University of New York Press, 2001), 91–113, 163–77; M. Cronin and D. Mayall, eds., *Sporting Nationalisms: Identity, Ethnicity, Immigration and Assimilation* (London: Frank Cass, 1998); John M. Hoberman, *Sport and Political Ideology* (Austin: University of Texas Press, 1984); Mike Marqusee, "World Games: The U.S. Tries to Colonize Sport," *Colorlines* 3:2 (July 31, 2000), 36; Gerald S. Gems, *The Athletic Crusade: Sport and American Cultural Imperialism* (Lincoln: University of Nebraska Press, 2006).

3. Stephen Kinzer, "In Politics as in Baseball," *The Guardian*, May 29, 2007, http://commentisfree.guardian.co.uk/Stephen_kinzer/2007/05/; Dean Chadwin, *Those Damn Yankees: The Secret Life of America's Greatest Franchise* (New York: Verso, 1999). Even worse, "there are several parallels between the New York Yankees and the People's Republic of China. They're both overpowering empires shrouded in mystery and nationalistic fervor." Will Leitch, "A Plague on the Yankees," *New York Times*, October 6, 2007.

4. Of Native Americans, African Americans, Japanese Americans, and Latino Americans. Bairner, *Sport, Nationalism, and Globalization*; G.H. Sage, *Power and Ideology in American Sport* (Champaign, IL: Human Kinetics Books, 1990), 41.

5. David Voigt, *America Through Baseball* (Chicago: Nelson Hall, 1976).

6. Berman, *Dark Ages America*; Morris Berman, *Twilight of American Culture* (New York: Norton, 2001).

7. In his recent trilogy, distinguished political analyst Chalmers Johnson sees U.S. foreign and domestic policies on a collision course with worldwide resentment and resistance. Johnson, *Nemesis*; Chalmers Johnson, *Blowback: The Causes and Consequences of American Empire* (New York: Holt, 2000); Chalmers Johnson, *The Sorrows of Empire: Militarism, Secrecy, and the End of the Republic* (New York: Metropolitan Books, 2004). See also Joseph Stiglitz and Linda Bilmes, *The Three Trillion Dollar War: The True Cost of the Iraq Conflict* (New York: Norton, 2008).

8. Some people have high hopes that the new Obama administration can change America's role in the world. Photographed prominently on the basketball court during the election campaign, Barack Obama also established his baseball credentials—as a fervent and vocal Chicago White Sox fan. As for his foreign policy, Obama has reduced Cold War antagonisms with Cuba and Venezuela, and promised to leave Iraq, but he's escalated U.S. military involvement in Afghanistan and thus far avoided dramatic changes elsewhere in American military policy. We'll have to see whether, under Barack Obama, U.S. foreign policy becomes a "whole new ball game."

9. Alan M. Klein, *Growing the Game: The Globalization of Major League Baseball* (New Haven, CT: Yale University Press, 2006).

10. Ibid. Thomas Friedman, *The Lexus and the Olive Tree* (New York: Farrar, Straus & Giroux, 2000).

11. David P. Fidler, "Baseball in the Global Era: Economic, Legal, and Cultural Perspectives," *Indiana Journal of Global Legal Studies* 8:1 (2000), 1–8; Charles P. Pierce, "The Goodwill Games: Billions of People Worldwide Are Getting Their Impressions of America Not from U.S. Economic and Military Might, but by Watching Its Sports on Television," *Boston Globe*, September 21, 2003, 10.

12. Junwei Yu, *Playing in Isolation: A History of Baseball in Taiwan* (Lincoln: University of Nebraska Press, 2007).

13. Peter C. Bjarkman, *Diamonds Around the Globe: The Encyclopedia of International Baseball* (Westport, CT: Greenwood Press, 2005); vii; William Kelly, "Is Baseball a Global Sport? America's 'National Pastime' as Global Field and International Sport," *Global Networks* 7:2 (2007), 187–201.

14. Jessica Skolnikoff and Robert Engvall, "Colonialism and Baseball: A Cultural Critique of Major League Baseball Academies," 18th Cooperstown Symposium on Baseball and American Culture, June 2006, 1–20; Bairner, *Sport, Nationalism, and Globalization*, 104.

15. Peter C. Bjarkman, "American Baseball Imperialism, Clashing National Cultures, and the Future of Samurai *Besuboru*," *Studies on Asia*, series 3, 3:2 (Fall 2006), 123–40; "The Whole World Is Watching," *Sports Illustrated*, June 14, 2004, 72–86.

16. George Gmelch, ed., *Baseball Without Borders: The International Pastime* (Lincoln: University of Nebraska Press, 2006); Kelly, "Is Baseball a Global Sport?"

17. Under the rubric of "sports diffusion," many theories have been offered about why a particular sport takes hold, or not, from one nation to another—and in particular, why baseball hasn't caught on in as many places as one might imagine. Robert Rydell and Rob Kroes, *Buffalo Bill in Bologna: The Americanization of the World, 1869–1922* (University of Chicago Press, 2005); John Blair, "Football in America," *Modular America: Cross-Cultural Perspectives on the Emergence of an American Way* (Westport, CT: Greenwood Press, 1988); Francis D. Cogliano, "Baseball and American Exceptionalism," in *Sport and National Identity*, ed. Dilwyn Porter and Adrian Smith (New York: Routledge, 2004), 145–67; Susan M. Matarese, *American Foreign Policy and the Utopian Imagination* (Amherst: University of Massachusetts Press, 2001).

18. Allen Guttmann, *Games and Empires: Modern Sports and Cultural Imperialism* (New York: Columbia University Press, 1994), 1–11; Richard C. Crepeau, "Pearl Harbor: A Failure of Baseball?" *Journal of Popular Culture* 15:4 (1982), 67–74; Bairner, *Sport, Nationalism, and Globalization*, 104; Kelly, "Is Baseball a Global Sport?"; Steven W. Pope, ed., *The New American Sport History: Recent Approaches and Perspectives* (Urbana: University of Illinois Press, 1997); Joseph L. Arbena, "Sport and the Study of Latin American Society," in *Sport and Society in Latin America*, ed. Joseph L. Arbena (New York: Greenwood Press, 1988), 1–14; Joseph A. Reaves, *Taking in a Game: A History of Baseball in Asia* (Lincoln: University of Nebraska Press, 2002).

19. Kelly, "Is Baseball a Global Sport?" Guttmann, *Games and Empires*; Gerald R. Gems, "Sports, Colonialism, and United States Imperialism," *Journal of Sport History* 33:1 (Spring 2006), 3–25.

20. Bjarkman, *Diamonds Around the Globe;* Bjarkman, "American Baseball Imperialism"; Andrew Zimbalist, *In the Best Interests of Baseball? The Revolutionary Reign of Bud Selig* (Hoboken, NJ: Wiley, 2006).

21. William Blum, *Rogue State: A Guide to the World's Only Superpower* (Monroe, ME: Common Courage Press, 2005); Noam Chomsky, *Rogue States: The Rule of Force in World Affairs* (Boston: South End Press, 2000); Ziauddin Sardar and Merryl Wyn Davies, *Why Do People Hate America?* (New York: Disinformation Books, 2003).

22. Marqusee, "World Games"; Bill Lee with Jim Prime, *The Little Red (Sox) Book* (Chicago: Triumph Books, 2003).

23. Joseph L. Price, "'What So Proudly We Hailed': National Crisis, the National Anthem, and the National Pastime," paper presented to the 16th Cooperstown Symposium on Baseball and American Culture, Cooperstown, NY, June 2004; Merritt

Clifton, "Where the Twain Shall Meet: What Baseball Means to Japan—and Humanity," *National Pastime* 4 (1985), 12–22. In his novel, David James Duncan suggests that baseball can "generate suspense and excitement on a national scale, just like war. And baseball can only be played in peace . . . pro ballplayers . . . are basically just a bunch of unusually well-coordinated guys working hard and artfully to prevent wars, by making peace more interesting." David James Duncan, *The Brothers K* (New York: Dial Press, 1996), 517.

24. Fidler, "Baseball in the Global Era," 1.

25. Gerald S. Gems, *For Pride, Profit, and Patriarchy: Football and the Incorporation of American Cultural Values* (Lanham, MD: Scarecrow Press, 2000).

26. Tim Wendel, *Castro's Curveball* (New York: Ballantine, 1999).

Index

Aaron, Hank, 199, 277, 357–58n20
Abbas II of Egypt, 70–71
Abreu, Bobby, 275
Acosta, Baldomero, 107
Adams, Brooks, 20
Adams, Doc, 6
Adams, Henry, 54–55
Adlesberg, Albert, 33
Afghanistan, baseball in, 272
Africa: baseball in the early 2000s, 272, 384n91; early baseball in, 314n56; post–World War I baseball, 112–13; and post–World War II baseball diplomacy, 168–69; World War II-era baseball, 151
African American players: and Berlin Olympics, 121; Cuban, 41, 108; and Cuban baseball, 40–42, 108, 303n40; declining opportunities in baseball, 232, 381n80; and Jim Crow, 41, 46, 57, 142, 163; and Mexican League, 165–66; and MLB color barrier, 41–42, 59, 96, 121, 163–64, 168–69, 180–81, 335n59; and origins of baseball/white American superiority, 49; and post–World War II baseball diplomacy, 168–69; and post–World War II military baseball, 170; the 25th Infantry Regiment team, 42, 45, 46; World War II-era baseball and military racism, 142–44, 335n59. *See also* Negro Leagues
African Baseball and Softball Association, 360n41
The Age of Baseball Fever (film), 173
Aguinaldo, Emilio, 44
Ainsmith, Eddie, 82
Albert, Alejandro, 46
Albom, Mitch, 254
Albright, Madeleine, 239, 242
Alderson, Sandy, 223, 274
Alemán, Miguel, 167

Alert America Convoy, 190
Alex Taylor & Co., 79
Alexander, Grover Cleveland, 81, 83, 214
Algeria, 151
Algiers Streetwalkers, 151
Ali, Muhammad, 206
Alien Enemies Act, 157
Alien Registration Act, 157
All-Africa Baseball Tournament, 384n91
All-American Girls Professional Baseball League (AAGPBL), 145–46, 162, 341n10
All-Army Baseball Championship (1957), 194
Allen, Jim, 270–71, 272
Allen, Maurice, 61
Allen, Newt, 113
All-Pacific Recreation Fund, 133
All-Star Army Team, 52–53
All-Star Games: Home Run Derby, 275; and Iraq War patriotic displays (2007), 260; [1969], 207; [1991], 222; [1997], 242; [2006], 268; World War II-era, 134–35, 144
All-Union Baseball Federation, 221
Almeida, Rafael, 41
Altizer, Dave, 60
Alvarez, Bernardo, 266–67
Amateur Baseball World Series, 107–8
Ambrose, Stephen, 298n38
America First Committee, 128
American Association, 17–19, 139
American Baseball Congress, 110
American Baseball Guild, 165
American Boy magazine, 86
American expansionism, nineteenth-century, 25–26, 37–47
American Indian Movement (AIM), 241
American League: and Ban Johnson, 73, 74; and baseball wars of early twentieth century, 73–75; and Vietnam War, 199

American Legion, 97–98, 146, 190, 192, 212, 322n13
American Legion Quarterly, 91
American Railroad Journal, 11
American Sports Publishing Company, 91
American Sugar Company, 109
American Veterans of World War II (AMVETS), 163, 177
Americanism and patriotic nationalism (post–World War I), 94–98
Americanization, 55–56, 108, 171–74
America's National Game (Spalding), 13, 48
Amsterdam Expos, 360n42
Ananicz, Tom, 139
Andelman, Bob, 376n60
Angelos, Peter, 237, 239–40, 277, 362n49
Anglo-American League, 90–91
Anson, Cap, 12, 21, 25
Antarctica, 349n10
Anti-Imperialist League, 45
Anti-Sweatshop Community Alliance, 268
Antonelli, Johnny, 178
Apple, Max, 350n23
Arce, Bill, 169
Argentina, 349n10
Arkin, William, 258, 373n35
Armed Forces Radio, 154, 179
Armstrong, Neil, 359n28
Army and Navy Life, 45–46
Army and Navy Relief Fund, 135
Army Flying Fortress, 136
Army-Navy baseball games, 47, 91, 92, 98, 262, 375n55
Arnett, Peter, 242
Arnett, Lt. Col. Roscoe, 153
Arnovich, Morrie, 139
Arocha, Rene, 237, 366n85
Arthur, Chester A., 12
Asahi baseball clubs (Japan), 43, 69, 133, 148
Asian Amateur Baseball Championships, 175, 180, 354n58
Asiatic Station Baseball League, 60–61
association football (soccer) clubs, 314n57
Atia, Tarek, 246
Atlanta Braves, 241–42
Atlantic League, 66
Atlantic Monthly, 46, 63, 280
AT&T Park (San Francisco), 260
Australia: baseball in the early 2000s, 385n96; baseball in the 1980s and 1990s, 358–59n27; Cold War-era baseball, 193–94; early leagues, 22–23, 70; and 1888 World Tour, 22–23; and McGraw-Comiskey world tour, 70; post–World War I baseball, 113
Australian Baseball Council, 70, 193–94
Australian Baseball League, 358–59n27
Australian National League, 113
Axelson, G.W., 69
Ayala, Carlos, 31

Babcock, Sgt. Dana, 154
Babe Ruth–Connie Mack All Star tour (1934), 119, 120, 329n85
Back to Africa Movement, 58
Bad Nauheim Baseball League, 155
Bad News Bears (film), 211
Bailey, Bob, 18
Bairner, Alan, 264
Baker, Dusty, 251, 371n22
Baker, Newton, 82
balata balls, 144, 335n65
Ball and Bat Funds, 135
Ball Four (Bouton), 205
Balmer, Randall, 374n42
Baltimore Elite Stars, 170–71
Baltimore Orioles: Cuban games, 237, 238–40, 292; and "Great Baseball War of 1901–1903," 73–74
Baltimore Sun, 98
Bancroft, Frank, 38
Bangkok Boys Baseball Association, 354n58
Bank, Col. Theodore, 131
Banks, Ernie, 178, 199, 201–2
Los Barbudos (the Bearded Ones), 195
Barnier, Alan, 282
Barrow, Ed, 84, 128, 136, 138
baseball academies, 233–35, 267, 287–88
Baseball and the Cold War (Senzel), 196
baseball cards, 133, 214, 268
Baseball Club of Africa (Tunis), 113
Baseball Digest, 133
Baseball Diplomacy Act, 240
Baseball for Italy, Inc., 171
Baseball for Peace tours, 217
Baseball Fraternity, 82
Baseball Magazine, 41, 115, 312n37; on home runs and the "power game" in 1920s, 101–2; and McGraw-Comiskey world tours, 69, 72–73, 103; and post–World War II baseball diplomacy, 168; and pre–World War I baseball militarism/imperialism, 52, 61, 64–65, 68, 69, 72–73; and World War I, 77, 79, 80, 88, 89–90, 320n44; and World War II–era baseball, 129

Baseball Reliquary, 202
Baseball Tomorrow Fund, 232
baseball wars: early twentieth-century,
    73–76; late nineteenth-century, 16–19
Baseball World Inc., 364n65
Baseball Writers' Association of America,
    131, 136, 351n25
Baseball/Beisbol: Latin American Baseball
    Project, 266
baseballs (equipment): Costa Rican,
    268–69; Cuban, 197; Haitian,
    231–32, 268; manufacturing and
    labor, 231–32, 268–69, 288;
    Nicaraguan, 217; and World War I,
    79; and World War II prisoner-of-war
    camps, 155–56; World War II–era
    balata balls, 144, 335n65
basketball, 14, 232, 272, 289, 387n108
Bass, Randy, 357n20
Batangas Normal School (Philippines),
    44
Bates, Albert, 28
Batista, Fulgencio, 108, 194
"Batter Up: Uncle Sam Is at the Plate"
    (song), 80
Batter Up (USO tour), 150–51
The Battle of Base Ball (Claudy), 51–52
Battle of the Bulge, 140, 150, 169
Bay of Pigs invasion, 196, 198
Bayard, Thomas, 22
Bearden, Gene, 140
Beatty, Jerome, 81, 85
Beazley, Johnny, 148
Bedingfield, Gary, 256
Beer and Whiskey League, 17
Beijing International, 221
El Beisbol (Krich), 217
Belgium, 360–61n42
Bell, Cool Papa, 165
Bell, Maj. Gen. Franklin, 44, 70
Beltré, Adrián, 234
Ben Cramer, Richard, 244
Bender, Albert "Chief," 75, 85, 98,
    241
Bendix, William, 132
Bennett, Eddie, 384n91
Bennett, Tony, 259
Benswanger, William, 164
Berg, Moe, 117, 151–53, 338n90
Berger, Victor, 100
Berlin Crisis (1961), 198
Berlin Wall, fall of, 222, 225
Berman, Morris, 284–85
Berra, Yogi, 140, 225, 282, 370n10
Bertman, Skip, 230

The Best Years of Our Lives (film), 162
Bethlehem Steel, 31, 84
Beveridge, Albert, 55
Beyond a Boundary (James), 32
bin Laden, Osama, 255
Birns, Larry, 266
Bjarkman, Peter, 30, 197, 228, 267–68,
    287–88, 290–91, 293
Black, Joe, 143
Black Sox scandal, 95–97, 100, 244,
    321n4, 323n23
Blair, Jeff, 359n31
Blanton, Joe, 261
Bloodgood, Clifford, 168
Bloom, John, 214
Bloomer, John, 37
Bob Hope Patriot Award, 372n32
Boggs, Kelly, 370n10
Bomb Bay Messenger, 153
Bonds, Barry, 246
Bonds, Bobby, 201
Bonura, Zeke, 151
Boone, Henry William, 60
Borges, Tomás, 217
Borstelmann, Thomas, 15, 144
Bosch, Juan, 67, 197
Bosnia-Herzegovina, 227
Boston Beaneaters, 40
Boston Braves, 136
Boston Globe, 112
Boston Herald, 27
Boston Red Sox, 94–95, 267
Boston Red Stockings, 17
Boston Transcript, 89
Boswell, Tom, 249, 262–63
Bourne, Randolph, 85
Bouton, Jim, 205, 353n44
Bowden, Jim, 245, 252
Bowman, John, 13, 20, 28, 79, 95
Boyington, Maj. Gregory (Pappy), 154
"Bracero Program," 166
Bradley, Alva, 145
Bradley, Omar, 52, 131, 151
Brazil, 112, 312–13n45, 327n61, 349n10,
    378n65
Brazilian Baseball Confederation, 363n62
Breadon, Sam, 138
Breneman, John, 255, 372–73n33
Breton, Marcos, 233
Brewer, Chet, 142
Bricker, John, 161, 184
Bridal Champion (film), 173
Briley, Ron, 177, 183, 185, 189, 198,
    204, 247, 349n13
Brissie, Lou, 140, 192, 257

British Baseball Association, 314n57
British Broadcasting Corporation (BBC),
    243
British National League, 360–61n42
Britt, Albert, 82
Brock, Darryl, 13
Broeg, Bob, 176
Brokaw, Tom, 216
Brooklyn Dodgers: and Cuban baseball,
    40–41, 193; move to LA, 194,
    349n13; 1951 season and "shot heard
    'round the world," 182; and post–
    World War II baseball diplomacy, 169;
    and Rickey's anti-radicalism, 190–91;
    Robinson and the baseball color
    barrier, 163–64, 168–69; World
    War II–era, 144, 150, 151
Brooklyn Royal Giants, 41
Brooks, Noah, 11
Brotherhood of Professional Baseball
    Players, 18, 82
Brotherhood War, 17–18
Brown, Bill, 27, 56
Brown, Elwood, 92, 114
Brown, Joe E., 133
Brown, Mordecai "Three Finger," 75
Brown, Robert "Bobby," 178, 215, 245,
    356n13
Brown, Willard, 170
Brownfield, William, 266
Bruce, Damon, 371n26
Brundage, Avery, 329n87
Brush, John, 39–40
Brush classification system, 24
Brutus, Dennis, 268
Bryson, Michael, 16
Buck, Jack, 248
Buck, Joe, 260, 375n50
Buffalo Bill Cody's Wild West Show, 25
Bull Durham (film), 253–54
Bullock, Steve, 138, 147, 194
"bullpen," 16
Bumbry, Al, 200
Bumiller, Elisabeth, 255
Bunau-Varilla, Philippe, 66
Burbage, Buddy, 139
Bureau of Educational and Cultural
    Affairs (U.S. State Department), 169
Burgos, Adrian, 30, 58, 192, 302n33
Burk, Robert, 138, 243
Burns, Ken, 298n38
Burns, Nicholas, 227, 362n49
Burnside, Pete, 210
Burr, Alex, 83
Burt, Gen. Andrew, 15

Busch Stadium (St. Louis), 248
Bush, George H.W., 127, 179, 215, 218,
    222, 227, 385n96
Bush, George W., 200, 246, 255–56;
    "Axis of Evil" speech, 251; as
    commissioner candidate, 223, 226,
    281, 362n47; and Cooperstown Hall
    of Fame, 253–54; and Iraq War, 260,
    273; and Little League baseball, 188,
    246; and 9/11 attacks, 129, 248–50,
    252; and Steinbrenner, 372–73n33;
    and Texas Rangers, 222, 224, 252,
    255; and 2004 reelection campaign,
    255–56; and U.S.-Cuba relations,
    265, 276, 378n66; and U.S.-Japanese
    relations, 270; and U.S.-Venezuela
    relations, 265–67, 379n71; and
    Vincent, 222, 223
Bush, William "Bucky," 222
Butler, Smedley, 57
Butte, Lt. Col. Charles, 171
Butts, Edmund, 35
Byrne, Tommy, 140
Byrnes, James F., 139, 165

Cabaleiro, Ricardo, 30
Cabrera, Miguel, 275
Cadore, Leon, 89
Caine, Hall, 71
California Angels, 207. *See also* Anaheim
    Angels
Calley, Lt. William, 211
Cambodia, 383n90
Cammeyer, William, 10
Campanella, Roy, 164, 165
Camus, Albert, 1, 291
Canada: baseball in the early 2000s,
    385n96; Civil War–era baseball, 13,
    297nn30–31; girls' baseball, 229;
    major-league teams, 225–26; and
    McGraw-Comiskey world tour, 69;
    reciprocity with American leagues,
    67; and singing of "God Bless
    America," 258–59; and World War I,
    77–78; World War II–era military
    baseball, 148–49
Canadian Reciprocity Bill, 67
Canel, Buck, 194–95
Cannon, Carl, 255
Cape Cod League, 262
Caple, Jim, 278
Caracas Base-Ball Club, 33
Cardenal, José, 213
Cardenas, Leo, 195
Carefree Father (film), 173

Caribbean baseball: and early twentieth-century American imperialism, 64–68, 312–13n45; and globalization, 228, 232–35, 265–69, 364n70, 381n80; late nineteenth-century, 30, 32–33, 302n33; and MLB baseball academies, 233–35, 267, 287–88; post–World War I, 107–13. *See also names of individual countries*
Caribbean Championships, 193
Carlin, George, 263
Carlisle School, 58
Carranza, Venustantio, 68, 111
Carresquel, Alejandro, 142
Carriere, Michael, 187
Carrillo Puerto, Felipe, 111–12
Carson, "Kit," 298n39
Carter, Jimmy, 214, 236
Carter, Thomas, 239
Cartwright, Alexander, 6, 15, 22, 148
Cartwright, Rosalind, 202
Casablanca Yankees, 151
"Casey at the Bat," 25, 38
Castro, Fidel, 192–93, 236–40, 265, 350n23, 365–66n82; and Cuban Revolution, 194–98; and WBC, 277, 388n109
Castro, Jud, 66
Cataneo, David, 154
Cava, Pete, 122
Caylor, Oliver, 18
CBS Clowns, 149
Center for International Exchange, 173
Central Intelligence Agency (CIA), 152, 180, 193, 216, 237, 255
Century magazine, 47
Cepeda, Orlando, 193
Ceylon, 22–23, 70
Chadwick, Henry, 18, 34–35, 47, 51, 73–74, 304n44
Chaillaux, H.L., 146
Chan Ho Park, 218
Chandler, Albert "Happy," 163–65, 166–68, 177, 184, 342n18
Changsha Field Ball Society, 61
Chapman, Ben, 145
Chapman, Sam, 147
Chappell, Larry, 83
Charleston, Oscar, 46, 83
Chase, Hal, 75
Chauncey, Henry, 118
Chávez, Hugo, 265–66, 378n66, 379n68
Chen, Joan, 64
Chen Shui-bian, 220–21
Cheney, Richard, 224–25

Chevez, Tony, 208–9
Chiang Kai-shek, 211
Chicago American, 51
Chicago Cubs, 94–95, 136, 144, 234
Chicago Daily News, 75
Chicago Herald American, 150
Chicago White Sox, 16, 67, 81, 266. *See also* Black Sox Scandal
Chicago White Stockings, 12, 16, 21, 69
Chicago World's Fair (1893), 302n25
Chien-ming Wang, 271
Chile, 312–13n45, 351n24, 378n65
China: baseball in the early 2000s, 271–72, 383n89; baseball in the 1980s and 1990s, 221; Chinese nationalists and Taiwan, 174–75, 210–11; Cold War–era baseball, 194, 354n58; Communist revolution, 174–75; and early twentieth-century baseball imperialism, 60–61; and McGraw-Comiskey world tour, 69–70; and nineteenth-century baseball imperialism, 28; Nixon and "Ping Pong diplomacy," 210; post–World War I tours, 119; post–World War II, 168, 174–75
China Relief Expedition, 60
China-Burma-India theater (World War II), 155
Chinese All-Star Game, 271
Chinese Baseball Association, 271
Chinese Exclusion Act (1882), 21, 60
Chinese Hawaiian baseball team, 42
Chinese Professional Baseball League (CPBL), 220, 271
Chisholm, Julian, 9
Chosen Amateur Athletic Association (Korea), 120
Chun Doo Hwan, 218
Churchill, Winston, 91
Cicotte, Eddie, 89
Cincinnati Red Stockings, 11, 12, 13, 16, 41, 60
Cincinnati Reds, 81, 110, 122, 190, 348n3
Cinco Estrellas team (Nicaragua), 111
Citgo Petroleum Corporation, 266
Civil Rights Game, 242
Civil War baseball, 7–11
Civil War Times, 10–11
Clancy, Tom, 387n106
Claudy, C.H., 51–52
Clemens, Roger, 252, 280, 371–72n26
Clemente, Roberto, 193, 209
Cleveland, Grover, 12, 21

Cleveland Indians, 59–60, 105, 164, 169, 241–42
Cleveland Naps, 59
Cleveland Plain Dealer, 60
Clifton, Merritt, 5, 118, 293
Clinton, Bill, 227, 233, 239, 243–44, 292, 358–59n27
Club Managua, 110
Cobb, Ty, 41, 52, 78, 83, 95, 116, 323n23
Cobbs, Thomas, 69
Cochrane, Mickey, 147
Cockcroft, James, 49, 57
Codrescu, Andre, 238
Cohen, Morris, 103, 324n30
Cold War politics and baseball, 175–88, 189–211; and American art/culture, 185–88, 347nn74–75; and the "American way," 186; baseball metaphors, 185; baseball's international initiatives, 189–94, 208–11, 355n59; collapse of service baseball, 194; and Frick as commissioner, 178, 189–92; and Little League, 187–88, 210–11, 348n80; rhetoric and indoctrination/ propaganda, 179–80, 189–94, 198; Robinson's HUAC testimony, 180–82, 190; Soviet bomb test and Thomson's "shot heard 'round the world," 182–84; and U.S.-Cuban relations, 192–93, 194–97, 350n23. *See also* Korean War; Vietnam War
Coleman, Jerry, 140, 178–79, 212, 215, 245, 257
Collier, Price, 56
Collier's magazine, 81, 172
Collins, Eddie, 82
Collins, Jimmy, 40
Collins, Terry, 362n49
Colombia, 66, 363n62, 378n65
Colombia Winter League, 363n62
colonial America, 5–6
color barrier and major league baseball, 41–42, 59, 96, 121, 163–64, 168–69, 180–81, 335n59
Columbia Brewing Company (St. Louis), 130
Comiskey, Charles, 46, 53, 69, 71, 78, 90, 103–4, 323n23
Committee on Baseball Integration, 163
Committee to Defend America by Aiding the Allies, 128
Communism/anticommunism: and the baseball color barrier, 163–64; post–World War I, 89–90, 95–96, 105;

Robeson's charges against America, 180–82
Communist Party of the USA (CPUSA), 163–64
Confederate Baseball Club, 9
Conigliaro, Tony, 199
Contras, Nicaraguan, 216–17
Cook, Beano, 213–14
Cooke, Alistair, 263
Cookson, Charles, 176
Cooper, Mort, 138
Cooperstown and Doubleday myth, 48
Cooperstown Hall of Fame, 226, 227, 372n28; the Baseball/Beisbol project, 266; canceled *Bull Durham* showing, 253–54; and Doubleday myth, 50; Film Festival (2007), 279; Petroskey and Republican Party, 253–54, 372n29, 372n31
Correa, Edwin, 380n76
Cosell, Howard, 236
Costa Rica and baseball manufacturing, 268–69
Coste, Guillaume, 273
Costello, Eddie, 346n54
Coubertin, Pierre de, 301n16
Coulter, Ann, 253
counterculture and Vietnam War, 202–8, 212–13, 353n42
Cousins, Norman, 172
Cousins, William, 186–87
Cramer, Emilio, 33
Crawford, Russell, 186, 203, 205
Crawford, Sam, 69
Creamer, Robert, 206
Creel Committee, 87
Crepeau, Richard, 98, 106, 122, 124, 136
cricket, 7, 32, 33, 34, 48–49, 70
Crissey, Harrington, 50, 139
Crocke, Erle, Jr., 165, 177
Cromartie, Warren, 357n20
Cronin, Joe, 154
Crow, Carl, 44
Crowder, Alvin, 80
Cuban American National Foundation, 240
Cuban baseball: African American players, 41, 108; and American baseball imperialism (nineteenth- and early twentieth-century), 30–33, 63, 65; and baseball colonialism, 228; and Bush administration, 265, 276, 378n66, 386n105; Cold War-era U.S.-Cuban relations, 192–97, 350n23; and Cuban Revolution,

194–97; goodwill tours, 367n90; and Mariel Boatlift, 237; MLB recruiting/defections and U.S.-Cuban relations, 235–40, 366n85, 367n89; and Negro Leagues, 40–41; and nineteenth-century nationalism/independence movement, 30–32, 38, 42, 290; and Olympic baseball, 230–31, 238, 240, 274; post–World War I, 107–8; and post–World War II Mexican League War, 342–43n19; Ruth's barnstorming visit (1920), 107; and Spanish-American War, 37–42, 305n9; style of, 365–66n82; and the WBC, 276–77, 278, 292, 387n106, 388n109; and World Baseball Cup, 274

Cuban Missile Crisis (1962), 198
Cuban Professional League, 30, 31, 40–41, 108
Cuban Revolution, 194–97
Cuban X Giants, 40
Curry, Jack, 224
"Curse of the Bambino," 255, 372n33
"Curve Ball" (Iraqi defector), 254–55
Custer, Gen. George, 15–16, 299n43
Czechoslovakia, 103, 168, 169, 324n31

Dai Nippon Tokyo Yakyu Kurabu (the Great Japan Tokyo Baseball Club), 117
Daisuke Matsuzaka, 270, 278
Daley, Robert, 194
Damon, Johnny, 261–62
Dandridge, Ray, 165
Daniel, Dan, 123–24, 129–30, 196
Dantos Sports Factory (Nicaragua), 217
Dark, Alvin, 189–90
Dark Ages America (Berman), 284–85
Davis, Jefferson, 12
Dawson, James, 137
Dawson Pact (1910), 66
Day, Leon, 165, 170
De Vries, Jack, 105
Dean, Dizzy, 98, 137
Dearborn, Henry, 6
Debs, Eugene, 100, 316n8
DeCasseres, Benjamin, 77, 78
Decatur Commies, 190
Deford, Frank, 263–64
Delahanty, Ed, 59
Delay, Janine, 239
Delgado, Carlos, 257–58, 386n105
DeLillo, Don, 182–84, 203
Dell, Rick, 273

Dennis, Pvt. David, 150
Denton, Jeremiah, 213
Depew, Chauncey, 26
Derby Baseball Club (England), 314n57
DeRosa, Christopher, 179, 180
Detroit News, 137
Detroit Tigers, 41
Detroit Times, 141
Dewey, Adm. George, 29, 39, 44, 70, 73
Dewey, Thomas, 331n22
Dickens, Irv, 138–39
Dickson, Murry, 140
Dihigo, Martin, 165, 197
Dilweg, La Vern, 132
DiMaggio, Dom, 148, 173, 257
DiMaggio, Giuseppe, 142
DiMaggio, Joe, 171, 360–61n42; and the baseball color barrier, 163; and Castro, 238; hitting streak, 127–29; Korean War tours, 178, 346n52; post–World War II Japanese tours, 173; and World War II–era baseball, 137, 140–42, 148, 162
DiMaggio, Vince, 147
Disabled American Veterans, 190
Dixie Chicks, 258
D&M Sporting Goods, 79
Doby, Larry, 46, 143, 164, 169
Dodger Stadium and Monday's "flag-rescue," 212–13, 259
Dole, Sanford, 22
Dole Corporation, 113
Dominican Republic: baseball in the early 2000s, 267; Cold War–era baseball, 192, 197–98; Dominican-style baseball, 109, 325n49; and early twentieth-century baseball imperialism, 66–67; Japanese recruiting in, 219, 233, 364n70; MLB recruiting and baseball academies, 233, 267; and nineteenth-century American imperialism, 32–33; and post–World War I baseball, 108–9; and Sandino, 326n55; winter leagues, 192, 197–98, 364n70
Donaldson, Carter, 65
Donlin, Mike, 69
Donnelly, Walter, 169, 191
Donoghue, Robert, 164–65
Donovan, Wild Bill, 152–53
Don't Take My Bat Away Coalition, 372n31
Dooley, Bill, 117
Doolittle, Lt. Col. Jimmy, 153
Doubleday, Abner, 7, 48
Doubleday myth, 47–50

Dougherty, Daniel, 26
Doulens, Maj. Roger, 175
Downs, John, 150
Doyle, Sir Arthur Conan, 103
Doyle, Larry, 69, 80
Dozer, Richard, 213
Dr. Strangelove (film), 203
Du Bois, W.E.B., 58
Ducat, Stephen, 251
Duffy, Hugh, 40
Duncan, David James, 390–91n23
Duncan, Frank, 143
Dunlap, George W., 44
Duquette, Dan, 384n92
Durocher, Leo, 102, 144, 150, 174, 194, 219, 341n10
Duvalier, "Baby Doc," 231
Duvall, Charles, 21
Duvall, John, 172–73, 182–84
Dyja, Thomas, 10
Dyreson, Mark, 101, 105, 122

Eanes, Louis, 132
East China Intercollegiate Athletic Association, 61
Eastern European baseball, 273, 360n42
Ebbets Field, 132, 136, 169, 177, 179, 190
Eckert, Gen. William, 198–200, 201, 355n59
Economist, 223
Eguchi, Saburo, 119
Egypt, 23–24, 70–71
Ehrenreich, Barbara, 231
Eisenhower, Dwight, 52, 151, 161, 165, 178, 210, 340n114, 348n1
Elfers, James, 69
Elkins, Stephen, 35
Ellis, Dock, 204
Ellis, John, 204
Elysian Fields (New Jersey), 6
Emeni, Aduaye, 169
Emmet, Robert, 147
End Zone (DeLillo), 183, 203
Enders, Eric, 253
Engelhardt, Tom, 160
Engelmann, Adolph, 7
England (Great Britain): association football (soccer) clubs, 314n57; baseball in the 1990s, 225, 360–61n42; and cricket, 7, 33, 48–49, 70; and disputed origins of baseball, 47–49, 71; early clubs, 314n57, 314n60; and the 1888 World Tour, 25; interwar baseball, 103–4, 324n33;

and McGraw–Comiskey world tours, 71–72, 104; World War I–era military baseball, 90–91; World War II–era military baseball, 148–49
Engvall, Robert, 288
Enoken's Home Run King (film), 173
Erlich, Blake, 171
Essegian, Chuck, 210
Estalella, Bobby, 142
Estrada y Palma, Tomás, 40, 41
ETO (European Theatre of Operations) World Series, 149
Etten, Nick, 150
European Baseball Championships, 222
European Baseball Confederation, 169
Evers, Johnny, 83
Everts, Thomas, 16
Ewing, George, 6
exceptionalism, American, 13, 48–49
Extra Bases Foundation, 258

Faber, Red, 69
Fairbanks, Douglas, 79
Fairly, Ron, 351n30
Faisal II, King, 169
Fall, Sen. Albert, 111
Far Eastern Games, 47, 61, 92, 114, 116, 120
"farm system," 228
Farrell, Warren, 203
Father Knows Best (television), 185
Feather River Bulletin, 122
Federal League, 19, 72, 75–76, 99
Federal League War of 1914–1915, 75–76
Feeney, Charles, 201
Fehr, Donald, 252
Feierstein, Mark, 378n66
Feldman, Jay, 158, 217
Feliciano, José, 205
Feller, Bob, 126–27, 137, 139, 147, 162, 166, 201, 255–57
Fellman, Elliott, 360n42
Felton, Happy, 190
Fenian Baseball Club, 13
Fenway Park, 178–79, 201, 224, 272
Ferri, Antonio, 152
Fidler, David, 234, 286
Field of Dreams (film), 1, 214, 387n108
Finland, 103, 324n31
Finnish Relief Fund, 135
First Association War, 17
First Pitch, 383n90
flags, American: Lasorda and anti-flag desecration amendment, 259; Monday's "flag-rescue" at Dodger

Stadium, 212–13, 259; and 9/11 attacks, 249; patriotic displays of late 1980s, 223; and Persian Gulf War, 224, 360n39
Flaherty, Pat, 68
Fleer, Josh, 256
Fleischer, Ari, 254, 372n31
Fleischman, Al, 202
Fletcher, Art, 80
Flood, Curt, 206, 214, 354n54
Florida Marlins, 220, 240
football, 2, 262–64, 293, 376n57; and African American players, 232; and Cold War–era baseball, 194; and Doubleday myth, 49–50; and Persian Gulf War, 224; post–Civil War, 14; and Reagan foreign policy, 214; and Roosevelt, 49–50; and Vietnam War, 198, 203; and war, 35, 49–50, 198, 203, 224, 263, 376–77n60
Forbes, Cameron, 46, 116
Ford, Gerald, 214
Ford, Henry, 95–96, 322n6
Ford, Whitey, 178, 245
A Foreign Affair (film), 170
Fort, Rodney, 229
Fort Wayne Capeharts, 176
Foster, John, 82
Fox Network, 224, 249, 257
Foxhole Circuit (USO tour), 150
Foxx, Jimmie, 117–18, 145
France: baseball in the early 2000s, 273; baseball in the 1990s, 360–61n42; and 1888 World Tour, 24, 301n16; and McGraw-Comiskey world tour, 71; post–World War I baseball, 324n31; World War I–era baseball, 90–93
Frank, Stanley, 133
Frank Merriwell sports novels, 56
Franks, Tommy, 251–52
Fraser, Ron, 363n60
Frazee, Harry, 322n6
free agency, 214, 242–43, 343n21, 368n96
Freeburg, Dwight, 144
Freedman, Andrew, 74
Freedom Alliance, 261
Freehan, Bill, 204
French, Larry, 178
French Baseball Federation, 113
Fresno Athletic Club, 157
Frick, Ford, 87, 134; Cold War rhetoric, 178, 189–92, 196; and Cuban baseball, 196, 197; and Eisenhower, 348n1
Friedman, Thomas, 286, 375n52

Friends of Greek Baseball, 362n49
Frisch, Frankie, 123, 151
From the Ballpark to the Battlefield: Baseball and World War II (television), 257
Fuhr, Eberhard "Zip," 339n104
Fukuyama, Francis, 223
Fullerton, Hugh, 55
Funston, Frederick, 44–45, 306n23

Gaddis, John Lewis, 246
Galeano, Eduardo, 54
Gallo, Bill, 250
Garbey, Barbaro, 237
Gardella, Danny, 167–68, 343n20
Garms, Debs, 316n8
Garrison, Lindley, 52
Garvey, Marcus, 58, 108
"Gas House Gang," 117
Gates, Clifton, 165
Gayo, Rene, 235
Gedeon, Elmer, 140
Gehrig, Lou, 116, 117–18, 137, 243, 329n85
Gehringer, Charlie, 117–18
Gems, Gerald, 29, 47, 115, 265, 282
Gentlemen's Agreement (U.S.-Japan), 62–63
George, David, 91
George V, King, 71, 91
Gergen, Joe, 224, 225
Germany: atomic weapons program, 152; and Landis's anti-German activities, 100; and 1936 Berlin Olympics, 121–22; post–World War I leagues, 92; post–World War II baseball diplomacy, 169–71; World War II prisoner-of-war camps, 155–57
GI World Series (1945), 170
Giamatti, Bart, 204, 215, 222
Gibson, Bob, 201
Gibson, Josh, 165
Gilbert, Thomas, 158, 159
Giles, Warren, 144
Gillett, Philip, 63–64
Gilmore, "Fighting Jim," 75
Giuliani, Rudy, 247, 248
Gleason, Roy, 200–201
Glenn, John, 179
Global Baseball League, 354n58
globalization and major league baseball, 1–2, 227–35, 273–81, 282–94; and All-Star Game home run derbies, 275; baseball academies and recruiting practices, 233–35, 267, 287–88; and baseball-equipment manufacturing,

globalization and major league baseball
(*continued*)
231–32, 268–69, 288; Caribbean and
Latin American players, 228, 232–35,
265–69, 381n80; and colonization/
neocolonialism, 227–29; and future of
MLB empire, 279–81, 282–94; and
Kuhn, 214–15, 236–37; and media-
baseball synergy, 230, 269, 288–89,
381n81; and multinational
corporations, 264, 286–87, 288; and
Olympic Games, 230–31; and Selig,
227, 230, 278, 370; and "separate but
equal" policies, 387n107; and the
WBC, 274–78, 287, 289, 292,
387n108
Gmelch, George, 200, 289
"God Bless America" (song), 257–59,
374nn41–42
Godfrey, Paul, 258
Goebbels, Joseph, 149
Goethels, Col. George, 66
Goewey, Ed, 93
Gold, Theodore, 206–7
Goldsmith Company, 156
Goldstein, Richard, 154
Gomez, Lefty, 139
Gomez, Preston, 236
Gómez, Rubén, 33
Gonzalez, Elian, 240
Gonzalez Echevarria, Roberto, 65, 293
Goodwill Games, 222
Gordon, Joe, 148
Gore, Kim, 381n80
Gorman, Bill, 37
Gould, James, 130, 133
Gould, William, 275
Gowdy, Hank, 83, 317n22
Graham, Billy, 205
Graham, Frank, 134
Grand Rapids Chicks, 145
Grant, Charlie, 59
Grant, Eddie, 83
Grant, Ulysses S., 12, 18, 32
Graves, Abner, 48
Graves, Danny, 383n90
Gray, Pete, 145
The Great American Novel (Roth), 185–86
"Great Baseball War of 1901–1903,"
73–74
Great Depression, 122
Great Lakes Training Center team, 147
Greece, 227, 362n49
Greenberg, Hank, 137, 140–42, 162, 166
Grey, Zane, 14

Griffith, Clark, 38, 75, 79, 92, 107, 134,
228, 342n16
Grimes, John, 16
Groat, Dick, 178
Groh, Heinie, 80
Growing the Game (Klein), 286
Guam, 42, 354n58, 383n90
Guam Major League, 354n58
Guerra, Fellito, 108
Guevara, Che, 197, 378n66
Guillen, Ozzie, 266
Guillo, Nemesio, 30
Gulf of Tonkin Resolution, 199
Gulick, Luther, 86
Guttmann, Allen, 290

Haak, Howie, 197
Haase, Bill, 253
Hairston, Hal, 143
Haiti, 108, 312–13n45, 325–26n49,
364n65; baseball manufacturing and
laborers, 231–32, 268
Hale, Creighton, 385n96
Hall, Donald, 376n57
Halsey, Adm. William "Bull," 340n114
Ham, Clifford, 110
Hamill, Pete, 349n13
Hand, Mark, 374n49
Haney, Michael, 242
Hankyu Braves, 174
Hanlon, Ned, 29
Hannity, Sean, 261
Harding, Warren, 111, 114, 322n8
Harmon, Tommy, 150
Harrelson, Bud, 201
Harridge, Will, 134
Harris, Bucky, 104
Harris, Vic, 139
Harrison, Benjamin, 12
Harvard University team, 10, 118
Harwell, Ernie, 45, 205
Hattig, John, 383n90
Havana Baseball Club, 30, 31
Havana Sugar Kings, 193, 195–96
Hawaii: baseball in the 1980s and 1990s,
358–59n27; and 1888 World Tour,
22, 300n9; and nineteenth-century
imperialism, 20; post–World War I
baseball, 113; U.S. annexation and
early leagues, 22, 42–43; World
War II–era military baseball, 147–48
Hawaiian League, 22, 42, 106, 147–48
Hayakawa, S.I., 66
Haywood, "Big Bill," 100
He Long, Marshal, 119, 175

Hearst, Bruce, 271
Hearst, William Randolph, 38
Heilman, Harry, 82
Heisenberg, Werner, 152
Heiser, Victor, 45
Helmig, Klaus and Hanjorg, 170–71
Helms, Jesse, 240
Hendrix, Jimi, 205
Herbert, Bob, 251
Herman, Babe, 145
Herman, Billy, 148
Hernandez, Chico, 67
Hernandez, Enzo, 215
Hernandez, Livan, 238
Hernandez, Orlando "El Duque," 238,
    366n85
Herrmann, Gary, 41, 72, 74
Hersh, Philip, 269
Hershel Islands (Alaska), 306n23
Hershiser, Orel, 224
Herter, Christian, 196
Herzog, Buck, 98
Herzog, Whitey, 245
Heydler, John, 117
Heylinger, William, 87
Hicks, Tom, 269
Hicks Sawyer Minstrel Company, 23
Hideo Nomo, 220
Higashi Hongwanji temple team (Japan),
    114–15
Higbe, Kirby, 338n93
Hildebrand, J.R., 329n89
Hillerich and Bradsby Company, 132–33
Hiroaka, Hiroshi, 29
Hirohito, Emperor, 116, 123, 173
Hiroshi Yamauchi, 253
Hiroshima Carp, 219, 364n70
Hitler, Adolf, 96, 121–22, 128, 130, 132,
    142–44, 152, 170, 322n6
Hobsbawm, Eric, 85
Holidays at Home, 149
Holland, John, 205
Holmberg, David, 184
Holmes, Oliver Wendell, 99
home runs and the "power game,"
    243–44; All-Star game home run
    derbies, 275; Bonds's record, 246;
    McGwire-Sosa race, 233, 243–44,
    251; Ruth and the 1920s game, 101–2
Homestead Grays, 143
Honda, Henry, 158
Hong Kong, 69–70
Hong Kong Baseball Association,
    221
Honolulu Bears, 143

Hoover, J. Edgar, 139, 165, 183, 187,
    341n10
Hopper, DeWolf, 25
Horatio Alger novels, 56, 101
Hornsby, Rogers, 95, 166
Houk, Ralph, 140
House Un-American Activities
    Committee (HUAC), 181, 184
Houston Astros, 236, 267
How to Play Base Ball (Chadwick), 34–35,
    51
Hoyt, Waite, 82, 115, 201
Huerta, Victoriano, 68
Hughes, Karen, 379n71
Hulbert, William, 17, 19
Hungary, 103, 324n31
Hunter, Herb, 113, 114, 115, 116, 119,
    120
Hunting a Detroit Tiger (Soos), 95, 96
Huston, Col. Tillinghast (Cap), 39, 78,
    87, 91
Hutchins, Capt. Richard, 188
Hutchinson, Fred, 147

Ichiko school (Japan), 29, 62
Ichiro Suzuki, 253, 270, 276
If I Never Get Back (Brock), 13
Iglesias, Angel, 387n106
imperialism, baseball: and early
    globalization, 26–27; early twentieth-
    century/pre–World War I, 54–76;
    interventionism and Americanization,
    54–57; nineteenth-century, 13–14,
    20–36; and racism, 21–24, 29, 57–60,
    300n9, 302n25
India, 383n90
Indian Wars, 14–16, 298n39, 299n43
Inter-Allied Games (Military Olympics),
    92–93
International Baseball Association, 180,
    221, 360–61n42
International Baseball Board of England
    and Wales, 104
International Baseball Federation, 104,
    274, 276
International League, 193, 195–96
International Olympic Committee (IOC),
    274, 329n87
Iranian hostage crisis, 213–14
Iraq, 169, 272–73. *See also* Persian Gulf
    War; war on terrorism (Iraq and
    Afghan wars)
Ireland, 25, 149
Irish Republican Army, 104
Irvin, Monte, 46, 143, 165, 348n2

Israel, 384n92
Isthmian Baseball League, 66
Italian Baseball Federation, 171
Italy: baseball in the early 2000s, 385n96;
    baseball in the 1990s, 360–61n42; and
    the 1888 World Tour, 24; and
    McGraw-Comiskey world tour, 71;
    post–World War I, 104; and post–
    World War II baseball diplomacy, 171;
    and World War I, 90
Itom, Bunshir, 116–17

Jackson, Joe, 84
Jackson, Reggie, 201
James, Bill, 87, 145
James, C.L.R., 32
James, Henry, 301n11
James, Weldon, 172
James, William, 103, 376n60
Japan: atomic bombings, 160, 180, 219,
    340n114; and Babe Ruth, 117–18,
    153, 159–60, 172, 328n76, 340n112,
    344n36; baseball and national identity,
    29, 61–62, 113–14, 124, 219, 311n26;
    baseball in the early 2000s, 270–71,
    382n85; baseball in the 1980s and
    1990s, 219–20; Berg's espionage in,
    152–53, 338n90; Brazilian
    community, 327n61; Cold War–era
    baseball, 188, 193, 209–10; and early
    twentieth-century American baseball
    imperialism, 61–64; and Filipino
    leagues, 46–47; and Hawaiian leagues,
    42–43; imperial ambitions, 63–64,
    119–20, 311n33; interwar baseball and
    tours, 113–18, 120, 153, 329n85; and
    Little League, 188, 210; and
    McGraw-Comiskey world tour, 69;
    mid-twentieth-century baseball
    diplomacy, 122–25, 171–74; MLB
    players, 209–10, 220, 252–53, 270,
    382n85; nineteenth-century teams,
    28–29; ownership of MLB teams,
    220; prisoner-of-war camps, 156,
    338n100; recruiting in Dominican
    Republic, 219, 233, 364n70; and
    Taiwan, 63–64, 119–20, 159; U.S.
    films tailored for, 173, 345n38; U.S.-
    Japanese relations, 42–43, 62–63,
    114–18, 120, 123–27, 129, 209–10,
    270–71, 381n83; and the WBC, 276,
    278, 386n104; and World War II,
    123–27, 129, 152–56, 158–60
Japan Central League, 172, 174
Japan World Series, 174

Japanese Americans: internment of,
    157–58, 339n105, 339n108; in
    Japanese leagues, 174
Japanese Baseball Hall of Fame, 174
Japanese Exclusion Act, 115
Japanese Pacific League, 174
Japanese Professional League, 118
Jefferson, Thomas, 6
Jenkins, Ferguson, 225
Jeter, Derek, 249
Jews, 95–96, 140–42, 329n87
Jim Crow practices, 41, 46, 57, 142, 163
Joe Robbie Stadium, 240
Johns Hopkins University team, 221–22
Johnson, Andrew, 12
Johnson, Ban: and American League, 73,
    74; and barnstorming, 41; and
    baseball wars of early twentieth
    century, 72, 73–74, 76; and baseball's
    military connections, 50–51; and
    McGraw-Comiskey world tour, 72;
    and 1918 World Series, 94; and post–
    World War I baseball in Mexico, 111;
    and World War I, 77–78, 79, 82, 84
Johnson, Chalmers, 389n7
Johnson, Davey, 385n96
Johnson, Josh, 143
Johnson, Lyndon, 198, 199–200
Johnson, Tim, 361n46
Johnson, Walter, 89, 137
Joint Civilian Orientation Conference,
    252, 371n22
Jordan, David Starr, 325n40
J.P. Morgan Company, 80
Junior Baseball, American Legion, 97–98,
    322n13
Junior World Series (1959), 195–96
Junwei Yu, 210, 287
Justice, David, 226

Kahn, Roger, 254
Kalas, Harry, 356n9
Kangaroo Club (Australia), 70
Kansas City Monarchs, 46, 135, 143
Kansas City Royals, 205–6, 384n91
Kansas State League, 161
Kataro, Tanaka, 116
Katsuyoshi Miwata, 358n23
Kauffman, Ewing, 205–6
Kazuhiro Sasaki, 253
Keating, Kenneth, 132
Keeler, Wee Willie, 29, 74
Keio University team (Japan), 63, 159,
    311n30
Kellogg, Frank, 110

Kelly, C. Guyer, 113
Kelly, John, 275, 277, 278, 387nn107–8
Kelly, Mike "King," 299n43
Kelly, William, 289
Kennedy, Bob, 245
Kennedy, John F., 198
Kennedy, Robert, 198, 201
Kennedy, William, 52
Kerry, John, 255–56, 373n35
Key West League, 31
Keys, Barbara, 105
Kibbey, W.G., 75–76
Killebrew, Harmon, 199
Kim Dae-Jung, 358n23
King, Cmdr. Ernest, 131
King, Martin Luther, Jr., 206
Kingwell, Mark, 226
Kinnosuke Adachi, 114
Kinsella, W.P., 282
Kinzer, Stephen, 283
Kipling, Rudyard, 44, 88
Kirsch, George, 8, 11
Kishi, Nobusuke, 193
Kissinger, Henry, 209, 236
Klein, Alan, 32–33, 108, 192, 233, 264, 278, 285–86
Klem, Bill, 123
Knapp, Gwen, 254
Knights of Columbus, 68, 83, 91, 92
Knothole Gang (television), 190
Koga, Heidi, 219
Koizumi, Junichiro, 270
Koosman, Jerry, 200
Korakuen Stadium (Japan), 172
Korea: Cold War–era baseball, 175–80, 354n58; and Japan's imperial ambitions, 63–64, 120; post–World War I baseball, 120; post–World War II baseball, 175–76
Korea, South: baseball and U.S-Korean relations in the 1980s, 218; baseball in the early 2000s, 270–71; Little League, 188; MLB television broadcasts, 230; post–Korean War teams, 180; and the WBC, 276, 278, 386n104
Korean Baseball Organization (KBO), 218
Korean League games, 64
Korean War, 175–80, 245
Kornheiser, Tony, 224
Kosovo war, 227
Kralick, Doug, 268
Kraus, Rebecca, 247
Krich, John, 215, 217
Kroh, Floyd "Rube," 67

Kuenster, John, 250
Kuhn, Bowie: and baseball's globalization, 214–15, 236–37; and Reagan administration, 213–14; and Vietnam War, 201, 203, 204–5, 207–8
Kuhn, Frederick, 191
Kuhn Directive of 1977 (amended 1991), 238
Kurtzer, Daniel, 384n92
Kushlan, James, 8
Kyojin Gun (Giant Troop), 159

LaGuardia, Fiorello, 136
Laird, Melvin, 352n38
Lajoie, Napoleon, 74
Lake, Anthony, 237
Lambert, William, 37
Lamoreaux, David, 11, 15, 34, 101
Lamster, Mark, 23, 27, 273
Lancaster Jet Hawks, 376n56
Landis, Kenesaw Mountain: and American Legion, 98; and American unilateralism, 164; and baseball wars of early twentieth-century, 76, 99; and Black Sox scandal, 97, 100, 244; and World War II–era baseball, 134, 136, 142, 144
Lane, F.C., 74, 76, 79, 84
Lane, Frank, 177, 190
Lange, Bill, 90
Langer, William, 145
laptá (Russian village sport), 104–5, 184, 221
Larsen, Don, 170, 245
Lasorda, Tommy, 193, 195, 257; and baseball academies, 234; and Monday's "flag-rescue" at Dodger Stadium, 213, 259; and Olympic baseball, 230–31, 240, 274; and Valenzuela, 215
Latin American baseball: Cold War–era, 191–93, 208–9; and globalization, 228, 232–35, 265–69, 364n70, 381n80; MLB recruiting practices and baseball academies, 233–35, 267, 287–88; and nineteenth-century American imperialism, 33. *See also* Caribbean baseball; *names of individual countries*
Lavagetto, Cookie, 141
Lawrence, Mark, 369n6
Lea, Capt. Luke, 102
Leach, Will, 242
Leahy, William, 160, 161
Lee, Bill, 152, 222, 292, 367n90
Lee, J.G., 91

Lee, Lawrence, 221
Lee, Leron, 219
Lee Gum Hong, 116
Lefebvre, Jim, 271
LeMay, Curtis, 185, 198
Lemon, Bob, 148
Lenin, Vladimir, 179
Leo, John, 104–5
Leonard, Dutch, 95, 151
Leonard, John, 68
Lesko, Jeanie Des Combes, 145
Letterman, David, 238
Levine, Peter, 20
Lewis, Buddy, 139–40
Lewis, Robert, 228
Lewis, Wade, 168
Liang Cheng, 60
Liang Funchu, 119
Lidge, Brad, 375n52
Lieb, Fred, 135, 172, 191
Lieven, Anatol, 279
Life magazine, 169
Limerick, Patricia, 349n13
Linares, Abel, 32
Linares, Omar, 237
Lincoln, Abraham, 7, 12
Lindbergh, Charles, 128–29
Lindenmuth, Mark, 178
Lindsay, John, 204
Lipsyte, Robert, 207
Lipton, Sir Thomas, 70
Literary Digest, 59, 114, 116
Little League baseball: and baseball
    diplomacy, 211; Bosnia-Herzegovina,
    227; and George W. Bush, 188, 246;
    and the Bush family, 385n96; and
    Cold War, 187–88, 210–11, 348n80;
    and Korean War, 178; post-9/11
    programs, 251; postwar Philippines,
    175; Russian teams, 221; South
    Korea, 218; Taiwan, 210–11, 220;
    Venezuela, 265; World Series, 210,
    211, 218, 265; World War II–era
    launching, 146–47
Littlefield, Bill, 245, 249, 259
Lobert, Hans, 98, 136
Lodge, Henry Cabot, 22, 50
Logan, Johnny, 210
London Baseball League, 314n57
London International Baseball League, 149
Longworth, Alice Roosevelt, 50
Look magazine, 134
Loomis, Francis, 55
López Portillo, José, 215
Los Angeles Coliseum, 194

Los Angeles Dodgers: and baseball
    academies, 234; and Chinese baseball,
    221; and Cuban players, 238;
    exhibition game in China, 272; move
    from Brooklyn, 194, 349n13; and
    Vietnam War, 200–201
Louisville Sluggers, 133, 155
Lowenstein, John, 353n42
Lucchino, Larry, 235
Lukas, Paul, 259
Lupien, Tony, 162
Lusitania, 72, 100
Lyons, Ted, 117, 151–52

M Fund, 172, 174
MacArthur, Douglas, 47, 154, 172, 173,
    176, 177–78, 190, 345n45
MacCambridge, Michael, 263
MacGregor Company (sporting goods), 231
Machado, Gerardo, 107–8
Mack, Connie, 117, 119, 120, 144, 150
Macmillan, Newton, 23
MacPhail, Larry, 102–3, 128, 131–32,
    135–36, 165, 166, 201
Maddox, Garry, 200, 356n9
Madritsch, Bobby, 227
Maduro, Bobby, 196, 208
Maestri, Orlando, 193
Maglie, Sal, 139
Maguire, Mickey, 146
Mahan, Alfred, 20
Mahler, Jonathan, 275
Major League Baseball Advanced Media,
    264
Major League Baseball International
    (MLBI), 229, 264
major league baseball (MLB): and African
    American players, 41–42, 232,
    381n80; and baseball academies,
    233–35, 267, 287–88; and baseball
    wars of early twentieth century,
    73–76; Cold War–era expansion and
    shifts to the west, 194, 349n13; color
    barrier, 41–42, 59, 96, 121, 163–64,
    168–69, 180–81, 335n59; foreign
    ownership of teams, 220; future of the
    MLB empire, 279–81, 282–94; and
    Mexican League, 166–68, 342–43n19,
    342n16; as multinational corporation,
    264; and 9/11 attacks, 247–54, 256,
    257, 259, 273–74, 369n6; player-
    owner fights of the 1980s, 242–44;
    post–Civil War nationalism, 12; post–
    World War I nationalism, 98; and
    raids on other leagues, 19, 46, 228,

342n16; and the WBC, 274–78, 287, 289, 292, 386n102, 387n108; and World War I mobilization, 78, 80. *See also* globalization and major league baseball

Major League Baseball Players Association, 229–30, 242, 267

Makepeace, Ray, 340n112

Malcolm, Don, 263

Manchuria, 116, 119

Mandelbaum, Michael, 263, 376n60

Manila Baseball Club, 46–47

Manila Baseball League, 45, 46

Manila Dodgers, 338n93

Mann, Arthur, 164

Mann, Leslie, 85, 108, 118, 121

Mao Tse-tung, 174–75

Maranville, Rabbit, 82

Marcano Guevara, Arturo, 234

Marchildron, Phil, 140

Marianas Islands, 155

Marichal, Juan, 192, 372n28

Maris, Roger, 243

Marquat, Maj. Gen. William, 172, 176

Marqusee, Mike, 230, 247, 292

Marsans, Armando, 41, 42, 75

Marshall, Gen. George C., 165

Marshall, Jim, 210

Marshall, Samuel, 204

Marshall, Thomas, 324n30

Martí, José, 32, 38

Martin, Billy, 178

Martin, Harold, 106

Martin, Morrie, 257

Martin, Pepper, 145

Martinez, Dennis, 208–9, 216, 218

Martinez, Pedro, 269

Martyrs of Chicago (Los Martires de Chicago), 111–12, 326n58

masculinity and sports, 14, 82–83, 203, 369n100, 376n60

M*A*S*H (television), 183

Mathews, Chris, 249

Mathews, Eddie, 178

Mathewson, Christy, 69, 80, 83, 91, 318n24

Matsumoto, Takizo, 172

Mauch, Gene, 195

Maui Athletic Association, 42

Maverick Media, 248

Mays, Willie, 178, 207, 245

Mazeroski, Bill, 196

McCain, John, 261

McCarthy, Eugene, 195, 237–38

McCarthy, Linda, 257

McClure, Col. A.K., 26

McClure, Capt. H.A., 147

McCormick, Moose, 98

McCoskey, Barney, 155

McCurry, Joseph, 16

McDowell, Sam, 202

McGlynn, Frank, 69, 70, 71, 72

McGovern, George, 236

McGraw, John, 46, 59, 69, 71, 74, 103–4

McGraw, Tug, 204

McGraw-Comiskey world tour: (1914), 46, 68–73, 311n32; (1924), 103–4

McGrory, Mary, 263

McGwire, Mark, 220, 233, 243–44, 246, 251

McKechnie, Bill, 163–64

McKenna, Dave, 259, 260

McKinley, William, 12, 43, 73

McLain, Denny, 201

McMurtry, John, 262

McNamara, Robert, 200

Mead, Tim, 252

Mead, William, 129

Means, Russell, 241

media-baseball synergy, 230, 269, 381n81

Medley, Calvin, 143

Medwick, Joe "Ducky," 150

Meiji Gakuin (American school in Japan), 29

Meiji University team, 113, 118

Mendez, José, 41

Merkle, Fred, 69

Merrill, Stump, 221

Metropolitan Baseball Association (Australia), 70

Mexican American leagues, post–World War II, 343n22

Mexican Baseball League, 19, 111, 112, 235

Mexican League War, 165–68, 277, 342n16, 342–43n19, 343n21

Mexican Revolution, 67–68

Mexican War, 6–7

Mexico: baseball in the early 2000s, 378n65; early baseball, 7, 67–68; and McGraw-Comiskey world tour, 69; Mexican League War, 165–68, 277, 342n16, 342–43n19, 343n21; MLB recruiting in, 235; and post–Civil War American nationalism, 297n31; post–World War I, 111–12; recruiting from MLB, 166–68, 342n16; recruiting from Negro League, 165–66; U.S. invasions (1914 and 1916), 67–68; and Valenzuela, 215, 235; Yucatán "resistance leagues," 111–12

Meyers, John "Chief," 59, 241
Miles, John "Mule," 335n59
Military Affairs Committees, 165
Military Athletic League, 52–53
military baseball: African American
   players, 170; Cold War and collapse
   of service baseball, 194; Negro
   League and 25th Infantry Regiment,
   46; post–World War I, 106–7; World
   War II service baseball in Europe,
   148–52; World War II stateside teams,
   147–48; Yankees and 1914 games
   against 22nd Infantry, 52
Military Baseball League, 52
Miller, Marvin, 242
Milligan, Marcus, 83
Mills, A.G., 9, 25, 47–48
Mills Commission, 47–49, 71
Milwaukee Brewers, 260
Milwaukee Chicks, 146
Minaya, Omar, 269, 384n91
Minneapolis Millers, 81, 195
minor leagues: and Caribbean baseball
   academies, 233; post–World War II
   Mexican League, 168; and visa
   requirements, 381n80; and World
   War I, 81; and World War II, 336n67
Minoso, Minnie, 341–42n10
Miranda, Aurelio, 31
Mitchell Report, 280
Mize, Johnny, 148
Mizuno (Japanese sporting goods
   company), 63
MLB Envoy Program, 229
MLB Inc., 222, 271
MLB Players Association, 215
Molina, Augustin, 31
Molloy, Paul, 351n25
Monday, Rick, 212–13, 259
Montreal Expos, 225, 259, 268, 354n58,
   360n42
Montville, Leigh, 178
Moore, Gene, 156–57
Moores, Sir John, 324n33
Mora, Melvin, 379n68
"The Moral Equivalent of War" (James),
   103
Morales, Eloy, 356n15
Moreland, Nate, 143
Moreno, Arturo, 378n65
Morris, Andrew, 64
Morris, Hal, 221
Morton, Frederic, 273
Moscow Red Devils, 222
Mr. Baseball (film), 219

Mulcahy, Hugh, 155
Mundt, Karl, 184
Munson, Thurman, 200
Murakami, Masonori, 209–10
Murcer, Bobby, 200
Murdoch, Rupert, 230, 381n81
Murphy, Charles, 85, 89, 91, 92
Murray, Richard, 367n90
"muscular Christianity," 14, 86, 283
Musial, Stan, 148, 166, 199
Mussolini, Benito, 104, 135
Myers, Hy, 82

Nahem, Sam, 170
Nankai Hawks, 209–10
Nash, Willard, 61
National Advisory Committee on
   Aeronautics, 152
National Agreement (1883), 17
National Agreement (1903), 74
National Amateur Athletic Federation
   (NAAF), 106
National Association of Base Ball Players
   (NABBP), 7, 12, 17
National Association of Professional Base
   Ball Players (NAPBBP), 17
National Baseball Commission, 69, 94, 99
National Baseball Congress (NBC), 110,
   121, 176, 213, 336n67
National Baseball League of Great Britain,
   25
National Basketball Association (NBA),
   272, 289, 387n108
National Coalition on Racism in Sports
   and Media, 242
National Guard, 98, 200, 260
National Guard Field at RFK Stadium,
   260
National League and baseball wars of early
   twentieth century, 73–76
National League of Professional Baseball
   Clubs, 17–19
"national pastime trade-off," 2, 81, 280,
   284, 291
National Security Act of 1947, 180
nationalism and Americanism of the
   1920s, 94–98
Native Americans, 6, 298nn38–39; Indian
   Wars and the U.S. military, 14–16,
   298n39, 299n43; and internal
   colonization/institutionalized racism,
   58–60; and team names/mascots,
   59–60, 241–42
NBC Fort Wayne–Japanese series, 176,
   193

Neal, Gen. Richard, 224

Nedzi, Lucien, 200

Negro Leagues: and Cuban baseball, 40–42, 108; and foreign teams, 40–42, 58, 112, 116; in Hawaii, 113; and Mexican League, 112, 165–66; MLB's raids on, 19, 46, 228; post–World War I, 109, 113; and 25th Infantry Regiment, 46; and World War II, 135, 143

Neighbors, Bob, 178

Netherlands, 278, 314–15n60, 360–61n42, 385n96

Nettles, Craig, 201

New China Baseball Tournament, 194

New England College Baseball League, 262

New Guinea, 155

New Orleans Statesman, 176

New York Baseball Writers Association, 261

New York City and Civil War–era baseball, 10

New York Clipper, 8, 10, 11–12

New York Daily News, 33

New York Giants, 31, 59, 69, 74, 81, 98, 104, 182, 191

New York Herald, 14, 25

New York Journal, 38

New York Mercury, 7

New York Mets, 202, 207, 258, 269, 357n17

New York Mirror, 184

New York Mutuals, 12

New York Post, 156, 177

New York Times, 22, 91, 99, 112, 117, 181, 182, 205, 232

New York Volunteer Regiment, 7

New York World, 40

New York Yankees: as baseball empire, 283, 389n3; and China, 272; Cuban games, 236; first spring training in Bermuda, 312–13n45; and "Great Baseball War of 1901–1903," 74; and Japan, 270; and Nicaragua, 357n17; Taiwanese players, 271; and 2001 World Series, 249–50; and World War I, 81; and World War I military baseball, 52; and World War II, 127–28, 149, 154

New Zealand, 22–23, 358–59n27, 385n96

Newark Eagles, 143

Newcombe, Don, 178, 245

Newhouser, Hal, 139

Newsweek, 230

Newton, C.H., 37

Nicaragua: baseball and crisis/revolution in, 216–18, 265, 290, 356n15, 357nn16–17; baseball in the early 2000s, 265, 379n71; Cold War–era baseball, 193, 208–9, 351n24; and early twentieth-century baseball imperialism, 65–66; and nineteenth-century baseball imperialism, 33; post–World War I, 110–11; team names, 65–66

Nicaraguan National Guard, 110–11

Nicaraguan National League, 66

Nicaraguan Professional League, 193, 265

Nicaraguan Winter League, 208

Niekro, Phil, 201

Nielsen, Lara, 10, 228, 230, 249

Nigeria, 169, 360n41

Nilsson, Dave, 358–59n27

Nimitz, Adm. Chester, 148

9/11 attacks and MLB response, 129, 246–59, 273–74. *See also* war on terrorism (Iraq and Afghan wars)

Nine Innings at Ground Zero (film), 250

nineteenth-century American baseball: baseball imperialism, 13–14, 20–36; baseball militarism, 34–36; Cuban and the Caribbean, 30–33, 40–41; and expansionism, 25–26, 37–47; foreign tours, 21–27, 31; Japan, 28–29; Latin America, 33; and racism, 21–24, 29, 300n9, 302n25

Ninety Days (play), 302n25

Nippon Professional Baseball Organization, 174

Nippon Professional League (NPL), 219–20, 230

Nixon, Richard, 191–92, 198, 207–8, 209, 210, 354n54

Norfolk Training Station team, 147

Norgren, Nels, 115

Noriega, Manuel, 217

North, Oliver, 216, 257, 261

North Africa World Series, 151

North American Free Trade Agreement, 227

North Carolina League, 81

Notari, Aldo, 387n108

Novak, Michael, 262

Nushida, Kenso, 116

Nuxhall, Joe, 145

Nye, Joseph, 229

Oahu Plantation League, 42

Oakland Oaks, 116

Obama, Barack, 285, 375n52, 389n8
Obregón, Alvaro, 111
O'Connor, Hap, 159
Odell, John, 247
O'Donnell, Maj. Gen. Emmett "Rosy," 178
O'Doul, Lefty, 116, 117, 118, 153, 173–74
Office of Strategic Services (OSS), 152
Office of War Information, 137
Oh, Sadaharu, 209, 274, 277, 357–58n20
Olds, Robert, 110
Olympic Games: Athens (2004), 274; Atlanta (1996), 238; Barcelona (1992), 220, 230; baseball's elimination from, 274, 289; and baseball's globalization/ international identity, 230–31; Beijing (2008), 271, 386n99; Berlin (1936), 121–22, 329n87; and de Coubertin, 301n16; Helsinki (1952), 363n60; interwar years, 120–22; Los Angeles (1984), 215, 230; Melbourne (1956), 363n60; Seoul (1988), 230; and Spalding, 56–57, 121; Sydney (2000), 230–31, 240, 274, 358n23; Tokyo (1964), 363n60
Omachi, George, 157
O'Malley, Peter, 360n41
O'Malley, Walter, 178, 191, 349n13
O'Neil, Buck, 143
O'Neill, Harry, 140
116th Infantry Regiment Yankees, 149
opening day celebrations: and Persian Gulf War, 224–25; and presidents' pitches, 12, 161, 177, 198, 224–25, 348n1, 355n6, 373n35
Operation Wetback, 168
origins of baseball: the Doubleday myth, 47–50; and *laptá* (Russian village sport), 104–5, 184, 221; and Latin Americans/African Americans, 49; Mills Commission, 47–49, 71; and rounders, 47–48, 71, 228; and white supremacy, 49
Ortega, Daniel, 218, 265
Ortega, Humberto, 217
Ortiz, Roberto, 142
Ott, Max, 90
Ott, Mel, 151
Our Base Ball Club and How It Won the Championship (Brooks), 11
Our Home Colony (Walker), 58
Outing magazine, 82
Outlook magazine, 44, 47
Over the Plate Circuit (USO tour), 155

Overseas Chinese Club (Hawaii), 42
Overseas Invasion Service Expedition All Stars, 170
Ozark, Danny, 208

Pacific Bell Park (San Francisco), 248, 259
Pacific Coast League, 81, 116, 336n67, 341n6
Paco Baseball Park (Philippines), 45
Paige, Satchel, 163
Paine, Phil, 174
Palmer, Harry, 21
Palmer, Mitchell, 96
Palmer Raids, 96, 100
Pan American Games, 193
Pan American League, 66
Panama, 33, 66, 112, 217–18, 378n65
Panama Canal (Zone), 65, 66, 112, 147, 327n60, 378n65
Pappas, Milt, 201
Paris Peace Conference, 93, 324n30
Parker, Alpheris, 8
Parker, Dan, 184
Parmley, Frederick, 85
Pasquel, Jorge, 165–68, 235, 277, 342n16, 342n18, 343nn20–21
Pastoriza, Jose, 30
Patriot Game (1942), 135
Patten, Gilbert, 56
Patterson, Robert, 164–65
Patton, Gen. George, 151, 250
Paul, Gabe, 236
Paxson, Frederick, 102
Peace Corps, 198, 229
Pearl Harbor attack (1941), 123–25, 126–27, 129
Pennock, Herb, 115
People's Liberation Army (PLA) (China), 119
Pepper, Al, 227
Perez, Rafael, 269
performance-enhancing drugs, 293–94; steroids scandal, 255, 280–81, 371–72n26, 380n75
Perkins, Owen, 239
Perry, Matthew, 28
Pershing, Gen. John, 68, 79, 87, 92, 99, 103
Pershing Stadium (France), 92
Persian Gulf War, 222–25
Person, Robert, 247
Pesky, Johnny, 148, 166, 257
Peterson, Harold, 48
Petraeus, Gen. David, 273, 281
Petroskey, Dale, 253–54, 372n29, 372n31

Pett, Jose, 363n62
Phelon, William, 72–73, 76, 85
Philadelphia Athletics, 12, 19, 21, 31, 112, 144
Philadelphia Bobbies, 115–16
Philadelphia Bulletin, 95
Philadelphia Phillies, 21, 41, 81, 136, 346n53
Philadelphia Royal Giants, 116
Philippine League, 45
Philippine War, 43–47, 306n19
Philippines: baseball in the early 2000s, 383n90; early Filipino baseball, 43–47, 306n22; the Filipino Insurrection, 43–47, 306n19; and Little League, 175; and McGraw-Comiskey world tour, 70; and nineteenth-century baseball imperialism, 28; post–World War I, 120, 329n85; post–World War II, 175; and World War II, 154, 156, 338n93
Philippines Baseball League, 106
Phillips, John, 166
Piazza, Mike, 358n23
Picinich, Val, 139
Pierce, Charles, 286–87
Pinder, Joe, 149
Pitch, Hit and Run program (MLBI), 229
Pittsburgh Courier, 163
Pittsburgh Crawfords, 143
Pittsburgh Pirates, 19, 164, 193, 197, 268
Pius XII, Pope, 131, 150
Platt Amendment, 40
Play for a Kingdom (Dyja), 10
Player's League (PL), 18
Players Protective Association, 74
Plessy v. Ferguson (1896), 57
PNC Park (Pittsburgh), 248
Podres, Johnny, 346n54
Polo Grounds, 52, 128, 135, 177
Pompez, Alejandro, 303n39
Ponce Massacre (Puerto Rico), 109–10
Pond, Arlie, 44, 70, 89
Poor, Henry, 11
Pope, Steven, 86, 93, 280
Porter's Spirit of the Times, 7
Porto Rican Baseball League, 109
post-Civil War baseball, 11–14
Povich, Shirley, 134
Powell, Colin, 225, 226, 255, 281
President's Committee on Civil Rights, 168
Price, Bryan, 168
Price, Byron, 292–93
Price, Melvin, 132

The Pride of the Yankees (film), 137, 173
Prince, Carl, 190, 191
prisoner-of-war baseball: American Civil War, 9; post–World War II, 175; World War II, 155–58, 338n98, 339n102, 339n104
Probst, Mark, 362n49
Prohibition, 100–101
Providence Grays, 77
Puerto, Carrillo, 67
Puerto Rican Baseball Academy and High School, 380n76
Puerto Rican Winter League, 110, 193, 268
Puerto Rican Workers Alliance, 109
Puerto Rico: baseball in the early 2000s, 267–68, 380n76; Cold War–era baseball, 193; and nineteenth-century U.S. imperialism, 33, 42; post–World War I, 109–10; Spanish-American War and U.S. occupation, 42; and the WBC, 276
Pulitzer, Joseph, 38
Pulliam, William, 44, 108
Punahou School (Hawaii), 22
Putnam, George, 9

Quayle, Dan, 224
Quebec League, 167
Quinn, Jack, 75
Quinn, Joseph, 23
Quirk, James, 229
Quiroz, Alexis, 234

Rable, George, 198
Rader, Benjamin, 73, 186
Radford, Mike, 372n32
radio technology, 90, 111, 137
railroads, transcontinental, 11
Ramirez, Sergio, 216
Rawlings Sporting Goods, 229, 231–32, 268–69
Razhigaev, Rudolf, 222
RBI (Reviving Baseball in the Inner City), 232
Reach, Al, 45, 49
Reach All-Americans, 63
Reach Athletic Goods, 79
Reagan, Ronald, 214, 216–18, 221
Reaves, Joseph, 63, 124, 218
Red, White, and Blue Tours of America, 262
Red Cross, 80, 135, 137, 149
Red Scares, 96, 164, 178, 182, 186, 187, 190

Reese, Pee Wee, 148
Regalado, Samuel, 65, 110, 157, 269
Reich, Otto, 265
Reich, Steve, 227
Reiner, Andres, 235
Reno, Marcus, 16
reserve clause, 84, 191, 206, 214, 299n52
Revolutionary War, 6, 13, 14
Reynolds, Gen. Burton, 338n93
Reynolds, Quentin, 132
Rice, Condoleezza, 222, 259–60, 261, 378n65
Rice, Jim, 231
Rice, Sam, 83
Richardson, Bill, 238
Richter, Francis, 22, 115
Rickenbacker, Eddie, 331n22
Rickey, Branch: the color barrier and Robinson's signing, 163–64; the Dodgers and Cold War anti-radicalism, 190–91; and Doubleday myth, 48; and "farm system," 228; and Mexican League War, 167, 342n16, 342–43n19; and post–World War I military baseball, 98; and Robinson's HUAC testimony, 181, 190; and World War I, 81, 82; and World War II, 153
Ridgeway, Gen. Matthew, 173
Rigney, Johnny, 155
Rijo, Jose, 380n74
Rikkyo University team (Japan), 116–17
Ring, Dave, 279
Ripken, Cal, 243, 261
Rivera, Mariano, 378n65
Rizzuto, Phil, 147, 166, 215
Robbins, Tim, 253–54
Robeson, Paul, 163, 180–82, 190
Robinson, Bill, 128
Robinson, Brooks, 199
Robinson, Jackie: on baseball and business, 228; Brooklyn Dodgers signing, 163–64; and Mexican League, 165; and 1936 Berlin Olympics, 121; and post–World War II baseball diplomacy, 168–69; on progress for blacks in organized baseball, 232; and Robeson's charges against America, 180–82, 190; signing, 46; testimony against Robeson, 180–82, 190; and Vietnam War, 206; and World War II military service, 143
Rochester Express, 8
Rochester Red Wings, 195

Rockefeller, John D., 80
Rocky Mountain Boys, 11
Roden, Donald, 62
Rodney, Lester, 163–64, 341n10
Rodriguez, Alex, 269, 372–73n33
Rogan, Wilber ("Bullet Joe"), 46, 68, 83, 113
Rogers, John, 26
Rogers, William, 236
Romulo, Carlos, 187
Roosevelt, Franklin, 118, 122, 126, 134, 149, 247
Roosevelt, Theodore, 25, 27–28, 37, 39, 43, 49–50, 60, 62–63, 102
Root, Elihu, 47
Rose, Pete, 199, 201
Rosenthal, Ken, 249
Ros-Lehtinen, Ileana, 239
Ross, Thom, 299n43
Roth, Philip, 185–86, 354n54
rounders, 47–48, 71, 228
Rowan, Carl, 181
Rowan, Jack, 55
Ruck, Rob, 65
Ruether, Walter, 98
Ruffing, Red, 139, 148
Rumsfeld, Donald, 226, 252
Rupert, Col. Jacob, 78
Russell, Harold, 162, 177
Russell, Marian, 251
Russia: baseball in the early 2000s, 385n96; and *laptá* (village game), 104–5, 184, 221; World War I and American anticommunism, 89–90. *See also* Soviet Union
Russo-Japanese War (1905), 60, 62, 63
Ruth, Babe, 77, 101–2; and "Curse of the Bambino," 255, 372n33; and Japan, 117–18, 153, 159–60, 172, 328n76, 340n112, 344n36; and Mexican League, 166; post–World War I barnstorming tours, 98, 107, 117–20, 153, 159, 328n76, 329n85; power baseball and home runs, 101–2, 244; and World War I, 84; as World War II–era baseball idol, 137
Ryan, Nolan, 372n31
Ryuji Suzuki, 172

Sabourin, Emilio, 32
Sacramento Senators, 116
Saigh, Fred, 178
salaries, players': Brush classification system, 24; and free agency, 242–43, 368n96; Japanese players' contracts,

270, 382n85; and Korean War, 178; and 1981 strike, 243; and World War I, 94; and World War II, 138
Salina Spurs, 219
Salsinger, H.G., 115
Salute the Soldier campaign, 149
Samoa, 306n18
Samsung Lions (South Korea), 218
San Diego Padres, 235, 260, 272
San Francisco Argonaut, 43
San Francisco earthquake (1989), 246
San Francisco Examiner, 38
San Francisco Giants, 194, 209, 251, 260, 355n60
San Francisco Seals, 173
San Juan Baseball Club (New York City), 109
Sanborn, Irving, 107
Sandinistas, 216–17, 265, 357n17
Sandino, Augusto César, 110–11, 326n55
Sangree, Allen, 314n56
Santana, Johan, 275
Santana, Pedro Julio, 65
Sarandon, Susan, 253
Sardar, Ziauddin, 246
Saturday Evening Post, 186
Savage, Bob, 140
Sawamura, Eiji, 117–18, 159, 328n77
Sawkard, Russell, 143
Scantlebury, Pat, 176
Schacht, Al, 150
Schaefer, Germany, 69
Scheller, Jason, 249
Schilling, Curt, 247, 257
Schott, Marge, 224
Schwarzkopf, Gen. Norman, 224, 226
Scientific American, 86
"scientific game" in baseball, 35, 101
Scribner's magazine, 44
Scully, Vin, 219
Seattle Mariners, 220, 252–53, 260, 270
Seaver, Tom, 204–5
Second American Association War, 18–19
Second Sino-Japanese War, 118
Seidel, Michael, 127–29
Selee, Frank, 40
Selig, Bud, 223, 226–27, 243–44, 245, 246; and baseball globalization, 227, 230, 278, 370; and baseball's response to 9/11 and war on terror, 247, 252, 257, 259, 261; and MLB empire, 280–81
Senzel, Howard, 196, 206–7
September 11, 2001. *See* 9/11 attacks and MLB response

Serrano, José, 240
service baseball. *See* military baseball
7th Cavalry baseball teams, 15–16
Seward, William, 8
Sewell, Joe, 83
Sewell, Luke, 155
Seymour, Harold, 34, 57–58, 93, 94, 97, 107
Shachin, Sergei, 221
Shafer, Tillie, 45, 63
Shanghai Amateur Baseball League, 69
Shanghai Baseball Club, 60
Shapiro, Walter, 252
Sharman, Ralph, 83
Shaw, George Bernard, 129
Sheldon, Lt. Col. Raymond, 78
Shelton, Henry, 245
Shepard, Bert, 140
Shigetoshi Hasegawa, 253
Shimkus, John, 273
Shinbashi Athletics, 29
Shinichi Ishimaru, 159
Shinzo Abe, 270
Shoriki, Matsutaro, 117
Shotton, Burt, 82
The Showdown (film), 279
Shriver, Sargent, 198
Shultz, Wallace, 77
Siegel, Lee, 376–77n60
Siger, Carl, 56
Silvestri, Ken, 155
Simmons, Bill, 357–58n20
Simmons, Curt, 178, 245, 346n53
Sinclair, Robert, 113, 114, 124
Singleton, Ken, 225
Sisler, George, 83, 128
Skolnikoff, Jessica, 288
Slaughter, Enos, 158–59, 162
Small, Jim, 271, 272
Smena [Change] (Russian magazine), 184
Smit, Alexander, 385n96
Smith, Clair, 212, 229
Smith, Gen. James, 45
Smith, Jay, 272
Smith, Kate, 136
Smith, Ken, 205
Smith, Leverett, 54
Smith, Red, 112
Smith, Theolic, 165–66
Smith, Wendell, 163
soccer, 264, 275, 289, 314n57, 377n62, 379n67
social Darwinism, 14, 20, 27, 41, 62
Sockalexis, Lou, 38, 59
Solaita, Tony, 354n58

Solomon Islands, 154
Someillan, Louis, 31–32
Somervell, Cmdr. Gen. Brehon, 131
Somoza, Anastasio, Jr., 208–9, 216
Somoza, Anastasio, Sr., 110–11
Somoza, Luis, 193
Soos, Troy, 95
Soriano, Alfonso, 364n70
Sosa, Elias, 378n65
Sosa, Sammy, 233, 243–44, 251, 380n75
South Africa, 168–69, 384n91
Southern Baseball Club, 9
Soviet Union: baseball in the 1980s and
    1990s, 221–22, 359n31; and Cold
    War, 182–84; interwar baseball, 104–5;
    the 1951 atomic bomb test, 182–83
Spahn, Warren, 140, 147, 162
Spain and nineteenth-century Cuban
    nationalism, 30–32, 38–39. *See also*
    Spanish-American War (War of 1898)
Spalding, Albert: and American
    nationalism/exceptionalism, 13,
    48–49; and baseball imperialism, 28,
    29, 55, 56–57, 61; and baseball
    militarism, 34; and baseball's early
    globalization, 26–27, 45; and Civil
    War, 8, 11; and late nineteenth-
    century baseball wars, 17–18; and
    Mills commission to investigate
    baseball's origins, 47–49; and Spanish-
    American War, 39; and U.S. Olympic
    Committee, 56–57, 121; World Tour
    (1888), 21–27, 69, 300n9, 301n11,
    302n25
Spalding Company (sporting goods), 27,
    49, 63, 231
Spanish-American War (War of 1898), 32,
    35, 37–43, 54, 55, 305n9
Speaker, Tris, 69, 83, 323n23
Spencer, Daryl, 210
Spencer, Herbert, 20
Spink, J. Taylor, 80, 123, 126, 161, 214
Sport magazine, 177
Sporting Life, 22, 31–32, 34, 38
Sporting News, 98, 108, 120, 213; and
    baseball diplomacy, 122, 123, 169,
    170; and baseball tours in Japan, 115,
    117, 118; and Cold War–era baseball,
    177, 194, 196, 209–10, 351n25; and
    Mexican League War, 166; and pre–
    World War II baseball, 122, 123, 127;
    support for American foreign policy,
    214, 355n5; and Vietnam War, 199,
    200, 202; and women's postwar
    return to household, 162; and World

War I, 80, 84, 90; and World War II,
    129, 133, 134, 138, 140, 142, 151,
    156
"sports diffusion," 390n17
Sports Illustrated, 288
Sports in Art exhibit (1956), 186
St. Louis Browns, 78, 145
St. Louis Cardinals, 81, 108, 117, 136,
    145, 149, 162, 193, 260
Stalag Luft III, 155
Stalin, Joseph, 105, 149, 176–77
Stallo, John, 24
Standard Oil Company, 109
Stanky, Eddie, 182
"The Star Spangled Banner" (national
    anthem), 94–95, 179; and Iraq War
    dissenters, 257–59; and 1918 World
    Series, 94–95; and Vietnam War
    dissenters, 205–6; World War II–era,
    122, 136, 146
Starfin, Victor, 118
Stargell, Willie, 201
Stark, Jason, 264
Stars and Stripes, 80, 84, 88–90, 91–92,
    149, 165
Staurowsky, Ellen, 59–60
Stead, William, 106
Stealing Lives (Marcano Guevara and
    Fidler), 234
Stein, Jeff, 239
Steinbrenner, George, 250, 251–52, 258,
    276, 372–73n33
Steininger, Edward, 75
Stengel, Casey, 83, 115, 173
steroids scandal, 255, 280–81, 371–72n26,
    380n75
Stewart, Charles, 51
Stewart, Jimmy, 185, 347n73
Stone, Larry, 101
Story, Ronald, 12
Stotz, Carl, 146–47
Strategic Air Command (film), 185
Stray Dog (film), 173
Streak (Seidel), 127
Strikeouts for Troops, 260–61
strikes, players', 243
Strong, Josiah, 20
Sugar (film), 267, 380n74
Suh Jyong-chul, 218
Suitcase Sefton and the American Dream
    (Feldman), 158
Sullivan, James, 47
Sullivan, Neil, 194
Sullivan, Ted, 71
Sumner, Jim, 81

Sun Yat-sen, 22, 61
Sunday, Billy, 84–85, 129
Sun-tzu's *The Art of War*, 250
Sutton, Don, 231
Swisher, Nick, 261
Swoboda, Ron, 204

Taft, William Howard, 75, 99
Taiwan: baseball in the early 2000s, 271;
    baseball in the 1980s and 1990s,
    220–21; and Chinese nationalists,
    174–75, 210–11; and Japanese impe-
    rialism, 63–64, 119–20, 159; Little
    League baseball, 210–11, 220
Taiwan Baseball Federation, 64
Taiwan Major League (TML), 220
Taiwanese Red Leafs, 210
Tampa Bay Devil Rays, 270
Tan Shin-ming, 355n60
Tandon, Shaun, 275
Tate, Steven, 225
Tawhan Baseball Association, 175
Taylor, Gen. Maxwell, 165, 178
Tearing Down the Spanish Flag (film), 38
television markets, 230, 288–89
Tener, John, 23, 72, 76, 79
Tenet, George, 255
Tet Offensive, 199–200
Texas Rangers, 222, 224, 252, 255, 269
Thailand, 354n58
Thayer, Ernest Lawrence, 38
Thiel, Art, 367n89
Thiessen, Mark, 240
Third U.S. Cavalry team, 67–68
13th Infantry baseball teams, 16
Thomas, Ira, 41
Thompson, Carson, 121
Thompson, F.C., 93
Thomson, Bobby, 182–84
Thoreau, Henry David, 7
Thorn, John, 294
Thorpe, Jim, 58, 69, 71, 72, 241, 329n87
Three Stripes in the Sun (film), 193
Tiant, Luis, Jr., 236
Tiant, Luis, Sr., 236
Tijerino, Edgardo, 217
Tillman, Kevin, 251
Tillman, Pat, 251, 371n21
Time magazine, 103, 104–5
Tinker, Joe, 75
Tobita, Suishu, 116
Todd, Capt. O.W., 153
Tokyo Giants, 118, 159, 173–74
Tokyo Six University League, 115–16
Toronto Blue Jays, 225–26

Torre, Joe, 199, 248
Torres, Gil, 142
Toru Shoriki, 173
Trading with the Enemies Act, 237, 276
Travis, Cecil, 162
Treaty of Cincinnati (1915), 76
Trosky, Hal, 105, 324n37
Trotsky, Leon, 105, 112
Trouppe, Quincy, 165–66
Troy, Robert, 83
Trucks, Virgil, 154
Trujillo, Rafael, 109, 192, 197, 326n55
Truk (island), 63, 311n33
Truman, Harry, 134, 160, 161, 177–78, 211
Tunisia, 113, 149, 169
Turner, Frederick, 20
Turner, Henry, 26
Turner, Ted, 222, 241, 381n81
Twain, Mark, 25–26, 45
26th of July Movement, 195
25th Infantry Regiment, 42, 45, 46
Twit, Grace, 381n80
Tygiel, Jules, 164, 182, 254

Ueberroth, Peter, 215, 216, 222
Ukraine, 385n96
UN Convention on the Rights of the
    Child, 234
Underworld (DeLillo), 182–84
Union Association War, 17
Union Club, 10
Union Grounds, 10
unions, players', 17–18, 74, 82
United Fruit Company, 33, 66, 192–93,
    196
University of Chicago team, 46, 63,
    114–15, 116, 311n32
University of Paris baseball club,
    360–61n42
University of Wisconsin team, 63
Uruguay, 33
U.S. Agency for International
    Development, 231–32
U.S. Air Force team, 148–49
U.S. Army Signal Corps, 188
U.S. Information Agency, 171, 197
U.S. Marines: and baseball in the
    Caribbean, 64–68, 312–13n45; and
    Iraq War enlistments, 260, 375n51;
    post–World War I baseball in Asia,
    116, 120, 153; World War II–era
    baseball, 154
U.S. Military Academy (West Point), 47,
    52, 98, 136, 345n45
U.S. Military All-Star Team, 262, 376n56

U.S. Naval Academy, 47, 98
U.S. Navy, 60, 63, 148, 260, 262, 375n51
U.S. Office of Latin American Affairs, 152
U.S. Olympic Committee, 56–57
U.S. Rubber Company, 187
USA Today, 256–57
USO (United Service Organizations), 135, 137, 150–51, 155, 201, 261

Valenzuela, Fernando, 215, 235
Van Slyke, Andy, 360n39
Van Smoot, Peter, 6
Vander Meer, Johnny, 163–64
Vargas, Angel, 234
Veeck, Bill, 153–54, 212
Venezuela: and the Cold War, 191; MLB recruiting and baseball academies, 233–34; nineteenth-century baseball, 33; post–World War I baseball, 109; and post–World War II baseball diplomacy, 169; U.S-Venezuelan relations in the early 2000s, 265–67, 379n71; and the WBC, 278
Venezuelan Baseball Players Association, 234
Veracruz Blues, 165
Verdi, Frank, 195
Vernon, Mickey, 155
Veterans Act of 1946, 162
Veterans of Foreign Wars, 135, 181, 190, 206, 212, 336n67, 367n90
Victoria Baseball League (Australia), 23
Vietnam, baseball in, 383n90
Vietnam Moratorium Day (1969), 204–5, 207
"Vietnam syndrome," 216, 223, 242
Vietnam War, 198–208; baseball and the military, 200–202; and counterculture protests, 202–8, 212–13, 353n42; drafted ballplayers, 200–201; and football, 198, 203; and national anthem, 205–6; players' draft-exemptions and deferments, 200; POWs, 207–8; and racism, 206
Villa, Pancho, 68
Vincent, Fay, 222–23, 247
Virgil, Ozzie, 191
Virgin Islands, 33, 109, 351n24, 363n62
Vitt, George, 324n37
Voigt, David, 20, 21, 35–36, 39, 55, 73, 95, 203, 284
Von Tilzer, Harry, 80

Wachtell, Dan, 251, 259
Wagner, Honus, 161

Waitkus, Capt. Eddie, 150, 337n80
Wakefield, Wanda, 88
Walker, Dixie, 155
Walker, Gee and Harvey, 11
Walker, Harry, 140
Walker, Levi, Jr., 241
Walker, Moses Fleetwood, 58
Walker, Welday, 58
Walker, William, 33
Wall Street Journal, 222, 236
Walters, Bucky, 151, 163
Waner, Paul, 155
Wang Chao, 271
Wang Liqiang, 383n89
War Is a Racket (Butler), 57
War of 1812, 6, 13
War of 1898. *See* Spanish-American War (War of 1898)
war on terrorism (Iraq and Afghan wars), 250–62, 370n10; Army-Navy baseball games, 262, 375n55; MLB team projects and patriotic displays, 259–61, 374–75n49, 375nn50–51; and patriotic jingoism, 257–62; service baseball within the armed forces, 262; and war dissenters, 257–59; World War II veterans' boosterism, 256–57
Ward, John Montgomery, 18, 21, 24, 27
Warlike Gods Society (Japan), 117
Waseda University team (Japan), 46, 116, 159, 311n30
Washington, George, 6
Washington Nationals, 12
Washington Nationals (new), 259–60, 274n49
Washington Post, 112
Washington Senators, 12, 73–74, 79, 82, 107, 135, 142
Weaver, Buck, 69, 71
Weaver, Harry, 81
Weaver, Monte, 149
Weeghman, Charles, 37, 53, 86
Weinberg, Mike, 369n6
Welcome Back Veterans campaign, 262
Wells, Col. W.H. "Cappy," 187
Wells, Willie, 112, 165
Welsh Baseball Union, 324n31
Wendel, Tim, 294, 372n30
Westmoreland, Gen. William, 199
White, Edward, 141
White Sea Baseball League, 148
Whiting, Robert, 124
Whitman, Walt, 13
Wilhelm II, Kaiser, 102
Will, George, 263

Williams, Albert, 216
Williams, Bernie, 378n65
Williams, John, 42
Williams, Capt. John Q., 201
Williams, Ramon, 31
Williams, Ted: Korean War service, 178–79, 245, 346n54; and Mexican League, 166; World War II service, 139, 148, 162
Wilson, Hack, 107
Wilson, Horace, 28
Wilson, Travis, 385n96
Wilson, Woodrow, 57, 67–68, 76, 77, 79, 80, 95
Wilson Sporting Goods Company, 130–31, 133, 231
Wings for Victory campaign, 149
winter leagues: Cold War–era, 192, 196, 197–98; Dominican, 192, 197–98, 364n70; and Mexican League War, 342–43n19; Nicaraguan, 208
Wolter, Tim, 155
Women's Army Corps, 146
women's baseball: nineteenth-century Cuba, 31; post–World War I Chinese teams, 119; post–World War I teams touring Japan, 115–16; and post–World War II return to households, 162, 185; post–World War II teams, 162, 341n10; World War II–era AAGPBL, 145–46, 162, 341n10; World War II–era army nurses, 147
Wood, Edward, 256
Wood, Gen. Leonard, 40, 99, 120, 128
Woodling, Gene, 155
Woodward, Stanley, 332n26
World Amateur Baseball Championship (WABC), 104, 209
World Baseball Classic (WBC), 274–78, 287, 289, 292, 386n102, 386n104, 387n106, 387n108, 388n109
World Baseball Cup, 273–74, 275
World Children's Baseball Fair, 270, 357–58n20
World Series: [1917], 79–80; [1918], 94–95; [1919 and Black Sox scandal], 95–97, 100, 244, 321n4, 323n23; [1942], 137; [1943], 149, 154; [1944 and the Service World Series], 148; [1945], 170, 171–72; [1946], 162; [1948], 140; [1969 and Vietnam Moratorium Day], 204–5; [1989], 246; [1992], 225–26, 241; [1994 and players' strike], 243; [1995], 241–42; [2001], 249–50; and sports militarism,

279–80; creation of, 74–75, 315n68; and Toronto Blue Jays, 225–26; and the WBC, 275–76; and World War I, 79–80, 82, 90, 92
World Trade Organization, 227
World War I, 77–93; ballpark recruitment campaigns, 80; and baseball/war metaphors, 88–90; and critics of the war, 316n8; and democracy/capitalism, 78–80; the draft, 81–82; enlisted players, 82–83; industrial leagues, 84; military displays at ballparks, 80; organized baseball and the war effort, 78–88; postwar American diplomacy and international relations, 102–3, 105–7, 324n30; and school athletics, 86; sporting press and baseball coverage, 77, 80, 84, 88–90, 320n44; stateside war production work, 84–85; war preparedness/mobilization, 77–78; wartime baseball in England and France, 90–93
World War II, 126–60, 247; ballplayers and military service, 138–40, 147–48, 153–54; baseball and militarism, 130–32, 136–37; and bombings of Hiroshima and Nagasaki, 160, 180, 219, 340n114; dissenters and resisters, 139; ethnic ballplayers/role models, 140–42; films/newsreels, 132, 137; the "Good War," 126–27, 160, 257; and injured GIs, 138; and Japanese baseball, 158–60; and jingoistic advertising, 130–33; and labor agitation, 138; Little League, 146–47; military baseball, stateside, 147–48; military baseball in Europe, 148–52; night baseball, 144; the 1941 season and wartime consciousness, 127–29; North African campaign, 151; the Pacific war, 152–55; Pearl Harbor attack, 123–25, 126–27, 129; and players' salaries, 138; prewar baseball diplomacy, 122–25; prisoner-of-war baseball, 155–58, 338n98, 339n102, 339n104; and racism, 142–44, 335n59; radio broadcasts and censorship, 137; Ruth as baseball idol, 137, 159–60; and sports equipment, 144, 335n65; team travel restrictions, 144; uniforms and patriotic symbols, 136; war production work, 139; warships and Liberty Ships, 148; wartime baseball's national

World War II (*continued*)
    importance, 129–34, 331n22,
    332n26; wartime relief efforts,
    134–36, 149; women's teams,
    145–46, 162; postwar, 162–75
World War II Veterans Committee, 256
Wounded Warrier Project, 261–62
W.R. Grace (agribusiness firm), 110
Wright, Harry, 21, 49, 69
Wrigley, Phil, 135
Wrigley Field, 146, 335n61

Yale University, 118, 215
Yamashita, Tomoyuki, 154
Yamauchi, Hiroshi, 220
"Yankee Doodle," 5–6
Yankee Stadium, 177, 248–49, 258,
    374nn41–42
Yao Ming, 240, 272
Yastrzemski, Carl, 200
Yokohama Athletic Club, 29
Yonamine, Wally, 174
Yoshiro Mori, 358n23
Young, Cy, 74

Young, Del, 173
Young, Dick, 199
Young, Nicholas, 17, 18–19, 28–29
Young Men's Christian Association
    (YMCA), 14, 42–43, 47, 55, 63–64,
    68, 86, 91, 106, 324n31
Yucatán Baseball League, 67

Zang, David, 202–3, 207, 210, 211
Zaun, Geoff, 258
Zeiler, Thomas, 24, 28
Zenimura, Howard, 157
Zenimura, Kenichi, 157–58
Zillgitt, Jeff, 256–57
Zimbabwe Baseball and Softball
    Association, 360n41
Zimmerman, Heinie, 80
Zinn, Howard, 258
Zirin, Dave, 258, 276
Zito, Barry, 260–61
Zoss, Joel, 13, 20, 28, 79, 95
Zuber, Bill, 139
Zuckert, Eugene, 198
Zúñiga, Yamil, 217